Shaping the Reading Field

The Impact of Early Reading Pioneers,
Scientific Research, and Progressive Ideas

Susan E. Israel   E. Jennifer Monaghan

EDITORS

INTERNATIONAL
Reading Association
800 BARKSDALE ROAD, PO BOX 8139
NEWARK, DE 19714-8139, USA
www.reading.org

The International Reading Association attempts, through its publications, to provide a forum for a wide spectrum of opinions on reading. This policy permits divergent viewpoints without implying the endorsement of the Association.

Executive Editor, Books   Corinne M. Mooney
Developmental Editor   Charlene M. Nichols
Developmental Editor   Tori Mello Bachman
Developmental Editor   Stacey Lynn Sharp
Editorial Production Manager   Shannon T. Fortner
Production Manager   Iona Muscella
Supervisor, Electronic Publishing   Anette Schuetz

Project Editor   Stacey L. Sharp

Cover Design   Linda Steere

Every effort has been made to contact copyright holders and publishers for permission to reprint. Any oversights that might have occurred will be rectified in future reprintings.

The publisher would appreciate notification where errors occur so that they may be corrected in subsequent printings and/or editions.

Library of Congress Cataloging-in-Publication Data
Shaping the reading field : the impact of early reading pioneers, scientific research, and progressive ideas / Susan E. Israel & E. Jennifer Monaghan, editors.
        p. cm.
Includes bibliographical references and index.
ISBN-13: 978-0-87207-598-6
1. Reading teachers--United States--Biography. 2. Reading--United States--History. 3. Progressive education--United States--History. 4. Educational psychology--History. I. Israel, Susan E. II. Monaghan, E. Jennifer, 1933-
LB1050.2.S44 2006
428.407'1073--dc22
                                                                        2006028836

This book is dedicated to Marguerite Vogler (1914–1994), my grandmother. Because Grandma Vogler valued the preservation of family history, I became inspired to continue the preservation of past knowledge in literacy and joined the History of Reading Special Interest Group (SIG) of the International Reading Association. She would have been pleased to know that I have been elected the SIG's new president for the year 2006–2007.

—SUSAN E. ISRAEL

CONTENTS

ABOUT THE EDITORS

S USAN E. ISRAEL, PHD, is an Assistant Professor of the Department of Teacher Education, University of Dayton, Ohio, USA. Her research agenda focuses on reading comprehension and child-mind development as it relates to literacy processes in reading and writing. She has worked with the Alliance for Catholic Education at the University of Notre Dame, and she provides literacy instruction to graduate and undergraduate students.

She was the 1998 recipient of the teacher-researcher grant from the International Reading Association, which she has served and been a member of for over a decade. She is currently the president of the Association's History of Reading Special Interest Group. She also was awarded the 2005 Panhellenic Council Outstanding Professor Award at the University of Dayton.

Her most recent publications include the edited volumes *Metacognition and Literacy Learning: Theory, Assessment, Instruction, and Professional Development* (Israel, Block, Bauserman, & Kinnucan-Welsch, Erlbaum, 2005) and *Poetic Possibilities: Using Poetry to Enhance Literacy Learning* (International Reading Association, 2006), and the coauthored texts *Reading First and Beyond: The Complete Guide for Teachers and Literacy Coaches* (Block & Israel, Corwin Press, 2005), *Collaborative Literacy: Using Gifted Strategies to Enrich Learning for Every Student* (Israel, Sisk, & Block, Corwin Press, 2006), and *Quotes to Inspire Great Reading Teachers: A Reflective Tool for Advancing Students' Literacy* (Block & Israel, Corwin Press, 2006). One other book will be published in 2008: *Handbook of Reading Comprehension* (Israel & Duffy, Erlbaum, in press).

In her free time, Susan enjoys quilting, reading best-selling nonfiction books, and bicycling.

E. JENNIFER MONAGHAN is Professor Emerita of the Department of English, Brooklyn College of The City University of New York. She taught reading in the Department of Educational Services for much of her 28 years at the college and also taught reading and composition to English-language learners and native speakers of English in the Department of English.

Born in Cambridge, England, Jennifer received a bachelor's and a master's degree in Literae Humaniores (i.e., classical literature, history, and philosophy) from Oxford University, England; another master's—in Greek—from the University of Illinois at Urbana-Champaign; and an EdD from Yeshiva University, New York. In 1975, with the aid of the late Ralph Staiger and Richard L. Venezky, she founded the History of Reading Special Interest Group of the International Reading Association. The group recently honored her by naming their triennial book prize in the history of literacy the E. Jennifer Monaghan Book Award. In 1997, Jennifer was the first plenary speaker at the Association's Reading Research Conference.

As an editor, Jennifer has compiled a special issue of *Visible Language* (1987), "Then and Now: Readers Learning to Write." As a historian, she is the author of *A Common Heritage: Noah Webster's Blue-Back Speller* (Archon Books, 1983), *Reading for the Enslaved, Writing for the Free: Reflections on Liberty and Literacy* (American Antiquarian Society, 2000), and *Learning to Read and Write in Colonial America* (University of Massachusetts Press, 2005). She has published numerous articles and book chapters on topics that include the literacy instruction of 17th-century Native Americans and 20th-century reading methodology, winning best-article awards from the American Studies Association and the History of Education Society. She is the senior author of the entry "History of Reading Instruction" in *Literacy in America: An Encyclopedia of History, Theory, and Practice* (Guzzetti, ABC-CLIO, 2002).

Jennifer and her husband, Charles, have retired to Charlottesville, Virginia, USA, where they greatly enjoy visiting the libraries of the University of Virginia and being grandparents.

CONTRIBUTORS

Marta K. Albert
Doctoral Candidate, Reading
    Department
University at Albany–State
    University of New York
Albany, New York, USA

Jackie Marshall Arnold
Project Coordinator, Department
    of Teacher Education
University of Dayton
Dayton, Ohio, USA

Arlene L. Barry
Associate Professor, Department
    of Curriculum and Teaching
University of Kansas
Lawrence, Kansas, USA

Allen Berger
Professor Emeritus and Heckert
    Professor of Reading and Writing
    (1998–2006)
Miami University
Oxford, Ohio, USA

Molly D. Dahl
Graduate Assistant, Department
    of Teacher Education
University of Dayton
Dayton, Ohio, USA

James Flood
Distinguished Professor
    of Education
San Diego State University
San Diego, California, USA

Edward Fry
Professor Emeritus
Rutgers University
New Brunswick, New Jersey, USA

Aviva Gray
Archival Consultant
Archival Management and
    Historical Editing Program
New York University
New York, New York, USA

Priscilla L. Griffith
Professor and Department Chair
Department of Instructional
    Leadership and Academic
    Curriculum
University of Oklahoma
Norman, Oklahoma, USA

Laurie A. Guthrie
Reading Intervention Teacher
San Diego State University–
    City Heights Collaborative
San Diego, California, USA

Douglas K. Hartman
Professor
University of Connecticut, Neag
   School of Education
Storrs, Connecticut, USA

Susan E. Israel
Assistant Professor, Department
   of Teacher Education
University of Dayton
Dayton, Ohio, USA

George Kamberelis
Associate Professor, Department
   of Reading, School of Education
University at Albany–State
   University of New York
Albany, New York, USA

Douglas Kaufman
Associate Professor of Curriculum
   and Instruction
University of Connecticut, Neag
   School of Education
Storrs, Connecticut, USA

James R. King
Professor, Childhood Education
University of South Florida
Tampa, Florida, USA

Diane Lapp
Distinguished Professor
   of Education
San Diego State University
San Diego, California, USA

Carol Lauritzen
Professor of Education
Eastern Oregon University
La Grande, Oregon, USA

Dixie D. Massey
Assistant Professor
University of Puget Sound
Orting, Washington, USA

Richard J. Meyer
Professor, Department of Language,
   Literacy, and Sociocultural
   Studies
University of New Mexico
Albuquerque, New Mexico, USA

Karla J. Möller
Assistant Professor of Language
   and Literacy
Department of Curriculum
   and Instruction
University of Illinois
Champaign, Illinois, USA

Charles Monaghan
Independent Scholar and Author
Charlottesville, Virginia, USA

E. Jennifer Monaghan
Professor Emerita
Brooklyn College of The City
   University of New York
Brooklyn, New York, USA

David W. Moore
Professor of Education, College
of Teacher Education
and Leadership
Arizona State University
Phoenix, Arizona, USA

Jolene B. Reed
K–3 Literacy Coordinator/Reading
Recovery Teacher Leader
Rio Rancho Public Schools
Rio Rancho, New Mexico, USA

Jiening Ruan
Associate Professor of
Reading/Literacy Education
Department of Instructional
Leadership and Academic
Curriculum
University of Oklahoma
Norman, Oklahoma, USA

Mary-Kate Sableski
Adjunct Faculty
University of Dayton
Dayton, Ohio, USA

Misty Sailors
Assistant Professor, College
of Education and Human
Development
University of Texas at San Antonio
San Antonio, Texas, USA

Lou Ann Sears
Director, Learning Resources
Center
University of Pittsburgh
at Greensburg
Greensburg, Pennsylvania, USA

Norman A. Stahl
Professor and Chair, Department
of Literacy Education
Northern Illinois University
DeKalb, Illinois, USA

Kristin Stoll
English Teacher
Mason High School
Mason, Ohio, USA

Arlette Ingram Willis
Professor, Department
of Curriculum and Instruction,
College of Education
University of Illinois at Urbana-
Champaign
Champaign, Illinois, USA

Joseph E. Zimmer
Director, MSED Literacy Programs
in the School of Education
St. Bonaventure University
St. Bonaventure, New York, USA

FOREWORD

$\mathcal{T}$HE HISTORY OF reading is an interesting subsection of the history of education. It has some colorful characters and significant movements in one of education's most controversial and important subjects. At one of the first reading conferences I ever attended, which was in the early 1950s in Los Angeles, California, USA, Emmett Betts was a featured speaker. One of the sidelights was that he arrived by flying his own airplane all the way across the United States from Philadelphia, Pennsylvania, USA. Now, this might not seem too remarkable today, but remember that it was only about 25 years after Charles Lindbergh had first flown across the Atlantic Ocean. However, it was not his flying that put Betts in the Reading Hall of Fame. It was more likely because he was the author of the most widely used college textbook on reading teaching methods in the United States, *Foundations of Reading Instruction* (1946), or possibly it was because of his idea of three levels of reading ability—(1) independent, (2) instructional, and (3) frustrational—that is still taught in many colleges and universities today.

Certainly, the history of reading is much older than the Reading Hall of Fame. In fact, the Reading Hall of Fame did not exist until 1973, when Russell Cassell, who was the editor of the journal *Reading Improvement*, started it. He and his staff selected four well-known founding members: (1) Helen Robinson, (2) Emmett Betts, (3) Donald Durrell, and (4) Nila Banton Smith. These founding members met and selected other distinctive contemporary reading leaders to become the original Reading Hall of Fame members. These were Miles Tinker, Edgar Dale, Constance McCullough, Guy Buswell, Guy Bond, George Spache, Marion Monroe, Paul Witty, Sterl Artley, and Nancy Larrick. Since 1973, the Reading Hall of Fame has added two to four living members in most years. However, the original members discovered that there were other important leaders in the reading field who had died before 1973 (such as William Scott Gray). As a result, the founding and original members generated a list of early reading pioneers, who are the subject of this book. In other words, the reading pioneers are persons who were quite eligible to be members of the Reading Hall of Fame but who had died before it was founded.

For the last several decades the Reading Hall of Fame has held a closed yearly meeting at the International Reading Association's annual conventions. In addition, the Reading Hall of Fame sponsors a meeting open to all Association convention attendees that features some of its members discoursing on timely topics. In recent years, the public meeting has featured newly elected members. In 2005, along with the Association's celebration of its 50th anniversary, the Reading Hall of Fame organized a series of programs during the annual convention in which the members spoke on topics for which they are known, providing a sort of living history.

However, the Reading Hall of Fame is not an official part of the International Reading Association. Most of its members belong to the Association, and some of its members are even past presidents of the Association, but the Reading Hall of Fame's membership, finances, governing rules, and customs are independent of it.

Scholars in the history of reading might be interested to know that the Reading Hall of Fame tries to keep in the Association library a personal file of those members who were elected after the original members. These files contain a photo, a vita, and a selected article or two.

The office of Historian of the Reading Hall of Fame was created by an amendment to the bylaws in 1994, and Alan Robinson served as the first Historian until his death in 2000. I became Historian succeeding him. I received the Reading Hall of Fame files from his widow and made arrangements to store them and succeeding files in the Association's library in Newark, Delaware, USA. They contained brief folders on most of the then-living members and some unsorted secretarial files. The files are a long way from being complete, but they are considerably better than nothing. My tenure of office ended in 2005 and the succeeding Historian is Dr. James Hoffman of the University of Texas at Austin. I should mention that Dr. Ira Aaron at the University of Georgia in Atlanta really served as unofficial historian before Alan Robinson, and I hope his personal files on the Reading Hall of Fame will someday be housed with the Reading Hall of Fame files.

The present project on the early reading pioneers was an attempt to fill in the gap of missing historical record on this group of people. The project started when I placed a call for help in the newsletter of the History of Reading Special Interest Group (SIG) of the International Reading Association (Fry,

2004) and Susan E. Israel responded. Our first intention was to have someone create files for the reading pioneers, but Susan saw bigger possibilities and transformed the files into the chapters of this book.

The book makes valuable information about the reading pioneers available to current and future scholars of the history of reading, much more so than do thin files about some important past leaders of the reading field.

The Reading Hall of Fame is greatly indebted to this book's editors, Susan E. Israel and E. Jennifer Monaghan, for selecting the chapter authors and putting the entire manuscript together. We are also indebted to each of the chapter authors for doing the research and writing. They have made an important contribution to the history of the reading field.

—*Edward Fry*

REFERENCES

Betts, E.A. (1946). *Foundations of reading instruction.* New York: American Book.
Fry, E. (2004). Call for biographies of reading pioneers. *History of Reading News*, 27(2), 7.

PREFACE

ECAUSE OF MY interest in learning about the past through story-telling and historical documents, I decided to join the History of Reading Special Interest Group of the International Reading Association in 2002. As a member I receive a biannual newsletter, the *History of Reading News*. When I received the spring 2004 issue, one particular announcement titled "Call for Biographies of Reading Pioneers" (Fry, 2004) caught my attention. The announcement reads as follows:

> Edward Fry, Professor Emeritus at Rutgers University, who is completing a four-year term as Historian for the Reading Hall of Fame,...has asked for the assistance of the History of Reading Special Interest Group in reconstructing vitae or brief biographies of those individuals identified as Reading Pioneers by the Hall of Fame....The list of Reading Pioneers is: May Hill Arbuthnot, James McKean [sic] Cattell, Walter F. Dearborn, Raymond Dodge, Arthur I. Gates, William S. Gray, Ernest Horn, Edmund Burke Huey, Charles Hubbard Judd, Bernice E. Leary, David H. Russell, Ruth Strang, Edward L. Thorndike, Douglas Waples, Robert S. Woodworth, and Laura Zirbes. Interested parties should contact Dr. Fry. (p. 7)

Although I was unfamiliar with the Reading Hall of Fame, I did know something about Edward Fry because "Ed Fry's Reading Autobiography" (2001) had appeared in the *History of Reading News*, and I was very curious to learn more about early reading pioneers. My response to the call for biographies of early reading pioneers began with a letter to Ed that expressed my interest in doing the research, which eventually led to our meeting at the International Reading Association's 49th Annual Convention in Reno, Nevada, USA. Our discussion fueled the ideas for this book. Some of our discussion included the following actions that I needed to take:

- Gather photos, articles, and so on—essentially any items owned by people who knew the pioneers and that could be shared.

- Ask veteran members of the Reading Hall of Fame, such as Kenneth and Yetta Goodman, for firsthand knowledge and stories about some of the pioneers.

- Conduct research to glean more knowledge to create a dialogue and discover how the field of reading has matured and developed.

- Learn lessons from the experiences of the pioneers that can be applied to the future.

- Understand the pioneers' major contributions: What were those contributions, and how are they related to the field of reading instruction?

Before our meeting ended, Ed gave me a brochure titled *Reading Hall of Fame*, which contains a list of the early reading pioneers. These pioneers were elected posthumously and as a group by members of the Reading Hall of Fame in 1973, the year the organization was established, for their contributions to the field of reading. The brochure also summarizes the purpose of the Reading Hall of Fame, which is to further improvement in reading instruction. According to its tenets, one way to accomplish this goal is to identify needed research and trends of the past that hold promise for the future. A remark by Bernice E. Cullinan sums up the lasting impact of these pioneers and of the Reading Hall of Fame members: "We walk among giants in the reading field."

Two emotions raced through me as I said goodbye to Ed after our meeting. The first was confidence about the value and purpose of "my" new research project. The second was a sense of urgency to begin gathering research about these giants in the field of reading.

At first the task of gathering research seemed overwhelming. I soon realized that it would be more efficacious to invite others to work with me on the project. I began a review of the literature on historical research to familiarize myself with others who had experience in writing about history. I contacted many of these authors, as well as a few new to the area of historical research, and urged them to join me in responding to Ed's call. The response was overwhelming. One of the researchers who responded asked me if I had contacted E. Jennifer Monaghan, who has published widely on the history of literacy. When I managed to do so, Jennifer was very supportive of the idea but at the same time asked many questions. From that time on, Jennifer's questions helped guide our conversations toward producing a better book. I was trying to integrate my knowledge of literacy and reading as it related to the teaching profession, and Jennifer was challenging me to pay very close attention to the dynamics of the historical research process. We collaborated on the book through e-mail for several weeks. Late one evening, when I was contemplating the book, I realized that Jennifer's strengths as an expert in historical research and her experience as an editor were needed for the book, and I invited her to be my coeditor.

As fast as the offers came to help, so did the questions about and objections to the choice of pioneers. Why weren't Emmett Betts and Nila Banton Smith included? (They were very much alive and already members of the Reading Hall of Fame.) Surely we should have included more women? (The choices made in 1973 reflect that time period, not my own opinions.) What happened to Ellen Cyr, who was the first woman in the United States to have a widely sold reading series? (The focus of the Reading Hall of Famers on research unquestionably neglected the authors of earlier reading series in general, and women authors in particular.) To all these questions, my answer was the same: The pioneers were not selected by me. Instead, they were a preselected group, chosen in 1973 by the existing members of the Reading Hall of Fame, as Ed Fry explains in this book's foreword.

If we were choosing the pioneers today, we might come up with a very different group, and certainly one that would include more women. We hope that *Shaping the Reading Field: The Impact of Early Reading Pioneers, Scientific Research, and Progressive Ideas* will encourage reading researchers to write about the lives of other pioneers in reading. Indeed, we hope that this book will be but the first of a series of biographies of those women and men who have made major contributions to reading instruction. We welcome accounts of the many other persons who were and are important to the reading field.

The Need to Document the Lives of Early Reading Pioneers

There is a compelling need to document the historical achievements—and failures—of those involved in the reading field. Members of the International Reading Association have acknowledged that need by passing two resolutions affirming the importance and value of historical research and the need to publish such research (Delegates Assembly of the International Reading Association, 1981, 1997). *Historical research* is defined as the technique used by historians to reconstruct and interpret the past (Harris & Hodges, 1995). Building on this definition, Stahl and Hartman (2004) state that history is about knowing the past and gathering pieces and parts of evidence while it remains (p. 175). The authors of the chapters in *Shaping the Reading Field* have used historical research based on qualitative, quantitative, and oral history approaches (Monaghan & Hartman, 2000) to interpret and sort the evidence of the past that relates to the field of reading and reading instruction.

Following the recommendations of Stahl and Hartman (2004) and Monaghan and Hartman (2000), and the rationale for how historical research should be written, *Shaping the Reading Field* has two main thrusts. The first and major thrust is to document the lives of the early reading pioneers, whose professional lives spanned the decades from the 1880s to the 1970s. Each of these 16 reading researchers, reading practitioners, and specialists in children's literature and adult reading has made a significant contribution to the field of reading. Well known in their own lifetimes, the pioneers' stories and contributions are now brought together in this book for the first time. In addition to filling a gap in the history of the field of reading, the second purpose is to demonstrate the process of biography itself. Contributors describe the joys, along with the trials and tribulations, of locating the sources for their accounts of the early reading pioneers. This book is, therefore, a valuable tool that offers models of the process of historical research as well as presenting its products.

Our contributors demonstrate that the present field of reading was grounded on scientific research from the first. With the possible exception of the children's literature chapters, virtually every chapter in this book reveals that those who taught the young to read based their practice on the scientific evidence available to them. Far from reading instruction having no basis in scientific research, it was precisely such exploration, beginning with eye-movement research, that led to the creation of the field as a discipline separate from both educational psychology and the study of education in general.

How to Use This Book

Shaping the Reading Field can be a valuable tool in many ways. First, the contributors to this book have organized historical research in a way that will help researchers and others in the field of reading think critically about the major contributions of the pioneers and their influences on the field of reading. Second, we hope the format of this book will appeal to a wide range of people who work in the field of reading, teachers as well as those devoted primarily to research. Each chapter includes questions that facilitate reflection and discussion about how the early reading pioneers have influenced the field of reading. Third, this book provides reading teachers with a resource that documents the scientific research base that guided much of reading practice during the first seven decades of the 20th century.

Organization of the Book

The introduction to this book anchors the pioneers firmly in the theoretical, cultural, social, and scientific contexts of their times. Jennifer (in the introduction) describes the emergence of psychology as a separate discipline, followed by the emergence of educational psychology as its own field. Educational psychology, in its turn, led to the formation of a field of scholarly endeavor specifically devoted to reading—the reading field as it is known today.

The next 16 chapters are devoted to the early reading pioneers themselves, with the chapters grouped into five parts. These groupings are necessarily somewhat arbitrary—certain pioneers might have been placed differently—but they represent our best judgment on the role that each pioneer played in "shaping" the field of reading.

Part I, The Psychologists: Researchers of Basic Reading Processes, focuses on the earliest form of research into reading processes—eye-movement research. Our contributors document the innovative experiments of three psychologists. James McKeen Cattell (Arlette Ingram Willis, chapter 1), who is documented as an unrelenting eugenicist, was the unflagging promoter of psychology as a science and the first to observe that readers perceive letters in words more speedily than isolated letters. His student, Robert Sessions Woodworth (Allen Berger, Dixie D. Massey, Kristin Stoll, and Aviva Gray, chapter 2), became highly regarded for his eclectic approach to psychological theory and his masterful textbooks. Raymond Dodge (Dixie D. Massey, chapter 3) emerges as the inventor of the tachistoscope and an experimenter whose rigorous observations of eye movements extended our knowledge of visual processes.

Part II, The Educational Psychologists: Researchers Applying Scientific Principles to Reading Instruction, moves the focus to those who saw the relevance of scientific research to educational progress. The key philosophical belief animating the life and work of Charles Hubbard Judd (Jackie Marshall Arnold and Mary-Kate Sableski, chapter 4) was his faith in the scientific study of education. Of particular concern to him were the roles to be played by silent and oral reading. In the work of Edward Lee Thorndike (Lou Ann Sears, chapter 5), we find educational psychology separating itself from psychology to become yet another discipline, with Thorndike's views on connectionism and of reading as reasoning wielding a vast influence on reading instruction. Cattell's student Walter Fenno Dearborn (Joseph E. Zimmer, chapter 6) focused on individual differences among learners, laying the groundwork for separate assessments of intelligence quotients and visual and auditory skills, along with differential treatment for different disabilities.

Part III, The Progressives: Researchers Committed to Progressive Education, presents a contrast to the sections that precede and follow it. It illuminates the tension between educational psychologists (particularly Thorndike) and educational progressives (such as John Dewey) concerning the direction that reading instruction should take. Edmund Burke Huey (Jolene B. Reed and Richard J. Meyer, chapter 7) was the first to synthesize the findings of psychological experiments in reading up to 1908. Yet he also portrayed what reading instruction looked like when conducted according to the progressive philosophy of Dewey. Laura Zirbes (David W. Moore, chapter 8) was in her day the leading practitioner and promoter of the progressive reading instruction admired by Huey.

The pioneers in Part IV, The Book Enthusiasts: Pioneers Engaged in Exploring Children's Books and Adult Reading, were all involved with books in some form. May Hill Arbuthnot (Charles Monaghan, Susan E. Israel, and Molly D. Dahl, chapter 9) was the first to write a comprehensive text for teachers about children's literature. It was published for decades. The adventurous Bernice Elizabeth Leary (Karla J. Möller, chapter 10), the only pioneer not to be a full-time member of a university, became an editor and leading anthologist of children's literature. Douglas Waples (George Kamberelis and Marta K. Albert, chapter 11) anticipated the relatively new field of the history of the book in his innovative inquiries as to what adults read and why.

The pioneers grouped together in Part V, The Reading and Spelling Experts: Researchers Engaged in Writing Texts for Teachers and Schoolbooks for Children, were united in establishing reading as a separate scholarly discipline with its own research, publications, and superstars. What the pioneers in this part have in common is that, in addition to their research into reading processes, they were all engaged in writing textbooks for teachers and schoolbooks for the elementary classroom. Spelling was included in this enterprise, and Ernest Horn (Jiening Ruan and Priscilla L. Griffith, chapter 12), admired for his early work on methods of teaching social sciences, became to spelling research and practice what William Scott Gray was to reading. Gray (Carol Lauritzen, chapter 13), a prolific writer and summarizer of reading research, was the leading author of the Scott Foresman basal reading series, widely known as the Dick and Jane readers. Lauritzen portrays Gray as the man most identified with creating the reading field as a separate field of research and practice. Arthur Irving Gates (Misty Sailors, chapter 14), a junior colleague of Thorndike at Columbia University, brought his gifts as an educational psychologist to the field, publishing vocabularies for the primary grades and books on reading disability, and becoming the senior author of a major reading series, Macmillan's Work-Play Books. Ruth May Strang (Diane Lapp, Laurie A. Guthrie, and James Flood, chapter 15) of Teachers College, Columbia University, became one of the best-known women in the reading field, excluding those still alive in 1973 when living members of the Reading Hall of Fame drew up the list of early reading pioneers. Like Gray, Gates, and Strang, David Harris Russell (Arlene L. Barry, chapter 16) authored children's readers (the Ginn Basic Readers) in addition to conducting his research and supervising his graduate students. Using a history-of-the-book approach (Darnton, 1989) Barry describes the attention Russell paid to every detail of the writing and publication process.

The book's conclusion, "Reflections on the Early Reading Pioneers and Their Biographers" by Douglas Kaufman and Douglas K. Hartman, offers a critical look at the pioneers, their achievements, and their flaws. The authors also reflect on how the pioneers are represented by their biographers, arguing that each chapter tells as much about the storyteller as about the pioneer.

Finally, in a brief afterword, Jennifer and I offer the reader a chance to reflect on the lessons of history and historical research, and on biography itself.

The appendixes switch from the products of biography to its processes. Joseph E. Zimmer (Appendix A) offers the reader hints on how to undertake biographical research, while Aviva Gray offers insights on finding sources from an archivist's perspective (Appendix B). Norman A. Stahl and James R. King (Appendix C) provide the reader with an overview of undertaking oral research projects, suggesting that literacy researchers at any level can undertake oral history. A matrix of the pioneers follows (Appendix D), providing a bird's-eye view of such features of the pioneers as where they were born; when and where they received their degrees; and how they related to one another as teachers, colleagues, and students.

We need to say a word here about our conception of this book and our decisions on documentation. We encouraged our authors to look for the pioneers' descendants, confident that pioneers' relatives would have personal reminiscences to contribute. Thanks to detective work on the Internet by our main researchers, Aviva Gray and Laurie A. Guthrie, our contributors were able to find a surprisingly large number of relatives willing to talk about their fathers, fathers-in-law, or grandfathers. (In the first half of the 20th century, women who became academics rarely married.) We hope you will agree that these memories greatly enrich the portraits of the pioneers as individuals.

Regarding documentation, our publisher, the International Reading Association, consistently uses American Psychological Association (APA) style for its publications. However, we had to make some adaptations to a style well suited to the reporting of scientific research but less well so to historiography. APA style insists only on providing page numbers for direct quotations. We, however, decided that it was crucial to document paraphrased material with page numbers as well. On all those occasions where historians would have supplied page numbers in footnotes, we required them of our contributors. This decision, in fact, conforms to APA guidelines, which encourage the inclusion of page numbers "when it would help an interested reader locate the relevant passage in a long or complex text" (APA, 2001, p. 121).

Organization of the Biographical Chapters

Each chapter in Parts I through V includes the following sections:

- "Historical Research Process": In this section the contributors describe their own experiences with undertaking the research. Many of our contributors were new to this kind of research, and we as editors asked them to share with readers the challenges that such research presents.

- "Personal and Professional Life": This section usually begins with the story of an incident in the subject's life before presenting an overview of his or her key activities, which include events such as marriage and major publications. Understanding the biographee's personal and professional experiences early on in the chapter humanizes the historical research journey.

- "Philosophical Beliefs and Guiding Principles": While summarizing the principles held by the subjects, contributors include brief descriptions of the subject's major contributions to fields other than reading. Our assumption is that the pioneers' contributions to the reading field can best be understood as flowing from their theoretical positions and interests in general.

- "Contributions to the Field of Reading": In this section, the contributors focus on the subject's most important contributions to the field of reading and his or her impact on the reading research and practice of the present as well as the past.

- "Lessons for the Future": In this section, the contributors not only identify lessons to be learned from the early reading pioneer but also offer a critique of the pioneer's theories and practices. Here the contributors offer readers insights into how and why the profession has moved on and what challenges still remain.

- "Reflection Questions": At the end of each chapter are additional reflection questions that the reader can use to think more deeply about the life of the biographee and how lessons of the past can apply to the future.

Our goal for this book is to help readers deepen their understanding of how the past has influenced the present. We also hope that the book will offer some practical benefits. If you are a reading researcher, you may wish to use the hints on how to undertake research that the contributors describe and the appendixes provide. If you are a university professor, you may consider using this text in a history of reading course. And if you are a teacher, perhaps the lives and contributions of those who have labored before you may inspire you in your own dedicated labors on behalf of children's reading education.

I personally have learned four valuable lessons from the early reading pioneers. First, we should value professional development. Second, service to one's profession is important to the future of that profession. Third, all teachers, not just reading teachers, should instill a love of literature in children. Finally, teachers and researchers alike should be passionate about the teaching of reading and use this passion to create positive literacy learning outcomes. I hope you, too, will appreciate how we still walk among giants in the field of reading.

—*Susan E. Israel*

REFERENCES

American Psychological Association. (2001). *Publication manual of the American Psychological Association* (5th ed.). Washington, DC: Author.

Darnton, R. (1989). What is the history of books? In C.N. Davidson (Ed.), *Reading in America: Literature and social history* (pp. 27–52). Baltimore: The Johns Hopkins University Press.

Delegates Assembly of the International Reading Association. (1981). *Resolution on the history of reading instruction*. Newark, DE: International Reading Association.

Delegates Assembly of the International Reading Association. (1997). *Resolution on the history of reading/literacy*. Newark, DE: International Reading Association.

Fry, E. (2001). Ed Fry's reading autobiography. *History of Reading News*, 24(2), 1–2, 5.

Fry, E. (2004). Call for biographies of reading pioneers. *History of Reading News*, 27(2), 7.

Harris, T.L., & Hodges, R.E. (1995). *The literacy dictionary: The vocabulary of reading and writing*. Newark, DE: International Reading Association.

Monaghan, E.J., & Hartman, D.K. (2000). Undertaking historical research in literacy. In M. Kamil, P. Mosenthal, P.D. Pearson, & R. Barr (Eds.), *Handbook of reading research* (Vol. III, pp. 109–121). Mahwah, NJ: Erlbaum.

Reading Hall of Fame. *Reading Hall of Fame* [Brochure]. (2004). Newark, DE: Author.

Stahl, N.A., & Hartman, D.K. (2004). Doing historical research on literacy. In N.K. Duke & M.H. Mallette (Eds.), *Literacy research methodologies* (pp. 170–196). New York: Guilford.

ACKNOWLEDGMENTS

Editors

Susan E. Israel

I am grateful to Ed Fry for his confidence in giving me the responsibility of researching the early reading pioneers and for his support of the idea of publishing a comprehensive volume highlighting their contributions. My thanks also go to Colleen Wildenhaus, Editorial Director at the University of Dayton, Dayton, Ohio, USA, for help with early reviews of the proposal.

E. Jennifer Monaghan

As your coeditor, I would like to thank you, Susan, for inviting me to share in the editing of this book. It has been an adventure I would not have missed.

Both Susan and I would like to address very special thanks to our contributors. Dixie Massey inspired us to add the "Historical Research Process" sections and aided us in other ways. Most of you were blissfully unaware of what a daunting task you would face in researching and writing a biography. We have been greatly impressed by your willingness to submerge yourselves in the often chilly waters of historical research and your devotion to the task. I am afraid I tried your patience to the limits with my unceasing demands for revisions, but you all surfaced with what was needed. Many of your comments in the "Historical Research Process" sections suggest that you acquired an enduring appreciation of our intellectual and pedagogic predecessors in the reading field and of the value of historiography itself.

Last, but by no means least, we would like to thank, at the International Reading Association, Corinne Mooney, Executive Editor, Books, for the care she has taken over this book. She has been a model of the good editor: insightful, efficient, prompt in her responses to our many queries, and courteous at all times. Special thanks, too, are owed to Stacey Sharp, Developmental Editor, Books, for her exemplary care and patience as the publication proceeded. We are also grateful to Shannon Fortner, Editorial Production Manager, for her valuable work.

Contributors

The following authors express their sincere thanks and appreciation to the people listed.

Arlene L. Barry (Russell, chapter 16)

David R. and Andrew Russell, sons of David Harris Russell; Isabel Robertson Barnsley, niece of David Russell; Robert Ruddell, professor emeritus of the University of California, Berkeley, and colleague of David Russell; Linda Long, Manuscripts Librarian, Division of Special Collections and University Archives, Knight Library, University of Oregon, Eugene; and Patrick Hayes, University Archives and Special Collections, University of Saskatchewan, Saskatoon, Canada.

Allen Berger and Kristin Stoll (Woodworth, chapter 2)

Patrick Deville, a graduate assistant at Miami University, Oxford, Ohio; Nina Rosner, Adult Services Librarian, Cuyahoga County Public Library, Beachwood, Ohio; and Tara C. Craig, Reference Services Supervisor, Rare Book & Manuscript Library, Butler Library, Columbia University, New York City.

Aviva Gray (Appendix B and Woodworth, chapter 2)

Jennifer Govan, Assistant Director of Collection and Curriculum Support Services at the Gottesman Libraries, Teachers College, Columbia University, New York City; Jeffrey Walker, Research Assistant, the Gottesman Libraries, Teachers College, Columbia University, New York City; Paul Schlotthauer, Reference Librarian and Archivist at Pratt Institute, New York City; and Gary Natriello, Professor of Sociology and Education, and Director of the Gottesman Libraries, Teachers College, Columbia University, New York City.

George Kamberelis and Marta K. Albert (Waples, chapter 11)

Carola Lacy and Terry Achelis, daughters of Douglas Waples, who shared memories and stories of their father that greatly enrich the chapter; Anita Lacy, granddaughter of Waples, who shared memories and photos and provided many leads for further research; and Steve Achelis, grandson of Waples, who sent us the digital photo used in the book.

Diane Lapp, Laurie A. Guthrie, and James Flood (Strang, chapter 15)
Aviva Gray, Archivist, New York, New York, for her invaluable research. (We can only imagine how impossible our quest for information about Strang would have been without her.) Pamela Hoagland, Strang's final doctoral student, Tucson, Arizona, who shared articles, stories, papers, letters, notes, photos, and treasured memories that brought Ruth Strang to life for us; and Patricia Anders, Professor of Education, University of Arizona, Tucson, Arizona, who shared personal insights about Strang for our chapter.

Carol Lauritzen (Gray, chapter 13)
Helen Huus, informant extraordinaire about Dr. Gray and the early history of the International Reading Association; William S. Gray III for sharing personal memories of his father.

Dixie D. Massey (Dodge, chapter 3)
Lizette Royer, The Archives of the History of American Psychology, Akron, Ohio.

Karla J. Möller (Leary, chapter 10)
Professor Nancy O'Brien and Librarian Joyce Berg, the Education and Social Science Library at the University of Illinois at Urbana-Champaign, who helped track down copies of Leary's anthologies; Special Collections Reader Services Liaison Katherine Hodson, Reference Librarian Christine Walters, and Library Assistant Janet Weaver of the Iowa Women's Archives at the University of Iowa Libraries, Iowa City, Iowa, who assisted in obtaining documents related to Leary's life and work; and Leary's family friend and librarian emeritus Mary Noble, University of Iowa Libraries, without whose research support and willingness to share memories of Leary my chapter would be missing its heart.

Charles Monaghan, Susan E. Israel, and Molly D. Dahl (Arbuthnot, chapter 9)
Beth Earley, Graduate Assistant for Curriculum and Website Development, Department of Teacher Education, University of Dayton, Ohio, for her help with the chapter in its early stages; Tom Steman, Archivist, and Heather Arnold Henderson, Technical Support Archivist, of the Case Western Reserve University Archives, Cleveland, Ohio; Aviva Gray, Archivist, New York, New York, for research; and Kayla Zimmer, St. Bonaventure University, for valuable suggestions on the chapter.

Jolene B. Reed and Richard J. Meyer (Huey, chapter 7)

Lauren Reed and Zoe Meyer, research assistants; and Douglas Hartman for sharing his unpublished research and guiding us to a portrait of Huey.

Jiening Ruan and Priscilla L. Griffith (Horn, chapter 12)

Diane Horn, Mrs. Thomas D. Horn, and the librarians and staff in the University of Iowa Archives, Iowa City, Iowa, for their assistance.

Misty Sailors (Gates, chapter 14)

Aviva Gray, Archivist, New York, New York; Dr. Walter MacGinitie, former Professor of Psychology and Education at Teachers College, Columbia University, New York, and Lansdowne Scholar and Professor of Education at the University of Victoria, British Columbia, Canada; and Dr. Joanne R. Nurss, Professor Emeritus of Educational Psychology at Georgia State University, Atlanta, Georgia.

Lou Ann Sears (Thorndike, chapter 5)

Ed Fry for thinking of this project, and Doug Hartman for the start he gave me in this field.

Arlette Ingram Willis (Cattell, chapter 1)

Reference librarians at the University of Illinois at Urbana-Champaign, Illinois; Kimberly N. Parker, graduate student at the University of Illinois at Urbana-Champaign; members of the United Kingdom Aristotelian Society; Professor Jonathan Baron, University of Pennsylvania, Philadelphia, Pennsylvania; and Patrick Kerwin, Manuscript Reference Librarian, the Library of Congress, Washington, DC.

Joseph E. Zimmer (Dearborn, chapter 6)

Natalie Cruickshank, Dearborn's daughter, who shared many happy stories about her family in the writing of the chapter.

Scientific Research and Progressive Education: Contexts for the Early Reading Pioneers, 1870–1956

□ ▪ ■

By E. Jennifer Monaghan

> And so to completely analyze what we do when we read
> would almost be the acme of a psychologist's
> achievements, for it would be to describe very many of the
> most intricate workings of the human mind, as well as to
> unravel the tangled story of the most remarkable specific
> performance that civilization has learned in all its history.
>
> —EDMUND BURKE HUEY (1908/1913, P. 6)

With these words, Edmund Burke Huey, in *The Psychology and Pedagogy of Reading*, depicts the complexity of the reading process and its relevance to psychology, the study of the mind. Both the first and second editions of *Theoretical Models and Processes of Reading* (Singer & Ruddell, 1970, p. xi; Singer & Ruddell, 1976, p. ix) use Huey's words to begin their prefaces. The connection Huey made between the reading process

---

Shaping the Reading Field: The Impact of Early Reading Pioneers, Scientific Research, and Progressive Ideas, edited by Susan E. Israel and E. Jennifer Monaghan. © 2007 by the International Reading Association.

and psychology was prescient: It foreshadowed the emergence of the reading field as a discipline separate from, but deeply rooted in, psychological investigation. (For Huey's biography, see Jolene B. Reed and Richard J. Meyer's account, chapter 7, this volume.)

Other paths might have been taken. The reading field and those claiming expertise in reading might have been embraced by the humanities, for instance, particularly by English departments, which had already laid claim to expertise in composition and in reading a particular class of reading material—literature. But that was not to be, and I attempt to explain the reasons for the path that was taken. I shall argue that the emergence of the reading field as a separate discipline is the climax of a story of three different academic groups that successively carved out separate intellectual and professional spaces for themselves. Psychology was the first to lay claim to its legitimacy as a science, creating itself from philosophy and physiology; then educational psychology hewed its own niche from psychology; and, finally, the reading field evolved in large part from educational psychology. All three fields were products of the scientific movement described in this introduction.

There is another aspect to this story, however. The early years of the reading field are also the tale of a contest between two competing approaches to reading education: the progressivism associated with John Dewey on the one hand, and the scientific movement in education on the other. The resounding victory of the second approach, the scientific movement, is evident from a list prepared in 1973 by leaders of the reading field as they attempted to identify the field's deceased luminaries and elect them as a group to the newly created Reading Hall of Fame. Those on the list are the early reading pioneers who are the subjects of this book. Of the 12 men and 4 women elected, Huey and Laura Zirbes were, as we shall see in the chapters that follow, the only two pioneers who were solidly at the progressive, Dewey-inspired end of the theoretical spectrum. (For Zirbes, see David W. Moore's account, chapter 8, this volume.)

In the discussion that follows I first review briefly the educational background to reading instruction at the end of the 19th century and the growth of progressive education. I then turn to the emergence of psychology, educational psychology, and, finally, the reading field itself. The theories held by specialists in any academic field become embodied in the materials they publish. Although reading series, and the reading methodologies on which they are based, do not necessarily play a large role in the chapters on the individual early reading pioneers, I use them as a point of entry into understanding where the history of the pioneers has led reading educators to the present day because it happened that basal readers and reading methods turned out to be a source of considerable conflict between professionals and laypersons.

At the end of each section, I take a look at relevant yearbooks of the National Society for the Study of Education (NSSE), an organization dedicated to the scientific study of education. The NSSE was reorganized in 1901 from the Herbart Society (founded in 1895) and became the key professional society for all involved in research in education. The first NSSE yearbook to deal exclusively with the teaching of reading, rather than with reading as just one component of elementary education, appeared in 1925 (Whipple, 1925). The topic was revisited at intervals of 12 years (Whipple, 1937; Henry, 1949). These three yearbooks, therefore, provide a convenient summary of how the theories and practices of reading professionals evolved over time.

Reading Instruction and the Rise of Progressive Education, 1870–1918

Schooling in the last quarter of the 19th century was largely conducted along traditional lines. In rural areas, teachers in one-room schools taught small or large classes of children of all ages; in the cities, sorting children by age into grades was well established. Rote learning played some role in most classrooms. No matter what the site was, the teaching of reading centered on *readers*—reading series that were later called *basal readers* to distinguish them from the children who read them. Once the principle was established that the school could dictate the textbooks to be used, the choice of a reading series largely controlled how reading was taught in that school.

Considerable experimentation in reading had taken place since 1825, when educational reformers began *The American Journal of Education* as a vehicle for ideas based on Pestalozzian principles. The Swiss educator Johann Pestalozzi (1746–1827) rejected harsh discipline and rote learning. He argued that young children learned from concrete experiences and should be taught from whole to part, instead of from part to whole as was the common practice. (Geography, for instance, should start not with descriptions of foreign countries but with the child's own home, street, and town, and only then spread to distant parts [Vinovskis & Moran, in press].) Central to all innovation was a new emphasis on understanding. Methodologically, the new ideas took a variety of forms: phonic, whole-word, and sentence approaches to reading instruction.

The old alphabetic method of preceding centuries, still in use in the 1870s in many schools, had required children to identify an unfamiliar word by saying aloud the names the letters of the word, syllable by syllable. Spoken letters and syllables were considered key to every aspect of the written language, to reading and writing as well as spelling. In contrast, the phonic approach, one of the post-1825 innovations, asked children to treat letters as sounds and successively "sound them" out and "blend" them. Whole-word (look-and-say, sight) instruction, another novelty, appeared first in 1828 in Samuel Worcester's *Primer of the English Language*, reappeared from time to time, particularly in primers, but did not have a major resurgence until about 1870. Whole-word teaching took two forms: (1) a word-to-letter approach that quickly moved to conventional instruction and (2) a later words-to-meaning approach that moved children directly to meaning, downplaying the role of letters (Mathews, 1966). The third and last of the innovations, the sentence method championed by George Farnham (1881), required children to proceed from a whole sentence down to its component words. All these approaches were clearly distinguished from each other in textbooks for teachers and survived a major consolidation of textbook publishers into the American Book Company in 1890 (Monaghan, Hartman, & Monaghan, 2002; Venezky, 1987).

Ever since its first publication in 1836, the field of 19th-century children's reading instructional texts had been dominated by the famous McGuffey Eclectic Readers series. Its publishers produced successive editions of the series to keep up with their rivals (Lindberg, 1976; Minnich, 1936, pp. 85–87; Vail, 1911, pp. 60–64). The series initially embodied the alphabet method, using a spelling book to help children practice word identification. The year 1879, however, marked a radical innovation in the series: The revised edition of that year moved to a "phonic-word" method (Vail, 1911, p. 59) and added diacritical marks to preparatory word lists. Other series began to put diacritical marks over words likely to be unfamiliar to children, whether or not they moved to a full phonic approach. Yet others offered systematic phonics (e.g., Monroe, 1877) or marked every word diacritically (e.g., Ward, 1896).

At the same time that systematic phonics was becoming popular, a countervailing force was gathering strength that privileged the whole-word approach. The so-called *object method* took advantage of objects familiar to children from their environment and used them as links to written words. It is not surprising that this whole-word approach found favor with the proponents of progressive education, the most important educational innovation of the late 19th and early 20th centuries. The new progressives of the late 19th century adopted and expanded the Pestalozzian principles first widely publicized in the United States in *The American Journal of Education*.

The progressive view was, and indeed still is, that children learn best by natural methods (which included moving from whole to part, rather than from part to whole). Children learn most easily, progressives believed, when they have a vital interest in a subject and act, rather than just talk. It was also a progressive axiom that subject matter should be adapted to the child, not the child to the subject matter. In terms of reading instruction, the whole-word approach provided whole units, not pieces such as letters. Any word of interest to a child was a teachable word, and whole words dodged all the vocabulary problems associated with the alphabet and phonic approaches, both of which were restricted to finding words that exhibited the elements taught to that point. In the eyes of many, the whole-word approach avoided the drill and drudgery associated with alphabetic and phonic instruction.

The educator most successful at translating progressive theory into progressive practice was Colonel Francis Wayland Parker (1837–1902). (His military title was a holdover from his Army service in the U.S. Civil War.) Parker first made his reputation as a progressive when he became superintendent of the schools of Quincy, Massachusetts, USA, from 1875 to 1881. He went on to hold the position of supervisor of Boston schools and then principal of Cook County Normal School in Chicago. In 1894 he published *Talks on Pedagogics* and five years later became the founder and principal of a private experimental school, the Chicago Institute (Kline, Moore, & Moore, 1987).

Parker believed that children should be connected to reading through (a) their interests and background knowledge, (b) content areas, and, at least initially, (c) written words linked to ideas (i.e., sight words). "Reading should be first of all," he wrote, "interesting to the learner" (quoted in Kline, Moore, & Moore, 1987, p. 143). Teachers in his schools used to draw pictures on the chalkboard of a familiar object, such as a hen, and ask the children to relate the written words *a hen* to the picture (p. 146). Reading, writing, listening, and speaking were all integrated into the lesson, and children's reading materials were those dictated or written by the pupils themselves: "Words are given children as they need them" (p. 147). Once children had a stock of sight words, Parker encouraged phonics to assist in word recognition, and the teachers modeled the slow pronunciation of a word: "Point to the c-l-o-ck" (p. 147). Parker even published a monograph, 21 pages long, consisting of word families (i.e., onsets and rimes), such as *flour, hour, sour, scour* (p. 147).

Parker's ideas were eagerly adopted by John Dewey (1859–1952), who had arrived in Chicago himself in 1894 to become chair of the Department of Philosophy at the University of Chicago. At his request, education was subsumed under philosophy, so he had the rare opportunity of uniting psychology, philosophy, and pedagogy under the same administrative umbrella at a time when, as Ellen Lagemann (2000) points out, increasing specialization in academic subjects was already the trend (p. 46). Dewey had become convinced that reforms in education would be most easily achieved in the naturalistic setting of a school. He believed that educational study should advance both social and scientific innovation and that educational efficiency would be improved by creating a more cohesive social system in which learning would be spread among many institutions as well as schools (Lagemann, 2000, pp. 48–49).

The promise of Dewey's Laboratory School, set up in January 1896, under the aegis of the University of Chicago, came to an abrupt end in 1904 when the university arranged to unite the Laboratory School with Parker's school and, because of misunderstandings over the role Dewey's wife was to play in the new school, Dewey resigned from the university (Lagemann, 2000, pp. 47, 55). Now called the Francis W. Parker School, the combined school was singled out by Huey in *The Psychology and Pedagogy of Reading* (1908/1913) as a model of the progressive approach to reading. Huey wrote, "The children learn to read as they learned to talk, 'from a desire to find out or tell something'" (p. 297). He continues, "Some work is done in phonics, but this is entirely distinct from reading" (p. 299).

After his departure from the University of Chicago, Dewey became a professor in the Philosophy Department at Columbia University, New York, but his direct involvement with experimental schooling was at an end. Nonetheless, his aura lived on. Lagemann (2000) puts it well:

> Frequently claimed to have been the father of progressive education and otherwise to have had a profound impact on American education, Dewey may have inspired all sorts of people to do all sorts of things as a result of

his ideas, but...few examples of "Deweyan education" were truly or accurately Deweyan. (p. 42)

Faithful to Dewey's ideas or not, examples of progressive education flourished, particularly at Teachers College, Columbia University, which was now Dewey's academic home. One articulate enthusiast was Dewey's colleague William Heard Kilpatrick, whose classes advocating his own "Project Method" (1918/1924), which "emphasized how one went about teaching and learning more than what one sought to teach and learn" (Lagemann, 2000, p. 109), were always packed with students.

Another influential force, one that had a direct impact on the content of children's readers, was a movement toward "cultivating a taste for good literature," as a course of study put it in 1901 (quoted in Smith, 1965/1986, p. 117). This goal, already apparent by 1880 (p. 116), emphasized the aesthetic value to children of reading literary masterpieces. The Herbartian movement, which highlighted aesthetics in general, boosted teachers' awareness of this aspect of reading as did a fiery article in 1891 by Charles Eliot, president of Harvard University, who castigated contemporary reading series for their being "not real literature...but mere scraps of literature," declaring that "we should substitute in all our schools real literature for [basal] readers" (quoted in Smith, 1965/1986, p. 120).

Yet another influence on the content of children's readers was that of G. Stanley Hall (1844–1924) and his child-study movement. Hall's underlying philosophy was that ontogeny recapitulates phylogeny—that is, that individual human beings retrace the history of their race as they mature into adulthood. In terms of reading instructional materials, Hall's philosophy encouraged the dismissal of the moralistic, child-centered stories found in earlier reading series and the substitution of stories that supposedly reflected the evolving beliefs of primitive people—myths, fables, nursery tales, and fairy tales. Publishers, embracing "sentence and story" methods, turned enthusiastically to printing readers composed of these tales, and The Little Red Hen graced many a first or second reader (Smith, 1965/1986, pp. 141, 143–145).

After the turn of the century, some reading series used various forms of phonics as they incorporated these new ideas—progressive, literary, and anthropological—into their series. An example is the story of Goldilocks, called "Silver-Hâir" in Edward Ward's Rational Method in Reading (Ward, 1896; see Monaghan & Barry, 1999, p. 23), a series that marks words diacritically throughout the text. Yet for many more series the whole-word method, with its much greater flexibility of word choice, now became the preferred method—easily identifiable today by the list at the end of each book of the sight words used in it (e.g., Bryce & Spaulding, 1906/1916; Monaghan & Barry, 1999, p. 34).

The role played, if any, by the sex of an author in adopting a whole-word approach is not clear. Up to about 1880, publishers had favored men over women as authors of their reading series. Since then, however, education had expanded massively at both the public and private level (Cremin, 1988, pp. 544–546), and women had increasingly predominated in classroom and supervisory positions. Women had been accepted as authors of books for girls as early as the 1840s; in the 1880s, now that nursery rhymes and fairy tales were considered appropriate for young children's readers, publishers turned to women for help (Monaghan, 1994, pp. 30–33). These new female authors for the most part enthusiastically supported the whole-word approach as one aspect of a reform movement.

Calls for reform in U.S. reading instruction were not restricted to Harvard presidents or professional educators of either sex. In 1896 one such call came from outside the educational establishment in the form of a series of stinging articles published in the *Forum* by Joseph Mayer Rice. Rice was a doctor in the United States who forsook medicine for education and spent two years abroad, part of them with the psychologist Wilhelm Wundt in Leipzig, Germany. After returning to the United States, he based his articles on the results of his surveys of U.S. schools located in 36 cities, where he personally examined some 125,000 children and talked to about 1,200 teachers (Adler & Porter, 2006; Lagemann, 2000, p. 79). Rice had, in fact, conducted one of the first large-scale surveys in the history of U.S. education.

School surveys subsequently became popular tools for examining the state of the educational enterprise. The best known example is the Cleveland survey, conducted in 1916. Thirty professional educators took part in it, among them Charles Hubbard Judd, director of the University of Chicago's School of Education (discussed by Jackie Marshall Arnold and Mary-Kate Sableski, chapter 4, this volume) and a youthful William Scott Gray (see Carol Lauritzen's biography of Gray, chapter 13, this volume), who was still a graduate student at the time (Lagemann, 2000, pp. 84–85).

By 1917, educators who were interested in improving education through fact finding had an organization to belong to: the NSSE which, as noted earlier, was the fruit of a 1901 reorganization of the Herbartian Society. The NSSE began publishing yearbooks in 1902, and its publications quickly became a magnet for scholars in a variety of academic and school-related disciplines. Its yearbooks focused on specific topics (such as "Adapting the Schools to Individual Differences") in the one or two volumes it issued annually. NSSE yearbooks became prestigious forums for scholars, young and old, who were pursuing the study of education through quantitative methods.

In short, between about 1870 and 1918, American reading education was exposed to a variety of novelties—a new focus on meaning, experimentation with different methodological approaches, the claims of the progressive education movement, and calls from outsiders for educational reform. Other developments, such as the children's literature and child-study movements, affected the content of children's readers. At the heart of all this turmoil was a respect for children and a desire to meet them at their own level.

Yet, parallel in time, a movement of a very different kind was developing, one that began wholly outside the arena of education—experimental scientific research. During those same decades, psychology was emerging as a distinct discipline, and its findings would eventually make a major contribution to the way the act of reading was conceptualized and taught.

The Emergence of the Field of Psychology, 1870–1918

Psychology itself grew from a blend of philosophy and physiology. Its creation was inspired, in part, by the strides scientists had made in understanding human physiology by the 1870s. Thanks to careful investigation, researchers were cracking open the secrets of the body. Surely cracking open the secrets of the mind by similarly careful study was a realistic possibility. The name for this new approach, "the scientific study of the mind" or "psychology," put it firmly in the scientific camp.

The first intellectual forebear of psychology was philosophy. In 1890 William James, who taught in the Philosophy Department at Harvard University and who was a brother of the novelist Henry James, finally published *Principles of Psychology*, a work that had taken him 12 years to write (Lagemann, 2000, 35–36). It was a book that intrigued hundreds of students over the year to come. In *Principles*, James identifies introspection as the key to understanding the workings of the human mind and introduced the concept of the "stream of consciousness."

The second intellectual parent of psychology was physiology, and it flourished in Europe. In the 1870s, physiologists—asking what readers perceived of the printed page and how fast they did so—turned their attention to the physical act of reading. By 1879, experiments undertaken by Emile Javal in France at the University of Paris had led to the discovery that the eyes of a reader do not move smoothly across a line of print, as one might think, but actually take little leaps across the line being read. (The French origin of this discovery explains why these movements are called today by their French term *saccades*, that is, *jerks*.) The question immediately arose as to whether the eyes of the reader take in visual impressions while they are moving as well as while they are at rest, to which the eventual answer was that they do not.

Yet it was to Germany, rather than to France, that aspiring young psychologists from the United States headed to obtain insights into this experimental work. The year that Javal first published his findings—1879—was also the year in which Wilhelm Wundt (1832–1920), whose name occurs frequently in the accounts that follow, opened the first fully functional psychological laboratory ever created. Wundt's career in psychology had itself begun in physiology and philosophy. After 18 years at other institutions, he had come to the University of Leipzig in 1875 as professor of philosophy (Boring, 1950, pp. 319–324).

The experimental method lay at the heart of Wundt's new laboratory, and adult readers were often used as subjects in the laboratory's experiments. Over the course of the following 20 years, Wundt, his assistants, and his students conducted about 100 experiments, studying, among other topics, sensation and perception (particularly vision), reaction experiments, and the role played by attention to a given task (Boring, 1950, pp. 339–344).

One of the many U.S. students to travel to Leipzig to work with Wundt was James McKeen Cattell, born in 1860, who served as Wundt's assistant for three years (Boring, 1950, p. 324). (For Arlette Ingram Willis's biography of Cattell, see chapter 1, this volume.) One of Cattell's experiments investigated readers' reaction time to briefly exposed letters. Using a drum with slits in which a letter or letters appeared, Cattell measured the time it took adults to read aloud the letters. He found that it took "twice as long to read (aloud, as fast as possible) words which have no connexion as words which make sentences, and letters which have no connexion as letters which make words" (quoted in chapter 1, this volume, p. 52). Cattell's experiment was probably the earliest example of research that demonstrated the importance of syntactics and semantics in word identification. In the years that followed, his findings would be frequently cited by reading educators as support for whole-word instruction (e.g., by Jenkins, 1913, p. 7).

At another German laboratory, Benno Erdmann of the University of Halle was also investigating perception. When Raymond Dodge, 11 years Cattell's junior, crossed the Atlantic and made his way to Germany, he chose to study at Halle, rather than Leipzig. Dodge's childhood skill at tinkering with objects, as Dixie D. Massey relates (see chapter 3, this volume), eventually helped him to invent the Erdmann-Dodge tachistoscope, a machine that controlled the length of time a subject was allowed to view stimuli such as letters. Dodge, too, concluded that readers focus on words as wholes, not on individual letters. The effect that his and Cattell's conclusions would have on the choice of the whole-word method as the preferred method of reading instruction would become apparent later.

In 1891, now back in the United States, Cattell was hired by Columbia University as professor of psychology and departmental chair. From this base, he became a leader in legitimizing psychology as a science, and his doctoral students fanned out to promote the new field. Robert Sessions Woodworth (see chapter 2 by Allen Berger and his colleagues, this volume) joined him at Columbia University in 1903; Edward Lee Thorndike (see Lou Ann Sears's discussion, chapter 5, this volume) rose up the ranks from an instructor in 1899 at Columbia's educational sister, Teachers College; and yet another former doctoral student, Walter Fenno Dearborn (described by Joseph E. Zimmer, chapter 6, this volume), began in 1912 to pursue a successful career in educational psychology at Harvard University. (See the matrix in Appendix D, which shows the teacher–student relationships of the early reading pioneers.)

As early as 1914 and the onset of World War I, psychology was already moving in an astonishing number of different theoretical directions that included psychoanalysis, Gestalt psychology, functionalism, and behaviorism. (As Cattell once put it, "Psychology is what psychologists do" [quoted in chapter 1, this volume, p. 44].) From an educational perspective, "intelligence" tests were already well known for their role in identifying individual differences. In 1906 Lewis Terman had published the Stanford Revision of the Binet-Simon Scale, which was soon hailed as the best of the individual intelligence tests on the market (Indiana University, 2006). When the United States entered World War I, psychologists found themselves in much demand for testing recruits. Dodge and Cattell both contributed their expertise to the armed services. Thorndike created the Alpha and Beta tests for evaluating the literacy of U.S. Army recruits. (It was an unpleasant surprise to discover during this war that large numbers of young recruits were functionally illiterate, unable to cope with the literacy demands of Army training.)

The contributions made by psychologists to the war effort helped clinch the role of psychology itself. By 1918, it was a self-confident discipline of its own. Yet its unity had already been challenged by the emergence from its ranks of a competing discipline, educational psychology.

The Emergence of the Field of Educational Psychology, 1900–1918

The separation of educational psychology from psychology in general had begun very early, in the first decade of the 20th century, and the new field was inextricably tied to the work of one man, Edward Lee Thorndike. Thorndike's first research was conducted on animals (cats and chickens), and his discovery that animals learned in a trial-and-error fashion was a major factor in his view on human learning. In a theory that became known as *connectionism*, he posited that adults as well as children responded to stimuli and that learning was a matter of acquiring useful habits. The connection between stimulus and reaction was reinforced, in his view, if the outcome were pleasurable and discouraged if it were disagreeable.

In 1903, Thorndike published *Educational Psychology*, a text whose title carved out a special space for the application of psychology to the classroom (1903; cf. Thorndike, 1925). Three years later, Thorndike produced one of the first monographs to discuss how successful teachers "can apply psychology, the science of human nature, to the problems of the school" (Thorndike, 1906, p. 10). Convinced by the eugenicist Francis Galton and others that individuals were born inherently different from one another (the catchphrase was "individual differences"), Thorndike saw education not as a way of overcoming the disadvantages of birth but as a means of training each person to his or her most suitable niche in the existing social structure. (John Dewey, in contrast, had hoped to change the social environment to suit the person [Lagemann, 2000, pp. 58, 62].) Books poured from Thorndike's prolific pen, and he developed a passion for counting. He is credited with the saying that everything that exists, exists in some measure and is, therefore, countable (Cremin, 1988, p. 234). Yet Thorndike's rigidly behavorist conception of human learning contrasts oddly with what is arguably his greatest contribution to the reading field—his study of those very mental events, misunderstandings in reading. His resulting conceptualization of "reading as reasoning" has influenced researchers for almost a century (Thorndike, 1917/1971).

Thorndike's passion for tabulation ranged from mental measurements to his famous *The Teacher's Word Book* (1921) and its successors, works that selected words for children on their usefulness. Usefulness itself was a concept behaviorally defined by the frequency with which the words had appeared earlier in certain well-known books. The equation of frequent use with utility led to an outpouring of word counting by researchers for a variety of different purposes. Whereas Thorndike counted words that he thought children most needed to read (Clifford, 1978), Ernest Horn (see his biography by Jiening Ruan and Priscilla L. Griffith, chapter 12, this volume) tabulated tens of thousands words from written work to find the ones most useful for children to know how to spell.

Yet another feature of psychology that was developing throughout this period should not be overlooked—the successful application of statistics to the social sciences. Statistics is a venerable discipline: By the early 19th century its theory had developed highly enough for astronomers to use its method of probability-based inference to estimate the role of error in their observations of the stars. But it took until 1860 for Gustav Fechner (1801–1887) to use statistical methods to explore the relationship between body and mind by means of data reported by introspection, such as an individual's sensation of which of two lifted weights was heavier (Stigler, 1999, pp. 189–193). In 1885 the existence of serial correlations was recognized (pp. 104–105), in 1893 Karl Pearson (1857–1936) first used the expression *standard deviation* in relation to the bell curve (p. 376), and in 1900 he introduced the chi-square test (p. 136). By the time Arthur Irving Gates wanted to compare, for example, children's reading ability with their success in detecting small differences between two drawings, he was able to identify group means and standard deviations, and provide multiple correlations from his data (Gates, 1922). (For Misty Sailors's biography of Gates, see chapter 14, this volume.)

The Scientific Movement and Its Impact on Reading Education, 1918–1925

The scientific movement in education and educational psychology were virtually synonymous, as far as a growing number of academics interested in reading and reading instruction were concerned. The year 1909 had been a key year: It was the date of Thorndike's first presentation of his handwriting scale, which Smith (1965/1986) identifies as the "birth of the scientific movement in education" (p. 157). Judd's study, *Reading: Its Nature and Development* (1918), was also an important one as psychologists turned their attention to reading.

In the 1920s, the impact of experimental evidence began to become visible. The experiments with eye movements had suggested that oral reading was slower and less efficient than silent reading; now basal reading series appeared that in some cases forebade children to read orally. One of these was The Silent Readers (Lewis & Rowland, 1920), which invoked the studies of Gray and Judd, among others, to support their insistence on silent reading (p. 1; cf. Watkins, 1922). Two years later, in *Silent Reading* (Judd & Buswell, 1922), Judd and his colleague disentangled the relation between oral and silent reading, concluding that there was a place for both in school at different stages of a child's development.

The year 1925 saw the publication of the first NSSE yearbook to devote an entire volume to the topic of reading instruction (Whipple, 1925). In this volume, the acceptance of progressive education in some form is still strong. John Dewey's *The School and Society* (1899) is invoked early in the yearbook by William S. Gray in support of libraries (Gray in Whipple, 1925, p. 1), and the term "progressive schools" (Rose Lees Hardy in Whipple, 1925, p. 293) is still a laudatory one. But the Thorndikean terminology of habits was creeping in, as evidenced in Gray's encouragement of "regular practice in reading each day for the purpose of developing attitudes, habits, and skills that are essential in all reading activities" (Gray in Whipple, 1925, p. 39).

It is fascinating to see how early and how clearly important features of contemporary reading instruction were established. Gray wrote the yearbook chapter titled "Essential Objectives of Instruction in Reading," and the entire committee on reading, which had organized the book, summarized its major recommendations. These included "a broad conception of the aims of reading instruction," a "vigorous emphasis from the beginning on reading as a thought-getting process" (with the "mechanics of reading" subordinated to "thoughtful interpretation"), an "emphasis on the enjoyment of literature," provision for individual differences ascertained by classroom tests, and the encouragement of students' permanent interest in reading (Whipple, 1925, pp. 305–306). Surely reading instructors would readily agree with these goals today, as they would with the yearbook's additional aim of providing a wide range of reading materials. Several of the objectives clearly derive from the tenets of educational psychologists as well as those of child-centered progressives.

What is less obvious than the objectives is the unquestioning assumption that the unit of reading instruction should be the word, not letters or syllables. One justification for using lessons based on children's "familiar experience[s] and activities" was that they would "introduce pupils to reading as a thought-getting process and...develop a sight vocabulary of frequently recurring words" (Gray, in Whipple, 1925, p. 36). "The word is a natural unit in reading because pupils are using words constantly to express ideas in oral language," said Frances Jenkins (in Whipple, 1925, p. 81), who was assistant professor of education at the University of Cincinnati and junior author of Houghton's Riverside Readers (1913).

Jenkins' chapter in the 1925 yearbook tackles the issue of phonics, apparently already a contentious one. "Conflicting opinions," she wrote, "regarding the place of phonetic training have prevailed for many years." She identified the "main controversy[:]...should phonetic training hold a place of primary or secondary importance in the teaching of reading?" (Jenkins in Whipple, 1925, pp. 85–86). Professional opinion came down firmly on the latter side. Jenkins drew on the findings of an unpublished 1920 master's thesis titled "The Present Status of the Teaching of Phonics" by Mabel Lucile Ducker at the University of Chicago. Ducker had summarized the phonics teaching described in 18 reading manuals published between 1900 and 1920. The manuals for most primers and first readers in these reading systems agreed that (a) the teaching of formal phonics should be deferred until children had mastered a sight vocabulary of 50 or 60 words; (b) phonic analysis should begin by analyzing sight words; and (c) the order of phonics instruction (in at least in two thirds of the manuals) ran from single consonants, through "compound" consonants, to long and short vowels and vowel combinations, deferring instruction on silent letters. The manuals also concurred on a list of what reading educators would now call *word families* or *rimes* (Jenkins, in Whipple, 1925, pp. 87–89). All in all, Jenkins recommended the adoption of a "definite system of training in phonetics" that was to be "carefully related to a rich reading program" (p. 90). She cautioned, however, that an "*overemphasis* [emphasis in original] on phonic analysis and mere word recognition encourages the development of 'word-callers'" (p. 89). No later yearbook on reading instruction would provide such a detailed list of the elements of phonics instruction. Arthur Gates, who was not on the NSSE committee on reading, took issue with Jenkins' declaration that "No separate work in phonetics should be done until the child…has a reasonable stock of sight words" (p. 90). While reviewing the yearbook at the NSSE's annual presentation, he criticized the delay, saying that words and letters should be taught simultaneously (MacGinitie, 1980, pp. 17–18). His caution went unheeded.

One novel feature of the 1925 yearbook (which became an NSSE bestseller, selling over 30,000 copies; Whipple, 1937, p. vii) was the introduction of the concepts of the diagnosis and remediation of reading failure. In three columns, labeled "Evidence of Deficiency," "Diagnosis," and "Remedial Suggestions," Laura Zirbes offers advice on providing for individual differences. One entry in the evidence column is, "Frequent halts and hesitations during oral reading." The source of the problem was diagnosed as a "Low stock of sight words," and the appropriate remedial suggestion was to "Provide incentive for accumulating a stock of sight words" (Zirbes, in Whipple, 1925, p. 278).

The years from 1920 to 1924 in general were the period when a few public schools began to incorporate remedial reading into their instruction and the first reading clinic was opened at a university (Smith, 1965/1986, pp. 190, 192–193). Smith notes that Gray and Gates had already published on the topic of diagnosis and remediation by 1925 (e.g., Gates, 1922; Gray, 1922).

As early as 1925, then, the scientific movement in education had made its mark. Men trained in experimental research techniques (i.e., Judd, Thorndike, Gates, Gray) had already published monographs on reading, found a publication outlet (NSSE yearbooks) where they could pool their knowledge, and had set out the parameters of a new field, reading education.

The Emergence of Reading and Spelling Experts, 1925–1937

The time between 1925 and 1937, when a new NSSE yearbook on reading appeared, was a period of international peace. Yet it was also a period that included the advent of the Great Depression in the United States and the threat of a Second World War. Despite the gloom of these national and international contexts, the educational enterprise did not falter. True, school expenditures for textbooks plummeted and the publication of new reading series was curtailed. The years 1933 and 1934 were known as a time of "book famine" (Willis Uhl, in Whipple, 1937, p. 248), but reading instruction continued to attract much interest and research among educational psychologists.

One focus was on a concern that had appeared in the previous decade—reading failure. In examining why some children failed to learn to read, an explanation that gained in popularity during the 1930s was that the failing child might have been introduced to reading before he or she was "ready" (see, e.g., Harrison, 1936; Morphett & Washburne, 1931). The concept of readiness hinged upon the discovery of children's differences in intelligence. All professionals had hailed the advances made in evaluating intelligence and allocating an intelligence quotient (IQ) to the tested child, and studies had revealed that children matured at different rates. Clearly, some maturation was necessary before children could be expected to master the complex task of reading. The reading researchers asked, When should children be introduced to reading? A commonly accepted answer was that reading instruction should be postponed until a child had reached the "mental age" of 6 and a half years (Morphett & Washburne, 1931). The cautions of Gray (in Whipple, 1937, p. 86) and Gates (1937), both of whom warned against accepting this dictum without taking into account the entire instructional context, fell on deaf ears.

This same period, 1925–1937, was also one in which several men and a handful of women solidified their status as the uncontested leaders of what was increasingly being defined as the field of reading. Two men in particular, both trained as educational psychologists, established themselves as important figures—Gates and Gray. Both had studied under Thorndike, but Gates, at Teachers College, was Thorndike's junior colleague and was chosen to revise Thorndike's college text on educational psychology (Thorndike & Gates, 1929). Gates's interest in psychology and education was matched by his research interests in reading. In addition to his publications on reading disability (1922, 1927/1935), noted earlier, Gates published his first word book for teachers, *A Reading Vocabulary for the Primary Grades*, in 1926 (1926/1935). It and similar works by Thorndike would be used by the creators of basal reading series as the uncontested authorities that determined which words should be included in their texts at each reading level.

Meanwhile, Gray had already become known as an indispensable voice in reading education, as his chairing of the NSSE's National Committee on Reading for the 1925 yearbook exemplified. In 1924 he had published the first of what would later become annual summaries of reading research; seven years later he presented an update in the newly founded *Review of Educational Research* (Gray, 1931). He was the first to quantify the amount of research on reading being undertaken, a number that increased every year except for the years of the Great Depression in the United States.

The year 1930, halfway between two NSSE yearbooks, was a turning point from several perspectives. From the vantage of children's basal reading series, this was the year when Gates became the senior author of Macmillan's Work-Play Books, which introduced the twins Peter and Peggy. It was also the date at which Gray became a junior coauthor of the Scott Foresman Elson Basic Readers, named for the series' leading author, William Elson. (Its first preprimer was titled *Dick and Jane*.) From another perspective, that of the sex of those who wrote basal readers, the advantage women had enjoyed from about 1880 on as the sole or senior authors of elementary readers for children would be steadily eroded because the nature of professionalism had changed. Expertise in the elementary classroom was no longer as highly valued by publishers as was experimental research. The new professionals held doctorates and, except for a very few women such as Ruth May Strang (see the biography by Diane Lapp, Laurie A. Guthrie, and James Flood, chapter 15, this volume), they were men (Monaghan, 1994, pp. 38–40).

When the NSSE decided to issue a second yearbook on the topic of reading instruction, its officers again turned unhesitatingly to Gray, already the acknowledged leader of these new professionals, to organize the book (Whipple, 1937, p. vii). With the aid of a committee that included Gates and Horn, Gray did so, writing the introduction, one chapter on the nature and types of reading, and another chapter on the nature and organization of the reading program. Gates authored chapters on testing reading achievement and on diagnosing and treating extreme reading disability, while Horn examined the role of reading in content areas of the curriculum.

The differences between this yearbook and the 1925 yearbook are not as large as might be imagined. Certainly, Gray was able to point to "striking evidence of the increasing importance of reading in social life" (Gray, in Whipple, 1937, p. 12), citing recent studies of the topic such as his and Ruth Munroe's *The Reading Interests and Habits of Adults* (1929), Douglas Waples and Ralph Tyler's *What People Want to Read About* (1931), and his and Bernice Elizabeth Leary's *What Makes a Book Readable* (1935). (For Waples's biography by George Kamberelis and Marta K. Albert, see chapter 11, this volume; for Leary's by Karla J. Möller, see chapter 10, this volume.) Contributors to the second NSSE yearbook were able to draw on a larger range of studies than their predecessors had, and they defined the goals of reading instruction more generously than ever.

New to the discussion was a tendency to shift the causes for a child's not learning to read from the school to the child, that is, to factors beyond the school's domain. Gray noted the general agreement that "successful reading at all grade levels is conditioned in large measure by the physical, mental, emotional, and social maturity of the learners and by proper adaptation of instruction to their needs" (Gray, in Whipple, 1937, p. 79). For the first time in a yearbook on reading, the phrase "reading readiness" occurs (Bess Goodykoontz, in Whipple, 1937, p. 60), in a footnote citing Arthur Gates and Guy Bond's article on the topic (Gates & Bond, 1936).

Another agreement was on word reduction in basal readers. As one yearbook contributor put it, "The days are gone when textbooks in reading are permitted to contain a large number of words that occur but once" (Willis Uhl, in Whipple, 1937, p. 224). Indeed, the need for constant repetition was already visible in the marked reduction in introducing "new" words to children's early readers, a trend that dated from the 1920s. In 1922, the average number of words in the vocabularies of 12 primers was 406; in 1928, of another 12 primers, 378; in 1931, in 7 new primers, 289. Meanwhile the repetitions of "new" words in first readers rose correspondingly (Smith, 1965/1986, pp. 216–217, 219).

As this reduction of new words suggests, the emphasis on learning words as wholes is as strong as in the preceding yearbook. While all agreed on the importance of word recognition—indeed, the 1937 yearbook dedicates an entire chapter to vocabulary development—the emphasis is still on identifying words by methods other than letter–sound correspondences. Children were to figure out words through their configuration; their larger component parts (such as in compound words like *policeman*); on occasion through smaller components, such as *th* in *that*; and a few letter sounds, most useful when they began a word (Paul McKee, in Whipple, 1937, p. 291). But "children need early [on] only the more obvious and frequent letter sounds," McKee wrote. Formal rules were "too complicated and too often inapplicable or misleading to be of value in the primary grades" (p. 293). Meanwhile, provisions were being made to help failing readers: Reading clinics had been opened in schools in several cities, and teachers were being trained in remedial reading (Gerald Yoakam, in Whipple, 1937, p. 431).

In other words, the reading field, still not identified as such, had coalesced. The level of agreement by its leaders on key educational points, such as reading readiness, the role phonics should play, and the need to help failing readers, would only be reinforced in the next 12-year period.

Professional Unanimity in the Reading Profession, 1937–1949

World War II (1939–1945) diminished the amount of research and new reading series being published. Reports of published research had averaged 110 a year between 1930 and 1940, but thanks to the Great Depression and the war, the numbers dropped by nearly half and did not fully recover until after 1950 (Smith, 1965/1986, p. 267). And whereas 16 new basal reading series had been published between 1925 and 1935, from 1940 to 1950 only 6 new series appeared (pp. 212–213, 277). Nonetheless, several reading series came to prominence, tending to swamp the others. Chief among them was Scott Foresman's reading series, the Basic Readers, headed since 1940 by Gray and his coauthor May Hill Arbuthnot. (For the biography of Arbuthnot by Charles Monaghan, Susan E. Israel, and Molly D. Dahl, see chapter 9, this volume.) In hot pursuit of the Scott Foresman Basic Readers was David Russell's Ginn Basic Readers, first published in 1948 and 1949. (For Arlene L. Barry's discussion of Russell's life, see chapter 16, this volume.) During this period, manuals for teachers using basal series increased in length and number (Smith, 1965/1986, pp. 275–276).

The social importance of reading was again a theme during this period. So was a novel threat—competition for children's leisure time. The radio, movies, and comics were now competing with books for children's attention (Smith, 1965/1986, p. 271). In the 1940s, more books for teachers appeared explaining the link between maturation and learning and offering hints on teaching children (dubbed *slow learners*) whose maturation was proceeding less quickly than the norm. The difficulties children encountered when tackling unfamiliar words were specifically addressed by Gray in his important but perhaps underappreciated work *On Their Own in Reading* (1948). World War II revealed, as the previous war had done, an alarming number of young recruits unable to read well enough to serve their country without additional instruction in reading (Smith, 1965/1986, p. 269).

Yet there was still no single organization devoted only to reading. This continued to be the case even when, during the late 1940s, two organizations related to reading instruction were formed. The first focused on remediation in all subject areas and was titled the National Association of Remedial Teachers (NART). Organized with the help of Walter Dearborn, it held its first organizational meeting in March 1947 (Jerrolds, 1977, pp. 20–21). The second of the young organizations was the International Council for the Improvement of Reading Instruction (ICIRI). (The *International* in the title was thanks to the request of two Canadians to join the council.) The ICIRI was organized in October 1947 and published its first newsletter, *The Bulletin of the International Council for the Improvement of Reading Instruction* (predecessor of *The Reading Teacher*), in November of the following year (Larrick, 1996, p. 1). The group's goals included the encouragement of research in remedial reading, diagnosis, text readability, and textbook construction (Jerrolds, 1977, pp. 1–5). The two groups had many members in common, including Gray, who had served as president of both associations by the time people's thoughts turned, in the early 1950s, to combining both organizations into one.

The medical metaphor that ran through the titles and constitutions of both groups is noteworthy. Good reading was regarded as a sign of health; poor reading was regarded as a kind of illness that needed the therapeutic intervention of specially trained personnel. Several more universities were now offering courses on helping children with reading problems. For decades, a course in diagnosis and remediation would be a standard one for any prospective teacher seeking a master's degree in reading.

In all of this, progressives and educational psychologists alike favored the whole-word method for teaching beginning reading. Progressives considered the word to be as "natural" and meaningful a feature of language as speaking, and educational psychologists followed the lead of Thorndike—who appreciated words because they could be counted—in elevating the word to the most basic unit of instruction. Indeed, the debate was not between phonics and the whole-word approach in the 1930s and 1940s but about which words should be taught as wholes.

In 1949 the NSSE published the third of its yearbooks devoted exclusively to reading, titling it *Reading in the Elementary School* (Henry, 1949). Nine men and five women contributed to the volume. Gates chaired the committee for the entire yearbook, while Gray chaired the society's Committee on Reading. Three others of our pioneers made contributions: (1) Russell, on the relation between child development and reading and on reading evaluation; (2) Horn, on the improvement of oral reading; and (3) Leary, on interpreting the reading program to the public. Meanwhile, a sixth pioneer, Ruth Strang, was serving on the NSSE Board of Directors.

The goals of a good reading program in a school were agreed upon by all the contributors to the 1949 NSSE report but articulated most clearly by Gertrude Whipple, supervisor of reading in the Detroit, Michigan, USA, public school system (Whipple, in Henry, 1949, pp. 34–38). They include the following:

1. "Rich and varied experiences through reading" (p. 34) and the ability to "comprehend and interpret what is read" (p. 34). Reading activities in the classroom are guided by these goals, "rather than being allowed to develop in a whimsical manner" (p. 34; clearly a jab at the serendipitous, progressive approach).

2. The reading program is coordinated with other aspects of child development such as enlarging children's experiential background, obtaining information on the child's community and home life, and talking with parents.

3. The program respects the relation between reading and the other language arts.

4. It is part of a larger program of reading instruction that stretches through all the grades.

5. It is able to adjust to the pupil's individual needs, such as by having flexible groups for reading.

6. It teaches all aspects of reading, including reading in content areas, literature, and for recreation.

7. It can provide for special cases of extreme reading disability by diagnosis and remediation, perhaps in a reading clinic.

8. It provides for regular evaluation of its programmatic outcomes.

Again, few teachers today would quarrel with these goals. However, although Smith (1965/1986), in her history of American reading instruction, characterizes these goals as "much broader" than those of 1937 (p. 272), in one sense they are narrower: While they set reading instruction within the larger school and neighborhood community and broaden the scope from learning to read to reading to learn, they actually promote reading instruction without end, one that lasts until graduation from high school and en route tries to make provision for students whom the earlier instruction has palpably failed. Moreover, despite the lip service acknowledgment of reading's close relation to other language arts, children's writing is virtually invisible within these goals.

The term *progressive education* had already acquired negative connotations by 1949, the date of the NSSE report (in fact, the Progressive Education Association would disband only six years later), and the term *progressive* never appears in the description of any school discussed in the yearbook. But progressive concepts still remained. One such concept was that of "readiness," which since the 1930s had become almost universally accepted as crucial to a child's academic success. In David Harris Russell's words, children develop better "if reading activities are keyed to maturing processes" (Russell in Henry, 1949, p. 29). He noted, however, that "there is child development *in* and *through* reading" (p. 10; emphasis in original). So widely accepted was the readiness concept that so-called number-readiness books were being tried out experimentally in some schools by 1949 (Whipple, in Henry, 1949, p. 157).

Another belief universally adopted by reading experts in the late 1940s—other than progressives—was that basal readers were the core of the reading curriculum. Reading professionals were united in designating good basal reading series as key to orderly, cumulative reading instruction. Again, they invoked scientific findings in support of their convictions. The language of "habits" is Thorndikean. As Gertrude Hildreth, a textbook author and an assistant professor at Brooklyn College, wrote,

> The basic reading series is regarded as a tool for giving pupils systematic training in reading habits....These scientifically constructed books with controlled vocabulary and careful gradation give pupils basic training in such skills as...practicing the skills of word recognition in context. (Hildreth, in Henry, 1949, pp. 77–78)

Her advice on using the manuals that accompanied reading series hinted at the role they played in dictating choices that rightfully belong to teachers: "Failure to use materials as the author intended," she warned, "may destroy much of the value" of carefully prepared textbooks (p. 78).

In a chapter on word recognition, Althea Beery sketched every element of what Jeanne Chall (1967/1996) of Harvard University later characterized as "the conventional wisdom" (pp. 13–15). After the child had acquired a basic sight vocabulary, the most helpful routes to word identification were, in Beery's view, context clues, picture clues, configuration clues, phonetic analysis, structural analysis (i.e., roots and suffixes), and the use of glossaries and dictionaries (Beery, in Henry, 1949, pp. 184–186). She warned that considerable mental maturity was necessary for "using the sounds of the letters and letter combinations" to figure out new words, invoking a much-cited 1937 study, "Phonic Readiness" by Dolch and Bloomster (Beery, in Henry, 1949, p. 185). (In the world of basal reading series, Arthur Gates's "intrinsic" phonics approach, in which speech sounds represented by letters were induced by children from known sight words, had already been incorporated into the reading schemes published by Scott Foresman, Macmillan, Ginn, and many others.) Beery herself thought that sounding and blending, the hallmarks of systematic phonics, could be used as a last resort, but "only in [the] most extreme cases, after more natural methods have been thoroughly tried" (Beery, in Henry, 1949, pp. 191–192).

As they had in the preceding yearbook, the experts realized that controlling the vocabulary of basal readers, in which the fundamental approach was recognizing words globally, was essential. "Acceptable" reading series were those that included "a sufficient number of new words, but not too many," which occurred "with reasonable uniformity and frequency" (Whipple, in Henry, 1949, p. 168).

One of the advantages of basal reading series often mentioned in the 1949 NSSE yearbook was the series' ability to offer small-group instruction. Each series now had so many books, from preprimers to eighth-grade readers, that different groups could be working on books of different levels at the same time. The discovery of individual differences justified the organization of reading groups (usually three per classroom) in which children were grouped according to their reading attainments. Yet, paradoxically, the 1949 yearbook, unlike its predecessors and despite its stated seventh goal of helping reading disabled children, has no chapters devoted to reading diagnosis and remediation.

No Longer at Ease: Attacks Against Professional Unanimity, 1949–1955

Several reading experts were already aware that the "conventional wisdom" of reading instruction and word attack (Chall, 1967/1996, pp. 13–15) that Beery described in the 1949 NSSE yearbook was not sitting well with some teachers and parents. In the same yearbook, Hildreth identified some of the questions that teachers were asking about the "new" reading approach—questions about the length of the readiness period, grouping students for beginning reading instruction, and the teaching of phonics (Hildreth, in Henry, 1949, p. 57). Some criticism had even been aimed at the basal reading series. The strict vocabulary control, according to Whipple, who called it the "scientific control of difficulties" (Whipple, in Henry, 1949, p. 151), "has been vigorously criticized...as leading to trivial content, stilted sentence structure, lack of story-telling quality, and failure to introduce children to varied vocabulary and superior modes of expression" (p. 151). It fell to Bernice Leary to tackle the problem of parents who were unreceptive to "natural" approaches to reading instruction. She wrote the yearbook's final chapter, titled "Interpreting the Reading Program to the Public." Leary reported that at a school in Portland, Oregon, USA, some years earlier, some parents had become vociferous: "A growing criticism of the shift from the 'phonetic method' to the 'word method' of teaching reading had approached the point of antagonism when the principal called upon the president of the P[arent] T[eachers] A[ssociation] for help" (Leary, in Henry, 1949, p. 335). A program of explanation at the next PTA meeting restored parents' confidence and goodwill.

Yet no early rumblings of this kind could have prepared the reading profession for the outburst of venom against their persons and their professional beliefs that was embodied in Rudolf Flesch's *Why Johnny Can't Read—*

And What You Can Do About It, published in 1955. Flesch's sarcastic pen spared none of the reading experts among the pioneers who were still at the peak of their profession at that date (i.e., Dearborn, Gates, Gray, Russell, and Strang) nor those long dead, such as Huey. He blamed them all for substituting the whole-word method for systematic phonics in early reading instruction and accused them of thereby causing massive reading failure among the young. The thousands of parents who bought his book apparently agreed with him. His book became (astonishingly, for a work devoted to reading methodology) a bestseller almost overnight and remained on the bestseller list for more than 30 weeks (Chall, 1967/1996, p. 3).

Flesch, who had learned to read his native German through systematic phonics, castigated every aspect of contemporary reading instruction. He flayed experience charts (1955/1986, pp. 97–99), Gates's intrinsic phonics method (pp. 53–57), reading readiness and phonic readiness (pp. 69–73), and the meager reading vocabulary (p. 80–82) and "artificial sequences of words" of basal readers (p. 84). But his most damaging criticism, for a field that claimed its practice was based solidly on scientific research, was that the reading professionals had ignored the results of their own research. *His* own research, he wrote, had found no experimental studies that favored the whole-word method over the systematic phonics approach but found 10 that displayed the superiority of systematic phonics over the whole-word method (pp. 60–68). He found only one experiment, by Gates (1927), that showed the superiority of the intrinsic phonics method over a systematic phonics approach (Flesch, 1955/1986, pp. 53–55), a result Flesch attributed to the timed nature of the tests. (When Jeanne Chall later reexamined the same evidence, she drew the same conclusion [1967/1996].)

Professional reaction was understandably angry and defensive. The experts countered by attacking Flesch's definition of reading: He had claimed that "reading means getting meaning from certain combinations of letters. Teach the child what each letter stands for and he can read" (Flesch, 1955/1986, pp. 2–3). Reading, the experts retorted, was not word calling but thought getting. *Why Johnny Can't Read* was arguably the catalyst for the creation of a new organization of reading experts that embraced the goals of its predecessors, NART and ICIRI. Discussions had already taken place before Flesch's book came out, but his searing attack erased any lingering hesitation, and the merger was opposed by only 7% of those voting (Jerrolds, 1977, p. 29). The International Reading Association, with Gray as its first president, began business on January 1, 1956, as a unified organization of reading professionals and of all others who cared about reading and reading instruction. The organization was officially impartial, open to all persons interested in reading and to views of all kinds.

The organization had been long in coming. Wundt had opened the first experimental psychology laboratory in 1879. His assistant, Cattell, with others, worked on establishing psychology as a separate academic discipline in the United States from the time Cattell was hired by Columbia University in 1891. The period from then until educational psychology parted from psychology was very brief: Thorndike's earliest publications on educational psychology date from the first decade of the 20th century. In contrast, the gap between, for instance, Gray's first publication on reading—his 1915 oral reading test—and his election as the Association's first president in 1956, was one of more than 40 years.

Part of the explanation of this large gap is that for many years reading and spelling experts were comfortable with NSSE and content to use its yearbooks as forums for issuing periodic summaries of the state of their art. But when the entire field was threatened, as it was by Flesch's attacks, the need for an organization devoted only to the interests of the reading community seemed more pressing.

Indeed, in the biographies that follow, we can track the emergence of the reading field by following the lives of individuals. The accounts begin with the contributions of psychologists who studied perceptual aspects of the reading process: James McKeen Cattell (chapter 1), Robert Sessions Woodworth (chapter 2), and Raymond Dodge (chapter 3). They then turn to those who used psychological research to understand education better, and by so doing helped define the new field of educational psychology: Charles Hubbard Judd (chapter 4), Edward Lee Thorndike (chapter 5), and Walter Fenno Dearborn (chapter 6). The lives of Edmund Burke Huey (chapter 7) and Laura Zirbes (chapter 8) exemplify the progressive end of the reading theoretical spectrum, which found itself on the losing side of its contest with basal reading instruction. The next group embraces those who were passionate about books—about children's books in the case of May Hill Arbuthnot (chapter 9) and books for adults in the case of Douglas Waples (chapter 11), while the adventurous Bernice Elizabeth Leary (chapter 10) had her hand in almost everything. The last group of biographees represents those who, up to the early 1970s, were crucial to the development of the reading field itself: Ernest Horn, the undisputed spelling expert (chapter 12); William Scott Gray, "Mr. Reading" (chapter 13); Arthur Irving Gates, the best of the reading researchers (chapter 14); Ruth May Strang, whose interests ranged from secondary reading to remedial reading (chapter 15); and David Harris Russell (chapter 16), whose life reflects the interplay between scholarship and the challenges of being the senior author of a basal reading series.

From Cattell to Russell, the lives of these men and women reveal how the reading profession achieved its own identity as a separate academic discipline, shaped by the early reading pioneers.

REFERENCES

Adler, C., & Porter, A. (2006). *Rice, Joseph Mayer*. Retrieved June 6, 2006, from http://www.jewishencyclopedia.com/view.jsp?artid=276&letter=R&search=joseph%20mayer%20rice

Boring, E.G. (1950). *A history of experimental psychology* (2nd ed.). New York: Appleton-Century-Crofts. (Original work published 1929)

Bryce, C.T., & Spaulding, F.E. (1916). *Aldine readers: Book one* (Rev. ed.). New York: Newsome. (Original work published 1906)

Chall, J.S. (1996). *Learning to read: The great debate* (3rd ed.). Forth Worth, TX: Harcourt Brace College. (Original work published 1967)

Clifford, G.J. (1978). Words for schools: The applications in education of the vocabulary researches of Edward L. Thorndike. In P. Suppes (Ed.), *Impact of research on education: Some case studies* (pp. 107–198). Washington, DC: National Academy of Education.

Cremin, L.A. (1988). *American education: The metropolitan experience, 1876–1980*. New York: Harper & Row.

Dewey, J. (1899). *The school and society*. Chicago: The University of Chicago Press.

Dolch, E.W., & Bloomster, M. (1937). Phonic readiness. *The Elementary School Journal, 37*, 201–205.

Farnham, G.L. (1881). *The sentence method of teaching reading, writing and spelling. A manual for teachers*. Syracuse, NY: C.W. Bardeen.

Flesch, R.F. (1985). *Why Johnny can't read—and what you can do about it*. New York: Harper & Row. (Original work published 1955)

Gates, A.I. (1922). *The psychology of reading and spelling, with special reference to disability*. New York: Teachers College, Columbia University.

Gates, A.I. (1927). Studies of phonetic training in beginning reading. *Journal of Educational Psychology, 18*, 217–226.

Gates, A.I. (1935). *A reading vocabulary for the primary grades*. New York: Teachers College, Columbia University. (Original work published 1926)

Gates, A.I. (1935). *The improvement of reading: A program of diagnostic and remedial methods* (Rev. ed.). New York: Macmillan. (Original work published 1927)

Gates, A.I. (1937). The necessary mental age for beginning reading. *The Elementary School Journal, 37*, 497–508.

Gates, A.I. & Bond, G.L. (1936). Reading readiness: A study of factors determining success and failure in beginning reading. *Teachers College Record, 37*, 679–685.

Gray, W.S. (1922). *Remedial cases in reading: Their diagnosis and treatment*. Chicago: University of Chicago.

Gray, W.S. (1931). Reading. *Review of Educational Research, 1*, 247–260, 328–336.

Gray, W.S. (1948). *On their own in reading: How to give children independence in attacking new words*. Chicago: Scott Foresman.

Gray, W. S., & Leary, B.E. (1935). *What makes a book readable: With special reference to adults of limited reading ability—An initial study*. Chicago: University of Chicago Press.

Gray, W.S., & Munroe, R. (1929). *The reading interests and habits of adults*. New York: Macmillan.

Harrison, M.L. (1936). *Reading readiness*. Boston: Houghton Mifflin.

Henry, N.B. (Ed.). (1949). *The forty-eighth yearbook of the National Society for the Study of Education. Part II. Reading in the elementary school*. Chicago: National Society for the Study of Education.

Huey, E.B. (1913). *The psychology and pedagogy of reading*. New York: Macmillan. (Original work published 1908)

Indiana University. (2006). *Lewis Madison Terman*. Retrieved June 6, 2006, from http://www.indiana.edu/~intell/terman.shtml

Jenkins, F. (1913). *How to teach reading: A manual for teachers using the Riverside Readers*. New York: Houghton Mifflin.

Jerrolds, B.W. (1977). *Reading reflections: The history of the International Reading Association*. Newark, DE: International Reading Association.

Judd, C.H. (1918). *Reading: Its nature and development*. Chicago: University of Chicago Press.

Judd, C.H., & Buswell, G.T. (1922). *Silent reading: A study of the various types*. Chicago: University of Chicago Press.

Kilpatrick, W.H. (1924). *The project method: The use of the purposeful act in the educative process*. New York: Teachers College, Columbia University. (Original work published 1918)

Kline, E., Moore, D.W., & Moore, S.A. (1987). Colonel Francis Parker and beginning reading instruction. *Reading Research and Instruction, 26*, 141–150.

Lagemann, E.C. (2000). *An elusive science: The troubling history of education research*. Chicago: University of Chicago Press.

Larrick, N. (1996). Nancy Larrick tells of early years at IRA. In *History of Reading News, 19*(2), 1. Available from http://www.historyliteracy.org/scripts/newsletters_list.php

Lewis, W.D., & Rowland, A.L. (1920). *The Silent Readers: Fourth reader*. Philadelphia: John C. Winston.

Lindberg, S.W. (1976). *The annotated McGuffey: Selections from the McGuffey Eclectic Readers, 1836–1920*. New York: Van Nostrand Reinhold.

MacGinitie, W.H. (1980, May). *The contributions of Arthur I. Gates*. A paper presented at the 25th Annual Convention of the International Reading Association, St. Louis, Missouri.

Mathews, M.M. (1966). *Teaching to read, historically considered*. Chicago: University of Chicago Press.

Minnich, H.C. (1936). *William Holmes McGuffey and his readers*. New York: American.

Monaghan, E.J. (1994). Gender and textbooks: Women writers of elementary readers, 1880–1950. *Publishing Research Quarterly, 10*, 28–46.

Monaghan, E.J., & Barry, A.L. (1999). *Writing the past: Teaching reading in colonial America and the United States, 1640–1940*. Newark, DE: International Reading Association.

Monaghan, E.J., Hartman, D.K., & Monaghan, C. (2002). History of reading instruction. In B.J. Guzzetti (Ed.), *Literacy in America: An encyclopedia of history, theory, and practice, Vol. 1*, (pp. 224–231). Santa Barbara, CA: ABC-CLIO.

Monroe, L.B. (1877). *The Chart-Primer, or first steps in reading*. Philadelphia: Cowperthwait.

Morphett, M.V., & Washburne, C. (1931). When should children begin to read? *The Elementary School Journal, 31*, 496–503.

Singer, H., & Ruddell, R.B. (1970). *Theoretical models and processes of reading*. Newark, DE: International Reading Association.

Singer, H., & Ruddell, R.B. (1976). *Theoretical models and processes of reading* (2nd ed.). Newark, DE: International Reading Association. (Original work published 1970)

Smith, N.B. (1986). *American reading instruction*. Newark, DE: International Reading Association. (Original work published 1965)

Stigler, S.M. (1999). *Statistics on the table: The history of statistical concepts and methods*. Cambridge, MA: Harvard University Press.

Thorndike, E.L. (1903). *Educational psychology*. New York: Teachers College Press.

Thorndike, E.L. (1906). *The principles of teaching: Based on psychology*. New York: AG Seiler.

Thorndike, E.L. (1921). *The teacher's word book*. New York: Teachers College, Columbia University.

Thorndike, E.L. (1925). *Educational psychology: Briefer course*. New York: Teachers College, Columbia University.

Thorndike, E.L. (1971). Reading as reasoning: A study of mistakes in paragraph reading. *Reading Research Quarterly*, 6, 425–434. (Original work published 1917)

Thorndike, E.L., & Gates, A.I. (1929). *Elementary principles of education*. New York: Macmillan.

Vail, H.H. (1911). *A history of the McGuffey readers*. Cleveland, OH: Burrows Brothers.

Venezky, R.L. (1987). A history of the American reading textbook. *The Elementary School Journal*, 87, 247–265.

Vinovskis, M., & Moran, G., with Monaghan, C., and Monaghan, E.J. (in press). Schools and print culture. In D.D. Hall (Series ed.) & R. Gross & M. Kelley (Vol. eds.), *An extensive republic: Books, culture, and society in the new nation, 1790–1840: Vol. 2. A history of the book in America*. Chapel Hill: University of North Carolina Press in cooperation with the American Antiquarian Society.

Waples, D., & Tyler, R.W. (1931). *What people want to read about: A study of group interests and a survey of problems in adult reading*. Chicago: University of Chicago Press.

Ward, E.G. (1896). *The rational method in reading. Second reader*. Boston: Silver, Burdett.

Watkins, E. (1922). *How to teach silent reading to beginners*. Philadelphia: J.B. Lippincott.

Whipple, G.M. (Ed.). (1925). *The twenty-fourth yearbook of the National Society for the Study of Education. Part I. Report of the National Committee on Reading*. Bloomington, IL: Public School Publishing Company.

Whipple, G.M. (Ed.). (1937). *The thirty-sixth yearbook of the National Society for the Study of Education. Part I. The teaching of reading: A second report*. Bloomington, IL: Public School Publishing.

FOR FURTHER READING

Adams, M.J. (1995). *Beginning to read: Thinking and learning about print*. Cambridge, MA: MIT Press. (Original work published 1990)

Balmuth, M. (1982). *The roots of phonics: A historical introduction*. New York: McGraw-Hill.

Capshew, J.H. (1999). *Psychologists on the march: Science, practice, and professional identity in America, 1929–1969*. Cambridge, MA: Cambridge University Press.

Monaghan, E.J. (1998). Phonics and whole word/whole language controversies, 1948–1998: An introductory history. In R.J. Telfer (Ed.), *Finding our literacy roots. Yearbook of the American Reading Forum* (Vol. 18, pp. 1–23). Whitewater, WI: American Reading Forum. Available online from http://www.americanreadingforum.org/98_yearbook/html/01_monaghan_98.htm

Monaghan, E.J., & Saul, E.W. (1987). The reader, the scribe, the thinker: A critical look at the history of American reading and writing instruction. In T.S. Popkewitz (Ed.), *The for-*

mation of school subjects: The struggle for creating an American institution (pp. 85–122). Philadelphia: Falmer.

Pressley, M. (2002). *Reading instruction that works: The case for balanced reading* (2nd ed.). New York: Guilford. (Original work published 1998)

Reeder, R.R. (1900). *The historical development of school readers and of method in teaching reading.* New York: Macmillan.

Schantz, P., & Zimmer, J. (2005). Why Johnny can't read: 50 years of controversy. *History of Reading News, 28*(2), 1–4.

Venezky, R.L. (1984). The history of reading research. In P.D. Pearson, R. Barr, M.L. Kamil, & P. Mosenthal (Eds.), *Handbook of reading research* (pp. 3–38). New York: Longman.

Worcester, S. (1828). *A primer of the English language, for the use of families and schools* (Stereotyped ed.). Boston: Hilliard, Gray, Little & Wilkins.

PART I

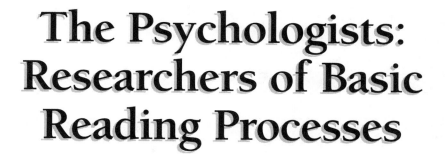

The Psychologists: Researchers of Basic Reading Processes

James McKeen Cattell (1860–1944): His Life and Contributions to Reading Research

By Arlette Ingram Willis

Historical Research Process

FOR ME THE process of writing biography began long before I ever heard of James McKeen Cattell. Growing up in the United States as an African American female shaped how I see and understand the world that includes, but is not limited to, the oppression I have experienced because of my race and gender. My race and gender consciousnesses took on a more critical stance once I entered graduate school, where the personal and the political

---

Shaping the Reading Field: The Impact of Early Reading Pioneers, Scientific Research, and Progressive Ideas, edited by Susan E. Israel and E. Jennifer Monaghan. © 2007 by the International Reading Association.
Photo: Courtesy of Dover Publications. By H. Cirker and B. Cirker, reproduced from *The Dictionary of American Portraits*, published by Dover Publicaitons, Inc., 1967.

were necessary to survive. For me, the process of documenting and writing history and biography begins within this consciousness and certainly informs my interpretation.

I became interested in the history of reading research when I entered the doctoral program at The Ohio State University from two separate but intersecting pathways. Before returning to graduate school I had been a stay-at-home mom. My life had centered not only around my family but also my interactions and conversations with other African American women. Every day we shared our lives and ongoing experiences as well as hopes and dreams for our future and the futures of our children. What I learned from these long conversations, in retrospect, is that I engaged in a collective system of caring, meaning making, and making sense of the daily oppression we faced, which in many ways was uniquely female and uniquely African American. What surprised me most about returning to graduate school was that my system of meaning making and understanding seemed out of place. In fact, I was told there was no place for this type of critical and womanist lens. The positivistic and scientistic forms of research presented to me did not fit into my frame of reference or system of meaning making.

Importantly, I read Venezky's (1984) chapter, "The History of Reading Research," in the *Handbook of Reading Research* (Pearson, Barr, Kamil, & Mosenthal, 1984). Although his handling of historical documents and ability to share this information in a succinct and cogent manner impressed me, I was dismayed that life in the United States and events in reading research—and in the lives of reading researchers—were unconnected. It is impossible to understand the history of reading research without a corollary discussion of the social and political contexts in which the research evolved. Venezky's 1984 chapter does not mention, for example, the histories of literacy among people of color or reading research conducted among people of color, points he mentions later (Venezky, 1987). Another shortcoming of his 1984 chapter is the lack of biographical information he supplies. Although he includes some biographical information, he argues, "One can deduce little about the direction or procedures of reading research from the personalities involved" (p. 4). Yet woven throughout the first half of the chapter are numerous, but oddly placed, commentaries about and references to the life and work of James McKeen Cattell that appear to contradict Venezky's statement. Like most readers, I might not have been aware of this inconsistency except for an assignment where, somewhat ironically, we were challenged to find the first published U.S. study in reading research by Cattell, "The Time It Takes to See and Name Objects" in *Mind* (1886). These experiences and countless others heightened my interest in re-presenting history in a more richly contextualized manner that includes sharing the influences on a person's life and showing how such influences can affect his or her research.

Throughout my career, I have been challenged to rewrite the history of reading research from a womanist and critical perspective and to include not only biographical information but also the histories of literacy among people of color in the United States. As I reconstruct the history of reading research in the United States, I use documents as evidence to illustrate how reading research has had an impact on the lives of people of color. Specifically, my process includes seeking to construct more inclusive and comprehensive portrayals of reading research and reading researchers within a racialized society, using all available evidence to help critically analyze the contexts in which individuals lived and in which research was conducted. Such a framework requires me to question, investigate, and deconstruct myriad intersections of the lives and research of individuals and to acknowledge researchers' strengths, weaknesses, limitations, challenges, and triumphs. In the United States this means a willingness to read broadly the texts and voices that have been silenced, marginalized, or ignored and to present alternative histories and biographies that neither lionize nor demonize reading research or researchers. For this particular biography, I have read broadly both primary and secondary sources as well as sources that challenge and oppose the views espoused by reading's royalty.

James McKeen Cattell (1860–1944) is among the many unsung heroes of psychology whose work has influenced reading research. The early histories of psychology and reading research are intricately interrelated and difficult to unravel (Venezky, 1984). It is equally difficult, if not impossible, to capture the entirety of a person's life in a few brief pages, and the task becomes even more difficult when you consider the legacy of a pioneer in an academic discipline. Cattell's myriad accomplishments include a career as a scholar, editor, publisher, and entrepreneur. His influence on the field of psychology is profound, although in his unpublished autobiography he implies that his role in the history of psychology had been slighted (Sokal, 1971). Nonetheless, Cattell's editorship and promotion of psychology did much to support the fledgling field. His early life and career are well documented, especially in Sokal's (1981) selective editing of the Cattell papers, so I only briefly sketch his early life.

Although Cattell's influence on psychology in the United States is unquestioned, his contributions to reading research are often overlooked. His most important contributions to reading research are (a) his belief that responses to stimuli reflect nervous system (brain) functioning and indicate intelligence; (b) his demonstration that the time it takes for an adult reader to read a single letter is similar to the time it takes to read a short familiar word; and (c) his idea that readers read more words in less time when words form sentences. Moreover, his crusade to legitimize psychology as a science, one useful to the field of education, helped to normalize the performance of English-dominant, European American males from middle to upper class environments as the standard group by which reading performance is measured.

Personal and Professional Life

James McKeen Cattell was born May 25, 1860, in Easton, Pennsylvania, USA, the first son of William C. Cattell (a Presbyterian minister) and Elizabeth (McKeen) Cattell. In his 1936 unpublished autobiography, Cattell outlines his ethnic heritage and attributes his success in the world to his inherited Scottish–Irish bloodlines and colonial spirit (Sokal, 1971). He also details the life of privilege into which he was born, his Presbyterian upbringing, and the wealth of his maternal grandfather, for whom he was named and from whom he later received a sizable inheritance that allowed him to spend time abroad in Europe in pursuit of pleasure and a doctoral degree (Sokal, 1981).

James and his younger brother, Henry, were taught at home by their father and tutors. During their father's business trips to Europe, the Cattell boys accompanied their parents, often spending brief stints in European schools. James attended Lafayette College in Easton, where his father was a professor of the classics and later president. After completing his undergraduate studies, focusing on literature, James graduated with highest honors in 1880.

When he received his master's degree in 1883, also from Lafayette College, it was again with highest honors. Like many U.S. students who sought graduate degrees, James traveled to Europe for an advanced education. Fortunately, in the voluminous papers left by him, there are excerpts of his correspondence with his family while abroad that help track his journey in Europe and eventual return to the United States.

Cattell's initial hope, to study philosophy with Rudolf Hermann Lotze (1817–1881) at the University of Göttingen in Germany, was altered when Lotze died shortly after Cattell's arrival. At this point, Cattell turned his attention to working with Wilhelm Wundt (1832–1920), founder of the first laboratory for experimental psychology, at Leipzig. Even without access to Lotze, Cattell wrote a prize-winning essay on Lotze's (1852/1966) philosophy, *Medicinishe Psychologie: Oder, Physiologie der Selle*, for which he won a fellowship for the academic year 1882–1883 to study at Johns Hopkins University in Baltimore, Maryland, USA. While there he began a series of studies on individual differences, one of which was designed

> to measure in milliseconds the time it took to recognize the letters of the Latin alphabet for each of nine subjects. This [sic] quantitative data was followed by the utilitarian recommendation that the least distinct letters be modified in certain ways to make them easier to read. (Sokal, 1987b, p. 25)

Cattell's nine subjects included Joseph Jastrow; John Dewey, soon to be considered a leading light in progressive education; G. Stanley Hall, future inaugurator of the child-study movement in the United States (Poffenberger, 1947, p. 13); and Cattell himself. He later published the results of this and further experiments in German (1885) and English (1886).

At Johns Hopkins University Cattell also conducted several experiments in which he used drugs or other substances (e.g., caffeine, cannabis, chocolate, ether, hashish, morphine, opium, etc.) to test his reactions. His drug use, although allegedly for scientific purposes, may also have been recreational but without the contemporary legal penalties. Cattell notes, with some embarrassment, that his youthful enthusiasm swayed his thinking. The following year his fellowship was withdrawn and awarded to John Dewey, who became a lifelong friend and supporter.

Cattell returned to Europe in 1883 to continue his reaction-time experiments as Wundt's assistant in his Leipzig laboratory. In his autobiography,

Cattell recalls that his professional relationship with Wundt was strained, in part because of Wundt's insistence that his students follow his line of research, experimenting on one or a few subjects, and in part because Cattell, who was fiercely independent, elected to follow his own line of inquiry. They both valued studies of reaction time: As Watson (1978) observes, "In Cattell's eyes it was a valuable tool for the study of the time necessary for mental operation and especially for the investigation of individual differences" (p. 408). Therefore, while at Leipzig under Wundt, Cattell's research was limited to two subjects. He also continued his experiments with drugs— "tobacco, caffeine, and chocolate, but after a while morphine and alcohol" (Sokal, 1981, p. 93). Cattell was awarded a doctorate from Leipzig in 1886.

During a 1886–1887 stay in Europe, Cattell worked in Sir Francis Galton's (1822–1911) anthropometric laboratory at London's South Kensington Museum. This was where Cattell's approach to psychology would take a more decided turn toward psychophysical measurement or anthropometric testing. Although Galton was an independent researcher, Cattell was in awe of him and referred to him as "the greatest man whom I have known" (Cattell, quoted in Woodworth, 1944, p. 203). Galton and Cattell shared an interest in individual differences, although Galton's focus was more overtly on heredity and racial differences. Thorndike (1914) observed, "Cattell refined Galton's methods and won recognition for such measurement of individuals as a standard division of psychology and of psychological training in universities" (p. 92).

Cattell returned to the United States, despite Galton's influence, and taught briefly at Bryn Mawr College in Pennsylvania. His father, however, used his considerable power in the academy to negotiate a lectureship for James at the University of Pennsylvania in Philadelphia, one that evolved rapidly into a full professorship. Cattell began his academic career in psychophysics in the Department of Philosophy in 1887. In addition to this position, the senior Cattell negotiated a laboratory for his son that was established in 1888 (Baron, 2004).

While at the University of Pennsylvania, Cattell created several psychological tests to measure individual differences and in 1890 coined the term "mental tests" (Cattell, 1890, p. 373). He recalled that his work at the university included teaching undergraduates in laboratory courses in psychology. He was most proud of this work and its role in solidifying psychology as a separate discipline, and years later he commented,

In this laboratory the research work and the courses for students were based on objective measurements of responses to the environment with special reference to individual and group differences and to the useful application of psychology, thus leading to the development of modern educational, clinical, and industrial psychology. (Cattell, 1928, p. 547)

In 1891, Cattell was hired by Columbia University, New York, as Professor of Psychology, and Department Head of Psychology, Anthropology, and Philosophy. He was a member of the faculty 1891–1917 where he taught courses in psychology and was renowned for his close relationships with graduate students. Cattell also enjoyed a full life away from the academy as he was a husband and father.

On December 11, 1888, Cattell had married Josephine Owens, who became his devoted wife and mother of their seven children. Josephine homeschooled the children until their later years when Cattell's graduate students assisted in their education. Josephine also served as an unofficial coeditor of many of the professional journals edited by Cattell (Sokal, 1981). Each of the Cattell children pursued professional endeavors; however, only his daughter Psyche Cattell (1893–1989) followed him into the field of psychology (becoming the creator of The Cattell Infant Intelligence Scale).

At the Cattells' house overlooking the Hudson River, Edward Lee Thorndike (see chapter 5, this volume) and his wife were frequent guests. When Bess (as Edward's fiancée) first met Cattell she described him as "the funniest little man...out of an old fashioned story book—white stockings, broad flat toed low shoes, little shifty eyes" (quoted in Joncich, 1968, p. 200). According to Robert Sessions Woodworth (1944; see chapter 2, this volume), the Cattells were welcoming hosts who shared their home with colleagues in what he called an "easy, friendly atmosphere...with [Cattell's] evident love of children and family life and his delight in the beauty and freedom of the outdoors" (p. 208).

In his academic life, Cattell was fond of identifying himself as the first American to achieve various honors. For example, despite his self-proclamation that he was the first U.S. citizen to obtain a doctorate, the history of psychology records Joseph Jastrow from Johns Hopkins University in 1886 as the first (Sokal, 1981, p. 11). Cattell also claimed to have been the first U. S. citizen to receive a doctorate in psychology from Leipzig, but this is also in error, for that honor belongs to James Thompson Bixby (p. 11). Finally, his claim to hold the first chair in psychology is an error because that distinction belongs to G. Stanley Hall, professor of psychology and pedagogics at Clark University (Sokal, 1971, p. 632; cf. p. 17). However, Cattell was indeed the first U.S. citizen to be awarded a doctorate (in 1886) in experimental psychology from Leipzig (Sokal, 1981, p. 11) and among the first to secure a U.S. university appointment in psychology. His dissertation, *Psychometrische untersuchungen* (*Psychometric investigation*) was translated and revised as *The time taken up by cerebral operations* (Sokal, 1987a).

From the outset of his academic career Cattell sought to legitimize psychology as a valid science that would earn respect as an academic discipline similar to the respect received within the academy for life and physical sciences. His sentiments were the focus of his 1895 presidential address (published in 1896) to the American Psychological Association: "In the struggle for existence that obtains among the sciences psychology is continually gaining ground...The academic growth of psychology in America during the past few years is almost without precedent" (Cattell, 1896, p. 1). Later, he claimed,

> I venture to maintain that the introduction of experiments and measures into psychology has added directly and indirectly new subject-matter and methods, has set a higher standard of accuracy and objectivity, has made some part of the subject an applied science with useful applications, and enlarged the field and improved the methods of teaching psychology. (pp. 13–14)

Cattell's approach to establishing psychology as a science was undertaken in a two-pronged attack. First, he promoted positivism, scientism, and the scientific method in his experimental research, which I will discuss later. Second, he insisted on teaching psychology to undergraduates. In his research he devoted his energies to trying to correlate subjects' reaction times with their mental abilities.

Cattell's position at Columbia would be his last academic post. This is not to suggest that his career and thinking were without controversy—quite the opposite. Although Cattell was an ardent supporter of experimental psychology, his career as a psychologist appeared doomed when, after years of experiments and "mental testing," his graduate student Clark Wissler, working with Franz Boaz (Sokal, 1981, p. 338), found that Cattell's experiments produced useless data that did not correlate with one another, with "mental power" (Lagemann, 2000, p. 88), or with academic success (Sokal, 1987a).

Early on, Cattell had realized that these experiments were flawed. Along with his colleague Livingston Farrand, he acknowledged that the experiments were better as "measurements of the body and of the senses" than of "higher mental processes" (Cattell & Farrand, 1896, p. 622–623). He and Farrand argued,

> As in other scientific work these tests have two chief ends, the one genetic, the other quantitative. We wish to study growth as dependent on environment and heredity, and the correlation of traits from the point of view of exact science. (p. 620)

Cattell continued his research on physical and mental measurements for several years until he was forced to abandon his experiments after coming under criticism by colleagues and after the publication of a dissertation by Emily Sharp that compared his work on mental tests (unfavorably) with that of Alfred Binet (Sokal, 1981, p. 338), whose tests were adapted for measuring intelligence, thereby discrediting Cattell's research on mental measurements.

During this period, however, Cattell, like many of his contemporaries, continued to express his interest in eugenics. In 1896 he was appointed a member of the American Association for the Advancement of Science's (AAAS) standing committee charged with "an ethnographic survey of the white race in the United States" (Cattell & Farrand, 1896, p. 619).

Due to ongoing conflicts, personal and professional, with the administration at Columbia University, Cattell appears to have been almost constantly at odds with his superiors. Biographers have differed on the source of Cattell's independence—whether it derived from his privileged background, incredible intellect, or his studies in Europe—but he was not known for his interpersonal skills. Watson (1978) remarks that Cattell once told the story of a visit to a phrenologist when he was a boy: After due inspection of the bumps on his head, the phrenologist proceeded to reel off characteristics that were laudatory with one distinguishing exception—"Cattell suffered from a deficiency in will power!" (p. 407). Those who knew Cattell found it laughable because he was known for his tenacity.

Cattell's troubled coexistence with the administration at Columbia University began in part when he moved his office space without prior approval, and in part when he built his home at Fort Defiance, a Revolutionary Army fort (Sokal, 1981, p. 340), and at a considerable distance from Columbia "overlooking the Hudson River opposite of West Point" (Joncich,

1968, p. 200). It was also known as Garrison-on-the-Hudson. The administration voiced concern that the distance between his home and the university would restrict his time on campus, although Cattell was comfortable working at home.

It seems that away from home Cattell was known for anything but an easygoing manner, especially during his tenure at Columbia University. In fact, he was much better known for his quick, piercing wit, which prompted Thorndike (1914) to consider him "the first rebel from within the ranks of psychologists" (p. 92). Another former student, Arthur Gates (1971) (see chapter 14, this volume), recalled in his autobiography Cattell's definition of the behaviors of psychologists: "Psychology is what psychologists do" (p. 198). He also remembered that Cattell was "a very strict perfectionist possessed of a piercing, caustic wit which made life miserable for many, notably [Columbia's] President Nicholas Murray Butler who he regarded as a bit pompous" (p. 198). Finally, Gates captured his own assessment of Cattell this way: "a very loving father, but a quite naughty child" (p. 198).

Cattell unflinchingly asserted himself against the university administration. On one occasion, he spoke in support of a greater role for faculty in the affairs of the university. On another occasion, he was threatened with dismissal when he drew attention to the Columbia University Trustees' policies on junior faculty members' salaries. Although the Trustees voted to dismiss him, the faculty supported his actions and the dismissal was withdrawn. Following the arrest of his son, Dana, for antiwar protest, Cattell's passionate protests against U.S. involvement in World War I led him to send the following letter to several Congressmen:

> Sir:
> I trust that you will support a measure against sending conscripts to fight in Europe against their will. The intent of the Constitution and our consistent national policy should not be reversed without the consent of the people. The President and the present Congress were not elected to send conscripts to Europe. (quoted in Joncich, 1968, pp. 377–378)

On this occasion, the University Trustees took action and charged him with treason and sedition (Dunlap-Smith, 1999). Cattell was dismissed from the university in 1917, without his pension.

Gruber (1972) notes that the American Association of University Professors, an organization Cattell helped to establish, supported Cattell's case. He took legal action against the university, winning his $40,000 suit to restore his pension. Cattell used the money to help establish the Psychological Corporation. Although reportedly reinstated by the university, Cattell never returned to Columbia University as a professor nor taught again (Dunlap-Smith, 1999). The importance of Cattell's suit can not be overstated: Because of his determination to have his voice heard, many universities created a tenure process as a means to protect "academic freedom," which allows professors to express potentially unpopular political views without fear of dismissal. It is one of Cattell's most enduring legacies.

His protest against conscription notwithstanding, Cattell helped the war cause through his work on psychological test development for U.S. Army recruits. In fact, in 1921 he addressed the first annual meeting of the Psychological Corporation, noting that

> The Army tests have put psychology on the map of the United States, extending in some cases beyond the limits into fairyland...even the pretensions of ignoramuses and charlatans may be voices of [those] crying from the wilderness to make strait the way for psychology. (quoted in Joncich, 1968, p. 385)

Cattell's enthusiastic public proclamations represent his way of verifying psychology's place in academia and U.S. society, although he successfully had been working toward this goal for decades. For example, Cattell advised numerous students in graduate school while at Columbia, and over 50 of them completed their doctoral degrees under his tutelage before 1917. Robert Woodworth (1944) recalled Cattell's "unfailing interest and generosity" (p. 208) and the personal interest he took in his students' lives. Specifically, he wrote, "He assisted them in many ways, tangible and intangible: guiding them into fellowships and assistantships, supporting their efforts to secure academic positions, and providing employment at scientific work during summer vacations" (p. 208). In addition to Woodworth himself, Cattell's students included Walter Dearborn (see chapter 6, this volume), Gates, Albert Poffenberger, Thorndike, Margaret Washburn, and the behaviorist John Watson. In 1914, Woodworth devoted an entire issue of the journal he edited, *Archives of Psychology*, to tributes to Cattell by former students, including Thorndike and Dearborn (Woodworth, 1914).

Cattell also served as president of the American Psychological Association (1895) and the Association for the Advancement of Sciences (1924). According to Woodworth (1944), at the age of 70 Cattell mentioned that his greatest honor was being chosen the president of the Ninth International Congress of Psychology (p. 208). Cattell's desire to establish psychology as a science continued throughout his life. In 1942, for example, he used 600 shares of stock in the Psychological Corporation to establish the James McKeen Cattell Fund: A Benevolent Foundation for Psychology in a gift to Duke University. The monies were given to support "scientific research and the dissemination of knowledge with the object of obtaining results beneficial to the development of the science of psychology and to the advancement of the useful application of psychology" (Duke University, 2005, n.p.).

Cattell's many accomplishments include his work as editor and publisher of several journals. As Woodworth (1944), Poffenberger (1947), and Sokal (1981, 1992) note, Cattell was the cofounder of *Psychological Review* (1894–1903) with James Mark Baldwin; publisher and editor of *Journal of Science* (1894–1944), having purchased it from Alexander Graham Bell; and editor of *Popular Science Monthly* (1900–1915), *Scientific Monthly* (1915–1943), *American Naturalists* (1907–1944), *School and Society* (1915–1920; with W. Ryan and R. Walters, 1921–1927), the *Psychological Bulletin* (1904) with Mark Baldwin, and *American Men of Science and Leaders in Education* (1906–1938). He was also, as noted earlier, the founder of the Psychological Corporation in 1921, and of a publishing company, the Science Press, in 1923.

This brief overview of Cattell's personal and professional life is under no circumstances complete, but offers a window onto the life of a man whose keen intellect supported the fledging field of psychology through his early research and scholarship. In addition, his entrepreneurial ventures helped to shape the publication of research in the field and continue to fund psychology and scholars. Moreover, Cattell was a devoted husband, father, and mentor who was deeply loved and admired.

Philosophical Beliefs and Guiding Principles

Cattell's philosophical beliefs were shaped initially by his Protestantism—his Presbyterian background—but evolved as he developed into a scientist. As an undergraduate he embraced theories that included Baconianism (inductive reasoning in which the emphasis is placed on collecting instances rather than testing theories), positivism (the theory that knowledge can be acquired only through direct observation and experimentation, rather than through metaphysics and theology), scientism (unquestioning trust in the value of the scientific method and its applicability to all investigations), and eugenics (the belief in the control and improvement of race through heredity).

Sokal (1971, 1981), Cattell's most cited biographer, observes that Auguste Comte's positivism, with its emphasis on the scientific method, experimentation, observation, and quantification, was important to Cattell. Sokal also explains that Comtean positivism "meshed well with Cattell's Baconianism, though he would add his own experimentalist and utilitarian twist. This scientific ideology formed the basis for Cattell's sixty year career" (Sokal, 1987b, p. 24). In other words, Cattell's notion of science evolved from his Baconian undergraduate orientation to his growing acceptance of positivism as he became more involved in experimental psychology, yet his religious grounding resurfaced in later writings.

Significantly, Cattell's description of his early experiments makes clear his devotion to Comtean ideas of observation, quantification, and the lack of introspection (Sokal, 1981). His positivistic zeal is demonstrated in his conviction that "quantifiable (and, hence, meaningful) results could be obtained if the stimulus causing the sensation and the subject's error in observing the stimulus were the only data measured" (Sokal, 1981, p. 335). For example, Cattell embraced the idea that measuring the reaction time of individuals and their differences could indicate intelligence as well as brain and nervous system functions. Although he was unsuccessful in proving his hypothesis, his notion of mental testing and the quantification of observable behavior remain cornerstones of psychology. In his 1890 article, "Mental Tests and Measurements," which illustrates the importance of the use of measurement, Cattell argues:

> Psychology cannot attain the certainty and exactness of the physical sciences unless it rests on a foundation of experiment and measurement. A step in this direction could be made by applying a series of mental tests and measurements to a large number of individuals. The results would be of considerable scientific value in discovering the constancy of mental process, their interdependence, and their variation under different circumstances. (p. 373)

The appendix to this article, written by Galton, attests to the like-mindedness of these researchers. Later, in an 1896 article, Cattell and Farrand write,

> What can we learn from the tests of elementary traits regarding the higher intellectual and emotional life?...We must use our measurements to study the development of the individual and of the [white] race, to disentangle the complex factors of heredity and environment. (p. 648)

Although Cattell's goals appear focused on improving the value of psychology as a science through positivistic means, he did not stray far from Galton's interest in eugenics.

In fact, Cattell's interest in individual differences and testing coalesced with Galton's notions of eugenics. Galton defined *eugenics* as "the study of the agencies under social control, that improve or impair the racial qualities of future generations either physically or mentally" (Eugenics Archive, 2005). The notion of race (i.e., ethnicity or national origin) as a social construct is seen very clearly in its shifting definitions and use by eugenicists, many of whom were leading psychologists and educational psychologists, including Cattell and many of his students. Galton referenced race by skin color and physical features, intellectual traits, and emotive or affective characteristics, which he believed were inherited. Likewise, Cattell believed that through a study of heredity, psychologists could trace intelligence.

Galton's eugenics movement, especially the concept of superior germ-plasm (the notion that people of Nordic ancestry had superior traits that were inheritable by their offspring) and Cattell's work on individual differences shaped much of Cattell's thought in the late 1890s. Cattell mentioned his use of Galton's germ-plasm theory in a description of his family lineage, praising his own strong Scottish–Irish germ-plasm, French–English and colonial bloodlines, and economically privileged background: "It was my fortune to find a birthplace in the sun. A germ-plasm fairly well compounded met circumstances to which it was unusually fit to react" (Sokal, 1971, p. 629). Cattell was so convinced of the role of germ-plasm in carrying on intellect and character that he supported the use of eugenics to breed only superior families. In fact, he promised his seven children a lucrative gift if they each married the child of a professor (Sokal, 1971, p. 630).

While some biographers attempt to distance Cattell from Galton's eugenics movement and soften Cattell's involvement in the eugenics movement in the United States, the influence of Galton, a cousin of Charles Darwin, on Cattell's life should not be overlooked. Sokal (1987b) reveals, "Galton provided [Cattell] with a scientific goal—the measurement of the psychological differences between people—that made use of the experimental procedures he had developed at Leipzig" (p. 27). Galton's view of individual differences, especially the role played by the inheritability of the intellect (that is, of the favored characteristics possessed by successful, white, male scholars) also became part of Cattell's agenda. According to Sokal (1987b), "Cattell devoted himself to an extension of Galton's anthropometric program into what he called mental testing" (p. 29).

Galton and Cattell believed that science could help them rank order any behaviors once a criterion was established. Cattell used the same thinking and method in his earliest experiments (1885), including the evaluation of response times used to name letters, colors, and pictures. According to one commentator:

> This method is applicable to any set of stimuli capable of being ranked according to some criterion, such as the relative brightness of shades of gray, the problem he first investigated.... A number of judges would be asked to arrange the items to be evaluated in order of merit. The average ranking for each item was then calculated and a final rank order obtained. (Watson, 1978, p. 410)

One such exercise involved ranking the traits of those whom Cattell considered the most intelligent of all men: scientists. In 1903, he estimated that there were some 4,000 "scientific men" (p. 569) in the United States and sought to complete a statistical study of their characteristics and to rank them "in order of merit" (p. 566). He constructed a list of their traits that included physical health, mental balance, and intellect, as well as independence, cheerfulness, and leadership (p. 568). He claimed, "I applied psychological classifications...[to classify] men of thought, men of action and men of feeling" (Cattell, 1914b, p. 515). Further, Cattell used these classifications to evaluate "character and... [arrange] individuals in the order of merit for different traits" (p. 515).

In 1913, Cattell's ideas of the nexus of race and intelligence resurfaced in an address to the AAAS. He drew on notions of eugenics and Social Darwinism to explain social stratification in the United States according to race, class, and gender as he claimed that the importance of education in a democratic society was to fit the individual to the job best suited to his abilities. From his viewpoint, psychology had "recreated the world" (1914b, p.

155). When his speech was published in *Science* as "Science, Education and Democracy" (1914b), it caused quite a stir among African American scholars. Cattell revised the nature versus nurture argument with several examples that sought to explain differences of race, class, and gender within a narrow understanding of historical, political, and social influences.

Cattell noted that people of mixed race inherit characteristics from both parents but are probably above average compared to either parent. Furthermore, he commented that "their social position as is that of the negroes, and their performance corresponds to their environment rather than their heredity" (1914b, pp. 158–159). Finally, he claimed, "There is not a single mulatto who has done creditable scientific work" (p. 159). Cattell's comments, although striking today, were not unlike those of many other white scientists in psychology and education, who in the early 1900s promoted the racial and intellectual superiority of whites (Manning, 1998). Cattell's unfounded claims of the dearth of mulatto scientists were challenged by W.E.B. DuBois (1914) in *The Crisis*.

Cattell's commitment to Galton's notion of the inheritability of traits and the ordering of merit consumed much of the rest of Cattell's research agenda, papers, and publications, which included several international and national presentations, book chapters, articles, and the multi-volume *Biographical Dictionary of American Men of Science* (now known as *American Men and Women of Science*). These volumes are often referenced as directories, psychology's "Who's Who," while the eugenics and racist roots that gave rise to the project are ignored.

Curiously, toward the end of his life Cattell's religious background reasserted itself. In many of the presentations he made late in his life (and subsequently published in one of the journals he edited), Cattell uses Biblical allusions reflective of his Presbyterian upbringing that draw connections to religion to justify the role of science, psychology, and eugenics in education and in maintaining a democracy. In short, Cattell's philosophical beliefs and guiding principles of his research reflect his commitment to positivism, scientism, and eugenics, as evinced throughout his early research, his promotions of experimental psychology to locate individual differences, and his decades-long search for the characteristics of men of science. His search was not conducted as a demonstration of altruism but was undertaken to prove, scientifically and statistically, the intellectual and moral superiority of white males.

These beliefs and principles were applied to his early experiments with reading. In a review of some of these experiments, Cattell (1924) recalled, "The reactions of an individual are determined by stimuli acting on a nervous system formed largely by preceding experiences, and in an environment which is largely a social heritage" (p. 510). He added, "My experiments on the rate of reading and its dependence on the method of presentation, published in 1885, were of the intelligence test type" (p. 512). In other words, Cattell believed that the mental processes that helped produce responses in his experiments were indicators of intelligence and were racially and ethnically attributable. He also believed that there was an irrefutable connection among reaction time (responses), intelligence, and race and ethnicity; that is, he maintained that there are biological and genetic arguments for differences in intellect as measured by performance on psychological tests. Given that the subjects in his early experiments were often other white male graduate students, Cattell surmised that their responses indicated their superior intellect. He further sought to normalize their characteristics—white, male, middle to upper class, and English-dominant—as standard.

One of his goals was to demonstrate the superior intellect of white males by comparing their results with subjects of different races and ethnicities and noting differences, not so much individual as racial and ethnic. (See, for instance, his early statistical analyses presented at the First National Conference on Race Betterment held in 1914.) It is important to acknowledge that most of the early reading researchers also were educational psychologists who had studied under Cattell or one of his students and who held similar beliefs, suggesting that his influence is immeasurable.

Contributions to the Field of Reading

Cattell's contributions to reading have been celebrated by historians of reading research since the turn of the last century, including Gibson and Levin (1976), Huey (1908), and Venezky (1984). Venezky's (1984) discussion of Cattell's contributions can be divided into two broad categories: (1) mental testing and (2) early reading experiments.

Mental Testing

Vivian Henmon (1914), a former student of Cattell, reviewed Cattell's early research in the United States on reaction time and observed that Cattell conducted a series of experiments on seeing and naming objects, believing they represented naturally occurring events in the lives of people. Significantly, she observes that Cattell sought to extend his research "to make experiments such as these on the lower races, as well as of persons of different age, sex, occupations, etc" (p. 19). Clearly, however, during his doctoral studies while working as Wundt's assistant, Cattell's research had focused on psychometry, or "measuring the rapidity of mental processes" of white males similar to himself (Cattell, 1886, p. 63). Cattell (1924) fondly labeled his early experiments the "Cattell-Columbia tests" (p. 514) after conducting numerous experiments on individual differences at Columbia University.

Early Reading Experiments

Of particular interest to this volume is Cattell's work with the measurement of mental abilities, even though these were restricted to the recognition of colors, letters, and words. His experiments with reading were limited to the reaction time of nine subjects in the first experiment and three in the second. Below are excerpts from Cattell's descriptions of these two experiments from his 1886 publication in *Mind*, on the time it takes to see and name objects:

(1) I pasted letters on a revolving drum (a physiological kymography) and determined at what rate they could be read aloud, as they passed by a slit in a screen. It was found that the time varied with the width of the slit. When the slit was 1 cm. wide (the letters being 1 cm. apart) one letter was always in view; as the first disappeared the second took its place, &c. In this case it took the nine persons experimented on (university teachers and students) [who included John Dewey, Stanley Hall, and Cattell himself] from 1/3 to 1/5 sec. to read each letter.... Of the nine persons experimented on four could read the letters faster when five were in view at once, but were not helped by a sixth letter; three were not helped by a fifth and two not by a fourth letter. This shows that while one idea is in the centre, two, three, or four additional ideas may be in the background of consciousness....

(2) I find it takes twice as long to read (aloud, as fast as possible) words which have no connexion as words which make sentences, and letters which have no connexion as letters which make words. When the words make sentences and the letters words, not only do the processes of seeing and naming overlap, but by one mental effort the subject can recognize a whole group of words or letters, and by one will-act choose

the motions to be made in naming them, so that the rate at which the words and letters are read is really only limited by the maximum rapidity at which the speech-organs can be moved...the time required to read each word when the words did not make sentences varying between 1/4 and 1/2 sec.... The rate at which a person reads a foreign language is proportional to his familiarity with the language.

(3) The time required to see and name colours and pictures of objects was determined the same way. The time was found to be about the same (over 1/2 sec.) for colours as for pictures, and about twice as long as for words and letters. Other experiments I have made show that we can recognize a single colour or picture in a slightly shorter time than a word or letter, but take longer to name it. This is because in the case of words and letters the association between the idea and name has taken place so often that the process has become automatic, whereas in the case of colours and pictures we must by a voluntary effort choose the name. (pp. 64–65)

Importantly, Cattell's findings indicate that readers appear to chunk information, reading words as opposed to letters. He found that (a) it takes longer to read some letters than words, (b) letters and familiar short words can be read in about the same amount of time, and (c) words in context are more easily read. Dearborn (1914), another former student of Cattell, summarizes these experiments as follows:

This observation that words are read as easily as letters had important bearings for the pedagogy of reading. The practise [sic] of teaching children to read words as words rather than as combinations of letters was already in common use, but this was the first experimental evidence tending to prove that words are read as wholes and to this extent gave justification for the change from the alphabet to the word method of teaching reading. (pp. 38–39)

Cattell's findings do indeed point to the importance of understanding that words are read as wholes, especially when they are placed in relation to other words or with pictures; however, he did not make clear, as do Gibson and Levin (1976), that his results were valid for adults (p. 197) and may have more to do with the familiarity of words and with redundancy than with reading (p. 215).

The comments by Henmon and Dearborn were part of a series of articles written by several of Cattell's former students in a volume of *Archives of Psychology* edited by Woodworth (1914). In addition to the comments mentioned above, Dearborn (1914) noted that two other of Cattell's former students—Josephine Horton Bowden (1911) and Myrtle Sholty (1912)—working at the University of Chicago's Laboratory School, had extended his research on reading to elementary school classrooms. Their experiments were subsequently published in *The Elementary School Journal* in 1911 and 1912. Both researchers conducted their experiments with children to determine if Cattell's experiments with adults were applicable (Dearborn, 1914, p. 40). Dearborn concluded that the results from the research of Bowden, Sholty, and others, including his own, indicated that (a) there are multiple types of readers who vary due to individual differences, (b) no one method of teaching beginning reading (word or phonetic) is effective for all readers, and (c) phonetic analysis was helpful for some beginning and early readers but not for others. Even though the word method was gaining in popularity among some educators, especially those at the University of Chicago's Laboratory School where Colonel Francis Parker (1883) endorsed the Quincy Method, Cattell is not known to have endorsed this method of instruction over others.

Cattell (1924) spoke before the AAAS and summarized his research on reading in this way:

> I found that a word could be read as easily as a single letter; that a subject might require about one half second to read a single word, about one fourth second each to read disconnected words in series and about one eighth second each to read words in sentences. (p. 512)

He continued by recalling his experiments in different languages and with colors and pictures. The texts were printed without spacing between words in English as well as in French, German, Italian, Latin, and Greek. An example begins as follows:

> IthappenededonedayaboutnoongoingtowardsmyboatIwasexceedinglysurpr isedwiththeprintofaman'snakedfootontheshore. (Cattell, 1886, p. 64)

He also claimed, "It took about twice as long to name a color or an object as the word designating it for those habitually engaged in reading, but not for others" (p. 512). In sum, Cattell's experiments and the reviews of his work revealed that reading is more efficient when letters are displayed as words than when they stand alone, and when there is some context for understanding the letters, words, or pictures.

Some scholars have linked the whole-word versus phonics debate to Cattell's research findings (Huey, 1908), while others—Gibson and Levin (1976) for example—note that instruction in letter and word-shape recognition does not significantly improve reading (p. 197). In short, decoding and whole-word recognition skills are not synonymous with reading. Currently, many reading researchers concede that while the alphabetic principle (phonemic awareness and phonics) supports some beginning readers, reading, as Cattell's findings indicate, is a nearly automatic recognition of letters and their accompanying sounds as familiar words. (Although we now know that many more unacknowledged skills and language features also support reading.) Cattell's idea that the brain works to form sentences or make meaning of groups of words that are presented suggests a search for meaning. In this view, the reading process involves the ability to use a variety of cueing systems, including world or prior knowledge, in order for words to be read and convey meaning. Cattell, however, used accomplished adult readers in his experiments. The use of his ideas by others among children, that is, the use of whole-word instruction, reflects use with nonreaders, or at least inexperienced readers. The leap from testing adults to teaching novices is, instructionally speaking, a huge one.

Linking Psychological Research and Education

In 1904, during an address at the International Congress of Arts and Sciences, later published in *Popular Science Monthly*, Cattell declared,

> I claim for psychology the freedom of the universe in its subject matter, so I believe that every method of science can be used by the psychologist. The two great achievements of science have been the elaboration of the quantitative method on the one hand and of the genetic on the other....It would be an irreparable limitation if either of these methods did not apply in psychology. (pp. 60–74)

Cattell, as a positivist, also envisioned a role for psychology in education. As a strong supporter of education, he believed in the importance of literacy in a democratic society. He put it this way: "Reading and writing have become, like air and water, the common heritage of all. This is the great achievement of democracy in the modern world" (1914b, p. 157). Furthermore, drawing on his positivistic and eugenic background, he qualified this statement by noting, "Children must learn to read, write, and calculate, but under proper conditions of family and society" (p. 157).

When asked to speak on the interpretation of intelligence tests—in part because of his support for eugenics and the role of intelligence testing in shaping education—Cattell delivered a speech that was soon published in *The Scientific Monthly* (1924). Ever the promoter of the role of psychology in education, Cattell noted that intelligence tests were based on psychological tests that could prove helpful in fitting people to their life's work. Although not a supporter of environmental or social influences, he declared that differences among Italian children and "[white] native American children may be more correctly identified as a lack of familiarity with language and directions when taking intelligence tests" (p. 516). Nonetheless, he concluded, "A great forward step has been taken when psychology is applied to useful purposes and the way is made straight for a profession that may become as serviceable as medicine or engineering" (p. 516).

In sum, Cattell's reading research drew upon his understanding of the mental and physical processes that produced varying reaction times which, he believed, were connected to intelligence and attributable to race and ethnicity. In addition, he sought to measure and identify differences between genders and races, while surreptitiously seeking to confirm his beliefs about the intellectual and moral superiority of white males. Cattell's experimental psychology and professional clout, in relation to reading research, center on his insistence on conflating individual and racial differences that have traditionally been used to support deficit notions about nonwhites, popular among some psychologists and reading researchers since the early 1900s. What is imperative to understand today is that Cattell set a precedent in reading research whereby positivism continues to underpin many research projects, especially those that seek to identify differences among students and to quantify them without consideration of historical, social, and political contexts.

Lessons for the Future

Cattell's role in intelligence and early reading research and testing was influential and continues to shape reading research. His life and work mirror the complex history of psychology and reading that is anchored to positivism, scientism, and eugenics (as well as racism). From Cattell we can learn the following lessons: (a) alternative ways of conceiving the reading research agenda are needed that do not center on positivism, scientism, eugenics, and racism; (b) reading research in the 21st century should reflect a wide range of philosophical underpinnings that are inclusive of multiple racial, ethnic, and cultural and linguistic epistemologies; and (c) reading research is only a small facet of the effect that one life can have on the field. His influence includes his work with his doctoral students, many of whom have also helped to shape the field of reading research, as has his extensive editorship of journals and his leadership of numerous professional organizations.

Reflection Questions

1. Given the current resurrection of positivism and the zeal to embrace scientism in federally and philanthropically funded reading research, is there also an unacknowledged acceptance of racism? Are reading researchers inadvertently, and, perhaps unwittingly, supporting positivism, scientism, and eugenics (as well as racism) by remaining silent about the philosophical basis of the current federal mandate and funding of scientifically and evidence-based reading research?

2. Dearborn's (1914) summary of Cattell's contribution to reading documents that there are individual differences among readers not limited to race and that there is no one method by which all children can learn to read. Why, then, are individual differences among readers categorized and tracked by reading researchers and the federal government (especially in light of annual yearly progress reports under the No Child Left Behind Act of 2001) under race, gender, and social class?

3. In 2005 the National Center for Educational Statistics and the National Assessment of Educational Progress issued reports on reading progress that include Cattell's notion of individual differences (i.e., racial, ethnic, gendered, linguistic, and social economic differences) among children in grades 4 and 8. Why has his notion of individual differences been retained? Are there other individual differences among students that may be more informative to reading researchers?

4. Cattell's normalization of psychological subjects continues to be the standard by which all school children's performance in reading is measured. As the public school population in the United States grows ever more racially, ethnically, and linguistically diverse, is it morally and ethically appropriate to retain this standard?

5. How can reading researchers draw from and build upon multiple epistemologies to effect a more socially just and morally impartial reading research agenda for all readers?

REFERENCES

Baron, J. (2004). *Cattell at Penn*. Retrieved December 21, 2004, from University of Pennsylvania, Department of Psychology website: http://www.psych.upenn.edu/history/cattelltext.htm

Bowden, J.H. (1911). Learning to read. *The Elementary School Teacher, 12*, 21–33.

Cattell, J.M. (1885). Ueber die Zeit der Erkennung und Benennung von Schriftzeichen, Bildern und Farben. *Philosophische Studien, 2*, 635–650. (Trans. R. Woodworth, 1886).

Cattell, J.M. (1886). The time it takes to see and name objects. *Mind, 11*, 63–65.

Cattell, J.M. (1890). Mental tests and measurements. *Mind, 15*, 373–381.

Cattell, J.M. (1896). Address of the president before the American Psychological Association, 1895. *Psychological Review, 3*(2), 1–15.

Cattell, J.M. (1903). Homo scientificus Americanus. *Science, 17*, 561–570.

Cattell, J.M. (1904). The conceptions and methods of psychology. *Popular Science Monthly*, 60–74.

Cattell, J.M. (1914a). The causes of the declining birth rate. In M. Robins (Ed). *Proceedings of the First National Conference on Race Betterment* (pp. 67–72). Battle Creek, MI: Race Betterment Foundation.

Cattell, J.M. (1914b). Science, education and democracy. *Science, 39*, 154–164.

Cattell, J.M. (1924). The interpretation of intelligence tests. *Scientific Monthly, 18*, 508–516.

Cattell, J.M. (1928). Early psychological laboratories. *Science, 67*, 543–548.

Cattell, J.M., & Farrand, L. (1896). Physical and mental measurements of the students at Columbia University. *Psychological Review, 3*, 618–648.

Dearborn, W.F. (1914). Professor Cattell's studies of reading and perception. *Archives of Psychology, 30*, 4–45.

DuBois, W.E.B. (1914). More correspondence. *The Crisis, 9*(2), 81.

Duke University. (2005). *James McKeen Cattell Fund*. Retrieved July 10, 2005, from http://www.cattell.duke.edu/index.html

Dunlap-Smith, A. (1999, September 17). Obscure perhaps, but this journal of philosophy is leader in its field. *Columbia University Record, 25*(3). Retrieved, December 21, 2004, from http://www.columbia.edu/cu/record/archives/vol25/03/2503_Philosophy_Journal.html

Eugenics Archive. (2005). *Image archive on the American eugenics movement*. Retrieved July 21, 2005, from http://www.eugenicsarchive.org/eugenics

Gates, A.I. (1971). An autobiography. In R. Havighurst (Ed.), *Leaders in American education: The seventieth yearbook of the National Society for the Study of Education. Part II* (pp. 189–217). Chicago: National Society for the Study of Education.

Gibson, E.J., & Levin H. (1976). *The psychology of reading*. Cambridge, MA: MIT Press.

Gruber, C. (1972, Autumn). Academic freedom at Columbia University: The case of James McKeen Cattell. *American Association of University Professors Bulletin*, 297–305.

Henmon, V.A. (1914). Professor Cattell's work on reaction time. *Archives of Psychology, 30*, 1–33.

Huey, E.B. (1908). *The psychology and pedagogy of reading*. New York: Macmillan.

Joncich, G.M. (1968). *The sane positivist: A biography of Edward L. Thorndike*. Middletown, CT: Wesleyan University Press.

Lagemann, E.C. (2000). *An elusive science: The troubling history of education research*. Chicago: University of Chicago Press.

Lotze, H. (1966). *Medicinische Psychologie: Oder, Physiologie der Seele*. Amsterdam: E.J. Bonset. (Original work published 1852)

Manning, K.R. (1998). Science and opportunity. *Science, 282*, 1037–1038.

No Child Left Behind Act of 2001, Pub. L. No. 107-110, 115 Stat. 1425 (2002).

Parker, F.W. (1883). *Notes of talks on teaching*. (Reported by L. Patridge). New York: E.L. Kellogg.

Pearson, P.D., Barr, R., Kamil, M.L., & Mosenthal, P. (Eds.). (1984). *Handbook of reading research*. New York: Longman.

Poffenberger, A.T. (Ed.). (1947). *James McKeen Cattell (1860–1944): Man of science*. Lancaster, PA: Science Press.

Sholty, M. (1912). A study of reading vocabulary of children. *The Elementary School Teacher, 12* (6), 272–277.

Sokal, M.M. (1971). The unpublished autobiography of James McKeen Cattell. *American Psychologist, 26*, 626–635.

Sokal, M.M. (Ed.). (1981). *An education in psychology: James McKeen Cattell's journal and letters from Germany and England, 1880–1888*. Cambridge, MA: MIT Press.

Sokal, M.M. (1987a). James McKeen Cattell and mental anthropometry: Nineteenth-century science and reform and the origins of psychological testing. In M.M. Sokal (Ed.), *Psychological testing and American society* (pp. 21–45). New Brunswick, NJ: Rutgers University Press.

Sokal, M.M. (Ed.). (1987b). *Psychological testing and American society*. New Brunswick, NJ: Rutgers University Press.

Sokal, M.M. (1992). Origin and early years of the American Psychological Association, 1890–1906. *The American Psychologist, 47*, 111–122.

Thorndike, E.L. (1914). Professor Cattell's relation to the study of individual differences. *Archives of Psychology, 30*, 92–101.

Venezky, R.L. (1984). The history of reading research. In P.D. Pearson, R. Barr, M.L. Kamil, and P. Mosenthal (Eds.), *Handbook of reading research* (pp. 3–38). New York: Longman.

Venezky, R.L. (1987). Steps toward a modern history of reading instruction. In E.Z. Rothkopf (Ed.), *Review of research in education* (Vol. 13, pp. 129–167). Washington, DC: American Educational Association.

Watson, R.I. (1978). *The great psychologists* (4th ed.). New York: Lippincott.

Woodworth, R.S. (Ed.) (1914). The psychological researches of James McKeen Cattell: A review by some of his pupils. *Archives of Psychology, 30*, 60–74.

Woodworth, R.S. (1944). James McKeen Cattell, 1840–1944. *Psychological Review, 51*, 201–209.

FOR FURTHER READING

Boring, E.G. (1950). *A history of experimental psychology* (2nd ed.). New York: Appleton-Century-Crofts. (Original work published 1929)

Cattell, J.M. (1895). Measurements of the accuracy of recollection. *Science, 2*, 761–766.

Cattell, J.M. (1929). Psychology in America. *Science, 70*, 335–347.

Charles, D.C. (1987). The emergence of educational psychology. In J.A. Glover & R.R. Ronning (Eds.), *Historical foundations of educational psychology* (pp. 17–38). New York: Plenum Press.

Gould, S.J. (1996). *The mismeasure of man* (Rev. ed.). New York: W.W. Norton.

Kline, E., Moore, D.W., & Moore, S.A. (1987). Colonel Francis Parker and beginning reading instruction. *Reading Research and Instruction, 26,* 141–150.

Lewontin, R.C., Rose, S.P., & Kamin, L.J. (1984). *Not in our genes: Biology, ideology, and human nature.* New York: Pantheon.

Mathews, M.M. (1967). *Teaching to read.* Chicago: University of Chicago Press.

O'Donnell, J.M. (1985). *The origins of behaviorism: American psychology, 1870–1920.* New York: New York University Press.

Sokal, M.M. (1980). Science and James McKeen Cattell, 1894–1945. *Science, 209,* 43–52.

CHAPTER 2

Robert Sessions Woodworth (1869–1962): Dean of Psychologists

By Allen Berger, Dixie D. Massey, Kristin Stoll, and Aviva Gray

Historical Research Process

HISTORICAL RESEARCH IS part hard work and part serendipity. While researching the life of Robert Sessions Woodworth, the senior author hosted a family during his university's Parents Weekend. By good fortune one of the parents turned out to be a librarian, and she provided additional hands-on help, delving into the research and coming up with opinion/editorials by and about Woodworth that had appeared in *The New York Times*. Next, we uncovered the vast collection of papers that Woodworth had amassed as a stu-

---

Shaping the Reading Field: The Impact of Early Reading Pioneers, Scientific Research, and Progressive Ideas, edited by Susan E. Israel and E. Jennifer Monaghan. © 2007 by the International Reading Association.
Photo: Courtesy of Columbia Archives.

dent and scholar, which are housed in the Rare Book and Manuscript Library—Manuscript and Archival Collections—at Columbia University. One would think this discovery would make our job of finding information about a pioneer in the field of reading much easier. However, the collection consists of 19 linear feet of approximately 12,500 items in 38 boxes extending from 1906 to 1962, all of which take research approval and at least a week's advance notice to transfer from the Rare Book and Manuscript Library archives to the main library. Because none of us were able to visit New York to track down relevant references, we had to rely on the assistance of master's degree students who were looking for additional college funds. One such master's degree student, Aviva Gray, just happened to be studying for her archivist's certificate and was thrilled to spend time with old letters and forgotten syllabi.

Personal and Professional Life

It is remarkable how famous Robert Sessions Woodworth was in his day considering how little he is known in our own. Here was a man who wrote the leading textbooks in psychology for at least two generations, who was elected president of the Social Science Research Council and the American Psychological Association (APA), and who received the first gold medal for achievement given by the APA. He was so healthy and active that on the day before his 87th birthday in 1956, "he put aside an examination he was stenciling for his class at Columbia and suspended work on a new book" to be interviewed by *The New York Times* (Harrison, 1956b).

Woodworth advanced the field of reading through his broad knowledge of physiology and eye movements. He not only focused on the physical activities of reading but he also carefully examined reading motivation and textual meaning. His willingness to learn from diverse fields set the stage for collaboration among many researchers.

Robert Sessions Woodworth was born October 17, 1869, in Belchertown, Massachusetts, USA, to Lydia Sessions Woodworth and William Walter Woodworth. Lydia was the third wife of William Woodworth. Robert was the eldest surviving son of Lydia and William's four children, with another four older half-brothers and -sisters from William's previous marriages. He was named after the Robert Sessions who participated in the Boston Tea Party (Poffenberger, 1962, p. 677), and the family was rather proud of their long American history. The first Woodworth on American soil—Walter—came to Scituate, Massachusetts, USA, in 1630, and later members of the family fought in the revolutionary war in New York and Connecticut (Woodworth, 1906–1962, Box 1).

Both of Robert's parents had college degrees. His mother graduated from what is now Mount Holyoke College and "became the 'founder' or first principal of a similar seminary in Ohio for young women" (Woodworth, 1932/1961, p. 359)—Lake Erie Female Seminary (now Lake Erie College) in Painesville, Ohio, USA. "She, then, was a teacher," Woodworth recalled, "and I might be said to have followed in her steps, since the subjects she taught included especially mathematics and 'mental philosophy'" (p. 359). Robert's father was a minister in the Congregational Church who had graduated from Yale College and Yale Divinity School (Poffenberger, 1962, p. 677).

When Robert Woodworth, at the age of 63, was asked to contribute to Carl Murchison's text (1932/1961), *A History of Psychology in Autobiography*, he reflected on his childhood and adolescence by analyzing his life as he would analyze a "problem child" for a psychological case study (p. 359). He described his household as strict. The family held prayers and read the Bible twice every day. In Woodworth's words, Lydia was self-sacrificing and devoted to her children but not coddling or sentimental. His father had a vast library, filled with volumes of Hebrew, Greek, and theology texts, but Robert commented in his memoir that he found little to read in his father's library:

> Absorbed in his study and the weekly writing of his sermons, intensely and rather sternly religious, [my father] permitted himself little relaxation with his children, except for afternoon drives about his country parish, when one or another of us was often delighted to accompany him. As I grew up during his mellowing later years, I became less and less afraid of him. He was aged fifty-five when I was born and died when I was twenty. (Woodworth, 1932/1961, p. 359)

In his autobiography Woodworth declares that to understand a person one should consider not merely parental influences but also influences within the neighborhood. So he mentions "the boys and girls I played with, the neighborhood bully who made me eat dirt, the men who would talk with me while doing their outdoor work" (Woodworth, 1932/1961, p. 360). His playmates' activities in and beyond his Connecticut village were "half-lawful" and resulted in his father "applying the birch," usually for staying out longer with his friends than he was given permission to do (p. 360). "Always, from the age of six or seven, I had a chum, I had a 'girl,' I had a group of friends" (p. 360), Woodworth remembered. These friends played a larger role in his life than what went on in his own home, he said. Woodworth even commented on his Oedipus complex (which he says was only represented in his life by his resistance to adult authority) and mother fixation (which he said did not exist for him) (p. 360). From the age of 12, he attended school in a Boston suburb. To do so, he stayed with his oldest half-sister, her husband, and their three daughters. He described his half-sister and husband as "second parents" and their daughters as "younger sisters" (p. 360).

Woodworth had many aspirations as a youth. His earliest intention was to become an astronomer. By the age of 14, he wanted to be a farmer. After graduating from high school, he asked his parents to allow him to go into music. Through high school and much of college he focused on classics and mathematics, "with some history, a little modern literature, and very little science" (Woodworth, 1932/1961, p. 363). He started college at Amherst in 1887 without a clear career goal, but music soon dropped out of sight and he became convinced that he would pursue some scholarly career instead. His parents hoped that he would enter the ministry, but they did not pressure him, and he settled on teaching as a career choice.

During his senior year at Amherst, he was scheduled to take a philosophy course, which then included psychology. The instructor, Charles Garman, was well respected and considered by many Amherst students to be the best teacher they had ever encountered (Woodworth, 1932/1961, p. 362). Woodworth recounts his initial encounter with Garman in great detail (p. 362). He first scheduled a meeting with Garman during the end of his junior year, and Garman took time to speak with him, inquiring into Woodworth's studies. He was appalled at how little science young Woodworth knew and suggested that he spend the summer gaining a scientific background. Garman even went with Woodworth to the library to select scientific texts and create a reading list for him. Woodworth wrote, "There is no doubt that that interview was an eye-opener to me, and a turning point in my career, for thenceforth I regarded science as the general field of my efforts" (p. 362). After the course, Woodworth said he was sure that his future work lay somewhere in the field of psychology. At the time, no textbooks in psychology existed. Years later, Woodworth's own texts would fill the gap.

Woodworth earned a Bachelor of Arts from Amherst College in 1891. Following his graduation, he taught high school mathematics and science for two years in Watertown, New York, USA, and then took a position as a mathematics instructor at Washburn College in Topeka, Kansas, USA, for another two years (Graham, 1967, p. 543). During these four years he was influenced by the writings of both the philosopher William James and of G. Stanley Hall, generally acknowledged to be the founder of the child-study movement in the United States. Woodworth was so enamored of Hall's views that after he heard Hall lecture he wrote the word INVESTIGATION on a large card and "suspended it by [his] desk" (Woodworth, 1932/1961, p. 364).

Woodworth next went to Harvard University, where he divided his interests between philosophy and psychology. James was one of his instructors, and Edward Lee Thorndike (see chapter 5, this volume) a fellow student. In 1896, Woodworth earned another BA and, a year later, an MA, both from Harvard University. When in 1897 James procured a position for him in the Harvard physiological laboratory, Woodworth finally abandoned the pursuit of philosophy to focus on psychology, a decision that involved spending five more years on physiology and just one on psychology. He spent the year on psychology under the tutelage of James McKeen Cattell (see chapter 1, this volume) at Columbia University, but he was also introduced to statistics and to the work of Franz Boas, from whom he gained "some appreciation of the value of anthropology to a psychologist" (Woodworth, 1932/1961, p. 367).

In 1899 Woodworth earned his PhD from Columbia University (Graham, 1967, p. 544). Upon his graduation, he accepted a position at Columbia University and Bellevue Hospital Medical College, teaching there until 1902, with a summer break spent at the University of Edinburgh, working with Charles Sherrington (Woodworth, 1932/1961, p. 368). Early in 1903, he made his way back to England for continued study with a physiologist in Liverpool. While in England, he met and married Gabrielle Schjoth, the daughter of the Danish consul (Poffenberger, 1962, p. 681). Later that year the couple returned to Columbia University, where Woodworth became an instructor of psychology.

Robert and Gabrielle Woodworth settled easily into university life, Woodworth recalled in his autobiography. Living deep in the woods some 40 miles up the Hudson River, they "soon became part of a small group of congenial young couples in the University" that included the Thorndikes (Woodworth, 1932/1961, p. 368). The Woodworths had four children: two sons, William and Robert; and two daughters, Greta and Virginia. According to Woodworth, although he "never attempted any systematic psychological study of [his] children," he kept his "eyes psychologically open" as he watched them grow up and learned much from them (p. 368).

Over the years, Woodworth's relationship with Gabrielle changed. Letters in the archives at Columbia University document that Gabrielle lived in Clinton, New York, USA, while Robert kept an apartment close to Columbia. The letters also indicated that Woodworth and his wife retained lawyers "to draw up an agreement and financial argument" (Woodworth to Poffenberger, 1931). Woodworth's files contain letters to two of his colleagues apologizing for anonymous, threatening notes that they had received. In the letters he explains that the notes were from his wife, who was slightly unbalanced, and that this was not the first time she had written such notes. They were written out of animosity toward him, he explains, and not toward the individuals who received the notes. In the same letters, he comments on what he believed to be "some mild condition of imbalance, manifested mostly by jealousy and hostility" (Woodworth to Warden, 1930; Woodworth to Poffenberger, 1931). Indeed, Gabrielle lived in nursing homes and at the Watrous Memorial Sanitarium many years before her death in 1960 ("Mrs. R.S. Woodworth," 1960).

Although the Woodworths never divorced, letters in the archives suggest that Robert went on to have some sort of relationship with Mrs. Enrica Tunnell, who served as his secretary while also working as the head of the Psychology Library (Graham, 1967, p. 556). Tunnell helped Woodworth establish his apartment office after his retirement. She also attended some family events with him. For example, an invitation for dinner prior to Woodworth's 75th birthday party is addressed to Robert, Mrs. Tunnell, and her daughter (B. Woodworth to R.S. Woodworth, 1946).

In spite of personal challenges, Woodworth's academic career prospered. At Columbia, Woodworth continued to work with Cattell, whom he recalled as "the chief of all my teachers in giving shape to my psychological thought and work" (Woodworth, 1932/1961, p. 367). In 1914, he devoted, as editor, an entire issue of *Archives of Psychology* to honoring Cattell. Six of Cattell's former pupils, who included Thorndike and Walter Fenno Dearborn (see chapter 6, this volume) as well as Woodworth himself, wrote glowingly about different aspects of Cattell's psychological research (Woodworth, 1914).

Thorndike and Woodworth joined with Cattell to form the Psychological Corporation in 1921, dedicated to creating psychological assessments. Harcourt Assessment, Inc. (2005) lists the Psychological Corporation as the point of origin for its psychological assessments. Cattell was dismissed from Columbia for his pacifism and criticism of the university administration after he wrote a letter to Congress arguing against the drafting of conscientious objectors during World War I, and he was even accused of treason by the university. Woodworth wrote letters to the university president and other high-ranking administrators in support of his friend, saying that losing Cattell would be a disservice to the field. Nonetheless, Cattell was dismissed. Woodworth retained copies of the letters and notes on the controversy (Woodworth to Butler, 1913; Woodworth to Howard, 1917), perhaps hoping to clear Cattell's name. Cattell never worked in higher education again.

Although Woodworth was greatly influenced by his mentor Cattell at Columbia University, Clarence Graham (1967), one of Woodworth's biographers, comments that any influence by Cattell and various others was balanced by Woodworth's own dedication to being his own man. "Woodworth's quiet and soft manner belied a streak of resistance, especially to what he took to be 'doctrinaire' attitudes" (p. 554), although once committed to a position he was its staunch advocate. Graham recalls that Woodworth's soft-spoken support of a position or student in faculty meetings was at first misleading, for his persistence and stubbornness could outlast any opponent (p. 555). As a result, students became his devoted supporters, even if access to him required an appointment made well in advance with his secretary.

Woodworth was active in a variety of professional activities and served as chair of his department at Columbia University, a task he did not like as much as teaching. In a letter dated May 7, 1925, Thorndike wrote to Woodworth, stating that Woodworth should give up his executive responsibilities in the department, passing them on to Poffenberger and "younger men" to free himself for his research and course work (Thorndike to Woodworth, 1925). It is interesting to note that in the letter Thorndike assumes that Woodworth would be dedicating 75 hours a week to the university, of which 10 were to be devoted to lecturing, 10 to consulting with instructors in the department and counseling students, and the rest to his laboratory work and research.

However, during his career Woodworth viewed teaching as his main work. Graham (1967) comments that Woodworth devoted great effort to teaching the course called Advanced Experimental Psychology. Graham writes, "This course was a major hurdle for all graduate students, and the amount of work was, as one said, 'frightening'" (p. 552), although students viewed Woodworth as a fair teacher. Expectations included the requirement that each student complete original experiments in the laboratory on each new topic introduced in class. Few students finished the course in the year it was given; in fact, some students needed several years to complete the course, but Woodworth was as careful with his grade records as he was with his experimental data, and no student completed the course without turning in all the required lab reports.

If all of his years as a teacher are included, Woodworth taught for 67 years. His commitment to his students is well documented. The journalist for *The New York Times* at the 1956 interview mentioned earlier reported that Woodworth was invited to attend dinner and a concert in celebration of his 87th birthday on the day following the interview. He refused to attend, saying that his class met on the night of his birthday and he would not miss class: "The students work hard and they pay a lot of money for the course. It costs them about $4 a night...they could go to a ball game for that" (Harrison, 1956b).

Although he had a firm commitment to his students, in his autobiography (1932/1961), Woodworth devotes a lengthy section to his activities outside the university. These activities provided him with research opportunities on an international scale. In 1905 he was put in charge of testing and analyzing the results of racial differences as represented by participants in the World's Fair (Poffenberger, 1962, p. 681). During World War I, Woodworth wished to participate in the Army testing service as many other psychologists did—Raymond Dodge, for instance (see chapter 3, this volume); however, as Woodworth wrote, "Conditions seemed to demand that I be the one to stay at home and carry on some semblance of psychological instruction in the University" (Woodworth, 1932/1961, pp. 373–374). It was during this time that the APA asked Woodworth to create a test for emotional stability, a test viewed as necessary because many of the soldiers who had returned from World War I were suffering from shell shock or war "neurosis" (Graham, 1967, p. 549).

Woodworth continued to carry on his "semblance of psychological instruction" and major work for many decades. He would stay at Columbia University for the rest of his career—through his first official retirement in

1945 and as professor emeritus until his final retirement in 1958, having taught at Columbia for 55 years. When he first retired, no space was allotted for him to maintain an office at Columbia, so he set up an office in his apartment, just a block from campus, with the help of his secretary, Tunnell. Graham (1967, p. 556) writes that Woodworth's most significant contributions to the psychological literature were made between the time of his retirement in 1945 and his death in 1962.

In addition to a rigorous writing and teaching schedule, Woodworth held many editorial positions (becoming editor of the *Archives of Psychology* and of the *Psychological Index*), held offices as president (of the APA, Social Science Research Council, and Psychological Corporation; "Dr. Woodworth honored," 1931), and received many awards and honorary doctorates (from the University of North Carolina and the University of Pennsylvania, among others). At the age of 86, at the 64th annual convention of the APA, Woodworth accepted the first gold medal for achievement ever to be awarded by the APA. Emily Harrison (1956a) interviewed him shortly after the award ceremony, and Woodworth remarked that he had attended a few sessions but that he wouldn't be staying for the duration of the conference because, she writes, "[He] says that in his 'age of maturity,' two days are 'quite enough.' His less mature colleagues will continue their meeting" (p. 16).

Woodworth's life was marked by an interest in many things, including gardening, academics, and music. As previously mentioned, before settling on psychology, he seriously considered pursuing academic careers in mathematics and physiology. Once he had chosen psychology, Woodworth was interested in "almost everything" within the field (Graham, 1967, p. 545), including perception of time, transfer of training, racial differences, motivation, psychophysics, and even the psychology of animals (Woodworth, 1932/1961, p. 372). What Woodworth called his "sad array of scattered interests" (p. 372), Graham referred to as his "encyclopedic background of information" (1967, p. 553). These many interests afforded Woodworth a perspective unique for many researchers. In the words of R.W. Rieber (1983), who wrote of Woodworth in *Thinkers of the Twentieth Century*, "Throughout his life, Woodworth moved freely throughout the field of psychology, unafraid of crossing boundaries and moving into new territory" (p. 628). Because of the breadth of his knowledge, Woodworth was asked to teach a variety of courses. Poffenberger (1962, p. 686) reports that a survey of what Woodworth taught included courses in physiology; experimental psychology; abnormal psychology; social psychology; tests and statistics; problems and methods; the theory, history, and applications of psychology; and a survey of contemporary psychology. As he taught, Woodworth often decided that a new or different textbook was needed, and so was born the variety of texts that he authored.

Robert Sessions Woodworth died in 1962 at the age of 92. Fittingly, for one who had given so much to his country and to his chosen field of psychology, he breathed his last on the Fourth of July ("Professor Woodworth," 1962).

Philosophical Beliefs and Guiding Principles

What Woodworth did and what he wanted to do were sometimes two separate achievements. As he observed,

> Though my ideal all along has been "investigation," and though I have been busy all along with research in an advisory capacity, I have done comparatively little investigation on my own account...I should have liked to be a discoverer, so that anyone asking, "What did Woodworth do?" would be promptly answered, "Why, he was the man who found out" this or that.... It seems as if real discoveries, on par with those in some of the other sciences, simply were not made in psychology. (Woodworth, 1932/1961, p. 376)

Although Woodworth expressed some regret over his lack of discovery, his contributions to the field of psychology were enormous, in part because of his broad view of the field. Balance and eclecticism were hallmarks of his philosophy. Even areas in which he was not directly involved benefited from his attention. For example, in the early 1920s he was invited to become a member of a committee organized by the National Research Council to look into child development. With his customary efficiency and creativity, he sent out letters to about 1,200 psychologists, asking if they were involved in research on child development in any way. The responses he received led to four conferences on child development between 1925 and 1933 and the creation of the Society for Research in Child Development (Lagemann, 2000, p. 133). According to his contemporary and colleague Laurence Shaffer,

"Much of today's psychology is Professor Woodworth's psychology. He has educated two generations of us to his ideal of a comprehensive, experimentally based science, which is wary of doctrines and looks insistently to the evidence for its answers" (Harrison, 1956a).

Woodworth's Textbooks

The scope of Woodworth's comprehensiveness and the evidence of his broad view of psychology can be seen in the books he wrote. One early publication, *Dynamic Psychology* (1918), consists of lectures that he gave at Columbia University from 1916 to 1917. Much more important was *Psychology* (1921). Initially subtitled *A Study of Mental Life*, it was testimony to the role Woodworth played in identifying and promoting psychology as an independent scholarly discipline that the book's later editions (e.g., 1940, its fourth edition) dropped the subtitle, no longer needing to define what psychology was. The titles of the book's chapters give a flavor of its breadth of coverage: "Intelligence," "Personality," "Learning," "Memory," "The Nervous System," "Thinking," "Feeling and Emotion," "Observation," "Individual Differences in Ability," "The Individual in His Environment," and "Heredity and Environment," among others. In each chapter Woodworth discusses the relation that all of these issues have to human behavior as well as to processes of thought.

Another successful publication was Woodworth's *Contemporary Schools of Psychology* (1931), its first edition a relatively small volume in which chapters are devoted to introspective psychology, behaviorism, Gestalt theory, psychoanalysis, and "Purposivism." In the book's final chapter, "The Middle of the Road," Woodworth asks which school of psychology should be followed, to which he answers, with a touch of humor,

> I should be inclined to advise you to stay in the middle of the road. We must remember that the middle-of-the-road group are not simply the leftovers or those who cannot make up their minds. Sometimes, with a slight change in the figure of speech, we middle-of-the-roaders are said to be sitting on the fence.... Well, in support of this position it may be said that it is cooler up here and one has a better view of all that is going on. (p. 216)

The work was still in print decades later, and its third edition was a coauthored one (Woodworth & Sheehan, 1964).

Yet another long-lived text was Woodworth's *Experimental Psychology* (1938), the text used by MacGinitie in graduate school. (Woodworth devoted a whole chapter of this 880-page book to reading; in it he revisits his earlier observations but has a section on the speed of reading, noting that speech movements can be a drag on rapid reading [pp. 713–745].) It was still in print in a revised and coauthored edition in 1954 (Woodworth & Schlosberg).

At the age of 89, Woodworth was the sole author of another volume of over 800 pages, *Dynamics of Behavior* (1958). This text was a modification of *Dynamic Psychology* (1918). Drawing on his experiences and the revision of his work with Schlosberg (Woodworth & Schlosberg, 1954), Woodworth continued to explain his so-called middle-of-the-road principles of psychology (Graham, 1967).

"Author of textbooks" was the summation of Woodworth's life in his obituary in *The New York Times* ("Professor Woodworth," 1962). Because many of his textbooks were also published in Great Britain (e.g., Woodworth, 1921, 1931, 1938), hundreds of thousands of students there as well as in the United States learned about psychology through reading them.

Themes in Woodworth's Work

Woodworth held a broad and varied view of psychology, as shown in an interview conducted by Emma Harrison, reporter for *The New York Times* (Harrison, 1956b). In the interview Woodworth reflected that the field of psychology was opting for a combination of theories, rather than divisions between experimental and applied psychologists. He saw this as a sign of maturity among the members of the field.

Various themes recur in Woodworth's theory and practice. The interest and areas that Graham (1967, p. 546) considered the most important were the experiments on the transfer of training that Woodworth conducted with Thorndike early in his career. These experiments did much to disprove a popular doctrine of formal discipline that held that practice and formal training in almost any intellectual field would transfer to other fields. Woodworth and Thorndike found instead that training in one area did not necessarily lead to increased abilities in another area. They wrote, "The mind is...a machine for making particular reactions to particular situations. It works in great detail, adapting itself to the special data of which it has had experience" (Thorndike & Woodworth, 1901, p. 250).

Another theme in Woodworth's work was motivation. Moving away from Thorndike's connectionism, he came to believe that a clear understanding of the desired outcome was a motivator that excluded the need for rewards or punishment:

> You get something you call a reward when your curiosity is aroused and you look and see. You don't have to give a child a piece of candy. Get a child's curiosity aroused and get him to satisfy it. He'll learn and there will be some retention of what he has learned." (Harrison, 1956b, p. 53)

Woodworth based most of his ideas about motivation on his work developing tests, such as the Association Tests (Woodworth & Wells, 1911). Later, Woodworth developed tests for screening military recruits for both World War I and World War II (Graham, 1967). All these tests were aimed at discovering individuals' inner motivations.

Intelligence was a third area of great interest to Woodworth. He long held that heredity and environment should be regarded as interacting and complementary influences (Graham, 1967, p. 552). In an opinion/editorial in *The New York Times* (1923), he wrote about "Aristocracy and Democracy Seen Through Intelligence Tests." After discussing the effects of heredity and environment on behavior, he observes, "No sound political philosophy can be built upon the fiction that all men, as adults at least, are equal in intelligence."

Far ahead of his time, Woodworth reminded readers to consider attributes other than intelligence:

> Intelligence is not the only thing to consider. There are the special aptitudes for music, art, mechanics and many others. There are the physical excellences, health and strength. There are temperamental excellences, as cheerfulness and steadiness. A man may have rather low intelligence, and be a man for all that. (Woodworth, 1923, p. X13)

As early as 1924 he stated that immigration tests should be based on the merits of the individual and have nothing to do with the individual's race or country of origin. In 1930, he encouraged the hiring of people regardless of age for factory work and that same year he developed tests to fit people to jobs when he was head of the Psychological Corporation ("Professor Woodworth," 1962).

On one point he appears to have lapsed, however: the intelligence of immigrants coming to the United States. Referring to the results of Army recruit tests, he stated, "The recent immigrants in the draft tested lower than the native born or than the immigrants who came here earlier. It appears that we have recently been receiving a rather unfavorable selection of Europeans in point of intelligence" (Woodworth, 1923, p. X13). He was apparently discounting the fact that the low scores of immigrants were a function of their taking the tests in an unfamiliar language.

A final area of continuing interest to Woodworth was what he called the "mind-body" problem, or the idea that thoughts were physically dependent on the brain (Woodworth, 1932/1961, pp. 376–377). Woodworth spent many years thinking about and researching this question, dissatisfied with the theory that posited that each mental activity paralleled a physiological one in the brain. What he concluded was summed up in a theory he called "levels of description" (p. 379). In this theory, he asserts that the same event can be given a description at two or more levels. For example, a psychologist might describe a conditioned reflex by discussing it in terms of a stimulus and its response, whereas a physiologist would characterize it by detailing its biological features such as nerve impulses. Both fields would be correct in their descriptions. Woodworth's own background in physiology came out in this theory: "The value of the theory, to me," he wrote, "is that it keeps all of psychology, introspective and behavioristic, within the bounds of natural science" (p. 379).

Woodworth's life was guided by his insatiable curiosity and his commitment to exploration. Some of his greatest insights came from looking at old dilemmas and researching them in new ways. His extensive knowledge of many fields brought together new ideas.

Contributions to the Field of Reading

Woodworth's contributions to the field of reading occurred within the much broader context of his discussions of psychology. His work included eye-movement study, but, as was true of other psychologists, he was well aware that the physiology of reading did not lead to understanding. Thus, he was also interested in how readers understood text.

Like other psychologists in the early 1900s, Woodworth studied the eye movements of readers, and his results, along with those of others, were reported by Edmund Burke Huey (see chapter 7, this volume; Huey, 1908, pp. 38–39). In 1921, when Woodworth published *Psychology: A Study of Mental Life*, he summarized the experimental evidence: Eyes, when reading, "advance along the line by a series of [saccadic] jumps.... In a newspaper line a good reader will pause or fixate about 3–6 times. Evidently his eyes are not responding to single letters" (p. 40). As others had, he concluded that since it did not appear that the eyes were seeing individual letters, words were being read as wholes:

> The reaction time...shows that a short, familiar word is read as a whole.... The reaction time is about 4/10 of a second for a single letter, and the same for a short, familiar word. Since it takes no more time to read a short word than a single letter, the word is certainly not read by a process of spelling. The word is seen as a whole. Even a long word, if familiar, is seen as a whole. A child can learn to read words before he knows his letters, and he can even recognize whole phrases and sentences before he has learned the separate words, just as he recognizes a face without analyzing it into its parts. (pp. 40–41)

Woodworth's shift here from the reading of skilled adults to the instruction of young novices is barely perceptible. It is clear how someone reading these and similar passages might come away convinced that beginning readers should focus on whole words, as the sight method of reading instruction requires, rather than on letters and syllables. Because of the popularity of Woodworth's texts, what he wrote regarding reading was considered by many of his contemporaries to be the best available description of reading.

Although his early work was on the physiological aspects of reading, Woodworth did not focus exclusively on the mechanics of reading. His interest in motivation further informed his views on the topic. In a chapter on attention in *Psychology: A Study of Mental Life* (1921), he describes the movement from external to internal rewards in reading:

> So, when the little child is learning to read, the printed characters have so little attractiveness in themselves that he naturally turns away from them after a brief exploration. But, because he is scolded when his mind wanders from those marks, because other children make fun of his blunders, because, when he reads correctly, he feels the glow of success and of applause,

he does hold himself to the printed page till he is able to read a little, after which his interest in what he is reading is sufficient, without extraneous motives, to keep his nose between the covers of the story book more, perhaps, than is good for him. (p. 258)

In the same chapter, Woodworth points to the important role played in understanding a text by what we would now call *story grammar* (e.g., Ruddell & Unrau, 2004) and *schema theory* (e.g., Anderson, 2004).

Reading may be called a kind of observation, since the reader is looking for what the author has to tell; and the rule that holds for other observation holds also for reading. That is to say that the reader finds the most when he knows just what he is looking for. (Woodworth, 1921, p. 267)

He provides examples from story reading—"You want to know how the hero gets out of the fix he is in" (p. 268)—and serious reading—"[Serious readers] get the author's questions and press on to find his answer" (p. 268). Couching his explanations in the language of stimulus and response, Woodworth comments on the role of context in determining word meaning: "Presented alone, a word may call up any of its meanings, according to frequency, etc.; but in context it usually brings to mind just the one meaning that fits the context" (p. 384).

Finally, Woodworth did not believe that this meaning resided solely in the text. Well before Rosenblatt (1976, 1978) depicted transactions between the reader and author as a negotiation and reading as an act of construction, Woodworth summarized a similar theory:

It requires imagination to enjoy art as well as to produce it. The producer of the work of art puts the stimuli before you, but you must make the response yourself, and it is an inventive response.... The novelist describes a character for you, and you must respond by putting together the items in the description so as to conceive of a character you have never met. (1921, p. 512)

Woodworth's contributions to the field of reading mirrored his interests in particular fields of study such as the areas of physiology and motivation, but he also described insightful thinking about comprehension and the transactional nature of the reading act.

Lessons for the Future

One characteristic shared by many of the early reading pioneers was their interest in a broad and eclectic array of fields. This was especially true of Woodworth. Throughout his career, he remained committed to physiology, statistics, psychology's many branches, and even his boyhood interests of gardening and agriculture. He set a fine example of the benefits other disciplines can provide to the field of reading.

Woodworth's commitment to excellence in research provides another example for reading researchers to follow. His mission statement was summarized in the poster he hung above his desk as a student—*INVESTIGATION*. Regardless of the field, the evidence was to be pursued and trusted above any theory:

> My bogey men, the men who most irritated me and from whose domination I was most eager to keep free, were those who assumed to prescribe in advance what type of results a psychologist must find, and within what limits he must remain. (Woodworth, 1932/1961, p. 376)

Instead, Woodworth believed that "fair-minded investigation can be trusted to show the way to better things" (quoted in Poffenberger, 1962, p. 688).

Woodworth's own words provide perhaps the best lesson for the future. Asked to offer advice for newcomers just entering the field of psychology, he responded by suggesting that newcomers balance what has already been done in the field while looking for new discoveries: "For getting on the trail of what will prove to be important and fundamental, there is no sure rule to be given...What we seem to need...is surprises" (Woodworth, 1932/1961, p. 380). His words ring equally true for the field of reading. As reading researchers, we would do well to follow Woodworth's advice—accepting what has been done before, pursuing that which does not match our long-held beliefs, and looking for surprises.

Reflection Questions

1. Woodworth was noted for his interests in a wide range of topics, a characteristic common to many reading pioneers. What were the impacts of such broad interests and research on the field of reading?

2. Do you think current reading research is marked by the same eclectic base of interests that marked Woodworth's work? Why or why not?

3. Woodworth stated, "I should have liked to be a discoverer, so that anyone asking, 'What did Woodworth do?' would be promptly answered, 'Why, he was the man who found out' this or that" (Woodworth, 1932/1961, p. 376). What has been discovered in the field of reading since the early reading pioneers worked? What do you think still needs to be discovered?

4. Consider the role of teaching evidenced in the life of Woodworth. How did teachers influence Woodworth's life?

5. What was Woodworth's commitment to teaching? Do you think these influences shaped his research? If so, how?

REFERENCES

Anderson, R.C. (2004). Role of the reader's schema in comprehension, learning, and memory. In R.B. Ruddell & N.J. Unrau (Eds.), *Theoretical models and processes of reading* (5th ed., pp. 594–606). Newark, DE: International Reading Association.

Dr. Woodworth honored: Is elected head of Social Science Research Council. (1931, March 20). *The New York Times*, p. 18.

Graham, C.H. (1967). Robert Sessions Woodworth, October 17, 1869–July 4, 1962. *National Academy of Sciences: Biographical Memoirs, 39*, 541–572.

Harcourt Assessment, Inc. (2005). Harcourt Assessment, Inc. Company History. Retrieved on August 26, 2005, from http://harcourtassessment.com/haiweb/Cultures/en-US/Company/History.htm

Harrison, E. (1956a, September 3). Woodworth gets scientific medal; Psychological Association honors pioneer—Three others get awards. *The New York Times*, p. 16.

Harrison, E. (1956b, October 16). Psychologist, 87, says field grows: Dr. Woodworth, at Columbia 57 years, thinks science approaches maturity. *The New York Times*, p. 53.

Huey, E.B. (1908). *Psychology and pedagogy of reading.* New York: Macmillan.

Lagemann, E.C. (2000). *An elusive science: The troubling history of education research.* Chicago: University of Chicago Press.

Mrs. R.S. Woodworth: Obituary notice. (1960, November 28). *The New York Times*, p. 31.

Murchison, C. (Ed.). (1961). *A history of psychology in autobiography* (Vol. 2). New York: Russell and Russell. (Original work published 1932)

Poffenberger, A.T. (1962). Robert Sessions Woodworth. *American Journal of Psychology, 75*, 677–692.

Professor Woodworth of Columbia dies: Retired psychologist was 92—Author of textbooks. (1962, July 5). *The New York Times*, p. 24.

Rieber, R.W. (1983). [Profile of R.S. Woodworth]. In E. Devine, M. Held, J. Vinson, & G. Walsh (Eds.), *Thinkers of the twentieth century: A biographical, bibliographical and critical dictionary* (pp. 627–628). Detroit, MI: Gale Research.

Rosenblatt, L.M. (1976). *Literature as exploration* (3rd ed.) New York: Noble & Noble.

Rosenblatt, L.M. (1978). *The reader, the text, the poem: The transactional theory of the literary work*. Carbondale: Southern Illinois University Press.

Ruddell, R.B., & Unrau, N.J. (2004). Reading as a meaning-construction process: The reader, the text, and the teacher. In R.B. Ruddell & N.J. Unrau (Eds.), *Theoretical models and processes of reading* (5th ed., pp. 1462–1521). Newark, DE: International Reading Association.

Thorndike, E.L., & Woodworth, R.S. (1901). The influence of improvement in one mental function upon the efficiency of other functions. *Psychological Review, 8*, 247–261.

Thorndike, E.L., to R.S. Woodworth. (1925, May 7). In Robert Sessions Woodworth papers, Box 20, Rare Book and Manuscript Library, Columbia University, New York.

Woodworth, B., to R.S. Woodworth. (1946). In Robert Sessions Woodworth papers, Box 1, Rare Book and Manuscript Library, Columbia University, New York.

Woodworth, R.S. (1906–1962). Robert Sessions Woodworth papers, Rare Book and Manuscript Library, Columbia University, New York.

Woodworth, R.S. (Ed.). (1914). The psychological researches of James McKeen Cattell: A review by some of his pupils. *Archives of Psychology, 30*, 1–101.

Woodworth, R.S. (1918). *Dynamic psychology*. New York: Columbia University Press.

Woodworth, R.S. (1921). *Psychology: A study of mental life*. New York: Henry Holt.

Woodworth, R.S. (1923, January 28). Aristocracy and democracy seen through intelligence tests. *The New York Times*, p. X13.

Woodworth, R.S. (1931). *Contemporary schools of psychology*. New York: Ronald Press.

Woodworth, R.S. (1938). *Experimental psychology*. New York: Henry Holt.

Woodworth, R.S. (1940). *Psychology* (4th ed.). New York: Henry Holt.

Woodworth, R.S. (1958). *Dynamics of behavior*. New York: Holt, Rinehart and Winston.

Woodworth, R.S. (1961). Robert S. Woodworth. In C. Murchison (Ed.), *A history of psychology in autobiography* (Vol. 2, pp. 359–380). New York: Russell and Russell. (Original work published 1932)

Woodworth, R.S., & Schlosberg, H. (1954). *Experimental psychology* (2nd ed.) New York: Holt, Rinehart & Winston.

Woodworth, R.S., & Sheehan, M. (1964). *Contemporary schools of psychology* (3rd ed.). New York: Ronald Press.

Woodworth, R.S., & Wells, F.L. (1911). Association tests. *Psychology Review Monographs, 13*(57), 1–85.

Woodworth, R.S., to President Butler (1913, May 13). In Robert Sessions Woodworth papers, Box 4, Rare Book and Manuscript Library, Columbia University, New York.

Woodworth, R.S., to L.O. Howard (1917, October 12). In Robert Sessions Woodworth papers, Box 4, Rare Book and Manuscript Library, Columbia University, New York.

Woodworth, R.S., to A.T. Poffenberger (1931, February 12). In Robert Sessions Woodworth papers, Box 4, Rare Book and Manuscript Library, Columbia University, New York.

Woodworth, R.S., to Dr. Warden (1930, February 12). In Robert Sessions Woodworth papers, Box 4, Rare Book and Manuscript Library, Columbia University, New York.

FOR FURTHER READING

Paulson, E.J. (2005). Viewing eye movements during reading through the lens of chaos theory: How reading is like the weather. *Reading Research Quarterly, 40*, 338–358.

CHAPTER 3

Raymond Dodge (1871–1942): Lessons From Observations of the Eye

By Dixie D. Massey

Historical Research Process

THE FIRST QUESTIONS about Raymond Dodge for new literacy researchers and historians like me are, Who was he and what does he have to do with literacy? For me, a member of a generation raised with the Internet and easy access to tomes of material, the traditional searches yielded books about human variability, cravings for superiority, and research on the effects of alcohol. Surely I had the wrong person. So I began asking my more knowledgeable colleagues about Raymond Dodge. "Raymond who?" asked one. "Who's that?" was another response from someone who had been in the field of lit-

Shaping the Reading Field: The Impact of Early Reading Pioneers, Scientific Research, and Progressive Ideas, edited by Susan E. Israel and E. Jennifer Monaghan. © 2007 by the International Reading Association.
Photo: Courtesy of the Archives of the History of American Psychology, University of Akron, Ohio.

eracy a long time. Their suggestions on how to find out more about Dodge involved getting to know and spend quantity time with the research librarian, and that is what I did. Actually, I spent time with not just one but several very talented research librarians. Their directions almost always involved actual books, rather than online resources. And the books were almost always in the dustier corners of the library—archives on the very top floor, at the back corner of the basement, and, as they described it, "Where we keep the old stuff." One helpful historian asked, "Do you speak German? These texts by Professor Dodge were written in German." Unfortunately, I do not speak German, and I did not think that I had time to learn in the short deadline I had to finish my research. The hunt only made me more curious about Raymond Dodge.

Personal and Professional Life

Born February 20, 1871, Raymond Dodge lived a life marked by wide interests in diverse fields, including reading. Dodge's invention of the tachistoscope—a device that projects an image for a given period of time—contributed to the careful study of eye movements when reading. Dodge was also interested in the processes of reading in primary and secondary languages. His questions have guided reading research for decades.

Dodge's father, George, owned a pharmacy in Woburn, Massachusetts, USA. He continued to study all his life and was awarded a Doctor of Medicine degree from Harvard University well after Raymond was born. Dodge's mother, Anna (née Pickering), was an invalid, and although Dodge is said to have favored her in looks, it was his father whom he most resembled in temperament. George Dodge has been described as "scholarly, speculative, socially minded and very religious" (Yerkes, 1942, p. 584). Raymond later described his father as "always studying something that seemed worth while" (Dodge, 1930, p. 99). George Dodge was eventually forced to retire from his pharmaceutical and medical careers due to failing health, but this did not mean that he was idle. He moved his family to West Acton, Massachusetts, USA, and began preaching in the Congregational Church.

Dodge inherited his father's interest in learning. One of Dodge's first interests was in mechanics, and he often could be found experimenting in the backyard toolshed. This interest and experience would serve him well in his development of scientific tools such as the ones he invented to measure eye movements. Dodge also read extensively from his father's vast collection of books. In 1889 Dodge began attending Williams College, in Williamstown, Massachusetts, USA, where he supported himself through school. He spent his Thanksgiving vacation during his freshman year reading *Darwinism: An Exposition of the Theory of Natural Selection, With Some of Its Applications* (Wallace, 1891) and *A Naturalist's Voyage Round the World* (Darwin, 1889). These were not assigned readings, but as Dodge recorded in his journal, "I wanted to get a deeper insight into Darwin's theories and didn't know when I could do it if not during this vacation" (quoted in Miles, 1956, p. 65). Such interest in a wide variety of subjects and his dogged pursuit of facts marked Dodge's professional pursuits for the rest of his life, including his contributions to the field of reading perception.

Dodge was known as a serious student with a sharp mind. One of his classmates, Charles Sewall, wrote,

> In our Junior year...when we were introduced to subjects fitted to the mentality of an upper-classman, such as logic and psychology, and more particularly in the Senior year, when we were subjected to philosophy, we began to realize that Dodge had one of the best minds in the class. His questions and his answers often amazed us...I think that all of us felt, when we graduated, that Dodge was likely to outstrip any of us in the field which peculiarly attracted him, because of his philosophical bent. His career since graduation has justified that opinion. (quoted in Yerkes, 1942, p. 585)

In Dodge's senior year, he met Henrietta Cutler at the railroad station while waiting for a train to West Acton, and they talked briefly. Their discussion was obviously important enough to cause them to exchange addresses because they began seven years of correspondence. They became engaged after Dodge finished his undergraduate studies but decided not to marry before he finished his graduate studies (Miles, 1956; Yerkes, 1942).

Dodge graduated from Williams College in 1893 with a Bachelor of Arts in philosophy. After graduation, he took a job as an assistant librarian at his alma mater to earn enough money to attend graduate school. While working at the library, he wrote a thesis on conceptions of space. This thesis was sent along with his letters of application to both Harvard University and Columbia University and was rejected by both institutions. Dodge decided to pursue other avenues of education and, less than a year after his graduation from Williams College, he traveled to Germany, where he attended the

University of Halle and studied with philosopher Benno Erdmann. Dodge (1930) describes this time:

> My decision to go to the University of Halle was determined by a misfortune, a conviction, and an accident. The misfortune seems instructive. During the year of graduate study at Williams I prepared a thesis on certain differences between psychological and philosophical conceptions of space, which I presented with applications for scholarship aid at both Harvard and Columbia. It was one of the few great disappointments of my life when I was refused at both institutions. That experience may be the background of my distrust of predictive tests. The conviction that influenced me was that if I was to become a philosopher I must know the German language, and if I was ever to learn the German language with my linguistic handicap [that German was not his native language] I must learn it where it was spoken. The argument was probably sound. It was an accident that the copy of Kant's *Kritik der reinen Vernunft* [1956] which was given to me by Professor Russell was edited by Benno Erdmann. After my disappointment, the conviction and the accident led me to Halle-an-der-Saale. (p. 101)

Once in Halle, Dodge's resources were very limited. He survived for two years with $500 he had saved during his time as an assistant librarian. But what he lacked in monetary means, he gained in professional resources (Dodge, 1930, pp. 100–101).

Dodge was focused on receiving a PhD in philosophy but changed to psychology through his work with his teacher and mentor Benno Erdmann, who was teaching a seminar in philosophy. Dodge described a paper that he wrote for Erdmann in which he missed some key points. Erdmann responded (kindly, as Dodge pointed out), "Herr Dodge, I fear you will never make a philosopher" (Dodge, 1930, p. 102). During the same semester, Dodge sat in on a seminar Erdmann taught on the psychology of reading. In this course, Erdmann began discussing a need in the newly emerging field of experimental psychology. He spoke to his students about the need for a tachistoscope, an instrument that could control the length of time that a stimulus was presented to a viewer. Erdmann followed his description of this need with the caveat that such a device was probably a physical impossibility. Yerkes (1942) writes of Dodge's reaction to this challenge,

> This problem and need fitted into the mechanical bent and immediate intellectual interest of the newly arrived American student, and, as he said,

"I adopted it as my own, lived with it, and gradually evolved the Erdmann/Dodge tachistoscope...My initiation into experimental psychology may be said to have started with that technical problem." (p. 587)

One may perhaps miss the importance of this event. Dodge (1930) wrote that he had resolved to leave graduate studies and return to his father's pharmacy, even reimbursing the college all funds, should the experiment fail (p. 104). But it did not fail. The Erdmann-Dodge tachistoscope was Dodge's first invention. This device could expose an object to a viewer for a brief period of time that could be precisely measured. The two men would conduct many research investigations together, and most of Dodge's initial publications were coauthored with Erdmann.

Dodge was awarded a PhD in psychology in 1896, following his dissertation *Die Motorischen Wortvorstellungen* (1896) (translated as *The Kinesthetic Imagination*). This project examined the relations between verbal imagery and the sensation of muscular movement (i.e., kinesthesia).

Dodge stayed in Halle for another year as assistant to Erdmann, with monetary assistance from the Berlin Academy of Sciences. He and Erdmann continue to collaborate on research and writing (Yerkes, 1942). Dodge returned to the United States in 1897, and he and Henrietta were married that August. Yerkes (1942) describes their marriage as a partnership that continued throughout their lives:

> To all who knew them early or late in their decades together, it was clear that each contributed more than a fair share to their contentment. Each evidently was enriched by giving. Crosses, physical ills, bitter disappointments came, but nothing seemed to upset the calm and serenity of their life. (p. 588)

Following their wedding, Dodge and his wife moved to Pennsylvania, USA, where he took his first job at Ursinus College in Collegeville. He was expected to carry a heavy teaching load in subjects outside his specialty, including logics, the history of philosophy, ethics, aesthetics, pedagogy, and the history of English literature. After one year, in the fall of 1898, Dodge took a position at Wesleyan University in Middletown, Connecticut, USA, where he was promoted to professor in only four years. He stayed at Wesleyan for the next 26 years. During this time, he served in a variety of roles at the local and national level, including serving as president of the American

Psychological Association in 1916 and chairman of the Division of Anthropology and Psychology of the National Research Council. Henrietta faithfully supported his work, even serving as his research assistant and a subject in his experiments (Miles, 1956, p. 79).

Although Dodge and Henrietta never had children of their own, they "adopted" many students from Wesleyan, frequently inviting them into their home. Students saw Dodge as playing an almost fatherly role. One student wrote of him, "His personality so impressed me in the introductory courses that I resolved to take as much work under him as I could" (quoted in Yerkes, 1942, p. 589). Another student reflected, "From my earliest contacts with the charming personality and the lucid teaching of Professor Dodge, together with the fascination of the subject as he developed the science of psychology, I found myself changing the entire course of my future" (p. 589). Yet another wrote,

> His kindliness in troubling moments, his inexhaustible patience with my periods of error and inactivity, the inspiration of his skill in laboratory technique and insight in experimental problems, the example of his utter caution in method and interpretation—these are but a few among those [qualities] I might enumerate. (p. 589)

Yerkes (1942) describes Dodge as a born teacher—sympathetic, patient, enthusiastic, and with a gentle sense of humor. He was also a man of great kindness and humility, facets of his personality that are reflected in his correspondence. Among the papers preserved at the Archives of the History of American Psychology are numerous notes by him of thanks and appreciation to colleagues regarding an article, accomplishment, or personal event (Archival Records, 2004).

Dodge's teaching at Wesleyan was interrupted by World War I, during which Dodge served in the U.S. Navy and also worked as a consultant with the Army. As Yerkes (1942) notes, "Few American psychologists rendered as valuable professional service to our military establishments in the war as did Raymond Dodge" (p. 593). While in the service, Dodge was again presented with a problem: Could a test be devised to select naval gunners? Dodge committed himself to this problem with as much enthusiasm as he had to creating the tachistoscope with Erdmann. Four days after the problem was presented to him, Dodge presented a solution. The result was a highly successful method not only of testing gunners but also of training them. He also served as a consultant psychologist to the Chemical Warfare Service and conducted a study of the effects of frequent gas mask wearing. This study reportedly influenced the subsequent design and development of new gas masks. Dodge was promoted to the rank of lieutenant commander as a result of his achievements. He was never able to publish the tests that he used, however, because they were classified.

As an interesting side note, during the 1930s Dodge was contacted by Neely Mashburn about the use of a test for selecting candidates for flight training (Mashburn to Dodge, 1934). He was quick to respond that he had no practical knowledge of flying but offered some suggestions for Mashburn to pursue regarding the creation of such a test (Dodge to Mashburn, 1934). When the United States entered World War II, the Navy tried to find Dodge's original tests again but failed to do so. Because this was around the time of Dodge's death, Dodge's tests remained a mystery to the public and to the Navy (Wesleyan University, n.d.).

Rather than being a pause in his professional career, Dodge's experience in World War I became a pivotal point in his thinking and work. For three years after returning to Wesleyan University, Dodge's publications focused on the application of science to military issues, including titles such as "Mental Engineering During the War" (1919a), "Mental Engineering After the War" (1919b), and "The Educational Significance of Army Intelligence Tests" (1920).

In 1924, Dodge accepted a professorship at Yale University. His appointment to the Institute of Psychology left no time for teaching but greater resources for research. As Yale expanded, he gained more elaborate laboratories, including his final office at the Yale Medical Center. Yerkes (1942) remarked, "I think that the elaborateness of his laboratories and their equipment, in contrast with what he had worked with for thirty-five years, somewhat disturbed him by offending his habitual frugality and economy of materials and space" (p. 595).

Parkinson's disease forced Dodge's retirement in 1936, and he and Henrietta moved to Tryon, North Carolina, USA. He had already been fighting the effects of the disease for at least six years, yet he had carried on his research. He died in Tryon on April 8, 1942.

Philosophical Beliefs and Guiding Principles

Dodge was guided by his interest in psychology and experimentation. As he reflected on his years of research, he wrote, "I still remain primarily an experimentalist," stating that all of his work was focused on an effort "to record with accuracy the behavior of normal and abnormal human organisms at various levels" (1930, p. 121). In his later years, however, he became more interested in the practical and theoretical implications of his experimental data. In spite of his focus on experimentation, Dodge consistently acknowledged the importance of meaning in reading. During his early work with Erdmann, he and Erdmann conceptualized reading as three processes: (1) the optical perception of the words, (2) the reproduction of sounds associated with the perceived words, and (3) the reproduction of meaning (Franz, 1900).

During the late 1800s and early 1900s, reading processes were beginning to be of interest to many researchers but only as a subset of psychological studies. Edmund Burke Huey (see chapter 7, this volume), a colleague of Dodge at the Wesleyan University of Western Pennsylvania, reviewed all of the research on reading at the time. In his single volume, *The Psychology and Pedagogy of Reading* (1908), Huey was easily able to cover the 40 studies published by other researchers up to that point, including Dodge's work on eye movements. In all the research, reading was seen as a visual process, which is why the research concentrated on this particular issue.

In his text, Huey extended the experimental data, including Dodge's work on eye movements, and concluded that the research supported practical pedagogical conclusions such as that the home is a natural place to learn to read, the school should focus on reading for meaning, reading should always be for the intrinsic interest of what is read—never for exercise—and speed drills should emphasize rate and reading for meaning. Still, neither Dodge nor Huey was able to make the immediate contributions to reading pedagogy that they believed were important. In spite of this, Dodge's research on eye movements formed the foundation for reading research and instruction.

Contributions to the Field of Reading

Dodge was perhaps best known as a psychologist. His most common works include *Conditions and Consequences of Human Variability* (1931) and *The Craving for Superiority* (Dodge & Kahn, 1931). His research included such topics as the effects of alcohol on human neuromuscular processes, the conditions for protracted happiness, and an experimental study of cancer. It was his early works that were focused on eye movement and perception. Yerkes (1942) believed that Dodge showed some regret later in his life over not pursuing the practical application of these eye-movement studies to the pedagogy of reading. Yerkes believed that had Dodge chosen to do so, the methods of teaching reading would have been revolutionized.

As it was, Dodge contributed much to the field of reading. During their time together in Halle, Dodge and Erdmann examined the way adults read, first through the mirror method of observation and later through the use of Dodge's tachistoscope. They observed the way readers looked at words and found that readers recognized words by whole parts, not by individual letters or syllables. They based their conclusion on the following observations. First, subjects recognized words that were printed in type too small for individual letters to be identified. Second, subjects recognized words that were too far into their peripheral vision for recognition of their individual letters. Third, readers recognized words at a distance from which individual letters could not be recognized. Dodge and Erdmann stated that it is the word form and shape that make a word recognizable, not the reader's recognition of individual letters (Tinker, 1965, p. 14). Today's practical application of this discovery is that vision is tested with isolated strings of letters, not words, because the mind naturally tries to group letters into words to make meaning.

Much of Dodge and Erdmann's early work on eye movements was conducted using the mirror method of observation. The reader held a mirror toward the page opposite to the one that he or she was reading. The researcher looked over the reader's shoulder and observed the eyes' movements along a line of text. During these observations, Dodge and Erdmann noted that the eyes did not move continuously from left to right across the page. Instead, they observed that the eyes moved in a short succession of movements toward the end of the line of text (movements called *saccades*) and then returned in one quick movement back to the left before sweeping to the next line. The movement toward the end of the line was broken up by pauses. The number of pauses per line did not change a great deal. Using themselves as subjects, the researchers noted that Dodge paused 3 to 5 times per line of text, while Erdmann averaged 5 to 7 pauses per line of text. The more familiar the reading material, the fewer pauses the reader required. They noted that pauses were also present in writing, except that pauses in writing seemed to be more frequent, making it hard to note all of the eye movements (Huey, 1908, pp. 20–21).

Dodge concluded that it was when the eyes paused, rather than when the eyes moved, that the reader was actually seeing and assimilating the letters into words and meaning:

In every change in the point of regard in a complex field of vision the eye distinguishes nothing during the actual movement. That this statement seems to be contradicted many times daily suffices to explain how the erroneous conceptions of the eye movements could have remained unchallenged so long and how so many false interpretations could have clustered around them...[These facts] explain the regular alternation of pause and movement in the reading eye. (Dodge, 1899, p. 477)

Dodge continued to refine the tachistoscope with mirrors (Dodge, 1930, p. 109) and create new instruments. Dodge and Erdmann recognized a need for "graphic registration" of eye movements (Dodge, 1930, p. 109) so interpretation of the eye movements was not reliant solely on immediate observation, but it was not until Dodge's time at Wesleyan University that he was able to develop a falling-plate camera with an air-cushion control that could record eye movements photographically. This instrument allowed a beam of light to be directed into the reader's eye. Once the light struck the eye, the light was reflected from the cornea's surface into a camera and the image was recorded on a photographic plate. From this image, the changes in the movement of the reader's eye could be interpreted from examining the changes in the direction of the beam of light. Timing data were obtained by interrupting the beam of light at regular intervals. Technological advances in film and cameras made Dodge's work widely used and repeated.

Dodge continued his own analysis of eye movements, in particular the saccadic eye movements, the rapid jerky movements of the eyes between pauses in reading and when shifting from one line to another. Dodge and Cline's (1901) published findings show that abductive saccadic movements were faster than adductive movements—that is, the eyes moved faster toward the temples than toward the nose. Dodge's studies of eye movements led him to conclude that readers focus on whole words, not letters; more specifically, readers focused most upon the middle of a word.

Dodge further examined the role of peripheral vision in reading (as described in Huey, 1908, pp. 17, 39). He believed that readers began seeing the words on a page indistinctly through peripheral vision, beginning the perceptual process before the actual direct reading of the words. Dodge found that persons with good peripheral vision had a greater reading speed and fewer and shorter fixation pauses during reading than those with decreased peripheral vision.

Still another area of interest for Dodge centered on increasing the speed of "intelligent reading" among adults. This work was never published, but in a letter to Magdalen Vernon of Cambridge, who was interested in experiments on reading speed, Dodge described his work:

Two particular methods seem to increase the speed of intelligent reading. One was by training to increase the span of reading at each fixation point, taking particular note of what could be seen on the page, on the line and in the immediate vicinity of the fixation point. The other method was to train the eye movements to a greater speed by first drawing lines down the page and seeing what one could remember of 4–5 fixation points per line, forcing the eye to move as rapidly as possible without waiting for the sense to clear up. The latter proved to be very much the better device for increasing the speed of reading and the subjects finally nearly doubled their normal speed with little loss of details in easy text. So much of our lives is spent in reading that I feel that the subject is worth investigation. (Dodge to Vernon, 1932)

Speed of reading was connected to inner speech in Dodge's work. Dodge found that in his own typical silent reading, almost every word was pronounced, but in his fastest silent reading, only the beginnings of words were pronounced. He felt that the speed of his reading seemed to be determined by the speed he could comprehend what he read. Huey (1908) commented,

The fact of inner speech forming a part of silent reading has not been disputed, so far as I am aware, by any one who has experimentally investigated the process of reading. Its presence has been established, for most readers, when adequate tests have been made.... Purely visual reading is quite possible, theoretically...yet it is perfectly certain that the inner hearing or pronouncing, or both, of what is read, is a constituent part of the reading of by far the most of people, as they ordinarily and actually read.... It is of the greatest service to the reader or listener that at each moment a considerable amount of what is being read should hang suspended in the primary memory of the inner speech.... [T]he attention [of the reader] may [thus] wander backward and forward to get a fuller meaning. (pp. 117, 148)

Dodge's work in the field of reading was primarily theoretical in scope. Yet he did speculate as to the practical application of his studies of visual processes. One unique example may be found in an exchange with his fellow researcher Miles Tinker in which Dodge discussed the matter of license plate identification:

> It seems to me that the use of numbers is based on a false assumption that numbers can be remembered better than letters. Four or five letters are probably much more easily remembered than six or seven numbers and four or five letters would give approximately nine million permutations and combinations. I have not put the matter before the authorities in Connecticut for the simple reason that I shall have to fight the uncritical use of capital letters. They would be correct in saying that the capital letter was more easily read than the small letter in isolation, but I believe that the small letter may have the advantage in combinations.... Of course, a good many combinations would have to be eliminated as being unsuitable for dignified people to use, but many words would be available and of course they would be easily read and remembered. Combinations that do not make words would often have some significance as abbreviations of longer words. In fact, as you know, letter combinations that have no significance are very rare and difficult to find for memory experiments. (Dodge to Tinker, 1934)

Dodge and Tinker continued to correspond about the use of letters and numbers on license plates, with Dodge advocating the use of letters on license plates and opposing the use of a combination of letters and numbers.

Through Dodge's commitment to the rigorous study of human behavior, particularly eye movements, others began making direct pedagogical suggestions that have influenced reading instruction for over a century.

Lessons for the Future

What is the significance of Dodge's work? Some emphasis on the role of visual processes in reading remains in many reading models. One of the most widely known models is the Laberge-Samuels model. This model consists of three memory systems: (1) the visual memory system, (2) the phonological memory system, and (3) the semantic memory system. The visual memory system includes the translation of incoming visual information from the words by the eye into meaningful letters. Coupled with the phonological memory system, the brain then makes sense of word parts or the whole word (the semantic memory system), depending on the familiarity with the word and/or parts of the word (Samuels, 2004). Samuels suggested that this model helps explain why students can recognize words but fail to comprehend text: They may spend so much attention focusing on visually processing words that they have little attention left for comprehension. Ken and Yetta Goodman and colleagues have coupled eye-movement research with miscue analysis (e.g,. Paulson, Flurkey, Goodman, & Goodman, 2003) to conclude that readers use syntactic and semantic context to predict and confirm words and contextual meaning.

There is some controversy regarding the utility of the eye-movement studies. On one hand, some current researchers view eye movements as an important area for further research. *The European Journal of Cognitive Psychology* recently dedicated an entire issue to reporting the current research on eye movements in reading. In their rationale, Radach, Kennedy, and Rayner (2004) state,

> The measurement and analysis of eye movements is one of the most powerful ways to study the workings of the human mind.... We believe that eye movements provide a unique opportunity to examine principles of human information processing in a well-structured visual environment while people engage in a natural cognitive task. At the same time oculomotor measures can be used as a tool to develop and test psycholinguistic hypotheses on the processing of written language. (p. 1)

Contributors to the journal suggest further research should include the analysis of word-based viewing time measures and fixations for dyslexic readers (Radach & Kennedy, 2004), speed reading (Radach & Kennedy, 2004), discourse processing (Rayner & Juhasz, 2004), and the eye movements of children (Rayner & Juhasz, 2004).

On the other hand, several researchers view eye-movement research as merely observational and not the basis for reading instruction. Tinker (1965) summarized his 30 years of eye movement studies by saying, "There is no evidence to support the view that eye-movements determine reading proficiency" (p. 111). Merely noting that one reader has more regressive eye movements than another does not indicate that one is a poor reader and the other is not. However, poor readers often have more regressive eye movements than more able readers. Regressive eye movements might be the result of a reader's failure to recognize the word. In 1970, Albert Harris wrote that if a reader's comprehension is acceptable, eye movements may be ignored. If eye movements are poor, remediation should stress comprehension instruction, not eye-movement training (pp. 492–493). Stanovich (2004) writes that eye-movement studies have been incorrectly interpreted as evidence that efficiency of eye movements indicate reading ability; that is, a more skilled reader has fewer pauses and fixations per line of text. Although poor readers do show inefficiency in eye movements, they are also poorly comprehending what they see. But an able reader also makes many pauses per line of text, with more pauses when the text becomes more difficult, so that he or she can focus on the comprehension of the text. Harris (1970) points out that eye movements "are not the cause of poor reading; they are symptoms of the fact that the reader is reading poorly" (p. 493) because the eyes are merely servants of the brain.

What has happened with the eye-movement studies is that they have been erroneously applied to programs that are touted as ways to improve reading speed by reducing the number of fixations and pauses (e.g., Stepware, Inc., 2004). Dodge's data seemingly contradict such programs in that he never claimed that certain eye movements made for a better or poorer reader. He recognized early on that there were more pauses when reading certain kinds of text (e.g., unfamiliar text or text in foreign languages) than when reading familiar material. The key for Dodge was so-called intelligent reading, or reading with comprehension.

Because of Dodge, inner speech is still considered an area for further research (Sadoski & Paivio, 2004). Although studies since Dodge's, and later Huey's, have demonstrated that inner speech is not necessary for comprehension, its role is recognized but not understood:

> Inner speech may serve a needed rehearsal function in an alternative modality without which reading could not optimally occur. Educationally, this implies that inner speech should be encouraged and taught, when in fact, many instructional programs have been introduced to eliminate it. (Sadoski & Paivio, 2004, p. 1351)

Another area pioneered by Dodge that remains largely unstudied is that of reading in a second language. Dodge and Erdmann studied the differences in eye movements when reading one's primary language and when reading a second language. They found that one's eye fixations and pauses increase when reading in the secondary language. Again, differences in rates and eye movements are to be expected when reading becomes more challenging. From the earliest pedagogical interpretations of reading, Huey

(1908) recommended that reading of primary and secondary languages should be for real purposes, with the focus on essential meanings. According to Huey, speed (which he equated to the efficiency of eye movements) was to be encouraged and practiced only if the student could understand the text (p. 381).

Although Dodge made no claim to be developing a pedagogy of reading through his experimental studies of eye movements, he did offer some ideas about pedagogy that have proved influential on those developing reading pedagogy:

> The importance of word form in reading has been exploited in the modern pedagogy of reading [i.e., the "whole word" or "sight" approach]—to my mind somewhat over-exploited. The participation of peripheral or pre-fixational vision in the reading process was determined in a later study but has been practically ignored in the psychologies of reading...I have also been disappointed that pedagogy has done so little to develop a better technique for adult reading. Exploratory, unpublished experiments convince me that such applications of our knowledge are entirely practicable and that with a little patience and ingenuity both the speed of reading and the understanding of what one reads could be notably improved for the average adult. (1930, p. 107)

The question remains as to why the field of reading in the United States has shifted away from eye-movement studies. One reason may be found in our ever-increasing technological advances. Sophisticated machines can now be used to measure eye movements while computers track each pause (e.g., Adams, 1990). Because we now understand the physiology of reading, which remains generally consistent in readers, we may turn our attention to the internal processes of reading, where there are many unexplained inconsistencies in word recognition and comprehension. Today's society requires a much greater level of literacy, and so our research has also had to change.

In spite of the changes, many of the tenets of Dodge's work can be seen in today's research on reading. Although the issue of visual perception may now focus less on how the eye moves than when Dodge was conducting research, thanks to Dodge's description of eye movements we now know that to obtain optimal comprehension readers need to be able to move visually through a text at varying rates. This awareness forms one basis of the current focus on metacognition and our decisions about how we can make students aware of their own thinking. Increasing instruction in decoding may enhance readers' abilities to move through a text at optimal rates. This premise forms the foundation for many of the current curricular phonics and direct instruction programs. Familiarity with text may also help readers move through a text, leading to the current look at fluency. Dodge would not argue against the emphasis of comprehension in the current literature, either. In his work, he was always mindful of the comprehension of text. One gets a sense that this was such a basic requirement for Dodge that he assumed one was not reading unless one understood what was being read.

Whether we believe that visual processes are crucial aspects of reading or we determine that much of the work is of historical significance only, Dodge provides an admirable model of high standards and rigor in reading research, caring in teaching, and service to the professional community.

Reflection Questions

1. Why do you think many of the early reading pioneers have been forgotten? Do you think this is positive or negative for the field of reading? If negative, what can be done to keep the early reading pioneers' work more visible?

2. How did Dodge's early interests in philosophy shape his research on reading?

3. Early reading researchers were interested less in practical pedagogy from their research and more in observing and collecting data on observable processes of reading. Is there a need for more formal experiments in the field of reading today? Why or why not?

4. Dodge identified reading in a second language as an important area of study. Why do you think his research was not pursued? Describe the current thoughts on reading in a second language.

5. Dodge emphasized "intelligent reading." What did he mean by this? Do you think this is still emphasized in the field of reading today?

REFERENCES

Adams, M.J. (1990). *Beginning to read: Thinking and learning about print*. Cambridge, MA: MIT Press.

Archival Records. (2004). *Raymond Dodge Papers*. Akron, OH: University of Akron.

Darwin, C. (1889). *A naturalist's voyage round the world*. London: John Murray.

Dodge, R. (1896). *Die motorischen Wortvorstellungen* [The kinesthetic imagination] (Abh. Philos. Gesch., no. 8, ed. by B. Erdmann). Halle a. S., Germany: Niemeyer.

Dodge, R. (1899). The reaction time of the eye. *Psychological Review, 6*, 477–483.

Dodge, R. (1919a). Mental engineering during the war. *American Review of Reviews, 59*, 504–508.

Dodge, R. (1919b). Mental engineering after the war. *American Review of Reviews, 59*, 606–610.

Dodge, R. (1920). The educational significance of Army intelligence tests. *Education, 40*, 417–428.

Dodge, R. (1930). Raymond Dodge. In C. Murchison (Ed.), *History of psychology in autobiography* (Vol. I, pp. 99–121). New York: Russell and Russell.

Dodge, R. (1931). *Conditions and consequences of human variability*. New Haven, CT: Yale University Press.

Dodge, R., & Cline, T.S. (1901). The angle velocity of eye movements. *Psychological Review, 8*, 145–157.

Dodge, R., & Kahn, E. (1931). *The craving for superiority*. New Haven, CT: Yale University Press.

Dodge, R., to N. Mashburn. (1934, September 29). In Archives of the History of American Psychology, University of Akron, Ohio.

Dodge, R., to M. Tinker. (1934, November 13). In Archives of the History of American Psychology, University of Akron, Ohio.

Dodge, R., to M. Vernon. (1932, March 1). In Archives of the History of American Psychology, University of Akron, Ohio.

Franz, S.I. (1900). Psychological literature [Review]. *Psychological Review, 7*, 188–191.

Harris, A.J. (1970). *How to increase reading ability* (5th ed.). New York: David McKay.

Huey, E.B. (1908). *The psychology and pedagogy of reading*. New York: Macmillan.

Kant, I. (1956). *Kritik der reinen Vernunft* [Critique of pure reason]. Frankfurt, Germany: Insel-Verlag. (Original work published 1781)

Mashburn, N., to R. Dodge. (1934, September 24). In Archives of the History of American Psychology, University of Akron, Ohio.

Miles, W.R. (1956). Raymond Dodge: A biographical memoir. In The National Academy of Sciences of the United States, *Biographical Memoirs, Volume XXIX*. New York: Columbia University Press.

Paulson, E.J., Flurkey, A.D., Goodman, Y.M., & Goodman, K.S. (2003). Eye movements and miscue analysis: Reading from a constructivist perspective. In C.M. Fairbanks, J. Worthy, B. Maloch, J.V. Hoffman, & D.L. Schallert (Eds.), *52nd yearbook of the National Reading Conference* (pp. 345–378). Oak Creek, WI: National Reading Conference.

Radach, R., & Kennedy, A. (2004). Theoretical perspectives on eye movements in reading: Past controversies, current issues, and an agenda for future research. *European Journal of Cognitive Psychology, 16*, 3–26.

Radach, R., Kennedy, A., & Rayner, K., (2004). Preface. *European Journal of Cognitive Psychology* (special issue), *16*, 1–2.

Rayner, K., & Juhasz, B.J. (2004). Eye movements in reading: Old questions and new directions. *European Journal of Cognitive Psychology, 16*, 340–352.

Sadoski, M., & Paivio, A. (2004). A dual coding theoretical model of reading. In R.B. Ruddell & N.J. Unrau (Eds.), *Theoretical models and processes of reading* (5th ed., pp. 1329–1362). Newark, DE: International Reading Association.

Samuels, S.J. (2004). Toward a theory of automatic information processing in reading, revisited. In R.B. Ruddell & N.J. Unrau (Eds.), *Theoretical models and processes of reading* (5th ed., pp. 1127–1148). Newark, DE: International Reading Association.

Stanovich, K.E. (2004). Matthew effects in reading: Some consequences of individual differences in the acquisition of literacy. In R.B. Ruddell and N.J. Unrau (Eds.), *Theoretical models and processes of reading* (5th ed., pp. 454–516). Newark, DE: International Reading Association.

Stepware, Inc. (2004). Ace Reader [Computer software]. Retrieved October 24, 2004, from http://www.acereader.com

Tinker, M.A. (1965). *Bases for effective reading*. Minneapolis: University of Minnesota Press.

Wallace, A.R. (1891). *Darwinism: An exposition of the theory of natural selection, with some of its applications*. London: Macmillan.

Wesleyan University. (n.d.). *History of the Wesleyan Science Department, Psychology*. Retrieved October 5, 2004, from http://www.wesleyan.edu/physics/history/psych.html

Yerkes, R.M. (1942). Raymond Dodge: 1871–1942. *The American Journal of Psychology, 55,* 584–600.

FOR FURTHER READING

Chaffin, R., Morris, R.K., & Seely, R.E. (2001). Learning new word meanings from context: A study of eye movements. *Journal of Experimental Psychology: Learning, Memory, & Cognition, 27,* 225–235.

Just, M.A., & Carpenter, P.A. (1987). *The psychology of reading and language comprehension*. Boston: Allyn & Bacon.

Paulson, E.J. (2005). Viewing eye movements during reading through the lens of chaos theory: How reading is like the weather. *Reading Research Quarterly, 40,* 338–358.

PART II

The Educational Psychologists: Researchers Applying Scientific Principles to Reading Instruction

CHAPTER 4

Charles Hubbard Judd (1873–1946): A Leader in Silent and Oral Reading Instruction

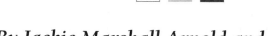

By Jackie Marshall Arnold and Mary-Kate Sableski

Historical Research Process

UNDERTAKING HISTORICAL RESEARCH was a new endeavor for both of us, and we entered into the process with wide-eyed innocence, in awe of the task ahead. Having never heard of Charles Hubbard Judd prior to this experience, we were uncertain what we would find and where the search would take us. However, as in many things in life, all the pieces fell into place as they needed to. Judd's work at the University of Chicago was a central component to his career, and we were able to spend some time with pri-

Shaping the Reading Field: The Impact of Early Reading Pioneers, Scientific Research, and Progressive Ideas, edited by Susan E. Israel and E. Jennifer Monaghan. © 2007 by the International Reading Association.
Photo: Courtesy of the archives of the History of American Psychology, University of Akron, Ohio.

mary source materials in the Special Collections Research Center of the University of Chicago Library. We conversed with librarians and historians via phone and e-mail, and we were struck by how much more accessible the people and resources that we needed were than they had been before the advent of the Internet.

As doctoral students immersed in reading widely in the field, we shared numerous intertextual connections between the work of Judd and our current research interests. We found that Judd's work on the scientific study of education, silent reading, and social aspects of reading is central to many issues today. This gave voice to the historical adage that those who do not learn from the past are condemned to repeat it. The life and work of Charles Hubbard Judd have influenced us both personally and professionally, and the work of historical research has left us with a new perspective on the foundations of the field of reading.

Personal and Professional Life

Charles Hubbard Judd has been referred to as having been a Caesar of his era (Pattison, 1994) because of his reputation for extreme determination, strength of conviction, and enduring leadership abilities. He inspired a generation of scholars to work tirelessly and relentlessly at the science of education. As one of his students, Ralph W. Tyler, aptly stated, "Charles Hubbard Judd was known throughout the western world as a great educational statesman. And he was. But I always think of him as an insightful teacher and a kindly mentor" (Tyler, 1996, p. 28). Judd's work on the scientific study of education, silent reading, and reading as a social process made him a key figure in reading education in the United States. He is a reading pioneer in the truest sense of the word because of his lasting impact not only on the practices of teaching reading but also on the people who continue to search for better methods of teaching children to read.

Judd's eyes are mentioned in many ways throughout the writings that document his lengthy career. In a speech given in 1973 at the Charles Hubbard Judd Centennial Celebration Dinner, Robert McCaul sketched Judd's physical appearance, stating,

> If he were addressing you tonight...he would be wearing steel-rimmed spectacles, but probably you would not notice them, for it would be his eyes that would catch and hold your attention. They were round and blue. His

friends said that he had a firm and steady gaze; his enemies said he tried to stare you down. (p. 1)

These eyes watched over a multitude of students throughout his lengthy career at many universities, including Wesleyan University, New York University, the University of Cincinnati, and the University of Chicago. Judd's students were required to meet high expectations because Judd was "intolerant of laziness or muddled thinking" (Tyler, 1996, p. 22). Students who were unable to meet Judd's expectations (or chose not to) were quickly removed from the program. Over time a sufficient number of students existed to "form a club called the 'FBJ Club', standing for 'Fired By Judd'" (Tyler, 1996, p. 23).

However, for students who worked to a higher standard, Judd was known as a mentor and a friend. In 1921, while Judd's student Floyd W. Reeves was presenting his final oral examinations, Reeves's appendix burst. After surgery Reeves's doctors informed Judd that Reeves must rest for several months for a full recovery. Judd recommended to Reeves's wife that she should take her husband back to their hometown; he provided them money for the trip and offered more money should they need it. He also arranged for Reeves to return, when ready, for a job that had been previously arranged for him. Tyler writes,

> Mr. Judd was always kind and helpful to me, and I knew a dozen of my fellow students who experienced his kindly encouragement and assistance. I believe that the notion of his coldness grew out of his intolerance of incompetence. (Tyler, 1996, p. 24)

In contrast to his kindness to young men who were his students, Judd seems not to have had much time for young women. Lagemann (2000, p. 70) reports that Judd felt there were differences in gender—that women should be teachers and men should be researchers. He also believed in a related manner that teachers (women) should not be required or encouraged to obtain advanced education, while researchers (men) should obtain their doctoral degrees.

Although he was referred to as a Caesar of his era (Pattison, 1994), Charles Hubbard Judd may also appropriately be compared to Horatio Alger.

His is a story of rags to riches in the truest sense. Born in 1873 in Bareilly, India, to missionary parents Charles Wesley and Sara Judd, Judd moved to Binghamton, New York, USA, at age 6 because his parents were in poor health. After returning to the United States, his father died within one year, and his mother died five years later. At age 11, Judd was left orphaned along with his younger sister, to be cared for by his eldest sister. He attended the Binghamton schools, from which he received a high school diploma in 1880.

Judd had an impressive academic genealogy that significantly influenced his future academic career. He made the acquaintance of several important figures during his elementary and high school years, including his science teacher, R.W. Griffiths, and the high school principal, Eliot R. Payson, who pushed him to achieve his full potential in the academic arena. Rev. George Murray Colville, a Methodist minister who lived across the street from Judd, took him under his wing and "did much—I hardly know how much—to arouse [Judd's] intellectual interests" (Judd, 1932/1961, p. 208). Colville used cunning in dealing with an unmotivated young Judd by informing him that his high school teachers had commented that he was not capable of high-quality intellectual work, and he suggested that Judd prove them wrong. Later, after Judd completed his undergraduate work at Wesleyan University, it was Colville who provided the funds for Judd to pursue his doctorate in Germany. It was an act of generosity to which Judd felt extremely indebted.

During his time at Wesleyan (1890–1894), Judd enrolled in several courses with Andrew Campbell Armstrong, a professor of psychology who introduced Judd to the field. Interestingly, another significant individual who studied with Professor Armstrong was Edward Lee Thorndike (see chapter 5, this volume). Armstrong was a caring mentor to the young Judd, providing him with individual attention, instilling in him the core values of academic life, and exposing him to the profession by taking him to the annual meeting of the American Psychological Association (APA). Here, Judd was able to hear from "a galaxy of psychologists" (Judd, 1932/1961, p. 211) and view a psychology laboratory. Even a cursory glance at the future academic career of Judd reveals the profound influence this experience had on him, through his work in the laboratory at Yale and his eventual presidency of the APA in 1909. Judd learned from Armstrong the importance of systematic, coherent thought, along with the need to take into account the thoughts of leaders in the field in any project. It is possible that the latter value was what influenced Judd to make such a careful listing in his autobiography (1932/1961) of those people who had made an impact on him throughout his career. Throughout his teaching life, Judd was referred to by his students as a master teacher, and the roots of this distinction can be found in the influence of Armstrong, whom Judd gratefully acknowledged as providing him with models of lectures and discussions that were better than those of any other teacher with whom he had studied (Judd, 1932/1961, pp. 210–211).

The seeds of Judd's academic career were planted during his time at Wesleyan University as an undergraduate student. Judd had the opportunity to participate in social activities, such as a fraternity, in which he demonstrated his strong leadership abilities and charisma, serving as manager of the football team. In his autobiography, Judd admits that his social experiences were limited and that his social ingenuity was taxed by the situations in which he found himself. However, as accounts of Judd's life would later suggest, he was engaging and dynamic in his personality, which helped him successfully navigate both the social and academic hurdles he encountered during this time.

Upon completion of his undergraduate work at Wesleyan University in 1894, Judd headed to Leipzig, Germany, to study under Wilhelm Wundt, a prominent psychologist of the time. Judd speaks of Wundt with great admiration in his autobiography, and there was clearly a mutual feeling on the part of Wundt, evidenced by the fact that he permitted Judd to translate a key text into English as *Outlines of Psychology* (Wundt, 1969), a task that he had repeatedly refused to allow others to do.

Wundt had a significant influence on the academic work of Judd. Judd is often credited with the expression, "Get the facts!" (McCaul, 1973, p. 10), and it is in his work with Wundt that one can find the origins of this idea. Wundt challenged Judd to support his claims with facts and to have a plentitude of facts from which to draw. Reading through Judd's account of Wundt in his autobiography, one is struck by the similarities that existed between Judd's and Wundt's work. The characteristics of strong work ethics, prodigious writing careers, and close work with students are similarities between the two men that cannot be ignored. Judd truly emulated and imitated his academic forebears, including Wundt, and he used their influence in positive ways to advance his own academic career after obtaining his doctorate at the University of Leipzig in 1896.

Judd's first position as an assistant professor was at his alma mater, Wesleyan University, working with his mentor, Armstrong, from 1896 to

1898. Here Judd obtained experience in teaching undergraduate courses in psychology and built a resume of published papers and conference presentations. He placed high value on academic productivity, a thread that runs throughout his career and that was a crucial aspect of the expectations he held for the faculty members under him in his future position at the University of Chicago.

In 1898, Judd accepted a position at New York University. At this time, he was also married for the first time, to Ella LeCompte, with whom he had one daughter, Dorothy. His work at New York University was one of his first entrées into education because he was asked to teach courses in pedagogy. According to Judd, "I was probably as ill-prepared to teach teachers as any young specialist in the theory of space perception and history of psychology could be" (Judd, 1932/1961, p. 221). During one of his lectures to a group of teachers, Judd was interrupted by a student asking, "How can we use this information in the teaching of children?" (p. 222). This comment made Judd rethink his understandings within the field of education, and he then set himself to learning as much about schools as possible so he could more effectively serve his students and improve the instruction of children.

Judd was asked to resign from New York University after two years because of his involvement with a group that was pressuring for a change in some of the administrative politics of the university and for higher standards in the School of Education (Lagemann, 2000, p. 67). Judd had a great respect for the institution of academia, and he held in high esteem the maintenance of suitable standards for scholarship, which he felt were not being met at the university (Freeman, 1927). This event instilled in the young professor a "great respect for an institution when its interests were in conflict with those of individuals," as William Scott Gray put it (1948, p. 20; see chapter 13, this volume). From the ordeal at New York University, Judd acquired a great respect for administrative officers and for expressing the strong convictions he had toward the improvement of education.

Judd continued to build his knowledge base in the field of education during a one-year stint (1900–1901) at the University of Cincinnati, Ohio, USA, as Professor of Psychology and Pedagogy. As he did in his previous position, Judd felt obligated to devote himself to the study of education to become well versed in the information he was being asked to teach. This one-year appointment, therefore, became instrumental in grounding Judd in the major activities of his future career.

While at the University of Cincinnati, Judd received an invitation to Yale University to teach courses and run the psychology laboratory. Although it involved a demotion in salary and rank, Judd eagerly accepted the invitation because of the excellent opportunity it afforded him to advance his academic career. While at Yale, where he arrived in 1901, Judd taught courses in psychology, including introductory courses and psychology courses for teachers, and, most significantly, he established Yale's psychology laboratory as one of the premier research facilities in the field. Judd continued his work in education while at Yale, publishing *Genetic Psychology for Teachers* (1903) and working with the school systems to develop courses for teachers. Judd focused his work on the nature of learning, specifically the difference between higher and lower mental processes, the influence of movement, and transfer of training. One of his most significant publications was a three-volume work on psychology, published in 1907 (1907a, 1907b, 1907c). His work at Yale helped to establish him as a leader in the field of education.

In 1909, Judd was appointed the director of the School of Education at the University of Chicago. It was at this institution that Judd spent most of his career, retiring in 1938. During his tenure, Judd succeeded in securing the University of Chicago's School of Education as one of the foremost schools in the country for teachers. The list of credits to his name during this time is lengthy and reveals his significant influence on the field of educational psychology and the scientific study of education. Judd's major lines of work included the psychology of high school subjects (1915), and, significantly, an introduction to the scientific study of education (1918a). He also authored or coauthored books on the nature of reading (1918b) and silent reading (Judd & Buswell, 1922). More general works on education include his study of national educational problems (1933).

Demonstrative of Judd's influence on his students and the field of education was the "Judd Club," as its members affectionately called it. This organization was composed of Chicago-area school administrators who admired Judd's work and wished to engage in discussions with this great educational statesman about the state of their schools and the field of education. Judd attended the meetings and provided support in the form of comments, reading material, and goodwill.

Judd's retirement from the University of Chicago in 1938 was met with a great sense of loss on the part of the educational community. He worked in school systems in California and continued to publish until his death in

1946. The tributes to Judd following his death were numerous. Most significant among them was the dedication of two buildings, the education building at the University of Chicago and an elementary school in Chicago, that were named after this forceful personality and honest leader. May Diehl, whom he had married in 1937, furnished flowers each February to the Charles Hubbard Judd building on the campus of the University of Chicago in memory of this man who is remembered not only for the "force of [his] personality, genius for leadership, capacity to inspire, utter integrity and ready wit" (Edwards, 1946, p. 11) but also for the enduring contributions he made to the field of education.

The academic career of Charles Hubbard Judd can perhaps best be summed up in the following quotation, taken from an exchange of letters between Judd and William S. Gray: "I am working away at the library. It is interesting to find out how much there is to be learned when one has spent a long life trying to learn" (Judd to Gray, 1930). Judd was truly a lifelong learner, and he inspired countless others to devote their lives to their own and others' learning.

Philosophical Beliefs and Guiding Principles

Judd has been described as having led two careers in different fields, one in psychology and the other in education (Freeman, 1947). Freeman attributes Judd's "extraordinary energy, force, and keenness of mind" (p. 60) to Judd's success throughout his life in these fields. Studying under Wundt in Germany formed many of Judd's philosophical beliefs and guiding principles. Judd's well-known belief in the importance of social psychology led him to "emphasize the significance of social institutions in shaping human thinking and behavior" (McCaul, 1973, p. 6).

The key element that defined Judd's work throughout his life was his belief in the scientific study of education. As Tyler (1996) so eloquently states, "That valid generalizations to guide education will come from investigations of the phenomena in practice was his central belief" (p. 22). Judd testified at the Scopes Trial to his beliefs in the power of scientific study because he was renowned for his unshaken belief in the power of this method of research in education. The Scopes Trial, held in Dayton, Tennessee, USA, in 1925, centered on the conflict regarding the teaching of evolution versus creationism in public schools. John T. Scopes, a high school biology teacher, was being prosecuted for refusing to follow the Butler Act of 1925, which "outlawed the teaching of the theory of evolution in Tennessee schools" (Olson, 2004, p. 7). Judd testified, although the jury was prevented from hearing it, that

> it would be impossible to obey the law [the Butler Act] without seriously depriving teachers in training of a proper view of the facts of human development.... It is quite impossible to make any adequate study of the mental development of children without taking into account the facts that have been learned from the study of comparative or animal psychology. (Scopes, 1997, p. 232)

This testimony is just one example of how Judd's belief in scientific studies saturated his work.

Judd believed that the "aim of education is to develop ideas and generalizations and by these humans can master all the problems of society and of life" (McCaul, 1973, p.12). In an early publication on the nature of reading (1918b), Judd articulates his foundational beliefs in the power of scientific study:

> The danger is that we shall go on experimenting without making the kind of study of results which will tend to bring experimentation to a definite issue in scientifically defensible methods. A scientific study of reading should point out the way in which the experiences of the school and the investigations of the educational laboratory may be combined to supply certain principles of procedure which will surely improve instruction. (p. 5)

Although Judd provided significant contributions to two different fields—psychology and education—he was consistent across all contexts in his central belief in the power of scientific study. Judd's major philosophical beliefs and guiding principles were based in this foundation that he served throughout his life.

Contributions to the Field of Reading

As Judd states in his *Introduction to the Scientific Study of Education* (1918a),

> Reading is the most important subject taught in schools; yet there are the widest differences in the results secured with different pupils. It is the duty of the schools to find out what constitutes the difference between good readers and bad readers, in order that both classes may be improved. (p. 9)

In his first published text, *Genetic Psychology for Teachers* (1903), Judd illustrates how the process of learning to read is a socially influenced, rather than an isolated, event. In a 1909 presidential address to the APA, Judd stated,

> I still hold that evolution has produced in human life a group of unique complex facts which cannot be adequately explained by resolving them into their elements. Human mental life is a unique product of organization. Through evolution certain complexes have been produced which are new and potent causes in the world; among these is human consciousness. (Judd, 1932/1961, p. 227)

As a social psychologist, the reading process for Judd held social implications as well as physical ones.

Judd summarizes a child's reading development in his text, *Reading: Its Nature and Development* (1918b), articulating in the process his beliefs about the instruction of reading. He speaks about children's education before entering school as a time when their education revolves predominately around acquiring oral language. He states that a young child is not ready to begin a formal education "in any proper sense until he has command of oral language" (p. 135). Judd believed that reading instruction should begin when children arrive at the world of school, opposing contemporary beliefs held by some that young children were not ready to be instructed in reading. Judd writes, "Pupils who do not learn to read early often have difficulty in learning to read in the upper grades" (p. 137). He draws an analogy between early reading instruction and the attempts of an older person to acquire a foreign language compared with those of a young child. The child, according to Judd, is "plastic in his habits" (p. 137) and can make a complete success of acquiring additional languages, while the adult will always be "handicapped" and "defective in pronunciation" (p. 137).

At this early stage of a young child's reading instruction, Judd believed in the power of oral reading instruction. Allowing a child to see the relation between oral language and the printed word was foundational to Judd's theory of the process of learning to read. A successful teacher, according to Judd's instruction, would take a child's familiar oral language and add the printed words and phrases to his or her instruction.

Nineteenth- and early 20th-century reading instruction focused predominately upon oral recitation as the determining instrument of proving one's reading capabilities. As articulated by Smith in *American Reading Instruction*

(2002), "The aim of developing eloquent oral reading [during that time span] was paramount to all others" (p. 37). However, Judd clearly states that successful oral recitation is not the end of reading instruction. In fact he writes, "Oral reading is a menace to intelligence when it emphasizes such matters as enunciation and forms of expression to such an extent as to eclipse the recognition of meanings" (1918b, p. 142). Judd then discusses the scientific path that would define the major component of his work in the field of reading throughout his life: "One of the major problems in the scientific study of reading is to discover the relation between reading and speech...and how far up the grades it is legitimate to emphasize oral methods" (p. 142).

Judd set out to explore and answer this question scientifically. Through photographing the reader's eyes as they scanned lines of print, Judd and his fellow researchers—Guy Buswell, Raymond Dodge (see chapter 3, this volume), and others—were able to examine the number and length of pauses that a reader's eyes made while he or she read orally in comparison to the number and length of pauses that occurred while the person was reading silently.

Judd believed the difference between oral and silent reading resided in the understanding that speech units control the process of oral reading. When a reader is reading orally, the eyes move to each word as the voice utters the particular speech units. In comparison, Judd asserted, silent reading is guided by units of visual perception. The mind searches for recognized phrases, and those phrases direct the movement of the eyes. Judd stated, "Silent reading consists of a series of pauses determined in number and length by the demands of recognition, while oral reading consists of a series of pauses dominated by articulation" (1918b, p. 24). Judd summarizes years of data collection and analysis in the following manner:

> The eye makes more pauses along a printed line when the reader is reading orally than when he is reading silently. Oral reading is therefore a more laborious, difficult form of reading. Furthermore, the time spent in each pause is greater in oral reading.... Figures show that oral reading is slow as well as laborious. (1918a, p. 10)

By examining the research and observing readers, Judd ascertained that a close relation exists between the ways that a reader's eyes move across the page and the ways in which the reader comprehends the meaning of the sentences. Judd's research, through the photographs taken of many subjects' eyes while reading, demonstrated that short eye movements and long pauses were indicative of the reader's experiencing difficulty in reading a text. Judd writes, "Among the fundamental discoveries which have been made, none is more important than the discovery that oral reading as contrasted with well-developed silent reading shows many of the characteristics of immature reading" (1933, p. 195).

Judd saw the implications of these findings as applicable to the classroom: "The significance of these results for practical class work is at once apparent. Methods which will promote fluent, rapid reading will contribute in general to clear understanding and increase in power of interpretation" (1930, p. 118). He felt strongly that teachers should be informed and educated about these results and their implications for teaching because, he said,

> books on methods are full of advice on the teaching of oral reading, but they pass silent reading with a casual mention. Yet silent reading is the only form of reading commonly employed in later life.... It is accordingly important that the distinction be impressed on teachers. (1930, p. 119)

Strong advocacy for the teaching of silent reading by Judd and other leaders in the field of reading (e.g., Buswell and Thorndike; for Thorndike, see chapter 5, this volume) affected the publishing of teachers' manuals and textbooks. In fact, as Smith (2002) states, "Emphasis upon the new silent reading procedures was responsible for bringing teachers' manuals into general use during this period [1910–1925]" (p. 159). These manuals include lessons, advice on the development of reading comprehension, directions for home application of the lessons, bibliographies, and more.

In a similar way, the focus on silent reading also made an impact on children's readers. Adapting to the call for silent reading instruction, the new readers, filled with factual and informational selections, reflected the reading that students would see in real life (Smith, 2002, p. 162). As Buswell and Wheeler (1923) state, the old readers had consisted of "fairy tales, folklore, myths, Mother Goose rhymes, and similar fanciful material" (p.10).

From his research Judd concluded,

> What is needed is...a clear understanding of the special demands of each type of reading and the special methods of each type of analysis. When teachers are clear on these matters, there will rapidly accumulate through school practice satisfactory methods of dealing with each situation. (Judd & Buswell, 1922, p. 89)

He had harsh words for schools and teachers that continue oral reading instruction too long: "Oral reading must be called sharply in question if it is overdone and carried into the upper grades" (1918b, p. 61) because, he continued,

> pupils outgrow oral reading just as infants outgrow creeping when they learn to stand up and walk....Oral reading should give way to silent reading and phonic analysis should give place to word analysis. Meanings should be emphasized and not the mechanical pronunciation of words. (pp. 146–151)

Judd understood the power of fluent silent reading to give students access to a lifelong ability to read and comprehend. Throughout his life he refused to stay silent, orally or in writing, about his findings and their importance to the lives of children.

Lessons for the Future

Lessons for those working in the field of reading can easily be drawn from such an enduring educational statesman. Judd's work in the area of reading has had both explicit and implicit influences on the current professional climate, and his work also has profound implications for the future of reading education.

The scientific study of education that Judd promoted has come back in vogue through mandates and funding by the U.S. federal government. The No Child Left Behind Act of 2001 has called for an increase in studies that focus on randomized, experimental designs, privileging the results of such studies over the results of ethnographic, qualitative designs (Glenn, 2004). Judd's life work was devoted to the promotion of the scientific study of education and the validation of its methods in the eyes of scientists. As with much in the field of reading, the pendulum has clearly swung from right to left and back again. Learning from the previous work of Charles Hubbard Judd, today's reading professionals can identify and discuss the origins of the scientific study of education and its roots in the field of reading. Judd hoped, as do current educational researchers, that his studies would influence the instruction of children in positive ways, and he felt that scientific study was the way to achieve that goal. As changing definitions of "science" emerge in the field (Anderson & Herr, 1999), what it means to undertake the scientific study of education can be informed by Judd's work.

Judd identified the propensity for the results of scientific studies to influence decisions about the nature of reading instruction, and he cautioned against making these decisions based on loosely connected facts or unreliable data. Almost as if he were speaking to the current debate over high-stakes assessment tools, Judd said,

> We have used reading tests but we have thought of the results of these tests merely as starting points. We believe that it is inherent in the nature of a test to reveal a present condition rather than to uncover a fundamental cause. A test may show, for example, that a certain individual is a poor reader, but the test does not tell what is the cause of the deficiency. The underlying cause of the present condition can be discovered only by painstaking analysis. (1932/1961, p. 230)

Judd invited further research that relied on experimental methods into the nature of reading. Through experimental work, he hoped to identify ways to uncover the causes of reading difficulties in individual children. This goal continues today, and Judd's belief that reading tests are to be used as starting points for analysis is a dominant tenet in the assessment of reading difficulties (Allington, 2000).

One of the major emphases of Judd's scientific studies was the movement of the eyes during oral and silent reading. The significance of eye-movement studies to current work in the field of reading is discussed elsewhere in this volume (see chapters 3 and 6). Silent reading is an integral part of today's classrooms, as evidenced by the proliferation of programs such as Drop Everything and Read (DEAR), Sustained Silent Reading (SSR), and Sustained Quiet Reading Time (SQRT). These programs are a result of the awareness, pointed out by Judd, that silent reading is the dominant reading form in everyday life. Oral reading still has a place in schools, as a way for students to perfect their listening skills, hone their ability to read with fluency, and provide a form of reading assessment (Clay, 1979; Goodman & Goodman, 2004). But Judd's study of the differences between oral and silent reading has contributed to modern understandings of how fluent reading is achieved, and fluency has become a "hot topic" (Cassidy & Cassidy, 2004/2005) because of its proven effect on reading comprehension (Rasinski, 2003). Illustrative of the significance of Judd's work in silent reading is the following comment by three modern reading researchers:

Perhaps the most significant shift in emphasis in reading comprehension instruction that is observable from published research reports occurred in the early part of the 20th century during which time educators shifted their emphasis from the improvement of oral reading as a method for "getting meaning" to an emphasis on improving comprehension during silent reading. (Flood, Lapp, & Fisher, 2003, p. 933)

Judd's theories of reading as a process of social acquisition, rather than academic transmission, are well documented in his research. The current climate of the field of reading promotes this view, through the work of psychologists Leo Vygotsky (e.g., 1934/1986), Marie Clay (e.g., 1979), and others. Reading, like learning in general, is believed to occur in social interaction, not through rote memorization of facts (Bransford, Brown, & Cocking, 2000). The work of Clay and the Reading Recovery program (Clay, 1979) also support Judd's emphasis on the connection between oral language and learning to read. Classroom instruction has moved away from exclusively direct instruction models to balanced approaches that focus on providing students with a variety of opportunities to interact with adults, peers, and resources to construct their understandings about reading. Current research with English-language learners, an International Reading Association "hot topic" for 2005 (Cassidy & Cassidy, 2004/2005), supports the need for social interaction to reinforce reading development (Gutierrez, 2004).

Interestingly, Judd addressed another issue that is of paramount importance to current reading professionals, that of the need to teach reading strategies to middle and high school students in addition to the instruction they receive in elementary school. In *Psychology of High-School Subjects*, Judd (1915) states, "It is assumed that the work of elementary education has been satisfactorily completed, and that elementary reading has prepared students for all their later work. The fact is, that the ordinary student does not know how to read economically" (p.169). Teachers of the English language arts in today's middle and high schools still deal with this dilemma, and it has been the cause for an increase in the professional literature on the subject (Robb, 2000; Tovani, 2000). As teachers now and in the future continue to struggle with how to ensure that middle and high school students possess the strategies they need to read effectively, helpful information may be gleaned from the work of the past.

The work of Charles Hubbard Judd was seen as of paramount importance in its own time, but it also has important lessons for the present and future of the field. Judd's work on the scientific study of education, silent reading, and reading as a social process can be seen running throughout the current research and practice of reading instruction, and the implications his work has for the future demonstrate that the significant influence of Charles Hubbard Judd will continue to be felt for ages to come.

Reflection Questions

1. Judd felt strongly that teachers should clearly understand the differences between oral and silent reading. How do you define for yourself the differences inherent in oral and silent reading? Reflect upon how you support instruction for students in both areas.
2. Judd articulated that reading is one of the most important subjects taught in schools but that students have different levels of success through their personal journeys of learning to read. Reflect and discuss with a colleague how you differentiate instruction for readers of all abilities.
3. Judd understood long ago the importance of social interaction in the process of learning to read. How can you incorporate additional social experiences into your instruction to support children's reading success?
4. Supporting reading instruction once a child shifts from oral to silent reading can be challenging for teachers when they cannot "hear" the child reading. What are ways that teachers can support instruction for silent readers?
5. Judd was an advocate of the scientific measurement of achievement in reading. However, he also cautioned against using the results of a single test to determine the course of a child's education. Articulate your own theory of reading assessment, in terms of both purposes and consequences, providing examples from your own practice.

REFERENCES

Allington, R.L. (2000). *What really matters for struggling readers: Designing research-based programs*. Boston: Allyn & Bacon.

Anderson, G.L., & Herr, K. (1999). The new paradigm wars: Is there room for rigorous practitioner knowledge in schools and universities? *Educational Researcher, 28*(1), 6, 12–21.

Bransford, J.D., Brown, A.L., & Cocking, R.R. (Eds.). (2000). *How people learn: Brain, mind, experience, and school*. Washington, DC: National Academies Press.

Buswell, G.T., & Wheeler, W.H. (1923). *The silent reading hour (Teacher's manual for the second reader)*. Chicago: Wheeler.

Butler Act of 1925, Public Act of the State of Tennessee, ch. 27, HB 125 (March 13, 1925).

Cassidy, J., & Cassidy, D. (2004/2005). What's hot, what's not for 2005. *Reading Today, 22*, 1.

Clay, M.M. (1979). *The early detection of reading difficulties: A diagnostic survey with recovery procedures* (2nd ed.). Auckland, New Zealand: Heinemann.

Edwards, N. (1946). Charles Hubbard Judd: 1873–1946. *The University of Chicago Magazine, 39*(1), 11.

Flood, J., Lapp, D., & Fisher, D. (2003). Reading comprehension instruction. In J. Flood, D. Lapp, J.R. Squire, J. & J. Jensen (Eds.), *Handbook of research on teaching English language arts* (2nd ed., pp. 931–941). Mahwah, NJ: Erlbaum.

Freeman, F.N. (1927). Biographical sketch of Dr. Judd to 1909. *Zeta News, 12*(3–4), 1–9.

Freeman, F. (1947). Charles Hubbard Judd. *Psychological Review, 54*(2), 59–65.

Glenn, D. (2004). No classroom left unstudied. *The Chronicle of Higher Education, 50*(38), A12.

Goodman, Y.M., & Goodman, K.S. (2004). To err is human: Learning about language processes by analyzing miscues. In R.B. Ruddell & N.J. Unrau (Eds.), *Theoretical models and processes of reading* (5th ed., pp. 620–639). Newark, DE: International Reading Association.

Gray, W.S. (1948, April 15). *Charles Hubbard Judd as a pioneer in the development of professional and graduate study in education*. Speech given at the Conference of Education of the University of Chicago.

Gutierrez, K.D. (2004). Literacy as laminated activity: Rethinking literacy for English learners. In C.M. Fairbanks, J. Worthy, B. Maloch, J.V. Hoffman, & D.L. Schallert (Eds.), *53rd Yearbook of the National Reading Conference* (pp. 101–114). Oak Creek, WI: National Reading Conference.

Judd, C.H. (1903). *Genetic psychology for teachers*. New York: Appleton.

Judd, C.H. (1907a). *Psychology: General introduction. Volume one of a series of textbooks designed to introduce the student to the methods and principles of scientific psychology*. New York: C. Scribner's Sons.

Judd, C.H. (1907b). *Laboratory manual for psychology: Volume two of a series of textbooks designed to introduce the student to the methods and principles of scientific psychology*. New York: C. Scribner's Sons.

Judd, C.H. (1907c). *Laboratory equipment for psychological experiments: Volume three of a series of textbooks designed to introduce the student to the methods and principles of scientific psychology*. New York: C. Scribner's Sons.

Judd, C.H. (1915). *Psychology of high-school subjects*. Boston: Ginn.

Judd, C.H. (1918a). *Introduction to the scientific study of education*. Boston: Ginn.

Judd, C.H. (1918b). *Reading: Its nature and development*. Chicago: University of Chicago Press.

Judd, C.H. (1930). Reading. In G.M. Whipple & G.D. Strayer (Eds.), *Standards and tests for the measurement of the efficiency of schools and school systems* (pp. 111–119). Bloomington, IL: Public School Publishing Company.

Judd, C.H. (1933). *Problems of education in the United States*. New York: McGraw-Hill.

Judd, C.H. (1961). Charles Hubbard Judd. In C. Murchison (Ed.), *A history of psychology in au-tobiography* (Vol. 2, pp. 207–235). New York: Russell & Russell. (Original work published 1932)

Judd, C.H., & Buswell, G.T. (1922). *Silent reading: A study of the various types.* Chicago: University of Chicago Press.

Judd, C.H., to W.S. Gray. (1930, June 30). Charles H. Judd Collection, Box 23, Folder 4, University of Chicago Archives, Chicago.

Lagemann, E.C. (2000). *An elusive science: The troubling history of education research.* Chicago: University of Chicago Press.

McCaul, R.L. (1973, February 18). *Charles Hubbard Judd: February 20, 1873–July 18, 1946.* Speech given at the Charles Hubbard Judd Centennial Celebration Dinner, Chicago.

No Child Left Behind Act of 2001, Pub. L. No. 107-110, 115 Stat. 1425 (2002).

Olson, S.P. (2004). *The trial of John T. Scopes: A primary source account.* New York: Rosen.

Pattison, W.D. (1994). *A Caesar in his day: Selected readings on the career and character of Charles Hubbard Judd.* Chicago: University of Chicago Department of Education.

Rasinski, T.V. (2003). *The fluent reader: Oral reading strategies for building word recognition, fluency, and comprehension.* New York: Scholastic.

Robb, L. (2000). *Teaching reading in middle school.* New York: Scholastic.

Scopes, J.T. (1997). *The world's most famous court trial: Tennessee evolution case.* Union, NJ: The Lawbook Exchange.

Smith, N.B. (2002). *American reading instruction: Special edition.* Newark, DE: International Reading Association.

Tovani, C. (2000). *I read it, but I don't get it: Comprehension strategies for adolescent readers.* York, ME: Stenhouse.

Tyler, R.W. (1996). Charles Hubbard Judd: As I came to know him. In C. Kridel, R.V. Bullough, and P. Shaker (Eds.), *Teachers and mentors: Profiles of distinguished twentieth-century professors of education* (pp. 19–28). New York: Garland.

Vygotsky, L.S. (1986). *Thought and language.* (A. Kozalin, Trans.). Cambridge, MA: MIT Press. (Original work published 1934)

Wundt, W. (1969). *Outlines of psychology.* (C.H. Judd, Trans.). St. Claire Shores, MI: Scholarly Press.

FOR FURTHER READING

Judd, C.H. (1918). *The evolution of a democratic school system.* Boston: Houghton Mifflin.

Judd, C.H. (1927). *Psychology of secondary education.* Boston: Ginn.

Judd, C.H. (1928). *The unique character of American secondary education.* Cambridge, MA: Harvard University Press.

Judd, C.H. (1939). *Educational psychology.* Boston: Houghton Mifflin.

CHAPTER 5

Edward Lee Thorndike (1874–1949): A Look at His Contributions to Learning and Reading

By Lou Ann Sears

Historical Research Process

THE BEGINNING OF my search for information about Edward Lee Thorndike, whose name I vaguely recalled from a graduate course called History of Reading Research and Instruction, was a bit like paddling a canoe into the Pacific. At some point, I realized that I had not been thinking big. It was time to get a stronger boat and drop anchor in Lake Thorndike. I thought I would examine first what Thorndike wrote, the primary sources. First, I

Shaping the Reading Field: The Impact of Early Reading Pioneers, Scientific Research, and Progressive Ideas, edited by Susan E. Israel and E. Jennifer Monaghan. © 2007 by the International Reading Association.
Photo: Courtesy of the National Library of Medicine.

would let him show me who he was. Later, I would take a look at his biography and other secondary sources. Only then would I know if my own conclusions, if the impression Thorndike made on me, would measure up to what others had to say.

I was to find that Thorndike's key contributions include a definition of "reading," the creation of reading tests, the obsessive compilation of vocabulary lists, the encouragement of adult reading and learning, a look at comprehension, and the development of easy-to-read classroom materials.

Personal and Professional Life

In 1938, Thorndike invited Robert Travers (1987) to sail to the United States to join the research team at the International Institute at Columbia University's Teachers College (p. 46). Travers, who later became "one of the world's foremost scholars in educational psychology and methodology of educational research" (Western Michigan University, 2004, n.p.), worked on his doctorate while working with Thorndike. Forty-nine years later, Travers (1987) recalled the experience:

> It has taken me a lifetime to understand the full significance of the model Thorndike presented. At the time I worked with him I viewed him as a scientist who managed to apply his scientific knowledge to the improvement of education. Such was the myth that surrounded Thorndike at Teachers College, a myth that historical accounts of Thorndike and his work have perpetuated. The myth has done much to hide the full significance of Thorndike and his work and has resulted in a failure of those who followed to benefit fully from the model he provided. From breakfast to dinner, Thorndike was a scientist concerned with the expansion and integration of knowledge. The second Thorndike came to life toward evening— Thorndike the inventor. Most of the materials he developed for schools he designed and constructed during the evening hours. That is what he did for relaxation, if one can call it that. (p. 47)

Edward Lee Thorndike was born on August 31, 1874, in Williamsburg, Massachusetts, USA, to Abigail Brewster Ladd and Edward R. Thorndike, a Methodist minister (Joncich, 1968, p. 19). With one older brother, Ashley, who would later become a fellow faculty member at Columbia University; a younger brother, Everett Lynn, who would earn a PhD in history at Columbia University (p. 209); and a younger sister, Mildred (p. 196), Thorndike was a dutiful middle child. Much was expected of the minister's children, and none disappointed.

Although he was not his parent's firstborn, Edward Thorndike would throughout his life earn the title "first." Thorndike stood apart from the crowd as early as the late 1880s when he was a student at the Lowell Massachusetts Common School. Prior to age 11 when he graduated from the eighth grade (Joncich, 1968, p. 46), he knew himself to be gifted and worried that he would be regarded as "teacher's pet" (p. 45) for his conscientious behavior and his abilities (p. 46). Like his brother Ashley before him, he began at this early age to win prizes and scholarships (p. 45).

Thorndike's capacity for standing out from the crowd extended to his secondary education. Unlike most of his peers, he went on to secondary school for several reasons. In 1886, common school was the end of the educational road for most, but Thorndike, son of a minister, won scholarships enabling him to carry on his parents' tradition of becoming more highly educated than most (Joncich, 1968, pp. 46–47). Another move related to his father's employment caused him to leave Lowell High School in 1887 and enroll in the Roxbury Latin School (p. 46), where he would earn the honor of being first or second in his class (p. 48). Another ministerial move caused him to attend the "rigid" Classical High School in Providence, Rhode Island, where he spent an extra year of high school to complete the school's requirements (p. 51).

For sons of Methodist ministers, Wesleyan University in Connecticut was a natural choice (Joncich, 1968, p. 52), and it was for Thorndike particularly because his brother Ashley had already set the precedent. There from 1891–1895, Edward won prizes in English literature, Latin, Greek, psychology, moral philosophy, English composition, junior exhibition, and junior debate. While there, he literally stood apart from the crowd because his antisocial feelings disturbed him (p. 59). At this time, he also quietly rejected his father's religion in favor of science, something that he told his future wife, Elizabeth Moulton, might ruin his chances of obtaining a faculty position at Wesleyan University (p. 63).

After graduating from Wesleyan University in 1895, Thorndike transferred to Harvard University, where he left behind his original aspirations of becoming an English teacher and obtained an AB degree in 1896 and an AM degree in 1897 (Adult Education History Project, 2002, para. 4). Teaching seemed like a means, rather than an end, to a man who felt the need to explore science and psychology (Joncich, 1968, p. 78). Studying under professor and mentor William James was so inspirational for Thorndike that he found his life turning in a new direction. Thorndike grew weary of the work at Harvard University and received a fellowship at Columbia University, where he could spend more time on research, although doing so meant another unwanted move (p. 103).

In 1897, Thorndike settled in at Columbia University and met James McKeen Cattell (see chapter 1, this volume), the man who became his second significant mentor (Joncich, 1968, pp. 104–105). In just a few years, Thorndike and the world's second man to hold the title of Professor of Psychology would be colleagues. Again seeking solace from his own antisocial tendencies, Thorndike accepted Cattell's offer to use the attic in one of the university halls for an animal experimentation lab (p. 118). Thorndike's 1898 thesis, "Animal Intelligence: An Experimental Study of the Associative Processes in Animals" (published in 1936 as an article in the *Columbia University Quarterly*) was "a classic...mark[ing] the real starting point of experimental animal psychology" (Joncich, 1968, p. 148). That year, he received his PhD.

Afterward, he accepted a low-paying position as Special Lecturer in Education at Western Reserve's College for Women in Cleveland, Ohio, USA. He viewed this offer as more appealing than the alternative of teaching in a normal school, mostly because his brother Ashley was on his way to the college and because it surely enjoyed a more impressive reputation than any normal school. There, he taught courses in what Arthur Irving Gates later called "the new world of pedagogy" (quoted in Joncich, 1968, p. 153).

After one year at Western Reserve's College for Women, Thorndike began the last and longest part of his 43-year career as instructor at Teachers College, Columbia University. He taught Elements of Psychology; School Hygiene, which was "the implication of physical and mental facts for school operations" (Joncich, 1968, p. 215); Child Study; Genetic Psychology; Educational Psychology; and the Psychology of School Subjects (pp. 215–218). By 1914, the university created a division of Educational Psychology, and Thorndike began to teach only at the graduate level (p. 217).

From his various experiences as student and professor, Thorndike had many colleagues but few friends. At Wesleyan, he met Charles Hubbard Judd (see chapter 4, this volume) but became better friends with Frederick Paul Keppel, a zoology classmate (Joncich, 1968, p. 105). At Columbia, he knew geography instructor R.E. Dodge; biologist Francis E. Lloyd; educational historian Paul Monroe, whose office was next door to his (p. 220); Elijah Bagster-Collins, a professor of German ("Prof. Bagster-Collins," 1954); and Nicholas Murray Butler, the president of Columbia at the time and someone who, like Thorndike, agreed that education was a subject worthy of study. Of course, the psychology department, "the most important center for psychological training in the U.S. because of Cattell" (Joncich, p. 220) was home to Cattell, Robert Sessions Woodworth (see chapter 2, this volume), and Albert Poffenberger (Joncich, p. 220). During the U.S. Great Depression, Thorndike awarded Abraham Maslow a Carnegie Fellowship to Teachers College, where he would do research (Joncich, p. 467).

Occasionally, Thorndike would engage in some type of collaborative work with colleagues. Thorndike and Virgil Prettyman, the principal of the Horace Mann School, opened an educational clinic in 1902 to provide special education and psychological services. Although the experience provided him with data, the business was quite possibly his only occupational failure in life. In a 1905 letter, Thorndike remembered the experience: "It was very valuable as a source of scientific data.... We got elaborate measurement of thirty defective children" (quoted in Joncich, 1968, p. 224). Woodworth and Thorndike would work together on "transfer of training," an aspect of connectionism (Cremin, 1968, p. 113) found in the next section of this chapter.

Although his relationships with colleagues may have been lacking, his relationships with family were rich and plentiful. At the beginning of his career at Columbia University, Thorndike finally married Elizabeth "Bess" Moulton. The Reverend Thorndike performed the ceremony in Lynn, Massachusetts, USA. Moving to New York City brought grief and joy for the couple: Bess was unhappy with city life but tolerated it for the next 60 years (Joncich, 1968, p. 198). Life with a workaholic left her alone much of the time, but childbearing would alleviate some of that loneliness. In 1902, Bess gave birth to Elizabeth Frances; in 1904, Virginia Moulton; in 1905, Edward Moulton; in 1910, Robert Ladd; and in 1918, Alan. Elizabeth Frances became a math teacher. Ten-day-old Virginia died of a poorly formed heart. Robert became a specialist in psychological measurement, and Edward and Alan became physicists.

Just as Thorndike the father had a rich influence on his children, Thorndike the professor had a significant impact on his students. Several of Thorndike's students would win fame in the educational world. Arthur Irving

Gates (see chapter 14, this volume) and William Scott Gray (see chapter 13, this volume) became, as Monaghan and Saul (1987) note, "perhaps the two most respected figures in reading education and research" (p. 98). Between 1913 and 1914, Gray had taken a few of Thorndike's courses at Teachers College, and Thorndike served as his master's thesis advisor. Thorndike was also a member of Gates's dissertation committee. Gates was hired by Thorndike to teach at Teachers College and was later permitted to revise Thorndike's educational psychology textbook. Test makers Henry Rinsland and B.R. Buckingham became significant word counters who "personified a coming together of vocabulary research and the testing movement" (Clifford, 1978, p. 114).

Before his death on August 9, 1949—nine years after he retired from Columbia University (Adult Education History Project, 2002, para. 5)—Thorndike had published over 500 books and articles, 75 of them pertaining to language (Clifford, 1978, p. 108). He was not, as some sources indicate, only a psychologist, only an experimenter in reading, only a prolific writer, only a teacher, only a scientist, only a researcher, only a workaholic. He was, in fact, all those things.

Philosophical Beliefs and Guiding Principles

Those who teach hope that their students will make connections among the things they learn and also make some sort of significant contribution to society. Thorndike was such a student. Even before he was William James's student, he had begun to read, absorb, and devour what James had to say about psychology. In his student days at Harvard University, he also studied under Franz Boas, an anthropologist who used numbers to prove points (Cremin, 1968, p. 110). Thorndike, who had earlier imagined himself as an English teacher, saw a chance for something more in his future. Suddenly, Thorndike, who had never had a course in algebra or calculus, saw that a blend of psychological concepts and numbers could change the world.

In 1910, he published his Handwriting Scale, an event that marked the beginning of the scientific movement in education (Smith, 2002, p. 148) that has continued until today. Thorndike began the movement that would repel John Dewey and others who sought "a more equal and cooperative America" and who denounced such practices as "testing, curriculum tracking, and the influence of business on schooling" (Cohen & Barnes, 1999, p. 19). Believing only in what he could see and measure, Thorndike "sought to create schools that would help to align the society with the economy by educating young members...for suitable positions" (p. 19).

Both Dewey and Thorndike sought a change in the educational climate that since the 1880s clearly needed rescuing (Cremin, 1968, p. 21). Largely due to the articles on schooling by the crusading reformer Joseph Mayer Rice, the United States realized the "national scope" (p. 22) of the education crisis: the corruption (p. 21), the overcrowding, the dull sameness of instructional techniques (p. 20). But as Lagemann (1989) notes, in the contest between philosophies, "Dewey lost and Thorndike won" (p. 184). With the one exception of his laboratory school concept, Dewey's ideas for improved quality of education in the United States remained in his head and on paper, while Thorndike put his plans into action. Cohen and Barnes (1999) explain: "Dewey's ideas never became a regular part of the research and graduate education mainstream.... Graduate research and education in education were instead largely defined by Thorndike's views, his agenda for inquiry, and his graduate students" (p. 20). Educational testing and measuring still drive the U.S. educational system.

From the study of animal behavior, a radically new concept at the time (Chance, 1999, p. 438), Thorndike developed his learning laws. Although he studied chickens in William James's basement (Joncich, 1968, p. 87) and monkeys that he kept in his own home (p. 267), Thorndike's best-known animal experimentation occurred in connection with his 1898 dissertation *Animal Intelligence*, a publication that "began the systematic search for fundamental behavioral processes and laid the foundation for an empirical science of behavior" (Chance, 1999, p. 433). From putting cats into wooden puzzle boxes and observing their behavior, Thorndike dispelled the associationist notion that animals understand their own behavior and presented his findings that (a) animals do not think; (b) producing a change in animal behavior is a gradual process; (c) animals do not have the ability to distinguish "between action and consequence" (p. 437); and (d) animals must act, rather than think, which leads them to use what Thorndike called "trial and accidental success" (p. 438).

Thorndike's new scientific movement came to be known as *connectionism* (Charles, 1987, p. 25). Connectionism explains the three-pronged process of learning as situation (the stimulus), response, and connection or bond (Joncich, 1968, p. 336). As Monaghan and Saul (1987) explain, "Learning in Thorndike's view was habit formation; habits tended to be stamped in by a 'satisfyer' and weakened by an 'annoyer'" (p. 96). To Thorndike, learning was first and foremost biological: "Therefore, it is in the neurons, and not in the body as a whole, that satisfaction and annoyance are defined" (Joncich, 1968, p. 353). Any person's ability to learn is, according to Thorndike, a "struggle of neurons to conduct" (quoted in Joncich, 1968, p. 354). In a letter to Thorndike, psychologist B.F. Skinner acknowledged Thorndike's work with animal behavior as a forerunner of his own: "It has always been obvious that I was merely carrying on your puzzle box experiments" (quoted in Joncich, 1968, p. 506).

In *Adult Interests* (1935) Thorndike explains that a teacher's job is to maneuver the student into a situation that will result in a response (p. 21). If a pupil is to make connections, he or she must become at least somewhat interested in learning. Thorndike, then, offered five strategies for increasing student interest: (1) contiguity, (2) suggestion, (3) imitation, (4) conditioning, and (5) selection by rewards and punishment. Contiguity involves the teacher's attempt to surround the topic at hand with pleasantries such as the teacher's attractive personal nature, other positive experiences, or both. Suggestion—trying to get students to like something by subtly encouraging them to try it—may sometimes be enough to get someone to like a topic (p. 21). Thorndike admitted that little was known about imitation (p. 24), yet it seemed to be a plan worth trying. Some students less inclined to make connections on their own may try to learn to be like the teacher and the model students in the class (p. 26). Conditioning resembles what happens when a dog is taught to beg (p. 28). Selection by rewards refers to offering praise, which made subjects more inclined to repeat certain behaviors (p. 30), and getting an answer wrong, a punishment, may provide incentive for learning (p. 66). In *Education: A First Book* (1914a), Thorndike explains: "Interest multiplies the satisfyingness of every success and inspires effort to discover the causes of every failure" (p. 112).

Also in *Education* (1914a), Thorndike summarizes his laws of learning. Based on Thorndike's findings, if we as educators wish to have a subject respond in a particular way, we need to provide multiple opportunities for the desirable response to occur. This is Thorndike's Law of Exercise (p. 95). The Law of Effect, he notes, "is the fundamental law of teaching and learning. It is the great weapon of all who wish to change men's responses, either by reinforcing old and adding new ones, or by getting rid of those that are undesirable" (p. 97). The Law of Effect, then, urges educators to make activities satisfying so students will want to respond favorably to them (p. 96). As a general rule, one aspect of a given situation may be "prepotent" (p. 98) in the eyes of the student. More specifically, Thorndike identifies the Law of Partial Activity and the Law of Selective Thinking—the former referring to the fact that a subject may develop connections to one aspect of the topic at hand or with the larger picture of the topic (p. 99). The latter pertains to the accumulation of new habits that are needed for learning to occur (p. 100).

What Thorndike did for the communities of psychology and education was truly "profound" (Cumming, 1999, p. 429), although Dewey's followers may argue that educators should not confuse "profound" with "positive." Levin (1991) notes that Thorndike brought the educational community

> a master plan for the whole class or the whole grade or cluster of grades, and the whole school or group of schools, the ubiquitous grade-level textbook accompanied by workbooks, timed tests and the underlying assumption that children should move at a certain rate through a "normal" agenda of academic exercises. (p. 74)

Fifty-seven years after Thorndike's death, his research is still frequently cited, and school districts at all levels across the nation still operate according to his agenda.

Contributions to the Field of Reading

Thorndike the behaviorist made significant and varied contributions to the field of reading. Holding to his habit of starting at the beginning, he first defined the term *reading*. Thorndike's research revealed that reading is not absence of thought, and it is not "word calling" (Joncich, 1968, p. 394). His research also found that focusing on oral reading may showcase how well a student can pronounce that which he or she does not comprehend (p. 394). As Thorndike writes in "Reading as Reasoning: A Study of Mistakes in Paragraph Reading" (1917b), "The vice of the poor reader is to say the words to himself without actually making judgments concerning what they reveal" (p. 332). He also discovered that meaningful reading is not synonymous with passive perception, and looking at a textbook and reading it for understanding are two entirely contrasting matters (1917c, p. 114). If reading, then, is not simply perceiving text or uttering words, how should we think of it?

In 1917, Thorndike's "Reading as Reasoning" and "The Understanding of Sentences: A Study of Errors in Reading" appeared. According to Singer (1994), Thorndike found reading to be a cognitive issue (p. 897), not merely the act of perceiving words on a page (Thorndike, 1917c, p. 114; Joncich, 1968, p. 394). Thorndike (1917b) explains,

> Reading is a very elaborate procedure, involving a weighing of each of many elements in a sentence, their organization in the proper relations to one another, the selection of certain of their connotations and the rejection of others, and the cooperation of many forces to determine final response. (p. 323)

When someone reads correctly, we are told, three things happen. First, the reader derives the intended meaning from each word. Second, he or she looks at all aspects of each word and decides which elements are most important. Finally, the reader considers the results to be sure they satisfy the purpose at hand (1917b, p. 326).

In the sophisticated scheme of things, thinking is less of a priority than comprehending. In "Reading as Reasoning" (1917b), Thorndike declares that it is common knowledge that more attention needs to be paid to "erroneous meaning" (p. 327) because some reader errors are slight, while others are drastic. So readers are wrong when they interpret terms differently. In *Adult Interests* (1935), which he wrote 18 years later, Thorndike says that people overestimate what they comprehend (p. 222), but what does *comprehend* mean?

Thorndike stresses that comprehension is not passive (1917c, p. 114). The mind has many jobs to do. It needs to make choices, turn attention to and away from certain elements, and both sort and arrange what it encounters (1917b, p. 329). As Joncich (1968) relates,

> Thorndike remain[ed] convinced that "mere word knowledge" [was] the most important teachable factor in comprehension of speech and books, and [was] related to interest because ignorance of the words one meets is a very important factor in preventing or reducing interest. (p. 577)

In "The Psychology of Thinking in the Case of Reading" (1917a), Thorndike considers the notion of underpotency and overpotency. Any one word encountered in reading, he notes, may carry too much (p. 221) or insufficient weight (p. 227). From respondents' answers to questions posed in a study, Thorndike determined that readers hone in on some particular word or line of thought and dwell on it (pp. 220–234). They can become stuck on the image of what they read, as occurred in Thorndike's Test M: Students in grades 7 and 8 were asked to read a paragraph and answer five questions. Incorrect responses to question 2—"In what respect is a prisoner in his cell like a man with a million dollars?" (p. 224)—show the overpotency of the prison image: "Because he is shut up in a cell," one subject replied. Another said, a "man in prison is sitting 8 hours daily with chains" (p. 225). Although the passage that students read did not indicate anything about a million dollars, it did mention a man in prison. The point is that, although no "right" answer exists and the responses the students gave do not answer the question, the students wrote anything they recalled. As they attempted to answer a question that contained unfamiliar information, they reached for scraps of understanding.

In "The Understanding of Sentences: A Study of Errors in Reading," Thorndike (1917c) detailed the process of understanding a paragraph. He asserted that looking at a word causes the reader to connect the word to past experience. A correct meaning situates itself within the context of the rest of the words that the readers know (p. 113).

Thorndike's study of comprehension logically extended to the examination of mistakes made in reading. He offered the following explanations of why pupils have difficulty answering questions about their reading: The generally untrustworthy student can be blamed for his own lack of understanding, his lack of control. In very few cases, pupils cannot or do not focus on the task at hand, the page, or the reading assignment (1917c, p. 99). They are liable to "follow whatever leads are offered by the shreds of meaning that [they do] see or by the mere words" (p. 108). A wrong answer to a question about the text, then, can be explained by too much attention to the wrong thing.

Reader error appears in other forms (Thorndike, 1917c):

- lack of focus on the appropriate passage and on the appropriate part of the passage (p. 102);
- failing to follow directions, or creating new directions (p. 100);
- grabbing too quickly at the first thing that pops into one's head (p. 107); and
- making questions overpotent (p. 105).

In the spirit of increasing reading comprehension and bettering the world, Thorndike invented educational materials. These significant contributions to reading created increased access to a successful education for pupils of all ages. One type of educational material that he invented was a reader-friendly statistics manual for college students. In *An Introduction to the Theory of Mental and Social Measurement* (1919), Thorndike invites those who share his lack of mathematical aptitude to venture into the territory of statistics: "It would be unfortunate if the ability to understand and use the newer methods of measurement were dependent upon the mathematical capacity and training which were required to derive and formulate them" (p. 1). He challenges readers to see that statistics are little more than "refined common sense" (p. 2).

Thorndike's son Robert remembered computing the algebra problems and constructing the answer keys for his father's invention, a common-sense algebra text that contained "realistic [problems] such as a child might meet rather than the absurd puzzles of the sort that had tended to appear in texts at that time" (R. Thorndike, 1991, p. 143). Thorndike expected that students might respond more favorably to a text that tapped into their prior knowledge, increased their chances of learning, and sounded sensible. *Thorndike Arithmetic*, a 1917 series, achieved bestseller status (Kappa Delta Pi, n.d., para. 8), a result, no doubt, of its practicality and reader friendliness.

In *The Teacher's Word Book* (Thorndike, 1927) and the updated *Teacher's Word Book of 30,000 Words* (Thorndike & Lorge, 1944), Thorndike and his coauthor and former student Irving Lorge switched to the topic of vocabulary. These texts, they believed, did the thinking for untrustworthy teachers and students, a particular necessity in the case of what he considered to be less capable female teachers and students. The preface to the 1927 book explains that the book

> enables a teacher to know not only the general importance of each word so far as frequency of occurrence measures that, but also its importance in current popular reading for adults...and its importance in such juvenile reading as schools and libraries approve. (p. xi)

After all, only some words deserve to be owned (p. xi). Both word books highlight the obsessive collecting, memorizing, and cataloging of words that students would be most likely to meet in their reading journeys (R. Thorndike, 1991, p. 143). The lists were used for vocabulary-building courses in college, radio announcements, dictionaries in other languages, school spelling lists, study skills booklets for college students, and typing and short-hand manuals (Joncich, 1968, p. 393). From these works, Thorndike created teacher manuals (Clifford, 2003, p. 2562).

Thorndike's scientific triumph over progressivism changed the course of reading instruction. *The Teacher's Word Book* (1927) added to the body of research on adult vocabulary size and continues to be respected today (Clifford, 1978, p. 110). The book "provide[d] vocabulary test-makers with a tool other than sheer, unaided judgment for selecting word series that better judge the precision of a child's comprehension of the words being tested." Thorndike also began a movement of "new" standardized vocabulary tests (p. 114). Others used his lists to devise tests based on words found in "reading materials more specific to children's interests" (p. 115).

Contemporary concern for "relevance and realism" in children's readers can be traced to Thorndike's 1917 breakthrough concept of reading as reasoning (Clifford, 1978, pp. 121–122). If reading could no longer be considered on an equal plane with word pronunciation, then "meaningful reading" (p. 121) required the teacher to tap into his or her students' background knowledge. By 1938, the number of students who made it to high school had nearly doubled since 1900; therefore, to have a chance at success, the larger student body needed more easy-to-read materials (p. 122).

The Thorndike-Barnhart dictionaries for children (Thorndike & Barnhart, 1929/1988), juniors (1935/1962), and high school students (1952/1957) are perhaps Thorndike's best-known and most significant contributions to the field of reading (R. Thorndike, 1991, p. 143). Ever since 1929, students have used the books to make more sense of their worlds, exactly what Thorndike intended. Clarence Barnhart summarizes the deliberate features used in the dictionaries to increase student interest: "language that pupils could understand, illustrative sentences, [and] sentences often written so that they force the meaning home to the pupil" (Thorndike & Barnhart, 1929/1988, pp. 6–7).

The world took notice when Thorndike, in his 1927 address to the Association for Adult Education, reported that people possess "a lifelong ability to learn" (quoted in Joncich, 1968, p. 484). Adults, he declared, may indeed have legitimate reasons for learning (1935, pp. 56–57). For example, studying adults in secretarial schools, he discovered no age-related difference in the success students had in learning shorthand and typing: Older students did just as well as younger students (Thorndike, Bregman, Tilton, &

Woodyard, 1928/1932, p. 79). Ever logical, Thorndike progressed to the study of why adults often do not learn, even though they are able to learn (p. 107). He found that adults do not realize their own potential for learning, care less about it than they should, and may, by learning, fall out of favor with their peers (p. 125). Through this study, Thorndike revealed a new audience for reading education.

His final contribution to the field of reading involved the creation of tests. In fact, the name Thorndike seems synonymous with *test*. The *Thorndike-McCall Reading Scale for the Understanding of Sentences* (1921) helped to elevate the status of reading instruction within the school curriculum. As a result, vocabulary and comprehension began to receive attention as valued components of the study of reading (Joncich, 1968, p. 394). In "The Measurement of Ability in Reading" (1914b) Thorndike included his three scales "meant to measur[e] school achievement" (p. 207): (1) Scale A for Visual Vocabulary, (2) a Scale for Measuring the Understanding of Sentences and Paragraphs, and (3) Scale Alpha for Measuring the Understanding of Sentences. Thorndike's Scale A for Visual Vocabulary measured whether or not fifth graders could classify words. A Scale for Measuring the Understanding of Sentences and Paragraphs holds more significance for educators because elementary education concerns itself most with students' comprehension of sentences and paragraphs (p. 238). For grades three to eight, the Scale Alpha for Measuring the Understanding of Sentences involved reading a passage and writing an answer to a question, underlining text, or crossing out a letter or number (p. 253). All three scales illustrate Thorndike's mission to promote silent-reading efficiency.

Throughout his versatile career, Thorndike created other intelligence tests as well as tests for college entry, law school entry, English usage, drawing, and geographical understanding. He helped to construct and later administered the 1917–1919 Alpha and Beta tests for literate and illiterate soldiers (Clifford, 2003, p. 2566). In 1925, he devised an intelligence test called the CAVD that concentrated on completion, arithmetic, vocabulary, and directions (Joncich, 1968, p. 390). In addition, he conducted the first major "study of ability tests and school records as predictors of later vocational performance" (R. Thorndike, 1991, p. 149).

Thorndike probably made more of a mark on the field of reading than anyone who came before him or anyone who came after him. He captured the elusive creature called *reading*, put it under a microscope, dissected it, introduced the world to its true nature and composition, created materials that would help the world understand it, and started the educational community on a quest for more information. His rich and varied research and practice have stood the test of time.

Lessons for the Future

Knowing about Thorndike is significant on several levels. From a critique of his assumptions about human behavior, learning, and teaching, educators can become more aware of our own. Despite his philosophical shortcomings, he provides two types of useful lessons: (1) the ones he specifies to us and (2) the ones we gather from a long, close look at his work. If we let him, he can help us to influence the future of reading education.

Many of Thorndike's assumptions would be characterized today as racist and sexist. Like Cattell and Judd, Thorndike carried his "hereditarian and racial determinist attitudes" (Lagemann, 1989, p. 212) with him at all times and, therefore, made assumptions about who could learn. Almost anyone can learn, but, Thorndike instructed, not everyone should bother (1935, pp. 111–112). One race cannot be taught, he believed, by the same methods as another (1914a, p. 32). After all, he warned, different races have different capabilities (p. 68). Thorndike was baffled by the early 20th-century trend toward prolonged education of the masses and was, therefore, amazed at what he considered the foolishness of spending much time on low- and average-ability students (p. 33). If teachers were being forced to try to reach students of varying abilities all sharing the same classroom, so be it, and with luck perhaps some of them could be taught "to want the right things" (p. 11). Thorndike felt that some women could become more than wives and mothers. However, he specified that if they must be educated, they should be taught home economics and child maintenance and be kept away from the more promising students (p. 3). Giving away the best to the least capable was, to Thorndike, poor practice (Seller, 1978, p. 9).

Thorndike assumed that the world, too, was not to be trusted. Changing the world for the better, something that he held dear (Cremin, 1968, p. 113), required taking control of as much as possible. Science, as opposed to his father's religion, dictated that everything can and should be measured. Everything must be scientifically observed, recorded, quantified, calculated (Clifford, 2003, p. 2564). God cannot be measured; therefore, Thorndike believed, he could not exist and could not be trusted. In addition, Thorndike felt that society had no idea what was good for it (1914a), so it could not be trusted either. He also believed that students certainly could not be trusted to do the right thing (1914a, pp. 165, 173). To determine what they want to learn and where to get that information, Thorndike believed that adult students would need an expert's advice (1936, pp. 131–132).

Teachers, too, would not survive without his assistance, Thorndike argued. Without his direction, he worried that they might mistakenly teach what is "nonexistent" rather than what is "real" (1914a, p. 128). The pages of Thorndike's texts are laden with teaching advice. For example, he mentioned that if teachers would only follow the word books they would be spared having to think about which words are important for students to learn. Eisner (1983) suggests that such examples show Thorndike's attempt to "create a better, more predictable world" (p. 6).

In addition to encouraging us to reexamine our own assumptions, Thorndike also left us with other lessons. The first lessons are specific ones. Researchers, historians, and teachers of all levels may find wisdom in Thorndike's teachings. The *Thorndike-Barnhart Children's Dictionary* (1929/1988) and *Education: A First Book* (1914a) challenge us to define our terms and start at the beginning. The children's dictionary asks us to visually demonstrate what we are saying. In *Education* (1914a), Thorndike issues a timeless warning: "We stay below our own possibilities in almost everything we do" (p. 108). In a sense, he asked educators to look for challenges and increased opportunities to make a difference in their field. His specific teaching tips also seem appropriate today. Students, he urged, need more practice in reading and studying (1917c, p. 112). Because students may not transfer what they have learned without help, educators might look for ways to create situations to assist them (Lagemann, 1989, p. 211). In itself, *Adult Interests* (1935) is a 200-page mini library of teaching methods.

The lessons we can learn from taking a long, close look at Thorndike's work indirectly challenge us to move the field of literacy forward. Like Thorndike, we should be open to new ideas and to the possibilities of tapping different disciplines. Robert Thorndike recalled his father's willingness to try new things and explore new territory: "He took whatever came his way that seemed to need doing and devoted himself wholeheartedly to it" (R. Thorndike, 1991, p. 151). Thorndike was one of the first researchers to be aware of the potential significance of educational psychology to education.

Although he did not invent educational psychology, he was key to its emergence as a "separate discipline" (Walberg & Haertel, 1992, p. 8).

Blending two disciplinary worlds came naturally to Thorndike. In his preface to the *Thorndike-Barnhart High School Dictionary* (Thorndike & Barnhart, 1952/1957), Barnhart notes, "Thorndike was the first lexicographer to apply statistical methods and the techniques of the psychology of learning to the making of dictionaries" (p. vi). Thorndike and his coauthors of *Adult Learning* (Thorndike et al., 1928/1932) assert, "If we keep on learning, we may expect to lose less of our ability to learn" (p. 133).

Why should we remember Edward Lee Thorndike? What was so significant about him? Some men are thinkers. Others are doers. Thorndike was both. His most significant contributions to learning and reading were multi-faceted, groundbreaking, and long lasting. From the perspective of later reading researchers, his Handwriting Scale of 1910 marked the beginning of the scientific movement in education (Smith, 2002, p. 148). He and Robert Sessions Woodworth conducted transfer-of-training studies that "shattered time-honored assumptions about the 'disciplinary' value of certain studies and thereby accelerated utilitarian tendencies already gaining in the schools" (Cremin, 1968, p. 113). His definition of reading forever changed the world's educational outlook. His work with word lists directly affected the instruction of reading (Monaghan & Saul, 1987, p. 97). His studies on learning and the wealth of learning material that he created raised awareness of the field of education as a serious profession (Cremin, 1968, p. 114). Overall, "Thorndike was never as interested in the acquisition of initial skill in reading as he was in improving the possibilities for long-term growth in reading" (Clifford, 1978, p. 182). He indeed had a far reach. As Cremin reports, "Certainly no aspect of public-school teaching during the first quarter of the twentieth-century remained unaffected by his influence" (p. 114).

In 2006, Thorndike's thoughts and practices continue to dominate the public schools, colleges, and universities. The current obsession with lectures, quickly scored tests, midterms, finals, SATs, ACTs, GREs, and memorization may be crowding out real learning; however, some teachers delight in the convenience of easy-to-check tests. Students who have not been taught how to study are only occasionally aware that they are memorizing in the hope of collecting the prize, the acceptable grade. What is often missing is the making of connections, the quest for the long term, and the genuine experiences that result in learning. Proponents of the No Child Left Behind Act of 2001 (2002) may argue that this method works because it has measurable outcomes, and if testing equals learning, this statement may well be true. Thorndike can have no better advertisement.

Reflection Questions

1. How does Thorndike's maxim "We stay far below our own possibilities in almost everything that we do" (1914a, p. 108) apply to ourselves and to our students?
2. Are we still using school district–prescribed vocabulary lists such as Thorndike's, and do they lead to "permanent knowledge" (Thorndike & Lorge, 1944, p. xi)?
3. How does Thorndike's theory of connectionism explain comprehension? Do you agree with this explanation?
4. What can we do to assess whether our students are aware of the active part they need to play in comprehending material?
5. In what ways does the U.S. educational structure still operate on Thorndike's themes of control, testing, and dependence on quantitative results? Is this a topic in need of examination? Why or why not?

REFERENCES

Adult Education History Project. (2002, May 5). Edward Lee Thorndike vita. Retrieved April 18, 2006, from http://www-distance.syr.edu/eltvita.html

Chance, P. (1999). Thorndike's puzzle boxes and the origins of the experimental analysis of behavior. *Journal of the Experimental Analysis of Behavior, 72,* 433–440.

Charles, D.C. (1987). The emergence of educational psychology. In J.A. Glover & R.R. Ronning (Eds.), *Historical foundations of educational psychology* (pp. 17–38). New York: Plenum.

Clifford, G.J. (1978). Words for schools: The applications in education of the vocabulary researches of Edward L. Thorndike. In P. Suppes (Ed.), *Impact of research on education: Some case studies* (pp. 107–198). Washington, DC: National Academy of Education.

Clifford, G.J. (2003). Thorndike, Edward L. In J.W. Guthrie (Ed.), *Encyclopedia of education, Vol. 7* (2nd ed., pp. 2562–2569). New York: Macmillan.

Cohen, D.K., & Barnes, C.A. (1999). Research and the purposes of education. In E.C. Lagemann & L.S. Shulman (Eds.), *Issues in education research* (pp. 17–41). San Francisco: Jossey-Bass.

Cremin, L.A. (1968). *The transformation of the school: Progressivism in American education, 1876–1957*. New York: Knopf.

Cumming, W.W. (1999). A review of Geraldine Joncich's *The sane positivist: A biography of Edward L. Thorndike*. *Journal of the Experimental Analysis of Behavior, 72*, 429–432.

Eisner, E.W. (1983). The art and craft of teaching. *Educational Leadership, 40*(4), 5–13.

Joncich, G.M. (1968). *The sane positivist: A biography of Edward L. Thorndike*. Middletown, CT: Wesleyan University Press.

Kappa Delta Pi. (n.d.). *Edward Lee Thorndike (1925)*. Retrieved January 8, 2005, from http://www.kdp.org/about/laureates/laureates/edwardthorndike.php

Lagemann, E.C. (1989). The plural worlds of educational research. *History of Education Quarterly, 29*, 183–214.

Levin, R.A. (1991). The debate over schooling: Influences of Dewey and Thorndike. *Childhood Education, 68*(2), 71–75.

Monaghan, E.J., & Saul, E.W. (1987). The reader, the scribe, the thinker: A critical look at the history of American reading and writing instruction. In T.S. Popkewitz (Ed.), *The formation of school subjects: The struggle for creating an American institution* (pp. 85–122). New York: Falmer.

No Child Left Behind Act of 2001, Pub. L. No. 107-110, 115 Stat. 1425 (2002).

Prof. Bagster-Collins rites in Peekskill. (1954, September 5). *NY Journal-American*. Retrieved July 10, 2006, from http://archiver.rootsweb.com/th/read/US-OBITS/2001-02/0983335573

Seller, M.S. (1978). G. Stanley Hall and Edward Thorndike on the education of women: Theory and policy in the Progressive Era. *Social Studies/Social Science Education*, 1–17.

Singer, H. (1994). The substrata-factor theory of reading. In R.B. Ruddell, M.R. Ruddell, & H. Singer (Eds.), *Theoretical models and processes of reading* (4th ed., pp. 895–927). Newark, DE: International Reading Association.

Smith, N.B. (2002). *American reading instruction: Special edition*. Newark, DE: International Reading Association.

Thorndike, E.L. (1914a). *Education: A first book*. New York: Macmillan.

Thorndike, E.L. (1914b). The measurement of ability in reading. *Teachers College Record, 15*(4), 207–277.

Thorndike, E.L. (1917a). The psychology of thinking in the case of reading. *Psychological Review, 24*, 220–234.

Thorndike, E.L. (1917b). Reading as reasoning: A study of mistakes in paragraph reading. *Journal of Educational Psychology, 8*(6), 323–332.

Thorndike, E.L. (1917c). The understanding of sentences: A study of errors in reading. *The Elementary School Journal, 18*, 98–114.

Thorndike, E.L. (1919). *An introduction to the theory of mental and social measurement* (2nd ed.). New York: Teachers College, Columbia University.

Thorndike, E.L. (1921). *Thorndike-McCall reading scale for the understanding of sentences*. New York: Columbia University.

Thorndike, E.L. (1927). *The teacher's word book* (2nd ed.). New York: Teachers College, Columbia University.

Thorndike, E.L. (1935). *Adult interests*. New York: Macmillan.

Thorndike, E.L., & Barnhart, C.L. (Eds.). (1957). *Thorndike-Barnhart high school dictionary*. Chicago: Scott Foresman. (Original work published 1952)

Thorndike, E.L., & Barnhart, C.L. (Eds.). (1962). *Thorndike-Barnhart junior dictionary*. Chicago: Scott Foresman. (Original work published 1935)

Thorndike, E.L., & Barnhart, C.L. (Eds.). (1988). *Thorndike-Barnhart children's dictionary*. Glenview, IL: Scott Foresman. (Original work published 1929)

Thorndike, E.L., Bregman, E.O., Tilton, J.W., & Woodyard, E. (1932). *Adult learning*. New York: Macmillan. (Original work published 1928)

Thorndike, E.L., & Lorge, I. (1944). *The teacher's word book of 30,000 words*. New York: Teachers College, Columbia University.

Thorndike, R.L. (1991). Edward L. Thorndike: A professional and personal appreciation. In G.A. Kimble, M. Wertheimer, & C.L. White (Eds.), *Portraits of pioneers in psychology* (pp. 139–151). Washington, DC: American Psychological Association.

Travers, R.M. (1987). Apprentice to Thorndike. *Teaching Education, 1*(1), 46–49.

Walberg, H.J., & Haertel, G.D. (1992). Educational psychology's first century. *Journal of Educational Psychology, 84*(1), 6–19.

Western Michigan University. (2004, October 29). Robert M.W. Travers. Retrieved July 10, 2006, from http://www.umich.edu/wmu/news/2004/10/093.html

FOR FURTHER READING

Glover, J.A., & Ronning, R.R. (Eds.). (1987). *Historical foundations of educational psychology*. New York: Plenum.

Lagemann, E.C. (2000). *An elusive science: The troubling history of education research*. Chicago: University of Chicago Press.

Moss, F.A. (Ed.). (1942). *Comparative psychology*. New York: Prentice.

National Society for the Study of Education. (1922). *Intelligence tests and their use: Pt. I. the nature, history, and general principles of intelligence testing*. Bloomington, IL: Public School Publishing.

Robinson, R.D. (Ed.). (2005). *Readings in reading instruction: Its history, theory, and development*. Boston: Pearson.

Thorndike, E.L. (1900). *The human nature club: An introduction to the study of mental life*. New York: Longmans, Green and Co.

Thorndike, E.L. (1906). *The principles of teaching: Based on psychology*. New York: AG Seiler.

Thorndike, E.L. (1911). *Individuality*. Boston: Houghton Mifflin.

Thorndike, E.L. (1913). *Educational psychology*. New York: Teachers College Press.

Thorndike, E.L. (1917). *The Thorndike arithmetics*. Chicago: Rand McNally.

Thorndike, E.L. (1920). *Exercises in arithmetic, no. 1–5, selected, graded, and arranged to meet the requirements of the hygiene of the eye and neuro-muscular apparatus*. Chicago: Rand McNally.

Thorndike, E.L. (1921a). *The new methods in arithmetic*. Chicago: Rand McNally.

Thorndike, E. L. (1921b). *The teacher's word book*. New York: Bureau of Publications, Teachers College, Columbia University.

Thorndike, E.L. (1922). *The psychology of arithmetic*. New York: Macmillan.

Thorndike, E.L. (1931). *Human learning*. New York: Century.

Thorndike, E.L. (1935). *The psychology of wants, interests and attitudes*. New York: D. Appleton-Century.

Thorndike, E.L. (1937). *The teaching of controversial subjects*. Cambridge, MA: Harvard University Press.

Thorndike, E.L. (1941). *The teaching of English suffixes*. New York: Teachers College, Columbia University.

Thorndike, E.L. (1943). *Man and his works*. Cambridge, MA: Harvard University Press.

Thorndike, E.L. (1949). *Selected writings from a connectionist's psychology*. New York: Appleton-Century-Crofts.

Thorndike, E.L., Bregman, E.O., Lorge, I., Metcalfe, Z.F., Robinson, E.E., & Woodyard, E. (1934). *Prediction of vocational success*. New York: The Commonwealth Fund.

Thorndike, E.L., Cobb, M.V., Orleans, J.S., Symonds, P.M., Wald, E., & Woodyard, E. (1923). *The psychology of algebra*. New York: Macmillan.

Thorndike, E.L., & Gates, A.I. (1929). *Elementary principles of education*. New York: Macmillan.

Thorndike, E.L., McCall, W.A., & Chapman, J.C. (1916). *Ventilation in relation to mental work*. New York: Teachers College, Columbia University.

Thorndike, E.L., Bregman, E.O., Cobb, M.V., & Woodyard, E. (1926). *The measurement of intelligence*. New York: Teachers College, Columbia University.

Thorndike, E.L., & the staff of the Division of Psychology of the Institute of Educational Research of Teachers College, Columbia University. (1932). *The fundamentals of learning*. New York: Teachers College, Columbia University.

Thorndike, E.L., & the staff of the Division of Psychology, Institute of Educational Research, Teachers College, Columbia University. (1933). *An experimental study of rewards*. New York: Teachers College, Columbia University.

CHAPTER 6

Walter Fenno Dearborn (1878–1955): Reading Through the Eyes of Each Child

By Joseph E. Zimmer

Historical Research Process

WHEN I BEGAN my study of Walter Fenno Dearborn, I only had a few bits and pieces of information about him. I remembered from my graduate studies that he had done work in eye movements and reading disabilities, and that he had conducted the Harvard Growth Studies, but beyond that, I knew very little about him. To look for clues, I began to read Dearborn's numerous books. Although his books taught me about his wide-ranging interests in reading and educational psychology, they are written in a very formal, scientific tone and offered very few clues to his home life. After several weeks of

Shaping the Reading Field: The Impact of Early Reading Pioneers, Scientific Research, and Progressive Ideas, edited by Susan E. Israel and E. Jennifer Monaghan. © 2007 by the International Reading Association.
Photo: Courtesy of Harvard University Archives, Call # Dearborn(1).

searching the Internet and talking to reference librarians both at my home institution of St. Bonaventure University and at Harvard University, I started to believe that I was never going to penetrate beyond Dearborn's professional works in compiling his biography.

Then, during an Internet search, I found that Dearborn has a school named after him in Arlington, Massachusetts, USA. This discovery was a ray of hope because I work at a private institution myself, and I realized that we have considerable information in our archives about the people for whom we have named things. When I contacted the school named for Dearborn, school officials told me they had a few items in the archives, but they astonished me by suggesting that it would be best if I talked with Dearborn's daughter, Natalie, with whom they kept regular contact. Thus began a three-month correspondence with Mrs. Natalie Cruickshank that has provided me with a much richer understanding and knowledge of the life of Walter Fenno Dearborn, a pioneer in the understanding of reading disabilities.

Personal and Professional Life

Walter Dearborn's academic career clearly elucidates the confluence of psychology, education, and medicine during the first half of the 20th century that fostered the birth and shaped the development of the field of reading education in the United States. His research, particularly in the area of reading disabilities, involved all of these fields, and much of what is now known about reading disabilities can be traced to Dearborn's work.

The son of a Methodist clergyman, Dearborn seemed destined from his youth to succeed academically. He was born in Marblehead, Massachusetts, USA, on July 19, 1878, and he was the oldest of his parents' three sons. His early years were strict and disciplined, and his parents stressed the importance of educational achievements. His daughter, Natalie, recalled that, much to her mother's chagrin, Dearborn never learned ballroom dancing in his youth because dancing was not deemed a necessary skill by his parents. Later in life, on social occasions, he cleverly improvised and cobbled together a foxtrot and Viennese waltz into quite a convincing dance (N. Cruickshank, personal communication, November 26, 2004).

Dearborn attended Boston public schools and graduated from Phillips-Exeter Academy in 1896. He received an AB degree in 1900 and an AM in 1903, both from his father's alma mater, Wesleyan University. To finance his graduate education while at Wesleyan, he served as vice principal and teacher of Latin and Greek at Middletown High School in Connecticut for three years (Langfield, 1955, p. 679).

In 1903, Dearborn started his PhD studies at Columbia University, and he quickly came under the tutelage of James McKeen Cattell (see chapter 1, this volume), a pioneer in psychology in the United States and a student of the German psychologist Wilhelm Wundt. At Columbia University, Dearborn met Edward Lee Thorndike (see chapter 5, this volume), also a clergyman's son and Wesleyan alumnus. Thorndike was a student of Cattell and then his fellow professor at Teachers College. Cattell and Thorndike's research focused on identifying individual differences in children, primarily in their intelligence. It was in this exciting new world of experimental psychology that Dearborn started his academic researches.

As the reader will see, the shadows of Wundt, Cattell, and Thorndike loomed large over the rest of Dearborn's career. Dearborn's dissertation, published as *The Psychology of Reading: An Experimental Study of the Reading Process and Eye-Movements* (Dearborn, 1906), foreshadowed his future contributions to the field of reading (Allport, Ulich, & Rulon, 1956). In his posthumous tribute to Dearborn, Herbert Langfeld of Princeton University says,

> It is significant that Dearborn's doctoral thesis was "The psychology of reading: an experimental study of the reading pauses and movements of the eye," for his first interest remained his most absorbing one and it was in this field that he made his greatest contribution to psychology. (Langfeld, 1955, p. 680)

Upon the receipt of his PhD in 1905, Dearborn accepted a position as Instructor in Educational Psychology at the University of Wisconsin in Madison, where he was promoted to assistant professor in 1907. He gained fame as he used educational psychology to solve practical problems. He also did some pioneering work in the prediction of success in college. This successful study precipitated an invitation to the University of Chicago, where he accepted a position as Associate Professor of Education in 1909. Here he was a pioneer again, this time in the field of intelligence testing. In 1912 Dearborn was invited by Harvard University President Abbott Lawrence Lowell to accept an associate professorship at the university, with the promise of a later promotion to the rank of professor (Langfeld, 1955, p. 679). Within the span of seven years, Dearborn had moved from being an instructor to being an associate professor at Harvard University, an astounding academic feat that is a testament to Dearborn's early work.

Dearborn's continuing interest in the physiology of reading and human growth prompted him to study medicine intermittently in Germany. He arranged his teaching schedule so that in 1904 he studied at the University of Göttingen, in 1911 he studied at the University of Heidelberg, and in 1913 he took a year off from Harvard University and completed his Doctor of Medicine degree at the University of Munich. This degree would be invaluable to him not only in his continuing studies of reading but also in his later direction of the Harvard Growth Studies. As his colleague and frequent collaborator, Leonard Carmichael (1957), noted in a tribute to Dearborn,

> After Dearborn returned to America from Germany with his medical degree, he was anxious to help the English-speaking world gain some of the new scientific insight that he had learned in the German universities of that day. He brought back with him, therefore, a number of books which were later translated and issued in this country as a result of his efforts. (p. 5)

In 1917, Dearborn established the Psycho-Educational Clinic at Harvard University and, commensurate with his promotion to professor, was named its director. In the same year Dearborn married Eileen Kedean, a native of Staffordshire, England, whom he had met several years earlier while at the University of Chicago. In 1918, the newlywed Dearborn was drafted into the United States Army and was ordered to France. On the day his ship left Boston, the ship's captain received word that the war was over, and the ship returned to port. Dearborn was immediately discharged (N. Cruickshank, personal communication, November 5, 2004).

On April 8, 1919, the Dearborns' first daughter, Elaine, was born. Natalie, their second daughter, was born on June 2, 1927. Although she remembers her father as being quite busy as a Harvard research professor, Natalie has vivid memories of Dearborn teaching Elaine and her to ski in Vermont in the winter and taking many pleasant vacations to Lake Winnipesaukee in New Hampshire:

> He was able to spend a great deal of time with us, and we knew he was genuinely interested in us. We also had wonderful travel experiences including a ship cruise through the Panama Canal when I was seven years

old. I have tried to emulate in our home environment, when the children were still with us, the atmosphere of our Cambridge home environment growing up. (N. Cruickshank, personal communication, November 5, 2004)

Natalie recalls her father as kind and caring, and he daily reminded his daughters to be thankful for what they had and to remember those who did not have as much as they did. At dinner each night, Walter and Eileen Dearborn would expect their children to tell them all about what they had learned in school that day. It is clear that the value of education instilled in Dearborn as a young man and the importance of nurturing children through their physical and mental development that he learned in his laboratory emerged in the parenting of his own children.

During the 1920s and 1930s, Dearborn enjoyed the life of a research professor at Harvard University, guiding many students through their graduate programs; directing the Harvard Growth Studies; and contributing research to the fields of reading, cognitive psychology, and educational psychology. The Harvard Growth Studies, a systematic series of longitudinal studies of the physical and mental growth of 3,000 schoolchildren over a period of 12 years, was one of Dearborn's major projects and remains one of the most comprehensive collections of data from children ever undertaken. These studies became the foundation for the academic careers of dozens of Dearborn's students, and many of the studies can be found under the general title of "Studies in Educational Psychology and Educational Measurement" in the *Harvard Monographs in Education*, which Dearborn edited from 1922 until 1926.

In his daughter Natalie's words:

My father's students *adored* him. He was, of course, very passionate about his subject. Our home was always filled with his students. My mother was a wonderful cook, and she would invite students unable to get home for the holidays to have dinners with us. When we went on vacation, he would invite one of the married students and his wife to stay at our home while we were gone. He didn't do it for security reasons. Students would tell us afterwards how much they appreciated being out of their "miserable graduate housing" and that it was like a vacation for them. Mother would leave meals for them while we were gone. (N. Cruickshank, personal communication, November 5, 2004)

Three of his Harvard colleagues—Gordon Allport, Robert Ulich, and Phillip Rulon—wrote in a tribute (1956),

> Dearborn's colleagues and students will remember him for the warmth and courtesy that marked all his human relationships. More than most teachers he kept himself informed concerning the needs of his students past and present, and often gave them timely assistance to advance their professional growth. (n.p.)

The Dearborn family seems what we would envision as a typical family of a Harvard professor in the first half of the 20th century. The Dearborns were devoted music lovers and regular subscribers to the Boston Symphony. Dearborn had also enjoyed football ever since witnessing the fierce rivalry between his alma mater, Phillips-Exeter, and Andover in his youth. From the time his daughters were deemed "able to behave properly," Dearborn took them to all the Harvard football games (N. Cruickshank, personal communication, November 26, 2004).

In 1942, Harvard University honored Dearborn with an honorary AM degree for his service to the university. Dearborn retired from Harvard as Professor Emeritus in 1947 and promptly became Professor of Education and Psychology at Lesley College (now Lesley University) in Cambridge, Massachusetts, USA, and Director of Lesley's Psycho-Educational Clinic. The W.F. Dearborn Laboratory School—a remedial school for children of average intelligence who struggled particularly in reading and mathematics—was one of three private day schools within the college. The establishment of the school was one of Dearborn's proudest accomplishments because it provided a place for Dearborn and the teachers to apply the research he did at Harvard in an authentic setting (N. Cruickshank, personal communication, November 5, 2004).

On November 14, 1953, at the age of 75, Dearborn suffered a severe cerebral hemorrhage that resulted in a crippling illness, forcing him to take a leave of absence from Lesley College. He died in his home in St. Petersburg, Florida, USA, on the morning of June 21, 1955, at the age of 76 (Langfeld, 1955, p. 681). His Harvard colleagues wrote of him, "For his humane qualities as well as for his scholarship and for his effective and lasting devotion to the Harvard Graduate School of Education we cherish his memory" (Allport, Ulich, & Rulon, 1956, n.p.).

Philosophical Beliefs and Guiding Principles

Walter Dearborn was not only a pioneer in the field of reading education, but he also was arguably a leading early player in the fields of cognitive psychology, educational assessment, and child development. His studies during his long career included intelligence testing (Dearborn, 1922) and examinations of visual fatigue in reading (Carmichael & Dearborn, 1947); the scholastic, economic and social backgrounds of unemployed youth (Dearborn & Rothney, 1938); and child development (Dearborn & Rothney, 1941).

As a student of the European pioneers of the scientific study of psychology and education, he spent much of his career using scientific methods to support or refute theories based on less formal observations that educators had made during previous decades. His beliefs about intelligence testing, reading disability, and child development will seem familiar to anyone who has studied these three fields extensively.

Dearborn strongly believed that intelligence tests were very useful tools for placing students in appropriate classrooms. His beliefs on this topic appear in the first few paragraphs of the introduction to *Psychological and Educational Tests in the Public Schools of Winchester, Virginia* (Dearborn & Inglis, 1921):

> No problem of education is more important than that which involves the adaptation of instruction to the capacities and needs of the children who are to be educated. Every parent, for the sake of his children, every citizen for the sake of society, every teacher for the sake of her pupils, and every school officer as a measure of the education provided should ask these questions: Is each child in the school located in the grade and class best suited to him? Are subject matter and methods of instruction properly adapted to his capacities and to his stage of progress? Is the school so organized that, within necessary limits, each child may progress in his education at the rate demanded by his individual abilities and needs? Have all reasonably possible means been employed to classify pupils in instructional groups according to their various capacities? (p. 5)

If the work of Wundt, Cattell, Thorndike, and Dearborn on the role of intelligence testing in schools could be summarized in one paragraph, this would be it. Modern educators reading this quotation need to realize that Dearborn was not stating the obvious. He was asserting the fairly novel idea that all children have individual differences that make educating them as a group a challenge.

In the area of reading disabilities, Dearborn was one of the first educational psychologists to attempt to refute the generally held conception of "congenital word blindness" (Harris & Sipay, 1990, p. 150). For years prior to Dearborn's work in reading education, other medical doctors and psychologists recognized dyslexia in children and presumed, in too many cases, that the problems were being caused by a congenital defect in the children that was preventing them from learning to read. In *Special Disabilities in Learning to Read and Write* (Lord, Carmichael, & Dearborn, 1925), Dearborn describes, approvingly, contemporary findings about reading disabilities and mirror writing:

> The educational psychologists who have more recently become interested in these conditions have come to hold much the same point of view in regard to extreme reading disability or word blindness, as has been generally held in regard to mirror writing. They have argued that disability or inability in reading forms simply "the fag end of the normal distribution" of the abilities in question, have questioned the existence of congenital factors, and have considered "the possibility that inhibiting habits, however acquired, may be at the bottom of the inability."
>
> There are quite possibly cases with no intellectual defect or shortcoming, either general or specific, where a combination of unfortunate circumstances with faulty learning may result in a disability as grave as that for which the term word blindness has been commonly reserved. (p. 1)

Dearborn and his associates did a great deal to open the diagnosis of reading disabilities to explanations that went beyond physical and congenital defects in children. He was among the first to recognize the wide range of abilities that normal children can have.

Through his direction of the Harvard Growth Studies, Dearborn was also instrumental in conceptually disentangling for future researchers the supposed correlation between physical and mental growth in children. In *Predicting the Child's Development* (1941), Dearborn and John Rothney use the results from the studies to dispel long-held beliefs about this relation:

> The cherished excuse of the parent that his or her child is growing so rapidly that his mental activities must suffer has...been challenged, if not negated. The fond hope of many that mental status may be predicted by means

of data on the physical characteristics of the individual has also been given little or no encouragement in the studies. (p. 57)

By scientifically examining cognitive and physical factors in longitudinal studies, Dearborn and his associates spent a good portion of their academic careers dispelling many of the misconceptions that people held about the educational and physical development of children.

Contributions to the Field of Reading

The researcher and literacy historian Richard Venezky credits Dearborn with several firsts in reading research (Venezky, 1984, pp. 7–10). Written within conceptual frameworks created with Cattell, Dearborn's dissertation at Columbia University, published in 1906, was one of the most comprehensive examinations of eye movements during reading that had been undertaken up to its time. According to Venezky (1984), Dearborn's dissertation "covered among other topics the number and duration of fixation pauses, refixations, perception during eye movements, span of attention, location of fixations, and eye fatigue in reading" (p. 8). Some of the questions Dearborn uncovered regarding the relation between the orthographic structure of words and their pronounceability remain unresolved today (Venezky, 1984, pp. 8–10).

The role played by the eye-movement studies of Dearborn, Edmund Burke Huey (see chapter 7, this volume), Cattell, J.F. Quantz, Raymond Dodge (see chapter 3, this volume), and many others laid the foundation of reading educators' understanding of the cognitive and perceptual nature of the reading process. Just as many reading educators today believe that miscue analysis is a key to understanding the mental processes of reading, so the researchers of Dearborn's era believed that an analysis of eye movements would give very important insights into the activities of the brain and eyes during reading. Much of what is known about optical effects of reading, visual perception, and information processing in reading is based upon the work of these early researchers.

When Dearborn started his research in the area of reading difficulties, there were considered to be very few causes of reading disabilities. Most researchers believed that the majority of reading disabilities had physical causes, either in the eyes and ears or the brains of children. As was previously mentioned, what we know now as dyslexia was referred to as *congenital word blindness* by Dearborn and his contemporaries. This was a condition that was presumed to have a physical cause and be genetically transferred from parent to child.

Although there were many children who suffered from physical disorders that prevented their acquisition of literacy, Dearborn worked hard to show that there was no physical or cognitive evidence of impairment for many of the children identified as having reading disabilities, and he also began the process of refining explanations for the different types of physical causes that could produce reading disabilities in children. The discrepancy model (Bond, Tinker, Wasson, & Wasson, 1994, pp. 42–45) for the diagnosis of reading difficulties, the separate assessment of intelligence quotient and auditory and visual perception skills in students, and the differential teaching of students with different types of reading difficulties can all be traced to the work of Dearborn.

The following statement from *Special Disabilities in Learning To Read and Write* (Lord, Carmichael, & Dearborn, 1925) encapsulates how Dearborn, in refuting through science the observed wisdom of the day, moved educators forward in their understanding of the multifaceted nature of reading disabilities: "The apparently equally successful use of these various pedagogical methods [word method, alphabet method, kinesthetic-tactile method] would seem to argue that, if there are specific defects, they are not confined to either the visual, auditory or motor processes" (p. 72). Dearborn goes on to describe eloquently how each reader has strengths and weaknesses in each of what educators would now call the *modalities*, and says that no one method will address the needs of all children with reading disabilities. In fact, Dearborn argued that teachers should not even use one modality-focused method to teach students with a deficit in that modality. For example, teachers should not focus exclusively on phonics for those students who show a deficit in phonics because it would not allow them to use strengths they may have in other modalities. By addressing the individual differences among children, Dearborn laid the groundwork for what educators would now call a *balanced literacy approach*, and in 1925 he was well ahead of others who later proclaimed that there was no one magic method for teaching children with reading disabilities.

Although his work on reading disabilities has had an important impact on reading research, Dearborn is perhaps best remembered for his collaboration later in his career with Irving H. Anderson on a textbook titled *The*

Psychology of Teaching Reading (Anderson & Dearborn, 1952), which was a staple in graduate reading programs for many years. The book is a wonderful compilation of all of Dearborn's work in the field of reading. It includes an in-depth look at how results from the Harvard Growth Studies on stages of intellectual development could be used to predict reading ability via a multiple causation model. It also explores reading readiness, eye movements, perception, teaching methods, and assessment. Throughout the book, Anderson and Dearborn continue Dearborn's mantra that the reading process is more complicated than was previously believed and that teachers and psychologists need to recognize and appreciate the complexities of the process, rather than try to find simple answers.

Anderson and Dearborn show a preference for whole-word methods in their book, which is not at all surprising for 1952, but some of their statements could have appeared just as easily in the 1990s as part of the whole language movement. In chapter 6 of their textbook, Anderson and Dearborn summarize their view of various reading methods:

> The alphabet and phonic methods are limited first and foremost by the fact that letter names and sound elements have no real meaning for the child. Learning to read is difficult without meaning, and much of the fun and enjoyment of reading is spoiled as well. Then, too, the alphabet and phonetic methods are mainly oral, which introduces the danger that the child will develop the habit of vocalization and word calling. (p. 256)

This text is full of such nuggets of wisdom based on all of the clinical psychological investigations in reading up to that point in time.

Dearborn was a scientist at heart and was very skilled at taking the results he learned through the scientific study of reading and applying them to reading instruction in schools. His pragmatic views of reading instruction appear to come from the breadth and depth of his scientific knowledge.

Lessons for the Future

Reading Walter Fenno Dearborn's work brings anyone who has studied reading education for more than 15 years back to what Venezky (1984) termed the "Golden Years" (p. 8) of reading research. Dearborn and his contemporaries showed the world that the new scientific methods of psychology could be and should be applied to the reading process, yielding a rich and abundant understanding of the complexities of cognition, perception, and child development with regard to literacy.

If I were to summarize Dearborn's work in two words, they would be *individual differences*. Dearborn, his colleagues, and his students spent their careers trying to convince teachers, school boards, departments of education, and the general public that close investigation of individual children reveals a vast complex of factors that interact to foster or prevent the acquisition of literacy, and that schools need to respond to these children by individualizing instruction as much as is practical. Dearborn rejected "silver bullet" theories about instructional methods throughout his career because they ran completely counter to his understanding of the child as an individual. The latest iteration of these beliefs is called *differentiated instruction*, and we can see from Dearborn's work that he would be very familiar with, and an advocate for, that conception of teaching were he alive today.

Dearborn also believed that each child grows and develops both mentally and physically at different rates and that schools cannot and should not disregard this fact. As one comes to appreciate the scope and importance of the work that Dearborn and others undertook to convince the world that each child is an individual, it is disturbing to see that the current standards movement, at several junctures, disregards this work and prefers to force all students to meet a standard for literacy. I believe that this idea would be repugnant to Dearborn, who would argue that, rather than forcing each child to meet a standard, schools should be providing all children with the instruction that would make them as successful as they could be within the constraints of their physical development and mental capacity.

There is a downside to individualizing instruction in the classroom setting. Stanovich's (1986) conception of Matthew Effects, in which grouping children according to their perceived capacity can create inequities in classrooms that increase over time, is probably the best recent discussion of this issue. However, as politics plays an ever-larger role in the education of children, the onus is on educators not to completely lose sight of the importance of the individualized instruction that Dearborn and other researchers championed.

Finally, throughout Dearborn's writings there is a reassurance, calmness, and open-mindedness about the reading process. There is very little in his writing that contemporary educators would consider wrong when considered alongside current standards and beliefs in the field. This is because Dearborn was a fine empirical scientist who calmly and clearly interpreted the data he found regarding cognition, perception, and the reading process. When he did make judgments on the data, it was frequently to dispel myths about reading. If he did go out on a limb in his interpretations, he would frequently follow the interpretation with a caveat about how more research was needed in the field to verify his judgment. Current readers would find his view of reading readiness, for instance, to be out of date because he was not privy to the concept of emergent literacy, but his views on the teaching of reading are remarkably on the mark with current best practices.

Dearborn's work on the connection of intelligence and reading paved the way for later work on schema theory and diagnostic models for university reading clinics. His work on child growth and development led to later developmental views of the reading process, and his work in defining the various forms of reading disability has shown us that everyone can learn to read if given instruction appropriate to his or her individual needs.

Reflection Questions

1. Dearborn devoted the first part of his professional life to the study of eye movements in reading. This connection continues to be studied using computers and more advanced technology than Dearborn had available to him. Why do we continue to study eye movements during reading?
2. Dearborn worked within the fields of psychology, medicine, educational psychology, child development, and reading education. Why does it seem impossible today to work within so many fields at the same time? What does this say about the future of educational research?
3. In *Why Johnny Can't Read—And What You Can Do About It* (1955), Rudolf Flesch criticizes visual reading methods taught in schools by pulling quotations out of context from teacher training textbooks of the day. The following is Flesch's selection from Anderson and Dearborn's *The Psychology of Teaching Reading* (1952):

> Little is gained by teaching the child his sounds and letters as a first step to reading. More rapid results are generally obtained by the direct method of simply showing the word to the child and telling him what it is (Anderson & Dearborn, 1952, as quoted in Flesch, 1955, p. 16).

Dearborn and his contemporaries were squarely in the sights of Flesch and his criticism of the "look-and-say" method for teaching reading. Evaluate this dispute in light of the focus of Dearborn's career.

4. Dearborn's life is very reflective of his contemporary faculty members at Harvard University and the other Ivy League schools during his era. Although there are still some who follow Dearborn's path to academia, there are still many more who do not follow that path. How has the professorate changed since the first half of the 20th century? How do these changes reflect changes in society?

5. A good portion of Dearborn's professional life was devoted to identifying individual differences among children. Although this research paved the way for separate programs for struggling students, the current trend in education is to end those separate programs and include students more in regular classrooms. This includes remedial reading programs where push-in programs appear to be preferable to pull-out programs. Do current school practices support or refute the work of Dearborn and his contemporaries? How can these differences be reconciled?

REFERENCES

Allport, G.W., Ulich, R., & Rulon, P.J. (1956, March 10). Walter Fenno Dearborn. *Harvard University Gazette*, n.p.

Anderson, I.H., & Dearborn, W.F. (1952). *The psychology of teaching reading*. New York: Ronald.

Bond, G., Tinker, M.A., Wasson, B.B., & Wasson, J.B. (1994). *Reading difficulties: Their diagnosis and correction* (7th ed.). Boston: Allyn & Bacon.

Carmichael, L. (1957). *Walter Fenno Dearborn and the scientific study of reading*. Unpublished transcript of a lecture delivered at Harvard Graduate School of Education, October 23, 1957 [private collection].

Carmichael, L., & Dearborn, W.F. (1947). *Reading and visual fatigue*. Boston: Houghton Mifflin.

Dearborn, W.F. (1906). *The psychology of reading: An experimental study of the reading process and eye-movements*. New York: The Science Press.

Dearborn, W.F. (1922). *Dearborn group tests, Series II*. Minneapolis, MN: Educational Test Bureau.

Dearborn, W.F., & Inglis, A.J. (1921). *Psychological and educational tests in the public schools of Winchester, Virginia*. Charlottesville: University of Virginia.

Dearborn, W.F., & Rothney, J.W.M. (1938). *Scholastic, economic, and social backgrounds of unemployed youth*. Cambridge, MA: Harvard University Press.

Dearborn, W.F., & Rothney, J.W.M. (1941). *Predicting the child's development*. Cambridge, MA: Sci-Art.

Flesch, R.F. (1955). *Why Johnny can't read—and what you can do about it*. New York: Harper.

Harris, A.J., & Sipay, E.R. (1990). *How to increase reading ability: A guide to developmental and remedial methods*. New York: Longman.

Langfeld, H.S. (1955). Walter Fenno Dearborn: 1978–1955. *American Journal of Psychology*, 68, 679–681.

Lord, E.E., Carmichael, L., & Dearborn, W.F. (1925). *Special disabilities in learning to read and write*. Cambridge, MA: Harvard University Press.

Stanovich, K.E. (1986). Matthew effects in reading: Some consequences of individual differences in the acquisition of literacy. *Reading Research Quarterly*, 21, 360–407.

Venezky, R.L. (1984). The history of reading research. In P.D. Pearson, R. Barr, M.L. Kamil, & P. Mosenthal (Eds.), *Handbook of reading research*, (pp. 3–38). New York: Longman.

FOR FURTHER READING

Dearborn, W.F. (1909). *The relative standing of pupils in the high school and in the university*. Bulletin of the University of Wisconsin, no. 312. Madison, WI: University of Wisconsin.

Dearborn, W.F. (1914). Professor Cattell's studies of reading and perception. *Archives of Psychology*, 4(30), 34–45.

Dearborn, W.F. (1924). Repeated measurements of the physical and mental development of school children. *School and Society*, 20, 515–518.

Dearborn, W.F. (1928). *Intelligence tests: Their significance for school and society*. Boston: Houghton Mifflin.

Dearborn, W.F. (1929). Teaching reading to nonreaders. *The Elementary School Journal*, 30, 266–269.

Dearborn, W.F. (1930). The nature of special abilities and disabilities. *School and Society*, 31, 623–636.

Dearborn, W.F. (1931). Ocular and manual dominance in dyslexia. *Psychological Bulletin*, 28, 704.

Dearborn, W.F. (1932). *Difficulties in learning*. Chicago: University of Chicago Press.

Dearborn, W.F. (1935). The mental and physical growth of public school children. *School and Society*, 41, 585–593.

Dearborn, W.F. (1936). The use of the tachistoscope in diagnostic and remedial reading. In *Psychological Studies of Human Variability* Psychological Monographs, 47(2), 1–19.

Dearborn, W.F. (1938, September). Motivation versus "control" in remedial reading. *Education*, 59, 1–6.

Dearborn, W.F. (1939a). Remedial reading: Case histories and recent experimentation. *Recent trends in reading*. Supplementary Educational Monographs, no. 49, pp. 110–113. Chicago: University of Chicago Press.

Dearborn, W.F. (1939b). The nature and causation of disabilities in reading. *Recent trends in reading*. Supplementary Educational Monographs, no. 49, pp. 103–110. Chicago: University of Chicago.

Dearborn, W.F. (1940). On the possible relations of visual fatigue to reading disabilities. *School and Society*, 52, 532–536.

Dearborn, W.F., & Anderson, I.H. (1937). A new method for teaching phrasing and for increasing the size of reading fixations. *Psychological Record*, 1, 459–475.

Dearborn, W.F., & Anderson, I.H. (1938a). Aniseikonia as related to disability in reading. *Journal of Experimental Psychology*, 23, 559–577.

Dearborn, W.F., & Anderson, I.H. (1938b). Controlled reading by means of a motion picture technique. *Psychological Record*, 2, 219–227.

Dearborn, W.F., & Comfort, F.D. (1935). Differences in size and shape of ocular images as related to defects in reading. *Third Annual Research Bulletin of the National Conference on Research in Elementary School English*, pp. 9–10.

Dearborn, W.F., & Gores, H.B. (1938, January). Adult reactions to silent reading test. *Harvard Educational Review*, 8, 38–43.

Dearborn, W.F., Johnston, P.W., & Carmichael, L. (1949, October 14). Oral stress and meaning in printed material. *Science*, 110, 404.

Dearborn, W.F., & Leverett, H.M. (1945). Visual defects and reading. *Journal of Experimental Education*, 13, 111–124.

Dearborn, W.F., & Long, H.H. (1928). On comparing IQ's at different age levels on the same scale. *Journal of Educational Research*, 18, 265–274.

Dearborn, W.F., Rothney, J.W.M., & Shuttleworth, F.K. (1938). *Data on the growth of public school children*. Monographs of the Society for Research in Child Development. Washington, DC: Society for Research in Child Development.

Dearborn, W.F., Shaw, E.A., & Lincoln, E.A. (1923). *A series of form board and performance tests of intelligence*. Studies in Educational Psychology and Educational Measurement, series 1, no. 4. Cambridge, MA: Graduate School of Education, Harvard University.

Dearborn, W.F., & Wilking, S.V. (1941). Improving the reading of college freshmen. *School Review*, 49, 668–678.

PART III

The Progressives: Researchers Committed to Progressive Education

CHAPTER 7

Edmund Burke Huey (1870–1913): A Brief Life With an Enduring Legacy

By Jolene B. Reed and Richard J. Meyer

Historical Research Process

LOCATING AND READING the work of Edmund Burke Huey, although requiring days of intensive searches in long-forgotten corners of the library, proved to be more easily accomplished than the search for the life of the man behind the words. Initially, John Carroll's foreword in the 1968 republication of Huey's seminal work *The Psychology and Pedagogy of Reading* (1908/1968) provided our sole source of biographical information on Huey. The facts of his life were sketchy and evoked more questions than answers. We wondered about his childhood and the factors that might have con-

---

Shaping the Reading Field: The Impact of Early Reading Pioneers, Scientific Research, and Progressive Ideas, edited by Susan E. Israel and E. Jennifer Monaghan. © 2007 by the International Reading Association.
Photo: Reproduced from *The Owl*, published by the University of Pittsburgh, 1909 (p. 19).

tributed to his professional interests. We wondered whether he had married and had a family. We were unsure of why his place of death was listed as Washington state and wondered what events had caused him to be there when his last place of employment had been Baltimore, Maryland, USA.

Our first course of action was to contact the Department of Vital Statistics in Olympia, Washington, USA, and request a copy of Huey's death certificate. This document proved to be a key beginning in the search for the personal side of Huey's life, providing a wealth of information previously unknown to us. From this certificate we learned who his parents were. We also found that what the certificate lists as the date and place of his birth as well as the date of his death contradicts what Carroll states. Carroll's foreword says that Huey was born December 1, 1870, in Curllsville, Pennsylvania, USA. This same birth date is recorded in obituaries announcing Huey's death ("Notes and News," 1914; "Scientific Notes," 1914). The 1910 United States Federal Census also shows Huey's year of birth as 1870. However, his death certificate lists his date and place of birth as December 2, 1871, in Rimersburg, Pennsylvania, USA (Department of Vital Statistics, 1913).

The death certificate also lists Huey as single—as opposed to widowed or divorced—at the time of his death, telling us that he had never married. Working backward from the information contained in his death certificate, we were able to reconstruct personal aspects of Huey's short life through the use of obituaries, census records, and existing fragmented biographical information. It is, indeed, ironic that the death certificate proved to be the catalyst in finding the life story of Edmund Burke Huey.

We would discover that Huey's interest in the teaching and learning of reading was short-lived—barely a decade—yet in that time he studied eye movements, reading as a cognitive process, and even health issues related to reading. His best known work, *The Psychology and Pedagogy of Reading* (1908/1968), serves as the first true compendium of reading research and also suggests areas of study that are thriving today.

Personal and Professional Life

Huey's parents were Robert B. and Matilda Fackender Huey of Rimersburg, Pennsylvania, USA. His father (whose primary occupation was that of physician) rented a building in which he served as the principal of a private school—the Clarion Collegiate Institute—in Rimersburg for about one year. The elder

Huey assumed this position because the regular management of the school had been suspended (Davis, 1887, p. 595). This one-time involvement by his father in educational administration may have been influential in young Huey's future decision to enter the field of education as a profession.

Huey's mother died in 1880, when he was only 9 years old (Eccles-Lesher, 2005). At about the time of his mother's death "Eddie," as he is referred to in the census and other documents at the time, went to live for an undetermined amount of time on the nearby farm of his paternal grandparents, Robert and Elizabeth Huey. This same year, Huey's father moved west to establish a medical practice in Birmingham, Illinois, USA (U.S. Federal Census, 1880).

Huey received his undergraduate education at Lafayette College in Easton, Pennsylvania, USA. He was awarded an AB in 1895. From 1895 through 1897, he taught at a private secondary academy in the northeastern Pennsylvania coal-mining community of Wilkes-Barre.

He pursued his doctoral studies at Clark University in Worcester, Massachusetts, USA. His focus on reading was nurtured at Clark University, where he studied under the university's first president, G. Stanley Hall, one of the fathers of American psychology and founder of the American Psychological Association. Hall's interests in learning, development, and the need for increasing the organization, numbers, and publications of scholarly works (Hall started many journals such as the *American Journal of Psychology* and the *Journal of Applied Psychology*) are reflected in Huey's 1908 tome.

Other professors at Clark University who influenced Huey's studies were W.H. Burnham, with his research on conceptions of memory; C.F. Hodge, with his investigations into the stimulation of nerve cells; and E.C. Sanford, who had published research on the relative legibility of small letters. Sanford was also Huey's academic advisor, and the influence of their association is evident in Huey's first published papers as well as in his later book, *The Psychology and Pedagogy of Reading* (1908/1968). In those publications Huey discusses the importance of font size, paper quality, and appropriate lighting to the reading process (Huey, 1900, 1907).

Huey's interests in the reading process were set in the context of many issues of human development and health. His concentration on the physiology of the eye was one facet of his interest in the eye–brain relation that is such an integral part of the reading process. While Huey was studying at Clark University, he developed an apparatus that allowed him to observe and track readers' eye movements. He describes the device in considerable detail in *The Psychology and Pedagogy of Reading* (1908/1968, pp. 25–27). It consisted of a small, rounded plaster of Paris cup that was shaped to attach directly to the eyeball of the reader. A very thin metal rod that acted as a pointer was connected to the cup by a light lever made of celloidin and glass. As the reader read, the pointer traced and recorded the movement of the eye by displacing a dot of soot on a cylindrical paper drum. Huey reduced or alleviated any possible discomfort his research subjects may have experienced by the administration of desensitizing agents—even, at times, cocaine.

Although his device was crude by modern standards, it was capable of recording landmark information regarding how the eye travels across the printed page. Until the research of Emile Javal (1839–1907), the French oculist, it had been believed that the eyes move across text in one continuous and smooth movement. Huey's work provided further evidence that this is not the case. Rather, the eye travels across the print in a series of quick movements and pauses. He conjectured, along with a few other researchers at the time, that the eye does not focus when it is in motion, but that "the visual field is unbroken to consciousness" (1908/1968, p. 36). Thus, he understood that the reading process involves interactions between the eyes and brain that are highly complex in nature. He surmised that the reader reads text using the largest, rather than the smallest, meaningful unit obtainable by the eye. This issue continues to be debated today in conflicting reports about the relation between what the eye captures and what the mind processes. Doubtless, Huey would have rejoiced at the technological advances that allow for more accurate measurements of the physiology of the eye during reading and the concomitant brain processes that occur during eye movements.

Huey completed his doctoral studies and was awarded his PhD by Clark University in 1899. His dissertation, "On the Psychology and Physiology of Reading," was soon published in two parts in *The American Journal of Psychology* (Huey, 1900, 1901). Following the completion of his studies at Clark University, Huey accepted a position teaching at a state normal school in Moorhead, Minnesota, USA. He remained there until 1901 (Carroll, 1968, p. vii; Cattell, 1910).

From 1901 through 1902, Huey availed himself of the opportunity to study in Europe. During this year, his time was divided between universities in Paris and Berlin. His travels allowed him to become better acquainted with the French oculist Javal and the German psychologist Benno Erdmann. Both these Europeans were gaining scientific fame for their pioneering studies regarding the visual processes involved during reading (Carroll, 1968, p. viii).

Huey returned to the United States in 1902 and taught genetic psychology at Miami University in Oxford, Ohio, USA, for a year. He then returned to Clark University in 1903 to become an assistant to E.C. Sanford, his former doctoral advisor, and help run the psychology laboratory. In 1904, Huey left Clark University to become a professor of psychology and education at the University of Western Pennsylvania in Pittsburgh. At this university, Huey was instrumental in organizing a joint department of psychology and education and in founding a laboratory of experimental psychology.

Huey continued his experiments and studies related to the psychology of reading while he was at the University of Western Pennsylvania (Carroll, 1968). It was during this time that he wrote his oft-cited book, *The Psychology and Pedagogy of Reading* (1908/1968). This book was an outcome of the research Huey had initiated while still a doctoral student at Clark University, but he was now able to draw upon the eye-movement research of investigators such as Raymond Dodge (see chapter 3, this volume) and Walter Fenno Dearborn (see chapter 6, this volume). His book is still referred to as a major contribution to the field of educational psychology (Charles, 1987, p. 26).

Huey left the University of Western Pennsylvania in 1908 to study abroad again. This time he spent a year studying with Pierre Janet, a renowned French psychiatrist whose acquaintance he probably had made during his prior trip to Europe. By this time, Huey's research interests were no longer focused on the field of reading pedagogy, and he was becoming more interested in research on the psychology of mental deficiency.

Upon his return to the United States in 1909, Huey accepted a position as a clinical psychologist at an institution for the "feeble-minded" in Lincoln, Illinois, USA. He resigned from this post in 1911 and accepted a position at Johns Hopkins University in Baltimore, Maryland, USA, to engage in clinical research with Adolf Meyer, founder of the mental hygiene movement. At Johns Hopkins University, Huey was a lecturer on mental development and an assistant in psychiatry at the Phipps Clinic ("Obituary," 1914).

Huey's second book, *Backward and Feeble-Minded Children: Clinical Studies in the Psychology of Defectives, With a Syllabus for the Clinical Examination and Testing of Children*, was published in 1912. By this time, Huey was recognized by his colleagues as one of the foremost leaders in the study of "mentally defective children" ("Notes and News," 1914). This second book contains his analysis of 32 children who were patients at the institution in Lincoln. Huey considered these documented cases to be borderline in their mental deficiency and surmised that their lack of development was due to "poor health, poor eyes, or improper home surroundings" (1912, p. 171). Huey felt that these students should receive training that would allow them to be self-supporting and advocated for the development of specialized occupational classes in schools to meet their needs.

Tragedy struck Huey in 1913 when the notes and manuscript of a third book, focusing on clinical psychology and culminating approximately 10 years of work, were destroyed by a fire. At this same time, Huey's health failed. He was diagnosed with tuberculosis, perhaps contracted during the time of his European studies. In the early 1900s, eastern Washington State was being touted as a place to recuperate from lung and respiratory ailments because of its dry climate. Huey moved to Connell, Washington, USA, in an effort to restore his health. Unfortunately, he succumbed to the disease on December 30, 1913.

Philosophical Beliefs and Guiding Principles

Edmund Burke Huey believed that reading is a complex process that involves the eyes, eye movements, the physiology of the brain, and the workings of the mind (Luria, 1979). He was convinced that issues of health, such as fatigue, glare, and print size, affect a reader's physical state of being (Huey, 1907). He also believed that his and others' findings about reading needed to be applied to reading pedagogy in schools in a timely and systematic way so research would inform pedagogy and pedagogy could inform the research agenda. He presented reading as a cognitive process rooted in an individual's construction of meaning, doing so around the time that cognitive views of learning were in their infancy.

Huey's work in reading research, spanning about 10 years, reflected the thinking of John Dewey, a progressive educator whom Huey admired and to whom he makes reference in some of his works. Huey supported Dewey's emphasis on the use of context, rather than drill, to introduce new words to young readers. He also admired Dewey's practice of teaching phonics separately from the reading lessons to keep the focus of reading instruction on obtaining the message of the text (Huey, 1908/1968, pp. 293–294).

Huey explained that reading is more than a collection of sounds or words. Reading is a perceptual process and, although readers do see words and sometimes use the sounds of individual letters to decide what a word is, the process of reading involves meaning making. This suggests, he argued, that the goal of reading instruction is for readers to learn to rely as little as possible on letters, sounds, and words. He understood these three elements to be visual "cues" (Huey, 1908/1968, p. 77), a word he used almost 60 years before research on miscue analysis was initiated by Kenneth Goodman (1967). Huey also believed that reading involves some tension between the building of images in the reader's mind and the use of inner speech as a way of understanding text. These beliefs were rooted in his research with readers who reported to him that they sometimes had mental images as they read, other times pronounced words silently in their minds, and on occasion sub-vocalized words (particularly if a text was challenging).

Huey explained reading as involving an individual actively predicting the sense of a text based upon perceptions of sounds, words, grammar, and meaning. He posed the idea that readers had "expectations" (Huey, 1908/1968, p. 157) of a text based upon what they read, their experiences, and their understanding of what language does in terms of its grammatical features both across texts in general and within a particular text.

The issue of fluency, quite popular now, was also studied by Huey. He concluded that readers' rates of reading varied across the type of text being read, an aspect of reading that researchers continue to study today (National Institute of Child Health and Human Development [NICHD], 2000, pp. 3–6). He also suggested that reading rate varies as a function of the physical state of the reader, prior experience with the subject matter being read, concentration, and the reader's strategies. He noted that some readers survey a text prior to reading and make decisions about how much to read, when to skip parts of the text, and which content words contribute to meaning making (1908/1968, p. 144). Huey's work on the phylogeny or development of the reading process parallels Vygotsky's (1934/1978) explanation of language development, although Huey did this work prior to Vygotsky's influence in the United States. Huey, like Vygotsky, discussed gestures, drawings, and scribbles as precursors to the written language development of individuals. Huey's interest in the development of the use of symbols for representation and the eventual evolution of an alphabet and conventions of printed language led him to suggest that alphabets are the most highly developed form of written language (1908/1968, p. 203).

Huey was dedicated to understanding effective reading pedagogy. After tracing the history of reading instruction programs and examining contemporary materials available for use in schools by teachers, he condemned most programs published specifically for reading instruction (1908/1968). He called them "most striking...[in] the inanity and disjointedness of their reading content" (pp. 278–279). Using what he had learned about the informal reading instruction that occurred in literate homes during his time, he suggested that reading be taught in a way that is natural, much the way oral language is taught, rather than as a "mechanical tool" (p. 306). He believed that children needed to be taught to read books that interested them and taught about the sound system of language (phonics) by using what they could already read. This led him to conclude that phonics is best taught when children are about 8 years old. This is consistent with the views of Montessori (1912), although Huey never cites her work.

It is apparent that Huey explored many of the critical issues we continue to face as scholars and teachers of reading. He recognized the complexity involved in the reading process and the essential role of meaning making in that process. He further advocated the use of instructional materials that drew from the interests and personal schemas of individual students.

Contributions to the Field of Reading

Edmund Burke Huey's remarkable volume *The Psychology and Pedagogy of Reading* (1908/1968) serves as the first compendium of research and thought on the reading process. We could find no other volume near the turn of the 20th century that served to summarize reading research as thoroughly as this one. Indeed, the book reminds us of volumes that appeared near the end of the 20th century and that claim to serve this summarizing purpose, such as those by Adams (1990) and Snow and her colleagues (Snow, Burns, & Griffin, 1998), and the report of the National Reading Panel (NICHD, 2000).

One measure of the influence of Huey's work is the extent to which it is cited in contemporary scholarship in the field. Nila Banton Smith (1965/1986), a historian of reading instruction, refers to Huey's work as "still considered a standard reference in this field" (p. 123). His work is cited in 9 of 25 chapters in the first volume of the *Handbook of Reading Research*

(Pearson, Barr, Kamil, & Mosenthal, 1984), in 10 of 25 in the second volume (Barr, Kamil, Mosenthal, & Pearson, 1991), and in 5 of 47 chapters in the third volume (Kamil, Mosenthal, Pearson, & Barr, 2000). Edfeldt (1990), in an article about dyslexia, writes, "Reading instruction at school must as soon as possible be changed radically in the direction which Edmund B. Huey was anticipating almost a hundred years ago" (p. 71). Such instruction would include emphasis on meaning making and comprehension. Huey felt that instruction should not be based on the view that learning to read is a formal process, but rather should find its basis in the intrinsic value of what is read (1908/1968, p. 380).

Historical studies of the place of psychology in education are not considered complete without mention of Huey's contributions (Hilgard, 1996, p. 998). Hiebert and Raphael (1996) point out that the shift to considerably more behaviorist views of the reading process, including the idea that reading involves automaticity rather than efficient cognitive processing, temporarily slowed interest in Huey's work. Still, in our present and tense times about what constitutes reading research and quality practice, scholars with differing approaches to reading instruction, such as Kenneth Goodman's meaning-based emphasis (1993) and Adams's phonetic-based methodology (1990), rely upon Huey's thinking about the reading process to support their own views.

A close look at Huey's work demonstrates that Huey had certain views of reading instruction and scholarship, including what needed to be studied as well as what the extant research suggested during his own time. In the following sections, we summarize some of his contributions to reading research and pedagogy. We find it extremely noteworthy that Huey's compilation (1908/1968) provides a broad consideration of the complexity of reading. He accomplished this task by setting the reading process in the context of such areas as language development, cognitive development, physical development, health and well-being, experiential background, the features of print making (paper quality, font size, etc.), and the close scrutiny of materials used for reading instruction in school as compared to literature available to children outside school.

Definition of Reading

The purpose of Huey's dissertation (published in 1900 and 1901) was to "analyze and describe the psycho-physiological processes involved in reading"

(1900, p. 283). In these two pieces and subsequently in the book (1908/1968) in which he elaborates upon his findings, Huey presents the physiological aspects of reading, which involve eye movements and fixation, and health and well-being. He presents reading as psychological, linguistic, and social in his discussions of language development, cognitive psychology, and meaning making.

Eye-Movement Research

In addition to what we discussed earlier, Huey found that eye movements did not differ significantly as a function of the reader's distance from the text but that smaller fonts caused an increase in eye fixations. He found that content words were often the site of fixations and readers did not fixate as often on function words. Huey (1898) lamented that the technology was not sufficiently developed to provide answers to important questions about eye movements.

Word Perception

Huey (1908/1968) reported that word perception was a function of the way that a reader was taught to read. For example, readers who are taught to focus on letters tend to focus on letters. Those readers whose instruction focuses on words tend to notice words more (pp. 103–104). He surmised that, over time, readers' experiences with reading influence their perception of words, in what was perhaps a foreshadowing of the Matthew Effect—good readers getting better and poor readers getting worse as time goes on (Stanovich, 1986). The sheer volume of words encountered by the skilled reader provides a cumulative advantage for that reader in learning to process text more efficiently and effectively.

Huey writes that visual perception cannot be separated from "the part played by inner speech and the consciousness of meaning" and that "meaning...dominates...the perception of words and phrases" (1908/1968, p. 116). He uses the word "predictable" throughout his work on word perception and suggests that readers use cues, such as their knowledge of the structure of language, to predict meaning. This is consistent with his assertion that language grows from meaning, which he credits to the well-known German researcher Wilhelm Wundt (1900).

Meaning

Huey (1908/1968) writes that meaning "belong[s] to the larger wholes, to the sentences and other large units" (p. 158). He reports that words within a continuous text (e.g., an article or story) are afforded "a rich context of associations" (p. 155) from within the text and because of the readers' experiences. Reflecting the opinions of another scholar, G.F. Stout, Huey boldly asserts that "apprehension of a whole, which takes place without the discernment of its parts...[reflects] the history of the individual" (1908/1968, p. 161). He also explains that readers need a sense of grammar to make meaning but that meaning is "deeper...we approach the pure meaning-consciousness as detached from articulation" (p. 165).

Huey seemed to know intuitively that a true understanding of the use of language demands a deep commitment to understanding structures of the brain and mind. Huey's influence can be seen in the present-day language researchers use to discuss meaning making—Huey describes meaning as something happening in the dark brain, away from the light that readers use to initially see words and sentences. Almost as if foretelling Frank Smith's ideas about "reading from behind the eye" (1997, p. 10), Huey writes, "The sentence-utterance, as we have seen, comes at some distance behind the eye" (p. 168).

History

In *The Psychology and Pedagogy of Reading*, Huey (1908/1968) provides a brief history of methods used in the teaching of reading, beginning with the early Greek and Roman civilizations. Although the alphabetic method of learning to read was predominantly used throughout the Western world, there were alternate methods being used in other areas such as the Far East. In that part of the world, beginning readers were given books and asked to repeat the text in unison until the readers knew the words and sentences.

The alphabetic method of instruction traveled to the United States with the Puritans, and that philosophy of learning was perpetuated over the next two centuries through the use of various reading primers. Huey notes that a change in this way of thinking did not occur until the publication of Worcester's *A Primer of the English Language, for the Use of Families and Schools* in 1828, which advocated learning to read by learning words first (Huey, 1908/1968, p. 258). This was Huey's favored method of teaching reading.

Pedagogy

As mentioned, Huey reviewed the history of materials and approaches available for reading instruction. Finding the materials and approaches rather dismal, he recommended exciting and interesting literature as a central part of reading instruction. He presented evidence of instruction based upon children's interests and typical out-of-school literature at Bank Street School in New York City and at Horace Mann in Chicago, two schools whose pedagogies were guided by the educational philosophy of John Dewey. Huey's view that phonics instruction should occur after the initial reading of books was confirmed at these schools.

Other Contributions

Huey's interest in the pedagogy of reading extended into many other facets of the field. His contributions to reading research also include descriptions of factors influencing reading rate. He suggested close study of children's reading to understand slow rates, but he attributed some slow reading to the effects of oral reading experiences in school. He was concerned about readers' fatigue because of poor lighting, muscle strain, and reading location. He called reading on a train "neurally expensive" (1908/1968, p. 390). He was an advocate of shorter lines of print in books so the eye might more easily view previously read lines and words. As a result, he preferred newspaper layouts to book layouts because of the narrow columns of the former and because more important items were printed in larger type in newspapers, helping readers to decide what to read. He proposed the use of a simpler alphabet with no silent letters and a consistent spelling system that had phonetic regularity. With a clarity that seems virtually prophetic, Huey called for specialists to study reading closely and to submit their findings to the government for the purpose of central supervision of optimal strategies that should be taught to readers (p. 430).

Huey also pointed out that reading and writing are related processes that inform the learner reciprocally. In *The Psychology and Pedagogy of Reading* (1908/1968), Huey summarizes his conclusions and recommendations on the essentials of quality reading instruction. He states that the home is the natural place for a child to learn to read by being introduced to literature through the storytelling and picture reading. He further states that little work should be done with phonics in the early years and that phonics instruction should be addressed separately from reading instruction. He believed that the reading process should never be viewed as an end in and of itself but that its value should be intrinsic and its purpose should be to gather meaning from the text (pp. 379–383).

Eventually, Huey's interest in reading waned and he shifted his attention to working with children with special needs (Huey, 1913). We have been interpreting and extending his contributions to reading research and pedagogy since the time he ended his research.

Lessons for the Future

The comprehensive view of reading that Huey studied and proposed made him unique in his time and, more importantly, influential on the thinking of reading researchers from his time to the present day. Former International Reading Association President Alan Robinson (1980) discusses five different periods of his life during which he read and reread Huey's 1908 tome: (1) as a reading specialist, (2) as a doctoral student, (3) as a beginning professor, (4) as an experienced professor, and (5) as Association president. Many of the ideas that we are studying as scholars and applying as practitioners in classrooms have roots that can be traced to this classic work. Although Huey studied and wrote about the reading process near the turn of the 20th century, his insights have endured the test of time. His thinking foreshadowed current debates regarding how best to teach reading and resulted in the 1968 republication of *The Psychology and Pedagogy of Reading*.

Eye-movement research (Paulson & Freeman, 2003) has reached a point that would excite Huey because technology is finally available that can track readers' eyes accurately as well as measure the length of fixations in exact fractions of a second. Brain research that focuses on what occurs physiologically during reading (Strauss, 2005) would also intrigue Huey. His interest in the brain and the mind would probably lead him to a serious consideration of multiple intelligences (Gardner, 1983) and of projects similar to the one with young children in Reggio Emilia, Italy (Edwards, Gandini, & Forman, 1998), where the curriculum is not taught in arbitrary time slots designed by adults. We the authors imagine that the scholarship on children as inquirers (Short, Harste, & Burke, 1996) would also be of interest to Huey.

Researchers continue to struggle with and argue about several basic questions as we near the centennial of Huey's book. We are still not in agreement about the role and placement of phonics in beginning reading instruction. We are still exploring comprehension, work that is complicated by issues such as second-language acquisition (Freeman & Freeman, 2004), cultural differences (Moll, 1990), resistance to learning (Krogness, 1995), and the influences of experiences on the making of meaning. There is also disagreement about the importance of fluency (words read per minute) when readers vary in speed within a text (Flurkey, 1997) or across different genres.

Huey's suggestion that the government rely upon experts to determine effective reading strategies, which are subsequently disseminated by the government, has come to fruition. He might have been surprised that the publication of the report of the National Reading Panel (NICHD, 2000) was met with a litany of scholarly protests and disagreements (Coles, 2000) as well as discussion in the popular press (Metcalf, 2002).

Huey's interest in teacher education, his kinship with John Dewey and progressive education, and his systematic study of reading as a contextualized process point to the contemporary theme of reflection (Schön, 1983) in teacher education and development. We conjecture that Huey would support the idea of teachers understanding their students' out-of-school experiences, available materials, and quality children's literature as vehicles for making instruction culturally responsive and relevant. His views of reading research and pedagogy are still present in the continuing debates about how best to teach children to read, the purposes of reading, and the connections between reading instruction and subsequent literacy activity within and beyond the walls of the school.

Reflection Questions

1. Huey believed that reading instruction should be based upon the interests and experiences of children. Because children enter schools with a wide variety of out-of-school experiences, how might classroom teachers develop reading programs that value the diversity of all students?

2. Huey emphasized the need for keeping phonics instruction separate from reading instruction. What might be the advantages and disadvantages of such instruction?

3. How might an emphasis on phonics during reading instruction have an impact on comprehension?
4. Given Huey's views on the importance of meaning making in reading instruction, how might Huey suggest that we assess comprehension?
5. What are some possible relations between a reader's use of visual cues and his or her use of syntax and semantics?

REFERENCES

Adams, M.J. (1990). *Beginning to read: Thinking and learning about print*. Cambridge, MA: MIT Press.

Barr, R., Kamil, M.L., Mosenthal, P.B., & Pearson, P.D. (Eds.). (1991). *Handbook of reading research (Vol. 2)*. Mahwah, NJ: Erlbaum.

Carroll, J. (1968). Foreword. In E.B. Huey, *The psychology and pedagogy of reading* (pp. vii–xii). Cambridge, MA: MIT Press. (Original work published 1908)

Cattell, J.M. (Ed.). (1910). *American men of science: A biographical directory* (2nd ed.). New York: Science Press.

Charles, D.C. (1987). The emergence of educational psychology. In J.A. Glover & R.R. Ronning (Eds.), *Historical foundations of educational psychology* (pp. 17–38). New York: Plenum.

Coles, G. (2000). *Misreading reading: The bad science that hurts children*. Portsmouth, NH: Heinemann.

Davis, A.J. (Ed.). (1887). *History of Clarion County, Pennsylvania: With illustrations and biographical sketches of some of its prominent men and pioneers*. Syracuse, NY: Mason.

Department of Vital Statistics. (1913). Certificate of death for Edmund Burke Huey. Olympia, Washington: Author.

Eccles-Lesher Memorial Library. *Cemetery records*. Retrieved January 10, 2005, from http://www.eccles-lesher.org/Cemetery/records.php?what=view

Edfeldt, A.W. (1990). The Huey legacy: A cognitive evaluation. *Early Child Development and Care, 59*, 53–72.

Edwards, C.P., Gandini, L., & Forman, G.E. (1998). *The hundred languages of children: The Reggio Emilia approach—advanced reflections*. London: Ablex.

Flurkey, A. (1997). *Reading as flow: A linguistic alternative to fluency*. Unpublished doctoral dissertation, University of Arizona, Tucson.

Freeman, D.E., & Freeman, Y.S. (2004). *Essential linguistics: What you need to know to teach reading, ESL, spelling, phonics, and grammar*. Portsmouth, NH: Heinemann.

Gardner, H. (1983). *Frames of mind: The theory of multiple intelligences*. New York: Basic Books.

Goodman, K. (1967, May). Reading: A psycholinguistic guessing game. *Journal of the Reading Specialist, 6*(4), 126–135.

Goodman, K.S. (1993). *Phonics phacts: A common-sense look at the most controversial issue affecting today's classrooms*. Portsmouth, NH: Heinemann.

Hiebert, E.H., & Raphael, T.E. (1996). Psychological perspectives on literacy and extensions to educational practice. In D.C. Berliner & R.C. Calfee (Eds.), *Handbook of educational psychology* (pp. 550–602). New York: Simon & Schuster Macmillan.

Hilgard, E.R. (1996). History of educational psychology. In D.C. Berliner & R.C. Calfee (Eds.), *Handbook of educational psychology* (pp. 990–1004). New York: Simon & Schuster Macmillan.

Huey, E.B. (1898). Preliminary experiments in the physiology and psychology of reading. *American Journal of Psychology, 9*(4), 575–586.

Huey, E.B. (1900). On the psychology and physiology of reading, I. *The American Journal of Psychology, 11*(3), 283–302.

Huey, E.B. (1901). On the psychology and physiology of reading, II. *The American Journal of Psychology, 12*(3), 292–312.

Huey, E.B. (1907, May). Hygienic requirements in the printing of books. *Popular Science, 20,* 542–548.

Huey, E.B. (1912). *Backward and feeble-minded children: Clinical studies in the psychology of defectives, with a syllabus for the clinical examination and testing of children.* Baltimore: Warwick and York.

Huey, E.B. (1913). The education of defectives and the training of teachers for special classes. *Journal of Educational Psychology, 4*(9), 545–550.

Huey, E.B. (1968). *The psychology and pedagogy of reading.* Cambridge, MA: MIT Press. (Original work published 1908)

Kamil, M.L., Mosenthal, P., Pearson, P.D., & Barr, R. (Eds.). (2000). *Handbook of reading research (Vol. 3).* Mahwah, NJ: Erlbaum.

Krogness, M.M. (1995). *Just teach me Mrs. K: Talking, reading, and writing with resistant adolescent learners.* Portsmouth: Heinemann.

Luria, A.R. (1979). *The making of mind: A personal account of Soviet psychology.* Cambridge, MA: Harvard University Press.

Metcalf, S. (2002, January 28). Reading between the lines. *Nation,* 18–22.

Moll, L.C. (Ed.). (1990). *Vygotsky and education: Instructional implications and applications of sociohistorical psychology.* Cambridge, England: Cambridge University Press.

Montessori, M. (1912). *The Montessori method.* New York: Frederick A. Stokes.

National Institute of Child Health and Human Development. (2000). *Report of the National Reading Panel. Teaching children to read: An evidence-based assessment of the scientific research literature on reading and its implications for reading instruction. Report of the subgroups.* (NIH Publication No. 00-4769). Washington, DC: U.S. Government Printing Office.

Notes and news. (1914, February 15). *Psychological Bulletin, 11,* 80.

Obituary. (1914, January 14). *American Journal of Psychology, 25,* 319.

Paulson, E.J., & Freeman, A.E. (2003). *Insight from the eyes: The science of effective reading instruction.* Portsmouth, NH: Heinemann.

Pearson, P.D., Barr, R., Kamil, M.L., & Mosenthal, P. (1984). *Handbook of reading research.* New York: Longman.

Robinson, H.A. (1980). Readings that made a difference: The book that made me flexible. *Journal of Reading, 23,* 296–299.

Schön, D. (1983). *The reflective practitioner: How professionals think in action.* New York: Basic Books.

Scientific notes and news. (1914, January 23). *Science, 39,* 136–138.

Short, K.G., Harste, J.C., & Burke, C.L. (1996). *Creating classrooms for authors and inquirers.* Portsmouth, NH: Heinemann.

Smith, F. (1997). Reading—from behind the eyes. In F. Smith, *Reading without nonsense* (pp. 10–30). New York: Teachers College Press.

Smith, N.B. (1986). *American reading instruction.* Newark, DE: International Reading Association. (Original work published 1965)

Snow, C.E., Burns, M.S., & Griffin, P. (Eds.). (1998). *Preventing reading difficulties in young children.* Washington, DC: National Academy Press.

Stanovich, K.E. (1986). Matthew effects in reading: Some consequences of individual differences in the acquisition of literacy. *Reading Research Quarterly*, *21*, 360–407.

Strauss, S.L. (2005). *The linguistics, neurology, and politics of phonics: Silent "E" speaks out.* Mahwah, NJ: Erlbaum.

United States Federal Census. (1910). Retrieved January 11, 2005, from http://ancestry.com

Vygotsky, L.S. (1978). *Mind in society: The development of higher psychological processes* (M. Cole, V. John-Steiner, S. Scribner, & E. Souberman, Eds. & Trans.). Cambridge, MA: Harvard University Press. (Original work published 1934)

Worcester, S. (1828). *A primer of the English language, for the use of families and schools* (Stereotyped ed.). Boston: Hilliard, Gray, Little & Wilkins.

Wundt, W.M. (1900). *Volkerpsychologie I.* Leipzig: Die Sprache.

FOR FURTHER READING

Clay, M.M. (1998). *By different paths to common outcomes.* York, ME: Stenhouse.

Dorn, L.J., & Soffos, C. (2001). *Shaping literate minds: Developing self-regulated learners.* Portland, ME: Stenhouse.

Krashen, S. (1993). *The power of reading: Insights from the research.* Englewood, CO: Libraries Unlimited.

Smith, F. (1988). *Joining the literacy club: Further essays into education.* Portsmouth, NH: Heinemann.

Weaver, C. (2002). *Reading process and practice* (3rd ed.). Portsmouth, NH: Heinemann.

CHAPTER 8

Laura Zirbes (1884–1967): A Premier Progressive Educator

By David W. Moore

Historical Research Process

I FIRST ENCOUNTERED Laura Zirbes's name while examining the beginnings of content area reading instruction. During an investigation of early 20th-century recommendations for reading and writing across the curriculum, I studied numerous reading education textbooks, professional association yearbooks, university monograph series, and journal articles of the time. While conducting this inquiry, I found Laura Zirbes's forthright advocacy of progressive education, which included linking reading instruction with subject matter instruction, to be remarkable. I cited her work as representing the progressive tradition in reading education (Moore, Readence, & Rickelman, 1983) and became interested in learning more about her.

Shaping the Reading Field: The Impact of Early Reading Pioneers, Scientific Research, and Progressive Ideas, edited by Susan E. Israel and E. Jennifer Monaghan. © 2007 by the International Reading Association.
Photo: Courtesy of the Association for Childhood Education International, Olney, Maryland.

When many of my reading education colleagues revealed only a limited knowledge of progressive reading education and practically no knowledge of Zirbes, I set out to explain her contributions to the field. I completed a brief intellectual history by spotlighting and contextualizing 32 of her more than 200 publications (Moore, 1986). Since then, noteworthy doctoral dissertations by Reid (1993) and Teel (2000) have contributed appreciably to my thinking about this extraordinary educator. My contention in my earlier report as well as here is that Zirbes's view of progressive reading education offers a productive reference point for examining other views; her conception of a sensible curriculum provides valuable perspective on today's reading curricula.

Personal and Professional Life

Born April 26, 1884, in Buffalo, New York, USA, Laura Zirbes spent her childhood in Sheboygan, Wisconsin, USA. (For a helpful chronology of Zirbes, see Reid, 1993, pp. 303–307.) The limited information available about her family reveals that she had a brother and sister (Teel, 2000, p. 118). Like many women of her generation who chose a career, she never married.

At the age of 14, Zirbes moved with her family to Cleveland, Ohio, USA, where her father served as pastor of the First German Baptist Church (Reid, 1993, pp. 48–49). Zirbes referred to her father a few times in her publications, telling how he left Catholic priesthood seminary training because he was harassed for disagreeing with the Church's teachings (Reid, 1993, pp. 48–49). On another occasion she told of his emotional goodbye while seeing her and her sister off to a trip to Europe (Teel, 2000, p. 118). In 1901 she completed a high school curriculum devoted to scientific and classical courses and graduated from the prestigious Central High School in Cleveland. Such a feat might seem somewhat commonplace today, but relatively few girls at the time completed a college preparation course of study and graduated from high school (Teel, 2000, pp. 76–81).

After her high school graduation, Zirbes entered the Cleveland Normal Training School and completed its teacher preparation program for the Cleveland public schools. She began teaching fourth grade in Cleveland at the age of 19. She later recounted two incidents with her teaching supervisors during her first year that characterize beliefs and principles she held throughout her career. After only a few weeks of teaching, she took her teacher's manual into her principal's office and informed him, "I didn't have to be told what to do by a book that was written by somebody I didn't know, and who never saw the children I was teaching" (as quoted in Reid, 1993, p. 23). She recalled that positive things happened in her classroom once she was allowed to put the manual aside, determine what the children needed in order to grow, and proceed straight for that growth (Reid, 1993, p. 23). The second incident involved arithmetic instruction. Zirbes retold this episode as follows:

> When I was still teaching in a fourth grade, I found a way of doing something about basic number learnings which enabled my pupils to make high test scores in arithmetic. The supervisor seemed to assume that those test scores were arrived at dishonestly. I was aware of her suspicion but said that I was not surprised at the high test results. I expected them to be high, because I thought what I was doing was better than what I had ever done before. When I explained what I had done and told her how I had deviated from procedures recommended in the course of study, she said, "My dear, you are too analytical." I wondered what was wrong about being analytical, but didn't say so. After reprimanding me for deviating from drill methods, she concluded her remarks by saying, "You certainly do not make a good cog." I could hardly believe my ears, I said, "Cog? Cog? I don't think the Lord intended me to be a cog!" (quoted in Teel, 2000, p. 93)

Zirbes requested to be transferred to a classroom where she was not expected to deliver cogwheeled teaching, so her superintendent assigned her to a class of slow learners where such teaching was failing. Once there, she began thoroughly documenting her innovative teaching practices and meticulously recording her students' test results so she could justify her actions to her new supervisor. Her supervisor turned out to be quite impressed and passed her records to Charles Hubbard Judd (see chapter 4, this volume), director of the University of Chicago's School of Education and a leading educational researcher. This led to the publication of her classroom report "Diagnostic Measurement as a Basis for Procedure" in *The Elementary School Journal* (Zirbes, 1918). Her report attracted attention by fusing the new scientific educational research procedures of the time, such as hypothesis testing and extensive data analyses, with emerging beliefs about child-centered instruction. Zirbes's findings supported her practices of accommodating individual differences by grouping students for instruction as well as emphasizing reading interests and attitudes along with achievement (Reid, 1993, pp. 27–31).

In 1920 Otis Caldwell, director of the Lincoln School of Teachers College, Columbia University, invited Zirbes to join his staff as a research associate (Reid, 1993, p. 31). Lincoln School was a well-funded and highly visible experimental center devoted to identifying effective instruction. Zirbes's professional identity flourished there as evidenced by her service on the National Society for the Study of Education's (NSSE) National Committee on Reading as well as her service on the National Education Association's Commission on the Curriculum Subcommittee on Reading. She wrote chapters for the NSSE's 24th yearbook on providing for individual differences, administering reading tests, and diagnosing and remediating reading problems (Whipple, 1925, pp. x, 227–289). She also served as an assistant editor of the *Journal of Educational Psychology* and the *Journal of Educational Research*.

During the time she was working as a research associate at Lincoln School, Zirbes enrolled as a student at Teachers College, eventually becoming a lecturer there while earning her bachelor's degree in 1925, master's degree in 1926, and doctoral degree in 1928. She interacted with the illustrious Columbia University educators of the time, such as John Dewey, Arthur Irving Gates (see chapter 14, this volume), William Heard Kilpatrick, and Edward Lee Thorndike (see chapter 5, this volume). She also began a long period of collaboration with the University of Chicago's William Scott Gray (see chapter 13, this volume). Her doctoral dissertation, "Comparative Studies of Current Practice in Reading, with Techniques for the Improvement of Teaching," was published as a *Teachers College Contributions to Education* (Zirbes, 1928a). Her dissertation was an important work, analyzing more than 600 reading research reports conducted since the turn of the century and framing their findings according to a progressive philosophy and set of beliefs.

Upon earning her doctorate in 1928, Zirbes joined The Ohio State University faculty. She contributed substantially to the elementary education program at Ohio State, which was called the Department of Principles and Practices when she arrived (Teel, 2000, p. 124), serving as the first permanent faculty member specializing in this area and helping to restructure the program and form it into a hub of progressive education (Reid, 1993, pp. 74–92). At the same time, she published widely on reading in scholarly journals and even turned her attention to writing for children, authoring or coauthoring five nonfiction children's books between 1926 and 1939.

Throughout her time at Ohio State, Zirbes maintained her early interests in and convictions about reading instruction while expanding her attention to other fields. For instance, she held several leadership positions within the Progressive Education Association (PEA). As this group declined and eventually dissolved in 1955, she became active in the Association for Supervision and Curriculum Development and the Association for Childhood Education International (ACEI), chairing the Board of Editors of this group's premier journal, *Childhood Education* (Reid, 1993, pp. 180–202). Interestingly, she never joined the International Reading Association—or its parent organizations prior to the Association's formation in 1956—disdaining a perceived narrowness in the Association and all other educational associations devoted to a single school subject (Reid, 1993, p. 265). She once told a friend that she stopped being a reading specialist right after publishing her dissertation in 1928 (Reid, 1993, p. 198), and she published only three articles in *The Reading Teacher* during her career (Zirbes, 1951, 1961, 1963).

In 1948 President Truman presented Zirbes with the National Women's Press Club's Woman of the Year Award for achievement in education, calling her a "teacher of teachers" (Reid, 1993, p. 109). In addition, the ACEI placed Zirbes's name on the Roll of Honor that the association displays in its Washington, DC, headquarters to recognize the outstanding accomplishments of selected people in childhood education. Zirbes retired from Ohio State as professor emeritus in 1954. Perhaps her most significant publication, *Spurs to Creative Teaching*, appeared in 1959. Stauffer's 1960 review of this book for *The Reading Teacher* characterizes it as follows:

> The many students who have sat at her feet, as well as the many, many more who have heard her lecture only a time or two, will recognize immediately the Laura Zirbes they admire and respect. She has written this, her book, with the sparkle, the warmth, and the soundness of an astute person who has lived a life dedicated to the proposition that man is creative by nature and that good teaching fosters courageous initiative or creative self-direction. (Stauffer, 1960, p. 315)

Zirbes remained a popular speaker after her retirement (Reid, 1993, pp. 314–319). She died on June 9, 1967, at the age of 83 in Columbus, Ohio, USA.

Philosophical Beliefs and Guiding Principles

Laura Zirbes was shaped by and helped shape many of the beliefs and principles espoused by progressive U.S. educators during the early 1900s. Her reaction against mechanistic, prescribed instruction as a first-year teacher suggests that she was predisposed toward progressive approaches, and she associated with progressive luminaries such as John Dewey and William Heard Kilpatrick during her formative experiences at the Lincoln School and Teachers College (Reid, 1993, pp. 38–41). Articles such as "Progressive Practice in Reading" (Zirbes, 1928b) and "Progressive Training for Elementary Teachers" (Zirbes, 1929a), along with her 1930 to 1942 Executive Committee service for the PEA (Reid, 1993, p. 183), attest to her unequivocal self-identification as a progressive educator. However, simply connecting Zirbes with progressivism does not describe her beliefs and principles because progressivism was not a unitary, cohesive system. Progressive educators promoted ideas ranging from individual freedom and social reconstruction to social efficiency and centralized school administration (Cremin, 1961).

Characterizing Zirbes's progressivism is knotty because she aspired to integration, enmeshing her thoughts and actions organically (Reid, 1993, p. 122). Pulling out separate pieces from her writings runs the risk of misrepresenting their ecological connections. Nevertheless, it seems safe to say that Zirbes adhered to a specific mode of progressivism that reacted against traditional reading instruction emphases on declamation, rote learning, and the literary canon. A personal statement she wrote at age 82 in a letter to a close friend mentions some key ideas that stand out as a fitting encapsulation of her beliefs and principles:

> While...many of those whom I was privileged to teach have *become* leaders, there is a new "breed" which is alien to them in midcareer, and alien to the faith in a creative developmental, personalized approach, which characterizes dedicated teachers. (cited in Reid, 1993, p. 311)

Zirbes's emphasis here on teaching indicates her lifelong focus and perhaps her greatest contribution. She took pride in her undergraduate teaching and graduate student advising at Ohio State as well as in her guest presentations, explaining how to enact progressive principles with groups of real children. She continually inquired into elementary school classroom concerns, maintaining a questioning perspective and seeking to find ways to best educate particular classrooms of children (Teel, 2000, pp. 171–172).

During the beginnings of the development of the elementary education program at Ohio State, Zirbes forthrightly stated that she intended to develop "a training program based upon a practical interpretation of progressive educational ideals" (Zirbes, 1929a, p. 250). She attended to her undergraduate teacher preparation classes and workshops passionately, always working to improve them. When her numerous graduate-level students and advisees campaigned to place her on the ACEI Roll of Honor, they characterized her with terms such as "one of the truly outstanding educators of our country" (Reid, 1993, p. 95) and "one of the most inspiring teachers that I was privileged to have" (p. 96), also saying that "she exemplified the highest quality as an educator" (p. 97). President Truman's citation of her as a teacher of teachers seems apt. In the excerpt from her letter cited previously, Zirbes's reference to a creative approach to teaching spotlights her beliefs about the importance of inventiveness and originality. She abhorred preset, lockstep, cogwheeled teaching, believing that it robbed learners as well as teachers of essential opportunities to form important understandings and attitudes.

Along this line, Zirbes continually advocated experimentation (Teel, 2000, pp. 123–173). She regularly tested ideas and instructional approaches, and she encouraged teachers to do the same. Indeed, she launched her career in academia by investigating and reporting her innovative classroom teaching practices with slow learners (Zirbes, 1918). She also tested workshop approaches to teaching, examining through trial and error how best to conduct small-group inquiries before recommending them to others.

Zirbes's adherence to creativity is also evident in her pioneering work with the technological innovations of her time, such as her use in the 1920s of lantern slides and stereographs to develop children's concepts (Zirbes, 1924b) and in the 1940s of voice recordings to present case studies, lectures, and panel discussions during professional development sessions (Reid, 1993, p. 87). Interestingly, one voice recording on education and mental health that was meant for Parent Teacher Association discussions contained an evaluation sheet for assessing how the session had gone in order to inform future sessions. Another aspect of creativity that Zirbes adhered to involved the arts (Klohr, 1996). She regularly infused the visual arts, music, dance, and drama into her teaching, and she expected teachers to do the same. She believed that intellectual and artistic processes were complementary.

In the personal letter excerpted earlier, Zirbes's mention of a developmental, personalized approach to teaching indicates her bedrock beliefs and principles. In line with the child-study research of G. Stanley Hall and Arnold Gesell, Zirbes believed that children progress through stages of growth characterized by emerging abilities to accomplish increasingly complex tasks. She also believed that children progress through these stages according to their own timetables and that educators should expect groups of children to display individual differences. Along with these realizations supported by scientific research, Zirbes held a deep, personal ethic of caring for each child as a unique individual (Reid, 1993, pp. 122–127). In brief, Zirbes's philosophical beliefs and guiding principles can be characterized in large part as a commitment to furnishing creative, developmental, and personalized attention to children's education. These beliefs and principles are apparent in her professional contributions to reading education.

Contributions to the Field of Reading

Laura Zirbes was first and foremost an educator. Her contributions to the field of reading mainly involve her applications of progressive thought to the goals and methods of elementary school reading instruction as well as elementary teacher education.

Goals of Reading Instruction

Zirbes regularly scorned reading programs that emphasized skill development over other important goals, advocating balanced reading development as the goal of instruction long before contemporary educators such as Pressley (2002) and Reutzel and Cooter (1999)—to name a few—began supporting it during the turn of the 21st century. As Zirbes wrote in the late 1920s, "We still find the market filled with prescriptive material for class room work in reading which ride roughshod over relative values and justifies itself in heightened power at the expense of all round, balanced growth" (1928b, p. 102). The goal of balanced reading growth that she prized combined skills with concepts, attitudes, and values (Moore, 1986).

Zirbes viewed reading as a vital tool for developing readers' concepts. Many educators considered that teaching students how to read to learn was appropriate only in the upper grades, but she embedded such reading in the lower grades: "Reading in the progressive classrooms of today begins not only with experience, but enriches experience by serving as a stimulus to creative expression and by concerning itself with content as well as skills" (Zirbes, 1928b, pp. 99–100). Zirbes advocated the use of informational texts in elementary schools so children could learn about the world while learning how to read. Evidence of her partiality to this type of reading material comes from the children's books she wrote or co-wrote throughout her career. All six of the children's books she produced were informational:

1. *The Story of Milk, for Boys and Girls Who Have Just Learned to Read* (Zirbes & Wesley, 1926)

2. *Workers: Written for Boys and Girls Who Want to Read About the Busy World* (Zirbes & Wesley, 1928)

3. *Animal Tales: True Stories for Boys and Girls Who Like to Read About Animals* (Keliher in collaboration with Zirbes, 1930)

4. *Little Journeys With Washington* (Zirbes, 1932a)

5. *The Book of Pets, for Boys and Girls Learning to Read* (Zirbes & Keliher, 1928)

6. *How Many Bears?* (Zirbes, 1960)

Along with concept development, Zirbes considered positive attitudes toward reading to be a legitimate instructional goal. She focused on students' feelings toward reading along with their abilities because she realized the connection: "Certain reading procedures which build skills at the expense of attitude have been prevalent and they too often eventuate by defeating their own ends" (Zirbes, 1925, p. 864). She acted on the belief that emphasizing skill over will was counterproductive. Moreover, Zirbes valued reading for what it could offer throughout a lifetime. She believed that those who would not read were as disadvantaged as those who could not read. She emphasized the power as well as the pleasure of reading: "If you are teaching reading creatively and developmentally, you are introducing children to satisfaction that will enrich their whole lives" (Zirbes, 1959, p. 172).

Zirbes also believed that developing students' personal values was an important goal of instruction. For example, she supplied The Ohio State University School's youngsters with cumbersome wooden blocks that were one- and two-feet square so the children playing with them would learn the value of cooperation along with geometric size relations (Reid, 1993, p. 146). In a manner similar to many of today's character education programs, she also advocated reading selections for children that portrayed desirable character traits such as respect and responsibility. And realizing that children developed their personalities through time, she planned active and purposeful reading engagements so children would become active and purposeful inside and outside of class with other activities. As she put it, "The modern reading program finds its true realization and justification in the contribution it makes to the development of personalities" (Zirbes, 1940, p. 155). In brief, the goals of reading instruction are malleable. U.S. schools over the years have emphasized reading as a means of achieving religious, moral, civic, and workforce ideals (Smith, 2002). Part of Laura Zirbes's contributions to the field of reading was in fleshing out how progressive thought informed the goals of reading instruction. Her application of creativity, developmentalism, and personalization led to the goal of balancing reading growth relative to skills, concepts, attitudes, and values.

Methods of Reading Instruction

Zirbes's applications of progressive thought to the methods of classroom reading instruction were consistent with her goals. The record of her teaching and publications shows the goal of balanced reading development being achieved largely through the methods of purposeful activity, functional instruction, language arts integration, and wide reading (Moore, 1986).

Purposeful activity. Traditional reading activities prior to the early 1900s mainly consisted of oral readings and recalls of texts (Cuban, 1993; Finkelstein, 1989). Although some reading texts of the time provided questions with the passages, and some of the questions required students to go beyond rote recall (Venezky, 1987), children generally were expected to reconstruct as faithfully as possible what the author wrote by reading aloud accurately and recalling text verbatim. As progressive thought began permeating classrooms, reading activities began to include more and more thinking about textual contents. Rather than being told to "speak distinctly and mind your stops" (Corson, 1895, p. 811), students were directed to read silently to "see how the story ends...see how many persons would be needed to play the story" or "find out whether the story could be true" (Zirbes, 1929b, pp. 95–96). Contemporary attention to reading as understanding "has been largely a feature of the twentieth century" (Monaghan & Saul, 1987, p. 88).

Expecting children to read and infer underlying ideas, rather than read and memorize surface details, was a substantial advance in terms of purposeful, meaningful activity, and having students answer thought-provoking questions after reading became a dominant mode of instruction. Zirbes's contribution to this type of reading is evident in her coauthored publication "Practice Exercises and Checks on Silent Reading in the Primary Grade" (Zirbes, Keelor, & Miner, 1927) that recommended the following types of questions for checking second-grade readers:

1. Yes–no questions
2. Questions of fact
3. Questions that involve judgment or interpretation
4. Questions that show a realization of sequence or organization
5. Questions that involve comprehension of correct relationship (between facts or phrases)
6. Questions to ascertain whether probable or possible answers are recognized when in contradiction to content or story
7. Questions in which the response leads to or indicates appreciation
8. Questions involving the assembling of a series of replies to a single question, to lead to thoroughness of comprehension and complete replies. (p. 45)

Pinpointing the cognitive processes that these types of questions tap is difficult without seeing the stimulus passages as well as the responses considered acceptable. On the surface, however, these questions seem to range along Bloom's revised taxonomy (Anderson & Krathwohl, 2001) from remembering (questions of fact) to creating (questions involving the assembling of a series of replies to lead to complete replies). In addition, this 1927 report reveals Zirbes's early advocacy of children reading short passages and then answering questions. Durkin's (1978/1979) landmark report of classroom observations 50 years later revealed the prevalence of this question-answering, comprehension-checking approach to reading instruction. Although contemporary constructivist perspectives (Kintsch, 2004) and sociocognitive perspectives (Gee, 2004) point to the shortcomings of this approach, it deserves credit for enhancing previous instructional activities.

Further, while initially believing that thought-provoking questions about short passages stimulated purposeful activity, Zirbes later pioneered new, more purposeful activity in the form of projects. She spent time with William Heard Kilpatrick at Teachers College and noted in one of her early publications that he was one of her "sources of insight and inspiration" (1924a, p.

150). Kilpatrick's (1918) well-known project method, which involved "wholehearted purposeful activity" (p. 320), involved children in self-directed inquiry projects, which Zirbes eventually promoted actively. According to Zirbes (1932b), "There is a vast difference between purposeful reading and assigned reading. The teacher who begins by saying, 'Now I want you to do thus and so,' is not getting purposeful reading. We must guide the reader to set up purposes for himself" (p. 6). Purposeful activity also played a role in Zirbes's elementary teacher preparation courses at The Ohio State University. Moving away from traditional lectures, assignments, and tests, she moved toward workshops that involved a "practical, hands on, analytical, problem-solving approach in which students were involved in group work for some common purpose" (Reid, 1993, p. 76). Moreover, preservice teachers at Ohio State were expected to visit social agencies such as orphanages and hospitals as well as recreational sites like summer camps and playgrounds to deepen their understandings of children's overall growth and development while engaged in purposeful activity (Reid, 1993, pp. 78–80).

During her years at Ohio State, Zirbes emphasized purposeful learning in all areas of the curriculum, advocating it for mathematics, science, and social studies as much as for reading and writing. She rejected skill instruction for its own sake, calling for instruction to be embedded in bona fide, relevant experiences and projects. Her celebrated advocacy of purposeful learning across the curriculum was one reason why Tanner and Tanner (1995) assert that she was "one of the pioneering women in the curriculum field" (p. 634).

Functional instruction. Zirbes opposed preset, systematic programs that were designed without knowledge of specific children, yet stipulated what they were to read, when they were to read, and what instruction they were to receive. As far as she was concerned, limiting reading instruction to a certain segment of the day disintegrated opportunities for effective instruction. She reported one incident that expressed her concerns well:

> I am thinking of a teaching situation where a teacher had used decorations to make the whole class-room radiate a Christmas spirit. There were Christmas pictures—one a Santa Claus—cutouts, chains and evergreens. It was just before Christmas and the children were flooded with Christmas, when she said, "Now children, forget all about Christmas and take out your readers; we are going to read *The Gray Cat* today." (Zirbes, 1932b, pp. 5–6)

In line with the celebrated progressive notion of teachable moments, Zirbes advocated functional instruction. She espoused the idea of involving children in purposeful activities and then providing appropriate resources and guidance as needed. She supported reading instruction that occurred across the curriculum, not just during a time set aside for it, and that provided specific instruction according to what students required to accomplish projects (Zirbes, 1928b).

Arguing against radical beliefs in a laissez faire approach, where children discovered knowledge entirely on their own, Zirbes championed guidance. Yet she believed that guidance needed to be contextualized functionally in purposeful activity. According to Zirbes, progressive practice "grants that there are places for specific training, but those places are on the way to broader outcomes, and should be determined with reference to specific needs and uses" (Zirbes, 1928a, p. 47).

Zirbes's commitment to functional instruction was firm. Even though she and William S. Gray had collaborated on the renowned 24th yearbook of the NSSE (Whipple, 1925), along with two other substantive projects (Gray & Zirbes, 1927–1928a, 1927–1928b), she declined several of his invitations to coauthor a basal reader program (Moore, 1986, p. 667). When she reviewed the 37th NSSE yearbook that Gray chaired, she criticized its "abiding and unquestioning faith in the 'systematic introduction of skills in an orderly arrangement of successively difficult steps'" (Zirbes, 1937, p. 221). She pointed out the yearbook's failure to present functional instruction, an alternative to systematic skills instruction.

Interestingly, in a 1949 interview Gray invoked the significance of progressivism with these words: "The formal instruction of previous decades no longer exists in classrooms which have adopted progressive methods. Instruction is highly motivated, carefully planned, and well adjusted to the varying needs and problems of children" (Robinson, 2005, p. 436). Despite this acknowledgment of progressivism, Gray's systematic views on when reading instruction should occur differed from Zirbes's functional views.

Language arts integration. Integrating language arts instruction is a predictable step for someone who advocated balanced development. As Zirbes (1940) put it, "Reading is to be conceived and treated as an integral phase or aspect of total language development" (p. 152). She early and often promoted instructional situations that included reading, writing, listening, and speaking. During the beginning of her career, she published illustrative units of problem-based instruction that connected the language arts (Zirbes, 1924a); later in her career, she helped break new ground by contributing to the language experience approach to beginning reading (Zirbes, 1951). Along this line, she had very little to say about initial reading instruction at the word level even in her pioneering article on language experience. She advocated the language experience approach's whole-to-part progression of examining words and their parts but recommended practically no additional practices beyond that. Especially after moving to The Ohio State University, she approached reading broadly, focusing on issues such as meaning, purpose, and value. She disdained basal readers that approached reading narrowly, focusing on the compilation of discrete phonic skills and sight words.

Project and experience approaches to instruction are similar in their emphases on student-centered, purposeful activity as well as on language arts connections. In addition, these approaches typically involve artistic and media representations, two forms of expression Zirbes frequently included in her instruction (Klohr, 1996). To illustrate, in the projects she designed for a health textbook (Bigelow & Broadhurst, 1924), Zirbes called for children to mount pictures from old magazines as a speech prop and to produce a safety-related picture book that included rules under each picture. When referring to the language experience approach, she noted its direct link with children's speech as well as its tendency to promote "dramatic play, vivid group discussion, and creative expression in various media" (Zirbes, 1951, p. 1).

Wide reading. At the middle of the 20th century, Zirbes (1950) reported that the new abundance of children's reading materials was "an educational achievement of note" (p. 2). She appreciated children's literature for its role in balanced development, believing that selections written at different levels of difficulty and addressing different topics provided children with optimal opportunities to grow. Wide reading necessarily occurred in classrooms in which children participated in projects. Children at different levels of proficiency inquiring into different topics required access to varied materials. Zirbes had great faith in the power of diverse materials to enable children to learn new vocabulary and ideas, develop positive feelings about books, enrich understandings of what was important to people, and increase reading proficiencies (Moore, 1986).

While Zirbes generally supported multiple materials being available, she had a special preference for informational books. As noted earlier, the children's books she wrote addressed animals, milk, and workers, presenting information about the world to children in an accessible fashion, and she recommended such materials for primary as well as higher grade levels. In addition, she championed meaningful materials that contributed to growth. In contrast with many of the book-buying public, she had particular disgust for Dr. Seuss' book *The Cat in the Hat* (Seuss, 1957) because of its nonsensical content and language and what she considered to be a "blatant attempt to write what would sell rather than what would be good for children" (cited in Reid, 1993, p. 147).

In sum, Zirbes's contributions to reading education involve her reading instruction goals that balanced skills with concepts, attitudes, and values. The methods of reading instruction that she advocated—purposeful activity, functional instruction, language arts integration, and wide reading—are additional professional offerings.

Lessons for the Future

Table 1, titled *Contemporary Reading Instruction Compared With Progressive Reading Instruction*, matches a recent U.S. survey's selected summary of actual present-day instruction (Baumann, Hoffman, Duffy-Hester, & Ro, 2000) with progressive recommendations for such instruction as articulated in this study of Laura Zirbes. Comparing contemporary elementary school reading instruction with progressive recommendations for such instruction provides perspective on the present and generates ideas for the future.

Table 1 shows that recent elementary school teachers and administrators generally embrace a balanced, eclectic set of philosophy and goals. Although this finding seems similar to progressive ideals, closer analysis reveals that the survey respondents were advocating a relatively narrow view of balance. They embraced goals such as "(a) to develop readers who are skillful and strategic in word identification, fluency, and reading comprehension and (b) to develop readers who are independent and motivated to choose, appreciate, and enjoy literature" (Baumann et al. 2000, p. 349). Progressive educators such as Zirbes probably would applaud the inclusion of skills and attitudes among the goals of reading instruction, but progressives likely would add concepts and values. As this chapter shows, Zirbes advocated reading selections and activities that would improve children's understandings of the world and enhance their regard for desirable personal values.

TABLE 1
TABLE 1
Contemporary Reading Instruction Compared With Progressive Reading Instruction

Category	Contemporary Reading Instruction	Progressive Reading Instruction
Philosophy and goals	• Balanced, eclectic perspective pervaded • Major theme of systematic instruction in decoding along with a literature-rich environment • Common goal was to produce skillful, fluent, motivated, independent readers	Balanced development based on • concepts • attitudes • values • skills
Instructional time and materials	• Considerable time dedicated to reading and language arts instruction and activities • Basals and trade books used in combination	• Purposeful activity • Functional instruction • Language arts integration • Wide reading

She viewed reading not as a destination by itself but as a vehicle for significant personal and social outcomes.

The table also shows recent elementary school teachers and administrators reporting "considerable time" being dedicated to reading and language arts instruction and activities. Closer analysis here reveals that on average 55 minutes per day is dedicated to teacher-directed strategy instruction; 42 minutes per day to applying and extending instruction in activities such as read alouds, sustained silent reading, and student led response groups; and 46 minutes per day to language arts instruction such as writing workshops, oral language activities, and spelling (Baumann et al., 2000, p. 350). Basals and trade books are said to be used in combination. Progressive educators like Zirbes probably would acknowledge today's apparent language arts integration and wide reading as appropriate, but they likely would raise questions about purposeful activity and functional instruction. Are today's children engaged only in assigned reading? When do they read for their own purposes? Do children inquire into issues and topics they find relevant and appealing? Are reading and language arts skills presented systematically or functionally?

Historical knowledge can inform people's views of the present (Moore, Monaghan, & Hartman, 1997). As this brief comparison between contemporary instruction and progressive recommendations shows, history can produce alternative views of mainstream practices and initiate possible directions for the future. Educators committed to the progressive value of purposeful activity might teach against the grain of dominant practice by incorporating inquiry projects. They might become politically active and advocate progressive educational policies at the local, state, and national levels. To be sure, educators can assess the present with historical standards other than progressive ones. Other historical points of view provide touchstones for viewing the present. Notwithstanding the possibilities of multiple perspectives on a topic, the central lesson of this report is this: Knowing where people have been sheds light on knowing where people might go.

Further analyses of Zirbes's exemplification of progressive reading instruction might set her contributions among those with similar beliefs and principles. To illustrate, foundations of education analyses frequently portray a series of well-known thinkers such as Froebel, Rousseau, Pestalozzi, Spencer, Dewey, Hall, and Piaget, to name a few, who articulated progressive philosophical beliefs and guiding principles (Egan, 2002). The fluctuation of these beliefs and principles in the U.S. reading curricula is evident over the years in the approach Laura Zirbes espoused as well as in the language experience (see, e.g., Allen, 1976; Lamoreaux & Lee, 1943), individualized reading (see, e.g., Fader, 1968; Veatch, 1959), and whole language approaches (see, e.g., Edelsky, Altwerger, & Flores, 1991; Goodman, 1986). Additional historical analyses might examine the social, cultural, and political conditions contributing to the emergence and demise of these specific approaches that are grounded in a common ideology.

In Laura Zirbes's 1966 personal statement cited earlier, wherein at age 82 she wrote about herself to a close friend, she included this commentary:

> I am beginning to conclude that education is going through a new and disconcerting *regressive* movement, at the same time that dynamic leadership could be moving things *ahead*. Where is that leadership? What can be done to challenge the young potential leaders whose insights and concerns could lead to a breakthrough and true advance? As for me, I am assumed to be wedded to the past, and am counted out by those who see themselves as innovators even when they are exponents of obsolete ideas. While I *am still a pioneer*...I know that *my* place is on the sidelines after

over 60 years of active involvement. (quoted in Reid, 1993, pp. 310–311; emphases in the original)

After breaking new ground for six decades as a progressive educator, Laura Zirbes rightfully considered herself to be a pioneer. Publicly including her among the ranks of early reading pioneers in this volume is a well-deserved honor.

Reflection Questions

1. What would Zirbes have contributed to the whole language approach to reading instruction that crested in the United States during the 1990s?
2. How would Zirbes react to the No Child Left Behind Act of 2001?
3. What other lessons for the future can be generated from this study of Zirbes?
4. Why is Zirbes not better known among today's reading educators?
5. Is there anyone who is enacting an educational role today that is similar to the role Zirbes enacted?

REFERENCES

Allen, R.V. (1976). *Language experiences in communication.* Boston: Houghton Mifflin.

Anderson, L.W., & Krathwohl, D.R. (2001). *A taxonomy for learning, teaching, and assessing.* New York: Longman.

Baumann, J.F., Hoffman, J.V., Duffy-Hester, A., & Ro, J.M. (2000). "The First R" yesterday and today: U.S. elementary reading instruction practices reported by teachers and administrators. *Reading Research Quarterly, 35,* 338–377.

Bigelow, M.A., & Broadhurst, J. (1924). *Health for every day.* New York: Silver Burdett.

Corson, H. (1895). Vocal culture in its relation to literary culture. *Atlantic Monthly, 75,* 810–816.

Cremin, L. (1961). *The transformation of the school: Progressivism in American education, 1876–1957.* New York: Knopf.

Cuban, L. (1993). *How teachers taught: Constancy and change in American classrooms, 1890–1990* (2nd ed.). New York: Teachers College Press.

Durkin, D. (1978/1979). What classroom observation reveals about reading comprehension instruction. *Reading Research Quarterly, 15,* 481–533.

Edelsky, C., Altwerger, B., & Flores, B. (1991). *Whole language: What's the difference?* Portsmouth, NH: Heinemann.

Egan, K. (2002). *Getting it wrong from the beginning: Our progressivist inheritance from Herbert Spencer, John Dewey, and Jean Piaget.* New Haven, CT: Yale University Press.

Fader, D. (1968). *Hooked on books.* New York: Putnam.

Finkelstein, B. (1989). *Governing the young: Teacher behavior in popular primary schools in the nineteenth century United States.* Philadelphia: Falmer.

Gee, J.P. (2004). Reading as situated language: A sociocognitive perspective. In R.B. Ruddell & N.J. Unrau (Eds.), *Theoretical models and processes of reading* (5th ed., pp. 116–132). Newark, DE: International Reading Association.

Goodman, K.S. (1986). *What's whole in whole language?* Portsmouth, NH: Heinemann.

Gray, W.S., & Zirbes, L. (1927–1928a). Primary reading. In M.B. Hillegas (Ed.), *The classroom teacher* (Vol. 2, pp. 39–386). Chicago: Classroom Teacher.

Gray, W.S., & Zirbes, L. (1927–1928b). Reading in the intermediate grades. In M.B. Hillegas (Ed.), *The classroom teacher* (Vol. 6, pp. 81–282). Chicago: Classroom Teacher.

Keliher, A.V., in collaboration with Zirbes, L. (1930). *Animal tales: True stories for boys and girls who like to read about animals.* Meadville, PA: Keystone View.

Kilpatrick, W.H. (1918). The project method. *Teachers College Record, 19,* 319–335.

Kintsch, W. (2004). The construction-integration model of text comprehension and its implications for instruction. In R.B. Ruddell & N.J. Unrau (Eds.), *Theoretical models and processes of reading* (5th ed., pp. 1270–1328). Newark, DE: International Reading Association.

Klohr, P.R. (1996). Laura Zirbes: A teacher of teachers. In C. Kridel, R.V. Bullough, Jr., & P. Shaker (Eds.), *Teachers and mentors: Profiles of distinguished twentieth-century professors of education* (pp. 139–145). New York: Garland.

Lamoreaux, D., & Lee, D.M. (1943). *Learning to read through experience.* New York: Appleton-Century-Crofts.

Monaghan, E.J., & Saul, E.W. (1987). The reader, the scribe, the thinker: A critical look at the history of American reading and writing instruction. In T.S. Popkewitz (Ed.), *The formation of school subjects: The struggle for creating an American institution* (pp. 85–122). Philadelphia: Falmer.

Moore, D.W. (1986). Laura Zirbes and progressive reading instruction. *The Elementary School Journal, 86,* 663–672.

Moore, D.W., Monaghan, E.J., & Hartman, D.K. (1997). Conversations: Values of literacy history. *Reading Research Quarterly, 32,* 90–102.

Moore, D.W., Readence, J.E., & Rickelman, R.J. (1983). An historical exploration of content area reading instruction. *Reading Research Quarterly, 18,* 419–438.

No Child Left Behind Act of 2001, Pub. L. No. 107-110, 115 Stat. 1425 (2002).

Pressley, M. (2002). *Reading instruction that works: The case for balanced teaching* (2nd ed.). New York: Guilford.

Reid, T. (1993). Towards creative teaching: The life and career of Laura Zirbes, 1884–1967. *Dissertation Abstracts International, 54* (07), 2460. (UMI No. 9400268)

Reutzel, D.R., & Cooter, R.B., Jr. (1999). *Balanced reading strategies and practices.* Upper Saddle River, NJ: Merrill Prentice Hall.

Robinson, R. (2005). Changes in the teaching of reading. *Reading Psychology, 26,* 433–440. (Reprinted from *School and Community,* September 1949, *35,* pp. 262–265, 267)

Seuss, Dr. (1957). *The cat in the hat.* New York: Random House.

Smith, N.B. (2002). *American reading instruction: Special edition.* Newark, DE: International Reading Association.

Stauffer, R.G. (1960). Thank you! [Review of *Spurs to creative teaching*]. *The Reading Teacher, 13,* 315.

Tanner, D., & Tanner, L. (1995). *Curriculum development: Theory into practice* (3rd ed.). Englewood Cliffs, NJ: Prentice Hall.

Teel, J. (2000). Laura Zirbes (1884–1967): An American progressive in an era of education conservatism. *Dissertation Abstracts International, 61* (11), 4280. (UMI No. 9993653).

Veatch, J. (1959). *Individualizing your reading program.* New York: G.P. Putnam's Sons.

Venezky, R.L. (1987). A history of the American reading textbook. *The Elementary School Journal, 87,* 246–265.

Whipple, G.M. (Ed.). (1925). *Report of the National Committee on Reading* (24th yearbook of the National Society for the Study of Education). Bloomington, IL: Public School Publishing.

Zirbes, L. (1918). Diagnostic measurement as a basis for procedure. *The Elementary School Journal, 18,* 205–522.

Zirbes, L. (1924a). *Illustrative units of reading activities for all grades or growth stages, with pertinent problems and reference readings* (Experimental ed.). New York: Columbia University, Teachers College.

Zirbes, L . (1924b). The relation of visual aids to educational objectives. In National Education Association of the United States, *Addresses and proceedings of the second annual meeting* (pp. 964–966). Washington, DC: National Educational Association.

Zirbes, L. (1925). Attacking the causes of reading deficiency. *Teachers College Record, 26,* 856–866.

Zirbes, L. (1928a). *Comparative studies of current practice in reading, with techniques for the improvement of teaching* (Teachers College Contributions to Education, No. 316). New York: Columbia University, Teachers College.

Zirbes, L. (1928b). Progressive practice in reading. *Progressive Education, 5,* 99–103.

Zirbes, L. (1929a). Progressive training for elementary teachers. *Educational Research Bulletin, 8,* 248–251.

Zirbes, L. (1929b). Purposeful reading. *Educational Research Bulletin, 8,* 94–97, 102–105.

Zirbes, L. (1932a). *Little journeys with Washington.* Richmond, VA: Johnson.

Zirbes, L. (1932b). Present practices in teaching reading as they affect child development. In A. Temple (Ed.), *A better beginning in reading for young children* (Bulletin of the Association for Early Childhood Education) (pp. 2–7). Washington, DC: Association for Early Childhood Education.

Zirbes, L. (1937). [Review of *The teaching of reading: A second report*]. *Curriculum Journal, 8,* 220–221.

Zirbes, L. (1940). What is a modern reading program? *Educational Method, 20,* 151–155.

Zirbes, L. (1950). *What is wrong with today's reading instruction?* Columbus: Ohio State University Press.

Zirbes, L. (1951). The experience approach in reading. *Bulletin of the International Council for the Improvement of Reading Instruction, 5*(2), 1–16.

Zirbes, L. (1959). *Spurs to creative teaching.* New York: Putnam.

Zirbes, L. (1960). *How many bears?* New York: Putnam.

Zirbes, L. (1961). Spurs to reading competence. *The Reading Teacher, 15,* 14–18.

Zirbes, L. (1963). The developmental approach to reading. *The Reading Teacher, 16,* 347–352.

Zirbes, L., Keelor, K., & Miner, P. (1927). *Practice exercises and checks on silent reading in the primary grade: Reports of experimentation.* New York: Columbia University, Teachers College.

Zirbes, L., & Keliher, A.V. (1928). *The book of pets, for boys and girls learning to read.* Meadville, PA: Keystone View.

Zirbes, L., & Wesley, M. (1926). *The story of milk, for boys and girls who have just learned to read.* Meadville, PA: Keystone View.

Zirbes, L., & Wesley, M.J. (1928). *Workers: Written for boys and girls who want to read about the busy world.* Meadville, PA: Keystone View.

FOR FURTHER READING

Cavanaugh, M.P. (1994). *A history of holistic literacy: Five major educators.* Westport, CT: Praeger.

Harris, A.J. (1964). Progressive education and reading instruction. *The Reading Teacher, 18*, 128–138.

Jacobs, L.B. (1967). Dedication to Laura Zirbes. *Childhood Education, 44*, 210–211, 216–217.

Shannon, P. (1990). *The struggle to continue: Progressive reading instruction in the United States.* Portsmouth, NH: Heinemann.

Zilversmit, A. (1993). *Changing schools: Progressive education theory and practice, 1930–1960.* Chicago: University of Chicago Press.

PART IV

The Book Enthusiasts: Pioneers Engaged in Exploring Children's Books and Adult Reading

CHAPTER 9

May Hill Arbuthnot (1884–1969): A Pioneer in the Field of Children's Literature

By Charles Monaghan, Susan E. Israel, and Molly D. Dahl

Historical Research Process

RESEARCH FOR THIS chapter, mainly conducted by Susan E. Israel, came from a variety of sources. The Internet provided material related to May Hill Arbuthnot's work and employment. The bulk of information came from follow-up inquiries to the archives of Case Western University, successor to Western Reserve University, where Arbuthnot taught from 1927 to 1946. Among the items provided by Case Western were autobiographical forms that Arbuthnot had filled out. In them, Arbuthnot said she had received her

Shaping the Reading Field: The Impact of Early Reading Pioneers, Scientific Research, and Progressive Ideas, edited by Susan E. Israel and E. Jennifer Monaghan. © 2007 by the International Reading Association.
Photo: Property of Case Western Reserve University Archives.

master's degree (under her maiden name, May Hill) from Columbia University in 1924. A problem appeared when it was discovered there was no record of such a degree in the class of 1924. Could this esteemed teacher have falsified such information? It turned out, on further inquiries to Columbia University, that the degree had been awarded in 1925. Filling out the form 14 years later, Arbuthnot had forgotten the exact date the degree was conferred. The lesson for the aspiring historian: Even primary-source information cannot always be taken at face value.

Another valuable cache of primary-source material came from the library of Arbuthnot's undergraduate alma mater, the University of Chicago. It contained a series of letters from Dean William Scott Gray (see chapter 13, this volume) concerning Arbuthnot's employment as a summer school teacher at the university, including such details as her salary. Such information, often hard to come by, provides a human touch amid a career of accomplishment. Among secondary sources, a notable help was a biographical article on her by her friend Zena Sutherland in *Notable American Women, the Modern Period: A Biographical Dictionary* (1980). Also of value was a biographical essay by Blue (1976) for an education seminar at the University of Akron.

Thanks to these various sources, we were able to gain a fairly clear picture of Arbuthnot's life and work. We were fortunate to be able to do so because Arbuthnot left no diaries. Nor, because she married late in life, did she have children who might have given us further insights into her passionate absorption in children's literature and her unwavering belief that children's books had an essential contribution to make to children's lives.

Personal and Professional Life

In June 1969, shortly prior to Arbuthnot's death, the American Library Association (ALA) decided to honor Arbuthnot by hosting an annual lecture named The May Hill Arbuthnot Honor Lectureship. Arbuthnot, in her acceptance speech, said that the award, funded by her long-time publisher Scott Foresman, was "one of the greatest surprises and honors of my long professional years" (1969b). She was delighted, she said, that the lecture series would be administered by what is now the Association for Library Service to Children of the ALA because she felt as if she had been indebted to librarians all her life. "It began long ago," she recalled, "in Newburyport, Massachusetts, in a small choice library where sympathetic librarians permitted a ten-year-old book-worm to browse happily in the adult sections and gave wise, patient guidance on the long road to more mature literacy" (1969b). She was to give wise, patient guidance herself for the next 75 years to those who cared about children and books.

The birthplace of May Hill (who became Arbuthnot through marriage in 1932) was in Mason City, Iowa, USA, but that was an accident: She appeared while her parents were on a visit there. She was raised in her early years in Newburyport, Massachusetts, USA, and testified that she had a happy childhood. One reason was her "absorption in books" (Sutherland, 1980, p. 30), strongly encouraged by her parents. She described her family as "cheerful, bookish [and] music-loving" (Corrigan & Corrigan, 1964, p. 337). Her mother introduced her to music, poetry, and literature, providing her with the works of Louisa May Alcott and, at an early age, the novels of Charles Dickens and Sir Walter Scott. Her father loved to read aloud books to his children, including works such as *Robinson Crusoe* (Defoe, 1719/2001), *The Swiss Family Robinson* (Wyss, 1812/1994), and *The Adventures of Tom Sawyer* (Twain, 1876/2001). One of May's favorite works was *The Book of Common Prayer* (1990), encountered as she regularly attended Episcopal Church services. She said it gave her "a sensitivity to the beauty and power of words" (quoted in Sutherland, 1980, p. 30). Arbuthnot remained a lifelong Episcopalian.

The family moved frequently, and May spent time in Minneapolis, Minnesota, USA, and Chicago, Illinois, USA, graduating from Chicago's Hyde Park High School. Her family's finances were too strained to permit her to advance immediately to college, but she seems to have dipped her toe into the waters of early education as a kindergarten teacher (Sutherland, 1980). It was a time when it was rare for those involved in early education to have a college degree. By 1912 she was on the faculty at the State Normal School at Superior, Wisconsin, USA (now the University of Wisconsin–Superior). The State Normal School had only graduated its first class in 1897 and in 1909 became the state's first institution to offer a full program devoted to the rapidly expanding kindergarten field (History of UW–Superior, 2005). Arbuthnot was associated with this effort, describing herself later in a vita as a "Demonstration & Training Teacher, Kindergarten-Primary" (Arbuthnot, circa 1947, p. 2).

At the same time, she began an association with the University of Chicago. In 1913, she received a kindergarten and primary-grade supervisor's certificate from the university, persevering to attain a Bachelor of Philosophy degree nine years later. Arbuthnot also became a fixture as a teacher in the School of Education's summer programs, giving courses in children's literature from 1913 to 1922 (Sutherland, 1980). One of her inspirations was the Chicago storyteller and folk tale translator Gudrun Thorne-Thomsen. Whenever Arbuthnot told any Norse folk tales, she testified, they always came out with Thorne-Thomsen's Norwegian accent (Blue, 1976, p. 3).

Arbuthnot had been recommended for the summer teaching post at the University of Chicago by Alice Temple, chair of the kindergarten and early education department there and a leading progressive educator. There is a record of Arbuthnot's salary for this job in her correspondence, as May Hill, with William Scott Gray, who was then Dean of the School of Education. Beginning in the first term of the summer quarter in 1917, she taught two courses for a salary of $200. In 1919, her salary was raised to $250. In 1920, it was $300, and in 1922 it was $350 for the two courses (Gray to Hill, 1916, 1919, 1920, 1922). (She was unable to teach in 1921 because of her mother's illness [Hill to Gray, 1921b].) The formal exchange of letters on her employment between Arbuthnot and Gray (Hill and Gray correspondence, 1916–1926) provides a small glimpse of her wit. One of Gray's letters was apparently addressed to West Superior, Wisconsin. "There is no West Superior," she replied. "At best and worst this is merely Superior" (Hill to Gray, 1918).

The University of Chicago connection also provided an opportunity to work closely with Gray, a rising star in education circles, that would yield benefits later when Arbuthnot became coauthor with him of the Scott Foresman Dick and Jane series. Indeed, at that moment in time, the University of Chicago was a perfect launching pad for a future career in education. Although it had only been founded in 1890 (backed by the largesse of John D. Rockefeller), the university had quickly developed a national reputation, enhanced in 1894 when John Dewey was lured there from the University of Michigan to head the new pedagogy department as well as the philosophy department.

One of Dewey's chief initiatives was the founding in 1896 of the University of Chicago Laboratory School. A landmark in progressive education, the Laboratory School was designed both for teaching and for conducting research in educational methods. Although Dewey had left the University of Chicago for Columbia University by the time Arbuthnot taught there, progressive education was still very much in favor there.

In 1918, Arbuthnot moved to New York City. There seem to have been two reasons. The first was so she could become a teacher trainer at the famous progressive institution the Ethical Culture School, where she remained until 1921. The second reason was to take graduate work at Teachers College, Columbia University. The experience at the Ethical Culture School brought her in contact with yet another set of reformers, mainly centered around Felix Adler, founder of the Ethical Culture Society. Adler had a longtime interest in early childhood education and in 1878 had started the Ethical Culture School as a free kindergarten. It became one of the best-known kindergartens in the United States.

Meanwhile, Arbuthnot caught up with John Dewey at Columbia University: Dewey now headed the philosophy department and held a joint professorship at Teachers College (Cremin, 1988, pp. 25, 77, 170–171, 625). Arbuthnot's transcripts show that she took courses on "Mental Adjustments" with one of the few female psychologists in the country, Leta Hollingworth; on "Foundations of Method" with the progressive enthusiast William Heard Kilpatrick; and with John Dewey, who awarded her the grade of A- for his course on "Historical Relations of Philosophy and Education." She received her master's degree in October 1925.

In 1922, Arbuthnot had moved to Cleveland, Ohio, USA, to be principal of the Cleveland Kindergarten-Primary Training School. One likely influence in her move was Charles Hubbard Judd (see chapter 4, this volume), who had become director of the School of Education at the University of Chicago in 1909 while Arbuthnot was a student there; Judd had conducted a "monumental study" of the Cleveland schools in 1916 (Cremin, 1988, pp. 233–234). In several of her letters to Gray, Arbuthnot mentions Judd with fondness (Hill to Gray, 1921a, 1921b, 1926). She would make her principal home in the Cleveland area for the rest of her life.

May Hill's first book was published in 1924, a compilation of children's stories and poems titled *The Child's Treasury*. In Cleveland, she became identified with yet another development in education, the establishment of pre-K nursery schools. She founded nursery schools that were the first both for Cleveland specifically and for the entire state of Ohio (Sutherland, 1980).

The nursery school movement had originated in England in 1911 with the opening of a school in a London slum by Rachel and Margaret McMillan. The first such school in the United States was in 1916 at the University of Chicago, established by faculty parents (Cremin, 1988, pp. 301–302). In 1927, the Cleveland Kindergarten-Primary Training School, with Arbuthnot as director, became part of the elementary education department of Western Reserve University. She was given the rank of associate professor of education (Sutherland, 1980).

A hallmark of the education provided at Western Reserve's nursery school was "parental education" (Blue, 1976, p. 3). The involvement of parents as well as teachers in the school was a leading tenet of the nursery school movement. Writing later, Arbuthnot commented that the school was "born of a desire of intelligent parents to know more about child care and was never, as one educator feared, 'a parking place for the children of bridge-playing women'" (quoted in Blue, 1976, p. 3). Rather, Arbuthnot's credo was her oft-reiterated belief that "the child and his needs come first" (quoted in Blue, 1976, p. 4).

In addition to her work with the nursery school and with parental education throughout the city of Cleveland, Arbuthnot taught regularly at Western Reserve such courses as "Principles of Teaching," "Psychology of Childhood," and "Parental Education" (Blue, 1976, p. 3). Later in her career, she extended her plea for inclusiveness by pointing out the importance of teacher involvement in school administration (Arbuthnot, 1948).

It was not long before Arbuthnot moved to the national scene. From 1927 to 1929 she served as national vice president of the International Kindergarten Union, later renamed the Association for Childhood Education. In 1930, under U.S. President Herbert Hoover, she was invited to become a member of the planning committee for the first White House Conference on Children. Subsequently, she served on a national committee on early childhood education that was responsible for establishing what were called "emergency nursery schools" during the U.S. Great Depression (Sutherland, 1980). The schools were authorized in October 1933 as part of the New Deal's emergency education projects, designed mainly to help unemployed teachers. Some 300 emergency nursery schools were opened for children 2 to 4 years of age, including a number for African American children, during the first year after the authorization. The schools were an extension downward of the public schools and were also an extension outward because they included such aspects of the child's development as health, physical growth and nutrition, play, social life, and mental hygiene. Providing an all-day program, including lunch and a nap, they became centers for medical care and the education of parents in the essentials of child growth and guidance (Cremin, 1988, pp. 302–303; Langdon, 1935). The parental component in particular may be a sign of Arbuthnot's influence on the program.

The 1930s were very busy years for May Hill. On her biographical data sheet at Western Reserve University in 1939, she reported being a member of Phi Beta Kappa, Pi Lambda Theta, the English Research Council, the Elementary English Council, and the Association for Childhood Education at both the national and local levels. A faculty data sheet in her handwriting at Western Reserve (circa 1947) provides additional information. (The manuscript is undated, but its latest internal date is 1947). In it, she reported giving speeches to education associations across the United States (in 48 cities in 18 states, she noted), including meetings in Dallas, San Antonio, and Denton, Texas; Raleigh, North Carolina; Nashville, Tennessee; Louisville, Kentucky; Washington, DC; Duluth, Minnesota; Grand Rapids, Michigan; New Haven, Connecticut; Milwaukee, Wisconsin; Indianapolis, Fort Wayne, South Bend, and Evansville, Indiana; and Cincinnati and Columbus, Ohio. For 10 years, beginning in 1930, she served as review editor for children's books for the *Journal of Childhood Education*. Her articles also appeared frequently in such venues as *Childhood Education* and *Parent's Magazine* (Arbuthnot, 1939, circa 1947).

In 1932, at the age of 48, Hill married a fellow faculty member at Western Reserve University, Charles Criswell Arbuthnot, a professor of economics. It proved to be a happy union, and Charles Arbuthnot fully supported his wife's work. The couple was much beloved on the Western Reserve campus and was noted for the gracious hospitality at their home. Their pet, Molly, a German shepherd, was also known on campus, and accompanied either Arbuthnot or her husband as they taught classes. (The couple maintained that a dog, just like a child, becomes too lonesome if left at home.) Charles Arbuthnot, who had taught economics at Western Reserve from 1908 to 1946, died in 1963 (Blue, 1976, p. 7).

In 1940, May Hill Arbuthnot embarked on another aspect of her varied career. She became coauthor with William Scott Gray, her mentor from the University of Chicago, of the Basic Readers in the Curriculum Foundation series, published by the house of Scott Foresman (Gray, Arbuthnot, et al.,

1940–1948). The series, better known as the Dick and Jane books, featured the youngsters Dick and Jane; their little sister, Sally; their parents; the dog, Spot; and the cat, Puff. The series reached its zenith in the 1950s when an estimated 80 percent of first graders were using Dick and Jane ("A. Sterl Artley," 1998). The series made Arbuthnot wealthy, and she retired from Western Reserve University as associate professor emeritus in 1946.

The following year, Scott Foresman published Arbuthnot's *Children and Books* (1947). In the early 1950s, she produced a series of anthologies (1951, 1952a, 1952b, 1953), gathered into one volume in 1961, to provide read-aloud matter to accompany and enhance reading instruction in elementary schools.

As her career drew to a close, Arbuthnot received numerous honors. The Women's National Book Association awarded her the Constance Lindsay Skinner Medal in 1959 for distinguished contributions to the field of books. In 1964, the Catholic Library Association gave her its Regina Medal for her distinguished contribution to the field of children's books (Corrigan & Corrigan, 1964). In June 1969, as previously mentioned, the American Library Association established an Honor Lectureship in her name. The lecture is delivered each April, published in the journal of the Association for Library Service to Children (ALSC), and made available on the ALSC website (May Hill Arbuthnot Honor Lecture Award, 2005). Case Western University gave Arbuthnot an honorary doctorate in the same year. (The honor may not have assuaged her. She resented being held at the associate professor level throughout her career [Blue, 1976, p. 8].) Her legacy was even formally recognized almost two decades after her death. In 1986, the International Reading Association established the Arbuthnot Award to honor an outstanding college or university teacher of children's and young adult literature (International Reading Association, 2005).

Even in her 80s, Arbuthnot was apparently still engaged in bringing books to children, although her coauthors were now probably in charge of the anthologies that drew upon her earlier work. The decade of the 1960s saw the reissue of *Children's Books Too Good To Miss* (a brief guide to children's literature for parents, librarians, and teachers; Arbuthnot, Clark, & Long, 1948/1963) and the publication of *Time for Biography* (Arbuthnot & Broderick, 1969) and *Time for Old Magic* (Arbuthnot & Taylor, 1970). In the year of her death Arbuthnot's last solo work appeared, reflecting her view of the importance of parents in education: *Children's Reading in the Home* (Arbuthnot, 1969a).

Arbuthnot died in a nursing home at the age of 85 on October 2, 1969. Her long and very full career had spanned several areas and eras in the education of children. As coauthor of the Dick and Jane readers, she helped produce an iconic reading series first revered and later reviled, but one that was certainly an enormous commercial success and part of the literacy education of decades of children. A pioneer in nursery school education in the United States, Arbuthnot also oversaw the training of decades of teachers in kindergarten and early childhood education. She served on several important national committees on education and held high office in national early childhood organizations. She spearheaded the acceptance of children's literature as an important course of study for teachers, the "kiddy lit" courses of today. And she performed her multitudinous tasks with a vivacity, wit, and warmth that endeared her to colleagues and students alike.

Philosophical Beliefs and Guiding Principles

What is most striking about May Hill Arbuthnot is the effect of her early academic education on her subsequent life and work. She came to adulthood in the first decade of the 20th century amid the fevered atmosphere spawned by progressive educational reform. At the University of Chicago and its Laboratory School, and later at that other center of progressivism, Columbia University, she came in contact with John Dewey and his ideas. Soon she was making her own contribution to progressive education at the Cleveland Kindergarten-Primary Training School. Hill's interest in the nursery school movement and in parental involvement in children's education as well as teachers' participation in school administration is an example of her creative adaptation of progressive ideas.

Arbuthnot's important work on children and literature in the latter part of her career may also reflect the rise of Herbartianism, which, like progressive education, held a positive view of children's potential. In the 1890s in the United States, as Nila Banton Smith notes, a wave of Herbartianism "swept the country" (1965/1986, p. 117). Herbartianism was based on the ideas of the German philosopher Johann Friedrich Herbart (1776–1841), himself a disciple of Johann H. Pestalozzi (1746–1847). The Swiss educator Pestalozzi held that educators should respect the principle that young children acquire knowledge through concrete experiences appropriate to their stage of development, not through rote memorization. Similarly, Herbart emphasized the duty of respecting and developing the individuality of the pupil, in particular capturing the child's interest in the world and his aesthetic appreciation of it, which in turn would help develop the child's moral character, while avoiding being didactic. "The intent to teach spoils children's books at once," Herbart wrote. "Interrupt a narrative with moral precepts and [children] will find you a wearisome narrator" (quoted in Smith, 1965/1986, p. 118). His ideas had undergone a revival with the establishment of a pedagogical seminary in Jena in 1874 that attracted visitors to Germany from around the world, including many U.S. citizens.

Herbart's books were translated into English, and the National Herbart Society was established in the United States in 1895. Herbart's ideas encouraged a movement that was already under way—Smith (1965/1986) calls it "Reading as a Cultural Asset" (pp. 115–156)—that emphasized the use of good literature in schools. Its adherents held that what children read (trash or uplifting literature) was as important as the fact that they read at all. These aesthetic and moral aspects of reading instruction differed both from progressivism's goal of integrating the child into society and from the didactic nature of earlier reading series. They fostered the publication of series such as The Heart of Oak series of readers, compiled by Charles Eliot Norton, professor of art at Harvard (e.g., Norton & Stephens, 1894), and Silver Burdett's Stepping Stones to Literature series, authored by Boston educator Sarah Louise Arnold (e.g., Arnold & Gilbert, 1897). These series and the theories that inspired them were much in vogue as Arbuthnot began her pedagogical training and surely contributed, decades later, to her enthusiasm for children's literature.

The influence of psychology can also be seen in Arbuthnot's work. In her introduction to the first edition of *Children and Books* (1947), Arbuthnot lays down a list of basic drives of children, listing the need of the child for material, emotional, and spiritual security; the need to belong; the need to love and be loved; the need to achieve; the need to know; the need for change (play); and the need for aesthetic satisfaction. The first group of these needs reflects Arbuthnot's adaptation of the "hierarchy of needs" philosophy of Abraham Maslow (1908–1970), but the last in particular is redolent of the Herbartianism of her youth. At the same time, the list also reflects a keen awareness of research and theories about children's cognitive abilities, psychosocial aspects, and moral and social development that were discussed by the social scientists and psychologists of her time, who may have included

Jean Piaget as well as Maslow. Maslow believed in the value of a humanistic education in helping individuals achieve self-actualization (e.g., Maslow, 1973), while Piaget explored children's moral growth as well as their cognitive development (e.g., Piaget, 1932). In her approach to children and literature, Arbuthnot seems effortlessly to incorporate this work, at least at the outset of her publications on children's books.

If progressivism, Herbartianism, and Maslow's hierarchy of needs played their part in the philosophical ideas and principles of Arbuthnot, so too did her convictions about the role reading should play in the lives of children. "Books," she wrote in her first edition of *Children and Books* (1947), "are no substitute for living, but they can add immeasurably to its richness" (p. 2). But, she continues,

> a book is a good book for children only when they enjoy it; a book is a poor book for children even when adults rate it a classic if children are unable to read it or are bored by its content. (p. 2)

(This statement perhaps reflects the Herbartian emphasis on the importance of the child's interest.)

Arbuthnot was equally convinced about the positive role to be played by oral presentations of stories and poetry to children and adults alike. She declared herself delighted when the ALA honored her by sponsoring an Honor Lectureship, rather than yet another book prize, because, as she put it, she was "a strong believer in the efficacy of direct speech, the spoken word. For poetry it is the only way, and for more people than we bookish ones like to admit, it is the best way" (Arbuthnot, 1969b). Arbuthnot believed that "saying or reading poetry" to children should continue from their extreme youth until they were 13 years old, and she in effect explains the total absence of poetry from the Dick and Jane readers by maintaining that children who have to struggle with reading a poem as part of a reading lesson get "baffled and discouraged" (Arbuthnot, 1947, p. 166). But listening to the same poem read or spoken aloud by an accomplished adult is another matter entirely: Then children can "respond with delight" and eventually read it easily for themselves (p. 166). In the first three editions of her *Children and Books* (1947, 1957, 1964), she makes it clear that reading to children from books was by no means the same as storytelling, instructing teachers on when they should read stories and when they should tell them (Arbuthnot, 1947, pp.

240–242). By her third edition, she was asking dramatically, "Is Storytelling Dead?" (1964, p. 376).

Arbuthnot's philosophy, then, was likely influenced by the important educational movements of her day—progressive education, Herbartianism, the emphasis on the cultural aspects of reading, and Maslow's hierarchy of needs. Yet one aspect of her beliefs was more salient than any other—her conviction that children's books could and should play a powerful role in the lives of their young readers.

Contributions to the Field of Reading

Arbuthnot's major contributions to the reading field took two forms. The first was unquestionably her coauthorship with William S. Gray of Scott Foresman's Dick and Jane series of elementary readers. The series had begun life as the Elson Basic Readers in 1930, with William Elson as the leading author and Gray as his coauthor. It was retitled the Elson-Gray Readers in its 1936–1938 revision, with Elson continuing as the leading author. In the revision of 1940–1948, however, the series became simply the Basic Readers, now with Gray as the leading author and Arbuthnot one of its coauthors (Stevenson, 1985, p. 71). Gray had urged his publishers to persuade Arbuthnot to join him because she provided important credentials as a teacher of young children, thanks to her nationally known work on nursery schools, kindergartens, and children's book reviews.

The Dick and Jane series was not without controversy, which came from two angles. Rudolf Flesch, in his best-selling Why Johnny Can't Read—And What You Can Do About It (1955), attacked the whole-word method that had dominated U.S. literacy education since the 1910s and that was employed as the basic approach in the Basic Readers, as well as in its look-alike competitors such as the Alice and Jerry books, published by Row, Peterson & Co. (later Harper & Row). Flesch maintained that the Dick and Jane books and their competitors had failed in the job of teaching children to read because they did not take a synthetic phonics approach (as opposed to an analytic/intrinsic phonics approach) that would have helped children deal with unfamiliar words. The second attack on the Dick and Jane books stemmed from the U.S. Civil Rights movements of the 1960s and 1970s. Critics of the series claimed that its vision of a "perfect" white, middle class, suburban household ignored the realities of the urban United States, particularly in its failure to include African

American and Hispanic children in the texts, and that it cast women and girls in roles that were overwhelmingly subordinate to men and boys (Women on Words and Images, 1972). These criticisms spelled the demise of the series in that form. However, thousands of children who had learned to read through the Dick and Jane books retained a great affection for the series, and old copies of Dick and Jane books have become collectors' items.

Arbuthnot's second and even greater contribution to the reading field was her massive review of children's literature, *Children and Books*. Its first edition, in 1947, was a substantial volume of 626 pages. Expanded by Arbuthnot in a revised edition to 684 pages (1957) and in the third edition to 688 pages (1964), *Children and Books* was a ground-breaking historical survey of children's literature that over the next five decades became the standard college-level text in schools of education. Arbuthnot wrote the first three editions of *Children and Books* alone. After her death in 1969, revised editions were published about twice a decade by Arbuthnot's friend and collaborator, a professor at the University of Chicago, Zena Sutherland (1915–2002). Sutherland was aged 82 when the ninth and final edition of *Children and Books* appeared in 1997. Even into the late 1970s, the revised editions remained the largest-selling texts on children's literature in the United States used extensively in schools of education.

The first and subsequent editions of the book alternate between analyses of genres of children's literature (such as picture stories, folk tales, epics, poetry, animal stories, and fantasies) and examinations of—and excerpts from—key children's books, with the addition of bibliographies. Illustrations graced the first edition, and more of them appeared with each edition, with the first colored illustrations appearing in the third edition. Arbuthnot's exploration of topics such as myth and fable contrast vividly with the contents of the Dick and Jane books: Gray had banished such exotic topics from his series in favor of stories based on (white) contemporary life, an approach that was in harmony with John Dewey's view of schooling as training for life.

Arbuthnot's next publication, *Time for Poetry* (1951), was designed to reintroduce poetry into the elementary classroom. Its subtitle reads, *A Teacher's Anthology to Accompany the New Basic Readers Curriculum Foundation Series.* Arbuthnot's *Time for Poetry* was followed by two other "Time for" books: *Time for Fairy Tales Old and New: A Representative Collection of Folk Tales, Myths, Epics, Fables, and Modern Fanciful Tales for Children* (1952) and *Time for True Tales and Almost True: A Representative Collection of Realistic Stories for Children* (1953).

The four books were later published together in one volume as the *Arbuthnot Anthology of Children's Literature* (1961). What both the Dick and Jane series and Arbuthnot's publications on children's literature have in common is their attempt to meet children at their own level and on their own terms.

Sutherland (1980) reports that Arbuthnot's first edition of *Children and Books* in 1947 was "not warmly welcomed" by critics (p. 31). The published reviews the work received, however, do not support this judgment. One of the few criticisms was voiced by A.C. Moore in the *Horn Book* (1948), who considered the index to the work inadequate. He was also concerned about "the lack of sustained historical and critical consideration" of children's books and of those involved in writing, illustrating, and publishing them (quoted in James & Brown, 1949, p. 20).

Children's librarians, in contrast, were almost uniformly enthusiastic about the book. Siddie Joe Johnson, a children's librarian for the Dallas (Texas) Public Library, correctly identified the book's purpose: It could be used, she wrote in the *Library Journal* (1948), "either as a basic text or supplementary reading by students in teachers' colleges, or in children's literature classes in library schools" (p. 53). She praised the amount of research put into its writing, and she particularly liked the chapter on history and trends, the Mother Goose chapter, and the section on storytellers. "As a reference book," she wrote, "this large volume is outstanding" (p. 53). She urged all medium and large public libraries to buy a copy for their children's reading rooms and encouraged colleges involved with education to purchase the book as well.

In *The Elementary School Journal* (1948), Eveline Colburn, who worked at the famously progressive University of Chicago Laboratory School, had nothing but praise for *Children and Books*. She called it a "comprehensive study of the reading interests and needs of children from two to fifteen years of age" and commended it for its wide coverage of "all types of literature except textbooks" (p. 585), from poetry and myths to nonfiction. Unlike Johnson, who was less confident of its usefulness to parents, Colburn thought it would be "of great value" (p. 585) to parents as well as professionals. Both reviewers welcomed the large number of illustrations and the excerpts from the stories, but Colburn also remarked on Arbuthnot's style: Perhaps "never before," she wrote, had children's literature been presented "with such complete understanding and in such an interest-impelling style." The "freshness" of the presentation "could have been achieved only by an expert" (p. 586).

Like the Dick and Jane series, *Children and Books* has come under criticism from a later generation of scholars and teachers. Arbuthnot's language is highly evaluative, succinctly described by Del Negro as "somewhat fulsome and dramatic but always apparently heartfelt" (1999, n.p.). Del Negro examined the two folk tale chapters in all nine editions of *Children and Books* and found Arbuthnot's prose in the first three editions to be Eurocentric and "rife with unacknowledged biases of the time, using paternalistic, sometimes racist, language that would be intolerable today" (1999, n.p.). Arbuthnot does indeed treat Native American folk tales severely, condemning them as "neither sufficiently dramatic nor well enough organized to command intense interest" (1947, p. 221). Del Negro also cites the phrase "heathenness of the Orient" used in the first three editions (e.g., Arbuthnot, 1947, p. 203). To be fair, however, the phrase is not Arbuthnot's but a quotation from another author concerning Asian influences on the development of pre-Christian European folk tales. And although Arbuthnot's discussion of works from Africa and Asia, as well as of African American material, is lamentably thin to the eyes of a contemporary reader, she was writing in a context where there was a paucity of books about children from those cultures.

An example of Arbuthnot's approach to different cultures may be found in her treatment of one of the most controversial children's books ever published—*The Story of Little Black Sambo* (Bannerman, 1899/1905). The problem with this work lies not in its story line (the young hero uses great ingenuity to prevent the tigers from eating him) but in Bannerman's illustrations, which to modern eyes are grotesque caricatures. Worse still, these early illustrations seem to have inspired ever more overtly racist ones by later illustrators: The pictures in later editions of the book—Bannerman lost the copyright early on—are rightly condemned as poster boys for cruel racial stereotyping (see, e.g., Hay, 1981, pp. 148–149, nos. 38–41), and in the 1970s *The Story of Little Black Sambo* was banned from many libraries and reading lists. Although she never used Bannerman's illustrations in her own book, Arbuthnot seems to have been wholly insensitive to their impact, ignoring them in her first two editions and labeling them, euphemistically, "stylized" in her third (1964, p. 336). Yet she was fully alert to the story's racial significance: "Isn't it desirable," she writes,

> that the first association of many children with people of a different color should be by way of a lovable character like *Little Black Sambo*? He has the

right kind of parents...[and] outwits the tigers over and over. He is happy and completely triumphant...That his euphonious name associates racial color with all these desirable attributes should be a basis for racial pride and interracial admiration. (1947, p. 288)

When Sutherland wrote the fourth edition of *Children and Books* after Arbuthnot's death, her much greater sensitivity to racially sensitive topics (Del Negro, 1999) led her to put the story in a new section titled "Books That Stir Controversy." She dropped Arbuthnot's description entirely and commented that the book was "offensive to many adults because of the illustrations and because the name 'Sambo' has derogatory connotations" (Arbuthnot & Sutherland, 1972, p. 263).

Another criticism of the three earliest editions of *Children and Books* is that neither Arbuthnot nor Sutherland (in later editions) kept up with the changing scholarship that lay behind various aspects of the work, such as the discussions and controversies over folk tales (Del Negro, 1999). Arbuthnot's rare contemporary critic, A.C. Moore, was on target when he objected to "the lack of sustained historical and critical consideration" of children's books (Moore, 1948, quoted in James & Brown, 1949, p. 20). Arbuthnot's works predate the interest that English department faculty began to take in children's literature as a legitimate scholarly enterprise, but once such criticism appeared, her work seemed further outdated.

Lessons for the Future

May Hill Arbuthnot's lessons for the future, and for all educators, parents, and those who work with children, is to develop a love for children's literature. This love of children's literature became an overarching theme in her life. Arbuthnot was devoted to the promotion of quality children's literature and believed that teachers were not the only ones responsible for its delivery but parents and librarians were as well. And she believed that immersion in good literature plays a key role in the development of the love of literature.

Another important lesson that educators can learn from Arbuthnot's work is her dedication to bringing the right books to the right child. This lesson still needs to be brought to classrooms, particularly today when curriculum standards guide textbook selections. Arbuthnot has taught us that children should guide textbook selections. She believed that children are engaged in a continuous process of learning about themselves and their world. As they get older, their world becomes much larger, with people along the way who have significant impacts on their growth and learning. For them to function successfully in society and achieve self-identity, children must first understand themselves. Books can greatly aid children in that task.

Arbuthnot's approaches to childhood education and children's literature were based on these philosophical beliefs. To be appreciated, she felt, literature should be shared. During her lectures she would remind her audience that each child must develop the inner resources needed to withstand the stresses of life. She used an analogy to describe the role of the teacher in furthering this goal: "The tree has roots to weather the storm. Educators must care for people, and grow in interests as the tree grows tall and wide" (quoted in Corrigan & Corrigan, 1964, p. 337). In her view, each of us must "make an effort to know life outside of his own immediate duties, to wave a little as do the topmost tree branches" (p. 337). Arbuthnot believed that the love of good books is acquired in childhood and the realm of children's literature should be made apparent to all children. Even textbooks should be satisfying experiences for every child, one child at a time.

The last lesson Arbuthnot has taught us is presented in the form of a goal. Toward the end of her acceptance speech at the announcement by the ALA of the May Hill Arbuthnot Honor Lectureship series, she fittingly acknowledged her contributions to the field of children's literature and education by giving a blessing to those who would continue the work she so dearly loved. She concluded her acceptance speech by saying,

> Nevertheless, ...there is not much to be said for old age, and what there is has been honestly said by William Butler Yeats in that remarkable poem, "Sailing to Byzantium." Here are just four lines from it:
>
> > An aged man is but a paltry thing,
> > A tattered coat upon a stick, unless
> > Soul clap its hands and sing and louder sing
> > For every tatter in its mortal dress. [Yeats, 1989, p. 301]
>
> And that is what I am going to do from now on, "sing and louder sing," for with this honor lecture Scott Foresman has lent dignity to the tatters and left the mortal dress with quite a jaunty air. (1969b)

The goal given to educators, parents, and children's literature lovers is to continue helping children develop a love of literature. We are to continue immersing children in books that they enjoy and can read at their developmental and interest levels, and continue growing professionally as educators so all children can have the opportunity to love literature throughout their lives.

Reflection Questions

1. How is Arbuthnot's work a reflection of the philosophical movements of the early 20th century? How was her writing influenced by the eminent educators she worked with and near?
2. Arbuthnot believed we should communicate to adults the importance of telling stories and reading aloud to children. Do you agree with her? If so, why? And how can we do this effectively?
3. What did May Hill Arbuthnot feel about the role parents should play in literacy developments at home? Are there ways, using Arbuthnot's wisdom, to inspire more parents to get involved?
4. What do you consider to be Arbuthnot's single greatest contribution to the reading field?
5. Considering the scathing criticisms of the Dick and Jane basal reading series that Arbuthnot coauthored with Gray, why have some of the stories been recently republished? What value do they have for today's classrooms?

REFERENCES

A. Sterl Artley, last surviving author of Dick and Jane, dies. (1998). *History of Reading News, 22*(1), 6.

Arbuthnot, M.H. (1939, September 19). *Biographical data*. In May Hill Arbuthnot manuscripts, Case Western Reserve University Archives, Cleveland, Ohio.

Arbuthnot, M.H. (1947). *Children and books*. Chicago: Scott Foresman.

Arbuthnot, M.H. (circa 1947). *Faculty data*. In May Hill Arbuthnot manuscripts, Case Western Reserve University Archives, Cleveland, Ohio.

Arbuthnot, M.H. (1948). Teachers—today and tomorrow. *NEA Journal, 37,* 214–215.

Arbuthnot, M.H. (Comp.). (1951). *Time for poetry: A teacher's anthology to accompany the New Basic Readers Curriculum Foundation series*. Chicago: Scott Foresman.

Arbuthnot, M.H. (Comp.). (1952). *Time for fairy tales old and new: A representative collection of folk tales, myths, epics, fables, and modern fanciful tales for children*. Chicago: Scott Foresman.

Arbuthnot, M.H. (Comp.). (1953). *Time for true tales and almost true: A representative collection of realistic stories for children*. Chicago: Scott Foresman.

Arbuthnot, M.H. (1957). *Children and books* (rev. ed.). Chicago: Scott Foresman.

Arbuthnot, M.H. (Comp.). (1961). *The Arbuthnot anthology of children's literature: Single-volume edition of time for poetry, time for fairy tales, and time for true tales*. Chicago: Scott Foresman.

Arbuthnot, M.H. (1964). *Children and books*. (3rd ed.). Chicago: Scott Foresman.

Arbuthnot, M.H.. (1969a). *Children's reading in the home*. Glenview, IL: Scott Foresman.

Arbuthnot, M.H. (1969b). May Hill Arbuthnot's acceptance speech. In *The May Hill Arbuthnot honor lectureship*. Chicago: Association for Library Service to Children, American Library Association.

Arbuthnot, M.H., & Broderick, D.M. (Comps.). (1969). *Time for biography*. Glenview, IL: Scott Foresman.

Arbuthnot, M.H., Clark, M.M., & Long, H.G. (1963). *Children's books too good to miss* (3rd rev. ed.). Cleveland, OH: The Press of Western Reserve University. (Original work published 1948)

Arbuthnot, M.H., & Sutherland, Z. (1972). *Children and books* (4th ed.). Glenview, IL: Scott Foresman.

Arbuthnot, M.H., & Taylor, M. (Comps.). (1970). *Time for old magic: A representative collection of folk tales, fables, myths, and epics to be used in the classroom, home or camp*. Glenview, IL: Scott Foresman.

Arnold, S.L., & Gilbert, C.B. (1897). *A second reader* [Stepping Stones to Literature series]. New York: Silver, Burdett.

Bannerman, H. (1905). *The story of little black Sambo*. Chicago: Reilly & Britton. (Originally published in 1899)

Blue, G.F. (1976). *Biographical essay on May Hill Arbuthnot*. Unpublished manuscript, University of Akron, Ohio, Case Western Reserve University Archives.

Book of common prayer. (1990). Oxford, England: Oxford University Press.

Colburn, E. (1948). [Review of the book *Children and books*]. *The Elementary School Journal, 48,* 585–586.

Corrigan, M.C., & Corrigan, A. (1964, February,). May Hill Arbuthnot: Regina Medal Award Winner, 1964. *Catholic Library World,* 336–339. Reproduction, in May Hill Arbuthnot manuscripts, Case Western Reserve University Archives, Cleveland, Ohio.

Cremin, L.A. (1988). *American education: The metropolitan experience, 1876–1980*. New York: Harper & Row.

Defoe, D. (2001). *Robinson Crusoe*. New York: Modern Library. (Original work published 1719)

Del Negro, J. (1999). A change of storyteller: Folktales in *Children and books*, from Arbuthnot to Sutherland [Electronic version]. *Library Trends, 47,* pp. 579–601.

Flesch, R.F. (1955). *Why Johnny can't read—and what you can do about it*. New York: Harper & Row.

Gray, W.S, Arbuthnot, M.H., et al. (1940–1948). Basic Readers [Curriculum foundation Series]. Chicago: Scott Foresman.

Gray, W.S., to M. Hill. (1916, December 18). In May Hill Arbuthnot manuscripts, Administrative Files, University of Chicago Library, Chicago, Illinois.

Gray, W.S., to M. Hill. (1919, February 21). In May Hill Arbuthnot manuscripts, Administrative Files, University of Chicago Library, Chicago, Illinois.

Gray, W.S., to M. Hill. (1920, March 13). In May Hill Arbuthnot manuscripts, Administrative Files, University of Chicago Library, Chicago, Illinois.

Gray, W.S., to M. Hill. (1922, January 27). In May Hill Arbuthnot manuscripts, Administrative Files, University of Chicago Library, Chicago, Illinois.

Hay, E. (1981). *Sambo Sahib: The story of little black Sambo and Helen Bannerman.* Totawa, NJ: Barnes & Noble.

Hill, M. (Ed.). (1924). *The child's treasury.* Chicago: Foundation Desk.

Hill, M., & Gray, W.S. (December 18, 1916, to January 27, 1926). *Correspondence.* In May Hill Arbuthnot manuscripts, Administrative Files, University of Chicago Library, Chicago, Illinois.

Hill, M., to W.S. Gray. (1918, March 14). In May Hill Arbuthnot manuscripts, Administrative Files, University of Chicago Library, Chicago, Illinois.

Hill, M., to W.S. Gray. (1921, January 22). In May Hill Arbuthnot manuscripts, Administrative Files, University of Chicago Library, Chicago, Illinois.

Hill, M., to W.S. Gray. (1921a, February 16). In May Hill Arbuthnot manuscripts, Administrative Files, University of Chicago Library, Chicago, Illinois.

Hill, M. to W.S. Gray. (1921b, February 16). In May Hill Arbuthnot manuscripts, Administrative Files, University of Chicago Library, Chicago, Illinois.

Hill, M., to W.S. Gray. (1926, January 27). In May Hill Arbuthnot manuscripts, Administrative Files, University of Chicago Library, Chicago, Illinois.

History of UW–Superior. Retrieved May 20, 2005, from University of Wisconsin–Superior website: http://www.uwsuper.edu/aboutuwsuperior/history

International Reading Association. *Arbuthnot award.* Retrieved June 14, 2005, from http://www.reading.org/association/awards/teachers_arbuthnot.html

James, M.M., & Brown, D. (Eds.). (1949). *Book review digest. Forty-fourth annual cumulation.* New York: H.W. Wilson.

Johnson, S.J. (1948). [Review of the book *Children and books*]. *Library Journal, 73,* 53.

Langdon, G. (1935). The emergency nursery school—A community agency [Electronic version]. *Opportunity, Journal of Negro Life, 13,* 49.

Maslow, A. (1973). *Dominance, self-esteem, self-actualization: Germinal papers of A.H. Maslow* (Richard J. Lowry, Ed.). Monterey, CA: Brooks/Cole.

May Hill Arbuthnot Honor Lecture Award. (2005). Association for Library Service to Children, American Library Association. Retrieved June 22, 2005, from http://www.ala.org/alsc/arbuth.html

Moore, A.C. (1948). [Review of the book *Children and books*]. *Horn Book, 24,* 174.

Norton, C.E., & Stephens, K. (Eds.). (1894). *Rhymes, jingles, and fables* [The Heart of Oak series]. Boston: D.C. Heath.

Piaget, J. (1932). *The moral judgment of the child.* London: K. Paul, Trench, & Trubner.

Smith, N.B. (1986). *American reading instruction.* Newark, DE: International Reading Association. (Original work published 1965)

Stevenson, J.A. (Ed). (1985). *William S. Gray: Teacher, scholar, leader.* Newark, DE: International Reading Association.

Sutherland, Z. (1980). May Hill Arbuthnot. In B. Sicherman & C.H. Green, with I. Kantov & H. Walker (Eds.), *Notable American women, the modern period: A biographical dictionary* (pp. 30–31). Cambridge, MA: Belknap Press of Harvard University Press.

Sutherland, Z. (1997). *Children and books* (9th ed.). White Plains, NY: Longman. (Original work published 1947)

Twain, M. (2001). *The adventures of Tom Sawyer.* New York: Modern Library. (Original work published 1876)

Women on Words and Images. (1972). *Dick and Jane as victims: Sex stereotyping in children's readers.* Princeton, NJ: Author.

Wyss, J.D. (1994). *The Swiss family Robinson.* London: David Campbell. (Original work published 1812)

Yeats, W.B. (1989). Sailing to Byzantium. In A.N. Jeffares (Ed.), *Yeats's poems* (p. 301). London: Macmillan.

FOR FURTHER READING

Avery, G. (1994). *Behold the child: American children and their books, 1621–1922*. Baltimore: Johns Hopkins University Press.

Huck, C.S., Kiefer, B.Z., Hepler, S., & Hickman, J. (2004). *Children's literature in the elementary school* (8th ed., rev. by B.Z. Kiefer). New York: McGraw-Hill. (Original work published 1961)

Lukens, R.J. (Ed.). (2006). *A critical handbook of children's literature* (8th ed.). Boston: Allyn & Bacon.

Meigs, C., Eaton, A.T., Nesbitt, E., & Viguers, R.H. (1969). *A critical history of children's literature* (rev. ed.). New York: Macmillan. (Original work published 1953)

Zipes, J., Paul, L., Vallone, L., Hunt, P., & Avery, G. (Eds.). (2005). *The Norton anthology of children's literature: The traditions in English*. New York: Norton.

CHAPTER 10

Bernice Elizabeth Leary (1890–1973): Reading Specialist, Curriculum Researcher, and Anthologist of Children's Literature

By Karla J. Möller

Historical Research Process

WHEN I WAS asked to choose an author from the list of early reading pioneers, I first undertook an Internet search of the reading researchers on the list so I could make an informed choice. Although most of their names were familiar to me, one stood out because (a) I did not know anything about her

Shaping the Reading Field: The Impact of Early Reading Pioneers, Scientific Research, and Progressive Ideas, edited by Susan E. Israel and E. Jennifer Monaghan. © 2007 by the International Reading Association.
Photo: Courtesy of Iowa Women's Archives at the Univeristy of Iowa Libraries, Iowa City, Iowa.

work, and, more important, (b) I discovered an article she had authored titled "Milestones in Children's Books" (Leary, 1970). I assumed that Bernice Elizabeth Leary's focal work, like mine, was in children's literature. She seemed a perfect match.

As I delved more deeply into the archival research, I learned that my children's literature colleagues had also never heard of Leary and that the "Milestones" paper I had found so quickly online turned out to be one of only two of her works that focused specifically on children's literature (the other being Leary, 1943). The only other easily available information was a two-page document on the Iowa Women's Archives website (Rymph, 1992) that contains basic facts about Leary's life. While my subsequent searches through my university's library system and online used-book sellers located over 100 titles attributed to Leary, her line of work became more confusing until I contacted the archival reference librarians at the University of Iowa. With their gracious help, I learned that, although collecting exemplars of children's literature was Leary's passion, her main work was as an editor of children's literature anthologies, as a curriculum development specialist for Madison (Wisconsin) Public Schools, and as an education specialist for the United States Department of the Interior and Office of Education. With further research I learned that Leary's dissertation had become one of the seminal books in the field of reading—*What Makes a Book Readable* (Gray & Leary, 1935)—coauthored by her doctoral advisor William Scott Gray (see chapter 13, this volume). I became fascinated with Leary's multifaceted career.

Unfortunately, materials that would have provided significant documentation of Leary's personal life are limited. There is no record of a diary or journal, and many documents that might have provided insights into her busy life are not available today. Written communications with her publisher were lost while Leary was still alive, as she lamented in a letter later in her life: "Even some of the delightful correspondence I had with dealers is no longer in my possession. The thought makes me sad" (Leary to Newsome, 1972). By the late 1970s, all her close relatives—her parents, sisters, brother-in-law, and lone niece—were dead. Leary never married nor had children. Only in the Main Library Special Collections Department and Iowa Women's Archives—both at the University of Iowa Libraries, Iowa City—have been preserved a few letters, some papers, and Leary's complete personal children's literature collection, along with her reminiscences on her family (1958) and later life (1964).

Personal and Professional Life

Born in 1890, Bernice (pronounced /Bər'-nĭs/) Elizabeth Leary challenged traditional gender roles by pursuing a professional career that offered her leadership opportunities in the fields of education and book publishing for over 40 years. Throughout her career Leary was a teacher, an adjunct professor in reading education, an author, a reading curriculum specialist, a literature anthology editor, and a world traveler—at a time when few such opportunities were afforded to women.

Although no biographies of this remarkable woman have been published previously and most of her personal and professional correspondence was not saved, her record as an educator in a range of settings and as a book editor, author, and anthologist leaves a fairly clear paper trail. Leary formed friendships around the world through her work on curricula and texts for both English-language learners and native English speakers, traveling and working in Thailand, the Philippines, India, and post–World War II Germany. Fortunately, in 1968, Leary offered the few letters and papers she had saved, as well as her personal children's literature collection (over 525 books—some 200 early children's books, 150 contemporary children's books, 175 foreign children's books, and over a dozen children's magazines), to the University of Iowa School of Library Science. Most of these materials, along with the acquisition correspondence between Leary and children's literature professor Louane L. Newsome, were sent to the rare books section of the University of Iowa Main Library Special Collections Department, where they are still housed. In 1973, a letter from attorneys for Leary's executor noted a bequest of 500–600 additional books, but requested that the books be left with Leary's sister Iva (then 90 years old) until her death so as not to disrupt Iva's daily routine (Tomasek to Dunlap, 1973). After the Iowa Women's Archives was created as a separate section of the Special Collections Department, the few letters, cards, and additional personal papers that remained were sent there in 1985 and were catalogued by 1992 into the Bernice E. Leary Papers collection (Rymph, 1992).

The openness with which Leary faced life and work shines through her letters, as does her adventurous spirit, love of learning, energy for teaching, compassion, and generosity. It is in one of these letters, in particular, mailed from the Philippines in 1964 when Leary was almost 74, that her approach to living is clearly shown. Leary describes not only the work she was doing with local educators (extending her visit and working through the weekend to complete the project), but also demonstrates her zest for life and her strong relationships with her students:

> There have been Phil. students who used to be in Madison to be entertained by, too. Yesterday one...[took] me to church at 9:30, to...dinner at noon, on a drive and to her home in the PM...(She's the one to whom I gave my electric sewing machine I'd never used, and furnished with winter clothes, blankets, etc. in a cold Madison winter.) It was good to see her in a new role as a college teacher...(She <u>always</u> had Sat. night supper at my Apt. with other foreign students who...sat on the floor and watched T.V.) I'll see more of them in Bangkok.... Friday and Saturday I spent in Baguio in the northern mountains.... It's...5 or 6 hours from here by trains...and then by car up a tortuous, hair-raising, narrow road, blocked here and there by landslides that we crept over and around, to some 4000 ft. elevation. I was relieved to be safely back...tho I'd loved going back to Baguio, wandering thru the markets, etc. (Leary to Helen, 1964, pp. 1–3)

Born in Ionia, Iowa, USA, on August 19, 1890, to James and Josephine Bell Leary, Leary was the youngest of three sisters, following five years after Iva (born in 1884) and almost three years after Leila May (born in 1887). Known as "Bernie" to her family, Leary grew up content and sheltered and later acknowledged that she and her sisters "owe [our parents] a debt of gratitude for a protected childhood and a parental devotion that few can equal" (Leary, 1958, p. 1). Her father, a first-generation Irish American, and her mother, a fourth-generation English American, moved to Riceville, Iowa, USA, in 1901, where Bernice entered the sixth grade. Her devotion to her parents was clear:

> My father, a tall young man with already graying hair at twenty-two, was one of nine children...My mother...was...an interesting contrast to my father, though she, too was one of a large family. Six years older than he, tiny—about 4 feet 10 inches in height and seldom, if ever, 100 pounds in weight, she was a power in our home—stern where my father was gay, prudent where he was extravagant. A rock-bound Protestant from a Presbyterian father and a Shaker mother, she held her children to the same firm faith. (1958, p. 1)

Leary describes Riceville life as "singularly satisfying" (1958, p. 2). She graduated from Riceville High and taught alongside her sister Leila at

Riceville Elementary until Leila's marriage and subsequent end to her teaching career in 1918. Leary (1958) writes of her early career:

> Teaching seemed an inevitable career...Perhaps because our Irish grandmother had been a teacher. Perhaps because it was the genteel thing to do in our growing up days. At any rate, it was the vocation that all of us pursued without question. (p. 2)

In 1919, Leary left her teaching post to study at Winona State Teachers College in Minnesota. When her mother died suddenly in 1923 after falling down the stairs, Leary returned home and to her teaching position.

Leary left Riceville a final time in 1926, enrolling at the University of Chicago and earning her Bachelor's of Philosophy (PhB) in 1930, her MA in 1931, and finally her PhD in Education on August 25, 1933. To support her studies, she had worked as an elementary school principal in LaGrange, Illinois, USA, and as a university research assistant. She had also received scholarships (Leary, 1964, pp. 1–2). Her dissertation, supervised by William Scott Gray, was titled *Elements of Reading Materials Contributing to Difficulties in Comprehension on the Part of Adults* (1933). When it was published as a book with Gray as first author, under the title *What Makes a Book Readable* (Gray & Leary, 1935), it was hailed as a seminal work and received an award from the National Research Association "for being the most outstanding research of the preceding five years" (Leary, 1964, p. 2). After this success, "opportunities for writing, editing, and publishing came fast," Leary added (p. 2).

Leary's career after her doctorate was rich and varied. She worked first in Washington, DC, as a curriculum specialist for the United States Office of Education. During the 1930s, she was active in survey research for United States Department of the Interior and the Office of Education, reviewing curricula (Leary, 1937) and documenting the organization and function of school systems, state departments of education, and institutions of higher education (Leary, 1938). Following these jobs, she worked on a survey of schools in New York state (Gray & Leary, 1939), "where for months I visited and evaluated schools in country, town, and city" (1964, p. 1).

From 1942 through 1955, "when she was not involved in government service" (Noble, n.d., p. 1), Leary was the Director of Curriculum for Madison Public Schools in Wisconsin (see Leary, 1943/1949a, 1947/1951).

She continued to publish on reading education, often in books associated with Gray. She wrote a chapter on difficulties in reading material for a book edited by Gray (Leary, 1940), an article on the role of literature in school instruction (Leary, 1943), and a couple of chapters for the prestigious yearbooks of the National Society for the Study of Education—one on problems associated with content (Leary, 1948) and the other on interpreting the reading program to the public (Leary, 1949b). The 1940s also saw Leary's first foray into children's literature in a coauthored book titled *Growing With Books: A Reading Guide* (Leary & Smith, 1947).

Professional recognition also came to Leary in the area of writing instruction. The National Conference on Research in English (NCRE; now NCRE/NCRLL) was an organization founded in 1932 by members of the National Council of Teachers of English (NCTE) in an effort to focus attention more squarely on English teaching at the elementary level, which some NCTE members felt had been neglected (Petty, 1983, pp. 5–6). While leading scholars in reading and English education were forming NCRE, Leary had been completing her doctorate with Gray. Gray, one of the few elementary-focused members of NCTE at the time, was heavily involved in NCRE. By the mid-1940s, Leary was already the author of many publications on elementary education. She was elected president of NCRE for the year 1947–1948, and at the NCRE's 1953 meeting she was a keynote speaker, presenting a paper entitled "Literature for Children in a Troubled World" (Petty, 1983, p. 49).

During this same period, Leary's interest in children's literature evolved into another facet of her career. As early as 1936 Leary had been a junior editor for Harcourt Brace's three-volume Discovery series for students in the middle and high school grades. By 1941, she was the sole editor of the seventh anthology of *Best Short Stories for Boys and Girls* for ages 10 and up (a Row, Peterson and Company imprint) that contains selections "from current juvenile magazines over a twelve-month period" (Row, Peterson, 1941, p. 3). Four years later, Leary became chairwoman of the editorial board for Cadmus Books, a division of the publishing house of E.M. Hale. During her tenure there, Leary coedited a 10-volume literature anthology series titled Through Golden Windows that was designed for use in U.S. public schools and covered five subject areas each for grades K through 4 and grades 5 through 8. While still chairing the editorial board for the E.M. Hale division, she also served as a junior editor for the 1950/1955 three-volume Row,

Peterson Reading-Literature series for high school students and as senior editor on six of the seven-volume J.B. Lippincott Time to Read series (1953–1957) geared toward elementary students.

During the 1940s and early 1950s, Leary traveled to Europe and Asia to work on "curriculum and textbook changes" (Leary, 1958, p. 3) that "led to the publication of much-needed books in the Far East…[and] promoted greater understanding of other people" (p. 3). Leary wrote in 1958, "Five assignments abroad—to Germany in 1947 and again in 1948, to Thailand, in 1954–5 and again in 1956–7 with shorter periods to India and Vietnam, and to the Philippines in 1955–6, have been extremely gratifying" (1958, p. 3). As family friend Mary Noble (n.d.) wrote in a brief overview of Leary's life, Leary spent the two postwar years in Germany "helping prepare new textbooks and setting up writers' workshops for children's books at the request of the military government" (p. 1). Leary (1964) emphasized the need for German writers and publishers after the war to have support preparing textbooks "for a new and more democratic school system" (p. 2). She extended her work preparing textbooks for schools during other foreign appointments for the U.S. State Department that required the long trips to, for example, Thailand (five months for one trip; a year for another), the Philippines (eight months), and India (five months).

Well after her formal retirement as a curriculum specialist for the Madison, Wisconsin, USA, school system in 1955, Leary was in demand for books on reading and writing instruction. In the early 1960s she continued writing curricular materials, including the New Reading Skilltext series, along with its workbooks and teacher's edition (Johnson, Young, Leary, & Myers, 1961; Young, Leary, & Myers, 1961a, 1961b, 1961c, 1961d, 1961e). From 1960 through 1964, she worked as an advisor for content on the English for Today series (Slager, 1962–1967)—a set of six books "for the teaching of English to junior and senior high school students in foreign countries" that was "sponsored by the National Council of Teachers of English (NCTE) for the United States Information Agency" (Leary, 1964, p. 2). After completing this project, Leary wrote that now her "retirement will really begin in earnest" (p. 2). However, through 1967 she remained chairman of the editorial board for Cadmus Books of E.M. Hale (p. 2).

Throughout these years of publishing and editing, Leary remained a teacher. She wrote,

All along the way there was the teaching of summer school in Emory University, the University of Chicago, Northwestern University, and the University of Wisconsin. Thousands of elementary school teachers received their training—good or bad, from me. I hope some of it was good. (1964, p. 1)

She also taught short courses and workshops in universities across the United States.

In 1961, Leary moved from Madison to live with her sister Iva, also a retired schoolteacher, in Webster City, Iowa, USA. Living a comfortable life "with church and civic responsibilities, gardening, and reading" (Leary, 1964, p. 3), Leary continued to travel in the United States, the Philippines, Thailand, and Hong Kong. She retired with Iva to the Mayflower Retirement Home in Grinnell, Iowa, USA, in late 1967 after a "nearly fatal automobile accident" (Wood, 1973, p. 3).

Family friend and librarian emeritus Mary Noble described Leary as a person of "great dignity" who also "didn't lack a sense of humor" (personal communication, July 29, 2005). Leary was tall and slender, always a "gracious hostess" whose "meals were very well organized and...more formal than [Noble] was used to. She had been accustomed to entertaining more extensively." Noble continued:

She had definite ideas about appropriate dress for certain occasions and often had clothes tailored for herself from fabrics she'd acquired in Thailand or wherever. She came to Iowa City once for a Friends of the Libraries annual dinner...and she arrived in what was to me a very attractive dress or suit which I assumed she'd wear to the dinner that evening, but she changed into something else for that and was mildly appalled to think I expected her to wear the traveling outfit. (personal communication, July, 29, 2005)

Despite this formality, Leary was not constrained by traditional notions of womanhood. She did not marry in a time when most women were expected to do so. And, as Noble shared with me,

A Bernice memory...came back to me over the weekend when I happened to see a bit of the 60's movie "Cleopatra" on...Saturday. This must have first come out when Bernice was living in Grinnell, and she invited my parents and me to visit her and drive to Des Moines to see it. What a big deal! I guess it had been pretty controversial in some ways, with some female nudity or near nudity. Anyway, after we'd seen the film, I remember being surprised that she commented that she didn't find the nudity offensive—she thought the bodies were beautiful. Good for her! (personal communication, October 3, 2005)

Leary died on March 20, 1973, and was buried in Riverside Cemetery, where her mother and father, and later Iva, were also interred.

Philosophical Beliefs and Guiding Principles

Leary's philosophy of reading is evident in her children's anthologies, her curriculum work, and her professional research. In the foreword to *Adventure Bound* (Persing & Leary, 1936a), the first book in the Discovery series, Leary and her coeditor Chester Persing mention that they hope their work will "answer the pressing need for special materials for pupils who, because of immaturity of interest or ability, react negatively to traditional literary content" (p. v). They continue with the hope that "the book will furnish remedial reading for the retarded pupil—the one who had grown book-shy from long struggling with traditional subject matter" (p. v). Although these volumes were written for middle class, European American children, the notion that reading materials should be geared toward children at all and the focus on reading with ease for understanding, pleasure, and participation in discussion were positive steps in reading instruction.

Adventure Bound (Persing & Leary, 1936b), the first book in the Discovery series, includes selections that were "chosen by the pupils themselves over a period of four years when their reading contacts were not restricted to the purely literary and when hundreds of books were always available in the classrooms for sampling or intensive reading" (p. v). The editors wrote: "*Adventure Bound* is an obvious departure from the usual literature text" in that it "provides no experience with literary masterpieces" but instead "builds upon the needs of pupils and upon those reading experiences which they have found interesting and desirable" (p. v). The book "is not concerned with the experiences which teachers have *thought* all pupils should enjoy" (p. vi; italics in original), but on texts recommended by readers for their peers.

Leary's later curriculum work—specifically monographs on developing word meaning (Leary, 1943/1949a) and a sight word vocabulary (Leary, 1942; Leary, 1947/1951)—built on her belief that teaching and learning reading should to be fun and engaging. Leary (1943/1949a) advocated learning experiences that allowed children to "taste, touch, hear, see, or manipulate the things for which a word stands" to give "the word reality and meaning." (p. 1). Emphasis was on "first-hand experiences, observations, and discussions" (p. 1). Use of visual aids, read-alouds, and projects centered on children's interests were encouraged. Leary's curriculum provided for "wide reading in library or classroom without subject-matter limitations" as well as "wide reading around a single center of interest" (p. 3). She highlighted promoting interest in words by encouraging students to use context clues to determine meaning and, in reverse, to illustrate multiple meanings of individual words by contextualizing the words in writing.

Vocabulary development was also furthered in Leary's work by studying the history of words; exploring figurative language; focusing on substituting more specific words for more general ones and less frequently used words for overused ones; and teaching word meanings directly by classifying, categorizing, chunking, and focusing on compounds, prefixes, suffixes, and analogies as well as synonyms and antonyms. Leary's group wrote, "Developing the habit of searching the context clues for meaning should begin early and continue throughout school, from sentence context to the context of a whole book or of a writer's total writings" (1943/1949a, p. 8).

In her later monograph on "sight vocabulary," Leary (1947/1951) emphasizes games that aid children's remembering of words already introduced through engaging literature in ways that would "stimulate most children to maximum effort" (p. 2). Leary supported first and foremost engaging children in reading and learning words through reading and being read to from "gay, lively, appealing stories" (p. 2). Although she believed that many words can and will be learned in the context of the stories, she acknowledged that children needed additional practice to develop fluency. In addition, she realized that quite a few words in English "have meanings that are vague and elusive" (p. 2), such as *who*, *of*, and others. These, as well as more concrete nouns, could be better remembered by children, Leary argued, if, after reading the words in a meaningful context, children played a range of games focused on vocabulary practice.

Leary (1943/1949a) clearly understood that multiple factors affect how a child creates meaning with text. She discussed factors such as

> the child himself, his home and environment, his experiences in life, his intelligence, his ability to organize experiences and give them meaning,

the kind of instruction he has had in school, the breadth of his reading, and a number of personal and school factors. (p. 1)

This work connected to her philosophy that learning should take children's interests into account to enhance motivation. It reinforced her commitment to supporting reading development by offering engaging structures for meaningful practice: "If the material is interesting and meaningful, or if the purpose for reading is important and vital, the likelihood of forgetting [vocabulary] is decreased" (1947/1951, p. 2).

Leary's philosophy overall was that (European American) children's interests and experiences must be included as an important part of the curriculum; that learning is best done in a fun and engaging atmosphere; that reading outside the "traditional" literary canon is potentially beneficial, especially for students who struggle with learning for a variety of reasons; and that material is most easily processed and learned when it is introduced within interesting reading materials and also practiced through language games and activities.

Although Leary did not author a monograph on word analysis, this omission was due to the fact that the committee had previously addressed word analysis prior to Leary's tenure in Madison. Rather than focusing on a single method—the look-and-say method, for example—Leary advocated a holistic method for teaching reading with extensive reading aloud, individual reading in a range of books, building meaning through context, practicing vocabulary with games and drills with words drawn from texts read, and using visual aids and children's experiences to enhance comprehension (including creating experiences with the children through hands-on projects and field trips). She advocated studying words with children, using categorization, dictionary use, analogy, direct teaching of meaning, attention to compound words and derivatives, and other methods. She seemed to be advocating true whole language teaching—teaching reading as a meaningful, complex system for creating and conferring ideas, some pieces of which can be absorbed through extensive reading and listening to texts and other parts that must at times be taught explicitly.

Contributions to the Field of Reading

Although Leary accomplished much in her life, this celebration of her contributions looks at three intertwined areas: her work as (1) an academic, (2) a curriculum specialist, and (3) a book editor. The connecting thread was her interest in engaged and meaningful learning. As a book editor she sought to produce reading materials for children that spoke to their needs, interests, and abilities so reading instruction would be both enjoyable and a learning experience. Her goal was very modern: to create lifelong, self-motivated readers.

Gray and Leary (1935) claimed that "objective evidence" had shown "the chief handicap to increasing the reading efficiency of new literates lies more often in a lack of readable materials than in serious disability of the learners" (p. 5). In *What Makes a Book Readable: With Special Reference to Adults of Limited Reading Ability—An Initial Study*, they report results of a survey asking reading professionals what they believed were the main factors significantly affecting a book's readability for an adult audience. Their question required a follow-up: "For whom?" (p. 5). The respondents agreed that the most important factor was a reader's high level of interest in the book's content. Next came the style of the text, then the format, and last the organization. The authors made it clear that the study focused only on one aspect of readability—text difficulty—and within that aspect only on "difficulty when reading is done for the purposes of obtaining a general impression of what is read" (p. 9). For this particular study, Gray and Leary noted that "classification of materials as 'easy' or 'difficult' for readers of limited ability is based solely on structural elements without regard for such qualifying factors as interestingness, familiarity of content, or purpose of reading" (p. 9). This study was an initial approach. Gray and Leary warned, "Whatever interpretations are made of the findings presented throughout the report must be in keeping with the qualifications already stated. Interpretations beyond these limitations are wholly unjustified" (p. 10).

Leary's later work focused on providing readers with material that was readable with regard to the vocabulary and structures used while also addressing key areas she did not investigate in her dissertation: interestingness, familiarity of content, and purpose. In an effort to motivate students to become readers, Leary eschewed a reliance on literary classics in favor of materials more popular from a child's perspective. Her emphasis was also on having an abundance of reading materials to promote fluent reading habits.

This emphasis had already appeared in a chapter on reading instruction in elementary schools, in which Gray and Leary (1939) had reported on a massive survey undertaken of schools in New York State. They argued that the school was responsible for providing "purposeful, challenging, and enriching" (p. 282) reading activities. The authors continue,

> [The school] should promote the development of habits of intelligent, fluent reading, including critical thinking and evaluation; it should develop power in applying what is read, thus contributing to intelligent self-direction and social reconstruction; it should broaden and deepen interests that will contribute to the wholesome use of leisure time and to enriched and stable personalities; and it should provide a broad common culture and an appreciation of finer elements in American life. (pp. 282–283)

For the survey, data were obtained on the reading achievement of sixth graders from elementary schools in 50 communities in New York State (Gray & Leary, 1939). More "intensive" (p. 283) follow-up surveys were undertaken of schools in seven communities. Gray and Leary examined New York State curricular materials; organization and methods of instruction and teacher preparation; use of materials and community resources such as library, radio, and so on; and observation of 310 classrooms in 72 schools whose "achievement in reading as revealed by the initial survey presented characteristics which merited special consideration" (p. 284).

Gray and Leary (1939) outlined five levels of elementary school reading instruction, ranging from Level I, representing "a narrow, formal type of instruction which...gave major emphasis to mastery of the mechanics of reading rather than to the broader ends which reading may serve in a child's life" (p. 285), to Level V, which provided the most integration with students' interests and cross-curricular reading. Level II "provided an enriched program of purposeful activities during the reading period in which the methods and materials used are adapted to the carrying needs and interests of pupils" (p. 285). Level III built on the previous level by adding wide reading across all school-based activities. Programs at Level IV added to these elements reading materials across subjects and activities that were organized "in terms of units, problems or centers of interest" (p. 286).

Most schools evaluated in this survey of 310 New York State elementary school classrooms were found to be at Level I (61.9%), while 19% were at Level II. Some schools deviated from the structure by incorporating advanced activities from, for example, Level IV, while neglecting rather than building on the formal guidance in reading that typified Level I. In their discussion of these results, Gray and Leary describe connections between instructional context, quality, and achievement and focused on issues that still needed to be addressed:

> Significant relationships were found between the level of achievement of the pupils and such factors as the breadth and vitality of the reading program, the quality of the teaching, the appropriateness and adequacy of the reading materials available, and the efficiency of the supervision.... *The fact that the achievements of the pupils varied largely with conditions that are subject to the control of the administrators, supervisors and teachers should prove a stimulus to constructive endeavor in every classroom.*... The vast majority of the schools have advanced somewhat beyond the traditional type of teaching which prevailed three decades ago and are making praiseworthy effort to improve the breadth and vitality of their teaching.... Unfortunately, the chief purpose of far too many of the reading activities that are provided is to improve the mastery of basic reading habits rather than to broaden the interests of pupils, extend their experiences, and stimulate good thinking. (Gray & Leary, 1939, pp. 287–288; emphasis added)

The authors discovered that a significant amount of what they labeled "reading deficiency" was related to "conditions which could be overcome or eliminated" (Gray & Leary, 1939, p. 288). Although they noted that some "deficiencies" were "due largely to conditions over which the schools could exercise no direct control, such as the home background and environment of the pupils, and limited learning capacity" (p. 287), they made it clear that this was the smaller factor and that the onus of teaching children to their capacity fell on the shoulders of the schools, which in turn needed more support from the state in the form of class reading materials, "stimulating and informative" professional development bulletins (p. 289), and a central professional education center that provided support for teachers as well as curricular and practical guidance from the normal schools in the state.

Avoiding a blame-the-home and a blame-the-teacher approach, Gray and Leary (1939) found classrooms with insufficient numbers of books, deficient housing facilities, and inadequate schooling opportunities for preschool 5-year-olds. They described the failure of some schools to become informed about students' needs and to modify instruction based on objective assessments. Another issue was "the more or less universal tendency to teach all pupils of a class as a unit, thus failing to adapt instruction to individual needs with resulting increase in the number of cases of reading deficiency" (p. 295). The coauthors offered suggestions for improvement, including broadening readers' visions, promoting "social enlightenment" (p. 296), and encouraging leisure-time reading. They expanded views of reading instruction to include wide reading and reading across the content areas—teaching basic instructional aspects along with guidance in reading literature, reading in other subject areas, and free-choice recreational reading. They called for teaching reading through high school and offering enriching activities and material tied to students' interests and needs, taught through differentiated instruction.

Another key suggestion Gray and Leary (1939) made was to move from a reading readiness model to one that works to prepare students: "The problem cannot be solved merely by postponing the time for beginning reading. The solution lies...in the provisions of training and experiences which prepare pupils to engage successfully in simple reading activities" (pp. 298–299). Although Gray and Leary argue for a wide array of reading materials in classrooms to create "more opportunities for extending the experience of pupils and for broadening their interests" (p. 300), there is no mention of diversifying the reading selections with respect to their portrayal of gender, race, or ethnicity.

In her 1949 chapter on "Interpreting the Reading Program to the Public," Leary discusses the need to create communication between schools and the communities they serve. Although a valuable goal, Leary's suggestions reveal a condescending attitude toward parents in poor districts and a blindness to the needs of families living in poverty. For example, instead of focusing on economic factors that might preclude parents being able to afford warm clothing and medical care, Leary seems to assume that parents living in poverty did not love and care for their children and suggested parents might

> need to be shown how important it is to take their children off the streets, to provide them with better food, clothing, and sleeping conditions, to give them needed medical care, love, and protection, and to insure them security and happiness. (1949b, p. 327)

Despite her biased approach, Leary's main focus was on educators translating the educational process so parents were included. She wanted families to be welcomed in the schools and classrooms, both through formal invitations and informal visits. In this chapter Leary also advocates the "three-track plan" (p. 331) that was begun in Madison schools around 1945. Although this system is still used in many schools today, it has been restructured by many others because of the obvious drawbacks of labeling children's reading ability as high, medium, or low so early in life. At the time, however, it was a move away from a one-size-fits-all approach to teaching reading.

Concerned with readability in her doctoral dissertation, Leary seemed afterward to focus much more intensely on engagement and motivation as central to efforts to teaching reading in schools. A critic of books published for children, Leary understood the appeal of the chapbooks of the early 18th century that although "filled with doggerel verse, and condensed crude, and vulgar stories,...were loved by children and eagerly bought for 'a penny plain, tup pence colored'" (1970, p. 4). In contrast, she branded the "reactionary publications of the Puritans" such as James Janeway's *Token for Children* (1676) as "cheap broadsides and fear-burdened" texts (p. 4) and wrote of *The New England Primer* (Ford, 1897/1962; Harris, pre-1690) of the late 1600s: "Through its miserable little pages the Puritans aimed to promote goodness on earth and joy in the Hereafter as well as to teach children to read" (p. 4). Leary preferred adventure stories that would capture children's imagination. This approach is clearly evident in her coedited literature anthologies.

Leary's (1955a) goal for her Reading-Literature series—and for her other anthologies—was for children to "gain some understandings of human nature by observing the ways of human beings through the eyes of observant authors" (p. 6). It was her hope that a young reader would see him- or herself as a "representative of humanity, trying to achieve better attitudes and higher ideals. Through materials that he can read and understand and enjoy, he will also acquire an at-homeness with books that will promote personal confidence and security" (p. 6). Leary created this series to be used as a tool that "stimulates rather than weakens creative teachers, that suggests rather than restricts, that is neither too much nor too little, that respects rather than disregards the ingenuity and sincerity of teachers" (p. 6). In her foreword to *Your World* (Reading-Literature series, book one; Leary, 1955a), Leary argues that the way to engage children with reading is to offer them material full of interesting experiences, variety, fun and laughter, and the security of friends (pp. 5–6). With regard to the final point, Leary writes,

> Does a child cherish inferiorities? Does he feel that life is not treating him right? Has he weak and tender spots that make him feel resentful? If so, he must come to see that there are real ways of solving problems, without bullet-proof body, anti-gravitational control, or super-dynamic energy. (p. 6)

In her foreword to the second Reading-Literature anthology (Eberhart, Swearingen, & Leary, 1955b), Leary (1955b) emphasizes the question, "What is America—for me?" (p. 6). She wanted children to "ask themselves this question, not with any superior, chauvinistic intent, but with an earnest desire to find an honest, inspiring answer" (p. 6). She felt the texts included would "help them to raise such a question and to arrive at a living, human way of thinking and feeling about America" (p. 6). Likewise in the third anthology (Eberhart, Swearingen, & Leary, 1955c), Leary (1955c) mentions her hope that "by reading about other people" a child would "grow in his understanding of them, their pattern of living, problems, and values. With this understanding will come sensitivity, sympathy, insight, tolerance, and the ability and willingness 'to put himself in the other person's shoes'" (p. 5).

Leary's interest in connecting to children's lives and focusing on engagement and readability were and are key issues in reading education, but missing was any demonstration of an understanding of diversity, even as applicable at the time. Her living, human approach was focused on whiteness and Christianity as the norms for goodness. In the second volume of the Discovery Series (Miller & Leary, 1936), a story is introduced as follows: "In your church or Sunday school you have been told of the men and women who have gone as missionaries to distant lands to carry the comforts of religion to heathen or backward peoples" (p. 167). In addition, Miller and Leary's (1936) selection of literature featuring heroes and adventurers in world travels and scientific study focuses exclusively on the achievements of white males. By the following year, in volume three of the Discovery Series, Persing and Leary (1937) did include both women and men who became champions in their time. (Ten of 24 chapters were by women about women.) However, none of the stories featured African Americans, and the one on Eddie Cantor depicted him in blackface on the first page. No later editions of this volume were published. In the third Reading-Literature anthology (Eberhart et al., 1955c), black African characters are subordinated to a white male child: "But I was white and must be obeyed, even though they knew I didn't know what I was doing" (p. 609). The interests addressed in the stories and the human relations furthered were those of white students exclusively and of males predominantly.

Selections for the anthologies emphasized the inevitability of progress within a white Eurocentric notion of superiority over native peoples, who were presented as savages who attacked unsuspecting whites and inevitably had to perish in the face of white progress and civilization (e.g., Eberhart, Swearingen, & Leary, 1955a, pp. 343–346). In another story, to demonstrate that a Native American male child had earned a white male child's acceptance, the former was stripped of his Native identity and labeled white: "He was white. It didn't matter how many Indian ancestors Monty had had, he was white clear through" (Eberheart et al., 1955b, p. 487).

Although forward-thinking in many ways, Leary failed to speak to the issues of race and racism prevalent in some selections she chose, taking instead a Eurocentric approach toward literature selection that Larrick (1965) describes in her groundbreaking article "The All-White World of Children's Books" (see also Larrick, 1995). Larrick's paper—inspired by a 5-year-old African American girl who asked the author why the children in the books she read were all white—remains a classic in the field. If Leary had extended her focus on understanding and personal growth to issues of racism, classism, and sexism, her work would fit well with many educators' understandings today. By 1955, when many of Leary's books had been published, the need for books to include positive images of African Americans was already clear. There had been loud calls for decades by African American and European American scholars for issues of diversity to be addressed directly in literature studies. However, in Leary's coedited anthologies, the maintenance of cultural and racist biases of the time was unquestioned.

This lack of focus on the social, historical, cultural, and political ramifications of reading and response in Leary's coedited work stands in contrast to writings of other scholars of the day (e.g., Rollins, 1941; Rosenblatt, 1938, 1946). Leary's contemporary Charlemae Hill Rollins, an African American library administrator and educator who lived from 1897 to 1979, attended and taught at Howard University and worked at the Chicago Public Library starting in 1926 (African American Registry, 2005). In charge of the children's department from 1932 through 1963, Rollins was in Chicago while Leary was enrolled at the University of Chicago. Rollins was an advocate for books featuring African Americans in nonracist ways and urged that they be published and used in schools. Rollins' edited book, *We Build Together: A Reader's Guide to Negro Life and Literature for Elementary and High School Use* (1941), offers an "unprecedented bibliography of acceptable depictions of minorities in children's books" (Chicago Public Library Digital Collections, n.d.).

Another Leary contemporary was European American English professor Louise Rosenblatt, a scholar who completed her doctoral work in 1931 and addressed issues of diversity directly in her 1946 issue of *English Education* that focused on the theme of intercultural education. Although most interculturalists promoted assimilation and did not go beyond a superficial implementation of multiculturalism in schools, a variety of authors wrote about the role that the "teaching of language and literature" could play in "nourishing the democratic appreciation of each human being as an individual, unobscured by any group label—racial, religious, national, social, or economic—which may be applied to him" (Rosenblatt, 1946, p. 285). In many respects interculturalists reinforced stereotypes, depicting people of color condescendingly and equating the prejudice they faced with that which white European voluntary immigrants faced. Despite their limitations, however, most interculturalists were aware of larger institutional forces and emphasized community outreach, honest portrayals of weaknesses in U.S. democracy, and the use of children's books to explore prejudice.

Despite emphasizing the use of literature that connected to students' lives and interests and engaged them in reflecting on their world, Leary did not refer to this then-current work, nor did she include any African American characters in the Time to Read series she edited (first published in 1953; see "For Further Reading" at the end of this chapter) until the revised 1968 edition. In Leary, Reichert, and Reely's 1968 edition of Finding Favorites, a few minor characters, such as a postal worker in one scene in a story and a child in the background on a carousel in another story, were drawn as African Americans, rather than as the European Americans of two earlier editions. In only one story, the last in the book, were the main characters changed from a middle class European American nuclear family to an African American one. This was one year after Rollins' book (1967) had been released in its third edition by the NCTE.

Lessons for the Future

Leary's lasting legacy could lie in our acknowledging how long the field has known, and not fully acted on, her understanding of why children struggle with reading: "The very existence of reading deficiencies is evidence of discord between reader and book—of failure to get the right book into the hands of the right pupil" (Leary, 1940, p. 273). She explored through her research and attempted to provide through her editorship reading material that might "attack the problem of fitting reading materials to the needs and abilities of each student" (p. 274).

Another part of Leary's legacy is that she was always questioning things, even aspects of conventional wisdom. For example, she suggested drawing on the judgment of experts to match books and readers but noted that even when experienced teachers are able to determine the relative difficulty of the material, "judging the suitability of particular materials for particular students" is quite another [matter]" (1940, p. 276). Leary understood that often books chosen as suitable by adults are not the books children would choose to read. Leary suggested drawing on quantitative measures of written text difficulty (often referred to as "readability formulas") but at the same time challenged the measures as by definition limited and at best partial solutions:

> The very nature of the method prevents [such measures] from going far enough. They are necessarily limited to those elements which lend themselves to quantitative analysis and statistical treatment, to the exclusion of other qualitative, intangible, and more or less subjective elements which seem inextricably involved in difficulty. To this extent, they fail to give a true picture of difficulty. Perhaps because they are quantitative and exact, these findings, more than any others, are open to misinterpretation. (p. 277)

Leary noted that often relationships of multiple variables are misunderstood, and even by using regression analysis there is no absolute to be discovered.

> Frequently, the index of difficulty obtained through the use of this device is interpreted as absolute, without regard to the individual reader whose interest and zeal in reading a given selection may compensate for inadequacies in his reading ability and carry him over some, if not all, of the difficulties inherent in the material. (Leary, 1940, p. 277)

Leary's main concern was to find ways to make "reading function more effectively...through a more harmonious relationship between readers and books" (1940, p. 300). This implies that teachers must "know student-readers—their reading abilities and habits, their reading interests and preferences, their previous reading experiences, their special interests, activities, and hobbies, their prejudices, opinions, and preconceptions, everything about them that may influence comprehension in reading" (p. 300). Knowing this, Leary suggested, a teacher could then explore the difficulty level of the book with a particular reader in mind.

If following Leary's guidelines in the "most logical order" (p. 300), a teacher would first "observe the format" of a text before considering "the type of subject matter and literary form" and evaluating the book's content for "the quality of ideas presented" (p. 301). The teacher would then "judge the degree of compactness of the ideas and the facts presented" (p. 301), determining whether there was too much information contained in any particular passage for the reader to process with ease. The teacher would also need to "observe the author's choice of words" (p. 301), assessing the linguistic complexity of the material at the word and sentence levels as well as its balance of literal and inferential or figurative meaning. The book's level of difficulty could be in part determined by "sampling the book, analyzing the passages for significant elements, and applying a formula of prediction" (p. 302) from among the early readability formulas available. Finally, and key to understanding the complex nature of the idea of "difficulty" in written text, a teacher must "synthesize the facts pertaining to the difficulty of the book under consideration and relate them to what is known about the reader in order to determine whether the book is suited to his interests, abilities, and purpose" (p. 302).

With regard to reading selections and talk around text, both Leary and Rosenblatt would be in tune with many literacy scholars today. In *Literature as Exploration*, first published in 1938, Rosenblatt (1938/1995) discusses the need to move away from a traditional, one-right-answer-provided-by-the-expert focus on literature and literary response. Leary repeatedly (in her forewords to her coedited Discovery Series and Reading-Literature anthologies) argued that children should have opportunities to read what interests them, even if it is not what adults would prefer children read. Leary's chosen reading material might qualify for what Rosenblatt calls "popular 'trashy' works" (1978/1994, p. 143):

> Despite the differences between the readings of great or technically complex works and the readings of popular "trashy" works, they share some common attributes: the aesthetic stance, the living-through, under guidance of the text, of feelings, ideas, actions, conflicts, and resolutions beyond the scope of the reader's own world. (p. 143)

In addition, although stuck in a prejudiced mindset with regard to race, gender, and class, Leary was forward-thinking in her emphasis on what Rosenblatt later called the transactional nature of response (Rosenblatt,

1938/1995, 1978/1994). Leary (1955c) emphasized repeatedly that readers must integrate what they read into their "own pattern of living" for reading to be a complete process (p. 6). This idea called for teachers to create spaces for students to "use what is read in floor talks, panel discussions, debates, conversations, themes, plays, and other forms of communication" to guide themselves to "more mature thinking and acting" (p. 6).

Interestingly, although many issues related to difficulties students face with regard to reading and studying literature are discussed in Leary's (1948) contribution to the National Society for the Study of Education's yearbook and in the chapter from which it was adapted that was coauthored with Gray (Leary & Gray, 1940), Rosenblatt's 1938 groundbreaking work on this topic—*Literature as Exploration*—is not cited in either paper.

After researching Leary's life and work, my clear impression of her is that she was a highly intelligent, hard-working, and generous woman who had a wonderful sense of adventure. She was a person who took responsibility for and reaped the rewards of making her own choices and following her own interests, while also maintaining close family ties and supporting students and teachers, whether they were in her classes, her community, or abroad. Family friend and librarian emeritus Mary Noble agrees (personal communication, July 29, 2005). Noble also emphasized Leary's sense of humor and proper etiquette, noting that Leary "was a close family friend during [her] later years and a kind of mentor to me as I was going through college and starting my job here in the Libraries" (personal communication, December 16, 2004).

Leary's blend of formality and adventure in her personal life may be used as a metaphor for her professional work as well. In many ways Leary clearly recognized dilemmas of her time, being adventurous in her recommendations to increase interest and motivation in children as readers by moving from traditional offerings to those selected by children for children. Her main concerns in her coedited anthologies were about interest level and readability, broadly defined: "The traditional literary selections offer three handicaps for a pupil who has reading difficulties: they often do not arouse his interest; they may be too mature in context or subtle in expressions; and they may be structurally too difficult" (Persing & Leary, 1936a, p. vi). Despite this forward-thinking approach to her understanding of readability as more than a quantitative measurement of words, Leary remained more constrained by the traditional race and class privileges afforded her throughout her career when it came to addressing specifically the racial injustices and sociopolitical dimensions of learning that were being discussed in her day and before her time.

Leary (1940) asked wonderful questions that would still today push the field of reading education further. (Below I have combined some of hers with my own.) These questions are relevant as increasing numbers of books today are leveled—marked by colored dots or numbers so making decisions about what to read is removed from the reader's sphere. Perhaps within our zeal over the No Child Left Behind Act of 2001, we are leaving past wisdom behind and disconnecting readers from personally and socially meaningful reasons to read. By overprogramming reading choices for children, we may be leaving their interests behind—as well as their rights and responsibilities as readers to know how to select books based on their interests, needs, and abilities, and how to extend those interests with material that may challenge their thinking.

Reflection Questions

1. "Do materials present the same degree of difficulty when read for different purposes" (Leary, 1940, p. 303), and how might this have an impact on students who are reading what may be familiar content but in the context of a high-stakes test?
2. "How is the absolute difficulty of a selection affected by a reader's impression that the selection is easy or hard" (Leary, 1940, p. 302), and "how may students be guided in choosing for themselves materials of appropriate degrees of usefulness?" (p. 303).
3. "To what extent is a reader's interest in a selection related to his [or her] ability to read the selection satisfactorily" (Leary, 1940, p. 303), and what is the precise nature of this relation?
4. How can both interest and ability be stimulated by texts that may be unfamiliar to a child of a particular cultural group in such a way that embracing the world's diversity through texts becomes increasingly possible in public school settings?
5. In what ways can we all as educators be aided in seeing and addressing our biases (with regard to race, class, gender, culture, ethnicity, sexual orientation, etc.) when they are by definition often transparent to us in their "normalcy" within our worldview?

REFERENCES

African American Registry. (2005). *Windy City educator, Charlemae Rollins*. Retrieved May 7, 2005, from http://www.aaregistry.com/african_american_history/935/Windy_city_ educa tor_Charlemae_Rollins

Chicago Public Library Digital Collections. (n.d.). *Charlemae Hill Rollins, 1950s*. Retrieved September 13, 2005, from http://www.chipublib.org/digital/chiren/instrollins.html

Eberhart, W., Swearingen, I.D., & Leary, B.E. (1955a). *Your world*. [Reading-Literature series, book one] (Rev. ed.). Evanston, IL: Row, Peterson.

Eberhart, W., Swearingen, I.D., & Leary, B.E. (1955b). *Your country* [Reading-Literature series, book two] (Rev. ed.). Evanston, IL: Row, Peterson.

Eberhart, W., Swearingen, I.D., & Leary, B.E. (1955c). *Your life* [Reading-Literature series, book three] (Rev. ed.). Evanston, IL: Row, Peterson.

Ford, P.L. (Ed.) (1962). *The New England primer: A history of its origin and development with a reprint of the unique copy of the earliest known edition and many facsimile illustrations and reproductions*. New York: Teachers College. (Original work published 1897)

Gray, W.S., & Leary, B.E. (1935). *What makes a book readable: With special reference to adults of limited reading ability—An initial study*. Chicago: University of Chicago Press.

Gray, W.S., & Leary, B.E. (1939). Reading instruction in elementary schools. In L.J. Brueckner *The changing elementary school* (pp. 282–305). New York: Inor.

Harris, B. (Comp.). (pre-1690). *The New-England primer* (20th-century reprint facsimile edition). Boston: Ginn.

Janeway, J. (1676). *A token for children: Being an exact account of the conversion, holy and exemplary lives, and joyful deaths of several young children*. London: Dorman Newman. (Reproduction of original in the Bodleian Library)

Johnson, E.M., Young, W.E., Leary, B.E., & Myers, E.A. (1961). *Pat, the pilot* [New Reading Skilltext series]. Columbus, OH: Charles E. Merrill.

Larrick, N. (1965, September 11). The all-white world of children's books. *Saturday Review, 48*, 63–65, 84–85.

Larrick, N. (1995). The all-white world of children's books. In O. Osa (Ed.), *The all-white world of children's books and African American children's literature* (pp. 1–12). Trenton, NJ: Africa World Press.

Leary, B.E. (1933). *Elements of reading materials contributing to difficulties in comprehension on the part of adults*. Unpublished doctoral dissertation, University of Chicago, Chicago.

Leary, B.E. (1937). *A survey of courses of study and other curriculum materials published since 1934* (Bulletin 1937, No.13 of the United States Department of the Interior and Office of Education). Washington, DC: U.S. Government Printing Office.

Leary, B.E. (1938). *Curriculum laboratories and divisions: Their organization and functions in state departments of education, city schools systems, and institutions of higher education* (Bulletin 1938, No. 7 of the United States Department of the Interior and Office of Education). Washington, DC: U.S. Government Printing Office.

Leary, B.E. (1940). Difficulties in reading material. In W.S. Gray (Ed.), *Reading in general education: An exploratory study* (pp. 272–306). Washington, DC: American Council on Education.

Leary, B.E. (Ed.). (1941). *Best short stories for boys and girls: Seventh collection*. Evanston, IL: Row, Peterson.

Leary, B.E. (1942). *Reading monograph, no. 30*. Evanston, IL: Row, Peterson.

Leary, B.E. (1943). Literature in school instruction. *Review of Educational Research, 13*, 88–101.

Leary, B.E. (1948). Meeting specific reading problems in the content fields. In N.B. Henry (Ed.), *Forty-seventh yearbook of the National Society for the Study of Education: Part II—Reading in the high school and college* (pp. 136–179). Chicago: University of Chicago Press.

Leary, B.E. (Ed.). (1949a). *Developing word meaning: A report by the Vocabulary Committee of the Madison Public Schools, 1942–1943*. Madison, WI: Curriculum Department of the Madison Public Schools. (Original work published 1943)

Leary, B.E. (1949b). Interpreting the reading program to the public. In N.B. Henry (Ed.), *Forty-eighth yearbook of the National Society for the Study of Education: Part II—Reading in the elementary school* (pp. 317–343). Chicago: University of Chicago Press.

Leary, B.E. (1951). *Word-games for developing a sight vocabulary*. Madison, WI: Curriculum Department of the Madison Public Schools. (Original work published 1947)

Leary, B.E. (1953, November). *Literature for children in a troubled world*. Paper presented as keynote speaker at the meeting of the National Conference on Research in English, Atlantic City, New Jersey.

Leary, B.E. (1955a). Foreword. In W. Eberhart, I.D. Swearingen, & B.E. Leary, *Your world* [Reading-Literature series, book one] (Rev. ed., pp. 5–6). Evanston, IL: Row, Peterson.

Leary, B.E. (1955b). Foreword. In W. Eberhart, I.D. Swearingen, & B.E. Leary, *Your country* [Reading-Literature series, book two] (Rev. ed., pp. 5–6). Evanston, IL: Row, Peterson.

Leary, B.E. (1955c). Foreword. In W. Eberhart, I.D. Swearingen, & B.E. Leary, *Your life* [Reading-Literature series, book three] (Rev. ed., pp. 5–6). Evanston, IL: Row, Peterson.

Leary, B.E., (1958). *The history of the Leary family*. Unpublished personal essay in Bernice Leary Papers, 1878–1977, Box 1, Iowa Women's Archives, University of Iowa Libraries, Iowa City, Iowa.

Leary, B.E. (1964). *Since 1924: A resume of the last forty years*. Unpublished personal essay in Bernice Leary Papers, 1878–1977, Box 1, Iowa Women's Archives, University of Iowa Libraries, Iowa City, Iowa.

Leary, B.E. (1970). Milestones in children's books. *Books at Iowa, 12*. Retrieved September 6, 2004, from http://www.lib.uiowa.edu/spec-coll/Bai/leary.htm

Leary, B.E. & Gray, W.S. (1940). Reading problems in content fields. In W.S. Gray (Ed.), *Reading in general education: An exploratory study* (pp. 113–185). Washington, DC: American Council on Education.

Leary, B.E. to Helen. (1964, February 24). In Bernice E. Leary Papers, 1878–1977, Box 1, Iowa Women's Archives, University of Iowa Libraries, Iowa City, Iowa.

Leary, B.E., to L.L. Newsome. (1972, March 25). In Bernice E. Leary, 1891–1973: To/from Mrs. Louane Leech Newsome. Ten Letters: 8 Jan 1968–25 March 1972, Main Library Special Collections Department, University of Iowa Libraries, Iowa City, Iowa.

Leary, B.E., & Smith., D.V. (Eds.). (1947). *Growing with books: A reading guide* (rev. ed.). Eau Claire, WI: E.M. Hale.

Leary, B.E., Reichert E.C., & Reely, M.K. (Eds.). (1953). *Finding favorites*. Chicago: J.B. Lippincott.

Leary, B.E., Reichert E.C., & Reely, M. K. (Eds.). (1968). *Finding favorites* (Rev. ed.). Philadelphia: J.B. Lippincott.

Miller, H.A., & Leary, B.E. (Eds.). (1936). *New horizons* [Discovery series, book two]. New York: Harcourt, Brace.

No Child Left Behind Act of 2001, Pub. L. No. 107-110, 115 Stat. 1425 (2002).

Noble, M.E. (n.d.). *The Leary family in Riceville*. Unpublished essay in Bernice E. Leary Papers, 1878–1977, Box 1, Iowa Women's Archives, University of Iowa Libraries, Iowa City, Iowa.

Persing, C.L., & Leary, B.E. (1936a). A preface for teachers. In C.L. Persing & B.E. Leary (Eds.), *Adventure bound* [Discovery series, book one] (pp. v–vii). New York: Harcourt, Brace.

Persing, C.L., & Leary, B.E. (Eds.). (1936b). *Adventure bound* [Discovery series, book one]. New York: Harcourt, Brace.

Persing, C.L., & Leary, B.E. (Eds.). (1937). *Champions* [Discovery series, book three]. New York: Harcourt, Brace.

Petty, W.T. (1983). *A history of the National Conference on Research in English*. Urbana, IL: National Council of Teachers of English. Retrieved December 10, 2004, from http://education.nyu.edu/teachlearn/research/ncrll/History/Petty.pdf

Rollins, C.H. (Ed.). (1941). *We build together: A reader's guide to Negro life and literature for elementary and high school use*. Chicago: National Council of Teachers of English.

Rollins, C.H. (Ed.). (1967). *We build together: A reader's guide to Negro life and literature for elementary and high school use* (3rd ed.). Champaign, IL: National Council of Teachers of English.

Rosenblatt, L.M. (1938). *Literature as exploration*. New York: D. Appleton-Century.

Rosenblatt, L.M. (1946). Foreword. *The English Journal, 35*, 285–287.

Rosenblatt, L.M. (1994). *The reader, the text, the poem: The transactional theory of the literary work*. Carbondale, IL: Southern Illinois University Press. (Original work published 1978)

Rosenblatt, L.M. (1995). *Literature as exploration* (5th ed.). New York: Modern Language Association of America. (Original work published 1938)

Row, Peterson. (1941). Preface (by the publishers). In B.E. Leary (Ed.), *Best short stories for boys and girls: Seventh collection* (p. 3). Evanston, IL: Author.

Rymph, C.E. (1992). *Finding aid to Bernice Leary Papers, 1878–1977, at Iowa Women's Archives*. Retrieved December 10, 2004, from http://sdrc.lib.uiowa.edu/iwa/findingaids/html/LearyBernice.htm

Slager, W.R. (Ed.). (1962–1967). *English for today series: Six volumes and teacher texts produced for the National Council of Teachers of English*. New York: McGraw-Hill.

Tomasek, F.W., to L.W. Dunlap. (1973, October 12). In University of Iowa Dunlap Gift Series, Main Library Special Collections Department, University of Iowa Libraries, Iowa City, Iowa.

Wood, A.A. (April 1973). *The Mayflower log, 17*, 1–4. In Bernice E. Leary Papers, 1878–1977, Box 1, Iowa Women's Archives, University of Iowa Libraries, Iowa City, Iowa.

Young, W.E., Leary, B.E., & Myers, E.A. (1961a). *Nicky* [New Reading Skilltext series, teacher's edition]. Columbus, OH: Merrill.

Young, W., Leary, B.E., & Myers, E.A. (1961b). *Nicky* [New Reading Skilltext series workbook]. Columbus, OH: Merrill.

Young, W.E., Leary, B.E., & Myers, E.A. (1961c). *Nicky* [New Reading Skilltext series]. Columbus, OH: Charles Merrill.

Young, W.E., Leary, B.E., & Myers, E.A. (1961d). *Uncle Funny Bunny* [New Reading Skilltext series workbook]. Columbus, OH: Merrill.

Young, W.E., Leary, B.E., & Myers, E.A. (1961e). *Uncle Funny Bunny* [New Reading Skilltext series, teacher's edition]. Columbus, OH: Merrill.

FOR FURTHER READING

Beust, N., Fenner, P., Leary, B.E., Reely, M.K., & Smith, D.V. (Eds.). (1958a). *Adventures here and there* [Through Golden Windows series, book four]. Eau Claire, WI: E.M. Hale.

Beust, N., Fenner, P., Leary, B.E., Reely, M.K., & Smith, D.V. (Eds.). (1958b). *American backgrounds*. [Through Golden Windows series, book eight]. Eau Claire, WI: E.M. Hale.

Beust, N., Fenner, P., Leary, B.E., Reely, M.K., & Smith, D.V. (Eds.). (1958c). *Children everywhere*. [Through Golden Windows series, book six]. Eau Claire, WI: E.M. Hale.

Beust, N., Fenner, P., Leary, B.E., Reely, M.K., & Smith, D.V. (Eds.). (1958d). *Fun and fantasy* [Through Golden Windows series, book two]. Eau Claire, WI: E.M. Hale.

Beust, N., Fenner, P., Leary, B.E., Reely, M.K., & Smith, D.V. (Eds.). (1958e). *Good times together: Stories and rhymes of fun and laughter* [Through Golden Windows series, book five]. Eau Claire, WI: E.M. Hale.

Beust, N., Fenner, P., Leary, B.E., Reely, M.K., & Smith, D.V. (Eds.). (1958f). *Man and his world* [Through Golden Windows series, book ten]. Eau Claire, WI: E.M. Hale.

Beust, N., Fenner, P., Leary, B.E., Reely, M.K., & Smith, D.V. (Eds.). (1958g). *Mostly magic: Best-loved fairy tales, folk tales and rhymes* [Through Golden Windows series, book one]. Eau Claire, WI: E.M. Hale.

Beust, N., Fenner, P., Leary, B.E., Reely, M.K., & Smith, D.V. (Eds.). (1958h). *Stories of early America: From before the white man came to Daniel Boone, Buffalo Bill and the winning of the West* [Through Golden Windows series, book seven]. Eau Claire, WI: E.M. Hale.

Beust, N., Fenner, P., Leary, B.E., Reely, M.K., & Smith, D.V. (Eds.). (1958i). *Through golden windows: Ten-volume set.* Eau Claire, WI: E.M. Hale.

Beust, N., Fenner, P., Leary, B.E., Reely, M.K., & Smith, D.V. (Eds.). (1958j). *Wide wonderful world: The wonders of nature* [Through Golden Windows series, book nine]. Eau Claire, WI: E.M. Hale.

Beust, N., Fenner, P., Leary, B.E., Reely, M.K., & Smith, D.V. (Eds.). (1958k). *Wonderful things happen: Adventures everywhere* [Through Golden Windows series, book three]. Eau Claire, WI: E.M. Hale.

Eberhart, W., Swearingen, I.D., & Leary, B.E. (1950a). *Your country* [Reading-Literature series, book two]. Evanston, IL: Row, Peterson.

Eberhart, W., Swearingen, I.D., & Leary, B.E. (1950b). *Your life* [Reading-Literature series, book three]. Evanston, IL: Row, Peterson.

Eberhart, W., Swearingen, I.D., & Leary, B.E. (1950c). *Your world* [Reading-Literature series, book one]. Evanston, IL: Row, Peterson.

Leary, B.E. (Ed.). (1941). *Best short stories for boys and girls: Seventh collection.* Evanston, IL: Row, Peterson.

Leary, B.E., Reichert E.C., & Reely, M.K. (Eds.). (1953). *Finding favorites.* [Time to Read series, book four]. Chicago: J.B. Lippincott.

Leary, B.E., Reichert E.C., & Reely, M.K. (Eds.). (1953). *Making friends.* [Time to Read series, book two]. Chicago: J.B. Lippincott.

Leary, B.E., Reichert E.C., & Reely, M.K. (Eds.). (1953). *Skipping along.* [Time to Read series, book three]. Chicago: J.B. Lippincott.

Leary, B.E., Reichert E.C., & Reely, M.K. (Eds.). (1954). *Helping others.* [Time to Read series, book five]. Chicago: J.B. Lippincott.

Leary, B.E., Reichert E.C., & Reely, M.K. (Eds.). (1954). *Sailing ahead.* [Time to Read series, book six]. Chicago: J.B. Lippincott.

Leary, B.E., Reichert, E.C., & Reely, M.K. (Eds.). (1954). *Moving forward.* [Time to Read series, book seven]. Chicago: J.B. Lippincott.

Miller, H.A., & Leary, B.E. (Eds.). (1936). *New horizons* [Discovery series, book two]. New York: Harcourt, Brace.

Persing, C.L., & Leary, B.E. (Eds.). (1936). *Adventure bound* [Discovery series, book one]. New York: Harcourt, Brace.

Persing, C.L., & Leary, B.E. (Eds.). (1937). *Champions* [Discovery series, book three]. New York: Harcourt, Brace.

Reichert, E.C., & Bracken, D.K. (1957). *Bucky's friends.* [Time to Read series, book one]. Chicago: J.B. Lippincott.

CHAPTER 11

Douglas Waples (1893–1978): Crafting the Well-Read Public

By George Kamberelis and Marta K. Albert

Historical Research Process

MOST READING RESEARCHERS are neither historians nor historiographers, and we are not exceptions in this regard. Yet while trying to understand the life and work of Douglas Waples (1893–1978), we learned some key lessons relevant to reading researchers everywhere, especially ones interested in history. Waples's most interesting work, for example, was thoroughly embedded within a particular historical moment that was informed by interdisciplinary impulses and especially influenced by communication studies. Perhaps for this reason, mention of Waples within the books and journals of the reading field hardly ever occurs, despite the fact that he was

Shaping the Reading Field: The Impact of Early Reading Pioneers, Scientific Research, and Progressive Ideas, edited by Susan E. Israel and E. Jennifer Monaghan. © 2007 by the International Reading Association.
*Photo:*Courtesy of Hester Waples Achelis.

connected to important scholars of his time in philology and literacy, education and library sciences, and communication studies and sociology. Partly because of this lacuna, we struggled to locate Waples historically in a way that captures the complexity of his intellectual positioning and the reach of his legacy in relation to a field where, ironically, he is centrally relevant but has no ostensible presence.

On a practical level, this dilemma caused us difficulties in building an evidence base from which to work. Waples spent almost his entire academic career at the University of Chicago. He came to Chicago in the late 1920s and was present during the remarkable social, intellectual, and political ferment that sedimented into what is now called the Chicago School of social thought. Recruited to direct the Library School at the university, he expressed criticism of the foundational purposes and methods that constituted the fields of library science and reading research. We know from his scholarship that Waples was determined to make these disciplines more effective, sound, and socially relevant during a time of social crisis and reform. Indeed, his push to cultivate a complex culture of research from his position in the Library School led to debate that lives on today among librarians and information scientists.

When Waples embarked on his Chicago career, he was the protégé and colleague of the prominent educational theorists Werrett W. Charters and Ralph W. Tyler. The more we read back and forth across Waples's major and minor texts, the more we saw threads that connected his questions about reading within library sciences to the educational scholarship that emerged from his collaborations with Charters and Tyler. A single passion stood out across all of this work: to help practitioners understand that the interests of multiple agents and relations among multiple forces affect all learning and reading practices, and shape learning and reading outcomes. Waples viewed scientific inquiry as essential a tool for teachers, school administrators, and librarians as it was for scholars, and the ways in which he focused his energies as administrator, cross-cultural researcher, and teacher reflected this belief.

To what extent, then, were Waples's motives, institutional roles, and research agendas materially linked to the scholars of the Chicago School? Or to the reading researchers who were his contemporaries? We are still left pondering these questions because little of the primary or secondary source material we found mentions Waples's direct connection to key Chicago scholars of the period. There are also many suggestions that his second wife,

Dorothy, played a central role in his postwar scholarship, but they remain mere suggestions in the extant material we found.

Finally, we struggled in our ability to connect Waples's cultural history and social science research contributions to relevant trajectories of reading research. Is it more accurate to position Waples as the "pioneer" of scientific studies of reading processes, motivation, and text accessibility as Damon-Moore and Kaestle (1991, p. 182) do? Or does he belong more squarely in the center of analysis related to the history of print culture, as a figure whose work foreshadowed recent scholarship on the history of the book (e.g., Darnton, 1989)? Or was Waples's symbolic contextual–interactional approach to research an avatar of intellectual trajectories in the field, such as reader response theory, situated learning, and critical discourse analysis? Perhaps the most revealing lesson we take from our effort to understand the complex figure of Douglas Waples is that the origins of what is called reading research lie in all of these fields, and others. We certainly finished this project with the feeling that it is to predecessors like Waples that we should turn to make sure our work puts forward complex questions about complex practices and their effects so we avoid the disciplinary provincialism that can too easily narrow and misguide our efforts.

Personal and Professional Life

In a *Library Quarterly* tribute published after Waples's death, his former student, Bernard Berelson, captures Waples's individuality and complexity as a person and scholar in this way:

> As for Douglas Waples the person, the quality that impressed us most as students and colleagues was how untraditional, how independent he was in virtually every way. His talk was different; often hard to fathom, surprising in where it began and where it ended, seemingly beside the point but always worth waiting for, listening to, and pondering over. One felt one was overhearing an internal puzzlement being worked through aloud. (Berelson, 1979, p. 2)

Among the interesting questions posed by Kenneth Adler, at a 1953 conference on "The Mass Media of Communication" at the University of Chicago that he and Waples helped to organize were the following:

> Is there such a thing as a critical reading skill? If there is, what specifically is it that a critical reader does which the casual reader does not do? How can

we guard against the danger that the student, in learning to reserve judgment and read critically, will come to regard the search for truth as too hopelessly complex and become cynical? ("Mass Media," 1953)

These are the kinds of questions that motivated Douglas Waples's scholarship throughout his life across disciplines as diverse as communication studies, teacher education, and library science—questions so pithy and counterintuitive that they often left audiences scratching their heads.

Much earlier, in a review of Huse's (1933) book, *The Illiteracy of the Literate: A Guide to the Art of Intelligent Reading*, Waples had praised the book's suggestion that "students can and should be taught to read with their tongues in their cheeks." He continued,

> To make the reading population more skeptical thus demands either that students read what is written by authors less clever than themselves (a dire possibility), or that the reading population be reduced to the small and courageous elite that honestly wants all the truth there is and all the shading necessary to give a fair perspective.... Apparently the human eagerness to have our legs pulled is an indispensable condition of mass writing and mass reading. (Waples, 1934, p. 343)

In connection with this claim, one aspect noted in Richardson's (1990) short biography of Waples was that the reading studies of the 1930s deliberately omitted fiction from their analyses because it was seen as too common and not related to the public improvement concerns of the time. Not until much later, when scholars such as Radway (e.g., 1991) began conducting historical research about popular fiction and group reading habits, did researchers begin to gain some understanding of the nature and functions of reading fiction during this period.

Douglas Waples was born on March 3, 1893, in Philadelphia, Pennsylvania, USA. He claimed more knowledge of his grandfather than his father. His grandfather was a federal judge during the Civil War and Reconstruction who wrote profusely to preserve his notes. His father, on the other hand, wrote almost nothing but personal letters. Although Waples described these letters as "literary masterpieces" (Waples & Waples, 1967, p. 1), he also noted that they contained no personal content. Waples traveled with his mother, who had tuberculosis, to Colorado Springs, Colorado, USA, in 1894 and then on to Mexico City and El Paso, Mexico, where he lived until his mother died in 1898. During this time, Waples's father, who worked for a New York company, visited when his schedule permitted. After his mother died, Waples moved to Wayne, Pennsylvania, USA, to live with his father, who remarried in 1901. Over the years, Waples attended religiously oriented grammar schools, where he studied and sang in the school choirs. He also gained two sisters from his father's second marriage (Waples & Waples, 1967, p. 1).

Waples attended Haverford School and Haverford College near Philadelphia, earning a BA in 1914. In college, he excelled as a musician; an athlete; and a student of English, Latin, and Greek. He remembered his undergraduate years as rewarding in several ways:

> Finished Haverford about second in the class, Phi Beta Kappa; won some literary prizes, did about as well in sports as I had in school. I won the all-round in intercollegiate gymnastics and a bid to the 1914 Olympics which were never held. I had real satisfaction in the local fraternity, The Triangle Society. Spent the summers of 1914 and 1915 helping Mitch and Hans Froelicher to run a boys camp at Pocono Lake, Pa., where I met Eleanor Cary of Baltimore [a Quaker], whom I married three years later. This camp and the Quaker community of Pocono Lake Preserve were both an experience in getting along with kids and with Quakers on intimate terms. (Waples & Waples, 1967, p. 2)

After earning an MA from Haverford College, Waples taught English at the Gilman School in Baltimore, Maryland, USA, for two years. He then moved to Cambridge, Massachusetts, USA, and earned a second MA from Harvard University. He and Eleanor, now married, traveled together to Europe on an international exchange through the first Friends Service Committee abroad program during World War I. While spending time in London during that period, Waples studied educational psychology, and when he returned to the United States in 1919, he earned a PhD in educational psychology in one year from the University of Pennsylvania. His dissertation was titled "An Approach to the Synthetic Study of Interest in Reading" (Richardson, 1990, p. 148).

Waples's first university position was at Tufts University in Boston, Massachusetts, USA. He soon moved, however, to the University of Pittsburgh in Pennsylvania, where he worked under Werrett W. Charters, a leader in curriculum theory, adult education, and educational research. Most of Waples's scholarship during the 1920s focused on the study of secondary school curriculum and administration. Among his major works in this area were *Procedures in High School Teaching* (Waples, 1924) and *The Commonwealth Teacher-Training Study* (Charters & Waples, 1929). In each text he and his coauthors were determined to stimulate readers' interest in methodological ideas, not to aid researchers so they might persist in practices of "'busy work' which [clog] graduate theses with masses of trivial data" (Waples, 1939, p. 51), but instead to inspire inquiry and methodological rigor so research might fulfill its ability to make "important contributions to theory" (p. 49).

When Charters accepted a position at the University of Chicago in 1925, he secured Waples a job as an education lecturer there as well. Because of his boundless energy and penetrating mind, Waples was soon recruited to become part of the Graduate Library School at Chicago, where he taught and conducted research until entering the U.S. Army in 1942. (He returned to the university in 1948.)

Community studies of reading, in which Waples attempted to link analytically the availability of diverse texts to particular reading publics, dominated his work during the 1930s. He became a staunch advocate of serious library research and scholarship, and he traveled abroad on a number of research trips, examining such issues as the impact on reading of the European economic downturn and "the obstacles restricting importation of foreign books in the social sciences" in Europe (Waples & Waples, 1967, p. 5). In Waples's view, librarians played a pivotal mediating role between the producers and suppliers of texts and ideas. They could and should move beyond standard research tasks, such as analyzing circulation records, to hypothesize the relation between trends and preferences among readers, their motivations for reading, demographic variables, and social trends. Waples's publications during this period included *What People Want to Read About: A Study of Group Interests and a Survey of Problems in Adult Reading* (Waples & Tyler, 1931) as well as *People and Print: Social Aspects of Reading in the Depression* (1938).

Waples's 1930s international research agenda always included Eleanor and the couple's three young daughters, Christine, Carola, and Hester (Terry), for extended travel. According to Terry, "We Waples kids were among the most fortunate in terms of childhood experiences" (personal communication, March 27, 2006). The girls attended boarding schools in Belgium and enjoyed formative educational and cultural experiences. Carola, who was 8, 12, and 15 years old during these yearlong research expeditions, recalled a three-week bicycling tour of the European countryside with her father in 1937—"my violin on my back, and an instrument on his" (personal communication, March 9, 2006). This proved to be a defining moment for her, a symbol of her close relationship with her father.

Terry remembers her father as thoughtful, driven about his work, and serious about a host of issues that mattered to him. Yet her father's "delicious light side," noted Terry, equally defined his character (personal communication, March 27, 2006). As Carola put it, "Dad was a dreamer, a musician and artist. His head was always sort of in the clouds" (personal communication, March 9, 2006). In recounting memories of her father, Terry added,

> Occasionally we'd open the front door, responding to a knock, and find him standing on his hands, coins falling out of his pockets. We'd scramble for the coins and he'd walk into the apartment upside down as though it were the most natural thing in the world. (personal communication, March 25, 2006)

Terry also described how, well before jogging and ecology became popular, Waples jogged on city streets "snagging litter as he came to it" (personal communication, March 25, 2006).

Public-minded in his scholarly stance as well as in his everyday life, Waples had no interest in organized religion, said both Carola and Terry. As Carola put it, "Nothing was rammed down our throats" (personal communication, March 9, 2006). And according to Terry,

> He scoffed at all organizations: religious, fraternal, birthdays (hard on young kids in foreign boarding schools), Mother's Day, even Christmas, though he produced wonderful cards. They were usually poems, some written by our cat, "Lemon Catsapig Higgenscat with a long tail and a very small brain," usually praising the value of the recipient's friendship and the worthlessness of the holiday. (personal communication, March 25, 2006)

Although life abroad presented complicated logistics often exacerbated by the geopolitical climates in which the Waples found themselves, family life seemed to fall into place, largely due to Eleanor, whom Terry portrayed as a "pragmatic and efficient" person who "kept the ship afloat, handling emergencies, finding necessary funds" (personal communication, March 27, 2006). Carola concurred, remembering that her mother also played an important role as secretary to Waples, supporting virtually all of the clerical needs of his research efforts (personal communication, March 9, 2006).

In the early 1940s, Douglas Waples shifted his attention fully to the war effort. Since his earlier European stint with the Friends Service Committee program, Waples had learned a great deal about topics such as foreign language training, learning and assessment, national intelligence, propaganda research, and international relations. His interest in reading as a sociopolitical practice resonated within the war context. As a U.S. Army major in 1942, for example, Waples found himself in Leipzig, Germany, just before it was taken over by the Russian army. He and several other officers

> went down to publishers row in that city and picked up the 10 publishers whom we considered the best compromise between the most important pre-war German publishers and those most likely to be cleared by [their] own Intelligence Branch, which had a veto on all of [their] recommendations to license. Those [they] picked were moved out of Leipzig...and across Germany by military convoy to Wiesbaden on the Rhine where they have prospered ever since. (Waples & Waples, 1967, p. 7)

Carola, who joined the Women's Army Corps in the early 1940s, noted that her father "was thrilled to be able to get some of the top German publishers, delighted to do his part in what he saw as beating the Russians" (personal communication, March 9, 2006).

In 1944, Waples was assigned to head the Office of Strategic Services Publications Branch in Paris, France, where he met Dorothy Blake, an Army employee whom Waples later described as a partner of "great congeniality in work and play" (Waples & Waples, 1967, p. 6). Dorothy later became a staff member in the Army's Publications Branch. In 1945, Douglas Waples and his staff (including Dorothy) were moved to Germany, where they remained for three years, establishing a functional infrastructure for the publication of German magazines and books. Following his divorce from Eleanor during this period, Waples married Dorothy Blake in 1947, and they returned to Chicago in 1948. Throughout the remainder of their lives together, Waples and Dorothy seem to have enjoyed a deep partnership that pervaded every aspect of their lives—intellectual, professional, and social.

On the heels of Bernard Berelson's resignation, Waples assumed the chair of the University of Chicago's Committee on Communication in 1951 and held that position until his retirement in 1958. The Committee was a program that supported graduate work and scholarship on communications theory and practice from across academic departments. Waples also conducted Fulbright research grant projects in India and Peru during the 1950s, hoping to gain understanding about the sources of high levels of illiteracy and the uneven distribution of access to reading and learning in these countries and others like them. Findings from his Fulbright investigations were published in various foundation monographs and academic books (Waples & Waples, 1967, p. 8).

As in his previous research endeavors, Waples tackled very practical problems in very practical ways while on the Fulbright fellowships. Of his work in India, for example, he wrote in a proto-postcolonial voice

> that present theories of international communication are so biased toward the value systems and public communication systems of western countries, and especially of the United States, that they are largely invalid as applied to Asian and presumably to other non-western nations and cultures. (Waples & Waples, 1967, p. 8)

He devoted himself to developing an ecologically valid theory of international communication equally applicable to nations and cultures as different as the United States, India, and Peru. Among other things, Waples argued that "the best means of telling people [in India] about birth control, agricultural improvements, government, or whatever, was through story tellers, singers and folk plays that introduced such information into the plots taken from the Indian classics" (Waples & Waples, 1967, p. 15).

In this regard, Dorothy Waples described her husband as a kind of classic anthropologist, making constant trips to visit students and colleagues in remote villages and frequently participating in various aspects of Indian culture (e.g., Muslim festivals, student riots, street fairs, family gatherings, and local swimming spots). Of one trip to visit a U.S. student in the village of Kumuwara, Dorothy Waples noted, "It meant riding [a bicycle] many miles on foot-wide dikes between the irrigation channels, over sandy patches, and around small huts. It was often easier to walk than ride" (Waples & Waples, 1967, p. 16). Perhaps the anthropologist in Waples was always afoot because, although "he scoffed at religion and rites of any sort" as daughter Terry saw it, "his keen interest in what makes for the rites, and his curiosity about man's needs were role model material" (personal communication, March 27, 2006).

Thinking back over his 30-odd years of scholarship at the University of Chicago—including research on teaching, reading and libraries, and public communication and social problems—Waples characterized it as a "progression" in coming to understand inquiry as more a matter of imagination than statistics (Waples & Waples, 1967, p. 5). Reading across his publications, we certainly got the sense that he came to view research as an effort to understand and explain broad human issues through broad and varied analytic lenses. Indeed, he praised the University of Chicago as a place that valued the cross-fertilization of philosophical beliefs and analytical approaches—all rigorous in the "insistence on excellence while allowing the individual complete freedom in the direction and methods of research in which excellence was expected" (p. 5).

Upon his retirement in 1958, Waples and Dorothy moved to Washington Island, Wisconsin, USA, where they gardened, fished, and socialized. Waples remained an active scholar and teacher, developing and teaching courses to Washington Island teachers sponsored by the University of Chicago and the University of Wisconsin at Madison. He suffered a debilitating stroke in 1960, which resulted in paralysis and expressive aphasia. Although he did learn to walk and, to an extent, talk again, Carola noted that "the stroke was devastating and he never really fully recovered" (personal communication, March 9, 2006). Carola's daughter, Anita, knew her grandfather only during this time of his life, when only Dorothy "was able to understand him...to [me] he was a mystery." Despite this, Douglas Waples was a source of inspiration, the person who encouraged Anita and her brothers "to read the dictionary for fun" and whose influence led her to believe that "all families were tri- or bilingual" (personal communication, March 11, 2006).

Many people, students and colleagues as well as family and friends, felt the imprint of Waples on their lives. In a moving *Library Quarterly* tribute published after Waples died, renowned behavioral scientist and former Waples student Bernard Berelson (1979), confirmed this sense when he noted,

Perhaps we can best appreciate Douglas in what he wrote about his own father on the occasion of his death: "He walked along the way, observing things curiously, as one who understands their purpose but finds no peace until he learns what each part does to make the whole. He picked up stones and turning them about would point out the precious and common ores by standards strange to us but clear to him since his own age-less youth." In memoriam, everybody is one of a kind, *sui generis*. Douglas truly was…those of us who knew him…cannot claim we always understood him—either his last paragraph or his full personhood—but none of us will ever forget him. (p. 2)

Philosophical Beliefs and Guiding Principles

The present intellectual moment in reading theory and research is in some ways a renewal of the life and work of Douglas Waples, especially the research he conducted while at the Graduate Library School of the University of Chicago. Importantly, this school was created during the emergence of the Chicago School of Sociology, an intellectual movement heavily influenced by a stunning range of scholars that included John Dewey, George Herbert Mead, Robert Park, Herbert Burgess, Herbert Blumer, William Foote Whyte, and Frederic Thrasher. Waples's most foundational and important line of research focused on why people read; what people read; and how reading affects individuals, social groups, and social institutions. He developed this research agenda largely through the study of institutions such as libraries and schools, analyses of reading pedagogies in secondary and postsecondary institutions, and analyses of situated reading practices. His work was fueled by two impulses: (1) a humanist's desire to improve society by generating widespread public interest in intellectual ideas and social advancement, and (2) a scientist's desire to improve the understanding of the formation and expansion of intellectual habits and of the role of reading in this process. As a scientist, Waples worked to identify discrete elements that were integral to reading, and, using both quantitative and qualitative analytic techniques, he decisively mapped and interrogated the relations he discovered among these elements. His theoretical and empirical work clearly paved the way for more current theories of reading, such as reader response theories, theories of motivation and engagement, situated learning theories, and critical discourse analysis.

Waples's work also seems a precursor of "history of the book" scholarship, an interdisciplinary approach designed to explore and understand the relations among readers, reading practices, publishers, authors, and media production technologies. Of particular interest here is the fact that we found Waples's work, especially *What People Want to Read About* (Waples & Tyler, 1931) and *What Reading Does to People* (Waples, Berelson, & Bradshaw, 1940), included in almost every "history of the book" syllabus we were able to locate in Internet searches. His legacy clearly had an impact on the birth and development of this domain of inquiry.

For scholars of style, Waples's writing is particularly interesting—simple yet elegant, complex yet crystal clear, prodigious yet efficient—a kind of writing that embodies the imperatives of stylists such as E.B. White and William Strunk. Perhaps this is because he held such firm convictions about the need for reading material to be accessible and useful, which required understanding the key relationships between the distributors and consumers of texts. In fact, Waples intended librarians, educators, and publishers—the stewards of social institutions whose influence regulated text production and use—to be the primary audiences for much of his scholarly writing. He argued across his many publications that these professionals needed to gain considerable theoretical and research proficiency to fulfill their role as intermediaries, rather than just viewing their work in narrow, administrative terms. Only if they were armed both with the tools to pose important questions about reading practices and the tools to investigate relevant hypotheses would librarians, educators, and publishers be able to provide more (and better) texts to their publics. And only if their publics had access to more (and better) texts could reading exert the desired effect of promoting liberalism and democracy.

As an intellectual and cultural icon, Waples remains both admirable and enigmatic, perhaps because he embodied the paradoxical and intellectual ferment of the times. As Kamberelis and Dimitriadis (2004) point out, the Chicago School of Sociology—the intellectual environment Waples inhabited—was constructed at an interdisciplinary intersection of multiple tensions—foundationalist and interpretivist epistemologies; structural, functional, and emergence theories; and descriptive and prescriptive social impulses. Not surprisingly, then, we are left with many questions about what animated Douglas Waples. Was he a behaviorist or a social constructionist? The answer seems to be that he was both. Was he a positivist or an interpretivist? The answer again seems to be that he was both. Was he a sociopolitical conservative or a sociopolitical radical? The answer yet again seems to be "yes" and "yes." It is perhaps this "both...and" quality about his thinking and his approach to research that makes him so intriguing and so remarkably contemporary. Moreover, a careful survey of his work across time—from studies of education and teaching to studies of libraries and then studies of public communication—suggests that his work became both increasingly complex and increasingly elegant—theoretically, methodologically, and substantively—as he developed as a scholar.

Waples's work thus remains interesting methodologically and theoretically for contemporary reading researchers. Methodologically, he created multimodal research designs that combined various kinds of quantitative and qualitative strategies in ways that were as principled as they were creative. Theoretically, Waples contributed to understanding readers and reading practices within their social and cultural contexts. It is to these issues that we now turn, after a look at Waples's research on teaching.

Investigation of Teaching Practices

Waples's attitude toward science as a mode of engaged, reflective practice applicable to the study of educational issues grew from his reading of Dewey (especially *How We Think* [Dewey, 1910/1997]) as well as his work with Charters on school evaluation and the study of teaching activities as a basis for developing pedagogical theory. *Procedures in High School Teaching* (Waples, 1924), for example, is a textbook that uses a problem-based approach to involve teacher education students in dialogue and critical reflection upon teaching practice and learning theory. Each chapter of the book uses a case study/scenario method to provoke theoretically oriented discussions and closes with references to significant theoretical works relevant to the chapter's central issues. Waples used this method because he believed that the goal of teacher education should be to lead students toward the construction of principles for effective teaching based on their growing theoretical understanding and expertise.

Waples, who had honed his research abilities under the guidance of Charters and in collaboration with theorist and researcher Ralph W. Tyler, coauthored with Charters the massive volume *The Commonwealth Teacher-Training Study* (Charters & Waples, 1929). Like many studies conducted in the social efficiency era of teacher education during the 1920s, its goal was to amass and analyze the pedagogical activities and characteristics of effective teachers to build grounded theories of learning and classroom practice. Like similar research of the time, *The Commonwealth Teacher-Training Study* exhibited "a faith in the power of science to provide a basis for building a teacher education curriculum" that became a recurring theme of the 20th century (Zeichner & Liston, 1990, p. 9).

The text's researchers collected data using teachers' self-reported checklists of teaching activities and researchers' observations of teachers' daily activities in public and experimental schools. Teachers, administrators, professors, and others were also asked to judge the "importance, difficulty of learning, and value of pre-service training" in relation to the activities enumerated in the initial surveys (p. 5). The trends and patterns that emerged from analyses of these data formed the basis for suggestions about improving teacher training. And indeed, Charters and Waples outlined ways to apply findings from their work to hypothesize about the motives underpinning the activities of the teachers with whom they worked, and provided examples and demonstrations of how readers might relate hypotheses about teachers' practices to institutional contexts and to the principles and theories that structured the field.

In this regard, the work done for *The Commonwealth Teacher-Training Study* was decidedly scientist. It was subsequently criticized for reducing the art of teaching to lists of correct behaviors and strategies (e.g., Lagemann, 2000, p. 108). There seems to be some truth to this criticism. Indeed, had Waples turned his attention to teaching and education a decade or two later, when his theoretical and methodological acumen was more fully developed, we suspect he would have carried out his research very differently and generated quite different conclusions and recommendations.

After completing work on *The Commonwealth Teacher-Training Study*, Waples extended the range, depth, and approach of his inquiry to include studies of community reading, reading interest and motivation, and theoretical aspects of library science. Waples referred to this decade-long stage of his scholarship—the 1930s—as the "who-reads-what-and-why?" period (Waples & Waples, 1967, p. 5). More important, it was the period during which Waples presided over the newly established Graduate Library School at the University of Chicago and brought to it a "critical, academic approach" (Rayward, 1986, pp. 349–350) that revolutionized the field—apparently to the consternation of many already in the field. Waples wanted an analytical and theoretical approach to take hold in the area of librarianship, which was overrun, in his opinion, with quantitative analyses that were difficult to use to address specific problems in specific locations.

Directly following the publication of *The Commonwealth Teacher-Training Study*, Waples wrote "Propaganda and Leisure Reading" (1930), an article published in the *Journal of Higher Education*. Its key themes reflected the problems he addressed as an educational researcher and prefigured his formative role in library science and communication studies. In the article, Waples urges educators to extend the scientific approaches that he elaborated in his earlier research on reading interests to the investigation of the "problem" of propaganda as it affected the information that college students gained about topics of great concern to them, topics not represented in the "collegiate curriculum...simply because the problems have no departmental classification; for example, sex, militarism, crime, business ethics, and personal ideals" (p. 73). How, Waples asked, could society help young people learn to critically engage the media they chose for leisure purposes if, indeed, these sources were influenced by propaganda?

One impetus for Waples to pose this question was an attempt by authorities "to restrict the supply of reading-matter within certain social and political limits" (1930, p. 74). This occurred, he claimed, because many people assumed that popular media emphasized aberrant behaviors, giving them acceptability and moral credence, and thus damaging young people who responded to such media based on the immediate interest they fostered, not the ideas represented or the potential truth value they held. Waples went on to argue that this assumption could stand only if it could be proven that a positive correlation existed among readers and the attitudes they might form as a result of consumption. His analysis suggested that the outrage of college authorities should not lead them to limit student access to controversial material. The ideas embodied in such material already permeated the lives of college students, and popular media could be used to encourage students to consider risqué ideas from multiple perspectives. In this regard, Waples urged colleges to become more active in providing diverse materials about issues not addressed through the formal curriculum:

> Commercialized exploitation of half-truths contains its own antidote when all half-truths are exploited. Hence efforts by authorities of the college to provide all the interesting material available on such issues are perhaps more effective than efforts to teach the whole truth by means of abstract

principles, when either method is applied separately. In the ideal solution, of course, the two are combined. (p. 77)

As Waples's interdisciplinary interests grew, he focused his attention on the need for solid scientific investigation and triangulation of reading problems to reflect the perspective embodied by the emergent theory of communication that interested him. That is, he argued that reading is a situated social practice that must be studied from the perspectives of institutions (initially schools, and later libraries, publishing houses, and political institutions); individuals and groups; and textual-ideological representations of information, ideas, and attitudes. His interest in the reading practices of the public was motivated by a desire to influence what libraries and other venues acquired and made available to their readers. One key goal underlying all of Waples's work was the production of an ever-increasing reading public. Another was to promote reading materials that led to socially desirable effects, which seems to have meant effects that promote a well-organized democratic society that is cooperative, enterprising, and socially just. The better library personnel understood their readers' interests and predilections, he claimed, the more successful they could be at stocking libraries with materials that would be read and would cultivate a particular kind of democratic reading public.

Research on Reading Practices

Perhaps the theory and research of Douglas Waples most likely to interest the community of reading scholars is his research on the nature, functions, and effects of people's reading practices. This work is contained in many of his many publications and is particularly well developed in the books *What People Want to Read About: A Study of Group Interests and a Survey of Problems in Adult Reading* (Waples & Tyler, 1931), *People and Print* (Waples, 1938), and *What Reading Does to People: A Summary of Evidence on the Social Effects of Reading and a Statement of Problems for Research* (Waples et al., 1940). This work embodied the Chicago School's productive tension between more modernist (positivist) and more interpretivist (ethnographic) approaches to social science. Indeed, Waples was a near classic functionalist, fundamentally concerned with the ways in which social institutions satisfy the biological and social needs of their members so social order and stability may prevail. He was also a consummate empirical scientist who conducted a remarkable number and array of empirical studies that often combined meticulous archival analysis, large-scale sociological surveys, face-to-face interviews, and case studies. In this regard, Margaret Monroe (1986) claimed in her brief biography of Waples that he was "a brilliant conceptualizer and skilled practitioner in research design" (p. 848) because of the ways he portrayed reading as social history while simultaneously constructing a treatise on methodology. Monroe notes that Waples "has not had his equal in the area of adult reading studies" (p. 848).

In 1931, Waples and Tyler published *What People Want to Read About*, precisely to explain the complexity of reading practices and their effects. Previous research, such as Edward Lee Thorndike's *Adult Learning* study (Thorndike, Bregman, Tilton, & Woodyard, 1928), had provided "evidence that adults can learn" (Waples & Tyler, 1931, p. 7), while William S. Gray and Ruth Munroe's collection, *The Reading Interests and Habits of Adults* (1929), had demonstrated that "adults read much trash" (p. 7). (For more information on Thorndike and Gray, see chapters 5 and 13, this volume, respectively.) Posing the question, "How far do differences in reading interest[s] affect group understanding and adjustment?" (Waples & Tyler, 1931, p. 147), the authors set out to explore how the findings of this earlier research could be expanded to discover more about "the character of adult reading," specifically the effects of adults' desires to learn more through reading (p. 7). If it were viewed as positive that more and more people read for a greater variety of purposes, and if reading were understood to influence "popular attitudes toward pressing social problems" (p. 1), then knowing what readers were interested in reading about was crucial for promoting the particular books that publishers and purveyors believed would best cultivate particular social effects such as creating an educated, democratic citizenry. In this regard, Waples and Tyler contended that "reading for adults is a public utility. Whether or not citizens have easy access to authentic material on social and personal problems is perhaps no less momentous than whether or not we have schools for children" (Waples & Tyler, 1931, p. 2).

Waples and Tyler realized it would be an enormous challenge to capture the diversity of interest in the reading public. They sought instead to capture group patterns, using the group rather than the individual as the central unit of analysis. Instead of relying upon circulation records and other secondary sources, they used survey methods to sample the population. Focusing on group data enabled them to look at patterns of reading about particular topics and subjects that appealed to definable groups of readers. They claimed group data were more reliable than individual data and better able to point toward feasible solutions to problems such as the lack of readable nonfiction on serious topics for "individuals beyond the pale of the 'cultured'" (Waples & Tyler, 1931, p. 65). The researchers found, for example, that the subject of "international attitudes and problems" appealed to all groups of readers, yet "readable and authentic material...is scarcely available to 'uncultured' groups except in a few general magazines" (p. 71). They continued,

> Unless such groups are informed on such topics, it is not likely that their congressional representatives will behave more intelligently. Nor is it likely that readable books will be written, published, sold, and placed in public libraries for such readers until both author and publisher can be assured of their interest in advance. (p. 71)

To promote research with broader utility and great acuity, Waples advanced a range of approaches. "Quantitative and qualitative analyses are mutually complementary, interdependent, and logically inseparable" in certain fields, he claimed, and library research was one of them (Waples, 1939, p. 52). Readers' interests and motivations, he argued, could not be inferred solely from circulation records, which ignored a range of data that could equally influence readers' tastes, such as the availability of particular sources. "Most reading," Waples argued, "like most conversation, probably occupies a region halfway between the extremes of any scale of values—halfway between useful and useless, altruistic and selfish, intelligent and stupid, artistic and careless, wholesome and morbid" (p. 92). Only sophisticated research techniques informed by a thorough understanding of the scientific method and an awareness of what counts as quality evidence were likely to capture the nuances embedded in any question posed as a reading research problem.

Waples's community reading studies culminated in 1937 with the publication of *Research Memorandum on Social Aspects of Reading in the Depression* (1937/1972; reprinted in 1938 as *People and Print: Social Aspects of Reading in the Depression*), commissioned by the Social Science Research Council as part of a series of investigations concerning changes to social organization and social life in the 1930s. As in previous texts, Waples stressed the need for synthesis in reading research, in part because he felt an emphasis on synthesis would force researchers to make explicit the assumptions that led them to form particular research questions. The proliferation of studies attached to other aspects of communication, such as radio and film, also made a synthetic approach desirable, both to account for a fuller range of sources and media available to the public and to make researchers more attentive to the warrants for their claims about reading behaviors and practices. In Waples's estimation, trying to separate the forces of supply from issues of demand often resulted in the "serious misinterpretation of reading behavior" (Waples, 1938, p. 4). For a useful "sociology of reading" to develop, one capable of speaking to a problem, such as the tendency for some groups in some places to access political journals while others stuck to light fiction, information about two key assumptions was required: (1) that people's attitudes toward social issues were reflected in their reading behaviors and (2) that people whose attitudes sociologists wanted to know about "read enough to reveal their attitudes" (p. 201). Scholars now take for granted the multidimensional nature of reading problems, which always involve readers, texts, and contexts, but in the 1930s the idea was revolutionary.

Waples drew upon an enormous range of sources in *People and Print*—census data, market analyses in printing and text distribution, community reading surveys and other research reports on libraries and reading or text circulation activity, and master's and doctoral theses. The report documents and analyzes trends. For example, during the early years of the U.S. Great Depression some readers in particular places tended to prefer rental libraries and bookstores to public libraries because public libraries restricted their offerings mainly to more serious literature. This trend did not seem to hold, however, in middle class areas, where people turned to public libraries, apparently finding reading material that suited their tastes. Based on his extensive cross-indexing of sources, Waples drew tentative conclusions such as these throughout the text. He claimed that no clear pattern existed between the production and consumption of reading matter, not because relations were non-existent but because different factors and events influenced patterns of production–publication–consumption differently for different groups. Again, specifying relations with precision mattered to Waples more than making grand claims that lacked validity. To move in this direction required collaboration with experts in other scholarly fields and an ability to conduct research on fundamental problems as a core practice of librarianship, a view that lives on today (Pollicino, 1999; Rayward, 1986; Svenonius & McGarry, 2001).

Waples's decade-long program of research on the reading practices of many social groups across gender, class, and occupational lines produced a theory of the nature, functions, and effects of reading that was fundamentally a theory of communication. This theory posited reading as communication having at least four key dimensions (or relevant units of analysis), each of which affects the others in constitutive ways. These four dimensions are (1) production, (2) distribution, (3) content, and (4) readers' predispositions and dispositions. We now examine each of these in terms of Waples's research.

Production. According to Waples, the amount and character of what is published each year go a long way toward explaining what various agencies have available to distribute. Significant changes in the books, magazines, newspapers, pamphlets, and so on have a radiating influence first on the shelves of distribution centers, such as libraries and stores, and then on readers. Forces influencing publication trends include gross population characteristics, changing educational levels of the reading public, changing age distributions of populations, reading competencies of the general public and various subgroups, the political climate of the nation and its regions, economic conditions, publishing costs, findings from market analyses, lobbying by special interest groups, technological innovations for producing printed texts, ideologies of publication houses, tastes of various social groups, popular trends or investments (e.g., fitness, self-help, and the creation of wealth), politics and competitiveness among publishers, and changing global relations. Because the kinds and amounts of texts published are largely driven by potential sales, socially and culturally privileged groups almost always have desirable reading materials in abundance, while socially and culturally marginalized groups almost always lack reading materials that they find interesting and thus desirable.

Distribution. Waples noted that the accessibility of reading materials is the single most important factor in determining what people read. To ensure their viability, then, systems of distribution (e.g., bookstores and libraries) attempt strategically to supply relevant publications to the various social groups they serve based on the kinds of reading effects such groups tend to desire: textbooks to students for their instrumental effects, women's magazines to housewives for their prestige and respite effects (note the sexism implicit in this claim), campaign literature to voters for their instrumental and reinforcement effects, specialized technical magazines to the various trades for their instrumental effects, belles-lettres to cultural aficionados for their aesthetic and respite effects, and newspapers to everyone for a wide variety of effects. Only a small subset of the total publications produced is available within any particular venue. Moreover, distribution agencies can be sites of, and for, surveillance and didacticism: "Whatever we know about the social effects of reading may be used to magnify the socially desirable effects, through the manipulation of the factor most readily controlled, namely the agencies of distribution" and "the effects of given kinds of reading may be traced back to the agencies which distribute the publications read" (Waples et al., 1940, p. 53). In addition, differences between people's desired versus actual reading practices may be traced to differences in accessibility of various kinds of reading materials, and differences in accessibility may be traced to specific patterns of distribution. Finally, just as with production, more desirable kinds of texts are almost always more available to mainstream cultural groups compared to nonmainstream ones.

Content. One key finding from Waples's many studies was that the single most important factor responsible for the social effects of reading was the content of publications read. Drawing on this finding, Waples insisted on conducting careful analyses of the thematic and rhetorical composition of texts because such analyses could help predict the ways that different texts were likely to attract and affect readers. Importantly, these were not content analyses per se but psychological and social analyses of transactions between readers and texts. The analyses were guided by two key questions (note that, as was characteristic of the time, male pronouns were used to refer to all readers independent of sex/gender): (1) "Who is the reader, and what does he do and want and get?" and (2) "What and how does the publication contribute to his wants? When the second question is answered in terms of the first, the resulting description of content will show the part it plays in whatever effects are inferred or observed" (Waples et al., 1940, p. 64). Even more fine-grained content analyses may be conducted if guided by questions derived from Waples's effects research:

> In a particular reading situation does a publication tend to relieve or intensify anxieties [the reader] may have about himself? Does it flatter or reproach 'his kind of people?' With what types of persons does it encourage him to identify? What goals are mentioned as desirable or undesirable, and what methods are proposed or opposed for attaining those goals? What popular symbols are approved or condemned?" (p. 65)

Using such questions, researchers can determine the precise ways in which content activates certain predispositions that tend to produce certain effects. Central factors in this process include the general style of texts, text coherence, and the rhetorical devices used by authors to persuade audiences. Interestingly, Waples's work showed that the topics or subjects of texts were far less responsible for social effects on readers than more stylistic and rhetorical factors. They reveal what the text is about, but not what it is likely to do to a reader.

Readers' predispositions and dispositions. Waples claimed that "readers' predispositions represent the least understood and probably the most important of the four major factors to which in combination we ascribe the social effects of reading" (Waples et al., 1940, p. 100). And perhaps his most pioneering and most important work was done in this domain. The predispositions that Waples found most influential on the social effects of reading may be grouped in four basic categories: (1) demographic traits such as age, gender, income, education, occupation, social loyalties, political inclinations, and current affinity groups; (2) psychosocial traits such as attitudes, beliefs, opinions, moral sensibilities, and sympathies relative to the subjects read about; (3) instrumental factors such as motives, expectations, and goals for reading; and (4) environmental factors such as the physical and emotional conditions of the reading moment. These various predispositions affect both the publications readers select and the interpretations they carry away from them. Importantly, and particularly nettlesome for research, readers' predispositions vary across reading contexts and change over time.

Finally, Waples did not stop at cataloguing the characteristics of text production, text distribution, text content, and reader characteristics. Instead, basing his conclusions on findings from many carefully conducted studies in many different social contexts, he theorized the precise ways in which these four dimensions come together to account for the amounts and kinds of reading readers do, as well as the personal, social, and political effects of their reading practices.

Waples also went on to insist that understanding the nature and effects of reading always requires attention to all four dimensions and that not doing so would lead scholars to serious misunderstandings that would have dire consequences in applied activities. In this regard, he criticized Adler's (1940) *How to Read a Book: The Art of Getting a Liberal Education* for its hopeless normativism and reductionism as well as its lack of empirical validation. He also attacked Mark Twain's (1883) "fulminations" in *Life on the Mississippi* about the effects of reading the works of Sir Walter Scott both because Twain imposed his own personal tastes and dispositions onto other readers and because he seemed to assume that text content or author's intention can account for the meanings readers will take from texts. All of these tendencies, Waples argued, perpetuate misguided folk theories rooted in popular assumptions by reducing effects to single (and usually assumed) factors, rather than attending to the complex set of social structures and processes (and the relations between and among them) that contribute to the production of complex and multiple effects. The only antidote to problems of bias and reductionism and the only way to understand the complexity of social effects of reading, according to Waples, was well-designed, scientifically rigorous, and meticulously conducted empirical research.

Indeed, his own theoretically grounded and meticulously crafted multimodal research designs seem to fit the bill, and based on findings generated by these designs Waples was able to posit several important and overlapping social effects of reading. These include (a) instrumental effects or increased knowledge that can be put into practice; (b) prestige effects, including the mitigation of low self-esteem or the affirmation of group identity; (c) reinforcement effects, or having one's attitudes validated or converted; (d) aesthetic effects, or feeling pleasure and gaining insight from literary icons such as poets, essayists, and novelists; and (e) respite effects, or escape from worldly tensions. Waples went on to map the ways in which certain kinds of texts (e.g., instruction manuals, novels, political pamphlets, and comic strips) tend to produce certain kinds of effects in relatively systematic ways (Waples, 1938; Waples et al., 1940).

In sum, although a certain elitism may be detected in Waples's work, he was a spirited intellectual maverick who produced a unique body of work over four decades, from the late 1910s through the 1950s. Within communication studies, Waples's intellectual legacy lives on in research agenda as varied as the nature and effects of library holdings, organization, and access (e.g., Svenonius & McGarry, 2001); the role of the mass media in social change (e.g., Shah, 2003); and how to reimagine and reinvigorate research and practice in library and information sciences in an electronic age (e.g., Pollicino, 1999).

The broad sweep of his research, robust both theoretically and methodologically, symbolizes much about Waples himself, a person variously described as "independent in virtually every way" (Berelson, quoted in Richardson, 1990, p. 148) yet fundamentally concerned "to make common sense more common" (Waples, 1931, p. 32). Contemporary reading researchers might find in Waples both a cutting intellectual figure and a model for pragmatic, interdisciplinary research practice.

Contributions to the Field of Reading

Douglas Waples outlined with great precision the importance of posing useful questions about reading and the public good. He was thorough in his approach to population sampling and data collection. In his empirical studies, Waples sought to demonstrate how individual reading habits intersect with group interests and relate to material forces, and to do this he considered multiple sources of data from an array of analytic approaches. Although the tone of this work comes across as more patient than pedantic, reading Waples's writing often does require a willingness to entertain ideas from several disciplinary perspectives, while keeping track of the complex and often counterintuitive articulations he and his coauthors make between theories and data—lots of data.

Although many of his colleagues praised the wide scope and rigor of Waples's scholarship, some found his exhaustive approach plainly exhausting, even forbidding. In a more laudatory tone, C. Wright Mills wrote of *What Reading Does to People* (Waples et al., 1940) that the "level of methodological awareness which the volume achieves, along with its systematic carefulness, should make [it] a model for future work" (Mills, 1942, p. 154). Yet Waples's Chicago School colleague, Robert Park, found his *People and Print* (1938) "extraordinarily and unnecessarily hard to read," an ironic finding "considering that this is a volume dealing with books and readers" (Park, 1938, p. 291). Some, like William S. Gray, celebrated the "wide and practical application" of Waples's research (Gray, 1932, p. 113). Others saw, at least in some of his work, the heart and sensibility of a cataloguer, a taxonomist who produced analyses that were "bloodless and utterly depersonalized...cold and unsympathetic...[and] appreciative of nothing but minute facts" (Thompson, quoted in Richardson, 1990, p. 150). In relation to a book he wrote with Ralph W. Tyler, *What People Want to Read About* (Waples & Tyler, 1931), still others offered a more balanced view, claiming "the investigators...apply their measuring instruments with courtesy, sensitivity, and with a respect for literary values. Measures and calculators that they are, they never lose sight of the personal and cultural nature of the situation with which they are dealing" (Harap, cited in Richardson, 1990, p. 150).

Across the academic landscape and against the internal disagreements that so often characterize schools of thought, Waples pressed forward, bringing what we view as a Chicago School approach to research about international concerns, public opinion and communications, the production of knowledge, the nature and functions of libraries, and how research institutions affect scholarship around the world. In short, he located himself in "reading" writ large and brought an iconoclastic and challenging vision to the field. Waples helped construct a vocabulary about how reading figures into people's roles and their participation in a democracy that remains vital and stimulating today. As controversial or difficult as his research might have been for some to understand or appreciate, it was in the service of this quite comprehensive and complex set of concerns about the roles of reading in public life that Waples came to sharpen his interdisciplinary vision and deepen his passion for scientific analysis.

Lessons for the Future

Among other things, Waples's work clearly demonstrates the key role played by motivation in reading practice. He posited several key motives based on his research on the social effects of reading that are outlined earlier in this chapter. Perhaps his most important finding about readers' predispositions from across a wide range of studies is that reading is primarily interest driven. While not a surprising conclusion, one has to wonder why this empirically derived social fact has taken so long to take hold in the reading field and why it is seldom used in decisions about reading materials within school literacy activities. Instead, these materials have typically been driven by assumptions about what is "good for" children based on one ideological regime or another (e.g., cultural literacy or whole language).

The second most important factor in determining why people read is the instrumental value of reading materials: Can people do anything with what they learn from reading? The accessibility of the content of reading materials is another key factor in whether people read on a regular basis or not. The prestige associated with reading particular kinds of texts contributes to regular reading practices as well: Do people like me do this? Readers are also motivated by a need for personal or social security. They seek validation for their behaviors, family situations, social status, occupational location, and so on. Many popular magazines and self-help books constitute responses to this motive. The extent to which reading affords escape or respite is another key motive that accounts for habitual reading. Reading allows people to explore possible selves and possible worlds (Bruner, 1987) and to experience the sublime or "the pleasurable experience in representation of that which would be painful or terrifying in reality" (Mirzoeff, 1999, p. 16). Finally, Waples insisted that motives almost never operate in isolation but that any reading practice almost always involves multiple motives—some more dominant, others less dominant. Parenthetically, this basic model of reading motives is very similar to Jakobson's (1960) famous model of language functions. More important, Waples's perspective on the nature and functions of motivation and engagement in reading is remarkably similar to much of the best theory and research on this topic being produced today (e.g., Guthrie & Cox, 2001; Guthrie, Wigfield, & Perencevich, 2004).

Perhaps less obvious, but equally significant, for the reading field is the way in which Waples embodied a particular view of intellectual work and research practice in every aspect of his professional life. His intensity seemed to strike some colleagues as a bit overwhelming, as he seemed to be animated by a kind of joy in the limitless possibilities that good science could bring to understanding social problems. But he never stopped at the level of naming the problems. Instead, he moved around, crossing disciplinary boundaries and cultural borders, trying to solve the problems that motivated his work. In addition, although he directed his work to practitioners, he did not prescribe solutions (except perhaps in his early studies of pedagogy). Instead, he encouraged practitioners to locate in their own domains the theoretical resources that would help them specify the key dimensions of problems they faced. This is indeed the same spirit that currently animates action research among teachers (e.g., Hollingsworth, 1994) and the so-called "teacher as reflective practitioner" movement (e.g., Schön, 1990).

What has been so striking to us as we have explored Waples's work is what Rayward (1986) refers to as Waples's "simple, extraordinarily generous conception of science" and research (p. 358). Reading and its role in the formation of attitudes and democratic behavior was fundamentally a social issue to Waples. And solving social problems, he argued, demanded not sophisticated techniques and derivative analyses but heightened awareness of the assumptions and biases that shape how a researcher poses a question, the ability to pose an important question, a feel for how to develop useful hypotheses to investigate it, a sense of what evidence might be useful or not, and a capacity to study how relations among elements and data might signal both key points of controversy and potential solutions. To do all this requires a critical frame of analysis and a commitment to look beyond the reaches of one's own field, where insularity and parochial tendencies impede progress and imagination. Legislative mandates about the need for and value of high-stakes testing notwithstanding, Waples's sentiments and impulses echo in various ways throughout the field of reading today under banners such as balanced approaches to teaching reading, situated learning, critical discourse analysis, and critical literacy and multiliteracies curricula.

Waples and his "internal puzzelement[s]" (Berelson, 1979, p. 2) were always grounded in external social realities, which he regularly pointed out and elaborated in his writing. Laced throughout the body of Waples's work are definitive statements about how research, and intellectual work more generally, ought to be conducted in relation to public interests. In this regard, his reading research is relevant to reading researchers and historians today, and his curriculum development work is relevant to curriculum theorists and historians.

Waples was also associated with the burgeoning mass communications field, key figures of which left a controversial legacy because they aligned themselves with pre-war and wartime governmental and foundation sponsors who studied reading habits, print cultures, and production and distribution processes to influence the messages encountered and negotiated by the public (Simpson, 1994). Waples himself pursued a number of military and intelligence assignments before, during, and after World War II, including war information, antisubversion, and "black propaganda" duties (Waples & Waples, 1967, pp. 5–6). The general thrust of all these research agendas—the necessary alignment of social scientific research and public interests and needs—is particularly relevant to reading researchers today as we struggle to have greater political impact on public agendas that affect the nature and scope of our work, as well as school curricula and classroom practice.

Although we have not fleshed out fully all angles of the Douglas Waples story, it is in the context of the sheer breadth of his projects and interests that we have come to appreciate Waples's influence on our thinking about literacy. His shift to library studies as an expansion of thought on the construction of reading via public institutions, his work to establish an interdisciplinary communications field, his collaboration with scholars and bureaucrats internationally to bring attention to issues of access to ideas as a fundamental democratic value—all of these endeavors constituted Waples's "reading" research. That he refused to restrict his research on any particular problem to one theoretical frame or another or to one methodological approach or another is perhaps the key strength of his legacy. He was a public intellectual who galvanized the public imagination and catalyzed social commentary—dialogue in the public sphere. Because the figure of the public intellectual seems difficult to sustain today, acknowledging Waples as an important predecessor of reading research and reminding ourselves of his legacy seem especially significant as we imagine and work toward a future we deem both possible and desirable (e.g., Goodman, Shannon, Goodman, & Rapoport, 2004; Willensky, 2005).

Reflection Questions

1. In an era marked by the privileging of standards-based programs and high-stakes testing, what might be gained by reimagining reading research in the expansive and multidimensional ways suggested by Waples's communication studies and his information and library sciences perspectives?

2. How might Waples's approach to reading research expand contemporary educators' and researchers' understanding of the relations among cognitive, cultural, and social dimensions of reading engagement and motivation?

3. In what ways does Waples's research about people and print (Waples, 1938) suggest the roles that schools might or should play in cultivating children's critical reading of the many media forms they encounter every day?

4. How might the teacher-research movement be "read" as an outgrowth of the work of Waples and other scholars concerned both with the value of evidence for informing practice and with making knowledge useful and relevant in and to people's lives?

5. In what important ways do oral histories and written histories complement each other as one attempts to reconstruct the life of a scholar, teacher, and public servant as dynamic and complex as Douglas Waples?

REFERENCES

Adler, M.J. (1940). *How to read a book: The art of getting a liberal education.* New York: Simon & Schuster.

Berelson, B. (1979). Douglas Waples, 1893–1978. *Library Quarterly, 49,* 1–2.

Bruner, J. (1987). *Actual minds, possible worlds.* Cambridge, MA: Harvard University Press.

Charters, W.W., & Waples, D. (1929). *The Commonwealth teacher-training study.* Chicago: University of Chicago Press.

Damon-Moore, H., & Kaestle, C.F. (1991). Surveying American readers. In C.F. Kaestle, H. Damon-Moore, K. Tinsley, & W.V. Trollinger, Jr. (Eds.), *Literacy in the United States: Readers and reading since 1880* (pp. 180–203). New Haven, CT: Yale University Press.

Darnton, R. (1989). What is the history of books? In C.N. Davidson (Ed.), *Reading in America: Literature and social history* (pp. 27–52). Baltimore: Johns Hopkins University Press.

Dewey, J. (1997). *How we think.* Mineola, NY: Dover. (Original work published 1910)

Goodman, K., Shannon, P., Goodman, Y., & Rapoport, R. (Eds.). (2004). *Saving our schools: The case for public education saying no to "No Child Left Behind."* Berkeley, CA: RDR Books.

Gray, W.S. (1932). What people wish to read [Review of the book *What People Want to Read About*]. *Journal of Higher Education, 3,* 112–113.

Gray, W.S., & Munroe, R. (1929). *The reading interests and habits of adults.* New York: Macmillan.

Guthrie, J.T., & Cox, K.E. (2001). Classroom conditions for motivation and engagement in reading. *Educational Psychology Review, 13,* 283–302.

Guthrie, J., Wigfield, A., & Perencevich, K.C. (Eds.). (2004). *Motivating reading comprehension: Concept-oriented reading instruction.* Mahwah, NJ: Erlbaum.

Hollingsworth, S. (1994). *Teacher research and urban literacy education: Lessons and conversations in a feminist key.* New York: Teachers College Press.

Huse, H.R. (1933). *The illiteracy of the literate: A guide to the art of intelligent reading.* New York: D. Appleton-Century.

Jakobson, R.O. (1960). Concluding statement: Linguistics and poetics. In T.A. Sebeok (Ed.), *Style in language* (pp. 350–377). Cambridge, MA: MIT Press.

Kamberelis, G., & Dimitriadis, G. (2004). *Qualitative inquiry: Approaches to language and literacy research.* New York: Teachers College Press.

Lagemann, E.C. (2000). *An elusive science: The troubling history of education research.* Chicago: University of Chicago Press.

Mass media of communication: The report of workshop no. 13. (1953). *College Composition and Communication, 4,* 100–102.

Mills, C.W. (1942). What reading does to people [Review of the book *What Reading Does to People*]. *American Sociological Review, 7,* 154.

Mirzoeff, N. (1999). *An introduction to visual culture.* London: Routledge.

Monroe, M. (1986). Waples, Douglas. In R. Wedgeworth (Ed.), *ALA World Encyclopedia of Library and Information Services* (pp. 847–848). Chicago: American Library Association.

Park, R.E. (1938). Interesting but obscure [Review of the book *People and Print*]. *Journal of Higher Education, 9,* 290–291.

Pollicino, E.B. (1999, January). *LIS education, academic libraries, and higher education research: Partnership for excellence.* Paper presented at the National Conference of the Association for Library and Information Science Association, Philadelphia, PA.

Radway, J. (1991). *Reading the romance: Women, patriarchy, and popular literature.* Chapel Hill: University of North Carolina Press.

Rayward, W.B. (1986). Research and education for library and information science: Waples in retrospect. *Library Quarterly, 56,* 348–359.

Richardson, J.V. (1990). Waples, Douglas (1893–1978). In W.A. Wiegand (Ed.), *Supplement to the Dictionary of American library bibliography* (pp. 148–151). Englewood, CO: Libraries Unlimited.

Schön, D. (1990). *Educating the reflective practitioner: Toward a new design for teaching and learning in the professions.* San Francisco: Jossey Bass.

Shah, H. (2003). Communication and nation building: Comparing US models of ethnic assimilation with "third world" modernization. *Gazette: The International Journal for Communication Studies, 65,* 165–181.

Simpson, C. (1994). *The science of coercion: Communication research and psychological warfare, 1945–1960.* New York: Oxford University Press.

Svenonius, E., & McGarry, D. (2001). An interview with Elaine Svenonius. *Cataloguing & Classification Quarterly, 29*(4), 5–17.

Thorndike, E.L., Bregman, E.O., Tilton, J.W., & Woodyard, E. (1928). *Adult learning.* New York: Macmillan.

Twain, M. (1883). *Life on the Mississippi.* Boston: James R. Osgood.

Waples, D. (1924). *Procedures in high school teaching.* New York: Macmillan.

Waples, D. (1930). Propaganda and leisure reading. *Journal of Higher Education, 1,* 73–77.

Waples, D. (1931). The graduate library school at Chicago. *Library Quarterly, 1,* 26–36.

Waples, D. (1934). A fundamental social problem [Review of the book *The illiteracy of the literate: A guide to the art of intelligent reading*]. *Journal of Higher Education, 5,* 343.

Waples, D. (1938). *People and print: Social aspects of reading in the Depression.* Chicago: University of Chicago Press.

Waples, D. (1939). *Investigating library problems.* Chicago: University of Chicago Press.

Waples, D. (1972). *Research memorandum on social aspects of reading in the Depression* (Studies in the social aspects of reading in the Depression, 11). New York: Arno. (Original work published 1937)

Waples, D., Berelson, B., & Bradshaw, F.R. (1940). *What reading does to people: A summary of evidence on the social effects of reading and a statement of problems for research.* Chicago: University of Chicago Press.

Waples, D., & Tyler, R.W. (1931). *What people want to read about: A study of group interests and a survey of problems in adult reading.* Chicago: The University of Chicago Press.

Waples, D., & Waples, D.B. (1967). *On the march: A short autobiography for friends and family [and] memories.* Washington Island, WI: Authors.

Willensky, J. (2005, March). *The access principle: The new economics of knowledge as a public good.* Lecture delivered at the Bahen Centre for Information Technology, University of Toronto, Toronto, Ontario.

Zeichner, K.M., & Liston, D.P. (1990). Traditions of reform in U.S. teacher education. IP90-1. Retrieved April 18, 2005, from http://ncrtl.msu.edu/http/ipapers/html/ip901.htm

FOR FURTHER READING

Barton, D., & Hamilton, M. (1998). *Local literacies: Reading and writing in one community.* New York: Routledge.

Brandt, D. (2001). *Literacy in American lives.* New York: Cambridge University Press.

Danky, J.P., & Wiegand, W.A. (Eds.). (1998). *Print culture in a diverse America.* Urbana: University of Illinois Press.

Davidson, C.N. (Ed.). (1989). *Reading in America: Literature and social history.* Baltimore: Johns Hopkins University Press.

Gere, A.R. (1997). *Intimate practices: Literacy and cultural work in U.S. women's clubs, 1880–1920.* Urbana: University of Illinois Press.

Kaestle, C.F., Damon-Moore, H., Stedman, L.C., Tinsley, K., & Trollinger, W.V., Jr. (1991). *Literacy in the United States: Readers and reading since 1880.* New Haven, CT: Yale University Press.

Manguel, A. (1996). *History of reading.* New York: Viking.

PART V

The Reading and Spelling Experts: Researchers Engaged in Writing Texts for Teachers and Schoolbooks for Children

CHAPTER 12

Ernest Horn (1882–1967): A Pioneer in Spelling Research and Instruction

By Jiening Ruan and Priscilla L. Griffith

Historical Research Process

ERNEST HORN WAS born on July 17, 1882, in Mercer County, Missouri, USA, to Asa and Lillie Mariah (Canady) Horn. He married Madeline Daggett Darrough in 1914, and they had two sons. Horn, widely regarded as the United States' greatest expert on spelling, died on November 9, 1967, in Iowa City, Iowa, USA. These few lines cannot possibly tell us who Ernest Horn was and why he was an important figure in U.S. reading education. It is now nearly four decades since Horn's death, and many people, even within the field of reading, may have forgotten his name. However, during his long ca-

Shaping the Reading Field: The Impact of Early Reading Pioneers, Scientific Research, and Progressive Ideas, edited by Susan E. Israel and E. Jennifer Monaghan. © 2007 by the International Reading Association.
Photo: Courtesy of Diane Horn.

reer, he had a large following and enjoyed an indisputable reputation as a highly respected educator, educational scientist, and statesman. He was considered the "Father of Spelling Research" for the rigorous research he conducted on spelling (Anonymous, n.d.) and was identified at the time of his death as an "educational statesman" ("Ernest Horn dies," 1967). He was known for not following the crowd and for standing by his beliefs when it came to controversial issues in education. His view that "social utility should be the basis of curriculum making and that scientific method should replace mere opinion in the selection of the content of the course of study" (Stein, 1973, pp. 50–51) also had a strong influence on curriculum design and instructional practices.

Who was Ernest Horn? Why was he such a respected, accomplished educator of the 20th century? What made him so special to so many people while he was alive? What do his works mean to us as reading educators? With these questions in mind, we embarked on our research undertaking, which turned out to be an exciting and intellectually fulfilling endeavor.

We started by identifying writings by and on Ernest Horn. A Google search of the Internet located the Ernest Horn Papers in the University of Iowa Archives, Iowa City, Iowa, USA. Most papers in the University of Iowa Archives were catalogued carefully by Horn himself and were then donated to the university. We spent several days reading the archival documents, which include his published books and articles, unpublished manuscripts, various kinds of notes, raw research data from his extensive spelling studies, newspaper clippings, and personal correspondence. We visited both the house on Kirkwood Avenue where Horn and his family lived for many years and Ernest Horn Elementary School on Koser Avenue in Iowa City. We interviewed Mrs. Thomas Horn, his daughter-in-law, and Diane Horn, his granddaughter. These research processes have enabled us to answer our questions.

Personal and Professional Life

The *Iowa Alumni Review* (Zielinski, 1966) called Ernest Horn a "word man" (n.p.). He had a collection of over 50 dictionaries that included several rare volumes, one of them published in 1578. He owned first editions of Samuel Johnson's dictionary, published in 1775, and Noah Webster's first dictionary, published in 1806. Horn is quoted as saying that dictionaries are "part of the history of words" (Zielinski, 1966, n.p.). Mrs. Thomas D. Horn, his daughter-in-law, shared a story with us that illustrates this point. In his later years, Horn developed arthritis, which was quite painful. With a chuckle he would quote from Samuel Johnson that the cause of arthritis was known only to God, and according to the physicians at the University of Iowa medical clinics, that was still the case (personal communication, January 28, 2005).

According to Mrs. Thomas D. Horn, Ernest Horn was a man with multiple interests as well as a good sense of humor (personal communication, January 28, 2005). In a letter to Professor C.W. Hunnicutt, Syracuse University, Horn provides a vita for his appointment to the Handwriting Foundation: "Among my interests are gardening, golf, collecting old books (especially dictionaries and collections of ballads and folksongs)" (Horn to Hunnicutt, 1961). The Horn family, which consisted of Horn; his wife, Madeline; and their sons, William and Thomas, enjoyed singing together. Diane Horn recalls walks with her grandfather, talking, and singing (personal communication, January 31, 2005). When Carl Sandburg was a guest in the Horns' home, Horn and Sandburg stayed up until 2:00 a.m., singing. Later, as a remembrance of the occasion, Sandburg sent Horn a copy of *The American Songbag* (Sandburg, 1927). The inscription read "To Ernest Horn, with thanks and all appreciation." Horn is believed to have added, "It is dedicated to those unknown singers who made songs out of love, fun, grief, and to those many other singers who kept those songs as living things of the heart and mind out of love, fun, grief" (Anonymous, 1967).

Diane Horn remembers that her grandfather loved birds and would put seed in the area outside the dining room to attract them. He had a bird book, and he taught Diane the names of those that came into the yard. In fact, one of those birds became so attached to Horn that it would land on his shoulder. Horn used to walk around the yard with this bird on his shoulder (Diane Horn, personal communication, January 31, 2005).

To fully understand Ernest Horn, one must go all the way back to his childhood in Mercer County, Missouri, USA. A newspaper clipping from his hometown newspaper, *The Fairfield Daily Ledger*, provides a picture of young Horn as an avid, self-driven student who was deeply devoted to learning.

> Earnie [sic] Horn was just one of the rest of us down in Princeton, Mo., in those days. His parents were not rich and he had no special advantages. He went to school along with the rest of the kids and he did very well, as did a lot of the others....

Young Horn kept on going to school, and people began to say that Earnie Horn was going to make something out of himself.

He went to school during the winter terms, and then he went down to the summer school at the state university at Columbia. He taught a little while in the schools down in the Mercer County, Mo., and then he was graduated from the university and from that time on his career was just a steady climb. ("Old Home Paper," 1923)

Horn was the oldest of 10 children, and he grew up on a farm (Diane Horn, personal communication, January 31, 2005). Music and folk songs were clearly part of his early experiences. In a personal communication with one of his brothers, Horn fondly mentioned the folk songs that their mother used to sing to them when they were young (Horn, n.d.). According to Diane Horn, at a young age Horn was also interested in being a farmer (personal communication, January 31, 2005). His upbringing in the farming community in Missouri might have played a role in his lifelong educational philosophy of social utility and practicality.

After graduating as valedictorian from Princeton High School in Mercer County in 1901 (Biographical information staff, 1965), Horn took a teaching job in a one-room public school in his home county (Mrs. Thomas D. Horn, personal communication, January 28, 2005). At age 19, he also became the superintendent of a local Sunday school. There he advocated a change to the curriculum to make it more meaningful to the children. The minister rejected Horn's recommendation, and Horn left the church and never returned to it (Anonymous, 1967).

Horn worked his way through the University of Missouri and received his BA degree in 1908 with a major in elementary education and minors in history, philosophy, and psychology. He received his MA degree in education in 1909 from the same university. While he was at the University of Missouri, he also served (from 1906 to 1908) as the principal of the university's elementary school (Stein, 1973, p. 9).

In 1909, Horn took a position at the Colorado State Normal School (known today as the University of Northern Colorado) in Greeley, Colorado, USA. Within a year, he was promoted to a professorship. There he won respect and admiration for his expertise in elementary education. Three years later, Horn went to Columbia University in New York to work on his PhD (where he took at least three courses with Edward Lee Thorndike; see chapter 5, this volume) and was offered a job as a lecturer at the university. For his

PhD thesis, *Distribution of Opportunity for Participation Among the Various Pupils in Classroom Recitations* (1914), Horn examined the distribution of the opportunities children had to respond to teachers' questions according to their ability groups.

From 1913 to 1915 Horn was principal of Speyer School, an experimental laboratory school run by Columbia University. Speyer School aimed at improving education by taking a middle-of-the-road position, emphasizing both curriculum improvement and the learning needs of children. The school aimed at improving public education, and it served as a facility where educators and researchers tested the effectiveness of new curricula, instructional approaches, and activities (Lagemann, 2000, pp. 115–116; Stein, 1973, pp. 12–13). It was at Speyer School that Horn came into his own as an educational scientist. A common thread running through his work from his time at Speyer School onward is the goal he set for the application of scientific methods of investigation to the development of curriculum. While at Speyer School he published an article advocating curriculum development that would be grounded in the nature and importance of its uses in life outside the school, rather than in an arbitrary selection of subject matter (Horn, 1915).

In 1915, Horn was invited to join the faculty of the State University of Iowa (now the University of Iowa) as an associate professor of education and to direct the newly conceived University Elementary School. Horn took as his models many of the approaches and practices used at Speyer School as he developed the laboratory school in Iowa. In a letter to Dr. W.A. Jessup, Dean of the College of Education at the State University of Iowa, prior to his move to Iowa, Horn outlined a program of experimental work to study problems of elementary schools (Horn to Jessup, 1915). It was at the University of Iowa and its laboratory school that Horn truly left his mark as an educational scientist, educator of educators, and leader in the field of elementary education.

During his long tenure at the University of Iowa, Horn conducted research projects on curricula and instructional practices in an effort to improve public education. His most extensive single research project was the identification of a basic writing vocabulary. The research was begun in 1922, and the findings were published as a University of Iowa monograph under the title *A Basic Writing Vocabulary: 10,000 Words Most Commonly Used in Writing* (Horn, 1926). To accomplish this feat, Horn and his associates conducted a content analysis of 5,000,000 words from the running text of various types of written communication. Horn was also recognized as the leading expert on spelling in the United States and was the developer of word lists for the national spelling bee (National Spelling Bee, circa 1928). His *5,000 Most-Used Shorthand Forms* (Horn, 1931), published by the Gregg Publishing Company, was based on his book of 10,000 basic words.

In 1937 another of Horn's most noted works, *Report of the Commission on the Social Studies: Methods of Instruction in the Social Studies*, was published. Horn was charged with writing this much-anticipated volume as a member of the Commission of the Social Studies of the American Historical Association. This book created a sensation among U.S. educators who were interested in and concerned about social studies education in public schools because it was the first book ever in the United States that systematically addressed significant issues in the curriculum and pedagogy of social studies education. Horn was, therefore, considered a pioneer in content area reading (Moore, Readence, & Rickelman, 1983). In his work with the Commission of the Social Studies, Horn again demonstrated his strength of character by refusing to sign the Commission's summary report. His reasoning was that he did not agree with the Commission's conclusion that the 1930s was a transitional period between a dying individualist age and the beginning of a collectivist era in the United States (Horn, circa 1933c). To Horn, this was a matter of principle because such a statement would have a significant impact on the content of various subjects and methods of instruction.

In 1947, Horn was elected to Kappa Delta Pi's Laureate Chapter. The chapter is composed of men and women who have made outstanding contributions to the field of education. (Past laureate members include Albert Einstein, Margaret Mead, and Jean Piaget.) Upon his retirement from the University of Iowa in 1952, he was named Professor Emeritus. During his retirement, he continued to participate in various educational organizations at the local, state, and national levels, such as the Handwriting Commission, and to give speeches to different interest groups to promote public education. Up until a year before his death, Horn taught a graduate course in curriculum and elementary education (Press release, 1967).

During his career Horn was highly productive, publishing numerous articles, books, book chapters, readers, and spellers (which are discussed in what follows). He held positions of leadership in several professional associations, serving as a member of the Board of Directors of the National Society for the Study of Education (1927–1948); vice president, Section Q, of the

American Association for the Advancement of Science (1932); president of the Association for Supervision and Curriculum Development (1932–1933); second vice president of the National Council for Social Studies (1939–1940); and president of the American Educational Research Association (1946–1947) (Biographical information staff, 1965; Haefner, Smith, & Spitzer, circa 1967). In 1940 he was awarded an honorary law degree from the University of Northern Colorado in Greeley. Moreover, to recognize his contributions to elementary education, the campus laboratory school was named Ernest Horn Elementary School. This is one of two schools named for Ernest Horn; the other is in Iowa City, Iowa, USA.

Philosophical Beliefs and Guiding Principles

In the contest between the progressive educational movement associated with John Dewey and the emerging group of educational psychologists such as Edward Lee Thorndike who were arguing for research-based curricula, Horn's work appears to have been more influenced by a drive for scientific methods. In one of the early spellers authored by Horn and Ashbaugh (1920), Horn made reference to a scientific analysis of vocabulary used to develop the graded word lists in their text. In addition, the speller contains standard scores that enabled students to compare their scores with those of children in other grades and in the United States at large. Thus one sees Horn leaning toward measurement and the related practice of establishing norms.

Our research on Horn has pointed to four major beliefs and principles that he held. First, Horn was a firm believer in public education. Second, he believed that the curriculum should be functional and relevant to children's needs and should be judged according to its social utility. Third, he felt that improvement in curricula and instruction should be based on rigorous research. Fourth, he held that competent teachers were critical to students' success in learning.

Horn devoted himself to the cause of improving public school curricula and public education. He committed his life to the betterment of public schools and was their tireless supporter and defender. This was evident in Horn's persistent emphasis on conducting research studies that could be duplicated in public school settings and could produce results to improve curriculum design and student learning in public schools. Unlike some of the other educational researchers of his time, he considered it less valuable to conduct research experiments in private school settings, where learning conditions were very different from most public schools and, therefore, the results were less widely applicable (Horn to Jessup, 1915; Stein, 1973). According to Horn (1929), the many desirable practices implemented in private, progressive schools would encounter challenges in most public schools, where class sizes were much bigger and funding was limited.

Horn vigorously refuted any allegations that schools did not teach reading or spelling as well as they had in the past. In a newspaper interview, the 71-year-old Horn replied to such an allegation with the retort, "This issue has whiskers on it. It certainly is as old as I am." He argued,

> We are doing a better job with more pupils than was done 50 years ago. We are doing a much better job in reading and, in addition, we are giving children many types of experience which were almost entirely absent in the earlier schools. ("Prof. Ernest Horn replies," 1953, n.p.)

Beginning with his master's thesis and continuing through his later works, Horn's scholarship focused on the progressive concepts of social utility and practicality (Ohles, Ohles, & Ramsay, 1997; Stein, 1973). His major concern was "developing courses of study based on their uses in life outside the school" (Stein, 1973, p. 23). He suggested that "one shall look in life outside of the school" to decide what should go into the curriculum (Horn, 1919, p. 762). In a personal communication with Dr. E.T. Peterson, Acting Dean of the College of Education at the University of Iowa, Horn stressed the importance of adopting a functional approach in which emphasis was put on helping students develop basic abilities in extracting meaning, rather than fostering skills such as rote memorization. Horn considered the goal of education to be to prepare students to become useful and contributing members of the larger society. He believed there was no economy in teaching students material that was socially irrelevant (Horn to Peterson, 1944).

Although following social utility as a major guiding principle of his work, Horn did not neglect student interests or individual differences in developing courses of study or providing instruction. On student interests, Horn pointed out that "interests and purposes are essential to the educational process" (Horn, 1929, p. 549). Horn was wary, however, of the tendency of some progressives to base curricular and instructional decisions solely on student interests. He argued that transient child interests should not be the center of the course of study. Rather, Horn wrote, "If interests and purposes are to have educational worth, they must be based on values, and the more universal and permanent the values, the better" (Horn, 1929, p. 549).

Horn was also keenly aware of the differences that exist among students in mental (cognitive) ability, their ability in a given subject, and rates of progress. He stressed the importance of providing individual instruction to students across the continuum. According to Horn (1920a), "We should have a renewed insistence that more of our school work be put on the basis of individual instruction" (p. 153).

During his lifetime, Horn actively promoted the concept of research-based curricular and instructional practices. Many considered him an educational scientist for the large amount of research he conducted to solve educational problems. He extolled the power and promise of educational research for the continued improvement of education (Stein, 1973). He used research results to inform decisions on instructional methods and on content selection in different subject areas. Stein (1973) commented that, according to Horn, "the technique for determining what subject matter was most socially useful was the scientific method. Scientific approach, or objectively secured evidence, would replace mere opinion in the selection of the content of the course of study" (p. 29). According to Horn, the scientific method is "the method of invoice" (Horn, 1919, p. 762), and "data should be objective and numerical" (p. 763). Indeed, Horn was faithful to this method of investigation. His research projects mostly involved methodical, laborious counting of the frequencies and occurrences of words and other items of interest. Although such methods might be considered a rather narrow definition of scientific research, they were state of the art in Horn's time (Stein, 1973, p. 83).

Horn was keenly aware of the various factors that impact student learning. However, among all factors, he placed the highest value on competent teachers when it came to effective instruction. He said, "There is no substitute for the teacher, either in stimulating and guiding the student's efforts, or in correcting and perfecting the ideas that he forms" (quoted in Stein, 1973, p. 56). He argued,

> No administrative device, no amount of instructional equipment, important as it is, and no paraphernalia of study aids and workbooks can take the teacher's place…it is critically important that teachers…should have the highest qualification. (Horn, 1937, p. 150)

Horn believed that differences in the achievement of classes were mostly due to "differences in the vitality and efficiency of teaching" (Horn as quoted in Stein, 1973, p. 56). He fully understood the complexity of teaching. He stated, "There is no such thing as a method of teaching that is good for all subject areas at all times and at all places" (Horn, 1937, p. 37). Teachers should select instructional methods according to the demand of the subject and the level of the students.

Apparently Horn lived by his words, as his papers bear witness. In his letter to Hunnicutt he says,

> My interests have always been in the development of my students. I believe I told you something of the careers of students who have been in my classes. Their marked success in varied lines of work has been a source of great satisfaction. (Horn to Hunnicutt, 1961)

Stein (1973, pp. 39–40) also reports that at the conclusion of each semester, Horn sent letters to his students, expressing his appreciation to them for participating in his class and highlighting their accomplishments.

Horn's views of teaching and learning were unique in his time. His beliefs and principles set him apart from his peers, and they are just as relevant in today's educational debates as they were several decades ago.

Contributions to the Field of Reading

Horn was a person of multiple talents, diverse interests, and intellectual curiosity (Mrs. Thomas D. Horn, personal communication, January 28, 2005). Although he was known for his erudition in all areas of elementary education, his most recognized works were in reading and language arts. Our research on Horn has allowed us to identify three major areas in which he made outstanding contributions and pushed the field of reading forward in both thinking and practice: (1) content area reading, (2) student assessment, and (3) vocabulary and spelling instruction.

Horn's Contributions to Content Area Reading

Horn's contributions to content area reading are indisputable. Along with Arthur Irving Gates (see chapter 14, this volume) and William Scott Gray (see chapter 13, this volume), Ernest Horn was named one of the most influential educators in the reading field whose works have shaped the field of content area reading (Moore et al., 1983). He considered it vital for students to be engaged in wide reading; he did not view reading as an isolated act to be acquired only in reading classes. Instead, he argued that reading must be practiced in all other subjects taught and that students should read with understanding their social science texts in geography, history, and civics. He wrote, "The more closely exercises in reading are integrated with the fields in which the reading is to be used, the more beneficial the results will be" (Horn, 1937, p. 201).

Horn was one of the first researchers to investigate ways to increase learning from text. According to Moore et al. (1983), Horn "played a dominant role in establishing and developing content area reading instruction" (p. 425). Consistent with his social utility view of education, Horn conducted investigations in which he closely examined the concepts in social studies textbooks for their relevance to students' lives and experiences. He paid careful attention to the difficulty level of concepts for students in specific grade levels. Basing them on the results of his research, he proposed recommendations for textbook revision so reading materials would be appropriate for students both in the amount and type of content and level of difficulty. Aided by his wife Madeline, Horn authored the Learning to Study reading series, which focuses on teaching children to learn from expository text (Horn, Cutright, & Horn, 1926a; Horn & McBroom, 1925). His recommendations that teachers use multiple instructional methods—such as visual aids, oral instruction, field trips, and constructive activities—to enhance student understanding of content area reading materials are reflected in the teachers' edition of the Learn to Study series (Horn, Cutright, & Horn, 1926b; Horn & McBroom, 1925). Horn emphasized that there was not one best method for all subject matter at all times and places (Horn, 1937) but that teachers should make decisions according to the demands of the subject.

Horn's (1937) *Methods of Instruction in the Social Studies* contains a chapter on the relation between reading and learning in the social studies. In that chapter Horn provides theory about the reading process and reading instruction that is pertinent today. We will focus our discussion of this chapter on three key points: (1) Reading is an active process, (2) background knowledge is critical to comprehension, and (3) reading must be viewed in a broad perspective.

Reading is an active process. Horn emphasized comprehension over memorization, and critical reflection that involved the evaluation of data. In his view "reading without comprehension was empty and futile" (1937, p. 151). In relation to social studies and his notion of "the continuing attack of social problems when school days are over" (p. 151), Horn advocated an inquiry method:

> Students must learn to locate dependable books and articles that deal with the problems at hand; to understand, appraise, and select data that bear on these problems; to organize these data often secured from a variety of references, so that they will contribute to the solution of the problems; and to provide for the retention, improvement, and use of what has been learned. (p. 151)

Horn also recognized the important role that reader interest in the topic and establishing a purpose played in reading comprehension: "Students who are much interested in a problem will get meaning out of a selection even though the selection...appears too hard to be read by them" (p. 177).

Background knowledge is critical to comprehension. Horn noted that reading was more than a transmission of the author's ideas:

> The author, moreover, does not merely convey ideas to the reader; he merely stimulates him to construct them out of his own experiences. If the concept is already in the reader's mind, the task is relatively easy,...but if it is new to the reader,...its construction more nearly approaches problem-solving. (Horn, 1937, p. 154)

He discussed the denseness of concepts presented in content area texts and the problem that this posed to a reader. He pointed out that ideas were presented in technical language and

> in the form of condensed and abstract statements that are readily understood only by those who have already formed the generalizations for which the statements stand. The background of experience, ideas, and interest that might make the statements intelligible are not provided. (p. 158)

This situation hinders intelligent reading.

Reading must be viewed in a broad perspective. In this regard, Horn was influenced by Thorndike's notion that reading is reasoning. According to Horn

(1937), it was difficult, if not impossible, to determine where "reading leaves off and only thought remains" (p. 153). In his view, the nature of reading in the content areas involves reading to get ideas, thinking about what the ideas mean, and studying those ideas to retain them for later problem solving.

In a discussion of reading disability, Horn provides insights that we can take to heart today. He expresses concern about the overly large role in both research and practice played by what he called the more technical and peripheral aspects of reading, including phonics and mechanical drill. He cautioned, "little improvement may be expected from formal drill in reading unless at the same time provision is made for the enrichment of experience, the development of language abilities, and the improvement of thinking" (1937, p. 156).

Horn has definitely left an indelible mark on the topic of content area reading. Many of his ideas are still in practice and will remain so in the foreseeable future.

Horn's Contributions to Student Assessment

The early part of the 20th century witnessed a rapid growth in the so-called objective testing movement. Three types of tests became highly popular in schools, namely (1) intelligence tests, (2) tests of personality traits, and (3) achievement tests. Although Horn was a strong supporter of using scientific methods in deciding the course of study for different subject matters, he was never too enthusiastic about the uncritical use of these new forms of testing, which had been developed by experts in experimental psychology and educational measurement without their linking the measurements to learning objectives. Horn pointed out the many negative effects of uncritical use of the new objective tests:

> [These tests were] full of technical imperfections; they reflected and perhaps exaggerated the current tendencies in teaching toward over-emphasis on verbal learning of isolated and poorly selected descriptive information... they failed...to measure the less tangible and perhaps most important outcomes of instruction; and in many instances they undoubtedly exercised an unfortunate reciprocal influence upon the content and methods of instruction and upon learning procedures. (Horn, circa 1933b)

Horn approved of using a variety of assessments (e.g., objective, subjective, personal, and indirect) to measure student learning in lieu of relying exclusively upon any single type of technique. He suggested that new forms of examination should complement but not substitute for the living, in-formed, and thoughtful judgment of the competent and thoroughly trained teacher. Horn argued eloquently, "Testing and learning are two aspects of a single process" (Horn, 1933a, n.p.). He further commented, "Although test-ing is commonly regarded as a separate operation, the process of learning is in itself a form of test" (Horn, 1933a, n.p.).

Horn (1920a) considered that an effective testing system is

> necessary for motivation as well as for the intelligent direction of the pupil's efforts in learning. If possible the pupil should know the gaps in his knowl-edge and the defects in his skill or habits before he begins to work on a given unit of materials. Certainly he must be shown the degree to which he has obtained his objectives. (p. 154)

Horn's ideas about testing focused on using it to help students understand where they were before and after instruction, and, therefore, testing served as a motivational tool to develop "[a] wholesome attitude and rigorous work" toward learning (p. 154). That is, Horn believed the test should be a metacognitive tool for increasing students' own awareness of their learning.

Horn proposed that students take responsibility for their own learning by engaging in self-assessment. On the subject of spelling, he considered that for students to achieve greater learning, they should accept responsibility for detecting their own spelling errors in writing (Frasch, 1965, p. 381). For example, students would start by finding out which spelling words they did not know in the beginning of the week, set a goal, study the words, and check their own progress at the end of the week.

Horn's Contributions to Vocabulary and Spelling Instruction

By 1928 Horn had completed his analysis of over 5,000,000 words in "every important type of writing that people commonly do in life outside of school" (Horn & Ashbaugh, 1928, p. vii). From this count he derived a list of 10,000 words, categorized by frequency, that he determined ought to be taught in school. His studies revealed that some 500 words make up 75% of people's writing, and a 1,000-word base vocabulary is what people use 90% of the time. In addition, he found that 50% of all the spelling mistakes made by col-lege freshmen concern less than 500 commonly used words ("They are spelling," 1954). Horn discussed the course of this research in a letter to E.T. Peterson, who at the time was the Dean of the College of Education at the University of Iowa:

> The first task undertaken was that of estimating which orders are most often used in writing. Under a grant from the Commonwealth Fund, a count was made of over five million running words of adult writing. The plan for this count was very carefully designed to include samplings of various types of business and personal letters. Letters from every state in the Union were sampled, and a measure of the quality of words was afforded by tabulation of the letters of gifted writers. This is the most extensive count ever made of adult writing in English-speaking countries....
>
> Having determined the words most likely to be written by adults, investigations were then instituted to discover the vocabulary needs of children at various ages. Data have now been accumulated which enable us to say for each age from six to fifteen which words are most likely to be written by children of that age. Research in learning has led to the gradual perfecting of methods of study which are now utilized by the great majority of the elementary schools of this country. Special emphasis has been placed upon investigations which attempted to discover and utilize [as many]...rational principles as exist in English spelling. (Horn to Peterson, 1944)

Although it is not entirely clear what the sources for all the texts used in his analyses were or how he obtained these samples of adult writing, what is certain is that Horn constructed his basic vocabulary list from the raw data he collected. Some indication of the sources is provided in a newspaper article that appeared in the *Des Moines Register* ("Iowa 'Prof.' indexes," circa 1928, n.p.). According to the article, some of the love letters used in the study came from University of Iowa collegians. Among the other types of letters were personal letters; letters written by "people of more than average literary ability," including preachers, state senators, and high school English teachers; letters printed in magazines and newspapers; minutes of meetings; letters from parents to teachers; and eight years of correspondence by one school district superintendent. *A Basic Writing Vocabulary: 10,000 Words Most Commonly Used in Writing* (Horn, 1926) was published based on the results of this writing vocabulary research.

Horn put his principles on spelling into practice in a series of spelling books for teachers and children (e.g., Horn & Ashbaugh, 1920, 1928, 1929, 1935a, 1935b; Horn & Peterson, 1945). It appears that these spellers were successful because versions of the original 1920 textbook continued to be published by the J.B. Lippincott Company at least until 1945. The 1929 version was adopted by the state of Kansas. Horn believed in the systematic study of graded lists of spelling words based on frequency counts (Horn, 1954; Horn & Ashbaugh, 1920, 1928, 1929, 1935a, 1935b; Horn & Peterson, 1945); however, he also believed that the time allotted to spelling instruction should be kept low, in most instances not more than 75 minutes per week (Horn, 1954). In an early speller, published in 1920 (Horn & Ashbaugh, 1920), Horn makes his philosophy explicit:

> One must insure that the pupils will study all words they are likely to use in life outside the school. One must also insure that the pupils' time will not be wasted through their being required to learn words which they will never use. (p. vii)

Specific criteria guided Horn's selection of vocabulary for his graded word lists. He placed great value on the application of scientific methods toward the construction of his spellers. In their general directions to teachers, Horn and Ashbaugh (1920) explain how the graded word lists in their speller were constructed:

> On the basis of Doctor Horn's compilation of correspondence vocabularies, all of the 4578 words were ranked according to the frequency with which they were used in correspondence. On the basis of Doctor Ashbaugh's study of the difficulty of these words in the various grades, the words were arranged in order of ease of spelling. With these two sources of data, the lessons are arranged so that in general the easiest words and those most commonly and frequently used are placed in the lower grades. In addition, on the basis of scientific analysis of the vocabulary of first, second, and third readers, the authors determined which words occurred most often in these readers. The words included in the lessons for the first three grades are not only easy and fairly common, but are found also in popular readers of the grades in which they are placed. (p. ix)

Although Horn refined his selection criteria and his database of words over subsequent editions of the spellers, his fidelity to social utility remained constant as evidenced by his emphasis in a monograph for teachers on selecting words of "high permanent value" for spelling study (Horn, 1954, p. 9).

For Horn, learning to spell was primarily a visual memory task that required the student to memorize correct spellings. His spelling texts introduced students to a plan for studying words that included five steps. Teachers were admonished to begin the year by teaching their students how to study. Horn's steps for how to learn to spell a word, introduced in an early speller (Horn & Ashbaugh, 1920) and reiterated in later versions (Horn & Ashbaugh, 1935a, 1935b), are summarized below based on the directions to pupils presented in the speller that was adopted by the state of Kansas (Horn & Ashbaugh, 1929):

Step 1—Pronounce the word, saying each syllable very distinctly, and looking closely at each syllable as you say it.

Step 2—With closed eyes try to see the word in your book, syllable by syllable, as you pronounce it in a whisper. Spell by syllables.

Step 3—Open your eyes and look at the word to see whether or not you had it right. If you did not have it right, do step one and step two over again. Keep trying until you can say the letters correctly with closed eyes.

Step 4—When you are sure that you have learned the word, write it without looking at your book, and then compare your attempt with the book in order to see whether or not you wrote it correctly. [As with step three, the unsuccessful student was to begin again at step one.]

Step 5—Now write the word again. See if it is right. If it is, cover it with your hand and write it again. [The student was to attempt three trials at writing the word. Successful students could consider they had learned the correct spelling for that day. Unsuccessful students were to start over at step one.] (pp. xxv–xxvi)

In addition to a method of study that incorporated a focus on repetition to achieve accuracy, as indicated in the steps above, Horn espoused other principles of spelling instruction. These principles included a weekly cycle of word study, review to eliminate error, provision for individual differences, the importance of the corrected test, and although not referred to as such, a focus on metacognition as it relates to individual regulation of learning to spell.

Horn's spellers contain lists of words for weekly study. The words were graded based on his frequency studies. However, across words in a list there was no attempt to represent common spelling patterns. Each week's word list consisted of 20 new words and 20 review words. The review words were those words that had been new four weeks previously. (The exception was grade 1 in which there were 10 new words and 10 review words.) A weekly unit began on Monday with students taking a pretest. Only those words missed on the pretest were targeted for individual study on Tuesday. Students were to use the five-step method outlined above as they studied the words they had missed. On Wednesday, students again were tested on all the words. The purpose of this test was to show the students the progress they had made in their study and to identify words for a second round of independent study on Thursday. On Friday students were tested on the words of the week and the review words.

Multiple testing during the weekly unit served two purposes. First, it enabled teachers and individual students to identify words not learned and, therefore, needing to be studied. Second, by having students correct their own tests, their individual attention was focused on each word misspelled as well as on the correct spelling of the word. In fact, Horn stated, "The test is the most fruitful single learning activity per unit of time that has yet been devised" (1954, p. 18).

Horn's spellers included standard scores that indicated the average number of words spelled correctly by children in general. Horn expected that over the weekly course of study students' scores should exceed the standard scores provided, with the ultimate idea being that students would regulate their study toward the goal of complete accuracy on the final test. Horn encouraged other forms of self-regulation in his general directions to pupils contained in his spellers. Students were advised in their spare time to review errors made on previous tests. Likewise, students were told to keep a spelling notebook of words missed on any test or composition. They were to look for frequently missed words to which they could devote special review.

Horn also discussed the concept of a spelling consciousness (i.e., the need for attention to accurate spelling) and the related idea that people are judged by their ability to spell correctly. In his "General Directions to Teachers" in *The Horn-Ashbaugh Fundamentals of Spelling: Grades One to Eight* (1928), Horn directs teachers to "show the pupils the importance of spelling in letters and in the written work done in the school. Give cases...where people have been discredited because of spelling errors in letters" (p. xiii).

The influence of Horn's work has had a continuing impact on spelling instruction. First, the notion that "pupils will study all the words which are frequently used in life outside the school" (Horn & Ashbaugh, 1928, p. vii) is reflected today in vocabulary instruction through the notion of selecting high-utility words (e.g., "tier" words) for instruction (Hickman, Pollard-Durodola, & Vaughn, 2004, p. 722). Furthermore, correct spelling is still considered a social marker, while poor spelling invites social disgrace. Finally, Horn's weekly cycle for spelling instruction, and his advice on learning how to spell words (i.e., the five-step test-study procedure), have been incorporated into many commercial spelling programs.

In 1953 Hanna and Moore published a paper that challenged Horn's belief that spelling was primarily a visual memory task. According to Hanna and Moore, an instructional program should "teach the child to 'hear' and to 'analyze' his speech in such a way as to facilitate the spelling of his speech" (p. 329). In contrast to Horn, these researchers believed that spelling involved mapping speech sounds through the use of letters that represented the sounds (p. 330). Yet Horn remained true to his belief that irregularity in English orthography made it challenging for children to learn to spell, and he continued to promote his belief that teachers needed to directly teach the large number of common words that do not conform to any phonetic or orthographic rule (Horn, 1957, p. 432). Prior to the article by Hanna and Moore (1953), Horn made almost no mention of the relation between the sounds of spoken language and the written forms. However, Hodges (1987) suggests that Horn's 1957 article in *The Elementary School Journal* was perhaps a rebuttal to Hanna and Moore.

On the issue of using phonics versus other approaches to spelling instruction, Horn argued in this article that it is critical for any plan of spelling instruction to be soundly grounded in scientific evidence. He wrote, "Some of the claims recently made for the contribution of phonics to spelling and the related proposal to spell by 'word analysis, sounding, and logical reasoning by analogy,' do not, unfortunately, appear to be so grounded" (Horn, 1957, p. 424). However, he agreed that "well-planned instruction in sound-to-letter and letter-to-sound associations in appropriate relation to other learning procedures may be of benefit both in spelling and in reading" (p. 424). Horn also acknowledged that some characteristics of English spelling exhibit considerable consistency and "most of these pertain to word patterns, syllables, meanings, word positions, the adding of suffixes and the influences of sounds or letters adjacent to the sound to be spelled" (p. 431). These consistencies could be pointed out for the students. However, the phonics approach in itself, he said, was not effective because of regional differences in speech. Therefore, due to the complexity of English orthography, according to Horn, "children should learn the *ways*, not *the* way, in which each sound is spelled" (p. 432).

Although Horn based his claims on the research evidence that existed at the time, his notions of spelling instruction might be disputed by current theorists, researchers, and practitioners in spelling. A significant challenge to Horn's theories is related to the developmental nature of children's understanding of English orthography. For Horn, a consideration of the developmental nature of spelling knowledge was to construct word lists for study based on the frequency of occurrence of words in the writing of adults and in the speaking and writing vocabularies of children. Words of the highest frequency were to be the words first taught under the assumption that they would be the words most used by children in their writing. Yet Read's (1971) landmark study of children's understanding of English phonology shifted the view on development from a curriculum content perspective to one of cognitive understanding. Specifically, Read's thesis was that children learn to spell by representing the individual sounds in words. Later, Henderson (1985) built on this notion through a spelling curriculum that focused on developmental stages that children follow as they master English orthography. Beginning with Read's work and fortified by Henderson's, understandings about spelling knowledge and instruction have expanded beyond the belief that learning to spell is primarily a visual memory process. Bear, Invernizzi, Templeton, and Johnston (2003) summed up by saying that word knowledge, although partly composed of information about high-frequency words, also includes understandings of letter–sound correspondences and spelling patterns.

Lessons for the Future

Horn's notions of the importance of the teacher, the relevancy of the curriculum, and the instrumental nature of methods of instruction are lessons that should continue to influence reading instruction. His emphasis on critical thinking combined with inquiry in the elementary school curriculum is as relevant now as it was when he proposed it in 1937.

Today, as Horn asserted decades earlier (Stein, 1973, p. 56), the teacher is the critical mediator between the subject matter and the learner. However,

Horn would argue that the teacher's competency in stimulating student learning must be juxtaposed with a socially useful curriculum (Stein, 1973, pp. 56–57). It is on this point that Horn's views of scientific method and social utility merge. His research investigations to determine what knowledge was most useful to learn have been criticized as an attempt to "mechanize" teaching (Brubacher, cited in Stein, 1973, p. 82). Nevertheless, Horn's idea that mastery of subject matter has to be weighed against the amount of time children spend in school, combined with his belief that learning, reading, and thinking are active processes, is relevant in the knowledge explosion of the 21st century. In sum, Horn eschewed general and abstract treatments of content or contrived school activities that emphasized superficial or irrelevant details (Horn, 1937). Thus, we suspect Horn would decry the use of motifs in the classroom that "organiz[e] content and activities together simply because they contain or mention a similar subject" (Barton & Smith, 2000, p. 55). (The reader is referred to the work of Barton and Smith [2000] for a discussion of the difference between motifs and themes, which are similar to our discussion below of Horn's notion of inquiry.)

Although he did not advocate that any one method should dominate instruction, Horn was a strong advocate of inquiry, or what he once referred to as a project—"a problematic act taken in its natural setting and involving something beyond mere thinking" (Horn, 1920b, p. 114)—to be incorporated into the course of study in elementary classrooms. According to Horn, differences in the thinking of the scholar and that of the immature student were simply a matter of degree. Horn (1937) indicated that "learning should be carried on in the spirit of discovery" and should incorporate a "search for sources of information...inquiry into their authenticity...selection, appraisal, and organization of data," along with interpretation "guided and safeguarded by the same principles that are used in scholarly research" (p. 23). He believed that the inquiry should be one with which children could identify and should involve the use of multiple hypotheses, the search for negative evidence, and reflection on the process to enable children to apply their method to future problems (Horn, 1937; Stein 1973). All these beliefs are relevant today.

In 1999 Duffy and Hoffman discussed the "flawed search for a perfect method" of teaching reading (p. 10). They asserted that reading instruction was under assault, an assault based on the public's belief that teachers do not teach in the right way, and that reading instruction could be fixed by legislating the perfect method of reading instruction (pp. 10, 12). Duffy and Hoffman's argument for the fallacy of this logic echoes Horn's (1937) position that "there is no such thing as a method of teaching that is good for all subject matter at all times and at all places" (pp. 37–38).

Based upon a review of the combined volume of Horn's writing, as well as commentaries about Horn's work, we have compiled the following list of accomplishments to which we believe Horn would want schools held accountable:

- Enable students to develop a sense of personal purpose.
- Develop habits of work.
- Provide a curriculum that focuses on social justice and the identification of social problems.
- Facilitate skill in inquiry, critical thinking, and scientific research methods.
- Ensure students are competent in both oral and written communication, in mathematical computation and problem solving, and in reading with comprehension.

Horn moved the field significantly through his contributions to spelling research and instruction. He chose to study the teaching of spelling because of its high objectivity. Up until 1920, the spelling curriculum covered a large number of words and also words of low usefulness. Those words were not developmentally appropriate, and the instructional methods were inefficient (Horn to Peterson, 1944). Through his spelling studies, Horn was able to identify fundamental principles of spelling and, therefore, inform curriculum making and improve methods of instruction in spelling. Under his leadership, the University of Iowa became an important center for research in spelling (Horn to Peterson, 1944).

However, the area of Horn's work that diverges most widely from contemporary theory and practice is also in the area of spelling instruction. Horn's belief in social utility resulted in a spelling curriculum that focused on frequency as the overarching principle to be used in determining vocabulary for word study. Although Horn made provisions for "word building" (Horn & Ashbaugh, 1928, p. viii), primarily the addition of inflectional endings to words, little emphasis was placed on teaching children to examine spelling patterns across words (e.g., words families formed by rime patterns such as -at, -et, -ake, etc.). Unlike the work of later researchers of spelling instruction (e.g., Henderson, 1985), who focused on children's spelling errors and what those errors meant in terms of a child's understanding of English orthography and general progression in spelling development, Horn's work focused on which words were of the highest utility and decreed that these were the ones to be learned.

The more we read about Ernest Horn, the more our respect and admiration for him grew. We wished we could have known him because we were sure we would have liked him. So many aspects of Horn's life impressed us. The way he carefully organized his papers for presentation to the University of Iowa Archives in the 1960s reflected how meticulously he must have approached the counting of over 5,000,000 words four decades earlier. We saw the artifacts of his efforts—alphabetized lists of handwritten words and tallies—all compiled without the benefits of today's technology. Ernest Horn was a man who up to the time of his death continued to do scholarly work and to teach. Although he was an emeritus professor for some 15 years, it is an extraordinary event that when he died his colleagues (Haefner et al., circa 1967) would write a tribute to his life to be incorporated into the minutes of a special meeting held at the College of Liberal Arts. Ernest Horn is a true pioneer in spelling research and instruction. His thoughts on curriculum development and instruction will also continue to inform and inspire educators for many years to come.

Reflection Questions

1. Do you agree with Horn's method of spelling and vocabulary research? How would yours be different or similar? Why?
2. Horn was a strong proponent of "social utility" when it comes to curriculum design and instruction. What are your responses to this approach?
3. How would Horn respond to the recent standards and accountability movement in education? Would he support it or go against it? Why?
4. If Horn were alive today, what would be his biggest concern(s) about reading education in the 21st century?

5. If Horn were alive today, what would you like to tell him about his contributions to reading education?

REFERENCES

Anonymous. (n.d.). About Horn. Retrieved July 16, 2006, from http://www.iowa-city.k12.ia.us/Schools/Horn/abouthorn.htm

Anonymous. (1967). Eulogy for Ernest Horn memorial service. In Ernest Horn Faculty File, University of Iowa Archives, Iowa City, Iowa.

Barton, K.C., & Smith, L.A. (2000). Themes or motifs? Aiming for coherence through interdisciplinary outlines. *The Reading Teacher, 54*, 54–63.

Bear, D.R., Invernizzi, M., Templeton, S., & Johnston, F. (2003). *Words their way: Word study for phonics, vocabulary, and spelling instruction* (3rd ed.). Upper Saddle River, NJ: Prentice Hall.

Biographical information staff. (1965, November 1). Ernest Horn. In Ernest Horn Faculty File, University of Iowa Archives, Iowa City, Iowa.

Duffy, G.G., & Hoffman, J.V. (1999). In pursuit of an illusion: The flawed search for a perfect method. *The Reading Teacher, 53*, 10–16.

Ernest Horn dies at 85: Organizer of UI School. (1967, November 10). *Iowa City Press-Citizen*. In Ernest Horn Papers, Box 28, University of Iowa Archives, Iowa City, Iowa.

Frasch, D.K. (1965). How well do six-graders proofread for spelling errors? *The Elementary School Journal, 65*, 381–385.

Haefner, J.H., Smith, L.L., & Spitzer, H.F. (circa 1967, November 9). Ernest Horn 1882–1967, incorporated into the minutes of the Liberal Arts faculty. In Ernest Horn Faculty file, University of Iowa Archives, Iowa City, Iowa.

Hanna, P.R., & Moore, J.T., Jr. (1953). Spelling: From spoken word to written symbol. *The Elementary School Journal, 53*, 329–337.

Henderson, E.H. (1985). *Teaching spelling*. Boston: Houghton Mifflin.

Hickman, P., Pollard-Durodola, S., & Vaughn, S. (2004). Storybook reading: Improving vocabulary and comprehension for English-language learners. *The Reading Teacher, 57*, 720–730.

Hodges, R.E. (1987). American spelling instruction: Retrospect and prospect. *Visible Language, 21*, 215–235.

Horn, E. (n.d.). Letter to brother. In Ernest Horn Papers, Box 28, University of Iowa Archives, Iowa City, Iowa.

Horn, E. (1914). *Distribution of opportunity for participation among the various pupils in classroom recitations* (Contributions to Education Monograph No. 67). New York: Teachers College, Columbia University.

Horn, E. (1915). Principles for making curricula in history. *Teachers College Record, 16*, 339–345.

Horn, E. (1919). The application of scientific method to making the course of study in civics. *The Elementary School Journal, 19*, 762–777.

Horn, E. (1920a). A suggestive plan of individual instruction in English. *The School Review, 28*(2), 153–154.

Horn, E. (1920b). What is a project? *The Elementary School Journal, 21*, 112–116.

Horn, E. (1926). A basic writing vocabulary: 10,000 words most commonly used in writing. *University of Iowa Monographs in Education, First series, No. 4*. Iowa City: University of Iowa.

Horn, E. (1929). The child-centered school: An appraisal of the new education. *The Elementary School Journal, 29*, 547–551.

Horn, E. (1931). *5,000 most-used shorthand forms*. New York: Gregg.

Horn, E. (circa 1933a). Chapter V on testing: Notes for the Chicago meeting. In Ernest Horn Papers, Box 2, University of Iowa Archives, Iowa City, Iowa.

Horn, E. (circa 1933b). Historical resume of the objective testing movement. In Ernest Horn Papers, Box 2, University of Iowa Archives, Iowa City, Iowa.

Horn, E. (circa 1933c). Reasons for not signing the summary volume. In Ernest Horn Papers, Box 3, University of Iowa Archives, Iowa City, Iowa.

Horn, E. (1937). *Report of the commission on the social studies: Methods of instruction in the social studies*. New York: Scribner.

Horn, E. (1954). *Teaching spelling* [What Research Says to Teachers series, book three]. Washington, DC: National Education Association.

Horn, E. (1957). Phonetics and spelling. *The Elementary School Journal, 57,* 424–432.

Horn, E., & Ashbaugh, E.J. (1920). *Lippincott's Horn-Ashbaugh speller for grades one to eight.* Philadelphia: J.B. Lippincott.

Horn, E., & Ashbaugh, E.J. (1928). *The Horn-Ashbaugh fundamentals of spelling: Grades one to eight incorporating the findings of tabular analysis of 5,100,000 words of ordinary writing.* Philadelphia: J.B. Lippincott.

Horn, E., & Ashbaugh, E.J. (1929). *The Horn-Ashbaugh fundamentals of spelling for grades one to eight incorporating the findings of 5,100,000 words of ordinary writing.* Topeka: The State of Kansas, B.P. Walker, State Printer.

Horn, E., & Ashbaugh, E.J. (1935a). *Progress in spelling grades one to four.* Philadelphia: J.B. Lippincott.

Horn, E., & Ashbaugh, E.J. (1935b). *Progress in spelling grades five to eight.* Philadelphia: J. B. Lippincott.

Horn, E., Cutright, P., & Horn, M.D. (1926a). *The learn to study readers: First lessons in learning to study.* Boston: Ginn.

Horn, E., Cutright, P., & Horn, M.D. (1926b). *Manual of directions for first lessons in learning to study.* Boston: Ginn.

Horn, E., & McBroom, M.M. (1925). *Manual of directions for the learn to study readers: Book three.* Boston: Ginn.

Horn, E., & Peterson, T. (1945). *Spelling you need.* Philadelphia: J. B. Lippincott.

Horn, E., to Professor C.W. Hunnicutt. (1961, November 16). In Ernest Horn Papers, Box 25, University of Iowa Archives, Iowa City, Iowa.

Horn, E., to Dr. W.A. Jessup. (1915, March 22). In Ernest Horn Papers, Box 23, University of Iowa Archives, Iowa City, Iowa.

Horn, E., to E.T. Peterson. (1944, September 4). In Ernest Horn Papers, Box 3, University of Iowa Archives, Iowa City, Iowa.

Iowa "Prof" indexes great American vocabulary. (circa 1928). *Des Moines Register.* In Ernest Horn Papers, Box 28, University of Iowa Archives, Iowa City, Iowa.

Lagemann, E.C. (2000). *An elusive science: The troubling history of education research.* Chicago: University of Chicago Press.

Moore, D.W., Readence, J.E., & Rickelman, R.J. (1983). An historical exploration of content area reading instruction. *Reading Research Quarterly, 18,* 419–438.

National Spelling Bee [multiple documents]. (circa 1928). In Ernest Horn Faculty File, Box 31, University of Iowa Archives, Iowa City, Iowa.

Ohles, F., Ohles, S.M., & Ramsay, J.G. (1997). *Biographical dictionary of modern American educators.* Westport, CT: Greenwood Press.

Old home paper and who's who. (1923, June 8). *The Fairfield Daily Ledger.* In Ernest Horn Papers, Box 28, University of Iowa Archives, Iowa City, Iowa.

Press release. (1967, November 11). In Ernest Horn Faculty File, University of Iowa Archives, Iowa City, Iowa.

Prof. Ernest Horn replies to criticism—Defends modern spelling instruction. (1953, December 2). *Iowa City Press-Citizen*. In Ernest Horn Papers, Box 28, University of Iowa Archives, Iowa City, Iowa.

Read, C. (1971). Preschool children's knowledge of English phonology. *Harvard Educational Review, 41*, 1–34.

Sandburg, C. (1927). *The American songbag*. Orlando, FL: Harcourt Brace.

Stein, F.J. (1973). *Ernest Horn's ideas on education within the context of the progressive education movement in America*. Unpublished doctoral dissertation, University of Iowa, Iowa City.

They are spelling better now. (1954, January 25). *The Daily Times Monday*. In Ernest Horn Papers, Box 28, University of Iowa Archives, Iowa City, Iowa.

Zielinski, M. (1966). Faces from the crowd: Word man. *Iowa Alumni Review*. In Ernest Horn Faculty File, University of Iowa Archives, Iowa City, Iowa.

FOR FURTHER READING

Ganske, K. (2000). *Word journeys: Assessment-guided phonics, spelling, and vocabulary instruction*. New York: Guilford.

Gentry, J.R., & Gillet, J.W. (1993). *Teaching kids to spell*. Portsmouth, NH: Heinemann.

Goswami, U., & Bryant, P. (1990). *Phonological skills and learning to read*. Hove, England: Erlbaum.

Horn, E. (1927). *Most-used shorthand forms: The 1,000 words of highest frequency*. New York: Gregg.

Horn, E. (1940). *Following new trails*. Boston: Ginn.

Horn, E., & Ashbaugh, E.J. (1928). *The Horn-Ashbaugh high school speller: Incorporating the findings of a tabular analysis of 5,100,000 words of ordinary writing and of over 1,000,000 running words of letters written by high school students*. Philadelphia: J.B. Lippincott.

Horn, E., Goodykoontz, B., & Snedaker, M.I. (1940). *Reaching our goals: Progress in reading*. Boston: Ginn.

Horn, E., McBroom, M.M., & Smith, K. (1940). *More adventures*. Boston: Ginn.

Pinnell, G.S., & Fountas, I.C. (1998). *Word matters: Teaching phonics and spelling in the reading/writing classroom*. Portsmouth, NH: Heinemann.

Rosencrans, G. (1998). *The spelling book: Teaching children how to spell, not what to spell*. Newark, DE: International Reading Association.

Treiman, R. (1993). *Beginning to spell: A study of first-grade children*. New York: Oxford University Press.

Venezky, R.L. (1999). *The American way of spelling: The structure and origins of American English orthography*. New York: Guilford.

CHAPTER 13

William Scott Gray
(1885–1960): Mr. Reading

By Carol Lauritzen

Historical Research Process

THROUGH THE 30 years that have passed since the completion of my doctoral program I have remained in contact with one of my professors and mentors, Helen Huus. In August 2004, I had the privilege of interviewing her to create a videotape for the International Reading Association's archive of memories of past Association presidents. For me it was a delight to visit with a woman whose clarity of thought was as impressive as it was when I was her student and whose keen memory and scrapbooks reached back to the founding of the Association. Much to my surprise and delight, I learned I was the "grand-student" of William Scott Gray, Dr. Huus's doctoral advisor. It was through our conversation that a famous name started to become a real per-

Shaping the Reading Field: The Impact of Early Reading Pioneers, Scientific Research, and Progressive Ideas, edited by Susan E. Israel and E. Jennifer Monaghan. © 2007 by the International Reading Association.
Photo: Courtesy of William S. Gray III.

son. When I volunteered to write a chapter for this book, I thought that, with my firsthand informant and my small knowledge of doing historical research (Jaeger & Lauritzen, 2004; Lauritzen, 2002), writing Gray's biography would not be too difficult. However, accessing primary sources and verifying information from more than 50 years ago proved to be challenging as I worked from my remote, rural small town. The Internet and excellent interlibrary loan facilities brought me most of the needed source material, but the handwritten letters from Dr. Huus as well as a phone conversation with William Scott Gray III, Dr. Gray's son, brought the finishing touches to this presentation of a man I have learned to respect and admire.

During my research, I discovered that at the third annual convention of the International Reading Association, in May 1958, William S. Gray was presented with a Citation of Merit that recognized his "distinguished service in the teaching of reading" and saluted him as a "scholar, teacher, teacher of teachers, author, lecturer, and critic who has given unceasing help and encouragement to classroom teachers and inspiring leadership in the organization of the International Reading Association" (Jerrolds, 1977, pp. 47–48). Gray is considered by some to be the founder of the field of reading education (Gilstad, 1985), and his contributions make him a preeminent figure in the field. It is fitting that the annual Citation of Merit now bears his name and that he was the second recipient. What made the presentation even more memorable was the awkward position in which Gray was placed. Because everyone wanted to see him when he received the citation, he was boosted on top of a table. Ralph Staiger suspected that the reason he remembers the incident "so vividly...is that Mr. Gray was decorous almost to a fault. The sight of him balancing on what is known in the hotel trade as a 'deuce' was completely out of character for him" (Staiger, quoted in Mavrogenes, 1985a, p. 6). One of Gray's doctoral students provided an extended description of Gray:

> I remember him as always wearing a dark suit, with a shirt collar that was crisp and having a conservative, foulard-type necktie. He was clean-shaven and never needed a haircut. He was always formal, dignified, and benign and often had a twinkle in his eyes. He never called his secretary or his students by their first names. [They all called him *Dr. Gray*.] He was truly a gentleman and a scholar. He was energetic and often walked to the University of Chicago from his home on the south side [two miles from 6910 Bennett Avenue], arriving at work at 8:00. (Helen Huus, personal communication, October 1, 2004)

"It was rumored that the 'S' in William S. Gray stood for 'systematic.' And so he was," said Huus, (personal communication, October 1, 2004). When Dr. Gray organized a conference, he gave specific instructions to the speakers because he was also planning a publication. Huus recalls, "Dr. Gray asked me to give a talk [at the first IRA conference], and I still remember he said, 'talk for 27 minutes'" (personal communication, August 24, 2004). Another example of his systematic ways was his attention to detail. Nancy Larrick told of editing the first proceedings of the International Reading Association conference with Gray. He said that one of his research assistants would first check every footnote. Larrick did not think that was necessary, considering the caliber of the authors, but she found that Gray was right as several distinguished presenters were found to have even misquoted their own works. Said Larrick,

> Dr. Gray...had a passion for detail. Just as no footnote was too slight to be questioned and corrected, no drugstore coffee-check was too small to be recorded at once in his little black expense book. This was like breathing in and breathing out to him. (Larrick, quoted in Mavrogenes, 1985a, p. 5)

Even Gray's handwriting revealed his nature: "He wrote much of his material in long hand [in a] miniaturized style...so he could get onto a sheet of paper probably 2 or 3 times as much as somebody writing in more normal sized script would do" (William S. Gray III, personal communication, October 26, 2005).

Gray's attention to detail also showed itself in his personal interactions. A prominent leader and a distinguished scholar, he is remembered as being serious yet approachable, demanding yet encouraging, knowledgeable yet humble. He was sensitive to the needs of others, offering opportunity, support, and encouragement: "Dr. Gray was always looking for young people to contribute to the teaching of reading and invited students and former students to important meetings" (Helen Huus, personal communication, October 1, 2004). These qualities explain why Gray was a "greatly respected, fondly remembered teacher, scholar and human being" (Stevenson, 1985, p. vii). His personal life also presented these qualities. His son derived "considerable benefit" from the environment created by his parents. The younger Gray said of his father that he "never (or my mother either) used alcohol.

They didn't smoke and they went to church regularly. It was a style of life." Dr. Gray also was, according to his son,

> conscientious and in every way a totally honest person, concerned for other people, very helpful.... He spent enormous amounts of time as a trustee of the church and as a member and leader on other committees.... He always had a willingness to drop at any moment whatever he was doing...to respond to somebody's need. (William S. Gray III, personal communication, October 26, 2005)

Personal and Professional Life

Born on June 5, 1885, to William Scott Gray and Anna Letitia Gilliland Gray, William Scott Gray, Jr., was the third of four children in a family that enjoyed life in the small town of Coatsburg, Illinois, USA. Gray's mother, whose father was a physician, came from an established Illinois family. His father's family had also been in Illinois for several generations, working as farmers and teachers. His father, in addition to being an educator, was a well-known businessman and state legislator. Gray seems to have had an idyllic childhood, attending the school where his father was principal. To attend high school, he walked four miles to the town of Camp Point, where he studied mathematics and the sciences and received his diploma in 1904. Between 1904 and 1908, he was a public school teacher in Adams County, Illinois, USA. His first job, at age 19, was in a one-room country school with students varying in age from 5 to 20. The job paid the handsome salary of about $400 for the year. Gray, Jr., became principal of the grade school in Fowler, Illinois, USA, serving from 1905 to 1908, during which time he decided to make education his career.

Because Gray had pledged to teach for a minimum of two years in Illinois, he was able to complete the two-year teacher-training course at Illinois State Normal University at no cost. He excelled in oratory and was involved in athletics (Mavrogenes, 1985b, p. 10). Because Normal University was the center of the North American Herbartian movement, Gray was immersed in its theories, beliefs, and methodologies, which emphasized starting from what the child knows and using an inductive approach (Mavrogenes, 1985d, p. 16). Following his graduation from Normal University in 1910, Gray became the principal of the university's model practice school for two years. The clinical aspect of teacher preparation was critical at the Normal Training School, as it was called, and Gray's selection as its principal indicated he had skills in leadership and critical analysis.

It is likely that during a visit to Normal University, Charles Hubbard Judd (see chapter 4, this volume), a prominent psychologist and professor, inspired Gray to go to the University of Chicago (Mavrogenes, 1985d, p. 11). Gray advanced his education, earning a baccalaureate in 1913, a degree intended for those preparing to teach biological sciences in secondary or normal schools. The following year he became a faculty member of the University of Chicago, hired as Assistant in Education. His path then led him to Teachers College, Columbia University, the largest school of education in the United States at the time. He received an MA in 1914 as well as the designation of Instructor in Education in Normal Schools.

Although Gray was only away from Illinois for one year, it was a significant time in his life. The standardized testing movement was blossoming under the direction of Edward Lee Thorndike (see chapter 5, this volume). For his master's thesis, Gray developed the Oral Reading Paragraphs (1915/1963), which were in essentially the same form for almost 50 years. Also while at Columbia, he met his future wife, Beatrice Warner Jardine: "She received an undergraduate degree in Home Economics from Teachers College in 1916 and then taught in a Massachusetts high school for several years" (Mavrogenes, 1985d, p. 14). They were married on September 14, 1921, and they had two children, Grace Warner and William Scott III.

Gray's scrupulous attention to detail and consistency was revealed in his family life as well as his professional life. According to his son, the Grays "had quite a close family." The family had breakfast and the evening meal together, "almost without exception." Dr. and Mrs. Gray maintained close contact with both sets of parents and their brothers and sisters: "It was very important to get together with them, with some regularity, and to correspond in written form during the periods in between" (William S. Gray III, personal communication, October 26, 2005).

After returning to the University of Chicago, Gray pursued a PhD, which was awarded in 1916. Nila Banton Smith (1965, p. 5) stated that Gray's was one of the three first doctoral dissertations in reading. His dissertation, titled *Studies of Elementary School Reading Through Standardized Tests*, was published as a University of Chicago monograph (Gray, 1917). While still a doctoral student, Gray had risen quickly in the academic ranks from assistant (1914) to instructor (1915) and was promoted to assistant professor in the year his doctorate was awarded. In 1916 he became assistant dean, and in 1917 he became dean of the College of Education, a position he held until 1931 when the College was abolished. He advanced to associate professor in 1918 and to full professor in 1922. He continued to lead the teacher education program until 1945, during which time he shaped the curriculum of the program, adding several courses, including one on the teaching of reading (Gilstad, 1985).

Gray had a strong work ethic. He generally worked each evening in his study at home as well as Saturday mornings at the university. However, he found time for other activities. He enjoyed working in his yard and taking his daily walks through the park as well as trips to the mountains, where he became interested in flyfishing (William S. Gray III, personal communication, October 26, 2005).

In 1929, Gray began an affiliation with the publishing house Scott Foresman that lasted throughout his life. The following year he became a coauthor of the Elson Basic Readers series (e.g., Elson & Gray, 1930), which introduced new trends into school readers, such as stories based on children's interests, varied content, and intrinsic (analytic) phonics (Mavrogenes, 1985b), as well as the characters of Dick and Jane. Here, as in all subsequent editions with which Gray was involved, the whole-word (sight) method of teaching reading was the underlying methodological approach, supported by such aids as context, configuration, structural, and phonic clues, along with the dictionary (Gray, 1960b, p. 16). The readers were revised again in 1936 as the Elson-Gray Basic Readers. The next revision, in the 1940s, called simply Basic Readers (Gray, Arbuthnot, et al., 1940–1948), was coauthored with May Hill Arbuthnot (see chapter 9, this volume). Gray was also named "Reader Director" of Scott Foresman's entire Curriculum Foundation series (Smith, 1965, p. 224).

Due to Gray's concern with supporting teachers, a substantial teachers' manual was written to accompany the Scott Foresman readers. It organized lessons into three parts—(1) preparation, (2) silent reading, and (3) follow-up activities—and recommended the use of three reading groups based on the children's reading abilities (Smith, 1965, p. 241). In addition, due to Gray's belief that reading should extend beyond the reading period into content learning, the Curriculum Foundation series grew to include readers in health, arithmetic, social studies, and science. Other additions at this time were the student workbook and books at the junior high school level.

Gray's last work on the readers in the series occurred in the 1950s with an author team that included Arbuthnot, A. Sterl Artley, and Marion Monroe. According to some accounts, the Scott Foresman series was used in 85% of U.S. schools ("Dick and Jane's Long-lost Dad!!!," 1998). Letters and other evidence indicate that Gray was more than a well-known name on the cover. Rather, as in all his endeavors, he played a significant role in terms of general guidance and specific suggestions about content and style (Mavrogenes, 1985c).

Upon his retirement from the University of Chicago in 1950, Gray was honored with the emeritus rank. For the next 10 years he remained active, authoring more than 100 publications, bringing his articles, monographs, books, and other publications to a total of over 500. At age 75, Gray died from injuries sustained when he fell from a horse on his annual vacation near Wolf, Wyoming, USA ("William S. Gray," 1960). Thus, the life and productive scholarship of the individual who was at the center of reading education for a half-century came to an untimely end. A chair—the William S. Gray Research Professorship in Reading—was established in his honor at the University of Chicago in 1960.

Philosophical Beliefs and Guiding Principles

In his 1941 summary of reading research, Gray identified three concepts of reading: (1) code based (word recognition), (2) meaning based (comprehension), and (3) response based (thinking about the significance of the meaning). He was able, therefore, to identify the ideologies that continue to be contentious. He cautioned,

> The fact that reading has been conceived narrowly by some investigators and broadly by others suggests that great care must be observed in comparing the results of different studies.... Obviously reading is a very complex art; furthermore, the need is urgent for a clear understanding of all that is involved in efficient reading. (Gray, 1941/1984, p. 18)

Gray defined reading broadly, viewing it as a thinking process with social implications. At the end of his career, he summed up this view:

> An analysis of research justifies two conclusions: First, reading is essential in the study and solution of serious personal and social problems that re-

quire deliberate thinking, penetrating interpretation, and sound judgment. Second, reading is indispensable in ensuring a balance in the content of vicarious experience, as a check on much that we hear and see, and in fostering substantial human values. (Gray, 1960c, pp. 56–57)

Gray realized that literacy is related to sociopolitical status. He believed that those seeking literacy for all people had focused too much on the skills of reading, while not giving enough attention to "welfare, social progress, and democratic growth.... [We] now realize that literacy as a skill is not enough; it must be viewed merely as an essential aid to individual and community welfare and inter-group understanding" (Gray, 1956, p. 9).

Within this broad view, Gray defined the reading process: "Although most of us probably think of reading as a kind of unified response to the visual stimulus of printed words, we can distinguish four main components in the interpretation of printed matter" (Gray, 1948, p. 10). He identified these essential components as word perception, "recognition and construing of meaning" (Gray, 1960c, p. 53), thoughtful reaction, and integration with previous experience and ideas. He believed that "it is of great importance that all four of these basic aspects of reading be cultivated from the earliest grades on" (Gray, 1960c, p. 54).

For Gray, phonics was only one aspect of his first component of reading, word perception, which also included memory of word forms, context clues, structural word analysis, and use of the dictionary (Gray, 1960a). Rather than emphasizing phonics, Gray insisted on

the primacy of meaning in reading instruction, on the necessity of interest and common experiences in his basal readers, on whole stories easy to read and varied in content, on a concern for the comfort and individual needs of readers, on functional and interesting drill in separate periods, and on the careful analysis of teaching procedures. (Mavrogenes, 1985c, p. 11)

Helen Huus, who taught with the Basic Readers, comments on Gray's views on word perception and describes his analytic phonics approach:

Gray saw phonics as an aid to learning to read, not an end in itself. While Dr. Gray was often criticized as the "look-and-say" proponent of learning to read, I found the method [advocated by Gray] to be a comprehensive approach: first children memorized a few words by sight, then developed the sight-sound relationship by using these words, but keeping the total word intact. For example, as children learned *see, so, some, Sally* by sight, the common initial *s* sound would be learned, but the capital *S* in *Sally* would be noted. Through a process of phonetic analysis, children learned the sounds that letters and groups of letters signify. In his book *On Their Own in Reading* [1948/1960b], Dr. Gray explained his method of helping readers become independent in recognizing the printed word. This book, in my opinion, never received the wide circulation it warranted. Certainly anyone who read it would not call Dr. Gray the "look-and say advocate." (personal communication, October 1, 2004)

Gray's beliefs in the four components of reading were the foundation of the pedagogy for the Basic Readers series and were the source of early acclamation and later criticism (Mavrogenes, 1985b). The criticism came from outside the reading profession, and the leading voice was that of Rudolf Flesch in *Why Johnny Can't Read—And What You Can Do About It* (1955). Flesch struck out against the conventional wisdom of the look-and-say (whole-word) method with its analytic phonics approach, calling the Dick and Jane readers "horrible, stupid, emasculated, pointless, tasteless" (p. 6). According to Gray's daughter, Grace, Gray "accepted criticism of the Dick and Jane readers graciously" (Mavrogenes, 1985b, p. 379).

Even though the pedagogy in the Curriculum Foundation series was the target of criticism, Gray can still be admired for his prescience in other aspects of reading. He believed that

> the ideas and vicarious experiences we acquire through reading form a large part of the background of meaning that we bring to the perception of words. In short, what we *take from* one reading experience gives us more to *take to* the next one. (Gray, 1948, pp. 12–13, emphases in original)

This recognition of the role of prior knowledge and experience in comprehension demonstrates that Gray anticipated what we now know as schema and reader response theories.

In addition, Gray was attentive to the aspect of maturity in reading and firmly believed that people have the capacity for growth and refinement of their reading interests, tastes, and habits throughout their lives (Gray, 1960c). Theodore Harris noted that Gray gave "continued attention to the teaching of reading beyond the elementary school level" (Mavrogenes, 1985a, p. 10). Gray thought there was a basic need to develop "a sound reading program in high schools and colleges" that recognized the continuous growth of reading and the need for teacher guidance and instruction at the appropriate level to move the students to their highest possible levels of achievement (quoted in Smith, 1965, p. 296). Gray also believed reading should move outside a designated reading period in the elementary school and should be taught in the content areas. In fact, the earliest reference to content area reading was in 1919 when Gray reported that he had asked high school teachers to list the uses that pupils made of reading in preparing assignments (Courtney, 1980, p. 2).

Finally, Gray was a strong proponent of the scientific study of reading and believed in the value of practice informed by research (Gray, 1984). He was not without caution, however:

> ...the progress achieved thus far is not without serious limitations. Unfortunately much of the scientific work relating to reading has been fragmentary in character...there is little or no coordination of effort among research workers...many of the studies reported have been conducted without adequate controls. (1941, p. 5)

These criticisms could well be written today.

Contributions to the Field of Reading

Just as the scientific study of education and Herbartianism were profound influences during Gray's formative education, Gray became a strong influence himself as a professor at the University of Chicago and a leader in the field of reading. He produced a steady stream of publications over an impressive range of topics. His interests and work addressed many aspects of teacher education and reading from preschool to adult levels at the national and international levels. Gray's work is characterized by its practical as well as scientific aspects. His contributions fit within a number of broad categories: (a) international studies, (b) the concept of reading, (c) measurements of reading, (d) diagnosis and remediation, (e) content area and adult reading, (f) summaries of research, (g) curriculum development, and (h) leadership.

Gray was one of the first researchers to study literacy on an international scale. As a graduate student he had worked on a massive survey of Cleveland, Ohio, USA, schools in 1917, and in 1939 he and Bernice Elizabeth Leary (see chapter 10, this volume) collaborated on a survey of New York State schools. Based on his success at conducting large surveys in the United States, Gray was asked to study literacy in Puerto Rico (1936) and Egypt (1949) and provide recommendations at the national level. His study for the United Nations Educational, Scientific, and Cultural Organization (UNESCO) of worldwide literacy remains his most monumental work. Over the course of four years of research, Gray reviewed world literacy programs by examining 500 sets of instructional readers, analyzing the results of questionnaires and interviews, and visiting eight countries. The resultant book, *The Teaching of Reading and Writing: An International Survey* (Gray, 1956), remains one of UNESCO's all-time bestsellers:

> Gray's book presents, as I see it, the most comprehensive and valid out-look hitherto made on the problems of promoting world literacy in its many varied aspects. It is a monumental piece of work—amazingly actual [sic] even today and still unsurpassed in many ways. (Malmquist, 1980, p. 395)

Gray's (1956) recommendations are still appropriate today. He called for the cooperation of competent leaders, more financial support, better training for teachers, sounder programs, more effective methods and access to libraries and readable materials (p. 274).

Another of Gray's concerns was the conceptualization of reading and the reading process. Although he refined his concept of reading over time, his definition of reading, as presented through the decades of his publications, always focused on meaning. Gray never referred to his concept of reading as a model, but he consistently advocated a four-part view of reading that emphasized the multiple aspects of word perception and increasing levels of comprehension and response to reading over a lifetime of development. Gray's consistent and persistent expression of this view helped set the stage for the acceptance of schema theory, reader response theory, and meaning-based models of reading.

Gray's interest and work in reading assessment began with his master's thesis in which he developed the Oral Reading Paragraphs (1915/1963). This test was significant not only because it was the first to measure a student's reading achievement through oral reading but also because it was based on a sequence of passages of gradually increasing difficulty. The test allowed for examining patterns of errors and led to further work in remediation based on individual student need. It also provided a ready instrument for conducting school surveys and other types of research on reading achievement. Because passages could be ordered in terms of difficulty, there was increased attention to the factors that affect readability.

Gray not only continued his study of assessment but also began using assessment to inform instruction. In 1922, Gray was senior author of *Remedial Cases in Reading: Their Diagnosis and Treatment* (Gray, Kibbe, Lucas, & Miller, 1922). He and his coauthors identified five categories of students and a broad listing of causes of difficulties in reading. This book legitimized the case study approach as well as the use of multiple methods of instruction. Another consequence of this work was the development of remedial reading as a specialty and the formation of reading clinics: As Gray stated, "Because the needs of many poor readers cannot be determined readily through classroom diagnosis, institutions and school systems in increasing numbers are establishing educational clinics" (quoted in Smith, 1965, pp. 258–259).

Applying his interest in measurement, Gray investigated the growth of reading maturity into adulthood. In 1929, after studying the interests and habits of adult readers, he concluded that reading instruction among children needed to change to result in lifelong readers. Gray also directly addressed the problem of adults with low literacy through manuals for teachers of adults and publications that defined illiteracy and its causes. His desire to assist adult learners led to the development of a readability formula, which used a variety of features such as content, style of writing, and format. After Gray, readability formulas became simplified, using only factors of sentence length and vocabulary difficulty, until recently returning to the factors that he identified 70 years ago. In *Maturity in Reading: Its Nature and Appraisal*, Gray and Bernice Rogers (1956) present a framework for defining reading maturity. This landmark in the field of adult reading contains admonitions that reading instruction should be directed at all students at the secondary level, not just the poor readers. Gray continually advocated a cross-curricular emphasis in reading, believing that reading was essential in every content subject. He also thought that good instruction was needed to guide students' progress in their reading skills and attitudes so they could make rapid progress in learning content area material.

One of the most remarkable aspects of Gray's scholarship was his thorough (some would say total) knowledge of the research in the field of reading. He published annual summaries of research in reading first in *The Elementary School Journal* (1926–1932) and then in the *Journal of Educational Research* (1932–1958). Gray's unparalleled ability not only to be knowledgeable about the research related to reading but also to synthesize and recognize trends made the annual summaries a boon for other scholars. He clarified what was known and also identified the areas that were in need of further research. Gray's annual summaries generally filled about 35 pages of print, and he would probably be surprised that each annual summary published by the International Reading Association until 1999 was a separate volume titled *Annual Summary of Investigations Related to Reading*, containing several hundred pages of reading-related research.

Gray's command of research findings, however, was not limited to the field of reading. He was active in producing the influential yearbooks of the National Society for the Study of Education. Gray was on the committee for the 20th yearbook, was chair and wrote three chapters for the 24th, and chaired the committees for the 36th and 47th. He also wrote a chapter on the role of teacher education in reading for the 60th. Through these yearbooks he broadened the definition of reading, encouraged the move to more silent reading, directed attention toward reading at the secondary and college levels, and considered the role of preparation in reading for preservice and in-service teachers. Gray's unequaled expertise in summarizing research was honored and recognized in 1984 through the republication of his entry on reading from the *Encyclopedia of Educational Research*, first published in 1941 (Monroe & Harris, 1941). In this text, he examines all the research on reading from ancient times until 1940. Gray also authored the entry on research in reading in the second (Monroe, 1950) and third (Monroe & Harris, 1960) editions of the encyclopedia in new and expanded formats. Comparisons across the three editions show the changes in reading research and information across the decades. Gray's research summaries thus provided guidance to his contemporaries as well as allowing for significant historical perspectives.

Although attention to Gray's scholarship is warranted, he may have been equally influential through his role in curriculum development. His earliest publications in 1911–1912 were articles with practical ideas about teaching geography. In 1929 he joined the authoring team of the Elson Basic Readers. By 1940 he was the lead author for Scott Foresman's Basic Readers, the centerpiece of their Curriculum Foundation series. Although Gray was not the "father" of Dick and Jane, the main characters of the readers, he could qualify as their "godfather," according to Gray's doctoral student Helen Huus: "The Dick and Jane readers became extremely popular, and a whole generation of children learned to read by using them. Children readily identified with the characters, and Dick and Jane became embedded in the national culture" (personal communication, October 1, 2004).

While several decades of children learned to read with the Dick and Jane readers, many teachers learned to teach reading through the teachers' manuals that accompanied them. Gray was at the forefront of the development of basal reading programs that had a significant impact on reading instruction in both public and parochial schools:

> By utilizing his wide familiarity with investigations in reading, by preparing highly useful and practical teachers' manuals, by testing and perfecting his material in actual classroom use, by sequentially and comprehensively providing for the development of reading skills as well as attitudes, and by coordinating content area material with basal material in a program which was more useful and complete than any other one on the market at the time, Gray produced a series of basal readers which became the most widely used reading books in the country and which consequently set the course of American reading instruction. (Mavrogenes, 1985c, p. 23)

Finally, one of Gray's most significant contributions was his leadership in reading when it was a new and upcoming field. He initiated the annual reading conferences at the University of Chicago in 1938 and directed them until 1952. The influence of Gray's leadership was evident in the organizations for reading professionals. As Helen Huus notes,

> Dr. Gray's eminence in the field of reading served to mobilize other experts and to get them to work together. When he was president of the International Council for the Improvement of Reading Instruction and it merged with the National Association of Remedial Teachers to form the International Reading Association, he became the first [Association] president. Its first convention was held in the Morrison Hotel in Chicago in 1956, with almost 2500 in attendance. On the program were nearly all the reading experts in the country. The excitement at this convention was tremendous, and the new association was launched in a splendid manner. (personal communication, October 1, 2004)

In his history of the International Reading Association, Bob Jerrolds (1977) commented on Gray as an architect of the Association: "One of Gray's avocations was the study of porticos and porches, but it was to the foundation and the superstructure that he addressed himself in his work with [the Association]" (p. 30). Nancy Larrick recalls Gray as a "relentless and indomitable steam roller.... Without raising his voice, without a harsh word...he pushed through decisions that left us gasping...and later proud" (quoted in Mavrogenes, 1985a, p. 3). He insisted, despite strong objections, that the organization hold its first convention within five months of its founding. He organized the event himself and attended to all the arrangements, including the publication of the proceedings. Gray was so committed to the success of the Association that he was willing to pay its bills from his own pocket. Larrick, the incoming Association president, was able to convince him that this was a precedent he should not set (Jerrolds, 1977, pp. 34–35). However, he continued to support the organization and its officers in other ways throughout the rest of his life.

The influence and contribution of William Scott Gray is hard to summarize because the scope of his work is so broad and without equal. He was the expert on reading in the first half of the 20th century. In his tribute to Gray, Arthur Irving Gates (see chapter 14, this volume), the only other man to come close to Gray's stature in the field, summarized Gray's life work: "Dr. Gray labored to improve the teaching of reading for a longer period of time (more than half a century) with a greater singleness of purpose and in a wider variety of enterprises than anyone else in history" (Gates, 1961, p. 73).

Lessons for the Future

Gray was a consummate scholar. We learn from his example that only through comprehensive scholarship can the past inform present practices and guide reading researchers and practitioners toward the future. Based on his comprehensive knowledge of the past, "Dr. Gray was always looking ahead to improve the total field of reading" (Helen Huus, personal communication, October 1, 2004). When preparing his 1941 review of research, he had indexed more than 2,000 publications on reading from the beginning of research in the field to the date of his report. This was prior to databases and computerized library resources. Gray's exhaustive approach reminds us that we have a serious responsibility to thoroughly understand the research and publications that have preceded us. We will then be able to follow his advice to "hold fast to that which has proved its worth, while marking out new trails and conquering new frontiers" (Gray, 1960c, p. 63).

Gray's work advises that reading professionals should use scientific research but realize its limitations. Gray was an advocate for the use of scientific research as the basis for instruction and practice. Yet he realized that much of scientific research showed flaws when held up to intense scrutiny. He cautioned, "Those who do research in reading should make every effort to avoid mistakes of the past" (quoted in Smith, 1965, p. 405). Most important, he would have urged current researchers to have open and inquiring minds and to accept the legitimacy of a broad range of investigations.

Gray emphasized that a broad definition of reading focused on meaning and thinking is essential:

> Any program of guidance in reading which is concerned primarily with the basic habits and skills involved in the recognition of words, and only secondarily with the meanings represented and the changes produced in the life of the reader, is in our opinion inadequate to meet contemporary needs. (Gray, 1940, pp. 20–21)

Thanks to Gray's example, those of us in the reading field know that we should emphasize reading across the content areas and throughout the life of the student: "I wish to refer again to the urgent need for improving reading in the content fields. Herein lies one of the greatest possibilities for developing mature, competent readers" (Gray, 1960c, p. 62). Gray also advised teachers to continue their efforts longer by offering instruction in reading throughout the upper grades, high school, and college.

Teachers should adjust this instruction to meet students' individual needs. Gray thought that "current efforts to adjust instruction to individual differences [should] be greatly extended.... Progress in reading [should] be paced far less in terms of age and grade norms and far more in terms of individual capabilities, motivation and needs" (Gray, 1960c, p. 59). He would admonish teachers to approach each child as an individual, rather than having common expectations and approaches for all children. As William S. Gray III said,

> My dad had an eclectic view about how people should learn to read. [We must] recognize that we all are different and therefore no single approach is really going to be the optimal solution to everybody's needs as far as learning how to read is concerned. (personal communication, October 26, 2005)

Gray also set an example for people in the reading field to be professional. He was scrupulous in separating his professional life from his commercial endeavors. As Huus reports,

Although I had more than one class with Dr. Gray, he never mentioned the Elson-Gray Readers at the University or tried to advertise them in any way. I did know that he spent many Wednesdays at the publishing company, but the readers and his teaching were kept separate. (personal communication, October 1, 2004)

Both in terms of personal attributes and scholarship, Gray provides a role model for us as teachers and human beings. His humility, dignity, perseverance, and energy are attributes to strive for as indicated by many testimonials from his contemporaries, including Albert Harris:

I tried to profit from his example of what a scholar in the field of reading could be.... The tradition that he began is being carried on today by the students of his students and the disciples of his disciples. (Harris, quoted in Mavrogenes, 1985a, p. 11)

Gray offered opportunities to his students and others to become part of the community of reading scholars and assisted many in being successful in the field. He reminds us that our work in the field of literacy can sustain us. Says his son, "He was genuinely involved in trying to help people get better educated, and reading was very central [to that purpose]. He was so deeply interested in this field of reading, it just made him a happy person" (personal communication, October 26, 2005).

According to Gray, teachers also should strive for quality and invest positively in the future. Gray believed in fostering important qualities of mind to bring about change—"an inquiring attitude, a willingness to probe deeply as one reads, and the capacity to deal imaginatively and creatively with the ideas acquired through reading" (Gray, 1960c, p. 58). This emphasis requires "the maximum use of the higher mental processes in reading and suggests new frontiers to conquer in future efforts to improve reading" (Gray, 1960c, p. 58).

Finally, Gray reminds adults that young people are growing up in a world different from the past because of the expansion of knowledge, the use of technology, and changes in world politics. He believed that increased levels of literacy are needed to engage in the "strategy of peace as contrasted with the strategy of war" and to preserve and improve "the way of life which, as a people, we cherish" (1960c, p. 57). He reminded all educators that "the hope of individual welfare and social progress in the future lies in a higher quality of educational process and product" (p. 57).

Reflection Questions

1. Gray was one of the creators of the Dick and Jane characters. Given what you know about Gray's personality and his professional commitments, what do you think Gray hoped to accomplish through these characters? Do you think he succeeded?

2. Gray was instrumental in creating teachers' guides and student workbooks for the basal readers he created. What impact have these tools had on the reading curriculum throughout the past several decades?

3. How does Gray's conception of reading compare with the concept of reading presented in the RAND Report (Snow, 1999)?

4. How might Gray caution modern reviewers of reading research? What might Gray recommend for future directions in reading research?

5. Gray recognized the micro- and macro-level influences on reading practices (e.g., students' interests, international political decisions). Do you see the same attention to both micro- and macro-level influences reflected in the field of reading today? What do you think educators in the field of reading should be giving more attention to in both practice and research?

REFERENCES

Courtney, L. (1980). *Content area reading in retrospect*. (ERIC Document Reproduction Service No. ED189546)

Dick and Jane's long-lost dad!!! [Electronic version]. (1998). *University of Chicago Magazine*. Retrieved January 15, 2005, from http://magazine.uchicago.edu/9812/html/enquirer2.htm

Elson, W.H., & Gray, W.S. (1930). Elson Basic Readers: Book one. Chicago: Scott Foresman.

Elson, W.H., Gray, W.S., et al. (1930, 1931, 1934). Elson Basic Readers series. Chicago: Scott Foresman.

Elson, W.H., Gray, W.S., et al. (1936–1938). Elson-Gray Basic Readers series. Chicago: Scott Foresman.

Flesch, R.F. (1955). *Why Johnny can't read—and what you can do about it*. New York: Harper & Row.

Gates, A.I. (1961). William Scott Gray 1885–1960: Results of teaching a system of phonics. *The Reading Teacher, 14*, 248–252.

Gilstad, J.R. (1985). Commentary: William S. Gray (1885–1960): First IRA president. *Reading Research Quarterly, 20*, 509–511.

Gray, W.S. (1917). *Studies of elementary school reading through standardized tests*. Supplementary Educational Monograph, No. 1. Chicago: University of Chicago Press.

Gray, W.S. (1940). *Reading in general education: An exploratory study. A report of the committee on reading in general education*. Washington, DC: American Council on Education.

Gray, W.S. (1956). *The teaching of reading and writing: An international survey*. Paris: UNESCO.

Gray, W.S. (1960a). The major aspects of reading. In H.M. Robinson (Ed.), *Sequential development of reading abilities* (pp. 8–24). Supplementary Educational Monographs, No. 90. Chicago: University of Chicago Press.

Gray, W.S. (1960b). *On their own in reading: How to give children independence in analyzing new words*. Chicago: Scott Foresman. (Original work published 1948)

Gray, W.S. (1960c). What lies ahead in reading? In *Education Looks Ahead, A symposium opening the 1959 general conference of Scott Foresman and Company, December 15* (pp. 53–63). Chicago: Scott Foresman.

Gray, W.S. (1963). *Gray oral reading tests*. Indianapolis, IN: Bobbs-Merrill. (Original work published 1915 as *Oral Reading Paragraphs*)

Gray, W.S. (1984). Reading. In J.T. Guthrie (Ed.)., *"Reading" by William S. Gray: A research retrospective, 1881–1941* (pp. 1–89). Newark, DE: International Reading Association. (Original work published 1941)

Gray, W.S., Arbuthnot, M.H., et al. (1940–1948). Basic Readers [Curriculum Foundation series]. Chicago: Scott Foresman.

Gray, W.S., Arbuthnot, M.H., Artley, A.S., Monroe, M., et al. (1951–1957). New Basic Readers [series]. Chicago: Scott Foresman.

Gray, W.S., Kibbe, D., Lucas, L., & Miller, L.W. (1922). *Remedial cases in reading: Their diagnosis and treatment* (Supplementary Educational Monographs, No. 22). Chicago: University of Chicago.

Gray, W.S., & Rogers, B. (1956). *Maturity in reading: Its nature and appraisal*. Chicago: University of Chicago Press.

Jaeger, M., & Lauritzen, C. (2004). *Memoirs of Thaddeus S. C. Lowe, chief of the aeronautic corps of the army of the United States during the Civil War: My balloons in peace and war*. Lewiston, NY: Edwin Mellen.

Jerrolds, B.W. (1977). *Reading reflections: The history of the International Reading Association*. Newark, DE: International Reading Association.

Lauritzen, C. (2002). *Portrait of a one-room school*. La Grande, OR: Caljae.

Malmquist, E. (1980). Readings that made a difference: Cooperating in the attack on illiteracy. *Journal of Reading, 23*, 392–396.

Mavrogenes, N.A. (1985a). *In memory of William S. Gray: Remarks at the Reading Hall of Fame's Gray centennial program, 1985*. (ERIC Document Reproduction Service No. ED268484)

Mavrogenes, N.A. (1985b). *William Scott Gray: Leader of teachers and shaper of American reading instruction*. Unpublished doctoral dissertation, University of Chicago.

Mavrogenes, N.A. (1985c). *William S. Gray and the Dick and Jane readers*. (ERIC Document Reproduction Service No. ED 269 722)

Mavrogenes, N.A. (1985d). William S. Gray: The person. In J.A. Stevenson (Ed.), *William S. Gray: Teacher, scholar, leader* (pp. 1–23). Newark, DE: International Reading Association.

Monroe, W.S. (Ed.). (1950). *Encyclopedia of educational research* (2nd ed.). New York: Macmillan.

Monroe, W.S., & Harris, C.W. (Eds.). (1941). *Encyclopedia of educational research*. New York: Macmillan.

Monroe, W.S., & Harris, C.W. (Eds.). (1960). *Encyclopedia of educational research* (3rd ed.). New York: Macmillan.

Smith, N.B. (1965). *American reading instruction*. Newark, DE: International Reading Association.

Snow, C.E. (1999). *Reading for understanding: Toward an R & D program in reading comprehension*. Santa Monica, CA: RAND. Available online at http://www.rand.org/pubs/mono graph_reports/MR1465/index.html

Stevenson, J.A. (1985). *William S. Gray: Teacher, scholar, leader*. Newark, DE: International Reading Association.

William S. Gray, reading expert. (1960, September 9). *The New York Times*, n.p.

FOR FURTHER READING

Gray, W.S., & Leary, B.E. (1939). Reading instruction in elementary schools [in New York State]. In L.J. Bruekner, *The changing elementary school* (pp. 282–305). New York: Inor.

Gray, W.S., & Munroe, R. (1929). *The reading interests and habits of adults*. New York: Macmillan.

Guthrie, J.T. (Ed.). (1984). *Reading: A research retrospective*. Newark, DE: International Reading Association.

Kismaric, C., & Heiferman, M. (1996). *Growing up with Dick and Jane: Learning and living the American dream*. New York: HarperCollins.

Maring, G.H. (1978). Freire, Gray and Robinson on reading. *Journal of Reading, 21*, 421–425.

O'Brien, J.A. (1942–1947). Cathedral Basic Readers [series]. Chicago: Scott Foresman.

O'Brien, J.A. (1952–1957). New Cathedral Basic Readers [series]. Chicago: Scott Foresman.

Robinson, R.D. (2002). William S. Gray (1885–1960). In *Classics in literacy education: Historical perspectives for today's teachers* (pp. 17–30). Newark, DE: International Reading Association.

Robinson, R.D. (2005). Changes in the teaching of reading. *Reading Psychology, 26*, 433–440.

CHAPTER 14

Arthur Irving Gates (1890–1972): Educational Psychology and the Study of Reading

By Misty Sailors

Historical Research Process

STUDENTS OF HISTORICAL research beware: While the Internet is an excellent source of information, personal information about someone you are researching often cannot be located there. Such was the case with my search for information on Arthur Irving Gates to find who he was and what he contributed to the field of reading. Being an avid user of the Internet, I began my search on Gates there to see what the larger community knew and thought

Shaping the Reading Field: The Impact of Early Reading Pioneers, Scientific Research, and Progressive Ideas, edited by Susan E. Israel and E. Jennifer Monaghan. © 2007 by the International Reading Association.
Photo: Courtesy of Teachers College, Columbia University.

about him. Using several search engines, many of the websites that I uncovered revolved around four elements: (1) links to the vitae of people who have held the Arthur I. Gates Endowed Chair at Columbia University; (2) Gates's writings that are archived by the *Teachers College Record* (http://www.tcrecord.org); (3) Gates's work that centered on perhaps his best-known products, his reading tests; and (4) links to bookstores that sell copies of the books that Gates authored. Although this was a helpful beginning, it did not lead to any significant personal information on Gates, not even a biography.

Because my Internet search left me with so little personal information, I did what all good researchers do. I e-mailed a colleague, Ed Fry, and asked, "Who in the world might have known Gates personally, and where in the world would I find that person?" Ed, known for his unfailing willingness to help, suggested that I get in touch with Walter MacGinitie because he had worked with Gates at Teachers College, Columbia University, in New York City, New York, USA. I called MacGinitie, and he was more than happy to accommodate my request, initially by sending me a paper he had presented at the 25th Annual Convention of the International Reading Association in 1980 (MacGinitie, 1980), and later by participating in a telephone interview. In this paper, MacGinitie speaks highly of Gates, calling him a "scholar and a gentleman" (p. 1). In the telephone interview, MacGinitie was more than helpful, giving me access to one of the only two other people I could locate who had actually worked with Gates. Walter's paper was, therefore, the first step along a trail that took me to Gates's autobiography and his many contributions to the field of reading and reading instruction.

Personal and Professional Life

Throughout his life, Gates was known to be a dignified and generous person, albeit a very private one. MacGinitie, a recipient of the Macmillan Fellowship at Gates's Language Arts Institute at Teachers College, described him as someone who was very meticulous about the quality of his work. For example, MacGinitie remembered one evening when he and his wife arrived at the Gates's apartment in New York City. They had been invited to join Gates and his wife at the Metropolitan Opera, a cultural event that Gates adored. However, upon arriving they discovered Gates busy at work on a set of proofs he had just received. His decision to edit his work at the expense of attending one of his favorite events was very much in keeping with other decisions that Gates made throughout his life (W.H. MacGinitie, personal communication, July 18, 2005).

The youngest son of William P. and Lenore (Gaylord) Gates, descendants of English and Scottish immigrants to New England, Arthur Irving Gates was born on September 22, 1890, in Red Wing, Minnesota, USA. After moving around for some time, his family settled in northwest California. His father supported a wife, a step-son (Lenore was a widow with a young son when she married William), and two younger sons by working in the lumbering business (Gates, 1971, p. 189).

Gates reported that his mother taught him to read just after his third birthday and it was reading that kept him out of trouble in school during his early years. One teacher allowed him to spend time in the so-called library, a dark attic room open only to teachers. He filled the remainder of his childhood and early adolescent years working on the family farm and at a local general store, organizing a baseball sandlot team, debating on the school debate team, and writing for the county's daily paper. Upon graduation from high school, Gates had to make a decision as to what career path he would take. He was offered a salary to play professional baseball, the chance to continue working at the general store with the promise of becoming a partner, and a scholarship to attend the University of California at Berkeley. At the insistence of his teachers, he chose the last option. During his spare time at Berkeley, Gates again played baseball and joined the debate team, and he wrote for the college newspaper (Gates, 1971, pp. 190–192).

Gates was uncertain as to what he would major in as he entered Berkeley. His teachers encouraged a career in teaching, medicine, or law. Gates, however, became very interested in psychology during his freshman year. Not caring that people at the time thought of psychologists as "vagrant mind readers" (Gates, 1964, p. 297), Gates followed his "compulsion to be a scientist" (p. 297) and study psychology. After a year off from college to recoup financially, Gates returned to Berkeley as a student assistant in the psychology department. His undergraduate work took a turn toward the unfamiliar when his advisor, Warner Brown, suggested that he read more and attend lectures less. Brown also suggested that Gates engage in research before his senior year. Gates followed this advice and during his senior year conducted two lines of research—laboratory experiments and group tests. The latter produced data that Gates evaluated statistically and then used for closer study of individuals from the group (Gates, 1971, pp. 192, 194–195). Three of his first experimental studies were published that year; he joked that his career was founded upon a yawn since in one of the three studies he demonstrated that most people get a little drowsy after lunch (Gates, 1964, p. 297). Gates received his bachelor's degree in 1914.

Although Gates began his first two years of graduate work in California, he found himself becoming increasingly attracted to the work of James McKeen Cattell (see chapter 1, this volume), Robert Sessions Woodworth (see chapter 2, this volume), and Edward Lee Thorndike (see chapter 5, this volume) at Columbia University. Once again, Gates found himself making a career-guiding decision: He was offered both a fellowship at Stanford University and a teaching assistantship at Columbia University. His attraction to the unfolding research at Columbia clinched the decision, and Gates chose the Columbia position (Gates, 1971, p. 195). While he was a graduate student at Columbia, Gates's primary appointment was spent assisting his mentor, Cattell, in his classes as well as tutoring Cattell's children in their home. He once described the Cattell children as full of life and told stories of how they would bring snakes in from the outdoors and place them under his chair (J. Nurss, personal communication, July 19, 2005).

It was during his graduate years at Columbia that Gates enrolled in one of Thorndike's general school psychology courses, which Gates (1971) described as "new, ingenious, exceedingly interesting, and often puzzling" (p. 196). After the completion of his dissertation in 1916, Gates was invited by Thorndike only a year later to join his department at Teachers College. Left speechless by the offer because he had never taught a day in his life, Gates quickly accepted the position. In an address made at the 50th anniversary celebration of a chapter of Phi Delta Kappa at Berkeley, Gates (1964) reported that in his early years as a professor at Columbia, he often struggled at times to "desperately get my head above the torrent for an occasional breath of sanity" (p. 298). His colleagues, whom he described as engaging in "enthusiastic, fearless, and wacky activity" (p. 298), included John Dewey, Woodworth, and Cattell at Columbia as well as Charles Hubbard Judd of the University of Chicago (see chapter 4, this volume). He reported that he enjoyed every minute of the work he did with these "extraordinarily brilliant, energetic, courageous, and well-informed thinkers" (p. 298).

Later Gates summarized his relation to progressive education, the school of thought led by John Dewey. For the first quarter-century of his professional life (from about 1917 to 1942), he said he had incurred criticism for not being a sufficiently enthusiastic supporter of Dewey. During his last quarter century, he was also criticized—but this time for being a naive supporter of Dewey's progressive ideas (Gates, 1971, p. 211).

One of Gates's most well-known early studies (Gates, Batchelder, & Betzner, 1926) was in effect critical of progressive education. Gates investigated the differences in the performance of children from a classroom in which a "systematic" method of teaching was employed and a classroom in which an "opportunistic" method of teaching was employed. He defined the "systematic" method as consisting of daily lessons that were defined, prescribed, and strictly adhered to, based on the nature of the subject matter (p. 681). He described the "opportunistic" method as a less definite program of studies and activities that was meant to conform to the inclinations and interests of the students in the class. The teacher in this classroom followed the "self-initiated urges of the pupils to learn to read, write, spell, etc." (p. 681), while still setting up a lesson and projects in which the students were encouraged to participate (such as writing a response to an invitation to a birthday party). These lessons were the impetus for necessary information and skills.

Through this yearlong study, Gates documented the differences in teaching methods and measured the differences in learning by the children in the two classes. He found that both groups were equally interested in school activities and that "opportunistic teaching" resulted in slightly higher achievements in the motor functions of children than "modern systematic teaching." However, "modern systematic teaching" resulted in considerably greater average achievements in the other school subjects—arithmetic, spelling, and silent and oral reading (p. 693). Herein lay what Gates described as the crux of the study; that is, one method achieved academic achievement results and the other paved the path for children to learn to like to read. Surely this study influenced the future work of this pioneer and others that followed him.

During World War I, Gates had begun teaching courses for and assisting Thorndike, who had been named chairman of the Committee on Classification of Personnel. In one of these classes Gates met his future wife, Georgina Stickland, who graduated with her PhD from the psychology department at Columbia University at the age of 22. The couple married in 1920 and had two children, a boy and a girl. Gates's son, Robert Gaylord, went on to earn a doctor of science degree in mechanical engineering and metallurgy. Gates's daughter, Katherine Blair, was awarded a PhD degree in English literature from Harvard-Radcliffe (Gates, 1971, pp. 197–200).

Although Gates (1971) reported that his most productive line of research occurred between 1920 and 1935 (p. 206)—and, indeed, he published numerous titles on psychology, vocabulary, reading tests, and reading improvement during these years (see later sections of this chapter)—his many years at Columbia gave him the opportunity to work with a number of outstanding graduate students who went on to be contributors to the field of reading. They included Ruth May Strang (see chapter 15, this volume), the future anthropologist Margaret Mead, Guy L. Bond (who became one of the founding members of the Reading Hall of Fame), David Harris Russell (see chapter 16, this volume), and Walter MacGinitie.

In addition to producing research and textbooks for psychology students, Gates is considered to be one of the two "giants" in the field of reading instruction (Smith, 1965, p. 222). Writing for Macmillan in the 1930s, Gates was the senior author of the Work-Play Books, which included the Peter and Peggy readers, the Nick and Dick readers (Gates & Huber, 1930, 1931), and other books. These books, very similar to their more memorable counterparts, the Dick and Jane readers written for Scott Foresman by William Scott Gray (see chapter 13, this volume) and May Hill Arbuthnot (see chapter 9, this volume) and the readers authored later for Ginn by Russell, operated under the same concept—present words as wholes, provide children with multiple opportunities to practice them, and introduce new words slowly. This approach, often referred to as the "look-and-say" or "whole-word" method, was the result of carefully sequenced steps designed to support reading progress through the elementary grades. These leveled readers consisted of preprimers, primers, and texts identified with grade levels. The basal texts were crafted to control for difficulty level primarily through the rate of introduction and repetition of key vocabulary. Gates's books, in conjunction with Gray's, Russell's, and similar series, became the mainstay of U.S. reading instruction, representing the formula for success in teaching reading and a consensus about beginning reading instruction from the 1930s to the 1950s (Chall, 1967).

During his time at Teachers College, Gates was also involved in social activism. For example, during the U.S. Great Depression of the 1930s, he devised a citywide remedial reading project, funded by the Federal Civil Works Administration, that employed about 200 previously unemployed New York teachers. These teachers, under the direction of Gates and 23 supervisors he had trained, went out and worked with children in the city schools who had severe reading problems. A second project, The Writers' Project, was designed to give unemployed writers the opportunity to construct small and relatively easy reading books with advanced interest levels (Gates, 1971, pp. 208–209).

Gates also offered advice to young scholars. In a speech at a Phi Delta Kappa meeting, Gates warned against yielding to the "pressure of the purse" (1964, p. 299). That is, because academics face poverty early in their career (a natural result of graduate school), the temptation to supplement an academic income through consultant work and the creation of educational materials is considerable. Gates cautioned young scientists to keep these enterprises within reason. He also warned them against becoming infected with "verbalism." This disease, he said, causes people to use "cumbersome expressions, loaded with professional clichés and technicalities" and is indicative of people whose "ideas are neither very clear nor very original" (p. 299). A rare glimpse of humor can be found in his last statement on this subject:

> To the young educator, especially the prospective scientist, I say most seriously: If you don't understand it clearly, don't say it or write it at all. And when you do say it or write it, avoid, as you would the plague, trying to speak or write it like a college professor. (p. 300)

Gates offered more frivolous advice to Joanne Nurss, who was helping him revise his reading tests. She must go, he said, to one of Nila Banton Smith's presentations at IRA because the hats that Smith wore were "absolutely wonderful" (J. Nurss, personal communication, July 19, 2005).

Gates retired in 1956 from the Department of Psychology and Research Methods at Teachers College. This mandated retirement did not stop him from doing what he loved best, researching and writing. He stayed active at Teachers College, being scrupulous about staying out of the affairs of the college, especially college politics. That same year, Gates was named supervisor of the Institute of Language Arts, an institute for research that he agreed to finance himself. The only external funding he received was through a fellowship that Macmillan agreed to support. He was provided with one graduate student per year under this fellowship. The first of several recipients of this fellowship, Walter MacGinitie, helped in the revision of the Gates Primary Reading Tests, first published in 1926 (1926a). Known as the Gates-MacGinitie reading tests, the first revised edition appeared in 1965, and it has been revised several times since then (MacGinitie, MacGinitie, Maria, & Dreyer, 2000).

MacGinitie (1980) notes that Gates continued to do personal research in the Institute. One of Gates's biggest interests at that time was exploring the ways in which children help each other. Although he was not considered to be a classroom teacher, in part because he was not very charismatic (W.H. MacGinitie, personal communication, July 18, 2005), Gates did enjoy working with children on this project, MacGinitie reported.

After his retirement, Gates was the recipient of several prestigious awards that reflected the substantial contributions he had made to the field of education. In 1961, the International Reading Association presented Gates with the William S. Gray Citation of Merit Award. In 1964, Gates was the first recipient of the Award for Distinguished Contributions to Educational Research, now given annually by the American Educational Research Association (AERA). The International Reading Association once again recognized Gates when the organization presented him in 1968 with its first International Citation of Merit for his service and contributions to understanding the reading process and reading instruction throughout the world. In addition, Gates received awards from outside the field of reading. For example, in 1971 the National Society for the Study of Education invited him to write his autobiography for their prestigious yearbook, *Leaders in American Education* (Gates, 1971).

Gates provided much service to his profession at the college, national, and international levels. In addition to other administrative positions he held at Teachers College, he was the executive officer of his department from 1933 to 1956. He served as chair of the educational section of the American Association of Applied Psychology (1940–1942). He was also the vice president (1942) and then president (1943) of the AERA. In addition, he was a member of the American Association of School Administrators, the American Association of University Professors, and the National Education Association. Gates became a council member and then the president of the Educational Psychology section of the American Psychological Association (1948–1949). He also held memberships in Sigma Xi, Alpha Sigma Phi, Phi Delta Kappa, and the Century Club ("Dr. Arthur Gates," 1972; Gates, 1971; Tostberg, 1971).

After many years of contributing to the fields of psychology and reading, Gates died on August 24, 1972, survived by his wife, daughter, son, and a grandchild. As with other aspects of his life, his funeral was private ("Dr.

Arthur Gates," 1972). The reading community honored Gates with a posthumous induction as a pioneer into the esteemed community of the Reading Hall of Fame (C. Harrison, personal communication, December 10, 2005).

Philosophical Beliefs and Guiding Principles

Coming of age at the same time that experimental psychology was gathering speed clearly influenced Gates's principles and the work he did. His research and pragmatic work were guided by the experimental nature of psychology and were heavily influenced by the works of the German psychologists (e.g., Wilhelm Wundt, H. von Helmholtz, and Ernst Meumann); the translated French reports of Alfred Binet and H. Bernheim; and the U.S. psychologists, including William James, Cattell, Woodworth, Judd, Lewis Terman, and Thorndike (Gates, 1971, p. 194).

In the field of educational psychology, Gates was a leader. He wrote his first book on the topic, *Psychology for Students of Education*, in 1923. His second book, *Elementary Psychology*, was published in 1925 and later revised in 1928 (1928a). He also revised Thorndike's 1912 version of *Education: A First Book* with a bit of trepidation, realizing that he himself deviated from Thorndike's terminology and systematic theories in his own work (Gates, 1971, p. 205). Gates reported that Thorndike was interested in discussing any differences that this exercise might bring forth. The book was published under the new title, *Elementary Principles of Education* (Thorndike & Gates, 1929). Gates's final contribution to the field of psychology came in 1942 with the revision of his *Psychology for Students of Education* (1923), now titled *Educational Psychology* (Gates, Jersild, McConnell, & Challman, 1942). It even had a Hebrew edition.

MacGinitie (1980) wrote that Gates went through a professional identity change during his career. Initially, when Gates came to Teachers College, he viewed himself as an experimental psychologist. Later, Gates began to divide his time between general psychological issues and pragmatic problems in education. He reported that he could do more for education by applying his "kit of scientific concepts and techniques" to the pragmatic problems teachers faced than to just confine them to the "typically narrow and artificial situations" of the experimental laboratory (Gates, 1971, p. 203). This was the beginning of a lifelong commitment to research and influence on reading instruction that spanned decades.

When this shift occurred is unclear, but it is clear that Gates's enrollment in Thorndike's Psychology of the School Subjects class during his first year as a student at Columbia University was instrumental in moving his interests away from laboratory tasks to the "multitude of complex and puzzling problems one must face in the daily tasks of teaching" (Gates, 1971, p. 203). Gates reported that his focus at Columbia changed when he became an administrator. As a result, he moved from analytical, experimental, and theoretical research in psychology to using the "mass-statistical approach" (Gates, quoted in Tostberg, 1971, p. 228), a move that he later regretted (Gates, 1964, p. 300). In short, Gates considered himself to be an educational psychologist who had contributed significantly to the fields of psychology and reading (MacGinitie, 1980).

And contribute significantly, he did. Five years before his forced retirement, Gates (1951/2002) summed up his philosophy of reading and reading instruction: "There can be but two real goals toward which we aim in teaching reading—...to teach children to read well and to love to read" (p. 49). Gates's work shows that he was deeply committed to improving the quality of living, both in individuals and in society, which is evident in his belief that formal education was the fundamental way to remake U.S. society (Tostberg, 1971, p. 229).

Contributions to the Field of Reading

Although Gates was considered to be, both by his colleagues and himself, an educational psychologist and not a reading researcher, the vast majority of his work, especially his later work, focused on reading and reading instruction. In this section, I will highlight the contributions that Gates made to the field of reading, especially in the areas of reading readiness, reading methodology, reading materials, and remedial reading instruction.

Reading Readiness

Gates contributed significantly to the movement of "reading readiness" (Harrison, 1936) with his seminal piece, *Methods of Determining Reading Readiness* (Gates, Bond, & Russell, 1939). He recognized that "pupils differ greatly in their interest and ability in learning to read" and that "failure in reading results from starting to teach a pupil to read before he is 'ready'" (p. 1), an inherently dangerous practice. Using tests on intelligence, auditory acuity and discrimination, visual function and discrimination, reading readiness (including tests of phonetic abilities), memory, visual perception of numbers and words, the alphabet, and types of errors in word recognition and the ability to complete stories, Gates and his colleagues demonstrated that "the most useful tests for predicting reading achievement in the primary grades are measures of reading attainments at the time" (p. 26). That is, the best way to predict how well a child will learn to read is to measure his reading abilities before he or she can read.

Although he later refused to use the term *readiness* when talking about early reading instruction (W.H. MacGinitie, personal communication, July 18, 2005), presumably because by then the term had fallen into disrepute, he, along with Guy Bond and David Russell, was well ahead of his time in recognizing that "the abilities directly involved in reading are acquired long before a child enters school" (Gates, et al., 1939, p. 26) and that reading readiness is "something to be taught and not a series of attributes for the development of which a teacher can do nothing but wait" (p. 53). The Gates reading readiness tests were a result of this work.

Reading Methodology

Gates's second significant contribution to the field of reading was a result of the work he began early in his career at Columbia University. He believed that reading should not be taught or learned as an isolated activity. Instead, he believed that it should be integrated into a "well-rounded program of linguistic, artistic, dramatic, constructive, and exploratory activities" (Gates, 1930, p. 193). In other words, reading should not be taught as an end in and of itself, but rather should be taught in the context of activities that children find interesting and essential to the expression of their interests. His first book on reading methodology, *New Methods in Primary Reading*, appeared in 1928 (1928b), soon followed by *Interest and Ability in Reading* (1930). He continued to write about this topic throughout his career. Titles that have influenced the field of reading instruction include *Reading for Public School Administrators* (1931), *Reading Attainment in Elementary Schools: 1957 and 1937* (1937/1961), and *Teaching Reading* (1953/1962).

In his seminal publication, *New Methods in Primary Reading*, Gates (1928b) introduced a new method of teaching (and learning) phonetics, as it was then termed. This method represented his growing aversion to the teaching (and learning) of phonics, which he considered a practice devoid of real reading—that is, of reading for meaning. In his *Interest and Ability in Reading* (1930), Gates expressed his belief that the development of all reading abilities should be the "natural and necessary result" of engagement in reading (p. 194). A reading vocabulary was not the result of artificial word study, he believed, but rather was acquired "more economically and effectively when the pupil repeatedly encounters the words in regular reading contexts" (p. 196). Simply stated, children should be provided with an increase in the amount of reading material based on the words they are to learn, and the words should be practiced within this context until they are learned.

Similarly, Gates believed that the traditional teaching of phonic skills was a "wasteful" way of providing children with useful techniques for recognizing new and unfamiliar words because the transfer of the skills was incomplete. He was convinced that these orthodox techniques provided "no experience in reading for the thought" (1930, p. 202) and that some children overused these habits until they were not able to see words as wholes. Further, and more alarming to Gates, was the fact that teaching by the traditional phonics methods does not allow children to see how the processes of reading interact with one another. He believed the best method of "attack" upon unfamiliar words in reading to be one in which context clues were used at the same time as a "quick perspective analysis of the word-form elements" (p. 202). He dubbed this new method the *intrinsic method* (p. 204) of developing phonic skills in word recognition and claimed that this method would develop them so that these skills would work when and where needed while a child was engaged in the act of reading. (He had already used the term "intrinsic" in earlier publications [e.g. Gates, 1928b, p. 40].)

Reading Materials

The new intrinsic method was presented to teachers and children in the reading materials created by Gates during the 1930s, 1940s, and 1950s, his third contribution to the reading field. Gates's Work-Play Books were the way in which his idea of the intrinsic method of teaching phonics instantiated itself. Immediately after children read their assigned passages in their basal reader, they encountered a series of questions that had as discriminators words that varied by onsets or rimes (to use today's terms):

Play you are a fairy's child.

1. What is around your garden?
   A light well.
   A high wall.
2. What is the wall made of?
   brown brick bright
3. How do you get into your garden?
   Through a little green gate.
   Through a little green great. (Gates & Huber, 1930, p. 32)

The purpose of these exercises was twofold. First, these questions were intended to tell the child if he or she had comprehended the main idea of the selection and to encourage rereading if necessary. Second, and perhaps most representative of Gates's work, these exercises were intended to help the child learn to distinguish between parts of words so he or she would be able to "distinguish the words which express the thought from other word forms that contain similar elements" (1930, p. 207). Reading instruction such as this, Gates believed, would help the child develop an insight into word-form structure and would be more useful than the traditional word study of the time. Through this method children would be unaware of learning phonics, and their minds would be focused on the thought of the passage. The method, Gates believed, provided for the transfer of skills and presented the opportunity for children to use both context clues and word-form clues simultaneously (p. 208).

Gates was innovative in his emphasis on the role that interest and ability played in reading. It was his book on this topic, *Interest and Ability in Reading* (1930), together with his book for public school administrators published the following year (1931) that led to the understanding that materials for reading instruction with children needed to be based on (a) experiences of children; (b) interests of children; (c) a wide range of topics; and (d) a wide variety of genres, including poetry, informative texts, stories, and what he called work-play texts—that is, texts that "direct or suggest to the reader some form of activity to be pursued" (1931, p. 16). In addition, Gates believed that materials in reading programs should be presented topically and followed for a period of two to four weeks. He also insisted that the illustrations in children's materials should be of "real art quality" (1931, p. 24) and that the work accompanying the basal reader should encourage individual and cooperative enterprises.

In 1930, Gates put his theories into practice in his own basal readers (with the help of Miriam Blanton Huber and Jean Ayer), published by Macmillan from the 1930s through the 1950s. The first series produced by Gates and his colleagues was the Work-Play books, published in 1930. Consisting of a teacher's manual and children's readers (grades 1–5), these books were written as a result of Gates's progressive ideas. The authors considered these materials to have a central place inside the reading program and to be a way of providing children with opportunities to engage in "work type" reading (Gates, Huber, & Ayer, 1932, p. 10).

In these readers, children's experiences with reading centered on following directions to complete a project. According to Gates, these books were the incentive for the children who read them to learn to do things. The books represented the research that demonstrated the conditions under which children learned to read, as espoused in Gates's intrinsic methods (Vance, 1985, p. 302). Gates published the Good Companion series in 1936 and revised the Work-Play Books series in 1939 (renamed the New Work-Play Books series) and again in 1945 (renamed Today's Work-Play Books series). Gates published another series in the early 1950s called the Macmillan Readers. Printed with the orange-and-black pictures that represented readers of that era, as the United States struggled out of the Great Depression, the Work-Play Book series of the 1930s was the first to have a design embossed on the back cover of the books (Smith, 1965, p. 223). The series' primer, *Peter and Peggy* (Gates & Huber, 1931), was "apparently the only one of that era to include pictures of literacy in context, such as print in public places or portrayals of parents reading to children" (E.J. Monaghan, personal communication, August 4, 2005).

Perhaps Gates's most significant contribution as a member of the basal reading establishment was the careful control of vocabulary in basal readers as a result of his work on vocabulary, his *A Reading Vocabulary for the Primary Grades* (Gates, 1926b). Gates described the appearance of too many and too difficult words in children's readers as a "burden" for young readers and discouraged the use of heavy vocabulary and the teaching of isolated elements of any sort (Gates, 1931, p. 53). The following excerpts summarize the characteristics of a reading program that Gates (1931) believed would ensure successful experiences with text:

1. Reading materials—story, informative, poetic, and work and play types— are used from the beginning in proper proportions and relations.

2. The various materials are organized...to make a given number of words most widely useful....

3. [Each new word must be introduced with] ample context clues [that] will enable the pupils to derive the meaning and pronunciation of the word with a high percentage of successes [sic]. (pp. 55–56)

In all of this—in his handling of reading readiness, methodology, and materials—Gates emphasized the importance of reading for meaning. His view was that the context of what was read should smooth the way to word identification.

Remedial Reading Instruction

A fourth contribution Gates made to reading and reading instruction centered on his work in the field of remedial reading instruction, or reading instruction with children who struggled with learning to read. (In keeping with the terminology used at the time of Gates's work, I will continue to use his words and phrases.) Gates published his first book in this area in 1922, *The Psychology of Reading and Spelling, with Special Reference to Disability. The Improvement of Reading: A Program of Diagnostic and Remedial Methods* was published in 1927 and revised in 1935 and 1947. Another book on remedial instruction was published in 1933, *Reversal Tendencies in Reading: Causes, Diagnosis, Prevention and Correction* (Gates & Bennett, 1933), and a fourth publication on this topic was available in 1942, *Teaching Reading to Slow-Learning Pupils* (Gates & Pritchard, 1942).

It was, perhaps, *The Improvement of Reading* (1927 and other editions) that demonstrated Gates's impressive contribution to the area of remedial instruction. In this book he defines remedial instruction as "first and primarily [an] individual prescription for individual needs" (Gates, 1927/1935, p. 25). Of the first edition of this book Miles A. Tinker wrote, in 1932,

> The development of a program of research dealing with materials and methods of the teaching of reading by Dr. A.I. Gates and his associates in the Institute of Educational Research of Teachers College has resulted in contributions that may be classified as among the most important appearing during the past decade. Dr. Gates gives an outline of what promises to become one of our most effective method[s] of teaching reading. (quoted in Tostberg, 1971, p. 223)

According to Gates (1927/1935), contemporary instruction for children who found learning to read difficult (or dull children, as they were referred to at the time) was radically different in type and intent from traditional reading instruction and was characterized by "stunts" that were "novel devices" (p. 26). He went on to remind his readers that the children with whom these devices were employed were the very children who were in the "most need of the best possible teaching [practices]" (p. 26). Gates argued that remedial teaching should follow the same principles that were used in any other type of instruction.

These guiding principles included the careful selection of reading materials, the careful scheduling of the program, and the careful identification of children's needs through a variety of reading tests. A major portion of Gates's work centered on the use of appropriate tests to gauge student abilities and needs because "reading is not a single ability which is utilized in every situation but, on the contrary, a number of abilities" (Gates, 1927/1935, p. 40). For the youngest of children, he espoused testing on word recognition, sentence reading, and paragraph reading. For the older children, he advocated four types of tests: (1) reading to appreciate the general significance (i.e., the main idea), (2) reading to predict the outcome of given events, (3) reading to understand precise directions, and (4) reading to note details.

Not only did Gates identify the types of tests that would be helpful in identifying the needs of students, he also offered suggestions for the instruction of such students. For each type of test listed above, teachers could take a number of approaches, all of which centered on the idea that good reading instruction for children with difficulties is just good reading instruction. Children who struggle with learning to read, Gates affirmed, need the same kind of instruction that other children need: They just need it more intensely and regularly.

During his career, Gates contributed to the publication of over 300 books, articles, and presentations (Tostberg, 1971, p. 226). He had a huge influence on the field of reading and reading instruction. His student, David Russell (quoted in Tostberg, 1971), summed up Gates's contributions:

> In the field of reading instruction Gates's original researches and wide-ranging writings have made him one of the most influential figures in the United

States and throughout the world. His [intrinsic phonics] method, with some later variations, has become standard practice in most American schools. It is no exaggeration to say that [Gates's] books largely changed reading from an isolated and mechanical exercise to a series of consecutive, meaningful, and zestful activities for American children. (p. 224)

Not everyone agreed with Russell's assessment. In 1955 Rudolf Flesch attacked Gates and other pioneers in the reading field for abandoning systematic phonics. A graduate of Teachers College himself, Flesch grouped the work of Gates among works that used the "look-and-say" method and blamed the works of Gates and Gray for the "alarming functional illiteracy" in the United States (Flesch, 1955/1985, p. viii).

Lessons for the Future

In many ways, Gates was ahead of his time because many of the topics he wrote about speak to reading educators today—so much so, that the International Reading Association chose to republish in 2002 an article that Gates originally wrote in 1951. Gates advocates several principles that are highly relevant today in this piece, titled "What should we teach in reading?"

First, he advocates that teachers teach children to read well and to love to read. He describes good reading as "something very different from being able merely to recognize printed phonograms and words or even to pronounce the series of words in a sentence" (Gates, 1951/2002, p. 50). Reading well, Gates argued, was a highly coordinated set of skills (how well the child reads) *and* how much he or she enjoys doing it. Teaching children to orchestrate the techniques involved in reading requires "shrewd guidance" by the teacher (p. 51). Teachers, he writes, can become pressured to "make a quick showing of some kind of skill in reading" (p. 51) through the use of programmed materials focused on phonic drills. Although he never supported the exclusion of phonics instruction—in fact, he addressed it as a necessary part of reading instruction in many of his writings—Gates did believe that children who were taught to read this way would not grow up to enjoy reading.

What is necessary, he wrote toward the end of his career at Teachers College, was the need to provide children with "an abundance of opportunity to read naturally and successfully" (Gates, 1951/2002, p. 51) in materials that are appropriate for their ability. That is, if we want children to learn to love to read, we must provide them with opportunities to engage in print experiences that are interesting, appropriate, and supported with high-quality instruction.

If we had been sitting in the audience at the 1968 Annual Convention of the International Reading Association, listening to Gates give his talk titled "The Tides of Time," here are the words we would have heard:

> The values of most reading materials and methods depend more upon what children do at the time in school and out, upon attitudes and abilities they possess, and upon the skills and habits of their teacher than upon any inherent, absolute virtue of the material or method itself. (quoted in MacGinitie, 1980, p. 14)

This speech has particular relevance to us as reading teachers today, given the highly politically charged climate of education.

Gates understood deeply the fact that all children come to school with different strengths and different instructional needs. He also understood that there are as many different ways to teach reading as there are children to be taught. In keeping with this fact, Gates advocated that a rigorous, systematic method of investigation be used to provide the basis for every program of reading instruction—no more, no less. We still have much to learn from the work of scholars like Arthur Irving Gates.

Reflection Questions

1. Although he has been described as apolitical and nonideological (Tostberg, 1971, p. 229), what would Gates say about reading instruction today, in general, and more specifically, with children who find learning to read difficult? Would he approve or disapprove of the use of highly scripted reading programs for such children?
2. What would Gates say about government mandates that require teachers to deliver a particular curriculum, rather than make their own choices of instruction and materials? What would he say about the way tests are being used today, in relation to identifying the instructional needs of students, wielding power over teachers and curricula, or both? What is your own opinion on the issues of government mandates and testing?
3. To what did Gates attribute his influence in the field of reading? What were his goals and purposes for working in the field of reading?

4. How was Gates's work similar to and different from the work of those other pioneers who were colleagues of Gates?
5. Do you agree or disagree with Gates's views on phonics instruction? How have his views informed and influenced the ways in which modern research addresses phonics instruction?

REFERENCES

Chall, J.S. (1967). *Learning to read: The great debate*. New York: McGraw-Hill.

Dr. Arthur Gates, a reading expert. (1972, August 25). *New York Times* [Electronic version]. Retrieved December 1, 2005, from http://pqasb.pqarchiver.com/nytimes/advancedsearch.html

Flesch, R.F. (1985). *Why Johnny can't read—and what you can do about it*. New York: Harper & Row. (Original work published 1955)

Gates, A.I. (1922). *The psychology of reading and spelling, with special reference to disability*. New York: Teachers College, Columbia University.

Gates, A.I. (1923). *Psychology for students of education*. New York: Macmillan.

Gates, A.I. (1925). *Elementary psychology*. New York: Macmillan.

Gates, A.I. (1926a). The Gates primary reading tests. *Teachers College Record, 28*, 146–178.

Gates, A.I. (1926b). *A reading vocabulary for the primary grades*. New York: Teachers College, Columbia University.

Gates, A.I. (1927). *The improvement of reading: A program of diagnostic and remedial methods*. New York: Macmillan.

Gates, A.I. (1928a). *Elementary psychology* (Rev. ed.). New York: Macmillan. (Original work published 1925)

Gates, A.I. (1928b). *New methods in primary reading*. New York: Macmillan.

Gates, A.I. (1930). *Interest and ability in reading*. New York: Macmillan.

Gates, A.I. (1931). *Reading for public school administrators*. New York: Teachers College.

Gates, A.I. (1935). *The improvement of reading: A program of diagnostic and remedial methods* (Rev. ed.). New York: Macmillan. (Original work published 1927)

Gates, A.I. (1947). *The improvement of reading: A program of diagnostic and remedial methods* (3rd ed.). New York: Macmillan. (Original work published 1927)

Gates, A.I. (1951). What should we teach in reading? *School and Community, 37*, 13–14.

Gates, A.I. (1961). *Reading attainment in elementary schools: 1957 and 1937*. New York: Teachers College, Columbia University. (Original work published 1937)

Gates, A.I. (1962). *Teaching reading*. Washington, DC: Deptartment of Classroom Teachers, American Education Research Association of the National Education Research Association. (Original work published 1953)

Gates, A.I. (1964). Science or sanity? *Phi Delta Kappan, 45*, 297–302.

Gates, A.I. (1971). Arthur I. Gates: An autobiography. In R.J. Havighurst (Ed.), *Leaders in American education: The seventieth yearbook of the National Society for the Study of Education, Part II* (pp. 189–216). Chicago: University of Chicago Press.

Gates, A.I. (2002). What should we teach in reading? In R.D. Robinson, *Classics in literacy education: Historical perspectives for today's teachers* (pp. 49–52). Newark, DE: International Reading Association. (Original work published 1951)

Gates, A.I., Batchelder, M.I., & Betzner, J. (1926). A modern systematic versus an opportunistic method of teaching: An experimental study. *Teachers College Record, 27*, 679–679. Retrieved December 21, 2005, from http://www.tcrecord.org, ID number: 5921.

Gates, A.I., & Bennett, C.C. (1933). *Reversal tendencies in reading: Causes, diagnosis, prevention and correction.* New York: Teachers College, Columbia University.

Gates, A.I., Bond, G.L., & Russell, D.H. (1939). *Methods of determining reading readiness.* New York: Teachers College, Columbia University.

Gates, A.I., & Huber, M.B. (1930). *Friendly stories* [Work-play books]. New York: Macmillan.

Gates, A.I., & Huber, M.B. (1931). *Peter and Peggy* [Work-play books]. New York: Macmillan.

Gates, A.I., Huber, M.B., & Ayer, J.Y. (1932). *The work-play books, first-grade manual.* New York: Macmillan.

Gates, A.I., Jersild, A.T., McConnell, T.R., & Challman, R.C. (1942). *Educational psychology.* New York: Macmillan.

Gates, A.I., & Pritchard, M.C. (1942). *Teaching reading to slow-learning pupils: A report on an experiment in New York City Public School 500 (Speyer School).* New York: Teachers College, Columbia University.

Harrison, M.L. (1936). *Reading readiness.* Boston: Houghton Mifflin.

MacGinitie, W.H. (1980, May). *The contributions of Arthur I. Gates.* A paper presented at the 25th Annual Convention of the International Reading Association, St. Louis, Missouri.

MacGinitie, W.H., MacGinitie, R.K., Maria, K., & Dreyer, L.G. (2000). *Gates-MacGinitie reading tests.* Itasca, IL: Riverside.

Smith, N.B. (1965). *American reading instruction.* Newark, DE: International Reading Association.

Thorndike, E.L., & Gates, A.I. (1929). *Elementary principles of education.* New York: Macmillan.

Tostberg, R.E. (1971). Biographical essay on Arthur I. Gates. In R.J. Havighurst (Ed.), *Leaders in American Education: The 70th yearbook of the National Society for the Study of Education, Part II* (pp. 222–230). Chicago: University of Chicago Press.

Vance, E. (1985). *Classroom reading and the work of Arthur Gates: 1921–1930.* Unpublished doctoral dissertation, Teachers College, Columbia University.

FOR FURTHER READING

Gates, A.I. (1927). Studies of phonetic training in beginning reading. *Journal of Educational Psychology, 18*, 217–226.

Gates, A.I. (1961). *Reading attainment in elementary schools: 1957 and 1937.* New York: Teachers College, Columbia University.

Monaghan, E.J., & Saul, E.W. (1987). The reader, the scribe, the thinker: A critical look at the history of American reading and writing instruction. In T.S. Popkewitz (Ed.), *The formation of school subjects: The struggle for creating an American institution* (pp. 85–122). New York: Falmer.

Robinson, R.D. (2002). *Classics in literacy education: Historical perspectives for today's teachers.* Newark, DE: International Reading Association.

Smith, N.B. (2002). *American reading instruction: Special edition.* Newark, DE: International Reading Association. (Original work published 1965)

CHAPTER 15

Ruth May Strang (1895–1971): The Legacy of a Reading Sage

By Diane Lapp, Laurie A. Guthrie, and James Flood

Historical Research Process

ONE MIGHT WONDER how difficult it would be for three literacy educators to locate information about Ruth May Strang, one of the early reading pioneers. Although we were very interested in our research, we must confess that our initial attempts were quite unsuccessful. We began searching for biographical information as many researchers would—we "Googled" her. However, this method of inquiry was not fruitful. After copying and pasting what we thought to be a treasure of information, a total of three pages of hodgepodge streamed from the printer. Next, we searched the library databases at our lo-

Shaping the Reading Field: The Impact of Early Reading Pioneers, Scientific Research, and Progressive Ideas, edited by Susan E. Israel and E. Jennifer Monaghan. © 2007 by the International Reading Association.
Photo: Courtesy of Pamela Hoagland.

cal university, only to find its holdings did not date back as far as we needed. Then we decided to call Ira Aaron, Edward Fry, Leo Fay, and Roger Farr
to get some insights about Strang. These literacy giants affirmed that, in addition to her stellar contributions, Strang was a lovely person. "What next?"
we asked.

Fortunately, with the assistance of E. Jennifer Monaghan and Susan E.
Israel, the resourceful editors of this text, we were able to enlist the assistance
of Aviva Gray, an extremely competent student in the Archival Management
and Historical Editing Program at New York University. Aviva's first attempt
to locate information was similar to ours; in fact the pages she sent to us
contained much of the same information. Yet Aviva eventually was able to
locate 258 articles by or about Strang.

We began to believe that a biography of Strang might become a reality.
Instead of sifting through dusty library archives, we now had an alternate
means of information retrieval. Together with Aviva, we selected some 60
articles that looked as if they might yield valuable information, and from
there Aviva began locating the accessible ones.

The dusty library archives of San Diego State University became unavoid-
able; otherwise our perusal of Strang's more notable books would not have
occurred. As a team of authors, we also became more competent with online searches, and a subscription to the *Teachers College Record*, an online
journal available from Columbia University, provided us with a valuable
archival treasure of articles by Strang. In addition, conversations with literacy leaders including Donna Alvermann, Patricia Anders, Cynthia Brock,
Doug Fisher, Lee Indrisano, Barbara Moss, Jeanne Paratore, Richard Vacca,
and Karen Wood, whose careers have been influenced by Strang's early work,
provided further insights that spoke to Strang's professional contributions.
And lastly, Pamela Hoagland, Strang's final doctoral student, was able to bring
life to Ruth Strang by sharing personal papers and memories.

As Eldon E. Ekwall, Assistant Professor of Education, University of
Arizona, commented,

> I really doubt if there are more than a very few, if any, school districts in
> Arizona [that] have not made a considerable amount of achievement in bet-

tering their reading programs either directly or indirectly as a result of Dr. Strang's program at the University of Arizona. (personal communication, May 27, 1968)

Ruth May Strang (1895–1971) lived a life devoted to developing diverse areas of education. Her almost 50 years of teaching at Columbia University and the University of Arizona earned her international respect for her ideas in five different fields of education: (1) nutrition, (2) health, (3) guidance and student personnel work, (4) child psychology, and (5) reading. Contributions to the field of reading education include her work with gifted students and students with special needs; the preparation of teachers who understood the complexities of teaching reading; and her insights about literacy instruction at the elementary, secondary, and college levels.

Personal and Professional Life

Born April 3, 1895, in Chatham, New Jersey, USA, Strang, the youngest of three children, had two brothers. The oldest by 15 years, Arthur Cornelius Strang (1880–1945), was described by Strang (1971) as "the most thoroughly kind person" she had ever known (p. 366). While serving in the 165th Infantry Division at the beginning of World War I he was severely wounded but survived.

Strang's second brother, Benjamin Bergen Strang (1889–1963), went to college and majored in mathematics. Although money was scarce in the home, Strang's parents were able to support his tuition. After graduating from Columbia University, he was given a position at the Georgia Institute of Technology in Atlanta, Georgia, USA, where he taught for three years. He then returned to New York, earned his master's degree from Teacher's College, and taught high school math (Strang, 1971, p. 366).

The dream of having his son graduate from college was of major importance to Strang's father, Charles Garret Strang (1854–1926), a New York City native whose hopes of becoming a lawyer were dashed after two years of college when his father requested his help in running a large, newly acquired farm in South Jamaica, Long Island, New York, USA. Since he was the only child, he felt obligated to give up college to help run the farm. During the years on the farm, Charles worked very hard to survive financially. Strang remembers her father as the disciplinarian in the family, while her mother, Anna Bergen Strang (1854–1927), was the gentle woman who "would be more likely to cry when [the children] were bad" than to scold them (Strang, 1971, p. 366).

Strang learned the details of her ancestry through research conducted by a cousin who was interested in the family's genealogy. The cousin had traced her father's ancestry to Louis XIV's reign in France, discovering her relationship to Daniel L'Estrange, who fled France during the Huguenot persecution. L'Estrange later settled in New York and, ironically, taught courses in French and philosophy at King's College, the predecessor of Columbia University. Strang's mother's ancestors emigrated from the Netherlands, having migrated originally, she believed, from Sweden. Both her father's and mother's ancestors arrived in North America during the colonial era (Kershner, 1980; Strang, 1971, p. 366). Strang (1971) facetiously attributed her "originality" and her "delight in a good theory" to her French background and her "exploration in the realm of thought" to her mother's Viking ancestry (p. 365).

Growing up with no clearly defined sense of self-image during her early childhood and adolescent years, Strang noted that during this time she was often filled with great anxiety (1971, pp. 366–367). There seemed to be no one with whom she identified, although she had a strong sense of determination, individuality, and originality. Although her family did not encourage this tendency toward originality, it and her independence influenced all of her later contributions to education.

Strang spent the first 10 years of her life on the Long Island farm. During her elementary years, she attended several different schools, the first of which was a one-room rural elementary school in Jamaica, New York, USA. Her next school experience was in Phoenix, Arizona, USA, where the family moved because of her father's bronchial illness. Missing the eastern United States after a couple of years, the family sold the farm, moved back to New York, and settled in Brooklyn, New York, USA (Strang, 1971, p. 368).

After graduating from elementary school, Strang enrolled at Adelphi Academy, a private high school in Brooklyn. She joined the walking club and played on the women's high school basketball team.

Aside from Strang's academic education, formal religion also had an impact on Strang's life. Her father read from the Bible every morning and evening. Strang maintains that she acquired her love of language during these readings, which helped her to develop a literary style that later supported her career (Strang, 1971, pp. 368, 371). An active churchgoer, she was inspired by two ministers, Dr. Cleveland B. McAfee and Dr. Charles C. Albertson, of the Lafayette Avenue Presbyterian Church in Brooklyn. She attributed her understanding of children to McAfee, while Albertson's love and inclusion of poetry during his sermons led to some of her deepest religious experiences. Strang's experiences with religion not only influenced her style of writing, her understanding of children, and her appreciation of literature but also instilled in her a sense of destiny and a belief that she was a part of a larger plan (p. 372).

Devoid of any educational guidance during her high school years, Strang had aspirations to continue her education. This was in conflict with the beliefs of her parents, who expected their only daughter to accept a domestic role in the family. Although she was not encouraged, expected, or supported financially to attend college, her determination led her to matriculate at Pratt Institute, which was two blocks from her home. In 1916 she completed Pratt's two-year normal program in household science and, with encouragement from her art and interior decorator professor, Mary Jane Quinn, embarked on a career in the field of interior decorating. This career choice was short-lived because she was forced to leave work to care for her ailing mother. While doing so, she began her career in education in 1917 in what she referred to as a "slum area" of New York, where she volunteered at a settlement house for Italian boys. In reflecting on this experience Strang remarked, "I learned much more [from them] than they learned from me" (1971, p. 371).

Resigning from her teaching position after three years to pursue her education, Strang met strong opposition from her parents, her brother Benjamin, and the school principal. Undaunted, she completed her bachelor's degree at Columbia University's Teachers College in 1922 with a major in nutrition. While at Columbia, Strang assisted Professor Mary Swartz Rose, her major advisor, in teaching an elementary course in nutrition.

Rose recommended Strang for a part-time graduate position in the Department of Health Education at Columbia, where Strang taught a large class of graduate students and supervised health education in the Horace Mann School. This experience provided her with the knowledge to coauthor, with Dr. Thomas D. Wood, a course of study in health education for the elementary school. While teaching at Columbia, she was also meeting the requirements for a doctoral degree, all the while commuting from Columbia to Brooklyn, where her family still lived (Strang, 1971, p. 369).

In 1924, after two years of working with Wood, Strang made the next move in her professional career because of two invitations from Dr. Arthur Irving Gates (see chapter 14, this volume) to prepare exercises for his primary reading test and to participate in an experiment that involved teaching beginning reading to deaf children. Feeling totally unprepared to work in the field of reading, Strang attended a double summer session at the University of Chicago, where she completed several courses that helped to prepare her for this endeavor. Using the 26 practice books Strang had written, Strang and Helen Thompson, professor of education at Columbia University, spent the next two years teaching and studying the reading processes of deaf children. While Strang prepared the reading material, Thompson did the teaching (Strang, 1971, pp. 369–370). As a result of this experience Strang concluded, "The reading processes of pupils of different abilities and background are only partially understood. Therefore, the training program should encourage the spirit of inquiry and scientific observation on the part of prospective teachers of reading and reading specialists" (1967b, section D).

While engaged in her graduate program, Strang also worked as a research assistant in psychology, coteaching with several other graduate students a class in psychological foundations to approximately 500 students. By 1926 she had completed all of the requirements for her PhD degree. The receipt of her degree came as quite a surprise to her family because she had never mentioned her doctoral studies to them; in fact, they learned of it from a newspaper announcement (Strang, 1971, p. 370).

While devoting her life to developing diverse areas of education, Strang's professional career followed many paths. Of notable importance are the contributions she made during the various phases of her life devoted to (a) counseling, (b) child development, (c) adolescent reading instruction, and (d) work at Teachers College and beyond.

Strang and Counseling

Because of her exemplary work during her graduate studies, Strang was offered by Dean James Russell of Teachers College a year's postdoctoral research fellowship in the newly developing field of student personnel administration. Her challenge was to increase the number of professional publications in the field.

Her contribution resulted in a review of theory and research on the major aspects of the field, which eventually took the form of three volumes: (1) *Behavior and Background of Students in College and Secondary Schools* (1937), (2) *Counseling Techniques in College and Secondary Schools* (1942a), and (3) *Group Activities in College and Secondary Schools* (1943). During the fellowship, Strang also worked as a teaching assistant for a Teachers College professor, Sarah Sturtevant, with whom she coauthored, in the late 1920s, two seminal studies on women deans in high schools and colleges (Strang, 1971, pp. 377–378).

Over the next few years, Strang's teaching responsibilities at Teachers College grew as she collaborated with Francis Wilson, who later became director of educational and vocational guidance in New York City, to develop courses in counseling techniques and group activities. One course for which she was solely responsible lasted for almost 30 years: The Role of the Teacher in Personnel Work. She believed that guidance counselors were not alone in their role of advising students; she was convinced that most teachers served as guidance counselors as well and should be trained accordingly. For use in this course, Strang wrote her textbook, *The Role of the Teacher in Personnel Work* (1932/1953). She said it was the first book of its kind "written at a time when the prevalent point of view was that guidance was the responsibility of specialists, not teachers" (1971, p. 378).

Strang and Child Development

A teacher, counselor, and woman of abundant energy and insight, Strang had also accepted summer positions elsewhere during her earlier years at Teachers College. For three summer sessions (1926, 1927, and 1928) she taught child study and child psychology at the Women's College of the University of North Carolina, Greensboro. It was during these summers that she developed an interest in the field of child growth and development and wrote *An Introduction to Child Study* (1930), which was grounded in her belief that "Reading is part of the total development of the child. Therefore, students should have a good foundation in child and adolescent psychology" (1967b, section D). *An Introduction to Child Study* appeared in four editions (1930, 1938a, 1951, and 1959) before going out of print. Strang held other summer positions as well, which she referred to as "stimulating and pleasant" (1971, p. 379), at the University of Maine in Orono, the University of Chicago, and the University of California at Berkeley.

Interested in the development and education of all students, Strang and her friend Pauline Williamson later cofounded the American Association for Gifted Children (AAGC) in 1946. It was the first voluntary nonprofit organization of its kind in the United States. The AAGC was incorporated in New York and was located at the University of the State of New York. Based on the belief that "the gifted were the most neglected children in our democracy," this organization was "devoted exclusively to the needs of gifted, talented and creative children" (AAGC, 1999). Strang identified practical strategies to help with the development of gifted children.

Strang and Adolescent Reading Instruction

Strang's interest in the improvement of reading occurred around 1930—she had been hired as a full-time assistant professor at Teachers College a year earlier—when she realized that many guidance problems involved reading issues. Because many courses already concentrated on the teaching of reading at the elementary level, Strang developed a reading program that focused on reading improvement for the high school and college levels. In 1932 she developed and directed the High School and College Reading Center at Teachers College. Until the time of her retirement from Teachers College in 1960 (she became a full professor in 1940), she continued to teach a heavy program of courses in both guidance and reading and remained active in the reading center (Strang, 1971, p. 378). Her texts, *Problems in the Improvement of Reading in High School and College* (1938b) and *Exploration in Reading Patterns* (1942b), were pioneering books on content area reading. Her work in this area "supported the development of reading and communication centers at many American schools and colleges" (Kershner, 1980, p. 663).

In addition to instructional texts, Strang wrote several volumes of juvenile literature for teenage readers. These included the Teen-Age Tales series (1954 and following), coauthored with Amelia Melnik, assistant professor at the University of Arizona, Tucson, and others (e.g., Strang & Roberts, 1959). This series, developed to motivate the adolescent reader, was a result of Strang's belief that "learning to read is a life-time process [and] courses in reading for teachers should include methods of reading throughout the school and college years, not just in the lower elementary grades," and an introduction to materials that keep students motivated to read (Strang, 1967b, section D).

Strang's Work at Teachers College and Beyond

Strang was the last president of the National Association for Remedial Teaching, which merged with the International Council for the Improvement of Reading Instruction to form the International Reading Association in 1956. Strang was a founding member of the new Association. William S. Gray, the Association's first president (see chapter 13, this volume), often teased her that she was the past-president of an organization before it existed.

Strang was highly regarded for her work at Columbia University, yet her rise to success has been noted as a rather slow process. Lederman (2000) describes Strang's rise through the ranks at Teachers College:

> Despite her prolific research (thirty books by 1960 and more than 300 articles), Strang rose slowly through the ranks at Teachers College, owing, she believed, to gender discrimination. She was assistant professor from 1929 to 1936, associate professor from 1936 to 1940, and full professor from 1940 to 1960. (section 9)

Burgess (1971) gave credibility to this idea of gender discrimination as having played a role in Strang's slow rise to success when he noted that she helped to form a "new minority of American Women—the female professor" (p. 398; also quoted in "Ruth May Strang," 2005a, section 8). He stated that it was "one thing to get through the door of academe and quite another thing for a woman to pass beyond the level of instructor or assistant professor," especially during a time when women "constituted only 18 percent of the faculties of institutions approved by the American Association of Universities" (p. 398; also quoted in "Ruth May Strang," 2005a, section 8). Strang did break the barriers; she was one of the few women at the time who succeeded.

While at Teachers College, Strang sponsored over 100 doctoral dissertations; edited the *Journal of the National Association of Women Deans and Counselors* from 1935 to 1960; and wrote articles, summaries of research, and chapters in yearbooks. A comprehensive bibliography of her writings was presented by Melnik (1960), who notes that Strang "never received any financial aid or special secretarial assistance in her research and writing, with the exception of one small grant in 1941" (p. 464), a grant from the Time-Life corporation that resulted in the publication of *Exploration in Reading Patterns* (Strang, 1942b).

Strang's key publications during her Teachers College years, all done before the invention of computer word processing, included the coauthored *Improvement of Reading* (Strang, McCullough, & Traxler, 1955), which was a revision of her earlier work *Problems in the Improvement of Reading* (McCullough, Strang, & Traxler, 1938/1946). In 1967 it would reach its fourth edition under the title *Improvement of Reading* (Strang, McCullough, & Traxler, 1967). Another important book Strang wrote while at Teachers College was *Making Better Readers* (Strang & Bracken, 1957).

Because the retirement policy at Columbia University was strictly enforced, Strang accepted mandatory retirement at the age of 65 in June of 1960. Fortunately for the education field, retirement did not end her multifaceted career. During the following summer she taught two courses at the University of California at Berkeley. In the fall of the same year, she began a professorship of education at the University of Arizona, Tucson, where she built a reading program for undergraduate and graduate students. This position appealed to her "because of the opportunity to build the reading program almost from scratch" (Strang, 1971, p. 387). While there, she established and directed the Reading Development Center, which "eventuated in the development of a Department of Reading at Arizona, one of the few such departments in the nation" ("Tribute," 1977, p. 161). She also found time to write two more books important to the reading field, *Diagnostic Teaching of Reading* (1964/1969), and *Reading Diagnosis and Remediation* (1968).

When the dean asked Strang to retire from the University of Arizona in 1968, hundreds of her students and many members of the faculty protested his request, but he was not to be deterred (Donovan, 1968). With her usual grace and elegance, she accepted the inevitable, retired for a brief moment, and went on to her next challenge—the Peter Sandiford Professorship at the Ontario Institute for Studies in Education of the University of Toronto in Canada.

The diversity of the professional associations Strang joined during her career reflects the breadth of her interests. She was a member of the International Reading Association, the National Society for the Study of Education (serving on its Board of Directors, 1948–54, 1958–61, and 1968–69), the AAGC, and the National Association of Deans of Women. She was also a fellow of the American Public Health Association, the American Association of Applied Psychology, and the Royal Society of Health in Great Britain ("Dr. Ruth Strang of Columbia," 1971; Lederman, 2000; "Ruth May Strang," 2005b; Strang, 1971).

Strang's Final Years

During her final years, while suffering from arteriosclerosis, Strang returned once again to New York and settled into retirement at her home in Amityville, Long Island, New York, USA (Kershner, 1980). Strang's complete devotion to work had ruled out any notion of marriage. She kept herself so completely absorbed in work that she was unable to entertain the idea of a social life. Strang (1971) noted that she "obtained much pleasure from professional associations. Work, when not carried to the point of fatigue and not frustrating, was not distinct from recreation" (pp. 379–380). Not long before her death, she reflected upon this thought:

> My work has always been so exacting and demanding that social activities other than those directly related to my own work have been crowded out. My chief satisfactions have been the responsiveness of classes and other audiences, the success and friendship of my students, the excitement of new ideas, and the "things of beauty" that John Keats describes. ("Dr. Ruth Strang of Columbia," 1971; "Ruth May Strang," 2005a, section 12)

Another factor that added to her lack of personal attachments outside her work was her state of health. Strang explains in "An Autobiographical Sketch" (1971) how illness affected her life and her career:

> My state of health has had a great influence on my career, surely contributing to my pessimistic outlook and my habitual fatigue. I was seriously ill as a baby, having malaria and typhoid fever in addition to the usual children's diseases. I've always been susceptible to headaches and respiratory diseases, have had three or four severe colds each winter, and flu whenever it came around. Then there was the serious, more recent operation for cancer.
>   How did these illnesses influence my career? Perhaps in two ways: by making me more introvert than I might have been, and by making it impossible for me physically to engage in the "normal" amount of social activities, thus giving me more time for reading and study. (p. 391)

After a long illness, Ruth May Strang died at the age of 75 on January 3, 1971, at Brunswick General Hospital, in Amityville ("Dr. Ruth Strang of Columbia," 1971). Her autobiography, biography, and selections from her bibliography were published in *Leaders in American Education: Seventieth Yearbook of the National Society for the Study of Education* (Havinghurst, 1971). Educators chosen for inclusion were those believed to have made the most significant impact on education since 1902. Ruth Strang was the only woman selected for inclusion.

Pamela R. Hoagland, Strang's final doctoral student, offers a moving, personal appraisal of Ruth Strang, the woman:

> Her interests were wide ranging. She treasured nature and poetry and being out-of-doors. She eschewed riding, always walking to and from the University of Arizona from her nearby home. As far as I know she never drove a car, and in the years I knew her, she certainly did not enjoy riding in them. This was proven to me one day, when, knowing of her love of nature, a fellow student and I invited her to go with us on a spring sojourn to see the beautiful panorama of wild flowers carpeting the Tucson desert. Warily, I maneuvered with the utmost care, avoiding bumps, sharp turns, and especially speed. She loved the stunning desert display, and we returned to the city safe and invigorated by our brief encounter with the desert's beauty. Of course, I received a follow-up note of appreciation and compliments on my driving.
>
> Ruth Strang had a great sense of humor and an incredible but soft laugh that was so contagious that you had to laugh, too. She did not hesitate to laugh at her own jokes, and we laughed, too. When something was amusing, the gentle laugh came forth, sometimes with a somewhat demur shrug, but always with playful, sparkling eyes. A picture I will always remember; a laugh I will always hear.
>
> Ruth Strang loved her life, her career, her students, her friends. We were all better for knowing her. (personal communication, January–February 2006)

Philosophical Beliefs and Guiding Principles

An educational pioneer, Strang lived her life according to a Puritan philosophy. As defined by U.S. essayist Agnes Repplier, a Puritan is one who understands "that life is neither a pleasure nor a calamity. It is a grave affair with which we are charged, and which we must conduct and terminate with honor" (quoted in Strang, 1971, p. 371). According to Strang (1971), this statement best expressed her own philosophy of life because, she said, "Judged by usual standards, I have had few pleasures. I have fulfilled every obligation that I have accepted" (p. 371). Guided by this philosophy, she was indeed "dedicated to work, duty, self improvement, and service" (Kershner, 1980, p. 663). As an educator, Strang embraced a number of beliefs and guiding principles that can offer practical direction to the course of education today.

Strang's belief that a teacher must be able to counsel as well as instruct appears in her statement on teacher qualifications:

> There is no one ideal teaching personality, but among the many qualities suggested as desirable, the following seem especially important:
>
> - Kindness and tact with both children and adults
> - Ability to arouse enthusiasm and interest
> - Skill in analyzing a learning situation and helping a pupil progress step-by-step without unnecessary failure
> - A tendency to accentuate the positive in individuals and situations
> - Personal enjoyment of reading and familiarity with books
> - A spirit of inquiry and desire to extend our knowledge of the reading process
> - Ingenuity in developing methods and materials to accomplish certain purposes. (Strang, 1967b, section E)

Strang's belief that counseling and instruction must be connected traits of the teacher presumably stems from her professional experience in the fields of both guidance and education. The teacher qualifications that she lists exemplify the traits that are expected of today's effective teachers.

Another quality that Strang believed is essential to being an effective teacher is continued education. Evidence of Strang's belief that an effective teacher is one who continues to be a lifelong learner in order to support student growth emerged during the 1967–1968 academic year. At this time she obtained federal grants to conduct an Experienced Teacher Fellowship program at the University of Arizona, which provided support for such teachers to advance their study of reading. The results of this program are best described by one participant in an anonymous evaluation at the end of the year that Strang reports in her 1971 autobiography:

> If any aspects of the program had been left out I would not feel I could do as effective a job of teaching and consulting as I now feel capable of doing. Each part seemed to complement the other and broaden our understanding of some facet—the lectures gave us ideas and suggestions; the field work permitted us to try them out, and the seminars encouraged an exchange of

ideas and how to best implement these ideas and the background obtained through the field work. I was exposed to theory and practical approaches to reading, one complementing the other. The theory in the classroom was put to practical use in our field work. The program was exceedingly well coordinated. The courses dovetailed into one another so that you came out with a clear picture of how to find out where a pupil was on the growth continuum and what and how you should teach him. (p. 388)

This belief holds true today. Professional development is an integral component of the teaching profession that gives teachers the support needed to stay abreast of the best practices available. These best practices are primarily effective research-based tools that teachers can use to help support student growth.

Strang also believed that, to be good teachers, educators need a rich background of courses that blend theory with practice. As director of the Reading Development Center at the University of Arizona from 1960 to 1968, Strang was responsible for preparing specialists in reading. A number of master's and doctoral degree candidates entered the program under her guidance. According to Strang (1971), this reading program "met the need for reading consultants in elementary and secondary schools, and it provided more adequate preparation for beginning teachers in self-contained classes and in subject areas" (p. 388).

Margaret J. Early, coeditor of the *Journal of Reading*, interviewed Strang about the University of Arizona reading program. During the interview, Strang described the extensive sequence of courses that master's and doctoral candidates needed to take:

> For all graduate students there is a core program in reading consisting of three basic experiences: first, a basic course that includes an overview of all aspects: theory, reading development, programs, and personnel. Next, a course in diagnosis recognizes levels of diagnosis and describes and demonstrates classroom and clinical procedures. The third part of this core program is a case study practicum in which students work with reading problems under supervision. The weekly sessions in which cases are reported provide a reservoir of concrete diagnostic and remedial procedures. Students gain experience in interpreting and synthesizing case data, formulating hypotheses, and suggesting remedial measures. (Early & Herber, 1968, p. 632)

Strang continued with her description of the program by noting other courses that supplemented the core program:

Teaching reading to the slow learner; further study of the reading process through efforts to improve the students' own reading; teaching of reading in the elementary school, and in the secondary school; learning theory applied to reading, review of research in the field of reading, advanced courses in diagnosis and case study, and internships in the Reading Center and the schools. (p. 632)

This interview was conducted at a time when the effectiveness of teachers of reading in secondary schools was under scrutiny. It was imperative during these times that reading instructors should be trained in a way that would allow them to demonstrate a breadth of knowledge and practical work experience. The responsibility for preparation of these teachers rested with programs such as this one. Strang designed the reading program's curriculum in a way that would assure the quality of the reading instructors trained at the center.

Strang believed that there was nothing "more important for the nation and for a better world than reducing illiteracy and helping every child develop his potentialities" (Strang, 1971, p. 386). From the beginning of her professional life in 1917, "her major interest [was] the development of children's potential during adolescence" ("Columbia to Lose Its Reading Sage," 1960, section 3). It was this interest that led her into the diverse fields of education. She commented, "My vocational history zigzagged from one apparently unrelated field to another. Yet each of the diverse kinds of work contributed in some way to my competency in subsequent positions" (Strang, 1971, p. 376).

The six fields that Strang embraced during her life include a brief period with interior decorating, and then more intense involvement in the five educational fields of nutrition, health education, guidance and student personnel work, child psychology, and reading. Although there were many turning points in her career, none of them were self-sought. "I've never planned anything," she said. "It seemed to me that a professional career elaborated itself, and that as you develop your abilities and interests, opportunities open. I've simply responded to the opportunities that offered themselves" ("Columbia to Lose Its Reading Sage," 1960, section 7).

Strang's research questions, which were initiated from her "work with children, from discussions in classes of graduate students, or from recognized need for the study" (Strang, 1971, p. 381), resulted in significant contributions to the fields of guidance, child development, and reading. When she identified questions that were unanswered, she felt a strong sense of commitment to find the answers. She affirmed that her motivation to write was never for financial gain or added prestige but invoked "by a sense of people's need for the information" (p. 380). Her sincere hope that in the course of her research she would be able to make "some small contribution to the world of today and tomorrow" (p. 386) was realized in myriad ways, as noted by Hoagland:

> In 1963 I was a 24 year-old second grade teacher with only three years of classroom experience when I enrolled in Ruth Strang's late afternoon "Word Recognition Skills" class. It was the first step on the path that would guide my teaching and my career for the next 40 years.
>
> Ruth Strang epitomized the "servant leader." She dedicated her life to developing her students' personal and professional growth by teaching, encouraging, mentoring, and challenging them to reach, to go beyond their own expectations. Her gentle manner, her exceptional intellect, and her amazing and vast storehouse of knowledge earned her the respect and affection of her students. She was generous in countless ways, but especially with her time. One didn't have to look far for her; she was in the Reading Center or in her adjacent office and was always willing to listen and advise. Ruth Strang did not post office hours; she didn't have to, as we always knew where we could find her.
>
> She was an indefatigable note writer sending messages of encouragement, thanks, congratulations, instruction...often with a bit of poetry, but always in teal-green ink. No ball point for Professor Strang!
>
> From Ruth Strang I learned the strategies of teaching reading and the techniques of "diagnostic teaching." But I also learned the most important lessons of all, lessons that became an indelible part of my teaching philosophy: focus on the learner, listen receptively and take your cues from the learner, teach by focusing on the learner's strengths, his or her reading proficiencies, difficulties, and interests. This principle was paramount: learn from your students.
>
> Ruth Strang's clearly articulated seven "Generally Accepted Principles" underlying reading instruction are as compelling today as they were in the 60s, when I first encountered them. They have directed my teaching career with children and adults. They are [the following]:
>
> (1) Let the child be the guide. Help him to proceed toward his potential as fast as he is able.
>
> (2) Nothing succeeds as well for children as *observed* success.
>
> (3) Respect for a child increases his self-esteem.

(4) Learning takes place in the relationship between the student and teacher.

(5) Success in working with children with reading needs depends on continuous assessment and understanding their needs.

(6) The dynamics of the instructional situation need to be continually changed to accommodate student success.

(7) Individualize instruction because children react differently and need a more personalized approach.... (personal communication, January–February 2006)

Hoagland also characterized Strang as "wise, selfless, [and] generous," of "impeccable character and one of the most ethical people" she had ever known. "Ruth Strang," she said, "gave of herself completely" (personal communication, January–February 2006).

Contributions to the Field of Reading

In addition to guidance and child development, Strang became a leader in the field of reading education. As Patricia Anders, a well-known educator in content area reading, noted,

> Ruth Strang laid the foundation for our current understanding of the complexities of adolescent developmental learning. She wasn't hesitant to investigate all dimensions of a student in order to understand and support his or her learning. Her legacy was a primary reason that I joined the faculty at the University of Arizona. Her work has greatly influenced mine. I believe her spirit and love of the adolescent, which has been shared through her writing and legacy, have contributed to the teacher and scholar I have become. Today's study of the multiple aspects of adolescent literacy is scaffolded on the shoulders of this early giant. (personal communication, January 16, 2006)

In *Making Better Readers* (1957), Strang and Bracken discuss the roles of the whole school staff in providing opportunities, as well as sharing responsibility, for every child's success. This "all-school" program sounds like a precursor to current Drop Everything And Read (DEAR) programs. The DEAR approach, designed to encourage students to read independently, is to set aside a regular time in the classroom schedule for both students and their teachers to stop all other activities and read. Likewise, Strang and

Bracken enlisted the support of the entire school faculty and staff to provide the emotional tone that models the importance of reading.

Strang's belief that students' engagement was a requisite to their becoming effective readers was so strong that she developed the Teen-Age Tales series, published in the 1950s as a collection of stories designed to (a) change students' negative attitudes toward reading, (b) develop their reading ability, and (c) facilitate their personal development through reading. Strang's details of how to use these stories to engage readers and make connections to their lives is illustrated by her statement, "Experience comes before reading" (Strang & Roberts, 1959, p. 2). She offers suggestions of how to make this concept a reality: "Some current event of local interest may make a particular story especially appropriate at a certain time. For example, the opening of the football season would be an appropriate time to read 'The Story of Football'" (p. 2), which is a story appearing in Book 1 of the Teen-Age Tales series. Making connections between reader and text as a way to support one's reading is a current practice being modeled for preservice teachers by teacher educators in classroom instruction and publications.

Even in her writing, Strang was the consummate teacher who provided instructional models of what she was attempting to teach. In the fourth edition of *The Improvement of Reading* (Strang, McCullough, & Traxler, 1967), Strang and her colleagues provide situations as examples of the reading behavior they are describing. These are currently referred to as *simulations* and are believed to situate instructional discussion in a reality-based model.

Strang's "Exploration of the Reading Process" (1967a), an article published in *Reading Research Quarterly*, reviews what researchers knew in the 1960s about underlying processes in reading, with special emphasis on the methodologies used to conduct research on processes of reading for different groups of readers, including struggling readers. Strang discusses in the article four dissertations conducted at the University of Arizona under her direction. Her noting of the multiple sources of data that were used in studies on reading processes foreshadows contemporary beliefs about the use of mixed methods, from observations and interviews to controlled experimental studies. In most of her writings on adolescent struggling readers, she emphasizes the need to "see" all aspects of students' performance, including their own perspectives on the processing of texts.

Strang's use of four dissertations on four different aspects of reading processes, an accepted methodological approach to analyzing the "big" questions in the late 1960s, provides additional evidence on her thinking. The findings of these four dissertations provide new information to readers on (a) processes that inhibit or facilitate reading achievement; (b) processes that severely struggling readers use; (c) relations between self-concept and reading; and (d) the effect of poor reading skills on self-concept, attitudes, and behavior (Strang, 1967a, pp. 37–44). Strang analyzes these themes in a way that illustrates the connections among these variables and foreshadows contemporary research traditions.

In *Reading Diagnosis and Remediation* (1968), Strang outlines her most important theme: that diagnosis and assessment must be linked to provide relevant, effective instruction to struggling readers. Her claims that diagnoses from multiple sources (e.g., tests, observations, and interviews) must be interpreted in light of everything else that is known about the student are as significant now as they were then. Her message of the 1960s is hauntingly familiar: Tie assessment to instruction so instruction is maximized. The message implied in this book—continually assess while you are instructing and use the instructional event as an opportunity to learn more—is still a new message for many teachers today, however.

In reviewing Strang's *Reading Diagnosis and Remediation*, Powell (1969) acknowledges the comprehensiveness and significance of her book, but he quickly adds that some of Strang's summaries include gross overgeneralizations about certain topics (such as her agreement with previous researchers about the relation between discrimination of sounds and reading), and he argues that she is quick to dismiss research that she perceives as insufficient to support further study on a specific topic that does not interest her (e.g., studies on laterality and reading).

Strang's belief that the child should be situated as the primary focus in any instructional plan is exemplified in her text, *Diagnostic Teaching of Reading* (1964/1969). While sounding so current, her 1969 description of the diagnostic process still provides the foundation of effective continuous diagnostic practice: "(1) getting facts about the individual and his reading, (2) synthesizing and interpreting the facts, (3) arriving at hypotheses that are modified as new information is obtained, and (4) using the understanding gained to help students improve their reading" (p. vi). Jeanne Paratore, whose work in the urban schools in Chelsea, Massachusetts, USA, was based on a model of tying assessment to instruction, comments on Strang's model of "diagnostic teaching":

Strang's clinical work in reading expanded our understanding of the importance of using engaging reading materials as a context for eliciting struggling
students' best reading performance; as well, Strang's work provided examples for supporting struggling readers by engaging their entire community—parents, teachers, and peers—in their routine reading activities.
(personal communication, February 21, 2006)

Strang cautioned that when interpreting performance data, an effective
teacher needed to consider many factors that might influence performance.
In addition to perceptual and motor areas, she noted that emotions, attitudes,
interests, language, and home and school conditions should be weighted
heavily when evaluating a child's reading performance. Her common sense
words ring true today as educators discuss reasons why English-language
learners are unable to pass standardized tests and why so many children receiving free lunches carry the label of *children with special needs*:

The education of the parents and their expectations of the child influence
his school achievement. In homes where there is little conversation or
where a foreign language is spoken, there is usually little opportunity for the
child to develop a meaningful vocabulary or to master English language
patterns. Children who have learned to think verbally and express themselves fluently naturally have the advantage in learning to read. (Strang,
1964/1969, p. 17)

These insights should guide teachers as they resist a one-size-fits-all assessment and instruction model that has become the implementation mode of
mandates from the No Child Left Behind Act of 2001.

Throughout her work, Strang also stressed that instruction was only as
effective as the teacher implementing it. To Strang (1964/1969), a well-prepared teacher was one who had a thorough understanding of reading:

Viewed as communication, the reading process involves the abilities (1) to
decode or decipher the author's printed words, (2) to associate them with
meaning gained through the reader's firsthand experience and previous
reading, and (3) to express the ideas thus acquired through speaking, drawing, writing, or other verbal or motor responses. (p. 5)

Lee Indrisano, noted expert in assessment and instruction, thought of
Strang as a pioneer in the improvement of assessment and instruction for all
children, adolescents, and adults with reading needs:

Her *Diagnostic Teaching of Reading* [1964/1969] was a gem for all of its forward thinking. She talked about the importance of collecting information from multiple, rich sources like group methods as well as individual methods, observations, interviews, and introspective and retrospective reports. She carefully called her section on tests "Contributions from Tests" to make her readers aware that tests were only one contributing factor in assessment and instruction. (personal communication, February 20, 2006)

Strang offered her own description of what she believed was the major movement in education in which she was engaged:

The movement toward improvement of reading in the secondary schools [evolved] from practically no recognition of the reading problem in junior and senior high school to the present increasing interest as evidenced by several magazines devoted to reading in high school and college, many articles in other magazines, large attendance at sections on high school reading at conferences and books and pamphlets on the subject. My contribution was through (a) *Problems in the Improvement of Reading in Secondary Schools and College*, first published in 1938 and subsequently revised and expanded four times; and (b) the high school and college programs begun at Teachers College in 1932 and at the University of Arizona in 1960. (1971, pp. 389–390)

In her autobiographical sketch, Strang (1971) describes what she believed to be her most significant achievement: "Whatever influence for good I have had on the lives and contributions of my students, I think there is no substitute for 'the impact of life upon life and personality upon personality'" (p. 382). In a comment Strang was never able to read, Sidney Rauch (1998), one of Strang's doctoral students at Teachers College, describes how his first professor of reading had an impact on his life:

This lovely lady and scholar, by word and example, enabled me and countless others to progress, as in my case, from teacher of English in a Brooklyn Vocational High School to a senior Professor of Reading and Education at Hofstra University, Hempstead, NY. She set standards as a person and teacher that I tried to emulate. Many times when faced with an academic or personal problem, I would ask myself, "How would Dr. Strang handle it?" Her words of comfort and praise were like Olympic medals. In her quiet, modest manner she motivated me as no other professor. Thank you, Ruth. (section 1)

Not long before her death, Strang (1971) contemplated her future: "The future is unknown and unknowable. Like Cezanne at Aix, I hope to keep on working to the end" (pp. 391–392). She wrote that she still wanted to use whatever wisdom she had acquired during 70 years "to make some further contribution to child development and guidance and to the more thoughtful and critical reading of adolescents. These seem to me two effective ways of making a better world" (p. 392).

Strang did indeed help to make a better world, and she received two awards of particular importance that illustrate how her work influenced others: (1) the William S. Gray Citation of Merit (1962) and (2) the award for Outstanding Contribution to the Literature of Higher Education. The International Reading Association's William S. Gray Citation of Merit is awarded to a nationally or internationally known person for outstanding contributions to the field of reading. The award for Outstanding Contribution to the Literature of Higher Education was extended to Strang posthumously on April 3, 1977, at the 59th Annual Conference of the National Association of Student Personnel Administrators. This date also marked the 82nd anniversary of her birth. The influence she had on others during her career of almost 50 years is highlighted in "Tribute to Dr. Ruth Strang" (1977):

> Her influence on the young people of the nation stemmed from the knowledge she made available to their teachers in the form of thirty-five books, 500 articles, and the 117 doctorates she directed.
>
> Whether teaching a settlement class of little Italian immigrant boys or her Sunday School class, whether teaching reading to deaf and mute children or talking with E.L. Thorndike or John Dewey, Ruth Strang was alert to the potentials of learning. To all who knew her, she was indeed a "presence." (section 2–3)

Lessons for the Future

Strang's many contributions to the academic world continue to be realized by contemporary educators in several areas of literacy education. Her pioneering work taught teachers to consider the importance of all dimensions of students. She stressed the importance of continuous professional development to address the needs of an ever-changing population of students. Cynthia Brock, noted for her work in teacher preparation, says that Strang's belief is relevant today:

A well-prepared teacher must be one who is open to learning more and more about language, culture, and psychology as these areas relate to the complexities of literacy teaching and learning. This is especially true in schools today when there is a mismatch between the backgrounds of the many students from nondominant backgrounds who populate U.S. schools and their predominantly white middle class teachers. (personal communication, February 6, 2006)

Strang's revolutionary leadership in introducing and teaching the first course in the improvement of reading in high school ever offered at Teachers College highlighted the importance of an expanded view of the types of texts that students must be taught to read if they are to experience lifelong literacy success. Karen Wood, whose groundbreaking work in middle school curriculum design has promoted educational innovations in middle-level learning, notes,

Ruth Strang's writings provided the foundational insights for threading all areas of literacy throughout the curriculum for students from the early elementary years through high school. I often return to her writings to add clarity to my work with middle school students, teachers, and curricul[a]. (personal communication, January 9, 2006)

Strang's belief that a teacher must understand the social, psychological, cognitive, and linguistic aspects of a student and his or her community, and the community's impact on the student's learning, was the basis for her Teen-Age Tales series (1954 and following), which modeled how to use appropriate texts to engage struggling readers. Donna Alvermann, well known for her insights that have advanced the field of secondary literacy, comments,

I first discovered Ruth Strang's work when I was conducting research on how a reader's proficiency can be inferred by the strategies he or she uses when processing text. Strang was writing back in the mid 1960s about a topic that intrigued researchers well into the 80s and beyond. Today, I frequently read studies that probably should cite Ruth Strang's pioneering work but don't.... I believe we lose something of value when we forget to inquire into the legacy of our academic predecessors. (personal communication, January 18, 2006)

Using high-level texts as a means to engage students is a common intervention at the secondary level. This is an integral component of a reading intervention program that has been initiated by Doug Fisher at the urban setting of Herbert Hoover High School in the San Diego City (California) Schools district. Fisher attributes Strang's forward thinking to much of the success for this program: "Strang's insights about the need to study the multiple complexities of first generation high school students when designing their education programs provided the foundation for what we have accomplished at Hoover High School" (personal communication, January 25, 2006). Strang's insights that many troubled children were also unsuccessful readers who could benefit from well-diagnosed instruction and engagement with appropriate materials showed us that something could be done to remedy this problem.

When considering content area reading and literacy, Anders admits that it is Strang to whom educators should turn:

> We would be wise to follow her advice by considering the learner's interests, emotional maturity, and instructional needs. While important, acquisition of strategies is just a small part of reading to learn and to engage ideas. She hasn't had the influence she might because so many current day scholars are intent on reading only the most recent literature. (personal communication, January 16, 2006)

Known for his instructional insights in content area reading, Richard Vacca affirmed that Strang's influence was far reaching when he said,

> Ruth Strang is one of the great 20th-century educational pioneers, not only in the field of reading but also in the fields of gifted education and the psychology of adolescence. Always ahead of her time, Strang's work on reading patterns was a precursor to text structure research and served me well as a fledgling researcher working on my dissertation. I wish I would have had the opportunity to...thank her for her remarkable contributions to the field of reading in general and adolescent literacy in particular. (personal communication, January 6, 2006)

Strang's development of curricula illustrated that reading is an integral part of the curriculum and, therefore, should be taught in connection with other subjects as well as independently. Barbara Moss, author of many articles and books about content area learning and instruction, believes that "Strang's early advocacy of the need for secondary as well as elementary students to engage with informational texts in preparation for school and the workplace demonstrates the extraordinary vision of this remarkable reading educator" (personal communication, February 19, 2006).

Constance McCullough, former president of the International Reading Association and a contemporary of Strang, answered all of our questions about Strang, the person, the educator, and the inspiring pioneer:

> How shall she be remembered? For the volume of production, the guidance (as advisor and committee member) of some 120 doctoral candidates, her thoroughness of scholarship, the clarity of her exposition, the insightfulness and circumspection of her observations, the brilliance of her insight and discoveries in pioneer fields? Some will surely remember her for her keen appreciation of Beauty—of literature and nature as manifestations of it, for her firm belief in the warmth of the individual, for her teacher's gift for the arousal of curiosity and confidence, for her sense of humor to relieve the tense moment, for the generosity in all aspects of her living, for her persistence in maintaining her integrity in whatever she tried or encountered; and for her devotion to the pursuit of ideals in the face of increasing encroachments of professional commitments upon her personal life.
>
> We, who are charged with the cultivation of the human potential, with its endless variety and limitless possibilities for excellence, are fortunate in the legacy of Ruth Strang, who chose selflessness as her fulfillment and the world as her family. (McCullough, 1971, p. E3)

Reflection Questions

1. What type of learning experiences must occur in teacher preparation classes for elementary and secondary teachers to understand that literacy learning is dependent on (a) how students perceive themselves as readers; (b) their interests; (c) the interactions they have with their family, teachers, and peers; (d) the classroom environments in which they learn; and (e) the institutional structures shaping their views of the significance of school?
2. What are the dimensions of content area lessons that support students as they develop skills, strategies, and the dispositions needed to achieve academic and functional literacies?
3. What factors do elementary and secondary students believe constitute an engaging read-aloud of fiction and nonfiction texts?
4. When students encounter difficulty reading a nonfiction text, what strategies do they most often use to support their comprehension?

5. As you reflect on the contributions made by Strang, think about the response she would have to a multiliteracies approach to adolescent learning. How do you think Strang might have replied if asked about this topic?

REFERENCES

American Association for Gifted Children. (1999). The history of AAGC. Retrieved October 11, 2005, from http://www.aagc.org/history.html

Burgess, C. (1971). Ruth Strang: A biographical sketch. *Yearbook of the National Society for the Study of Education, 70,* 398–411.

Columbia to lose its reading sage [Retirement notice]. (1960, June 19). *The New York Times,* p. 50.

Donovan, J. (1968, May 28). Rift aired at reading center: IRA officials meet with UA students. *Arizona Daily Star,* p. A1.

Dr. Ruth Strang of Columbia, 75: Retired Teachers College professor is dead [Obituary]. (1971, January 5). *The New York Times,* p. 39. ProQuest Historical Newspapers: The New York Times (1851–2001).

Early, M.J., & Herber, H.L. (Eds.). (1968, May). An interview with...Ruth Strang. *Journal of Reading, 11,* 630–633.

Havinghurst, R.J. (Ed.). (1971). *Leaders in American education: Seventieth yearbook of the National Society for the Study of Education, part II.* Chicago: University of Chicago Press.

International Reading Association. (2006). William S. Gray citation of merit. Retrieved October 10, 2005, from http://www.reading.org/association/awards/service_gray.html

Kershner, F.D. (1980). Strang, Ruth May. In B. Sicherman, I. Kantrov, & C.H. Green (Eds.), *Notable American women: The modern period: A biographical dictionary* (pp. 662–663). Cambridge, MA: The Belknap Press of Harvard University Press.

Lederman, S.H. (2000). Ruth May Strang. *American National Biography Online Feb. 2000.* Retrieved November 17, 2005, from http://www.anb.org/articles/09/09-00721.html

McCullough, C.M. (1971, February 3). In memoriam: Ruth Strang, 1895–1971. *Arizona Daily Star,* p. E3.

McCullough, C.M., Strang, R.M., & Traxler, A.E. (1946). *Problems in the improvement of reading.* New York: McGraw-Hill. (Original work published 1938)

Melnik, A. (1960). The writings of Ruth Strang. *Teachers College Record, 61,* 464–476.

No Child Left Behind Act of 2001, Pub. L. No. 107-110, 115 Stat. 1425 (2002).

Powell, W.R. (1969, Summer). A review. *Reading Research Quarterly, 4,* 560–565.

Rauch, S.J. (1998, Fall). Fifty years a reading teacher: Looking back. *History of Reading News,* 22(1). Retrieved October 11, 2005, from http://www.historyliteracy.org/scripts/search_display.php?Article_ID=138

Ruth May Strang. (2005a). In *Encyclopedia of world biography* (2nd ed., Vol. 17). Reproduced in *Biography Resource Center.* Farmington Hills, MI: Thomson Gale. (Document No: K1631006296: http://galenet.galegroup.com/ servlet/BioRC)

Ruth May Strang. (2005b). In *Contemporary authors online.* Reproduced in *Biography Resource Center.* Farmington Hills, MI: Thomson Gale 2005. (Document No. H1000095825: http://galenet.galegroup.com/servlet/BioRC)

Strang, R.M. (1930). *An introduction to child study.* New York: Macmillan Company.

Strang, R.M. (1937). *Behavior and background of students in college and secondary schools.* New York: Harper & Brothers.

Strang, R.M. (1938a). *An introduction to child study* (2nd ed.). New York: Macmillan.

Strang, R.M. (1938b). *Problems in the improvement of reading in high school and college.* Lancaster, PA: Science Press Printing.

Strang, R.M. (1942a). *Counseling techniques in college and secondary schools.* New York: Harper.

Strang, R.M. (1942b). *Exploration in reading patterns.* Chicago: University of Chicago Press.

Strang, R.M. (1943). *Group activities in college and secondary school.* New York: Harper.

Strang, R.M. (1951). *An introduction to child study* (3rd ed.). New York: Macmillan.

Strang, R.M. (1953). *The role of the teacher in personnel work* (4th ed.). New York: Bureau of Publications, Teachers College, Columbia University. (Original work published 1932)

Strang, R.M. (1959). *An introduction to child study* (4th ed.). New York: Macmillan.

Strang R.M. (1967a). Exploration of the reading process. *Reading Research Quarterly, 2,* 33–45.

Strang, R.M. (1967b). *Programs for the preparation of reading teachers, supervisors, and specialists.* Paper presented at the Reading Development Center, College of Education, Tucson, AZ.

Strang, R.M. (1968). *Reading diagnosis and remediation.* Newark, DE: International Reading Association.

Strang R.M. (1969). *Diagnostic teaching of reading* (2nd ed.). New York: McGraw-Hill. (Original work published 1964)

Strang, R.M. (1971). An autobiographical sketch. *Yearbook of the National Society for the Study of Education, 70,* 365–397.

Strang, R.M., & Bracken, D.K. (1957). *Making better readers.* Boston: Heath.

Strang, R.M., McCullough, C.M., & Traxler, A.E. (1955). *Problems in the improvement of reading* (2nd ed.). New York: McGraw-Hill.

Strang, R.M., McCullough, C.M., & Traxler, A.E. (1967). *Improvement of reading* (4th ed.). New York: McGraw-Hill.

Strang, R.M., & Roberts, R. (1959). Teen-age Tales (Book 1, 2nd ed.). Boston: D.C. Heath.

Tribute to Dr. Ruth Strang. (1977). *Journal of the National Association for Women Deans, Administrators, & Counselors, 40,* 161.

FOR FURTHER READING

Barry, R.E., & Wolf, B. (1955). *A history of the guidance-personnel movement in education.* New York: Teachers College, Columbia University.

Cremin, L.A., Shannon, D.A., & Townsend, M.E. (1954). *A history of Teachers College, Columbia University.* New York: Columbia University Press.

Strang, R.M., & Sturtevant, S.M. (1929). *A personnel study of deans of girls in high schools.* New York: Bureau of Publications, Teachers College, Columbia University.

Strang, R.M. (1940). *Problems in the improvement of reading in high school and college* (2nd ed., rev.). Lancaster, PA: Science Press.

Strang, R.M. (1960). *The administrator and improvement of reading.* New York: Appleton-Century-Crofts.

Strang, R.M. (Ed.). (1965). *Understanding and helping the retarded reader.* Tucson: University of Arizona Press.

Strang, R.M., Phelps, E., & Withrow D. (1966). *Gateways to readable books: An annotated graded list of books in many fields for adolescents who find reading difficult* (4th ed.). New York: H.W. Wilson.

Strang, R.M. (1970). *Learning to read: Insights for educators* (J. McInnes, Ed.). Toronto: Ontario Institute for Studies in Education.

Sturtevant, S.M., & Strang, R.M. (1928). *A personnel study of deans of women in teachers colleges and normal schools.* New York: Bureau of Publications, Teachers College, Columbia University.

CHAPTER 16

David Harris Russell (1906–1965): A Man Who Loved Learning and Teaching

By Arlene L. Barry

Historical Research Process

ONE RICH DATA source in biographical research is the family of the subject. The process of collecting information from descendants is interesting indeed. Genealogical databases, family newsletters, People Search (https://people.yahoo.com), alumni associations, and advertisements in newspapers all help locate individuals who possess pieces of the puzzle. As a bit of an introvert, I admit that I find it awkward to contact complete strangers and essentially say, "Hello, you don't know me, but may I come over and dig in your attic?" The

Shaping the Reading Field: The Impact of Early Reading Pioneers, Scientific Research, and Progressive Ideas, edited by Susan E. Israel and E. Jennifer Monaghan. © 2007 by the International Reading Association.
Photo: Courtesy of Russell sons, David R. and Andrew Russell.

most surprising thing about this process is how willingly family members assist and how gracious they are about sharing private moments and mementos.

However, while I have always found individuals to have the best intentions, sometimes their sense of timing is far different from my own. When I was researching the life of Ellen Cyr, for example (Barry, 2005), one great-granddaughter committed herself to helping but then just couldn't get around to digging out the materials she had promised. I called, then e-mailed, then wrote letters, and finally resorted to sending reminders by Federal Express to make sure that she received my request. When those means did not work, I sent flowers with a gentle reminder. After a year of waiting, it took the threat of my arriving on her doorstep to nudge the process along. I felt worse than a telemarketer, but it did the trick. Ellen Cyr's great-granddaughter came through.

During my research on David Harris Russell (1906–1965), several relatives who were wonderfully prompt provided invaluable assistance for this study: Russell's two sons, David Robert and Andrew; and Russell's niece, Isabel Robertson Barnsley. Russell's sons were most generous with their time and in loaning such family artifacts as photographs, newspaper clippings, an album, memoirs of their grandmother and grandfather, family histories, a family tree, publisher's pamphlets, and their father's lectures. A former colleague, Robert Ruddell, professor emeritus from the University of California at Berkeley, graciously shared university records, a eulogy, and personal memories of Russell's research and teaching. Even a former graduate student, Ed Farrell, willingly offered his reminiscences.

A picture of a superb professor, one who excelled in all areas required of his profession—research, teaching, and service—emerged. A prolific researcher, Russell published widely "in the field of education and psychology includ[ing] teaching guides, essays on educational problems, college textbooks, yearbook contributions, research articles and monographs, reviews for encyclopedias, and diverse leaflets and pamphlets on curriculum development and instruction" (Buswell, Michaelis, & Parker, 1966, p. 99). Russell's love of research resulted in his contribution of scientifically based and developmentally appropriate reading instruction in the form of the Ginn Basic Readers. With more than 60,000,000 copies sold before his death, these readers affected many teachers as well as children. Russell's passionate commitment to both teaching and service afforded him the opportunity to spread the philosophies developed through his upbringing and his research across the United States and around the world.

Personal and Professional Life

"Teaching is an art," explained David Russell, "but more and more it is an art being influenced by scientific facts" (1953, p. 10). Russell's passion for teaching is a quality that is clear when examining this early reading pioneer's life. Even early in his career, Russell realized the important place research played in guiding one's teaching. His zeal for the role of research must have been infectious. "Those were the days," he recalled, referring to 1929 when he began work on his Bachelor of Education degree at the University of Saskatchewan (Saskatoon, Saskatchewan, Canada),

> when the scientific study of education was an open sesame to the solution of most of our problems and doubt....Those were the days when we discovered with Dean [Frank] Quance that educational problems had been studied scientifically since about the turn of the century.... Then we found with Dr. Laycock that children were different, that mental ability could be measured.... I'll never forget, for example, my thrill as I first saw Dr. Laycock demonstrate the giving of a Stanford-Binet Intelligence Examination to a child. It was beautiful to see. (1953, pp. 23–24)

Russell's unusual enthusiasm for research and his ability to share what he knew with other educators continued for decades. This eagerness to teach was still evident in Russell's work in the schools, even as a full professor at the University of California at Berkeley. Despite the fact that the workshop began on a Friday afternoon at 3:45 p.m., Russell met with Long Beach, California, teachers of grades 9 to 12 to address the titular question, "How Can We Improve Our Language Usage Program?" On Saturday at 10:00 a.m. he was back to help tackle "Newer Trends in Reading in Secondary Schools." Saturday afternoon he worked with both elementary and secondary teachers on the question, "How Can We Improve Spelling?" ("Teachers' Parley," n.d.).

The love of learning exhibited by Russell was fostered at home during his childhood. Russell was born on May 22, 1906, in Ottawa, Ontario, Canada. He was the son of Reverend Andrew Russell, a Presbyterian minister who received degrees from McGill University (Montreal, Quebec, Canada) and did postgraduate work at Princeton University in New Jersey, USA, and Yale

University in New Haven, Connecticut, USA (A. Russell, Memoirs, n.d.). Russell's parents, Andrew and Janet, valued schooling and made sure that both of their children were well educated. Russell's sister, Rhoda, 10 years his senior, graduated from the University of Saskatchewan in 1919. She became a teacher and continued teaching for several years until she met and married Charlie Robertson in Bradwell, Saskatchewan, Canada, where she taught (Bradwell-Clavet Historical Society, 1986).

Because he grew up in a family where father, mother, sister, and three aunts had been teachers, Russell also aspired to teach. He attended Regina Normal School in Regina, Saskatchewan, Canada, and taught in the Saskatchewan schools. He described himself, however, as being the "product of a peculiar system then in force...which said that the younger the teacher was, the less training he should have" (Russell, 1953, p. 20). By this Russell meant that after high school, he was required to attend normal school for only four months, after which he was awarded a Third Class teacher's certificate by the Saskatchewan Department of Education. Then, in 1923, at the ripe old age of 17, he became the principal of a rural, one-room school called Tipperary (I. Barnsley, personal communication, January 9, 2005). "The only rationale for this peculiar system," Russell (1953) explained, was that "presumably the younger normal students were nearer their own childhood and therefore had less to learn about children and teaching." He reported in his self-deprecating fashion, "This was an optimistic view in my case" (p. 21). "Life had its bright spots in the Tipperary pursuit of alphabets, fractions, and Gray's elegy," he continued, "but it is clear, I think, that I knew nothing about classroom procedures, much less the scientific study of education" (p. 22).

To remedy his lack of preparation, Russell took courses in the College of Education at the University of Saskatchewan in the summer of 1929. Always eager to learn and committed to the notion that research should guide practice, Russell referred to his studies as "an exciting time." "We students all probably underestimated the complexity of the usual classroom situation," he admitted later, "but it was thrilling to know that we had the powerful key of scientific research to open new classroom doors" (1953, pp. 23–25).

After receiving his BEd with "great distinction" in 1931 and in 1932 the first MEd given by the University of Saskatchewan, Russell accepted another principalship, this time at Melfort High School, Saskatchewan. Still in search of answers and needing to be challenged, he attended Columbia

University, New York, USA, where he received his PhD in Educational Psychology in 1937. During his time there, he was appointed Associate in Educational Psychology and Research Assistant to the distinguished scholar Arthur Irving Gates (see chapter 14, this volume) (Laycock, 1965, p. 40). Russell worked with Gates in the field of children's reading, and Gates spoke about him in glowing terms:

> David Russell, who as you know, is staying at our house this summer, is a source of continual satisfaction to all here. He is a most charming young man imaginable and stands at the very top in all of his work. (Gates to Quance, 1936)

While attending Teachers College, David met Elizabeth Fatherson, a doctoral student in the speech department. Their "summer friendship ripened into love," Russell explained (Russell to Quance, 1938), and they became engaged. Ever the serious academics, however, they postponed their wedding for a semester so Elizabeth could finish "her teaching in the speech department, her dissertation and a joint writing project" (Russell to Quance, 1938).

As Elizabeth completed her obligations, Russell accepted an appointment to the Faculty of Education at the University of Saskatchewan. While there, he published his Columbia University dissertation, *Characteristics of Good and Poor Spellers: A Diagnostic Study* (1937), published *Diagnostic and Remedial Spelling Manual* with Gates (Gates & Russell, 1937), and found time to coauthor yet another book, *Reading Aids Through the Grades: Two-Hundred and Twenty-Five Remedial Reading Activities* (Russell, Karp, & Kelly, 1938). Another collaborative effort with Gates and Bond was to follow, a book titled *Method of Determining Reading Readiness* (Gates, Bond, & Russell, 1939). Despite their busy academic schedules, David Russell and Elizabeth Fatherson gathered family and friends in May of 1939 for their wedding.

Several months later, Russell was offered a position at the University of British Columbia (Vancouver, British Columbia, Canada) for the "substantial" salary of $3,400 a year (Russell to Quance, 1940). Delighted by the opportunity but truly sorry to leave friends in Saskatchewan and New York, the couple packed up and headed for Vancouver. Their first child, Russell's namesake, was born in Vancouver in 1941.

The next year the Russells moved to Berkeley, California, USA, where Russell was appointed associate and then professor of education at the

University of California. A second son, Andrew, named after his paternal grandfather, was born in 1944. Elizabeth Russell was hired to teach in Berkeley's Speech Department and did so for 15 years. A lifelong colleague and helpmate, she also traveled with her husband to collect data and attend conferences. She would later coauthor Ginn's preprimers. Perhaps indicative of the Russells' close relationship is a comment on a conference photo from an album lent to me by one of Russell's sons. In this photo, Russell and Elizabeth gaze at each other, though separated by another conference participant. The back of the photo reads, "It has been recorded that the Russell's [sic] make eyes at each other. Isn't it wonderful?" (signed, Bernard, December 12, 1947).

This close pair continued their academic productivity throughout the next two decades. Having made a name for himself with his publications and presentations, and with some prior experience developing Canadian readers, Russell was hired by the publishing house Ginn & Co. to serve as senior author on its basic reading series. A Carnegie Fellowship to the University of London in 1948 coincided with the debut of Russell's work as senior author of the new Ginn series, the Ginn Basic Readers. His research in London later appeared in his book, *Children's Thinking* (1956).

Philosophical Beliefs and Guiding Principles

Because he was a firm believer in the scientific study of education, Russell laid the groundwork for the Ginn Basic Readers series with a study. He began with a questionnaire to 400 individuals across the United States who had "special competence in the field of primary-grade reading" (Russell, 1944, p. 602). Russell specifically asked the respondents to provide information regarding what they believed to be the best "general organization, content, vocabulary controls, methods, and accessories" for the first three grades of a basal reading program (p. 602). Summary recommendations from this august group were as follows: First, include multiple books per grade level that contain children's classics, poems, study activities, and "common experience" (p. 604) materials. Next, keep the same characters throughout a book and group stories by units. Regarding teaching methods, respondents favored either the "combination [sentence, word, and phonics] or the sentence method of teaching, some form of phonics instruction, and a variety of methods for motivating reading activities" (p. 609). Workbooks and wall charts were the preferred supplementary materials. With this information as a starting point,

Russell used additional research to further refine his beliefs about appropriate reading instruction. He shared these beliefs in the Ginn Basic Readers series, in his reading textbook *Children Learn to Read* (1949a), and in pamphlets distributed by the University of California (e.g., 1955).

The last of these pamphlets, titled *Johnny Can Read*, was written in response to Rudolf Flesch's attack on the reading profession. Flesch's book, *Why Johnny Can't Read—And What You Can Do About It* (1955; later followed by *Why Johnny Still Can't Read: A New Look at the Scandal of Our Schools*, 1981) attacked the reading programs, reading methods books, and the authors whom he believed neglected phonics. Flesch specifically criticized Russell and his book *Children Learn to Read* (1949a). This interaction clearly left its mark. Andrew Russell referred to *Why Johnny Can't Read* as his father's "*most hated*" book (personal communication, November 11, 2004). Russell countered Flesch's attacks with *Johnny Can Read* (1955), which was distributed by the Department of Education at the University of California at Berkeley that same year. In it Russell claims that "the truth is distorted in the Flesch book" (p. 1) and systematically points out what he calls Flesch's "misstatements" to which he provides "factual replies" (p. 4). He emphatically tells the public that Flesch's exhortation to "teach the child what each letter stands for and he can read" (p. 3) was wrong. "Grasp of meaning," Russell responded, "depends upon knowledge of words and phrases, not of individual letters" (p. 5).

Russell believed that the purpose of reading is to get meaning, that "the ideas behind the printed page are more important than the black-and-white symbols on it" (Russell, 1955, pp. 2–3). He referred to studies by Edward Lee Thorndike (1917) (see chapter 5, this volume) and Eva Bond (1938) to support this emphasis on meaning. Russell also advocated instruction in word identification via a multimethod approach: context clues, sight words (including such visual techniques as the "perception" of similarities and differences of words and the use of a picture dictionary), structural clues, and phonics. "There is probably no one 'best' method of identifying a word or of reading a story or paragraph," Russell explained (1955, p. 4). Regarding phonics, he said, "There is no justification in modern psychologies of learning for a completely synthetic approach of building up words from sounds of individual letters" (p. 6). He referred his readers to the work of Buswell (1922) and Smith (1955) as support for this position. Instead of synthetic phonics, he believed that Hildreth (1954) and Smith (1955) provided evidence "that the procedure from the whole, to the parts, back to the whole again is an efficient one in early reading" (p. 5). This emphasis on meaning through using quality literature and multiple approaches for word recognition was already evident in the Ginn Basic Readers series.

Russell later took his belief in a meaning-centered approach a step further to examine the effect that reading has on people. He focused on what he called "creative reading—for implied and inferred meanings, for appreciative reactions, for critical evaluations of what is read, and sometimes for individual changes in ideas and personality" (1970, p. 16). It was essentially what we would now call a reader response theory that guided the thinking for his book *The Dynamics of Reading* (published posthumously in 1970). In it Russell describes the reading process as a set of interactions among the "content of the material," "the person doing the reading," and the "setting in which it is done" (p. 113). Russell also includes specific discussions on text types, so-called schema reader response, and reader interest. Because three chapters were incomplete when Russell died, these chapters and the editing of the book were finished by Russell's former student Isabel Lewis and colleagues Robert Ruddell, Virginia Reid, and James Squire. Ruddell notes, "Their efforts and my own, in effect represent a memorial to a dear friend and colleague" (1970, p. vii).

Another body of knowledge that guided Russell's work was that of child development. As a matter of fact, in *Manual for Teaching the Reading-Readiness Program* (Russell & Ousley, 1948a) Russell introduced the Ginn Basic Readers series as "a product of research" in child development. This meant, for example, that Russell used studies conducted by Lewis Terman and Margaret Lima (1935) on developmental changes in reading interests to demonstrate that a 5-year-old was interested in Mother Goose rhymes or jingles; therefore, the readiness book included "Old Mother Hubbard" and "Here We Go Round the Mulberry Bush." Because a 10-year-old was reportedly interested in "stories of other lands," such stories were included in the Ginn middle-grade readers.

A more unusual developmental component included by Russell was his broad view of readiness. He explained that children enter school with wide differences in language acquisition, in "knowledge of stories," and "visual perception" (Russell, 1949a, p. 138). The teacher was directed to assess a child's readiness and then "build a background of concepts" (p. 139) and provide instruction as needed. At the upper grade levels Russell suggested that teachers examine student readiness to "understand the sequence of events" (p.

171), interpret maps or charts, or read "abstract mathematical symbols" (p. 171). Methods recommended in *Children Learn to Read* to diagnose and develop readiness at any grade include (a) building background concepts, (b) stimulating interest in reading, (c) providing a "mental set" for material, (d) setting a purpose for reading and helping students adjust their reading to the text's type and purpose, and (e) focusing on basic reading skills (p. 137).

Some of Russell's own work in the area of child development was published by the National Society for the Study of Education—"Reading and Child Development" (1949c) and "Evaluation of Pupil Growth in and Through Reading" (1949b). After several more years of thought and study on the topic, Russell collected his writings in *Children's Thinking* (1956). In the preface to this text, Russell notes that the information within was supported with a "thousand research references" (p. vii). This text represents another example of Russell's love of learning because he said that he started it simply because he "wanted to know much more about the topic" (p. vi). This project embodies Russell's belief "that at least once every seven years one should undertake a task different from what one has been doing—that one should have a sort of mental sabbatical leave" (p. vi). *Children's Thinking* (1956) and *The Dynamics of Reading* (1970) were what colleague Robert Ruddell noted as Russell's "two major contributions to theory" (personal communication, November 8, 2004).

Taken as a whole, then, Russell's faith in the scientific study of education and in the research produced by the movement in the areas of child development (related broadly to literacy), reading as a meaning-making process (using interesting, appropriate, relevant text and multiple literacies), attainment of word identification through a multiple-method approach, and certain aspects of reader response served to mold the Ginn Basic Readers series.

While Russell believed that research should guide instruction, his upbringing guided the affective and moral components of his work and life. It is perhaps no surprise that when asked about the principles that guided Russell's work, his colleague Ruddell focused on the humanitarianism of the man who was the son of a minister. In a similar vein, other colleagues mentioned Russell's "respect for the inherent dignity of all men" (Laycock, 1965, p. 39) and his efforts to "promote harmony in all relationships" (Buswell et al., 1966, p. 100). Russell tried to integrate the concept of harmony into the schools through the stories and themes in the Ginn Basic Readers. This intention comes across in correspondence related to the readers. Regarding the seventh reader, coauthor Doris Gates (no relation to Arthur Gates), a former librarian with expertise in children's literature, told Russell,

> I shall try to find stories that tie into your idea of getting along with others. I don't think it will be easy, but perhaps it can be done. Anyway, I'll make a search and let you know the results. (D. Gates to Russell, 1948)

Referring to the sixth reader, Russell raised a question about the title, "Ours to Keep." He queried, "Doesn't it have a selfish sound in days when we all share?" (Russell to Medary, 1949).

In a more overt fashion Russell's presentations urged teachers to educate for understanding. He explained, "If children and youth are to understand their world, they must learn something of how people work together in small groups, in communities, in nations and in international affairs" ("Russell says school's task," 1951). Modeling that kind of community collaboration, Russell wrote, "I have also just been on a panel on defacto segregation in Berkeley schools and gave a paper last night on book censorship—so you see I am trying to do my duty" (Russell to D. Gates, January 12, 1964). Concerned about integration being reflected in the Ginn Basic Readers series, Russell noted, "We have definitely introduced some children of other racial groups on the playground" (Russell to Anderson, 1964). This change was not apparent until after Russell's death in Ginn's 1966 "100 Edition."

In retrospect, some considered these changes insufficient and criticized aspects of race and gender in basals produced during the 1950s and 1960s (e.g., Larrick, 1965; Lipton, 1976; Women on Words and Images, 1975). It is true, as Lipton comments, that the Ginn Basic Readers and other basals portrayed the "well-scrubbed Negro family" and essentially "colored white characters brown" (1976, pp. 14–15). But of course these books mirror their times. Clearly, Russell and others at Ginn wanted to do the right thing in all respects and struggled with the tacit messages they sent to children. Father's occupation, the story setting, use of terms such as "slim waist" or "poor Ben" and countless others were scrutinized and debated. There was a lengthy discussion, for example, about the appropriateness of a story in which children played in a vacant lot. The authors concluded that it was important for children to "avoid vacant lots and similar places where not only danger but also trespass are involved" (Anderson to Russell, 1963). The complex tightrope of accuracy, censorship, and sales is one still walked today by publishers and their authors.

Closer to home, Russell's connection to family, friends, and students was evident. Despite the fact that he was overextended with presentations, executive obligations, publishing deadlines, and a heavy teaching load, Russell seemed to find time for his family. He mentioned sailing with his sons and "trying to do a little writing in the mornings but baseball games with the boys and some attempts at fishing have interfered" (Russell to D. Gates, 1951). While Russell never heard Jim Trelease encourage fathers to read to their sons, he appeared to do so regularly:

> It was sweet of you to send *River Ranch* to the boys. We have already enjoyed the first three chapters of it as the bedtime story (only one chapter a night of course), and we all can hardly wait to know what will happen next. (Russell to D. Gates, December 19, 1949)

"His friends were legion," remarked Frank Quance, as further testimony to Russell's connection with humanity, "and he prized highly the friendships he made" (Quance, 1965, p. 40). Russell's willingness to put others first caused him to pay particular attention to his teaching and advising. His teaching load was substantial, as was evident in this comment to Doris Gates: "I have 220 in my course in reading, about 100 of whom have not taught before. What are your suggestions for teaching a course like that?" (Russell to D. Gates, June 29, 1949). Doris's response was a tribute to the care and detail with which Russell developed the teacher's manuals for the basic reading series: "Give your class the Ginn manuals and forget your troubles. Even I could teach reading with them" (D. Gates to Russell, 1949).

Contributions to the Field of Reading

According to Ruddell, the Ginn Basic Readers represented a "major contribution to teaching" because they "were at one time used in about 50% of classrooms across the country" (personal correspondence, November 8, 2004). During Russell's tenure as the series' senior author (from 1948 until his death in 1960) the "elementary division became the second largest in the country—and in some years the first" (Madison, 1966, p. 447). By the 1960s the series had sold 60,000,000 copies. California (Russell's home state) adopted the readers "with an order amounting to $3,140,000—the largest ever received by a textbook publisher" (p. 447). Indeed, these readers made an impact.

The Ginn Basic Readers series presented a comprehensive reading program. It consisted of two reading-readiness books, three preprimers, a primer, and eight readers, several with multiple levels. In addition, a Big Book, picture and word cards, workbooks, teachers' manuals, and a testing program were all part of the package. Russell frequently coauthored books in the series with Odille Ousley—a "lifelong teacher"—and Doris Gates. This kind of authorship, a balance between those with public school experience and those from universities with research knowledge, was a characteristic of basal readers produced between 1940 and 1950 (Smith, 1965/1986, p. 279). Russell's broad knowledge of research was evident from his numerous articles, chapters, and books, and it clearly served as the backbone for the Ginn Basic Readers.

Another characteristic of reading programs that developed during the 1940s was the introduction of reading-readiness books and the acceptance of the readiness concept (Smith, 1965/1986, p. 277). This concept was one Russell had pioneered with his mentor Arthur Gates and Gates's colleague Guy Bond almost a decade earlier (Gates et al., 1939). Bond had identified factors they believed determined success or failure for beginning readers (Gates & Bond, 1936).

Russell's belief in using children's common experiences led to an emphasis on the improved quality of realistic stories. To ensure realism in the preprimer zoo and transportation units, coauthor Doris Gates told Russell, "My plan is to go to the [children's] zoo in Griffith Park in Los Angeles and if this doesn't offer enough, I will go to San Diego" (D. Gates to Russell, November 5, 1964). After checking information for the zoo stories, Doris planned to investigate the helicopter: "I will be riding the helicopter to and from Riverside, and am hopeful that this first experience of such transportation will yield up a gem-like insight that can be handled in ten words" (D. Gates to Russell, November 5, 1964).

A characteristic unique to the Ginn Basic Readers was Russell's use of *vertical organization*. "If the realities of child development are respected," Russell explained, the series needed "an arrangement which cuts across grade lines and emphasizes, both within and between grades, the continuity of growth in reading abilities" (Russell & Ousley, 1948a, p. 13). An example of vertical organization (which today might be called the *spiral curriculum*) was Russell's inclusion of reading readiness from "the first year through the eighth" (p. 10) and then into the secondary school.

Another "distinctive feature" of the 1948 Ginn series was the provision for "language and speech activities to be integrated with the reading activities" (Smith, 1965/1986, p. 285). This communication feature clearly reflected Russell's self-described research "interest in the field of the language arts, that group of abilities essentially concerned with the communication of ideas...speaking, handwriting, spelling, composition, listening, and reading" (1953, p. 76).

The thoughtfulness with which Russell guided the production of the Ginn Basic Readers was culled from hundreds of pages of author correspondence available at the Knight Special Collections at the University of Oregon Libraries. At the middle and junior high level, for example, Russell's expertise in the field of English (he served as president of the National Council of Teachers of English [NCTE]) and his research on adolescent reading interests—shown in articles such as "The Magazines They Read" (Russell & Black, 1940) and "Reading Preferences of Younger Adolescents in Saskatchewan," (Russell, 1941)—served him well in gauging student reading preferences. Throughout the Ginn Basic Readers, connecting reading to children's interests and experiences was a guiding principle. At the primary level, stories were written within the parameters of graded vocabulary lists; that is, the vocabulary was restricted to words previously introduced and to a previously determined number of new words. Because the emphasis in the primary-level books was on word meaning, sight vocabulary was supported with context clues via both illustrations and text. Phonics was stressed in the program after mastery of sight vocabulary "in all books of grades 4-5-6"; structural analysis rounded out the word recognition program (Ginn, 1952).

Due to Russell's belief in the importance of meaning, a broad range of literacy components as well as supplementary reading materials were included in the Ginn Basic Readers. Russell (n.d.) advocated "using materials of community interest, thus stimulating pupils to read materials important to them" (p. 5). Poetry was added to complement units.

The process of choosing reading materials for the upper grades was thorough: Only reputable authors and prose or poetry with strong "literary qualities" (Russell to D. Gates, July 14, 1949) were considered, critiques of works under consideration were checked in resources such as the *Elementary English Review*, material was field tested with various student groups in a variety of settings, and consideration was given to diversity in terms of geography and gender (but not, at this time, in terms of race or socioeconomic status). Stories that portrayed various regions of the United States—"city life," "suburban life," and "the cultural life of people in many lands" (Russell & Wulfing, 1948, p. 7)—were noted in the readers' manuals and included in the readers. Russell regularly advocated the inclusion of a "girl as central character," yet worried about both girl and boy interests. Finally, Russell told his coauthors that there should be "humor" and "fun" in the books (Russell to D. Gates & Snedaker, 1949).

Once material was chosen at the middle and upper levels, it was adapted (i.e., paragraphs were cut and sentences added) and the content analyzed in such a way that explanations for unusual terms like *jib* or *chaps* were included in context. Also, Russell and his coauthors read and commented on each other's work and recommendations constantly.

After the reading series was produced, Russell took it to teachers in the field to help them use it and listened to those teachers so he knew their needs. In a 1953 lecture presented in Canada, Russell described the interactions between the producer of a reading series and its consumers:

> Work on a course of study for the language arts [was] planned on a continuous basis from kindergarten through high school...each member [of the language arts committee] was taking problems and then decisions back to his own school for discussion and try-out. Examples of materials and methods from many classrooms have been incorporated into a tentative teachers' guide, which will be revised after teachers use it for a couple of years and evaluate its contents.... The junior high group has...some effective procedures for reducing...reading retardation...such projects may be influencing practice more than the scientific article in a journal of limited circulation. (pp. 79–81)

Even though there was input on the Ginn Basic Readers from classroom teachers, coauthors, and editors, Russell had the final say. In any major decision, such as in moving to more decodable text in the mid-1960s (which would have required a change in the names of familiar characters), editorial department director Marion Anderson told Russell, "the decision must be yours" (Anderson to Russell, March 4, 1964). Perhaps Russell did not have much choice on this issue because pressure to move from whole-word methods of beginning reading instruction came from many sources: "Most school people want[ed] a major revision" (Anderson to Russell & Clymer, 1964); there were "criticisms from linguists" (Clymer to Russell, 1964), and "linguistic practices were being included in state board criteria" (D. Gates to Elizabeth Russell, 1964). The writings of a vocal critic like Rudolf Flesch were not mentioned in any Ginn correspondence as a catalyst for change, but the work of linguistics professor Henry Lee Smith (1956) was noted. (In the linguistic readers, vocabulary control is based on spelling regularity or spelling patterns, rather than sounding and blending.) Other influences mentioned in correspondence on the choice of decodable words (such as the use of *dad* instead of *father*) were Henry Rinsland's *A Basic Vocabulary of Elementary School Children* (1945), Helen Murphy's *The Spontaneous Speaking Vocabulary of Children in Primary Grades* (1957), and Carl Lefevre's *Linguistics and the Teaching of Reading* (1964). (See Clymer to Russell, 1964, for more on the shift from sight words to decodable text.) Russell did not live to see the changes these works promoted.

Implementing any change was difficult, as Russell found when he tried to address the issue of the struggling reader. One of Russell's suggestions, to broaden awareness, was to include stories about children who had difficulty reading. Reaction from one of the reviewers was that the issue should not even be broached in a story: "Do children...have a sympathetic understanding of this problem?" or "Might there not be a kind of contempt for a boy who cannot handle words as simple as 'help' and 'safe?'" (Robinson to Russell, 1955). Another of Russell's suggestions was "to get more books which are high in level of interest but low in level of difficulty" into the reading series (Russell to D. Gates, October 17, 1955). This collection of easy supplementary books was euphemistically referred to as the *enrichment series*. This solution was accepted, but with reservations:

> Marion [editorial department director Marion Anderson] has hinted that some of the Ginn offices are only moderately enthusiastic. This does not surprise me in the least because the enrichment series is a new venture in textbook publication. I should think that it would take at least two or three years to develop the idea fully with agents and school people." (Russell to D. Gates, October 17, 1955, p. 2)

Another innovative idea Russell proposed for the sixth- to eighth-grade level was "moving from the reading of short selections in readers to whole books" (Russell to D. Gates, October 17, 1955, p. 2). This idea was later embraced, and Russell was regularly on the lookout for books written by new authors whose stories met the needs and interests of the audiences whom they served. Diverse authors such as the "Indian teacher of Indian children in...Jemez Pueblo in New Mexico" (D. Gates to Russell, 1963) were included.

Russell worked tirelessly on the Ginn Basic Readers and as an effective manager was capable of inspiring others to do the same. He was a taskmaster who got the job done in a professional and timely manner. Despite the problems experienced by his coauthors—bronchitis, pneumonia, exhaustion, and physical injuries—Russell kept everything on schedule. Perhaps others pushed themselves for him because he pushed himself harder than anyone else. Only months before his death, Russell was still editing Preprimer II and apologizing for his "detailed" and "picayunish" comments (Russell to D. Gates, August 30, 1964). Thin and weak from chemotherapy, he still "worried about first grade books...in [the] hospital" (Russell to D. Gates, August 30, 1964).

Russell was clearly more than an author and editor for Ginn; he appears to have been a catalyst and innovator as well. In a June 13, 1960, letter addressed "To the authors of the Ginn Basic Readers," he wrote, "Now is the time to think about 1970.... I have discussed the possibility of an exploratory conference" (Russell to the authors, p. 1). His idea was to get people together (e.g., authors, sales representatives, and school people) who "have some ideas about reading" to brainstorm and make short presentations of a "topic or problem" (p. 1). Some of the topics mentioned later were "current trends in reading" and "major changes in the middle-grade program" (p. x).

Other less tangible contributions to the reading field include Russell's selfless donation of time to both teaching and service. Russell served as president of the California School Supervisors' Association from 1947 to 1948; president of the National Conference on Research in English from 1952 to 1953; vice president and president of the NCTE from 1955 to 1956 and 1963 to 1964, respectively; and vice president of the American Educational Research Association from 1957 to 1958 and then president of that organization from 1958 to 1959. Russell gave countless presentations to professional associations (e.g., the International Reading Association in North America and in Australia when he was a Fulbright Research Fellow there), community groups such as Parent Teacher Associations, and school districts across the United States. Evidently these organizations felt his contributions were significant enough to name numerous awards after him. For example, the Alameda County (California) chapter of the International Reading

Association still gives out the David H. Russell Award for Excellence in Reading Instruction. The David H. Russell Award for Distinguished Research in English is currently administered by the NCTE.

Russell remained as president, for the second time, of NCTE up until his death, even though his poor health made the job difficult. His correspondence with Doris Gates indicated that he was already being hospitalized and feeling the effects of the rare bone marrow disorder that was to take his life. Professional that he was, however, he did not slow down and apparently did not want others to know that he was ill. Doris assured him, "I will not mention this to anyone" (D. Gates to Russell, January 2, 1963). The 1964 NCTE conference was in Cleveland, Ohio, USA, and Russell confided to Doris, "I have been feeling a little less chipper for three or four days and my spleen is definitely larger again. However, NCTE means the fun of seeing friends and I think we'll go" (Russell to D. Gates, November 16, 1964). A month later, unfortunately, Russell was quite ill. Doris wrote,

> I talked with Elizabeth yesterday and David is bad. He was in great pain; she used the word 'anguish.' She told me that their doctor had got hold of a new medicine not yet on the market from Bethesda Naval Hospital and had it flown out to give to David. (D. Gates to Anderson, 1964)

David Russell died an untimely death on January 28, 1965, at the age of 59.

Lessons for the Future

Reflection on Russell's substantial work on the Ginn Basic Readers brings to mind his contemporary and competitor from Scott Foresman publishing, William Scott Gray (see chapter 13, this volume). Similar to Mavrogenes's (1985) conclusions about Gray, it appears that Russell's strong point was not originality but that he took what existed and made it better. As Ruddell explained, "One of the Russell hallmarks [was] the ability to synthesize and summarize significant research in a meaningful and interesting fashion" (1970, preface to *The Dynamics of Reading*, p. vi). Undoubtedly, these communication skills helped Russell connect with those teachers and administrators who had adopted the Ginn Basic Readers and assure them that they had purchased a quality product, one that was research based. However, Russell remained open minded, willing to learn from other researchers and teachers alike. Comfortable in the classroom himself, he maintained regular contact with teachers in the field and was guided by their input. Therefore, research guided practice, and practice guided the questions to be researched. This is a process I myself have found essential to maintaining one's credibility.

Russell's belief in reading as a meaning-making process drove the kind of reading instruction the Ginn Basic Readers present, and his beliefs were not altered by the vitriolic chastisement of critics like Rudolf Flesch. Changes in approach were discussed, but they were not implemented in Russell's lifetime. Although I have worked with struggling readers long enough to value a more balanced approach to reading instruction, a firm conviction in a model of the reading process is essential for anyone who teaches reading. As the parent of a child with dyslexia, I know that one approach to reading instruction does not work for everyone, so a variety of models offers a variety of options. I respect Russell's convictions.

I have also affirmed my understanding that to shepherd a basal reading series, one must possess a multitude of talents, willingness to work around the clock, good managerial skills, and the ability to multitask. It appears that one needs to be a big-picture person to be senior author of a successful reading series. These are qualities many professors (myself included) do not possess.

Reflecting on my engagement in historical biography brought to mind my obligations and the process of fulfilling them. Telling this story about David Harris Russell brought me in contact with his family, friends, and colleagues. While true for all research, these personal contacts intensified my concerns for accuracy. This issue (which might also be referred to as *validity*) was especially challenging in this study, perhaps because of the recency of the subject's life. Although I love doing historical research and find the search and discovery exciting, validation of information is the true grind, yet necessity, of this work. This study brought that fact to light more clearly for me than any other I have done because there were so many contradictory pieces of data about Russell: Graduation dates, award dates, and even his wedding date were reported differently in different sources. Validating the correct wedding date, a small yet important piece of information, required finding and checking multiple obituaries and newspaper announcements, writing to Russell's family members, and finally requesting a copy of the marriage license from the New York City Marriage Bureau. I honestly questioned the amount of time I spent validating this and other data issues, especially in an era in which experimental research is the methodology de jour. However, in writing the story of a man whose life exemplified professionalism, hard work, and attention to detail, I could certainly do no less. Perhaps that is one of the goals of biography—to inspire others by the lives we portray.

Reflection Questions

1. Compare and contrast Russell and the other early reading pioneers. What characteristics or qualities are possessed by all the early reading pioneers? What qualities are unique?
2. What role was played by the spouses of the early reading pioneers?
3. Rudolf Flesch specifically attacked Russell and other early reading pioneers. How much influence did Flesch's books have on changing methods of initial reading instruction during the 1960s? Would methods have changed if Flesch had not written *Why Johnny Can't Read*?
4. It would appear that William Scott Gray and David Harris Russell, senior authors of two of the most widely sold reading series, were not particularly original. Are originality and sales inversely related over short-term cycles when it comes to reading programs? Can original or unique ideas be found in current reading programs?
5. Examine one of Russell's studies or his dissertation. How would the "scientifically based" research conducted by Russell be viewed today?

REFERENCES

Anderson, M., to E. Russell. (1963, October 4). In Knight Special Collections, University of Oregon Libraries, Eugene, Oregon.

Anderson, M., to D.H. Russell. (1964, March 4). In Knight Special Collections, University of Oregon Libraries, Eugene, Oregon.

Anderson, M., to D.H. Russell. (1964, March 17). In Knight Special Collections, University of Oregon Libraries, Eugene, Oregon.

Anderson, M., to D.H. Russell & T. Clymer. (1964, March 4). In Knight Special Collections, University of Oregon Libraries, Eugene, Oregon.

Barry, A.L. (2005). Ellen Cyr: Forgotten author of a best-selling reading series. *Paradigm: Journal of the Textbook Colloquium, 3*(1), 10–23.

Bond, E. (1938). *Reading and ninth-grade achievement.* Contributions to Education No. 756. Bureau of Publications, Teachers College, Columbia University.

Bradwell-Clavet Historical Society. (1986). *Echoes of our past.* Bradwell, Saskatchewan: Brigdens.

Buswell, G.T. (1922). *Fundamental reading habits: A study of their development* (Supplementary Educational Monographs, No. 21). Chicago: University of Chicago Press.

Buswell, G.T., Michaelis, J.U., & Parker, J.C. (1966). In memoriam. University of California, Berkeley, School of Education, Office of the Dean.

Clymer, T., to D.H. Russell. (1964, March 13). In Knight Special Collections, University of Oregon Libraries, Eugene, Oregon.

Flesch, R.F. (1955). *Why Johnny can't read—and what you can do about it*. New York: Harper.

Flesch, R.F. (1981). *Why Johnny still can't read: A new look at the scandal of our schools*. New York: HarperCollins.

Gates, A.I., & Bond, G.L. (1936). Reading readiness—A study of factors determining success and failure in beginning reading. *Teacher's College Record*, 37, 679–685.

Gates, A.I., Bond, G.L., & Russell, D.H. (1939). *Method of determining reading readiness*. New York: Teachers College, Columbia.

Gates, A.I., & Russell, D.H. (1937). *Diagnostic and remedial spelling manual*. New York: Teachers College, Columbia University.

Gates, A.I., to F. Quance. (1936, July 20). In University of Saskatchewan Archives, Saskatoon, Saskatchewan.

Gates, D., to M. Anderson. (1964, December 15). In Knight Special Collections, University of Oregon Libraries, Eugene, Oregon.

Gates, D., to D.H. Russell. (1948, December 15). In Knight Special Collections, University of Oregon Libraries, Eugene, Oregon.

Gates, D., to D.H. Russell. (1949, June 30). In Knight Special Collections, University of Oregon Libraries, Eugene, Oregon.

Gates, D., to D.H. Russell. (1963, January 2). In Knight Special Collections, University of Oregon Libraries, Eugene, Oregon.

Gates, D., to D.H. Russell. (1963, March 12). In Knight Special Collections, University of Oregon Libraries, Eugene, Oregon.

Gates, D., to D.H. Russell. (1964, November 5). In Knight Special Collections, University of Oregon Libraries, Eugene, Oregon.

Gates, D., to E. Russell. (1964, August 7). In Knight Special Collections, University of Oregon Libraries, Eugene, Oregon.

Ginn [Publisher's letter to customers]. (1952, January). In Knight Special Collections, University of Oregon Libraries, Eugene, Oregon.

Hildreth, G.H. (1954). The role of pronouncing and sounding in learning to read. *The Elementary School Journal*, 55, 141–147.

Larrick, N. (1965). The all-white world of children's books. *Saturday Review*, 48(3), 63–64, 84–85.

Laycock, S. (1965). A tribute to Dr. David Harris Russell. *Arbos*, 2, 39–44.

Lefevre, C.A. (1964). *Linguistics and the teaching of reading*. New York: McGraw-Hill.

Lipton, M.J. (1976). *Sexism and racism in popular basal readers 1964–1976*. New York: Racism and Sexism Resource Center for Educators. (ERIC Document Reproduction Service No. ED123307)

Madison, C.A. (1966). *Book publishing in America*. New York: McGraw-Hill.

Mavrogenes, N.A. (1985). *William Scott Gray: Leader of teachers and shaper of American reading instruction*. Unpublished dissertation, University of Chicago. Chicago, Illinois.

Murphy, H.A. (1957). The spontaneous speaking vocabulary of children in primary grades. *Journal of Education*, 140, 1–105.

Quance, F. (1965). A tribute to Dr. David Harris Russell. *Arbos*, 2, 39–44.

Rinsland, H.D. (1945). *A basic vocabulary of elementary school children*. New York: Macmillan.

Robinson, B., to D.H. Russell. (1955, July). In Knight Special Collections, University of Oregon Libraries, Eugene, Oregon.

Ruddell, R.B. (1970). Preface. In D.H. Russell, *The dynamics of reading*. Waltham, MA: Ginn.

Russell, A. (n.d.) Memoirs. Private collection.

Russell, D.H. (n.d.). *The basic reading program in the modern school.* [Ginn and Company Contributions in Reading No.1]. Boston: Ginn. (Source: Andrew Russell's private collection.)

Russell, D.H. (1937). *Characteristics of good and poor spellers: A diagnostic study.* New York: Teachers College, Columbia University.

Russell, D.H. (1941). Reading preferences of younger adolescents in Saskatchewan. *The English Journal, 30,* 131–136.

Russell, D.H. (1944). Opinions of experts about primary-grade basic reading programs. *The Elementary School Journal, 44,* 602–609.

Russell, D.H. (1949a). *Children learn to read.* Boston: Ginn.

Russell, D.H. (1949b). Evaluation of child growth in and through reading. In N.B. Henry (Series Ed.) and A. Beery, E. Betts, D. Durrell, A.I. Gates, & G. Whipple (Vol. Eds.), *Forty-eighth yearbook of the National Society for the Study of Education: Part II. Reading in the elementary school* (pp. 284–301). Chicago: University of Chicago Press.

Russell, D.H. (1949c). Reading and child development. In N.B. Henry (Series Ed.) and A. Beery, E. Betts, D. Durrell, A.I. Gates, & G. Whipple (Vol. Eds.), *Forty-eighth yearbook of the National Society for the study of Education: Part II. Reading in the elementary school* (pp. 10–32). Chicago: University of Chicago Press.

Russell, D.H. (1953). *Implications of research for Canadian practices.* Toronto, ON: W.J. Gage.

Russell, D.H. (1955). *Johnny can read* (Field Service leaflet no. 5). Berkeley: University Of California, Berkeley, Department of Education.

Russell, D.H. (1956). *Children's thinking.* Boston: Ginn.

Russell, D.H. (1970). *The dynamics of reading.* Waltham, MA: Ginn.

Russell, D.H., & Black, W. (1940). The magazines they read. *The School: Ontario, 29,* 245–250.

Russell, D.H., Karp, E.E., & Kelly, E.I. (1938). *Reading aids through the grades: Two-hundred and twenty-five remedial reading activities.* New York: Teachers College, Columbia University.

Russell, D.H., & Ousley, O. (1948a). *Manual for teaching the reading-readiness program.* Boston: Ginn.

Russell, D.H., & Ousley, O. (1948b). *Manual for teaching* We are neighbors. Boston: Ginn.

Russell, D.H., & Wulfing, G. (1948). *Manual for teaching* Friends far and near. Boston: Ginn.

Russell, D.H., to M. Anderson. (1964, March 9). In Knight Special Collections, University of Oregon Libraries, Eugene, Oregon.

Russell, D.H., to the authors of the Ginn Basic Readers. (1960, June 13). In Knight Special Collections, University of Oregon Libraries, Eugene, Oregon.

Russell, D.H., to D. Gates. (1949, June 29). In Knight Special Collections, University of Oregon Libraries, Eugene, Oregon.

Russell, D.H., to D. Gates. (1949, July 14). In Knight Special Collections, University of Oregon Libraries, Eugene, Oregon.

Russell, D.H., to D. Gates. (1949, December 19). In Knight Special Collections, University of Oregon Libraries, Eugene, Oregon.

Russell, D.H., to D. Gates. (1951, August 17). In Knight Special Collections, University of Oregon Libraries, Eugene, Oregon.

Russell, D.H., to D. Gates. (1955, June 27). In Knight Special Collections, University of Oregon Libraries, Eugene, Oregon.

Russell, D.H., to D. Gates. (1955, October 17). In Knight Special Collections, University of Oregon Libraries, Eugene, Oregon.

Russell, D.H., to D. Gates. (1964, January 12). In Knight Special Collections, University of Oregon Libraries, Eugene, Oregon.

Russell, D.H., to D. Gates. (1964, May 2). In Knight Special Collections, University of Oregon Libraries, Eugene, Oregon.

Russell, D.H., to D. Gates. (1964, May 31). In Knight Special Collections, University of Oregon Libraries, Eugene, Oregon.

Russell, D.H., to D. Gates. (1964, August 30). In Knight Special Collections, University of Oregon Libraries, Eugene, Oregon..

Russell, D.H., to D. Gates. (1964, November 16). In Knight Special Collections, University of Oregon Libraries, Eugene, Oregon.

Russell, D.H., to D. Gates & M. Snedaker. (1949, March 23). In Knight Special Collections, University of Oregon Libraries, Eugene, Oregon.

Russell, D.H., to M. Medary. (1949, January 18). In Knight Special Collections, University of Oregon Libraries, Eugene, Oregon.

Russell, D.H., to F. Quance. (1938, August 18). In University of Saskatchewan Archives, Saskatoon, Saskatchewan.

Russell, D.H., to F. Quance. (1940, May 17). In University of Saskatchewan Archives, Saskatoon, Saskatchewan.

Russell says school's task to build human resources. (1951, April 4). *The Ashville Citizen*, B1.

Smith, H.L. (1956). *Linguistic science and the teaching of English*. Cambridge, MA: Harvard University Press.

Smith, N.B. (1955). What research tells us about word recognition. *The Elementary School Journal, 55*, 440–446.

Smith, N.B. (1986). *American reading instruction*. Newark, DE: International Reading Association. (Original work published 1965)

Teachers' parley called to stiffen reading, spelling. (n.d.). *The LongBeach Gazette*. n.p.

Terman, L.M., & Lima, M. (1935). *Children's reading: A guide for parents and teachers*. New York: Appleton-Century.

Thorndike, E.L. (1917). Reading as reasoning: A study of mistakes in paragraph reading. *Journal of Educational Psychology, 8*, 322–332.

Women on Words and Images. (1975). *Dick and Jane as victims: Sex stereotyping in children's readers*. Princeton, NJ: Author.

FOR FURTHER READING

Breines, W. (1992). *Young, white and miserable: Growing up female in the fifties*. Boston: Beacon Press.

Chall, J.S. (1967). *Learning to read: The great debate*. New York: McGraw-Hill.

Gates, A.I. (1953). *Teaching reading: What research says to the teacher*. Washington, DC: National Education Association.

Ravitch, D. (1983). *The troubled crusade: American education, 1945–1980*. New York: Basic Books.

Robinson, R.D. (Ed.). (2000). *Historical sources in U.S. reading education, 1900–1970*. Newark, DE: International Reading Association.

CONCLUSION

Reflections on the Early Reading Pioneers and Their Biographers

□ ▨ ▪

By Douglas Kaufman and Douglas K. Hartman

BEFORE WE BECAME involved with this project we were barely aware of the existence of a group called the early reading pioneers who were inducted posthumously in 1973 into the Reading Hall of Fame, nor were we familiar with several of the individual pioneers. Figures such as the independent and original Douglas Waples, for instance, introduced themselves to us for the first time. What to make of them as a group proved fascinating. What does it mean, for instance, that of the 13 figures whose parents' occupations are described, 7 had fathers who were members of the clergy (including one set of missionary parents)? What are we to make of their professional incestuousness? A small number of universities dominated their experiences: At least 12 of the early reading pioneers were associated with Columbia University or its affiliate, Teachers College, at some point in their careers; at least 7 with the University of Chicago; at least 4 with Harvard; and at least 4 with Wesleyan University in Connecticut. At least 6 focused heavily on eye-movement studies. In short, this was a group of researchers and educators—colleagues, mentors, and protégés—who directly and heavily influenced one another, perhaps excluding other potentially influential figures outside the walls of these few institutions who might have brought a broader spectrum of ideas to the research table.

Shaping the Reading Field: The Impact of Early Reading Pioneers, Scientific Research, and Progressive Ideas, edited by Susan E. Israel and E. Jennifer Monaghan. © 2007 by the International Reading Association.

As we compared and contrasted the works and lives of researchers whom we already knew with those who had previously been strangers, our conceptions of all their interests and activities evolved. We left our reading of these chapters with a more comprehensive and holistic sense of how our field got to where it is today. These reading pioneers profoundly affected the ways in which we currently conduct research in reading education; introduced the research, initiatives, and materials that still guide almost every literacy practice conducted in schools today; and either predicted or fomented the seemingly contradictory theories that fuel the most enduring, ongoing debates in our field. However, we also left the pages with a very interesting sense of dissonance, and that is what we choose to meditate on in this chapter.

Dissonances Encountered While Reading About the Early Reading Pioneers

The astounding contributions of these pioneers to the fields of reading and literacy are obvious; here we will not belabor what has already been said so eloquently in the previous chapters. Instead, we will focus on two particular and acute dissonances we experienced as we read these biographies, the first being between the pioneers' philosophical positions and their research activities and products, and the second being between the biographers' representations of the pioneers and the pioneers' actual research activities and products.

Pioneers' Philosophical Positions Versus Their Research Activities and Products

One of the most fascinating aspects of these figures, when looked at as an interrelated group who together charted a direction that still guides the profession, is a clear contrast between many of their general philosophical statements and guiding principles (as attributed to them by the chapters' authors), and the kinds of research they conducted and the educational products arising from their work.

In her introductory chapter to this volume, E. Jennifer Monaghan states that the early years of the reading field were "the tale of a contest between two competing approaches to reading education: the progressivism associated with John Dewey on the one hand, and the scientific movement in education on the other" (see Introduction, this volume, p. 2). For Monaghan, the selection of these particular figures as early reading pioneers indicates the "re-sounding victory of the second approach" (p. 2). Monaghan, in fact, identi-fies Laura Zirbes and Edmund Burke Huey as the only 2 of the 16 pioneers "who were solidly at the progressive, Dewey-inspired end of the theoretical spectrum" (Introduction, p. 2), and their respective chapters bear out their philosophical bent. Jolene B. Reed and Richard J. Meyer clarify how Huey re-flected Dewey's thinking in his valuing of "authentic" literacy experiences, and David W. Moore portrays Zirbes as a champion of "inventiveness and originality" (chapter 8, p. 182) who accounted for children's innate creativi-ty and individual development while she promoted individualized instruc-tion. She "abhorred preset, lockstep, cogwheeled teaching, believing that it robbed learners as well as teachers of essential opportunities to form impor-tant understandings and attitudes" (p. 182).

But the rest of the pioneers, Monaghan suggests, were scientists in a tra-ditional sense of the word, rooted in studying the more quantifiable aspects of human endeavor and gravitating toward behaviorism as a theory that would unlock the secrets of reading acquisition. Their approach to the study of reading, she claims, has influenced subsequent research more heavily than any other factor.

We believe, however, that the pages of this book reveal an even more complex and interesting phenomenon. It is true that the pioneers' research methodologies, the findings they produced, and the instructional tactics and materials they created clearly favor the values of the scientific manage-ment movement that was prevalent during many of their careers, and they give credence to Monaghan's claim. However, what is equally striking is how often in the midst of their researcher-centered approaches, which often de-fined their subjects outside their social situation, so many of them expressed clearly progressive—*Deweyan*—ideals. There are exceptions, of course. James McKeen Cattell's embrace of eugenics and Edward Lee Thorndike's rigid be-haviorism clearly place them outside a perspective that identifies learning as a constructive act heavily influenced by sociocultural and political forces. But time and again the reader hears—through the pioneers' own words and through the interpretations of their chapters' authors—an articulated need to individualize instruction, facilitate student construction of meaning, learn the whole background of the reader to teach most effectively, and create an edu-cational arena where children's voices were heard and valued. The following examples illustrate this:

- Allen Berger, Dixie D. Massey, Kristin Stoll, and Aviva Gray identify a portion of Robert Sessions Woodworth's work as a precursor to schema theory.

- Jackie Marshall Arnold and Mary-Kate Sableski claim that Charles Hubbard Judd's focus on the social influences of reading is a premonition of the work of Vygotsky and Clay.

- Walter Fenno Dearborn advocated schools where the child can "progress in his education at the rate demanded by his individual abilities and needs" (Dearborn & Inglis, 1921, p. 5).

- May Hill Arbuthnot advises that "the child and his needs come first" (quoted in Blue, 1976, pp. 3–4).

- Karla J. Möller describes Bernice Elizabeth Leary as "advocating true whole language teaching" (chapter 10, p. 230).

- As George Kamberelis and Marta K. Albert state, Douglas Waples defined the goal of teacher education as leading students "toward the construction of principles for effective teaching based upon their own growing theoretical understanding and expertise" (chapter 11, p. 259).

- Ernest Horn took into account student interest, student background knowledge, and the importance of both qualitative teacher assessment and student self-assessment.

- William Scott Gray defined *reading* broadly. According to Carol Lauritzen (chapter 13, p. 314), he believed

  that literacy is related to sociopolitical status. He believed that those seeking literacy for all people had focused too much on the skills of reading, while not giving enough attention to "welfare, social progress, and democratic growth.... [W]e now realize that literacy as a skill is not enough; it must be viewed merely as an essential aid to individual and community welfare and inter-group understanding" (Gray, 1956, p. 9).

- Misty Sailors lauds Arthur Irving Gates for his focus on the child and the teacher, rather than the educational material, as the foundation of learning. Gates himself discussed the criticism he received later in his career for supposedly being a naïve supporter of Dewey's progressive ideas (Gates, 1971, p. 211).

- Diane Lapp, Laurie A. Guthrie, and James Flood offer Ruth May Strang's list of "Generally Accepted Principles" of teaching, which include letting the child guide the teacher toward educational success, developing respectful relationships between the teacher and student, and adapting and individualizing instruction according to dynamic situations and children's individual needs.
- Arlene L. Barry describes David Harris Russell's "creative reading" (Russell, 1970, p. 16) as a precursor to reader response theory and highlights Russell's attempts to inject children's common experiences into the Ginn readers.

So, while Monaghan's original assertion that the scientific movement clearly won the day cannot be ignored, the journey toward that seeming victory appears interesting and complex. A powerful dissonance emerges in almost every chapter. The research questions that most of the early pioneers asked, and the approaches they adopted to answer those questions, do not appear to lead them toward these more progressive philosophical constructions to which they lay claim in their more general discussions about education. Most of their research was heavily influenced by new innovations in scientific methodology. The pioneers' research examines reading from perspectives that shed little light on (a) the individual construction of meaning, (b) the effect of a student-centered literacy curriculum, or (c) the sociopolitical aspects of the reading act. Two aspects of the pioneers' work, in particular, seem to belie the progressive characterizations of effective reading instruction and learning that their chapters' authors attribute to them: (1) their research and (2) their conceptions of the social milieu that influences schooling.

Regarding research. The early reading pioneers rarely engaged in ethnographic, anthropological, or sociological research approaches. What they researched, they researched well. They clearly and enthusiastically embraced innovations in statistical research and the new trends of the scientific movement, and the authors of the chapters in this volume consistently cite the meticulous research approaches of their subjects. The quality of the early reading pioneers' scholarship, particularly the rigor of their methodology, is well documented. However, the scope of their research designs, at least in contemporary terms, appears to be fairly narrow. While they created a trend to study, perhaps for the first time, the actual *behaviors* of readers, the focus was almost purely on the physiological—with their particular focus on eye movement—rather than on the social, cultural, or anthropological aspects of reading.

Research paradigms that approached these elements were certainly in existence at this time, if in more nascent forms. Anthropology and sociology were clearly recognized as disciplines by the middle of the 19th century. Ethnographic studies in which researchers examined the everyday lives of cultural and social groups gained a stronghold in the 1920s with Robert Parks's work at the University of Chicago (Erickson, 1986). However, the training and the research agendas of most of the pioneers did not appear to lend themselves to the study of the progressive themes that they were beginning to support. While many called for instruction that recognized the whole child and that took into account individual talents, tastes, and needs—characteristics of the educational milieu that reside more on the social end of the spectrum—few of the pioneers appear to have studied to any great degree what this instruction might look like in actual working classrooms or to have asked the big qualitative question, What is going on here? in the natural setting. Moreover, while many of the pioneers appeared to view the voices of teachers and children as essential to effective literacy learning, they apparently did not view them as essential to effective literacy learning *research*. With a few exceptions (see some of the work of Gates, Huey, and Waples), we do not see the pioneers asking teachers and students about their perceptions or understandings of the literacy classroom. Instead, we see more historically traditional approaches in which the researcher enters a setting (natural or artificially constructed), imposes some kind of condition outside the normal routine, and then measures the effect of that variable on the more easily observable facets of reading—eye movements, numbers of words read in a given time period, or performance on standardized tests.

In just one example of the tension between the early reading pioneers' more progressive statements and their identities as leaders in the scientific movement, Jackie Marshall Arnold and Mary-Kate Sableski introduce Charles Hubbard Judd as a man who "illustrate[d] how the process of learning to read is socially influenced rather than an isolated event" (chapter 4, p. 110). At the same time, the authors describe Judd's promotion of very specific "scientific" methods of reading research as a harbinger of the intense focus on randomized, experimental designs, privileging the results of such studies over the results of ethnographic, qualitative designs (Glenn, 2004) that have been marginalized by the No Child Left Behind (NCLB) Act of 2001. One of the primary criticisms of NCLB has been, of course, that its language limits the definition of legitimate research to those designs that are "scientifically based," and that these particular designs have a notoriously difficult time unearthing the complex social, cultural, and political influences on learning as people interact in naturalistic settings. The dissonance between Arnold and Sableski's depiction of Judd as a predecessor to Vygotsky and Clay (chapter 4, p. 115) on the one hand, and Judd's fairly rigid experimental approach and his focus on eye-movement research on the other, gives the reader pause. Although his studies led him to call for instruction that favored oral reading over silent reading, he did not do so to exploit the social nature of the act but because his eye-movement studies suggested that it was more physiologically efficient.

Regarding the social milieu of the classroom and schooling. The early reading pioneers held a myopic view of diversity, particularly regarding issues of race, culture, and gender. This is perhaps not unexpected given the era in which these figures prospered. The majority of the early reading pioneers conducted their most significant work before the beginning of the modern U.S. Civil Rights movement (jumpstarted by Brown v. Board of Education in 1954) and the modern U.S. women's movement of the 1960s and 1970s (which gained strength through, among other events, the Food and Drug Administration's approval of birth control pills in 1960 and the publishing of Betty Friedan's *The Feminine Mystique* in 1963). Nevertheless, many of the pioneers held what our society would now characterize as openly racist, sexist, and culturally elitist views, which must have also disturbed more socially progressive thinkers in their own eras.

Some of this bigotry is obvious. In her chapter on James McKeen Cattell, Arlette Ingram Willis vividly describes Cattell's embrace of Galton's eugenics movement, the suppositions of which he used to attempt to prove the intellectual superiority of white European males. Lou Ann Sears, in her chapter on Edward Lee Thorndike, attributes to both Thorndike and Cattell "hereditarian and racial determinist attitudes" (Lagemann, 1989, p. 212) that discouraged the formal education of women and of specific racial groups. Their racism has been documented in other publications, and anyone who reads some of their work today would be horrified by some of their more blatant positions.

However, a form of racial and cultural myopia appears in more subtle, and, therefore, perhaps more insidious, forms in the materials proposed and created by some other pioneers. If a continuum of philosophical leaning were created, figures such as Arbuthnot, Leary, Gates, Gray, and Russell might occupy a place more toward the "progressive" side than would other pioneers. These are the figures who speak most articulately about the need to individualize instruction, to learn the background of the reader to teach most effectively, and to create an educational arena where children's voices are heard and valued. While one can make a strong case that the basal series and the educational materials that arose from their work were part of their attempt to meet the specific social and academic needs of children on a more direct basis, it is striking that the materials' creators still completely controlled what would be taught and how it would be taught. The pioneers retained a traditional, paternalistic, antiprogressive vision of how education works, thereby contradicting many of their own admonitions about finding ways to bring the voices of children into the curriculum.

At the same time, the pioneers' conceptions of the interests, tastes, and learning styles of their constituency were, by modern standards, astoundingly narrow. Beginning in the 1960s, basal readers began to receive justified criticism for their racial insensitivity, their narrow definition of the "typical" child, and their one-size-fits-all approach that actually *does not* individualize instruction well. This volume's chapters reveal a pattern of indifference toward—or, at the least, an ignorance of—people of color, the poor, and the culturally disenfranchised. The lack of racial and cultural diversity in Gray and Arbuthnot's Dick and Jane series is legendary, and it was not until after their publishers had received heated criticism from civil rights groups that the series began to include African American characters in 1965. These characters, however, continued to live in an Anglo-dominant suburban world, and nothing other than their skin color indicated any differences between them and the sterilized representation of their European neighbors. Authentic address of much more complex racial and social issues did not occur. (Toni Morrison uses to powerful effect interspersed parodies of passages from Dick and Jane to underscore racial tension in her novel The Bluest Eye [1970].)

In her chapter, Karla J. Möller does an excellent job of placing the work of Bernice Elizabeth Leary in a historical context that shows Leary's insensitivity to issues of race, color, gender, poverty, and special needs, particularly when compared with the work of contemporaries like Louise Rosenblatt. A very narrow, white, Eurocentric view of the world dominates Leary's work. The reader sees similar charges leveled against David Harris Russell's Ginn readers. While Russell "urged teachers to educate for understanding" (Barry, chapter 16, p. 383) by learning "how people work together in small groups, in communities, in nations and in international affairs" ("Russell says school's task," 1951), his Ginn readers, nonetheless, represented a similar homogeneity. Like the Dick and Jane authors, Russell made moves to diversify the characters in his readers. However, as Barry points out, even then many groups considered these moves insufficient. Although the books may have offered the reader a character or two with a darker skin color, they did not offer any examples of cultural diversity through character development, examples of culturally influenced behavior, or social settings that might enrich and complicate the text.

This common belief, perhaps subconscious, in a homogenized United States is one of the most disturbing descriptive features of the early reading pioneers when we look at their work as a group. Whether or not their attitudes were a product of their times, their estimation of the breadth of U.S. children's backgrounds, interests, values, and needs was severely narrow. Although apparently understanding intellectually the need to bring the children's lives into the curriculum, their *depiction* of children's lives through their readers and other materials indicates that they were not able to look beyond their vision of an idealized neighborhood in which everyone literally had the same interests. This explanation may be the only way to mediate the schism between their stated progressive philosophies and their narrow views of the educational context: If one assumes that the spectrum of talents, interests, and needs of the constituency are narrow, then one can create reading materials with narrowly prescribed boundaries without worrying that something necessary is missing.

In trying to come to terms with this perceived schism between pioneers' statements that support a Deweyan vision of progressive schooling and the actions and products arising from their work that support an opposing vision of scientific management, we ask the question, Is there a ubiquitous lag time between the intellectual embrace of innovative educational constructs and our actual ability to research them well and implement them into the classroom effectively? Is there an inevitable "window of hypocrisy" in which we can conceive, as Dewey and others did, of new ways of thinking but not yet internalize them so they actually influence practice? Our immediate sense—and we may be wrong—is that most of the early reading pioneers were sincere in calling for classroom conditions that would facilitate both individual and social constructions of meaning, embrace the social and political aspects of learning, and diversify the curriculum to account for unique talents and needs. They may have been, more than some would have cared to admit, heavily influenced by the progressive philosophy while still being unable to incorporate its ideas into the scientific examination of education into which they had been indoctrinated. Their narrow training in psychology and physiology may not have lent itself to studying, or even recognizing, an educational approach that appears on the surface to be so diametrically opposed to the norm.

It may be reasonably argued that every era is dominated by the research that is most quantifiable and gives the most discrete results. Today, for instance, NCLB initiatives limit the scope of what is deemed to be acceptable research largely to empirical studies that yield statistical results. Currently, we also see another return to research on fluency, which measures fluidity and words read per minute. Eye movement, to give the most prominent example of the pioneers' era, could, thanks to Raymond Dodge, be measured by a machine and compared to the eye movements of others in similar or different situations. Social conditions, on the other hand, are inherently difficult to quantify, and any conclusions drawn from research that involves observation of real-world events to the exclusion of imposed variables will always be called into question, rightly or not, as overly subjective. Yet this fascination with the social aspects of education seems to be held by most of the pioneers despite their so-called scientific bents. They did not incorporate these views into a consistent vision of education that included both a philosophy and rigorous research that examined the practices and materials arising from the philosophy. However, this does not negate the importance that these scientific minds could still recognize a place for the social—for the *progressive*.

On good days, our conception of who has won the alleged war between "progressivism" and the "scientific movement" may be a little more optimistic than that of Monaghan. We have been identified on occasion as scholars who hold many classically "progressive" ideals, and our work often focuses on how the progressive principles of authentic experience and social growth can be translated to practical classroom applications. Our take on what constitutes a positive direction in education and what does not has its own subjectivities. However, many will agree that several current educational methods, techniques, and strategies—readers' workshops, writers' workshops, Readers Theatre, literature circles, phonics instruction contextualized by the commensurate promotion of real reading experiences and supporting explications of reading as a meaning-making event, interdisciplinary units, and so on—have clearly arisen from Deweyan conceptions of experiential, social education. Despite mounting pressures from Reading First and NCLB mandates, the above practices make many elementary classrooms look vastly different than they did even 30 years ago. Yet the limitations revealed in the work of the early reading pioneers suggests that our work continues. Some of the tensions that still exist in the reading community are not necessary. The work of those who succeeded the early reading pioneers, and the work of those who will succeed the successors, is not nearly done.

The Biographers' Representations of the Pioneers Versus the Pioneers' Actual Research Activities and Products

Another fascinating aspect of the pioneering figures in this volume is how they are represented by their biographers. Each chapter not only tells us a great deal about the pioneer but also about the person or people telling us the story about that pioneer. In fact, there is a long history about the people who write about the pioneers in their profession, field, organization, society, culture, and so on. Some of the earliest literature we have in this genre is the Christian writings concerning saints—which are called *hagiography* (from the Greek for *holy writing*).

To a large extent, this hagiographic literature hallowed, venerated, idolized, idealized, and revered these people of the Church. Because these biographies presented over-the-top accounts of the canonized saints, the meaning of hagiography took a turn—a pejorative turn—so in the professional nomenclature of historians today a hagiographic account of a person means that the biographers lose all sense of a critical eye. As Osborn (2004) says,

> Biographers fall in love with their subjects. Because they get to know and perhaps understand a person, and maybe because they feel that they know this person better than anyone else...there's a temptation to be uncritical, or at least less critical in their analysis. (p. 15)

The point of this background about hagiography is that it is the larger story behind the pioneer stories in this book. To us, the story of hagiography is the kind of story that raises questions such as, How hagiographic are the biographies in this book? How enamored are the researchers with their subjects? Are the researchers critical when there's reason and evidence to be so?

Questions such as these remind us of how some believers in the Christian church responded to the sanitized, hallowed, hagiographic images of the saints: They challenged the accounts and deconstructed the halos. These challengers and deconstructors were called *iconoclasts* (from the Greek *image breakers*). Part of the work to be done by the biographers who wrote for this volume is to make sure that the iconoclastic questions get asked, too; the project of historians—biographers among them—is to be both an *iconodule* (a reverer and venerator of pioneer images) as well as an iconoclast.

One of the morals of the story behind the stories in this book is to be an iconoclast, as well as an iconodule, when writing and reading these chapters. That is, the authors were to break the pioneers' image as well as make it.

What Should All This Mean for Future Research About Reading and "New Pioneers"?

To learn from the early reading pioneers and then use what we have learned to promote a richer and more dynamic research agenda, we must ask both what we have been given by, and what is missing from, the work of the pioneers. As two readers who have assumed multiple roles as literacy researchers, classroom teachers, and historians during our careers, we constructed many valuable lessons from these chapters. We will leave it to the previous chapters to offer the most comprehensive account of the contributions of these figures. However, even a brief summation impresses.

A few primary themes stood out as we read the biographical chapters. First, we were struck by how the reading pioneers were at the forefront of proving the value of systematic, rigorous, detailed research. Indeed, these chapters' authors make a strong case that many of the pioneers were among the first to adopt the wide-scale use of the scientific method. They approached educational practices, learning processes, the human psyche, and human behavior as phenomena that could—and should—be observed and measured systematically, in ways that could confound previous generations of policy shaped by anecdote and opinion. Certainly our profession now knows that any research design cannot always overcome the blindness and prejudices of some of its users. (See, in just two instances within this volume, Cattell's scientific measurements that he interpreted to "prove" the superiority of white males and many of the pioneers' research that seemed to indicate the advantages of whole-word learning.) Nevertheless, the pioneers helped show the world the attributes of detailed empirical research when used to measure certain phenomena.

Second, while we point out the gaps in of some of the pioneers' research approaches and perspectives, we were also impressed by the variety of questions that they asked and answered, a variety that we suspect far surpasses the research conducted in previous decades. The sheer breadth of the work of even individual figures, such as Thorndike or Gray, is astonishing. Reading through the chapters one sees research designs arising from a variety of fields: physiology, psychology, biology, and even, in some rare cases (see Waples, chapter 16), anthropology and sociology. The pioneers used experimental and quasi-experimental designs, surveys, direct observation, and a host of other methodologies to approach their questions. Their work speaks to the necessity of eclecticism when asking a number of very different questions.

Third, in one way or another, the pioneers touched upon almost every reading concept, method, or movement that we teach or research today. An incomplete but still staggeringly long list of the themes and topics they covered gives a sense of their importance to modern reading research and practice:

Adult reading

Background knowledge and prior experience

Biological and cognitive components of learning

Child development

Communication studies

Comprehension

Connection between oral language and learning to read

Constructions of meaning

Content area texts and reading

Correlations between physical and mental growth

Cueing systems

Curriculum development

Curriculum tracking

Definitions of reading

Development of classroom materials

Differences between higher and lower mental processes

Differences between reading disabilities and intelligence quotient

Educational leadership

Eye movements

Fluency

Health issues related to reading

Human variability

Individual differences

Influence of movement

Intelligence

Intelligence testing

Library science

Linguistics

Motivation

"Opportunistic" versus "systematic" reading

Phonics analysis

Prediction

Psychology of mental deficiency

Racial differences

Readers' conceptions of textual meaning

Readers' perception of time

Reading assessments

Reading environments

Reading habits and practices

Reading readiness

Sight vocabulary

Silent versus oral reading

Spelling

Standardized tests

Teacher effectiveness

Textual features

Transfer of training

Visual fatigue

Vocabulary

Word analysis

Word meaning

Word perceptions

Writing vocabulary

This list also clearly has profound implications for the teacher. Looking at the pedagogical initiatives that arose from the pioneers' work, we find that only the whole-word method of teaching reading seems to have dropped by the wayside as a legitimate approach. The rest of the initiatives still have a strong hold, especially those at the center of some of our greatest debates. Explicit phonics instruction, literature-rich classroom environments, formal professional development, anthology-based teaching, and constructivist approaches all have roots in the research of the pioneers. They have created our legacy and we, as historians, need to look much more carefully at their work, in the ways that the authors of these chapters have, to gain a clearer understanding of the temporal landscape within which we operate.

At the same time, those involved in the field of reading need to examine the areas that the pioneers' work did not touch, which perhaps can only be revealed by us because of our existence in another place and time. We engage in this examination not as criticism but as a valuable approach in which anyone in any subsequent era might engage when examining the work of predecessors. This work further develops the understanding of our profession's landscape, illuminating not only where we have been and where we are now but also into what previously uncharted territories we might venture in the future. We asked, "Where might we go to build upon the work that has come before?" The following speculative initiatives—all related—arose as we read.

Bridging Progressive Thinking and Science

We can examine the confluences between traditional notions of "progressivism" and "science." Although the early reading pioneers did not always bridge the "scientific" and "progressive" aspects of their thinking and their research, the fact that readers can recognize a dualistic mindset on these pages suggests that we may yet be able to discover relations between them. Dewey himself recognized that we regularly create artificial oppositional constructs (e.g., "progressive" versus "scientific," "phonics" versus "whole language," etc.) for the sake of finding a comfortable identity in a camp (Dewey, 1938/1963). He also argued for the elimination of such polarized thinking. However, currently there appears to be little scholarly effort toward systematically studying either the psychology behind the knee-jerk categorization of ideas into oppositional camps or the inherent relations between seemingly disparate notions. Many teachers and researchers today advocate a "balanced approach" to reading instruction (Adams & Bruck, 1995; Aihara, Au, Carroll, Nakanishi, Scheu, & Wong-Kam, 2000; Fitzgerald & Cunningham, 2002; Pressley, 2005), but until we understand more clearly the *relationships* between the elements that balance the scale, we may not be able to achieve a fully coherent, efficient, and effective educational system.

Instead of reiterating age-old arguments about approach, we might begin to ask questions such as, How close can we get to identifying all the intellectual, social, cultural, emotional, political, physiological, biological, environmental, and linguistic factors that influence the way each child learns in the classroom? What are the interrelations among these factors? How do they affect one another in any given learning situation? How might they fit into a unified theory of literacy education, instead of simply becoming a hodgepodge of disparate, eclectic approaches? These are difficult, complex questions that were not asked by the early reading pioneers. If we want to create a truly balanced approach, rather than an approach of inclusive appeasement, they are questions that we need to ask now.

Considering Alternative Research Methodologies

To do this, of course, we need a complementary set of research methodologies to approach vastly more complex questions. We should officially recognize sociological, anthropological, and action research as legitimate forms of reading research at the policy level. Politicians and public policy favor simple numbers, regardless of the actual value that those numbers have in making positive educational change. Conducting experimental research that tests the efficacy of new innovations in practice and measures the discrete physical, biological, or neurological qualities of any human endeavor is undeniably essential, but it will tell only part of the story. The fuller story also reveals what occurs in naturalistic settings outside the world of the classic experiment, depicting the extravagantly complex relations within any social event, thus allowing teachers and researchers to navigate more effectively within it. The qualitative researcher's elegant basic question, What is going on here? is hard for one to answer using only a traditional experimental design because as soon as we introduce an outside variable into a setting, the setting changes. Our ability to know what it is like when we are not there evaporates.

In short, we need both *forest* research and *trees* research: We need to look at specific reading events, strategies, and methods—and the data that result from them—but we need to do so from a variety of positions and perspectives, never ignoring our learning of the multifaceted contexts within which they occur. The early reading pioneers rarely appeared to engage in systematic, trustworthy qualitative research; their schooling did not train them to do so, and the interests of their eras did not lead them to learn how. Subsequently, their contributions, no matter how important, were necessarily incomplete.

Including Teachers' and Students' Voices in the Research

When one begins to engage the world with more socially and culturally inclusive viewpoints, the voices of those who comprise a given culture or social group become louder and more important. In fact, the way they conduct themselves—their words, actions, products, and shared relationships—creates the sum total of the ethnographer's research data. The researcher takes on a new role that is more passive than the one he or she assumes in a more traditional experimental study that involves the introduction of isolated variables into a situation to determine their specific effects. The researcher becomes the listener rather than the leader. He or she is no longer granted the power to decide which independent variable to inject into the experiment. Now the researcher must perform inductively, trying to make sense of things over which he or she has little control. For this to work, the researcher must make a radical turn of self-identification, positioning the teacher and student of reading as the givers of knowledge rather than simply as subjects.

To create this holistic conception of reading research, we must rid ourselves of a narrow idea of researcher as expert. This is a role that the early reading pioneers might have had great difficulty assuming. It is thus an area in which we can extend and complete their work. Along with this new recognition of the teacher as expert should be recognition of their grassroots contributions as fundamental agents of change in the worlds of reading and literacy. The two types of recognition would feed off each other, validating the professionalism of teaching that gets lost in the frenzied blame game that we call *accountability*. With recognition comes responsibility, and when teachers assume the responsibility of a leadership role, they become models for all their colleagues. One name that springs to mind when we think of practicing teachers who have internationally influenced literacy instruction is Nancie Atwell, whose book *In the Middle* (1987, 1998) has perhaps changed classroom literacy practice as much as the work of any single one of the reading pioneers.

Final Thoughts

The dissonances found within the chapters of this volume are often profound, and they lead the reader to wonder whether the authors, with their own contemporary takes on what is important in literacy research, have subconsciously searched for connections between their beliefs and those of their subjects. Are the seeming contradictions we find here simply a matter of laying a more liberal 21st-century academic viewpoint on a researcher's early work in such a way that it undermines the researcher's own original intentions? Perhaps this is the case to some extent. Every biography is influenced by the time within which it is written, stymied by the writer's own proscribed life and conceptions of the world from achieving a truly objective story. However, many of the depictions of the pioneers as having at least a smidgen of a progressive bent appear to be supported by the pioneers' own words.

It is also essential for the profession to articulate some of the contradictions and limitations of the early reading pioneers' work. We do not intend to diminish their significant contributions to the field. Their influences have been outlined in this volume and in other publications, and that is why it is important to approach their work from a different perspective. Although their research has largely had a positive impact on the reading field, it was also defined and limited by the era within which it was conducted. However, our goal is not only to learn from the early reading pioneers' accomplishments, building upon the substantial foundation of their work, but also to illuminate the unexplored spaces defined by the boundaries of their accomplishments. By directing our gaze into these uncharted territories, we can envision new possibilities for research and educational reform that might otherwise have remained inchoate. We intend that our meditations here invigorate the conversation about these issues.

REFERENCES

Adams, M.J., & Bruck, M. (1995). Resolving the "great debate." *American Educator, 19*(2), 7, 10–20.

Aihara, K., Au, K., Carroll, J., Nakanishi, P., Scheu, J., & Wong-Kam, J.A. (2000). Skill instruction within a balanced approach to reading. *The Reading Teacher, 53,* 496–498.

Atwell, N. (1987). *In the middle: Writing, reading, and learning with adolescents.* Portsmouth: Boynton/Cook.

Atwell, N. (1998). *In the middle: New understandings about writing, reading, and learning.* Portsmouth: Boynton/Cook.

Blue, G.F. (1976). *Biographical essay on May Hill Arbuthnot.* Unpublished manuscript, University of Akron, Ohio, Case Western Reserve University Archives.

Brown v. Board of Education., 347 U.S. 483 (1954).

Dearborn, W.F., & Inglis, A.J. (1921). *Psychological and educational tests in the public schools of Winchester, Virginia.* Charlottesville: University of Virginia.

Dewey, J. (1963). *Experience and education.* New York: Collier. (Original work published 1938)

Erickson, F. (1986). Qualitative methods in research on teaching. In M.C. Wittrock (Ed.), *Handbook of Research on Teaching* (3rd ed., pp. 119–161). New York: Macmillan.

Fitzgerald, J., & Cunningham, J.W. (2002). Balance in teaching reading: An instructional approach based on a particular epistemological outlook. *Reading and Writing Quarterly: Overcoming Learning Difficulties, 18,* 353–364.

Friedan, B. (1963). *The feminine mystique.* New York: Norton.

Gates, A.I. (1971). Arthur I. Gates: An autobiography. In R.J. Havighurst (Ed.), *Leaders in American education: The seventieth yearbook of the National Society for the Study of Education, Part II* (pp. 189–216). Chicago: University of Chicago Press.

Glenn, D. (2004). No classroom left unstudied. *The Chronicle of Higher Education, 50*(38), A12.

Gray, W.S. (1956). *The teaching of reading and writing: An international survey.* Paris: UNESCO.

Lagemann, E.C. (1989). The plural worlds of educational research. *History of Education Quarterly, 29,* 183–214.

Morrison, T. (1970). *The bluest eye.* New York: Holt, Rinehart and Winston.

No Child Left Behind Act of 2001, Pub. L. No. 107-110, 115 Stat. 1425 (2002).

Osborne, B.D. (2004). *Writing biography and autobiography.* London: A & C Black.

Pressley, M. (2005). *Reading instruction that works: The case for balanced teaching* (3rd ed.). New York: Guilford.

Russell, D.H. (1970). *The dynamics of reading.* Waltham, MA; Ginn.

Russell says school's task to build human resources. (1951, April 4). *The Ashville Citizen,* B1.

The Uses of History

By Susan E. Israel and E. Jennifer Monaghan

*W*e would like to close this book by reflecting on historical writing and its uses. Neither of us believes that history is useful only for antiquarian reasons, for nostalgic glances over our shoulders at the past. Rather, we feel that the history of where we have been provides considerable information on where we are today. Indeed, it serves, often in a cautionary manner, as an exemplar of where we might end up tomorrow.

Reporting on the lives of individuals, in biographies as this book's contributors have done, serves several purposes. The first and obvious one is that it captures the lives of those who were very important in diverse ways during their own time. But their lives are also important to our own. We can learn directly from them by inferring what we should not do as well as what we should do. Another lesson is that disagreement in an academic field is healthy. Tensions between alternate points of view can be enlightening because they require us as educators to reexamine our own underlying assumptions as we think about the next steps to take. All of us share the same goal—the improvement of reading instruction. As we look again at means to attain this goal, we would be wise to look backward for examples of past theories and practices and their consequences.

The researching and writing of history is itself a salutary, sometimes humbling, exercise. The requirement to review the historical literature, the necessity of looking for both qualitative and quantitative data, the need to

---

Shaping the Reading Field: The Impact of Early Reading Pioneers, Scientific Research, and Progressive Ideas, edited by Susan E. Israel and E. Jennifer Monaghan. © 2007 by the International Reading Association.

search for primary sources, the obligation to assess them with care, and the consequent shaping of them into narrative form are the same stringent demands made upon us by other kinds of research. Historiography is an intellectual challenge, and writing good history is not easy. Novices to biographical and other historical research, as many of our contributors were, should consider joining the International Reading Association's History of Reading Special Interest Group and take advantage of what its Web page (History of Reading Special Interest Group, 2002) has to offer.

We accept that we cannot write "unbiased" history. All of us are ourselves products of a historical process. But we can identify our own perspectives candidly and alert our readers (who themselves bring a series of preconceptions to their reading) about the viewpoint from which we come. Change for the better is not preordained: It is achieved by imagination and effort. Our new insights today on the need for equity in areas such as gender, class, and race are the product of hard-fought battles in the 1960s and 1970s over civil rights. Writing history provides not only a new perspective on the past but invites us, as Douglas Kaufman and Douglas Hartman suggest (p. 413, this volume), to imagine new futures.

This book illustrates another use of history. The pioneers, so revered in their own time, left uneven legacies. It was easier to locate their books than to unearth their lives and personalities. We encourage our readers to think about their own legacies and choose archives suitable for their papers, publications, and memorabilia. Autobiographies, along with the memories of family members, proved to be a key source for this book. Those who have worked so hard in the reading field should consider recording their personal and professional lives for posterity in essays, journals, diaries, on the Internet, and as oral histories.

We greatly appreciate the Association's decision to publish this book. We hope that it will be but the first in a series of biographies, and perhaps autobiographies, not only of the "elite" of the reading field, as Norman Stahl and James King term the pioneers (p. 427, this volume), who have shaped the field of reading, but of all who have dedicated themselves to teaching children worldwide the crucial skill of reading.

REFERENCES

History of Reading Special Interest Group. (2002). History of Literacy Web page. Available from http://www.historyliteracy.org

APPENDIX A

Hints on Gathering Biographical Data

◻ ▨ ◼

By Joseph E. Zimmer

S I COMPLETED the chapter on Walter Fenno Dearborn, I discovered some tips and tricks for doing this type of biography that might prove useful to future biographers. There are several challenges to researching people who were famous within their fields but not well known outside them. In nearly all cases, the reading pioneers were honorable people who lived quiet lives, did their work, and did it exceptionally well. Most loved their families, did not see themselves as special, and were not embroiled in controversies. Hence, the historical record on many of these people is thin. The following are some suggestions that future researchers may find useful.

Find basic biographies and autobiographies. With luck, your subject was famous enough to be listed in a compendium such as *Who's Who in American Education* (2006–2007). This and similar publications can provide you with at least the basic facts about a person's birth, education, professional work, and death. In researching Dearborn, for example, I also found a few biographical dictionaries of psychologists in which he appears, such as the *Biographical Dictionary of Psychology* (Sheehy, Chapman, & Conroy, 1997). Gathering these kinds of facts will allow you to put some parameters on your study and narrow your searches in other venues.

Shaping the Reading Field: The Impact of Early Reading Pioneers, Scientific Research, and Progressive Ideas, edited by Susan E. Israel and E. Jennifer Monaghan. © 2007 by the International Reading Association.

Finding a person's autobiography is a goldmine. Several of the contributors to this volume were able to use the autobiographies found in *A History of Psychology in Autobiography* (1931) for their research. Unfortunately, the International Reading Association has no comparable resource, with the exception of the autobiographies found in *Distinguished Educators on Reading: Contributions That Have Shaped Effective Literacy Instruction* (Padak, Rasinski, Peck, Church, Fawcett, Hendershot, et al., 2000). The History of Reading Special Interest Group, however, has published a number of autobiographies and biographies of reading experts in its newsletter, the *History of Reading News*. (These texts are available on the Web via www.historyliteracy.org/news_auto.html.) Remember to consult *Dissertations Abstracts International* as well. Other researchers may have done much of your work for you. Laura Zirbes, for instance, has two dissertations written on her.

Ask a reference librarian. Although you may know the resources in your field, there are many more biographical resources that a good reference librarian can help you with, including specialized biographical dictionaries. These resources can be found in a well-stocked university library and online.

Look for collections of papers, and consult university archives. Many professors leave their offices for retirement and shred or discard all of their papers, but some more established researchers will leave a collection of their papers to the archives of the university at which they worked. In Dearborn's case, the Harvard University library system houses all of his papers in a collection. (You should be aware that many of these collections are in closed stacks, and you will need to make special arrangements to view them.) Although, tragically, many universities do not maintain archives, many do, and these can be excellent sources of information about your subject.

In addition to the subject's own files, you might find in the archives the formal faculty file maintained by the university. The authors of the Ernest Horn chapter report that in Horn's faculty file at the University of Iowa they found many newspaper clippings, the obituary read at his funeral, and even his annual faculty evaluations. In general, university archives are usually the best place to locate pictures, newspaper clippings, and the campus activities of your subject.

Purchase the subject's writings. In researching the 20th century, some researchers find www.abebooks.com, the website of the Advanced Book Exchange, a very helpful resource—more so than www.amazon.com—for finding old textbooks and publications by the person they are researching. The texts usually cost only a few dollars to purchase.

Look for tributes. It may be profitable to look in professional journals and other publications that were released around the time of the subject's death. These sources can quite often provide tributes to the subject made by former students, colleagues, and friends. For example, the authors of the Ernest Horn chapter found a tribute to him written by his dean that appeared in *The Elementary School Journal*.

Search online. There are many online services available for genealogical research. For example, I have used www.ancestry.com fairly successfully for my research. I found census records (which can give clues about spouses and children), military records, death notices, and even pictures of gravestones on this site. The USGenWeb Project (www.usgenweb.org) and Family Search (www.familysearch.org) are two other websites that can help you do genealogical searches. Although many such services charge a fee, some also have free trials that give you enough time to get what you need for free.

Talk to other researchers. During my research for this book, I contacted some of our friends in the History of Reading Special Interest Group of the International Reading Association whom I know have done similar research before. They were very helpful in providing me with any information they had on my subject. The International Reading Association maintains an e-mail distribution list for the History of Reading at hrsig@bookmark.reading. org. Readers with historical questions frequently get good responses about the history of reading by submitting an e-mail message to this list.

Find a relative of your subject. As a professor at a private college, I realized that when we name a building or a scholarship after someone, we usually maintain contact with the family of that person. When I was researching Dearborn, I found on the Internet that there is a school in Massachusetts that is named after him. I contacted the school, and sure enough, they maintain contact with one of Dearborn's daughters. I was able to work closely with her to verify all the nonacademic statements I made about Dearborn.

Find colleagues or students of the subject. Professors have many contacts, especially within their own university communities. Former students and colleagues of your subject could provide some rich background about his or her personality and teaching style. As you go farther into history, however, it will be more difficult to locate people who worked alongside or studied under your subject.

Find a departmental historian and speak with faculty friends in the history department. At many universities, one or more faculty members have a sense of history about the department in which they work. In some cases, they even write brief departmental histories for webpages and other projects. These people can be valuable sources of information and documents for your research. It was very helpful to me, for example, to describe my study to a faculty friend in the history department at my university. He was able to give me several tips about how to use the library and online archives to my advantage in my research.

Consult the university's student newspaper or other publications. Most universities maintain collections of the student newspaper and press releases of the university. If you are lucky, these will be searchable in some way. For example, Dearborn taught at Harvard University, and the archives of the *Harvard Crimson* are online and can be searched by keyword. These texts gave me a glimpse of campus life and the work of Dearborn as a faculty member and an administrator.

Use interlibrary loan. If your university library is not complete with regard to your subject's works, you should consider visiting a larger library or using interlibrary loan to gather the professional materials you will need to complete your study.

REFERENCES

A history of psychology in autobiography (Vols. 1–8). (1931). Stanford, CA: Stanford University Press.

Padak, N.D., Rasinski, T.V., Peck, J.K, Church, B.W., Fawcett, G., Hendershot, J., et al. (Eds.). (2000). *Distinguished educators on reading: Contributions that have shaped effective literacy instruction*. Newark, DE: International Reading Association.

Sheehy, N., Chapman, A.J., & Conroy, W. (1997). *Biographical dictionary of psychology*. New York: Routledge.

Who's who in American education? (2006–2007). New Providence, NJ: Marquis.

Searching for Biographical Sources: An Archivist's Perspective

By Aviva Gray

When I agreed to assist Diane Lapp with her research for the chapter on Ruth May Strang, I imagined that this process would entail contacting relevant institutions to gain access to archival holdings, making appointments to visit and examine collections, and then selecting and reviewing materials of interest. In the case of Strang, I would soon find that this conventional approach to archival searching would yield few results because only limited primary resources are available that document her life and work. My most fruitful results instead would come from searching available bibliographic data and examining these documents for any light they could shed on her career.

In what follows, I describe some approaches to biographical research from an archival perspective, using my research on Strang as a basis for demonstrating some useful methods. Strang is an important example of a major scholar whose contributions to the field are often acknowledged, yet whose biographical details have largely been lost from the historical and documentary record. This loss may be due in part to the general attitude toward women scholars in academe at the time, and in part to her remaining unmarried, leaving no direct descendants as informants.

Shaping the Reading Field: The Impact of Early Reading Pioneers, Scientific Research, and Progressive Ideas, edited by Susan E. Israel and E. Jennifer Monaghan. © 2007 by the International Reading Association.

I began the project by conducting a basic Internet search on Strang. This search yielded only a few relevant hits, which provided limited, piece-meal biographical information, but it did give me an initial sense of the immediate resources available. It also helped me to target several significant organizations with which Strang was affiliated that had the potential to offer useful leads for future research. For example, Strang is mentioned as a founder and important contributor to early research at the American Association for Gifted Children. On another website she is acknowledged for her influence on the life and career of the late Sydney Rauch, a senior Professor of Reading and Education at Hofstra University in New York. A Google search also revealed that the International Reading Association awarded Strang the William S. Gray Citation of Merit for 1962 and that the National Association for Women in Education confers a Ruth Strang Research Award each year. It seemed reasonable that future inquiries by the chapter authors could perhaps yield additional information about the details about Strang's career or character.

Basic online searching also retrieved a host of bibliographic citations that yielded more detailed listings of Strang's scholarly works and even, at times, access to the full text of certain materials. The online index of *Teachers College Record* at www.tcrecord.org also provided a list of 27 of Strang's contributions to the publication between 1924 and 1955. (The *Teachers College Record* index includes abstracts of articles as well as online access through a paid subscription.) Another source for information retrieved through this initial search was the Education Resources Information Center (ERIC) at www.eric.ed.gov, a database sponsored by the U.S. Department of Education that lists citations to education literature going back to 1966, offering full-text access to articles when the material is available. In the ERIC database I found references to a tribute to Strang, presented by her students at the University of Arizona, titled "Ruth Strang's Diagnostic Legacy." A further search of the ERIC database for Strang as both an author and a keyword retrieved additional hits, including some of her later monographs. Because the ERIC database only covers works published after 1965, however, the majority of Strang's publications are too early to be included.

This situation brings up the important point that when using bibliographic databases it is always essential to check first that the scope of information indexed corresponds with the date limitations of your research because even many long-running publications only have data available online for their later volumes. Also, searching for the name of your subject using combinations of the full name and last name, as well as by author, title, and keyword, may yield better results than a simple subject search. Using Boolean search options such as "and," "or," and "and not," when available, can help narrow searches that retrieve a large number of hits.

When I was starting my research, I also performed Internet searches on topics and keywords related to the subject of my research to familiarize myself with the wider history of the field and any broader issues that might be significant when examining collections and requesting materials in the archives. In Strang's case these included searches on the history of gifted and talented education, the history of education, and studies of reading. My introductory research also included a search of the ProQuest Historical Newspapers database (see www.proquest.com), which provided a number of newspaper clippings on Strang, and most significantly, two obituaries that revealed important information about her personal and professional life. The ProQuest Historical Newspapers database indexes major newspapers from across the United States since their establishment, providing articles and obituaries in PDF format beginning in the mid-19th century. Later newspapers can also be searched using a separate ProQuest database that indexes a wider selection of more recent periodicals.

After conducting this preliminary Internet and database research, I felt prepared to begin examining local area collections individually. I started by focusing on the archival holdings of institutions with which Strang had been closely affiliated, including Teachers College and Columbia University. At Teachers College, I was put in contact with Gary Natriello, a professor in the Sociology and Education program, and Director of the Gottesman Libraries. I had hoped that Strang's personal papers had been maintained by the college, but he informed me that there was no record of such a collection having ever been deposited in the library. Although this discovery was disappointing, considering Strang's long and active tenure at the school as a professor and her attendance at the college as a student, I hoped that it would be possible to find information by searching subject or chronological files and any accessible administrative records. Searching more general records in the Teachers College's archives, even in the absence of Strang's personal papers, might still have offered better information about what classes Strang taught and when, and what school groups or extracurricular activities she might have participated in, and it might possibly have provided school photographs from her yearbook portrait or graduation, or correspondence with other significant members of the school community.

A major complication in accessing information at Teachers College was that the archives had been closed to the public for renovation since 2002. So before I contacted Teachers College a second time, I expanded my search of outside sources to see what might be found in other New York collections. I visited the Rare Books and Manuscripts Library at Columbia University, which holds many of the early records of Teachers College, particularly those of the Sociology and Psychology departments. However, neither this search nor a review of the holdings at other institutions such as The New York Public Library yielded any information.

I then began a more detailed online search of bibliographic and archival databases. One resource I had often found useful was ArchivesUSA, at http://archives.chadwyck.com, a subscription directory of manuscripts repositories in the United States that indexes over 154,000 collections containing primary-source material. Most academic institutions and many public libraries make these resources, which can be purchased only through subscription, available to users. The most comprehensive listing of online archival resources can be found on the Ready, 'Net, Go! Internet Archival Resources site maintained by Tulane University (2006).

In my nationwide search of archival collections via electronic databases I found no relevant information on Strang. One of the difficulties of such archival searching is that for the majority of repositories only a small percentage of any collection is represented online. An archival finding aid, or guide to a collection, contains an inventory and summary of the records held by a repository on a particular subject, usually with some additional background information, but even when the finding aid is available online, it may not list files individually. In addition, not every name appearing within a set of records is likely to be indexed for most collections. So although this type of broad online searching was a necessary step in the process of seeking information on Strang, it may not have uncovered all existing data. The best approach for finding primary resources on subjects like Strang is still to persistently contact archivists, librarians, and other appropriate individuals at the institutions with which the subject was associated.

Having had no luck finding additional sources around New York, I contacted Teachers College again. This time I corresponded with Jennifer Govan, Assistant Director of Collection and Curriculum Support Services at the Gottesman Libraries. Jennifer sent me a list of archival collections at Teachers College and offered to help me gain access to them, as major reorganization of collections within the libraries eliminated the possibility of casual browsing and subject searching. None of the resources available at Teachers College seemed to provide any significant information about Strang's life, other than what was held in her published works. Jennifer kindly offered me access to Strang's publications and also sent some biographical information about Strang drawn from online sources, including the Biography Resource Center at www.gale.com/BiographyRC and American National Biography Online at www.anb.org/biooftheday.html that proved very useful.

Beyond examining Strang's major monographic publications, I began a search for other scholarly contributions by or about my subject. I was particularly interested in looking at the reception of Strang's work at the time of its publication. The best way to find this information was by searching contemporary review articles published in peer-reviewed journals. Particularly in the sciences, many publishers do not index early volumes of their periodicals electronically, so it can be difficult to find this type of information online. However, bound indexes issued at regular intervals can be accessed for this type of information. In our research, it was necessary to search these bound volumes when reviewing journals from the field of education. One excellent online resource for bibliographic searching is the WilsonWeb database (see www.hwwilson.com). Using this resource, which allows a single search to be conducted across multiple databases within relevant fields, I discovered 258 relevant citations. Because WilsonWeb offers abstracts for each article, and full-text links when available, I was able to make a preliminary selection of 60 articles that appeared to be valuable, trying to choose those that would reflect the broad scope of Strang's research and accomplishments. I then began to retrieve these articles, either from the Columbia University libraries or through interlibrary loan (ILL) requests. Because many libraries will be found by researchers that do not carry early or obscure publications, ILL will be a key part of any research project.

During the final stage of the project I was asked to assist with locating a portrait of Strang. Her obituary published in *The New York Times* was accompanied by an excellent portrait that we hoped to use, taken by Bradford Bachrach. (Famous women photographed by Bachrach include the Duchess of Windsor and Indira Gandhi, and the Bachrach Studios were noted for taking portraits of every U.S. President since Lincoln.) Yet because the policy of the studios was to keep photo negatives for only 10 years, and Strang had no easily contactable family, it seemed unlikely that a copy of the image would be found through relatives. I checked with the photo archives of *The New York Times*, but they only maintain select images for sale. The rest of its newspapers are simply scanned and available for purchase as PDF files through ProQuest. These images are not suitable for reproduction because they are simply low-quality scans of the entire newspaper page upon which the image appears. I contacted Jennifer Govan of the Alumni Office and also various other administrative offices at Teachers College to inquire about the possibility of finding yearbook photos of Strang, but none were available. Paul Schlotthauer, Reference Librarian and Archivist at Pratt Institute in New York did find a small image of Strang from her 1916 yearbook, but otherwise I seemed to have reached a dead end. Fortunately, Diane Lapp was able to find a portrait at the University of Arizona.

My work on the Strang chapter entailed searching for primary sources, or original records and photographic materials related to her life and work; reviewing secondary resources such as subject encyclopedias, including *American Women: The Official Who's Who Among the Women of the Nation* (Howes, 1939); and a careful search of what are know as tertiary resources, or indexes and abstracts that serve to locate secondary and primary sources.

The various steps to archival searching detailed here are only a few suggested methods for how to approach a research project. They are selected not only to lay out a basic process and technique but also to demonstrate that when the quest for biographical data presents challenges and gaps in information, it can encourage us as researchers to ask new questions and take new approaches to our research. Although a clear path to finding information is ideal, sometimes stumbling blocks may force us to explore new avenues and examine a topic in new and significant ways.

REFERENCES

Howes, D. (1939). *American women: The official who's who among the women of the nation*. Los Angeles: American Publications.

Tulane University (2006). *Ready, 'Net, Go!* Retrieved October 31, 2005, from http://www.tulane.edu/~lmiller/ArchivesResources.html

Oral History Projects for the Literacy Profession

By Norman A. Stahl and James R. King

Foundations for Oral History

THE BIOGRAPHIES IN this text have allowed you the opportunity to learn about early pioneers in the reading field. Portrayed through narratives that were built upon both primary and secondary sources, the biographies focus on each individual's contributions to, and place them within, the historical and professional moment. The methodologies used for these biographies within the literacy field are well described in guides authored by Gilstad (1981), Monaghan and Hartman (2000), and Stahl and Hartman (2004).

Literacy pioneers, whether they are classified as members of the elite or the nonelite, now belong to the ages. But what of those individuals who are now the senior leaders of the profession, or those individuals who are experienced practitioners of the current moment? As our profession continues moving forward, the scholars and teachers of the present professional moment will become the field's historical figures to future generations.

This book has presented the opportunity to read about the contributions of the field's elite. The members of the elite will always leave a legacy of historical traces such as texts, articles, curricular materials, and even professional progeny that will provide them with a certain professional immortality. However, for those who might be seen as the nonelite, it is unlikely that

Shaping the Reading Field: The Impact of Early Reading Pioneers, Scientific Research, and Progressive Ideas, edited by Susan E. Israel and E. Jennifer Monaghan. © 2007 by the International Reading Association.

they will leave such traces for the historical record. Further, those artifacts that do exist (e.g., grade books, diaries, and instructional planners) will likely be fugitive documents that will not be preserved for future generations.

Yet for individuals, elite or nonelite, there is a historical method that captures the knowledge, memories, and wisdom of our future pioneers for perpetuity. Such a method is the oral history or life history interview as preserved through the oral history project. Although it is not possible to provide an in-depth guide to the oral history method in the limited confines of this appendix, we can reiterate our recommendations from across the past decade in which we have on numerous occasions (e.g., Stahl & King, 2000; Stahl, King, Dillon, & Walker, 1994) prompted the profession to preserve its historical roots through oral history interviews. We can also steer colleagues toward appropriate guides for undertaking oral history projects.

The oral history interview is a focused form of interview that draws upon the memories and expertise of the members of a particular community or generation. For instance, in the literacy profession it would be particularly timely to focus an oral history project on the generation of professionals who entered the field either to teach the baby boomers to read or to train the teachers who would be in that role. Many of those who have been retired for up to two decades still have vivid memories, insider information, and community perspectives about the following:

1. Instructional methods (e.g., the language experience approach, Initial Teaching Alphabet, linguistic models, phonics, and whole-word approaches);

2. Curricular materials (e.g., Scott Foresman's Dick and Jane readers, Science Resource Associates reading kits, controlled readers, experience charts, and Bank Street Readers); and

3. Policies and programs (e.g., the Elementary and Secondary Education Act of 1965, the Emergency School Assistance Act, the Right to Read commitment, and the Bilingual Education Act) that influenced the profession across the latter half of the 20th century.

This same cadre of reading professionals was also instrumental in initiating many of the field's current professional associations.

While the previous suggestions focus on the profession and on era-oriented theory, research, and best practices, literacy oral histories can also focus on the role of literacy within individuals' lives and their memories of learning to read. Brandt's *Literacy in American Lives* (2001) with its focus on individuals in Wisconsin is a particularly good example of this avenue for literacy research.

An Approach to Conducting Oral Histories

Before conducting an oral history interview, you should address the legal and ethical issues associated with it and determine whether you need to ask your Institutional Review Board (IRB) for clearance. Generally speaking, oral history interviews do not fall within the regulatory definition of research in the Department of Health and Human Services Regulations for the Protection of Human Subjects (45 CFR 46.102-d), so oral history interviews are excluded from an IRB review without exemption. Yet there is a caveat: If the project is "a systematic investigation, including research development, testing and evaluation, designed to develop or contribute to generalizable knowledge" (Ritchie & Shopes, n.d.), then you should submit the project for IRB review. Err on the side of conservatism because internal IRB policies and procedures for oral history interviews differ from institution to institution, regardless of nationally accepted policies. (For further explication of this issue, refer to the Oral History Association's update on the exclusion of oral history from IRB review at http://omega.dickinson.edu/organizations/oha.)

Procedures and sample consent forms for interviews and later archival activities can be found in Baum (1987), Sommer and Quinlan (2002), and Yow (1994). Whether you request IRB clearance or not, professional ethics suggest that you should get written permission from the interviewee to conduct the interview and use the results.

To recapture an individual's recollections and expertise about an event or era, the oral history process moves through a succession of stages. The first stage includes the conceptualization of the topic and purpose of the project, followed by the development of the interviewer's working knowledge of the times, the locale, and those events that are central to the topic(s) under review. The focus statement underlying the project (whether explicitly stated or implicitly understood) gives readers information as to whether the interview subject was a member of society's (or the profession's) elite or nonelite status groups. The selecting, screening, and contacting of the informant for each interview will include explaining the nature of the project to the interviewee and scheduling the interview session. This overall readiness stage will include the development of a preliminary interview guide with well-crafted, open-ended questions based on background research undertaken earlier.

The second stage of the process focuses on the interview. As an interviewer, you should be both directive, through the use of an interview guide, yet also flexible enough to capture serendipitous discoveries. Sample questions for generic interviews can be found in Howarth (1998), for literacy interviews of the general populace in Brandt (2001), and for the literacy profession in Stahl and King (2000). Baum (1987) provides a particularly cogent set of guidelines for the neophyte on the steps of conducting an interview. More theoretical and scholarly discussions can be found in texts by McMahan and Rogers (1994) and Yow (1994). Finally, technology is an intrinsic part of the interview process. It is imperative that an interviewer be a master of the technology used to capture the interview. Discussions on the role of technology and the types of technology available for the oral history interview can be found in both Howarth (1998) and Sommer and Quinlan (2002).

The post-interview process, or third stage, includes an initial review of the tapes and any field notes. At this time you should copy the tape for safekeeping. Next, undertake a verbatim transcription of the tape. Give a copy of the transcription to the interviewee so he or she can review it for accuracy and personal comfort with the content.

Archival activities as well as practices for the interpretation of data are described in Thompson (2000). You or your students may undertake to publish your findings in professional journals (e.g., Dillon, 1985; King, 1991) or books (e.g., Brandt, 2001; Clegg, 1997). Consider approaching local or state historical societies, professional organizations, or university libraries for long-term archival services. More recent innovations in media technology may provide online storage of audio, visual, and textual (transcript) data.

Classroom Oral History Projects

Oral history projects in classrooms from elementary schools through graduate programs in literacy education are powerful teaching contexts. The methodology has been a proven tool for integrating the language arts with the content fields and building upon what are now called *funds of knowledge*. The most famous of these curricular oral histories was Wigginton's seminal Foxfire Project (see Wigginton, 1986, for a discussion of the project). Educators may consult any of several texts designed to support classroom oral history projects at the elementary or secondary school levels (Brown, 2000; Sitton, Mehaffy, & Davis, 1983), the undergraduate level for potential use with both developmental reading programs and literacy methods courses (Hoopes, 1979), and the graduate level for master's projects and doctoral dissertations (Butchart, 1986; King, 1991; McCulloch & Richardson, 2000). Still, experience shows that for all the positive aspects and outcomes for such projects, there is a set of situational, interpretive, and representational cautions associated with the pedagogical praxis and methodological grounding of oral history (King & Stahl, 1991) that educators should consider carefully in planning a project.

Professional Organizations

Professional organizations in the field of oral history can provide both valuable resources and opportunities for networking with fellow oral historians. In North America, consider joining either the Oral History Association (OHA; http://omega.dickinson.edu/organizations/oha/about.html) or the Canadian Oral History Association (COHA; http://oral-history.ncf.ca). You will probably want to refer regularly to either the *Oral History Review* (the official journal of the OHA) or to *Forum* (the publication of the COHA).

Conclusion

In closing, we can rejoice over the publication of this text that shares with the profession the lives and contributions of these early reading pioneers. Yet we fully understand that our previous call for the preservation of roots of the profession through oral history projects (Stahl, et al., 1994), whether focused on elite or nonelite members, has yet to be answered in a serious and meaningful manner. Oral history projects (Stahl & King, 2000) offer a viable avenue down which local and state reading councils, graduate degree programs, special interest groups, and national organizations can begin toward the preservation of the heritage that is our profession's legacy.

REFERENCES
Baum, W.K. (1987). *Oral history for the local historical society*. Lanham, MD: AltaMira.
Brandt, D. (2001). *Literacy in American lives*. New York: Cambridge University Press.

Brown, C.S. (2000). *Like it was—A complete guide to writing oral history*. New York: Teachers and Writers Collaborative.

Butchart, R.E. (1986). *Local schools: Exploring their history*. Lanham, MD: AltaMira.

Clegg, L.B. (1997). *The empty schoolhouse*. College Station: Texas A&M University Press.

Dillon, D. (1985). Ira E. Aaron: A qualitative case study of a career history. *Georgia Journal of Reading, 11*(1), 18–25.

Elementary and Secondary Education Act of 1965, 20 U.S.C. 6301 *et seq.*

Elementary and Secondary Education Amendments of 1967, P.L. 90-247, 81 Stat. 783, Title VII—Bilingual Education Programs.

Gilstad, J.R. (1981). Methodology of historical research of reading instruction: Principles and criteria. *Reading World, 20*, 185–196.

Hoopes, J. (1979). *Oral history: An introduction for students*. Chapel Hill: University of North Carolina Press.

Howarth, K. (1998). *Oral history: A handbook*. Bridgend, England: Sutton.

King, J.R. (1991). Collaborative life history narratives: Heroes in reading teachers' tales. *Qualitative Studies in Education, 4*, 45–60.

King, J.R., & Stahl, N.A. (1991). Oral history as a critical pedagogy: Some cautionary issues. In B.L. Hayes & K. Camperell (Eds.), *Eleventh yearbook of the American Reading Forum* (pp. 219–226). Logan, UT: American Reading Forum. (ERIC Document Reproduction Service No. ED333492)

McCulloch, G., & Richardson, W. (2000). *Historical research in educational settings*. Buckingham, England: Open University Press.

McMahan, E.M., & Rogers, K.L. (1994). *Interactive oral history interviewing*. Hillsdale, NJ: Erlbaum.

Monaghan, E.J., & Hartman, D.K. (2000). Undertaking historical research in literacy. In M. Kamil, P. Mosenthal, P.D. Pearson, & R. Barr (Eds.), *Handbook of reading research* (Vol. 3, pp. 109–121). Mahwah, NJ: Erlbaum.

Report of Forum 7. (1970). The Right to Read commitment, White House Conference of Children. Washington, DC: Superintendent of Documents, U.S. Government Printing Office.

Ritchie, D.A., & Shopes, L. (n.d.). *Oral history excluded from IRB review*. Retrieved October 11, 2005, from http://www.dickinson.edu/oha/org_irb.html

Sitton, T., Mehaffy, G.L., & Davis, O.L., Jr. (1983). *Oral history: A guide for teachers (and others)*. Austin: University of Texas Press.

Sommer, B.W., & Quinlan, M.K. (2002). *The oral history manual*. Walnut Creek, CA: AltaMira.

Stahl, N.A., & Hartman, D.K. (2004). Doing historical research on literacy. In N.K. Duke & M.H. Mallette (Eds.), *Literacy research methodologies* (pp. 170–196). New York: Guilford.

Stahl, N.A., & King, J.R. (2000). Preserving the heritage of a profession through California Reading Association oral history projects. *The California Reader, 34*(1), 14–19.

Stahl, N.A., King, J.R., Dillon, D., & Walker, J.R. (1994). The roots of reading: Preserving the heritage of a profession through oral history projects. In E.G. Sturtevant & W.M. Linek (Eds.), *Pathways for literacy: Learners teach and teachers learn* (16th yearbook of the College Reading Association; pp. 15–24). Commerce, TX: College Reading Association.

Thompson, P.R. (2000). *The voice of the past: Oral history*. New York: Oxford University Press.

Wigginton, E. (1986). *Sometimes a shining moment: The Foxfire experience*. New York: Anchor Press/Doubleday.

Yow, V.R. (1994). *Recording oral history: A practical guide for social scientists*. Thousand Oaks, CA: Sage.

APPENDIX D

Matrix of Early Reading Pioneers

By Susan E. Israel and E. Jennifer Monaghan

Matrix of Early Reading Pioneers

Early Reading Pioneer	Year and Institution of Bachelor's Degree Earned	Year and Institution of Doctoral Degree Earned	Influenced By	Studied Under	Year and Institution of Most Important Faculty Position(s)	Colleagues	Students	First Significant Reading-Related Publication
Chapter 1: **James McKeen Cattell** (1860–1944) b. Easton, Pennsylvania, USA	1880, Lafayette College	1886, University of Leipzig, Germany	Sir Francis Galton, Rudolf Hermann Lotze	Wilhelm Wundt	1891–1917, Columbia University	Livingston Farrand, Edward Lee Thorndike, Roberts Sessions Woodworth	Walter Fenno Dearborn, Arthur Irving Gates, Edward Lee Thorndike, John B. Watson, Robert Sessions Woodworth	"The Time it Takes to See and Name Objects," in *Mind*, 1886
Chapter 2: **Robert Sessions Woodworth** (1869–1962) b. Belchertown, Massachusetts, USA	1891, Amherst College	1899, Columbia University	Franz Boas, G. Stanley Hall	James McKeen Cattell, Charles Garman, William James	1903–1945, Columbia University	James McKeen Cattell, Arthur Irving Gates, Edward Lee Thorndike	Albert T. Poffenberger	*Psychology: A Study of Mental Life*, 1921

(continued)

Matrix of Early Reading Pioneers

Early Reading Pioneer	Year and Institution of Bachelor's Degree Earned	Year and Institution of Doctoral Degree Earned	Influenced By	Studied Under	Year and Institution of Most Important Faculty Position(s)	Colleagues	Students	First Significant Reading-Related Publication
Chapter 3: Raymond Dodge (1871–1942) b. Woburn, Massachusetts, USA	1893, Williams College	1896, University of Halle, Germany	Charles Darwin	Benno Erdmann	1898–1924, Wesleyan University; 1924–1936, Yale University		T.S. Cline	"The Reaction Time of the Eye," in *Psychological Review*, 1899
Chapter 4: Charles Hubbard Judd (1873–1946) b. Bareilly, India	1894, Wesleyan University	1896, University of Leipzig, Germany	Rev. George Murray Colville	Andrew Campbell Armstrong, Wilhelm Wundt	1909–1938, University of Chicago	Guy Buswell, William Scott Gray	May Hill Arbuthnot, William Scott Gray, Ralph W. Tyler	*Reading: Its Nature and Development*, 1918

(continued)

Matrix of Early Reading Pioneers

Early Reading Pioneer	Year and Institution of Bachelor's Degree Earned	Year and Institution of Doctoral Degree Earned	Influenced By	Studied Under	Year and Institution of Most Important Faculty Position(s)	Colleagues	Students	First Significant Reading-Related Publication
Chapter 5: Edward Lee Thorndike (1874–1949) b. Williamsburg, Massachusetts, USA	1895, Wesleyan University 1896, Harvard University	1898, Columbia University		Franz Boas, James McKeen Cattell, William James	1899–1940, Columbia University	James McKeen Cattell, John Dewey, Arthur Irving Gates, Leta S. Hollingworth, Robert Sessions Woodworth	Arthur Irving Gates, William Scott Gray, Ernest Horn, Ruth May Strang, Laura Zirbes	"Reading as Reasoning," in *Journal of Educational Psychology*, 1917
Chapter 6: Walter Fenno Dearborn (1878–1955) b. Marblehead, Massachusetts, USA	1900, Wesleyan University	1905, Columbia University	Edward Lee Thorndike, Wilhelm Wundt	James McKeen Cattell	1912–1947, Harvard University	Leonard Carmichael	Leonard Carmichael	*The Psychology of Reading: An Experimental Study of the Reading Process and Eye-Movements*, 1906

(continued)

Matrix of Early Reading Pioneers

Early Reading Pioneer	Year and Institution of Bachelor's Degree Earned	Year and Institution of Doctoral Degree Earned	Influenced By	Studied Under	Year and Institution of Most Important Faculty Position(s)	Colleagues	Students	First Significant Reading-Related Publication
Chapter 7: **Edmund Burke Huey** (1870–1913) b. Curllsville, Pennsylvania, USA	1895, Lafayette College	1899, Clark University	Walter Fenno Dearborn, John Dewey, Raymond Dodge, Adolf Meyer, Wilhelm Wundt	Benno Erdmann, G. Stanley Hall, Pierre Janet, Emile Javal, E.C. Sanford	1904–1908, University of Western Pennsylvania			"On the Psychology and Physiology of Reading," in The American Journal of Psychology, 1900, 1901
Chapter 8: **Laura Zirbes** (1884–1967) b. Buffalo, New York, USA	1925, Teachers College, Columbia University	1928, Teachers College, Columbia University	Otis Caldwell, Arnold Gesell, William Scott Gray, G. Stanley Hall	John Dewey, William Heard Kilpatrick, Edward Lee Thorndike	1928–1954, The Ohio State University		Leland Jacobs	*Comparative Studies of Current Practice in Reading*, 1928

(continued)

Matrix of Early Reading Pioneers

Early Reading Pioneer	Year and Institution of Bachelor's Degree Earned	Year and Institution of Doctoral Degree Earned	Influenced By	Studied Under	Year and Institution of Most Important Faculty Position(s)	Colleagues	Students	First Significant Reading-Related Publication
Chapter 9: **May Hill Arbuthnot** **(1884–1969)** b. Mason City, Iowa, USA	1922, University of Chicago	1969, Honorary Doctorate, University of Chicago	Felix Adler, Abraham Maslow, Alice Temple Herbartianism	John Dewey, Arthur Irving Gates, Patty S. Hill, Leta S. Hollingworth, Charles Hubbard Judd, William Heard Kilpatrick	1927–1950, Western Reserve University (now Case Western University)			(As May Hill), The Child's Treasury, 1924
Chapter 10: **Bernice Elizabeth Leary** **(1890–1973)** b. Ionia, Iowa, USA	1930, University of Chicago	1933, University of Chicago		William Scott Gray	1942–1955, Director of Curriculum, Madison (Wisconsin) Public Schools			(With Gray as senior author), What Makes a Book Readable, 1935

(continued)

Matrix of Early Reading Pioneers

Early Reading Pioneer	Year and Institution of Bachelor's Degree Earned	Year and Institution of Doctoral Degree Earned	Influenced By	Studied Under	Year and Institution of Most Important Faculty Position(s)	Colleagues	Students	First Significant Reading-Related Publication
Chapter 11: Douglas Waples (1893–1978) b. Philadelphia, Pennsylvania, USA	1914, Haverford College	1920, University of Pennsylvania	Werrett W. Charters, John Dewey, Ralph W. Tyler		1925–1958, University of Chicago	Kenneth Adler, William Scott Gray	Bernard Berelson	*What People Want to Read About*, 1931 (With Tyler as junior author)
Chapter 12: Ernest Horn (1882–1967) b. Mercer County, Missouri, USA	1908, University of Missouri	1914, Columbia University		Edward Lee Thorndike	1915–1952, State University of Iowa (now the University of Iowa)	John H. Haefner, Lloyd L. Smith, Herbert F. Spitzner	Paul G. McKee, Gerald Yoakam	*A Basic Writing Vocabulary: 10,000 Words Most Commonly Used in Writing*, 1926

(continued)

Matrix of Early Reading Pioneers

Early Reading Pioneer	Year and Institution of Bachelor's Degree Earned	Year and Institution of Doctoral Degree Earned	Influenced By	Studied Under	Year and Institution of Most Important Faculty Position(s)	Colleagues	Students	First Significant Reading-Related Publication
Chapter 13: William Scott Gray (1885–1960) b. Coatsburg, Illinois, USA	1913, University of Chicago	1916, University of Chicago		Charles Hubbard Judd, Edward Lee Thorndike	1914–1950, University of Chicago	Charles Hubbard Judd, Douglas Waples	Helen Huus, Bernice Elizabeth Leary	Oral Reading Paragraphs, 1915
Chapter 14: Arthur Irving Gates (1890–1972) b. Red Wing, Minnesota, USA	1914, University of California, Berkeley	1917, Columbia University	Alfred Binet, William James, Charles Hubbard Judd, Lewis Terman, Wilhelm Wundt	James McKeen Cattell, Edward Lee Thorndike, Robert Sessions Woodworth	1917–1956, Teachers College, Columbia University	James McKeen Cattell, John Dewey, Joann Nurss, Edward Lee Thorndike	Guy L. Bond, Walter H. MacGinitie, Margaret Mead, David Harris Russell, Ruth May Strang	The Psychology of Reading and Spelling, with Special Reference to Disability, 1922

(continued)

Matrix of Early Reading Pioneers

Early Reading Pioneer	Year and Institution of Bachelor's Degree Earned	Year and Institution of Doctoral Degree Earned	Influenced By	Studied Under	Year and Institution of Most Important Faculty Position(s)	Colleagues	Students	First Significant Reading-Related Publication
Chapter 15: Ruth May Strang (1895–1971) b. Chatham, New Jersey, USA	1922, Teachers College, Columbia University	1926, Columbia University	Helen Thompson, Pauline Williamson	Arthur Irving Gates, Mary Swartz Rose, Edward Lee Thorndike	1929–1960, Teachers College, Columbia University	John Dewey, Leta S. Hollingworth, James Russell, Sarah Sturtevant, Edward Lee Thorndike, Francis Wilson	Virginia Ballard, Marian Brown, Rachel Burkholder, Eldone E. Ekwall, Pamela R. Hoagland, Sidney J. Rauch	*Problems in the Improvement of Reading in High School and College,* 1938
Chapter 16: David Harris Russell (1906–1965) b. Ottawa, Ontario, Canada	1931, University of Saskatchewan	1937, Columbia University	Guy Bond, Margaret Lima, Frank Quance, Elizabeth Russell, Lewis Terman	Arthur Irving Gates, Gertrude Hildreth, Leta S. Hollingworth, Ruth May Strang, Edward Lee Thorndike	1942–1965, University of California at Berkeley	Robert Ruddell	Isabel Lewis	*Characteristics of Good and Poor Spellers: A Diagnostic Study,* 1937

AUTHOR INDEX

GEE, J.P., 186
GIBSON, E.J., 51, 53, 55
GILBERT, C.B., 208
GILSTAD, J.R., 308, 312, 427
GINN, 386
GLENN, D., 113, 401
GOODMAN, K., 165
GOODMAN, K.S., 92, 114, 167, 192, 274
GOODMAN, Y.M., 92, 114, 274
GRAHAM, C.H., 65–69, 72–73
GRAY, W.S., 16, 18–19, 21, 106, 188, 202, 205, 221, 224, 231–234, 241, 263, 270, 311–318, 321–323, 399
GRAY, W.S. III, 309–312, 322–323
GRAY, W.S., TO M. HILL, 202
GRIFFIN, P., 166
GRUBER, C., 44
GUTHRIE, J., 272
GUTHRIE, J.T., 272
GUTIERREZ, K.D., 115

H

HAEFNER, J.H., 287, 303
HAERTEL, G.D., 135
HANNA, P.R., 299
HARCOURT ASSESSMENT, INC., 67
HARRIS, A.J., 92–93, 147
HARRIS, B., 235
HARRIS, C.W., 319
HARRIS, T.L., xxii
HARRISON, C., 335
HARRISON, E., 62, 68–69, 71–73
HARRISON, M.L., 17, 336
HARSTE, J.C., 171
HARTMAN, D.K., xxii, 4, 192, 427
HAVINGHURST, R.J., 358
HAY, E., 213
HENDERSHOT, J., 418
HENDERSON, E.H., 300, 303
HENMON, V.A., 51
HENRY, N.B., 3, 22–25
HERBER, H.L., 360
HERR, K., 113
HICKMAN, P., 299
HIEBERT, E.H., 167
HILDRETH, G.H., 380
HILGARD, E.R., 167
HILL, M., 202. See also Arbuthnot, M.H.
HILL, M., TO W.S. GRAY, 202–203
HISTORY OF READING SPECIAL INTEREST GROUP, 416
HISTORY OF UW–SUPERIOR, 201
HOAGLAND, P.R., 358, 362–363
HODGES, R.E., xxii, 286, 299
HOFFMAN, J.V., 301
HOLLINGSWORTH, S., 272
HOOPES, J., 431

HORN, D., 283–284
HORN, E., 285, 287–299, 301–302
HORN, E., TO DR. W.A. JESSUP, 285, 288
HORN, E., TO E.T. PETERSON, 288, 295, 302
HORN, E., TO PROFESSOR C.W. HUNNICUTT, 283, 290
HORN, M.D., 291
HORN, MRS. THOMAS D., 283–284, 290
HOWARTH, K., 430
HOWES, D., 426
HUBER, M.B., 332, 339–340
HUEY, E.B., 1, 6, 51, 55, 75, 87–90, 94, 159–171
HUSE, H.R., 250
HUUS, H., 308–309, 315, 320–321, 323

I

INDIANA UNIVERSITY, 12
INDRISANO, L., 367
INGLIS, A.J., 146, 399
INTERNATIONAL READING ASSOCIATION, 206, 368
INVERNIZZI, M., 300

J

JAEGER, M., 308
JAKOBSON, R.O., 272
JAMES, M.M., 212, 214
JANEWAY, J., 235
JENKINS, F., 11
JERROLDS, B.W., 21, 26, 308, 320–321, 416
JERSILD, A.T., 335
JOHNSON, E.M., 226
JOHNSON, S.J., 212
JOHNSTON, F., 300
JONCICH, G.M., 41, 43–45, 120–123, 125–128, 131–132
JUDD, C.H., 14, 104–107, 109–115
JUDD, C.H., TO W.S. GRAY, 108
JUHASZ, B.J., 92

K

KAESTLE, C.F., 249
KAHN, E., 87
KAMBERELIS, G., 258
KAMIL, M.L., 36, 167
KANT, I., 83
KAPPA DELTA PI, 130
KARP, E.E., 378
KEELOR, K., 186
KELIHER, A.V., 184
KELLY, E.I., 378
KENNEDY, A., 92
KERSHNER, F.D., 350, 357, 359
KIBBE, D., 318
KILPATRICK, W.H., 7, 187
KING, J.R., 428, 430–431
KINTSCH, W., 186

SUBJECT INDEX

Note. Page numbers followed by *t* indicate tables.

writing and, 418–419. *See also* historical research

BIOGRAPHIES, 417–418
BIXBY, JAMES THOMPSON, 41
BLAKE, DOROTHY. *See* Waples, Dorothy
BOAS, FRANZ, 42, 65
BOND, GUY, xv, 332
BOOK ENTHUSIASTS, 197–277
BOOK OF COMMON PRAYER, 201
BUCKINGHAM, B.R., 124
BURNHAM, W.H., 161
BUSWELL, GUY, xv
BUTLER, NICHOLAS MURRAY, 44, 123

C

CALDWELL, OTIS, 179
CANADIAN ORAL HISTORY ASSOCIATION, 431
CASSELL, RUSSELL, xv
CATTELL, DANA, 44
CATTELL, JAMES MCKEEN, 10–12, 27, 35–60, 434t; contributions to reading field, 51–56; and Dearborn, 142; and Gates, 330, 335; personal and professional life of, 38–46; philosophical beliefs of, 46–51; and Thorndike, 122; and Woodworth, 65–67
CATTELL, JOSEPHINE OWENS, 41
CATTELL, PSYCHE, 41
CHARTERS, WERRETT W., 248, 252, 259
CHICAGO SCHOOL, 248, 257–258, 262, 271
CHILD DEVELOPMENT: Dearborn and, 146; Russell and, 381; Strang and, 353–354; Woodworth and, 70
CHILDREN'S LITERATURE: Arbuthnot and, 199–219; Leary and, 220–246
CHILD-STUDY MOVEMENT, 7
CLARK UNIVERSITY, 161–163
CLEVELAND SURVEY, 8
COLLEAGUES: and biographical research, 419
"COLUMBIA TO LOSE ITS READING SAGE," 361
COLUMBIA UNIVERSITY, 7, 44, 396; Arbuthnot at, 203; Cattell at, 41–42, 44–45; Dearborn at, 142; Gates at, 330, 332–333, 336; Horn at, 284–285; Russell at, 377–378; Strang at, 349, 351–352, 355–357; Thorndike at, 120, 122; Woodworth at, 65–67, 69; Zirbes at, 179
COLVILLE, GEORGE MURRAY, 104
COMPREHENSION: Dodge on, 90, 93; Thorndike on, 128–130
COMTE, AUGUSTE, 47
CONNECTIONISM, 12; Thorndike on, 123, 125–126
CONTENT: of reading matter, Waples on, 267–268
CONTENT AREA READING: Gray and, 322; Horn and, 290–293; Strang and, 370
CONTINUING EDUCATION: Strang on, 359–360

COUNSELING: Strang and, 352–353, 359
CREATIVITY: Zirbes and, 182
CULLINAN, BERNICE E., xx
CULTURE ISSUES: reading pioneers and, 402–406
CURRICULUM DEVELOPMENT: Gray and, 319–320; Horn and, 285, 287–288; Strang and, 370
CUTLER, HENRIETTA. *See* Dodge, Henrietta Cutler
CYR, ELLEN, xxi

D

DALE, EDGAR, xv
DARROUGH, MADELINE. *See* Horn, Madeline Daggett Darrough
DATABASE SEARCHING, 422–423
DEARBORN, EILEEN KEDEAN, 143–144
DEARBORN, WALTER FENNO, 11, 21, 140–155, 436t; contributions to reading field, 148–150; personal and professional life of, 141–145; philosophical beliefs of, 146–148
DEPARTMENTAL HISTORIAN: and biographical research, 420
DEWEY, JOHN, 6–7, 12–13, 124–125, 202–203; Cattell and, 39; Gates and, 330–331; Huey and, 164
DIAGNOSIS, 16; Strang and, 365
DICK AND JANE BOOKS, 18, 205–207, 210–211, 312, 315, 319–320
"DICK AND JANE'S LONG-LOST DAD," 313
DIEHL, MAY, 108
DIFFERENTIATED INSTRUCTION: Dearborn and, 151; Gray and, 322; Horn on, 289; reading pioneers and, 403
DIRECT INSTRUCTION: Horn on, 299
DISABILITIES, READING, 21, 25; Dearborn and, 147–149; Huey and, 163–164
DISTRIBUTION: of reading matter, Waples on, 266–267
DIVERSITY. *See* gender issues; race issues
DODGE, HENRIETTA CUTLER, 82, 84–86
DODGE, R.E., 123
DODGE, RAYMOND, 11–12, 80–97, 435t; contributions to reading field, 87–91; personal and professional life of, 81–86; philosophical beliefs of, 86–87
"DR. ARTHUR GATES, A READING EXPERT," 334–335
DROP EVERYTHING AND READ PROGRAMS, 363–364
"DR. RUTH STRANG OF COLUMBIA," 357
"DR. WOODWORTH HONORED," 69
DUCKER, MABEL LUCILE, 15
DUKE UNIVERSITY: Cattell and, 46
DURRELL, DONALD, xv
DYSLEXIA: Dearborn and, 147

HOLLINGWORTH, LETA, 203
HOME–SCHOOL CONNECTIONS: Leary on, 234
HOOVER, HERBERT, 204
HORN, ERNEST, 13, 22, 281–306, 439*t*;
  contributions to reading field, 290–300;
  personal and professional life of, 282–287;
  philosophical beliefs of, 287–290
HORN, MADELINE DAGGETT DARROUGH, 281,
  283, 291
HUEY, EDMUND BURKE, 159–175, 437*t*;
  contributions to reading field, 166–171;
  personal and professional life of, 160–164;
  philosophical beliefs of, 164–166
HUUS, HELEN, 307–310, 319–320

I

ICONOCLASTS, 407
ILLINOIS STATE NORMAL UNIVERSITY, 310–311
INNER SPEECH: Dodge on, 90, 93; Huey on, 165
INSTITUTE OF LANGUAGE ARTS, 333
INSTITUTIONAL REVIEW BOARD: and oral history,
  429
INTELLIGENCE TESTS, 11–12, 17; Dearborn and,
  142, 146–147; Thorndike and, 132
INTERLIBRARY LOAN: and biographical research,
  420, 425
INTERNATIONAL COUNCIL FOR THE IMPROVEMENT
  OF READING INSTRUCTION, 21
INTERNATIONAL READING ASSOCIATION (IRA),
  26–27; Arbuthnot Award, 206; Gray and,
  308, 320–321; History of Reading Special
  Interest Group, xix, 416; Russell and,
  389–390; Strang and, 355–356; William
  S. Gray Citation of Merit Award, 308, 334,
  368
INTERNATIONAL STUDIES OF LITERACY: Gray and,
  316–317
INTERNET: and biographical research, 419,
  422–423
INTERVIEWS: in oral history, 429–430
INTRINSIC METHOD: Gates on, 338
INVESTIGATION: Waples and, 259–262;
  Woodworth and, 65, 70, 77
"IOWA 'PROF' INDEXES GREAT AMERICAN
  VOCABULARY," 295
IRA. *See* International Reading Association

J

JAMES, WILLIAM, 9, 65, 122, 335
JANET, PIERRE, 163
JARDINE, BEATRICE WARNER, 311
JARGON: Gates on, 333
JASTROW, JOSEPH, 39, 41
JAVAL, EMILE, 10, 162–163
JENKINS, FRANCES, 15–16
JOHNS HOPKINS UNIVERSITY, 163

JUDD, CHARLES HUBBARD, 8, 14, 101–118,
  435*t*; and Arbuthnot, 203; contributions
  to reading field, 109–113; and Gates, 335;
  and Gray, 311; personal and professional
  life of, 102–108; philosophical beliefs of,
  108–109; and Zirbes, 178
JUDD, ELLA LECOMPTE, 106
JUDD, MAY DIEHL, 108

K

KAPPA DELTA PI: Laureate Chapter, 286
KEDEAN, EILEEN. *See* Dearborn, Eileen Kedean
KEPPEL, FREDERICK PAUL, 122
KILPATRICK, WILLIAM HEARD, 181, 186–187, 203
KING, JAMES R., 427–432
KNOWLEDGE: funds of, 430

L

LABERGE-SAMUELS MODEL, 91
LAFAYETTE COLLEGE, 38–39, 161
LANGUAGE ARTS INTEGRATION: Zirbes and,
  188–189
LAPP, DIANE, 426
LARRICK, NANCY, xv, 309, 320–321
LEADERSHIP: Gray and, 320; Strang and, 369;
  Zirbes and, 192
LEARNING DISABILITIES. *See* disabilities, reading
LEARY, BERNICE ELIZABETH, 22, 25, 220–246,
  438*t*; contributions to reading field,
  230–238; and Gray, 316; personal and
  professional life of, 222–228;
  philosophical beliefs of, 228–230
LECOMPTE, ELLA, 106
LESLEY COLLEGE, 145
LICENSE PLATES: Dodge on, 91
LIFE HISTORY INTERVIEW, 428
LINCOLN SCHOOL, TEACHERS COLLEGE,
  COLUMBIA UNIVERSITY, 179
LLOYD, FRANCIS E., 123
LOTZE, RUDOLF HERMANN, 39
LOWELL, ABBOTT LAWRENCE, 142

M

MACGINITIE, WALTER, 328–329, 332–333
MASHBURN, NEELY, 86
MASLOW, ABRAHAM, 123, 208
MATTHEW EFFECTS, 151, 168
MCAFEE, CLEVELAND B., 351
MCCULLOUGH, CONSTANCE, xv
MCGUFFEY ECLECTIC READERS, 4
MCKEE, PAUL, 20
MCMILLAN, RACHEL AND MARGARET, 204
MEAD, MARGARET, 332
MEANING: Flesch on, 26; Huey on, 165, 169;
  Leary on, 229–230; Russell on, 380–381,
  386; Woodworth on, 76
MEDICAL METAPHORS, 21

SCHLOTTHAUER, PAUL, 426
SCHOOL SURVEYS, 8
SCIENTIFIC MOVEMENT: and reading education, 14–16; Thorndike and, 124–125
"SCIENTIFIC NOTES AND NEWS," 160
SCIENTIFIC RESEARCH, 1–31; Cattell and, 52–56; Dearborn and, 146; Dodge and, 86–87; Flesch on, 26; Gates and, 329–331; Gray and, 316, 321–322; Horn and, 285, 287, 289; Huey and, 163; Judd and, 108–109; need for research on, 410; reading pioneers and, xxii; Russell and, 379–380; Thorndike and, 123; Waples and, 260, 262, 272–273; Woodworth and, 72–73, 75; Zirbes and, 178, 182
SCIENTISM: Cattell and, 47
SCOPES TRIAL: Judd and, 108–109
SECOND-LANGUAGE READING: Dodge on, 93–94
SELECTIVE THINKING: Thorndike on, 127
SEMANTIC MEMORY SYSTEM, 91
SENTENCE METHOD, 4
SEWALL, CHARLES, 82
SEX OF AUTHOR: and basal readers, 18; and instructional methods, 8; Judd on, 103. See also gender issues
SHAFFER, LAURENCE, 70–71
SHARP, EMILY, 43
SHERRINGTON, CHARLES, 65
SILENT READING, 14; Judd on, 111–114
SKINNER, B.F., 126
SMALL-GROUP INSTRUCTION, 24–25
SMITH, NILA BANTON, xv
SOCIAL ACTIVISM: Gates and, 332–333
SOCIAL EFFECTS: of reading, Waples on, 269
SOCIAL LEARNING: Judd on, 110, 115
SOCIAL MILIEU: reading pioneers on, 402–406
SOCIAL STUDIES: Horn on, 286, 291
SOCIETY FOR RESEARCH IN CHILD DEVELOPMENT, 70
SPACHE, GEORGE, xv
SPELLING EXPERTS: emergence of, 17–20; Horn as, 281–306
SPEYER SCHOOL, 285
STAHL, NORMAN A., 427–432
STAIGER, RALPH, 308
STATISTICS, 13–14; Thorndike on, 130
STICKLAND, GEORGINA, 331
STORY GRAMMAR: Woodworth and, 76
STOUT, G.F., 169
STRANG, ARTHUR CORNELIUS, 349
STRANG, BENJAMIN BERGEN, 349
STRANG, RUTH MAY, 22, 347–373, 441t; contributions to reading field, 363–368; and Gates, 332; personal and professional life of, 349–358; philosophical beliefs of, 358–363
STRATEGY INSTRUCTION: Judd on, 115

STUDENTS: and biographical research, 419–420; voices of, in research, need for, 411–412
STURTEVANT, SARAH, 353
SUTHERLAND, ZENA, 200, 211, 214

T
TACHISTOSCOPE: Erdmann-Dodge, 11, 84, 87–89
TEACHER VOICES: in research, need for, 411–412
"TEACHERS' PARLEY CALLED," 376
TEACHING PRACTICES: investigation of, Waples and, 259–262
TEMPLE, ALICE, 202
TENURE: Cattell and, 45
TERMAN, LEWIS, 11–12, 335
TESTING. See assessment
TEXT SELECTION: Arbuthnot and, 214–215; Leary and, 238–239
TEXTBOOKS. See pedagogy
"THEY ARE SPELLING BETTER NOW," 294
THOMPSON, HELEN, 352
THORNDIKE, EDWARD LEE, 11–14, 17, 27, 119–139, 436t; and Cattell, 44; contributions to reading field, 127–133; and Dearborn, 142; and Gates, 330, 335–336; and Horn, 284; personal and professional life of, 120–124; philosophical beliefs of, 124–127; and Woodworth, 65, 67
THORNDIKE, ELIZABETH, 41
THORNE-THOMSEN, GUDRUN, 202
TINKER, MILES, xv, 91
TRIBUTES: for biographical research, 419, 425–426
"TRIBUTE TO DR. RUTH STRANG," 356, 368
TRUMAN, HARRY S., 180
TUFTS UNIVERSITY, 252
TUNNELL, ENRICA, 66, 69
TYLER, RALPH W., 248, 259

U
UHL, WILLIS, 17, 19
UNITED NATIONS EDUCATIONAL, SCIENTIFIC AND CULTURAL ORGANIZATION (UNESCO), 317
UNIVERSITY OF ARIZONA, 349, 356, 360
UNIVERSITY OF BRITISH COLUMBIA, 378
UNIVERSITY OF CALIFORNIA AT BERKELEY: Gates at, 329; Russell at, 376, 378–379; Strang at, 356
UNIVERSITY OF CHICAGO, 6–7, 396; Arbuthnot at, 200, 202–204; Dearborn at, 142; Gray at, 308, 311–313; Judd at, 107; Leary at, 224; Waples at, 248, 252, 255–257
UNIVERSITY OF IOWA, 285–286, 295
UNIVERSITY OF MISSOURI, 284